SEVENTH EDITION

Infants & Toddlers
CURRICULUM AND TEACHING

Terri Jo Swim
Linda Watson

Australia • Brazil • Japan • Korea • Mexico • Singapore • Spain • United Kingdom • United States

**Infants and Toddlers
Curriculum and Teaching
Seventh Edition**
Terri Jo Swim
Linda Watson

Executive Editor: Linda Schreiber-Ganster

Developmental Editor: Robert Jucha

Assistant Editor: Rebecca Dashiell

Editorial Assistant: Linda Stewart

Media Editor: Dennis Fitzgerald

Marketing Manager: Kara Kindstrom-Parsons

Marketing Assistant: Dimitri Hagnéré

Marketing Communications Manager: Martha Pfeiffer

Content Project Manager: Samen Iqbal

Creative Director: Rob Hugel

Art Director: Maria Epes

Print Buyer: Karen Hunt

Rights Acquisitions Account Manager, Text: Roberta Broyer

Rights Acquisitions Account Manager, Image: Leitha Etheridge-Sims

Production Service: Mary Stone, Pre-PressPMG

Text Designer: Susan Schmidler

Photo Researcher: Martha Hall

Copy Editor: Carol Ann Ellis

Compositor: Pre-PressPMG

Cover Designer: Denise Davidson

Cover Image: © Cengage Learning, ECE Photo Library

© 2011, 2008 Wadsworth, Cengage Learning

ALL RIGHTS RESERVED. No part of this work covered by the copyright herein may be reproduced, transmitted, stored, or used in any form or by any means graphic, electronic, or mechanical, including but not limited to photocopying, recording, scanning, digitizing, taping, Web distribution, information networks, or information storage and retrieval systems, except as permitted under Section 107 or 108 of the 1976 United States Copyright Act, without the prior written permission of the publisher.

For product information and technology assistance, contact us at
Cengage Learning Customer & Sales Support, 1-800-354-9706.
For permission to use material from this text or product, submit all requests online at **www.cengage.com/permissions.**
Further permissions questions can be emailed to
permissionrequest@cengage.com

International Student Edition:
ISBN-13: 978-0-495-80822-0

ISBN-10: 0-495-80822-9

Wadsworth
20 Davis Drive
Belmont, CA 94002-3098
USA

Cengage Learning is a leading provider of customized learning solutions with office locations around the globe, including Singapore, the United Kingdom, Australia, Mexico, Brazil, and Japan. Locate your local office at **www.cengage.com/global**

Cengage Learning products are represented in Canada by Nelson Education, Ltd.

To learn more about Wadsworth, visit **www.cengage.com/wadsworth**

Purchase any of our products at your local college store or at our preferred online store **www.cengagebrain.com**

Printed in the United States of America
1 2 3 4 5 6 7 13 12 11 10

Brief Contents

PART 1 Infant-Toddler Development and Professional Educator Preparation 1

chapter 1 A DEVELOPMENTAL PERSPECTIVE ON EDUCATING INFANTS AND TODDLERS 3

chapter 2 BIRTH TO THIRTY-SIX MONTHS: PHYSICAL AND COGNITIVE/LANGUAGE DEVELOPMENTAL PATTERNS 28

chapter 3 BIRTH TO THIRTY-SIX MONTHS: SOCIAL AND EMOTIONAL DEVELOPMENTAL PATTERNS 66

chapter 4 THE THREE As: THE MASTER TOOLS FOR QUALITY CARE AND EDUCATION 103

chapter 5 EFFECTIVE PREPARATION AND TOOLS FOR PROFESSIONAL EDUCATORS 120

PART 2 Establishing a Positive Learning Environment 149

chapter 6 BUILDING RELATIONSHIPS WITH AND GUIDING THE BEHAVIORS OF INFANTS AND TODDLERS 151

chapter 7 SUPPORTIVE COMMUNICATION WITH FAMILIES AND COLLEAGUES 175

chapter 8 THE INDOOR AND OUTDOOR LEARNING ENVIRONMENTS 205

chapter 9 DESIGNING THE CURRICULUM 251

PART 3 Matching Caregiver Strategies, Materials, and Experiences to the Child's Development 285

chapter 10 THE CHILD FROM BIRTH TO FOUR MONTHS OF AGE 287

chapter 11 THE CHILD FROM FOUR TO EIGHT MONTHS OF AGE 312

chapter 12 THE CHILD FROM EIGHT TO TWELVE MONTHS OF AGE 333

chapter 13 THE CHILD FROM TWELVE TO EIGHTEEN MONTHS OF AGE 355

chapter 14 THE CHILD FROM EIGHTEEN TO TWENTY-FOUR MONTHS OF AGE 376

chapter 15 THE CHILD FROM TWENTY-FOUR TO THIRTY MONTHS OF AGE 398

chapter 16 THE CHILD FROM THIRTY TO THIRTY-SIX MONTHS OF AGE 419

appendix A TOOLS FOR OBSERVING AND RECORDING 441

appendix B DEVELOPMENTAL PROFILE AND INSTRUCTIONS 474

appendix C STANDARDS FOR INFANT/TODDLER CAREGIVERS 477

Glossary 483

Index 493

Contents

Preface xvii
Supplements xxi
About the Author xxiii

PART 1 Infant-Toddler Development and Professional Educator Preparation 1

chapter 1 A DEVELOPMENTAL PERSPECTIVE ON EDUCATING INFANTS AND TODDLERS 3

Introduction 4
Taking a Developmental Perspective 5
Using a Developmental Profile 7
Theories of Child Development 9
   Current Trends in Development and Education 15
Valuing Cultural Diversity 21
CASE STUDY: Trisha 24

chapter 2 BIRTH TO THIRTY-SIX MONTHS: PHYSICAL AND COGNITIVE/LANGUAGE DEVELOPMENTAL PATTERNS 28

Differences Between Development and Learning 29
Patterns of Physical Development 29
Patterns of Cognitive/Language Development 42
Children with Special Rights 54
CASE STUDY: Sasha 60

chapter 3 BIRTH TO THIRTY-SIX MONTHS: SOCIAL AND EMOTIONAL DEVELOPMENTAL PATTERNS   66

Patterns of Emotional Development   67
Patterns of Social Development   82
Children with Special Rights   93
CASE STUDY: Marcus   96

chapter 4 THE THREE As: THE MASTER TOOLS FOR QUALITY CARE AND EDUCATION   103

Introduction   104
The Three As: Attention, Approval, and Attunement as Tools   105
The Attachment Debate and the Roles of Caregivers   106
Understanding the Three As   109
- Attention   109
- Approval   111
- Attunement   112

Using the Three As Successfully with Infants and Toddlers   114
CASE STUDY: Rangina   116

chapter 5 EFFECTIVE PREPARATION AND TOOLS FOR PROFESSIONAL EDUCATORS   120

Introduction   121
Characteristics of a Competent Early Childhood Educator   121
Acquiring Knowledge   123
- About Yourself   123
- About Children   123
- About Families   123
- About Early Child Care and Education   123
- About Program Implementation   124
- About Partnerships   124
- About Advocacy   125

Professional Preparation of the Early Childhood Educator   126
Impact of Teacher Education on Quality of Care and Education   128

Observing Young Children to Make Educational Decisions   130
   Observe and Record   130
   Assess and Evaluate   141
   Using Data Gathered   142
CASE STUDY: Audrey   144

PART 2   Establishing a Positive Learning Environment   149

chapter 6   BUILDING RELATIONSHIPS WITH AND GUIDING THE BEHAVIORS OF INFANTS AND TODDLERS   151

Introduction   152
Reggio Emilia Approach to Infant-Toddler Education   153
   History   153
   Philosophy   153
   Image of the Child   154
   Inserimento   155
A Developmental View of Discipline   157
   Mental Models   158
Strategies for Respectfully Guiding Children's Behavior   160
   Labeling Expressed Emotions   160
   Teaching Emotional Regulation   163
Building the Foundations for Perspective-Taking   164
   Setting Limits   166
   Establishing Consequences   168
   Providing Choices   168
   Redirecting Actions   169
   Solving Problems   169
CASE STUDY: Enrique   171

chapter 7   SUPPORTIVE COMMUNICATION WITH FAMILIES AND COLLEAGUES   175

Introduction   176
Skills for Effective Communication   177
   Rapport Building   177
   I Statements versus You Statements   178

Active Listening: The "How" in Communication   179
Mirroring   180

Communicating with Families   181
Teacher Beliefs   181
Using Active Listening with Families   182
Partnering with Families   187
Family Education   188
Family-Caregiver Conferences   188
Home Visits   190

Family Situations Requiring Additional Support   191
Grandparents as Parents   191
At-Risk Families and Children   192
Teenage Parents   195

Communicating with Colleagues   198
Listening to Colleagues   198
Collaborating with Colleagues   199
Supporting Colleagues   199
Making Decisions   200

CASE STUDY: Sheila   201

chapter 8 THE INDOOR AND OUTDOOR LEARNING ENVIRONMENTS   205

Introduction to Principles of Environmental Design   206

The Teacher's Perspective   206
Learning Centers   207
Use of Space   210
Calm, Safe Learning Environment   212
Basic Needs   213

The Child's Perspective   215
Transparency   216
Flexibility   218
Relationships   218
Identity   219
Movement   221
Documentation   221

Senses 222
Representation 223
Independence 223
Discovery 224
Society's Perspective 226
Environmental Changes 226
Curricular Changes 227
Partnerships and Advocacy 228
Ongoing Reflection on the Physical Environment 229
Selecting Equipment and Materials 230
Age-Appropriate Materials 230
Homemade Materials 233
Protecting the Children's Health and Safety 235
Emergency Procedures 235
Immunization Schedule 236
Signs and Symptoms of Possible Severe Illness 236
First Aid 236
Universal Precautions 241
Injuries 243
CASE STUDY: Ena 246

chapter 9 DESIGNING THE CURRICULUM 251
Infant-Toddler Curriculum 252
Influences on the Curriculum 253
Influences of Society 253
Influences from Cultural Expectations 255
Influences from the Care Setting 259
Influences from the Child 261
Routine Care Times 262
Flexible Schedule 263
Planned Learning Experiences 273
Daily Plans 275
Weekly Plans 275
CASE STUDY: Lukaz 282

PART 3 Matching Caregiver Strategies, Materials, and Experiences to the Child's Development 285

chapter 10 THE CHILD FROM BIRTH TO FOUR MONTHS OF AGE 287

Kierston's Story 288
Materials 288
Types of Materials 289
Examples of Homemade Materials 289
Caregiver Strategies to Enhance Development 290
Physical Development 291
Cognitive/Language Development 297
Emotional Development 303
Social Development 307
CASE STUDY: Kierston 309

chapter 11 THE CHILD FROM FOUR TO EIGHT MONTHS OF AGE 312

Theresa's Story 313
Materials and Activities 313
Types of Materials 313
Examples of Homemade Materials 313
Caregiver Strategies To Enhance Development 315
Physical Development 316
Cognitive/Language Development 321
Emotional Development 326
Social Development 328
CASE STUDY: Theresa 331

chapter 12 THE CHILD FROM EIGHT TO TWELVE MONTHS OF AGE 333

Marcel's Story 334
Materials and Activities 334
Types of Materials 334
Examples of Homemade Materials 334

Caregiver Strategies to Enhance Development   336
  Physical Development   336
  Cognitive/Language Development   341
  Emotional Development   347
  Social Development   349
CASE STUDY: Marcel   352

chapter 13 THE CHILD FROM TWELVE TO EIGHTEEN MONTHS OF AGE   355

Caregivers of Toddlers   356
  Andrea   356
Materials and Activities   356
  Types of Materials   357
  Examples of Homemade Materials   358
Caregiver Strategies to Enhance Development   359
  Physical Development   359
  Cognitive/Language Development   362
  Emotional Development   367
  Social Development   371
CASE STUDY: Andrea   373

chapter 14 THE CHILD FROM EIGHTEEN TO TWENTY-FOUR MONTHS OF AGE   376

  Lennie's Story   377
Materials and Activities   377
  Types of Materials   377
  Examples of Homemade Materials   378
Caregiver Strategies to Enhance Development   379
  Physical Development   379
  Cognitive/Language Development   382
  Emotional Development   389
  Social Development   391
CASE STUDY: Lennie   395

chapter 15 THE CHILD FROM TWENTY-FOUR TO THIRTY MONTHS OF AGE 398

Ming's Story 399

Materials and Activities 399

Types of Materials 400

Examples of Homemade Materials 400

Activity Ideas 403

Caregiver Strategies to Enhance Development 403

Physical Development 403

Cognitive/Language Development 406

Emotional Development 412

Social Development 414

CASE STUDY: Ming 417

chapter 16 THE CHILD FROM THIRTY TO THIRTY-SIX MONTHS OF AGE 419

Juan's Story 420

Materials and Activities 420

Types of Materials 420

Examples of Homemade Materials 420

Activity Ideas 421

Caregiver Strategies to Enhance Development 422

Physical Development 422

Cognitive/Language Development 424

Emotional Development 431

Social Development 434

CASE STUDY: Juan 436

SUMMARY: CLOSING NOTE 439

appendix A TOOLS FOR OBSERVING AND RECORDING 441

Running Record 442

Anecdotal Record 443

Developmental Prescriptions (Combination of Checklist and Rating Scale) 444

Indoor Safety Checklist 468

Playground Safety Checklist 471

appendix B DEVELOPMENTAL PROFILE AND INSTRUCTIONS   474

Instructions   474

appendix C STANDARDS FOR INFANT/TODDLER CAREGIVERS   477

CDA Competency Standards for Infant/Toddler Caregivers in Center-Based Programs   477

NAEYC Standards for Early Childhood Professional Preparation: Initial Licensure Programs   481

NAEYC Initial Licensure Standards Summary   482

Glossary   483

Index   493

Preface

This revised, expanded, and updated edition was developed by Terri Jo Swim with the intention of guiding the reader through the acquisition of skills necessary to provide high-quality care for infants and toddlers in any educational setting. Information based on current theories and research, as well as standards for infant/toddler teacher preparation, is reflected throughout the book. It provides appropriate caregiving and educational techniques along with curriculum ideas for groups of very young children and the individual children within those groups. Early childhood educators, administrators, advocates, and parents will find practical information that can be put to immediate use to promote the highest-quality care and education possible for all children.

TEXT ORGANIZATION

Part I Infant and Toddler Development and Caregiver Preparation

This section presents an overview of the theories and research in the fields of child development and early childhood education, including new information on brain development, to prepare the reader as a professional educator who possesses the skills necessary to meet the developmental and learning needs of infants and toddlers effectively. Chapter 1 highlights the importance of taking a developmental perspective when working with infants and toddlers as well as an overview of environmental, social, cultural, and governmental influences in child care. Chapter 2 creates a framework for understanding the growth and development of physical and cognitive/language areas from birth to 36 months. Chapter 3 focuses on growth and development in the emotional and social areas from birth to 36 months. In both Chapters 2 and 3 there is information on children with special rights. Chapter 4 presents the master tools of caregiving: Attention, Approval, and Attunement as a model of conscious caregiving, combining practical principles and techniques from current theories and research in the field. Chapter 5 describes specific knowledge

xvii

bases that professional educators acquire through informal and formal educational opportunities. One such knowledge base involves the appropriate assessment of children. This chapter, then, focuses on various observational tools for tracking development and learning, and how to use the data as the groundwork for other aspects of the caregiver's work.

Part 2 Establishing a Positive Learning Environment

Four chapters provide the reader with details about how to create appropriate environments for very young children. Learning environments include not only attending to the physical arrangement by carefully selecting equipment and materials but also to the socio-emotional and intellectual climates created among adults and children.

Chapter 6 utilizes key components of educational philosophy found in the schools in the Reggio Emilia, Italy, as the foundation for creating a caring community of learners. Respectful and effective communication and guidance strategies are outlined. Chapter 7 is devoted to appropriate communication strategies to use when creating reciprocal relationships with family members and colleagues. Family situations that may require additional support from the caregiver, the program, or community agencies are presented. Chapter 8 covers components of high-quality and developmentally appropriate indoor and outdoor learning environments from the teachers', children's, and society's perspectives and presents common safety issues for children. Chapter 9 presents practical techniques for designing the intellectual environment. Curriculum—both routine care times and planned learning experiences—must be specially designed to enhance the development and learning of all the children, including those with special needs.

Part 3 Matching Caregiver Strategies and Child Development

Seven developmental levels are defined within the age range of birth through 36 months. Tasks, materials, and specific learning experiences to enhance development are provided in Chapters 10 through 16. This practical section provides specific techniques, teaching strategies, and solutions to many of the common problems confronted when addressing the rapid growth and development of infants and toddlers.

Major Revisions in the Seventh Edition
The seventh edition of *Infants and Toddlers: Curriculum and Teaching* further attempts to bridge the gap between theory and practice. As scholar-practitioners, teachers need to use theory to inform their practice and use their practice to inform theoretical understanding. Building from the strong foundation of previous editions, the text has been updated, reorganized, and thoroughly revised. While notable differences set apart this edition, points of continuity remain. For example, in this seventh edition, the child continues to be, rightfully so, at the center of care and education. Defining infants and toddlers as engaging, decision-making forces within their environments sets a tone of excitement and enthusiasm. No longer can we afford to agree with the description of toddlerhood as the "terrible twos." Rather, we need to embrace the image of the child as capable, competent, and creative.

Doing so opens a number of educational options that were unavailable previously. Results of research on social and emotional development, for example, and attachment behaviors, have been expanded as foundations for this edition. In addition, incorporating key components of the high-quality infant-toddler and preschool programs in Reggio Emilia, Italy, has improved our understanding of what developmentally appropriate practice looks like in action. Respecting children, designing effective physical, social, and intellectual environments, building partnerships with families, and planning individually appropriate curricula are discussed throughout this edition. Major content revisions in this edition also include the following:

- Results of new research and scholarly articles have been incorporated into each chapter. For example, new research on prosocial behaviors can be found in Chapter 3; new information regarding attention from a sociocultural perspective was added to Chapter 4; current thoughts about examining the intellectual integrity of the caregiver's work is now included in Chapter 9 and Chapter 15 was expanded to include hints for selecting high-quality, culturally diverse books for young children.
- Chapter 1 was significantly reorganized, based on reviewer feedback, to provide an overview of developmental theories as a rationale for taking a developmental perspective in our work with infants and toddlers. Now the practical applications of developmental theories for early childhood programs—family grouping, continuity of care, and the primary caregiving system—are more clearly grounded in this theoretical approach to infant-toddler care and education.
- Chapters 2 and 3 focus on typical and unique patterns of development. Chapter 2 now concentrates on physical, cognitive, and language development, while Chapter 3 covers emotional and social development. Dividing the areas of development in this way allowed for more research for each area to be included.
- Based on this author's professional knowledge and preferences, the observing and assessing sections of Chapter 5 have been reorganized and updated.
- Chapter 6 includes a new section, using the results of recent research, on using mental models to inform discipline practices. Also, the strategies for guiding the behavior of very young children are expanded to include labeling expressed emotions and solving problems.
- "Green" principles for environmental design, such as relying on natural light or changing to compact fluorescent lighting, and curriculum inputs such as recycling and gardening, for example, are explored in Chapter 8.
- Based on reviewer feedback, a clearer focus on care of infants and toddlers with special rights has been provided throughout the book.
- Chapters 10–16 have been reorganized so that the information presented parallels the order in Chapters 2 and 3. In other words, the areas of development are discussed in the following order: physical, cognitive and language, emotional, and social.

NEW INSTRUCTIONAL FEATURES FOUND IN THE SEVENTH EDITION

To Help Aid the Student's Comprehension and Understanding of Infant-Toddler Development and Learning, Several New Instructional Features Have Been Created for the Seventh Edition.

- New features "Spotlighting" research, professional organizations, and voices from the field can be found throughout the text. For example, Chapter 2 features a "Spotlight on Research" box which contains current information on how father-child interactions impact children's developmental outcomes. The Infant-Toddler Specialists of Indiana (ITSI) organization is highlighted in Chapter 5. In Chapters 10–16, "Voices from the Field" can be found. To illustrate, in Chapter 11, a teacher discusses how she created learning experiences to promote understanding of object permanence and learned to appreciate individual differences in performances for children of the same age.
- To improve students' comprehension, Reading Checkpoints containing review questions can be found in each chapter.

CONTINUED USE OF INSTRUCTIONAL FEATURES FOUND IN PRIOR EDITIONS

- Chapter overviews, objectives, and a specific chapter outline are included.
- Revised case studies present real-life examples of the concepts and principles discussed.
- References as well as questions and experiences for reflection are given at the end of each chapter.
- Numerous photos and illustrations are included throughout to illustrate the concepts and materials presented.
- A comprehensive Developmental Prescription of behavioral expectations for children from birth to 36 months is provided for the four major areas of development to assist the caregiver in establishing Developmental Profiles and Developmental Prescriptions for each child.
- The text is comprehensive so that caregivers acquire the essential skills necessary to function at nationally accepted standards of quality.
- The level of the language used is easy to follow and offers practical examples for self-study by caregivers-in-training.

Questions or discussions on any topics covered in the book can be sent to me at the e-mail address below.

TERRI JO SWIM
swimt@ipfw.edu

Supplements

INSTRUCTOR'S MANUAL
The instructor's manual includes tools for facilitating learning, questions for generating discussion, lecture notes, and suggested projects for constructing knowledge for instructors of classes on infant and toddler care and development. The test bank includes multiple choice, true/false, completion, short answer, and essay questions.

PowerLecture
This one-stop digital library and presentation tool includes preassembled Microsoft® PowerPoint® lecture slides. In addition to a full Instructor's Manual and Test Bank, PowerLecture™ also includes ExamView® testing software with all the test items from the Test Bank in electronic format, enabling you to create customized tests in print or online.

Premium Website
The Premium Website offers access to TeachSource Videos including Video Cases with exercises, transcripts, artifacts, and bonus videos. You'll also find other study tools and resources such as links to related websites for each chapter of the text, tutorial quizzes, glossary/flashcards, and more. Go to www.cengage.com/login to register using your access code.

WebTutor™ Toolbox on WebCT™ and Blackboard
Jumpstart your course with customizable, rich, text-specific content for use within your course management system. Whether you want to Web-enable your class or put an entire course online, WebTutor™ delivers.

ACKNOWLEDGMENTS

This seventh edition of *Infants and Toddlers: Curriculum and Teaching* would not have been possible without the influence, loyalty, and positive influence of the following very exceptional people.

To my parents and grandparents, thanks for intuitively knowing all about the three *A*s when I was growing up. Special thanks goes to my family: Danny, Savannah, Randy, and Justin – you have taught me much about the importance of strong attachments.

T. J. S.

To Chris Shortt, Robert Jucha, and the rest of the staff at Wadsworth Cengage Learning for continued support and guidance.

To the following reviewers of the *seventh* and previous editions, we thank you for your candid feedback and support:

Suzanne Adinolfi, Gulf Coast Community College
Wendy Bertoli, Lancaster County Career & Technology Center
Susan Bowers, Northern Illinois University
Eileen Brittain, Houghton College
Sue Davies, Ivy Tech Community College
Phyllis Gilbert, Stephen F. Austin State University
Janet Imel, Ivy Tech Community College
Ruth Saur, Lorain County Community College
Gwen Sherman, Gulf Coast Community College
Jennifer Volkers, Baker College

About the Author

TERRI JO SWIM, Ph.D., is an Associate Professor and Program Director of Early Childhood/Elementary Education at Indiana University—Purdue University in Fort Wayne, Indiana. She has been in the field of early childhood education for over 15 years. She has worked in private child care centers, university-based laboratory programs, and summer camps with children from birth to 13 years of age. Terri is the coauthor of *Creative Resources for Infants and Toddlers* (2nd ed.) with Dr. Judy Herr. Current research interests include infant-toddler and preschool curriculum, Reggio Emilia, documentation, and teacher education.

PART 1

Infant-Toddler Development and Professional Educator Preparation

Since publication of the previous edition, the information explosion in child development and caregiving has continued. As a result, early childhood educators need to learn more theories, principles, and skills to keep pace with the demands of their profession.

Child care settings are powerful contexts for influencing the development and learning of very young children. High standards of care require that teachers learn to take good care of both themselves and the children, and to be aware of the interests, abilities, and desires of the child, family, community, and society as a whole. This section provides current trends in caring for infants and toddlers, theories and principles of child development, and a structure for caregiving that helps prepare the caregiver for the challenging and rewarding profession of early childhood education.

This edition continues to emphasize science and new discoveries by researchers (for example, on brain development and attachment), as well as the influences these findings have on caregiver behavior when working with very young children. By closely observing and recording

part 1 INFANT-TODDLER DEVELOPMENT AND PROFESSIONAL EDUCATOR PREPARATION

the behaviors of children, the child care specialist will create a powerful framework to use in caring for and educating infants and toddlers.

When you finish this section, you will have the knowledge and principles necessary to care for children effectively and enhance the development of each child through your direct, intentional interactions. The following sections build on this base of knowledge to give you all the specific skills, techniques, strategies, and activities needed to function confidently as a professional.

chapter 1

A DEVELOPMENTAL PERSPECTIVE ON EDUCATING INFANTS AND TODDLERS

learning objectives

After reading this chapter, you should be able to:

- Identify the four major developmental areas for assessment, and discuss how they differ from one another.
- Grasp the use of developmental profiles.
- Compare theories of child development.
- Justify how Bronfenbrenner's ecological systems theory can be used to explain current trends in development and education.

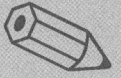

chapter outline

- Introduction
- Taking a Developmental Perspective
- Using a Developmental Profile
- Theories on Child Development
- Current Trends in Development and Education
- Valuing Cultural Diversity
- Chapter Summary
- Case Study: Trisha

3

INTRODUCTION

What do people who work with young children need to know and what do they need to be able to do? Early childhood educators* have long debated these questions. For almost 100 years, people from all areas of the field and all corners of the world have gathered together to come to a consensus in answering these two key questions. Current research has helped early childhood specialists to clearly define a core body of knowledge, as well as standards for quality in both teacher preparation and in programming for young children. Scholarly research has validated what early childhood professionals have always known intuitively: the quality of young children's experience in early care and education settings is directly related to the knowledge, skills, and dispositions of the adults caring for them. Scientific evidence through the latest brain research clearly brings to light the importance of the "disposition" part of the equation in creating quality care and education for all young children, but most importantly in the care of infants and toddlers. This validation of our work allows us to more clearly assume an advocacy or leadership role in sharing this information with others.

For the past 75 years, the National Association for the Education of Young Children (NAEYC) has worked to develop standards for the educational preparation of early care and education teachers (Hyson, 2003) as well as children's programs (accreditation). Many other professional organizations, such as the NFCCA (National Family Child Care Association), the NACCRRA (National Association of Child Care Resource and Referral Agencies), and the Council for Professional Recognition, have articulated professional values and desired outcomes for both teachers and children. These standards provide the definition of quality and support for both young people and programs as they work to improve the quality of care and education for young children.

Recent brain research has provided evidence of the connection between early care and education and a baby's ability to develop the capacity to incorporate all of the skills that any human being has ever developed. The philosophical grounding of this text is supported by the findings that "warm, responsive care is not only comforting for an infant; it is critical to healthy development" (Shore, 2003, 27).

A common theme in both the results of the brain research and in the standards mentioned previously is the importance of building strong, respectful, reciprocal relationships with infants, toddlers, and their families. Family members have much to tell us about their child(ren) in our care. Educators must come to understand quickly that the needs of the infants and toddlers are best met when partnerships are formed to support the clear, open exchange of ideas. Viewing infants, toddlers, and family members as competent, capable, and caring assists in promoting optimal

---

*In this book, the terms *early childhood educator, teacher, caregiver,* and *primary caregiver* will be used interchangeably to describe adults who care for and educate infants and toddlers. Other terms, such as early childhood specialist, educarer, practitioner, staff, child care teacher, Head Teacher, Assistant Teacher, or family child care provider, might also be familiar. The use of these four terms is not intended to narrow the focus of professionals discussed in this text or to minimize a particular title, rather the purpose is to provide some consistency in language.

development and learning for everyone involved. Today's theories and philosophies regarding child development and learning have evolved over time and have been influenced by both ancient and modern society and thought. They are the direct result of the early childhood professionals and scientists building upon previous theories and research in order to better understand children today.

How teachers use and apply the developmental theories depend not only on their understanding of those theories and associated research but also on their personal beliefs and dispositions. Being unable to attend to every aspect of an interaction, our mind filters and categorizes information at astonishing speeds. Our beliefs impact not only how our brain does this work but also how we make sense of the information once it is available. Matusov, DePalma, & Drye (2007) suggest that adults' responses constantly and actively impact the trajectory of development of children. Thus, teachers participate in "... co-constructing the observed phenomenon of development" (p. 410) such that "development defines an observer no less than the observed" (p. 419). In other words, what we observe and what we think the observations mean are as much a reflection of us (our beliefs and knowledge bases) as it is a reflection of the child we observed. This is illustrated in conversations between two adults after observing the same event. They each describe the actions, behaviors, and implications of the phenomenon differently. Thus, recognizing how teachers shape the development of children must subsequently result in the opening of dialogue and communication.

These points are made so that you will take an active role in reflecting on your own beliefs and how they are changing as you read this book and interact with infants and toddlers. Developing the "habit of mind" for careful professional and personal reflection will assist you in thinking about your role as an educator.

TAKING A DEVELOPMENTAL PERSPECTIVE

The structure of this book allows for the philosophy that the authors believe is most helpful in child care settings. The major contributions of early childhood theorists are presented within this structure. This philosophy, which follows a *Developmental Perspective*, states that teachers and other adults must be consciously aware of how a child is progressing in each area in order to create environments that assist with the development of *all* the skills that any human being has ever developed. Unlike the tabula rasa theory of the past, which claimed that children are molded to parental or societal specifications, current research indicates that each child's genetic code interacts with environmental factors to result in the realization (or not) of her full potential.

A child born with a physical disability such as spina bifida may not realize as much potential in certain areas as a child born neurologically intact, and a child whose ancestry dictates adult height less than five feet will most likely not realize the potential to play professional basketball. However, within these limiting genetic and environmental factors, every child has the potential for a fulfilling and productive life, depending on how well his or her abilities are satisfied and challenged and to what extent the skills necessary to become a happy and successful adult are fostered by family members and caregivers.

As you can see, from the moment of birth, the child and the people around the child affect each other. This dynamic interaction is sometimes deliberate and controlled and sometimes unconscious behavior. Caregivers working with infants and toddlers plan many experiences for children. Simultaneous with these planned experiences are the thousands of actions that are spontaneous, that stimulate new actions and reactions and challenge both the child and the caregiver. Teachers must learn to be mindful in all of their interactions.

Magda Gerber (e.g., Gerber & Weaver, 1998) has established an approach and structure for child care that emphasizes mindful interaction between child and caregiver. This approach is illustrated through her "10 principles of caregiving."

1. Involve children in activities and things that concern them.
2. Invest in quality time with each child.
3. Learn the unique ways each child communicates with you and teach him or her the way you communicate.
4. Invest the time and energy necessary with each child to build a total person.
5. Respect infants and toddlers as worthy people.
6. Model specific behaviors before you teach them.
7. Always be honest with children about your feelings.
8. View problems as learning opportunities and allow children to solve their own problems where possible.
9. Build security with children by teaching trust.
10. Be concerned about the quality of development each child has at each stage.

These types of interactions focus on the development of the whole child. Thinking about all of the areas at once can be an overwhelming task for people who are new to the profession. Child development knowledge, in this situation, can be divided into distinct, yet interrelated, areas for easy understanding. It is important to note that no area of development functions in isolation from another. This division is arbitrary and is done for the ease of the learner, you. For children, the areas of development come together and operate as a whole, producing an entirely unique

TABLE 1–1	DEVELOPMENTAL DOMAINS
AREA I	**Physical:** height, weight, general motor coordination, brain development, visual and auditory acuity, and so on
AREA II	**Emotional:** feelings, self-perception, perception of others related to self, confidence, security, and so on
AREA III	**Social:** interactions with peers, elders, and youngsters, both one on one and in a group, social perspective-taking, and so on
AREA IV	**Cognitive/Language:** reasoning, problem solving, concept formation, imagination, verbal communication, and so on

chapter 1 A DEVELOPMENTAL PERSPECTIVE ON EDUCATING INFANTS AND TODDLERS   7

individual. Table 1–1 lists the four developmental domains that will be used in this book. Coming to understand the four individual areas well is necessary for you to promote optimal development for each child in your care.

A major goal of this book is to help caregivers understand normal sequences and patterns of development and to become familiar with learning tools that enhance development in the four major developmental areas. Once you understand the normative patterns or **milestones**, you can more easily recognize and honor the unique patterns that each child demonstrates. Throughout this book, you will learn to evaluate the development of an individual child by comparing milestone behaviors with the larger group that was used to establish normative behavior for that age. Therefore, necessary aspects of preparing to be an infant/toddler teacher are learning to observe children carefully, record that observational data, and analyze separate skills, learning, or behaviors. Once individual parts are understood, early childhood educators can apply the knowledge to care for the whole, constantly changing child in a competent manner.

USING A DEVELOPMENTAL PROFILE

Use the Developmental Prescription in Appendix A or another developmental hierarchy to evaluate which behaviors and skills the child can perform successfully and the point in the hierarchy at which the child can't perform higher-level behaviors (refer to Appendix B for Profile Construction). The last point at which the child performs with success is translated into an estimate of age in months indicating the level of development in that skill area. For example, in evaluating a 12-month-old in Area I (Physical), the Developmental Prescription in Appendix A for 8 to 12 months lists six behaviors under "Muscular Control, Trunk and Leg." If the child being observed can successfully perform the first three behaviors, his or her development is estimated to be 10 months (half of the age range between 8 and 12 months). Evaluate each child in all the skill behaviors of the age range in order to establish an average age level for each of the four developmental areas on the profile. Remember that these are average estimates of ages and not specific tests.

Figure 1–1 graphically illustrates the assessment of a 12-month-old compared to age norms on a Developmental Profile. The heavy line at 12 months indicates Juan's chronological age (C. A.) and each point indicates his development in each of the four areas. To make up the points on the profile, specific skills under each area from the Developmental Prescription in Appendix A were evaluated. By comparing relative strengths and weaknesses, a program can be implemented to enhance his development (refer to Appendix B for instructions on Developmental Profile construction and Appendix A for specific age expectations). In the example, Juan is above his age in responding to adult attention and below age expectancy in interacting in a group. From this profile we can see that activities should be done to help Juan feel more secure in a group setting and to help him function more independently in one-on-one interactions. Since his language skills are good, talking to Juan while he is in a group might help.

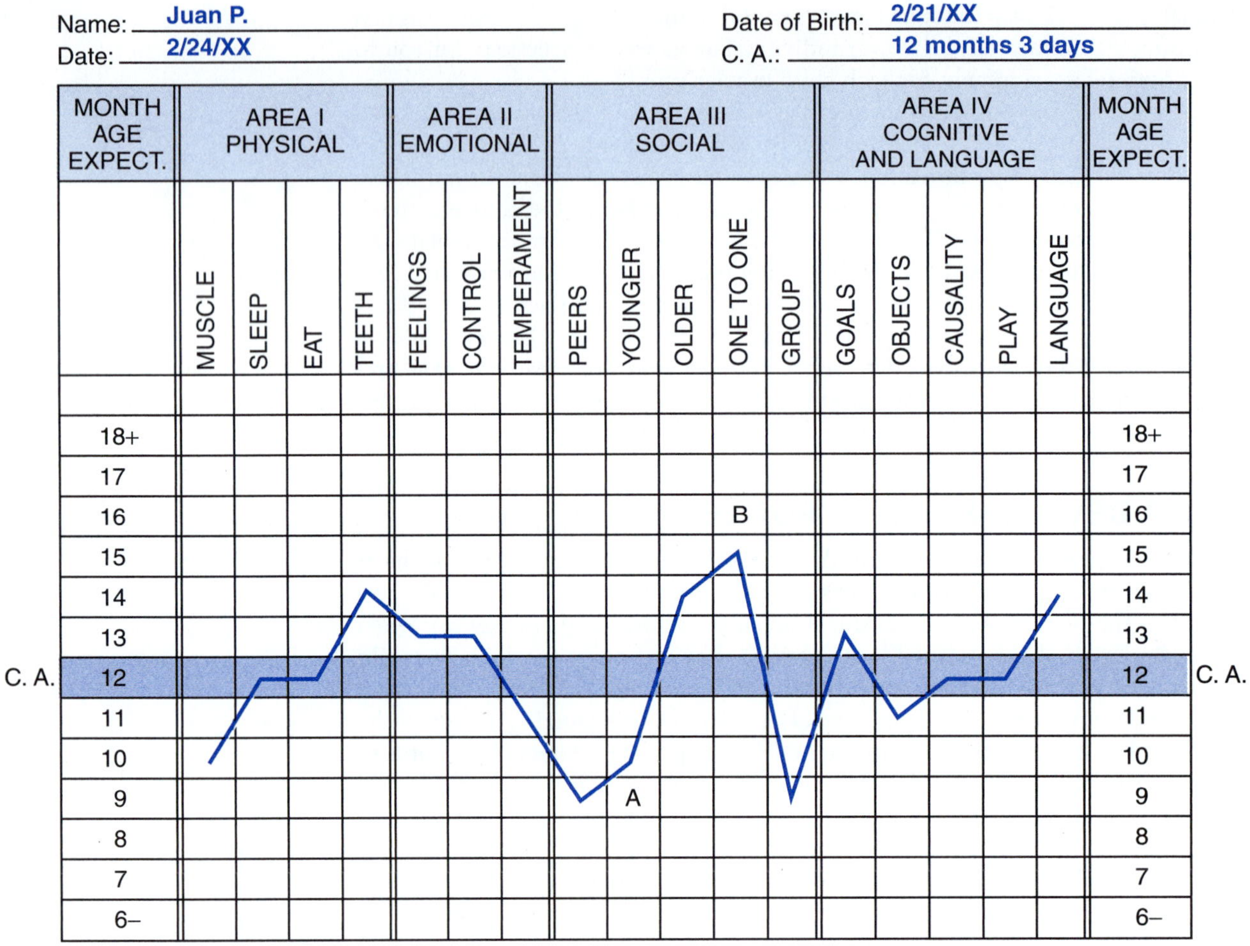

Name: **Juan P.**
Date: **2/24/XX**

Date of Birth: **2/21/XX**
C. A.: **12 months 3 days**

MONTH AGE EXPECT.	AREA I PHYSICAL				AREA II EMOTIONAL			AREA III SOCIAL					AREA IV COGNITIVE AND LANGUAGE					MONTH AGE EXPECT.
	MUSCLE	SLEEP	EAT	TEETH	FEELINGS	CONTROL	TEMPERAMENT	PEERS	YOUNGER	OLDER	ONE TO ONE	GROUP	GOALS	OBJECTS	CAUSALITY	PLAY	LANGUAGE	

Age scale: 18+, 17, 16, 15, 14, 13, **C.A. 12**, 11, 10, 9, 8, 7, 6–

Notes: A = Juan has a little problem dealing with a group—sometimes is overwhelmed.
B = He responds very well to one-on-one adult attention.

FIGURE 1-1 Sample Developmental Profile

A word of caution is in order here. Although needs and skills must be measured to provide a structure for promoting development, estimates of skill development are used only to determine goals and not to label children as better or worse. If several skills are significantly below age expectations, it can provide valuable information to share with other professionals who specialize in diagnosing special needs for infants and toddlers. Development varies widely, especially for babies and young children, so you should assess needs and skill levels on an ongoing basis and be timely in changing your goals to keep up with the rapidly changing child. Development is a continuing process wherein people grow in the same direction at different rates. This idea regarding individual differences will be discussed later in this chapter. But first, our discussion will turn to some of the theories of child development that informed the creation of the Developmental Prescription.

THEORIES OF CHILD DEVELOPMENT

Before the Reformation in sixteenth-century Europe, little importance was placed on children; they were considered little adults. With the Reformation and the Puritan belief in *original sin* came harsh, restrictive child-rearing practices and the idea that the depraved child needed to be tamed (Shahar, 1990).

The seventeenth-century Enlightenment brought new theories of human dignity and respect. Young children were viewed much more humanely. For example, John Locke, a British philosopher, advanced the theory that a child is a *tabula rasa*, or blank slate. According to his theory, children were not basically evil but were completely molded and formed by their early experiences with the adults around them (Locke, 1690/1892).

An important philosopher of the eighteenth century, Jean-Jacques Rousseau, viewed young children as *noble savages* who are naturally born with a sense of right and wrong and an innate ability for orderly, healthy growth (1762/1955). His theory, the first child-centered approach, advanced an important concept still accepted today: the idea of *stages* of child development.

During the late 1800s Charles Darwin's theories of *natural selection* and *survival of the fittest* strongly influenced ideas on child development and care (1859/1936). Darwin's research on many animal species led him to hypothesize that all animals were descendants of a few common ancestors. Darwin's careful observations of child behaviors resulted in the birth of the science of child study.

At the turn of the twentieth century, G. Stanley Hall was inspired by Darwin. Hall worked with one of Darwin's students, Arnold Gesell, to advance the *maturational perspective* that child development is genetically determined and unfolds automatically – leading to universal characteristics or events during particular time periods (Gesell, 1928). Thus, Hall and Gesell are considered founders of the child study movement because of their *normative approach* of observing large numbers of children to establish average or normal expectations (Berk, 1997). At the same time, in France, Alfred Binet was establishing the first operational definition of intelligence by using the normative approach to standardize his intelligence test.

At the turn of the 20th Century, Sigmund Freud was also working on a *theory* of development. His **psychoanalytic theory** explained that infants and toddlers are unique individuals, whose earliest experiences and relationships form the foundation for self-concept, self-esteem, and personality, and are the basis for why we experience life as adults the way that we do (Freud, 1938/1973).

A proponent of Freud, Erik Erikson, expanded Freud's concepts into what became known as the *psychosocial theory* of child development. Erikson's (1950) theory, which is still used in child care today, predicted several stages of development,

Responsive caregivers assist very young children in dealing with strong emotions.

including the development of trust, autonomy, identity, and intimacy. How these stages are dealt with by child development specialists determines individual capacity to contribute to society and experience a happy, successful life.

While Freud and his disciples greatly influenced the fields of child development and care, a parallel approach was being studied, called **behaviorism**. John Watson, who is considered the father of behaviorism, in a historic experiment, taught an 11-month-old named Albert to fear a neutral stimulus (a soft white rat) by presenting the rat several times accompanied by loud noises. Watson and his followers used experiments in **classical conditioning** to promote the idea that the environment is the primary factor determining the growth and development of children. B. F. Skinner and coauthor Belmont (1993) expanded Watson's theories of classical conditioning to demonstrate that child behaviors can be increased or decreased by applying **positive reinforcers** (rewards), such as food and praise, and **negative reinforcers** (punishment), such as criticism and withdrawal of attention.

During the 1950s, social learning theories became popular. Proponents of these theories, led by Albert Bandura, accepted the principles of behaviorism and enlarged on conditioning to include social influences such as modeling, imitation, and observational learning to explain how children develop (Grusec, 1992).

The theorist who has influenced the modern fields of child development and care more than any other is Jean Piaget. Piaget's cognitive developmental theory predicts that children construct knowledge and awareness through manipulation and exploration of the environment, and that cognitive development occurs through observable stages (Beilin, 1992). Piaget's stages of cognitive development have stimulated more research on children than any other theory, and his influences have helped child development specialists view young children as active participants in their own growth and development. Piaget's contributions are clear and have many practical applications for teachers.

Attachment theory also examines how early care, especially relationships between adults and children, impacts later development. Bowlby (1969/2000), after observing children between the ages of one and four years in post–World War II hospitals and institutions who had been separated from their families concluded that "the infant and young child should experience a warm and continuous relationship with his mother (or permanent mother substitute) in which both find satisfaction and enjoyment" in order to grow up mentally healthy (p. 13). Relying heavily on ethological concepts, he proposed that a baby's attachment behaviors (e.g., smiling, crying, clinging) are innate and that they mature at various times during the first two years of life (Bowlby, 1958). The ethological purpose of these behaviors is to keep the infant close to the mother, who keeps the child out of harm's way (Honig, 2002). However, the quality of attachment is not just determined by the infant's behavior. The caregiver's responses to the attachment behaviors serve to create a foundation for their relationship to develop (see, for example, Oppenheim & Koren-Karie, 2002). Attachment history has been associated with emotional, social, and learning outcomes later in life (see Honig, 2002, and Thompson, 2000, for reviews) and has been very influential on classroom practices.

New technologies, such as innovations in noninvasive neuroscience imaging techniques, have begun to significantly impact on our understanding of brain development (Acredolo & Goodwyn, 2000; Shore, 2003). It was once believed that nature, or the basic genetic makeup of a child, played a dominant role in determining both short- and long-term cognitive developmental outcomes. But now, new technologies allow for close examination of nurture, or environmental impacts, on the same outcomes. Scientists have found that harmful, stressful, or neglectful behaviors early in life can affect the development of the brain, potentially leading to lifelong difficulties (Gunnar & Cheatham, 2003; Gunnar, 2006; Legendre, 2003; Morgan et al., 2002; cf. Johnson, 2003). The quality and consistency of early care will affect how a child develops, learns, and copes with and handles life. The more quality interactions you have with the children in your care, the more opportunities there are for positive development.

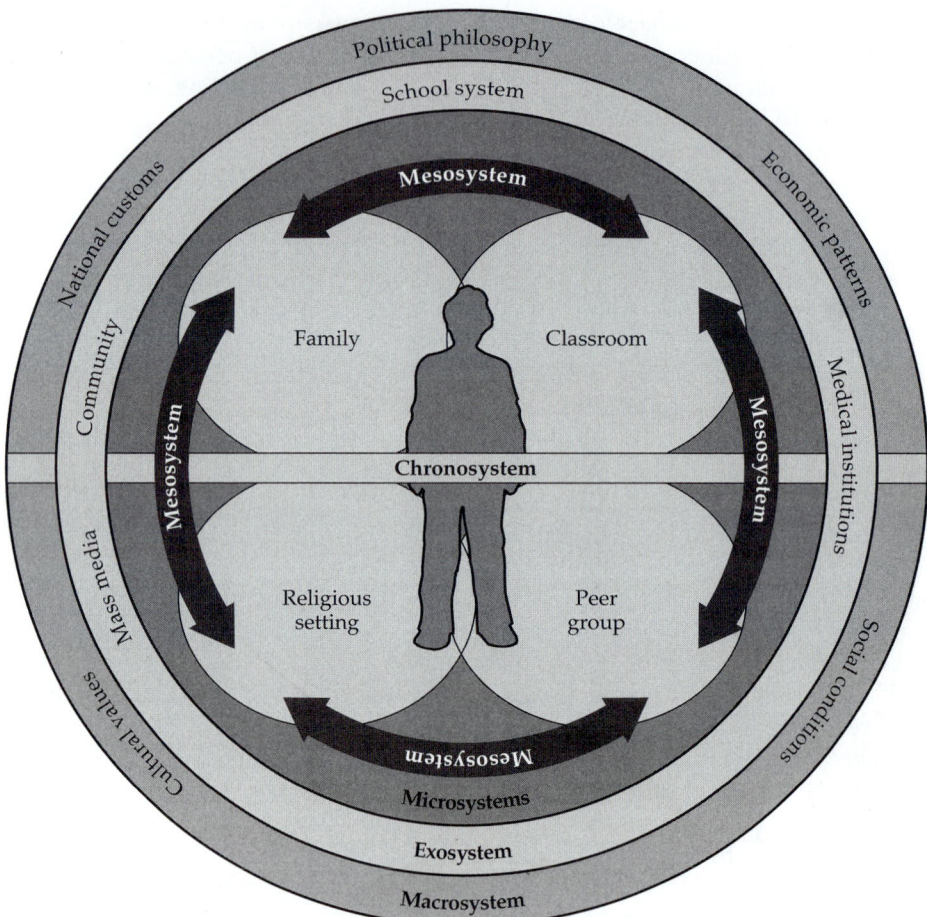

FIGURE 1-2 Model of Urie Bronfenbrenner's ecological systems theory

Another recent theory of child development is the **ecological systems theory** developed by Urie Bronfenbrenner, an American psychologist. Bronfenbrenner (1995) has expanded the view of influences on young children by hypothesizing four nested structures that affect development (see Figure 1–1). At the innermost level is the **microsystem**, which comprises patterns of interactions within the immediate surroundings of the child. This system includes families, early childhood educators, direct influences on the child, and the child's influence on the immediate environment. The **mesosystem** is the next level of influence and includes interactions among the various microsystems. For example, family and teacher interactions in the child care setting represent connections between home and school that impact the child's development. The **exosystem** includes influences with which the child is not directly involved that affect development and care, such as parent education, parent workplace, and the quality and availability of health and social services. The macrosystem consists of the values, laws, resources, and customs of the general culture in which a child is raised. This theory has wide applications in understanding and categorizing the factors that affect child care.

The final developmental theory to be discussed here is the sociocultural theory. A Russian psychologist, Lev Semenovich Vygotsky, hypothesized that culture, meaning the values, beliefs, and customs of a social group, is passed on to the next generation through social interactions between children and their elders (1986). Those social interactions must be at the appropriate level for learning to occur. Adults must observe and assess each child's individual levels of performance as well as her assisted levels of performance on a given task in order to judge what supports (also known as scaffolding) are necessary for promoting learning (Berk & Winsler, 1995; Bodrova & Leong, 2007; Wink & Putney, 2002). Cross-cultural research has supported this theory through findings that young children from various cultures develop unique skills and abilities that are not present in other cultures (Berk, 1997).

Unique Patterns of Development

The theories reviewed above differ in how they view various controversies in development (McDevitt & Ormrod, 2010). For the purposes of this chapter, we will talk about the controversy of universal versus unique patterns of development. Theories on the universal end of the continuum (see Figure 1-3) state that development stages or accomplishments are common to all children. As you can tell from the descriptions above, some theorists such as Piaget and Gesell describe development as occurring in set patterns for all children. In other words, there are universal trends in cognitive reasoning and physical development. From these perspectives, if you know a child's age, you can predict with some degree of confidence how that child might think or act.

On the other end of the controversy, theories espousing a unique view of development suggest that patterns of development cannot be determined or predicted because environmental factors impact each child differently. Ecological systems and sociocultural theories are both examples on this end of the continuum. These theorists did not believe that teachers could predict a child's behaviors or abilities by knowing a child's age or where they are in their development. Each child is unique in his or her progression of skills, knowledge, and behaviors.

Some theories of development are at neither end of the continuum. Rather, they fall somewhere in the middle, suggesting that development is representative of both controversies. Attachment theory, for example, believes that all children experience similar phases; yet, the relationship each child has with her caregivers greatly impacts the type of attachment displayed. Erikson, for another example, suggests that all young

FIGURE 1-3 Continuum for the controversy of universal versus unique development

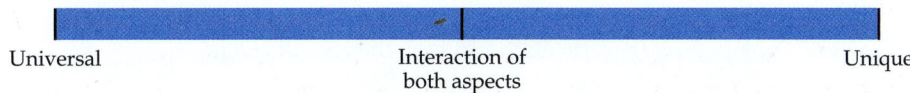

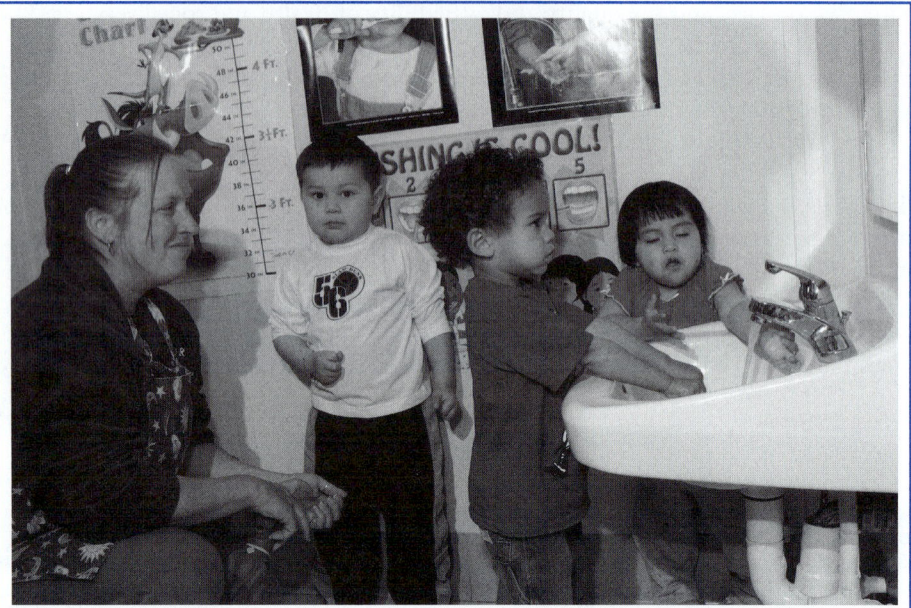

Toddlers share many characteristics, yet they are all developmentally unique.

children experience a series of developmental crises. How each crisis is resolved is associated with environmental factors such as the responsiveness of caregivers.

It must be kept in mind that the United States is a world leader in the fields of child development and care, but we cannot assume that research findings on developmental skills and abilities from primarily Caucasian American children directly apply to other cultures outside, or subcultures within, the United States (Diaz Soto & Swadener, 2002; Matusov, DePalma, and Drye, 2007). Only through taking a developmental perspective and paying close attention to both universal and unique patterns of development will we be able to determine the practices to optimally enhance the growth and development of individual infants and toddlers.

✓ reading checkpoint

Before moving on with your reading, make sure that you can answer the following questions about the material discussed so far.

1. Justify why an infant-toddler teacher should employ a developmental perspective in his work.

2. Explain what the four developmental domains are and why it is useful, yet artificial, to divide development in this manner.

3. Select two developmental theories. Compare and contrast them; in other words, explain how they are alike and how they are different.

Current Trends in Development and Education

Current child care trends considered in this section reflect the research being completed concerning brain development, attachment theory, and sociocultural theory. All of these trends are discussed within the framework of the ecological system of Urie Bronfenbrenner (1995): microsystem, mesosystem, exosystem, and macrosystem. In this system, human relationships are described as bidirectional and reciprocal. *Relating* is the act of being with someone and sharing the same space and setting, expressing needs and accepting responsibility for interacting with each other. Interactions are respectful to all parties involved.

The recommendation to respect children is also expressed by other authorities in child development such as Magda Gerber, who feels that one of the most important aspects of relating to infants is an adult's respect for the child as an individual. The educational leaders of the municipal infant, toddler, and preschool centers of Reggio Emilia, Italy have clearly communicated their beliefs about the rights of children, which include, among other things, the right to be held in high regard and treated respectfully. Similarly, previous editions of this text emphasize that the reader be mindful of positive intentions toward the child and engage in reflective, careful planning, resulting in good outcomes for both.

Trends in the microsystem involve effects that adults and children have on each other. For example, an adult who consciously uses attention, approval, and

A grandparent can share in caring for an infant.

attunement with children elicits a positive response from them. Any third party who is present may also be affected. How this person is affected is determined by whether or not the reciprocal relationship is positive or negative. If the people interacting are supportive, the quality of the relationship is enhanced. An example of how an early childhood educator can enhance an interaction as a third party is explained in detail later in the text.

The microsystem is the closest system to the child. It contains the child, the immediate nuclear family, and others directly relating to the child. There are more children who receive non-familial care in the United States, with many vastly different backgrounds, than ever before. In 2005, 42 percent of U.S. infants and 53 percent of toddlers were cared for regularly—at least once a week—by someone other than a parent (U.S. Department of Education, 2006). These children have widespread cultural differences in customs, family structure, and parenting styles. For example, children experience living with one parent, two parents, grandparents and other extended family members. In addition, more and more children grow up experiencing poverty (see Table 1–2). Respectful, mindful teachers are necessary in all child care settings to promote interest, acceptance, and pride among children and families.

The mesosystem includes child care settings. In the past, it was thought that the immediate family (microsystem) had the greatest single impact on a child's life. However, with so many more people entering the workforce today, the need for child care is so great that this is no longer true. Many young children spend more waking hours with caregivers than they do with their primary families. While initially this was of great concern for many child development experts, they are no longer concerned as long as best practices are adopted by child care programs. Family grouping, continuity of care, primary caregiving, and creating partnerships with families are ways to minimize the effects on children of long hours away from family members.

Family grouping for infants and toddlers involves having a small number of children of different ages in the same classroom. Such living arrangements reproduce relationships that children naturally have in a home setting. For example, families often have siblings who are two or fewer years apart in age. Organizing the program so that the six children who share the room vary in age from a very young infant (e.g., six weeks) to three years of age provides opportunities for interactions that are similar to those that may be found more naturally.

Attachment theory suggests that infants, toddlers, and adults need time to create positive emotional bonds with one another. Having the same teachers work with the same children for a three-year period is one way to promote strong attachments (Bernhardt, 2000; Essa, Favre, Thweatt, & Waugh, 1999; Honig, 2002; Miller, 1999). This type of arrangement is often referred to as **continuity of care**. As this term suggests, emphasis is placed on maintaining relationships for long periods of time. With older children, this is often referred to as *looping*. Continuity of care can appear in several different forms in practice. For example, a teacher and her group

TABLE 1–2 FACTS AND FIGURES ON FAMILIES IN THE UNITED STATES WITH INFANTS AND TODDLERS

ALL INFANTS AND TODDLERS

There are about 12 million infants and toddlers in the United States. Every minute a baby is born to a teen mother.[a]

Every two minutes a baby is born at low birth weight. Black babies are about twice as likely as White or Hispanic babies to have low birth weight.

The infant mortality rate is 6.9 per 1000 live births in the United States, which ranks 25th among industrialized countries on this statistic.

Among two-year olds, one in three children are not fully immunized.

10.5 percent of children age birth – five in the United States do not have health insurance. More than half of those children live in six states: Texas, California, Florida, New York, Georgia, and Illinois.

Thirty-eight percent of infants and toddlers with working mothers spend an average of 35 hours or more a week in child care.

INFANTS AND TODDLERS IN POVERTY

Every 35 seconds a baby is born into poverty.[a] Forty-three percent of infants and toddlers are in families living below or near the federal poverty line. Poverty, however, is related to race and ethnicity with African American, American Indian, and Hispanic infants and toddlers being more than twice as likely to live in poverty as young White children. In addition, 61 percent of infants and toddlers with immigrant parents live in low-income families.

Forty-nine percent of infants and toddlers in urban areas and 53 percent in rural areas live in low-income families.

Most poor infants and toddlers live in families where at least one adult works. Seventy-nine percent of low-income families have at least one parent who works part-time or full-time, part of the year.

Fifty-four percent of infants and toddlers in low-income families live with a single mother.

Only about 3 percent of eligible infants and toddlers are enrolled in the Early Head Start program. Yet, an average of 8.7 million women, infants, and children participated in the WIC program each month in 2008. Data for April 2009 showed more than 9.1 million participants; this number is expected to rise as the recession continues.

Children under age three in low-income families with employed mothers were less likely to be in some kind of regular nonparental child care arrangement (62 percent) than higher-income children (68 percent).

[a]Based on calculations per school day (180 days of seven hours each).

Sources: National Center for Children in Poverty (2008) *Basic Facts About Low-Income Children: Birth to Age 3* (retrieved December 31, 2008, from http://www.nccp.org/); Children's Defense Fund (2008) *State of America's Children* (retrieved December 31, 2008, from http://childrensdefense.org); and United States Department of Agriculture (2009) Monthly Data (retrieved August 10, 2009, from http://www.fns.usda.gov/pd/37WIC_Monthly.htm).

of children could remain in one classroom for the infant and toddler years, changing furniture, instructional tools, and supplies as needed to respond to the developing capabilities of the children. In contrast, a teacher and her group of children could move each year into a new classroom which already is equipped with age-appropriate furniture, supplies, and materials.

Another way to help adults bond with infants is to divide the work using a **primary caregiving system** (Kovach & De Ros, 1998). In this method, one teacher in the room is primarily responsible for half of the children, and the other teacher is primarily responsible for the rest. While a teacher would never ignore the expressed needs of any infant or toddler, she is able to invest time and energy into coming to understand a smaller group of children and their families. Frequently, the primary caregiver is the person responsible for providing assistance during routine care times such as diapering, feeding, or napping.

Keep in mind that caregiving factors at the mesosystem level exert bidirectional influences. Of particular importance at this level is the relationship that teachers

Infants, toddlers, and adults need time to create positive emotional bonds with one another.

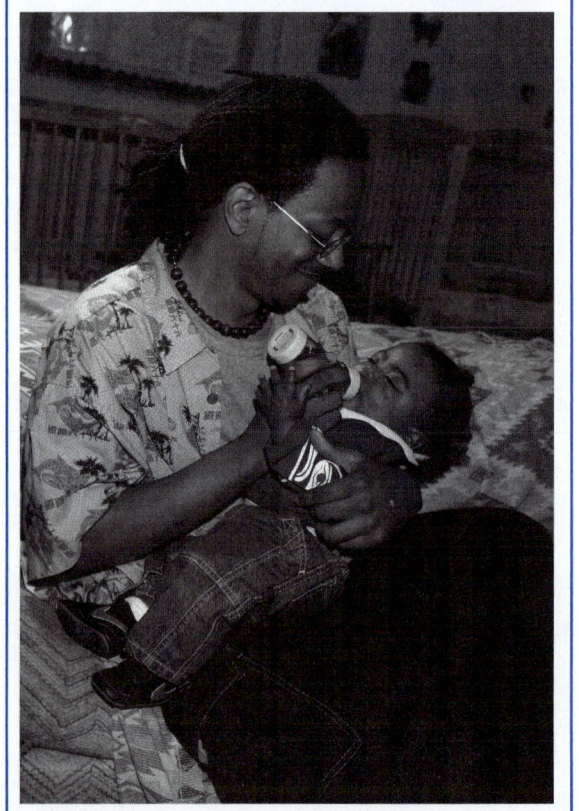

have with families. The transition between home and school should be smooth and continuous. The only pathway for achieving that is through *partnering* with families. Families are experts on their children. Recognizing, supporting, and utilizing this can significantly improve your effectiveness as a caregiver and educator. On the other hand, you are an expert on this time period—infancy and toddlerhood—given your vast experiences with numerous children of this age and your intentional studying of child development. Help each person bring his or her strengths to the relationship. Valuing each family's childrearing practices while helping them to understand child development is not only respectful but also part of your ethical responsibility (NAEYC, 2005a).

Another trend in the mesosystem of child care bears mentioning. Due to the many recent, highly publicized, violent acts by school-age children against peers, there has been renewed interest in violence among children throughout the United States. This interest can be a positive trend because social pressure to understand and stop the causes of violence among young children can result in better parenting and child care practices. Many movements against violence are aimed at the care of preschool-age children. For example, NAEYC has established ACT (Adults and Children Together) Against Violence, "a campaign in conjunction with the American Psychological Association and the Ad Council to teach young children positive, nonviolent ways to respond to conflict, anger, and frustration" (NAEYC, 2001). Teaching young children to become more emotionally intelligent instead of merely cognitively intelligent is one of the most important trends in child development and care today; a trend that will become even more important as people live closer together.

All of these factors at the mesosystem level have been shown to result in positive outcomes for children, families, teachers, and programs. Used in combination, the effects can be particularly strong. Our purpose in highlighting the relationships between the nested systems is to help you understand that the purpose of child care is not to replace familial influences on very young children but rather to enhance them.

The exosystem refers to social settings that do not contain the child but still directly affect the child's development, such as community health services and other public agencies. This structure manifests itself in the work of grassroots groups and professional organizations who lobby and advocate for quality child care services.

Many local, regional, and national organizations stress child care advocacy that sets higher standards of care, along with education that touches each child in the community. NAEYC, for example, has created standards defining high quality early educational programs. The accreditation process, recently revised, is a way for programs to demonstrate they are providing exceptional care and educational experiences for young children. Hence, this organization, while a part of the exosystem, can directly impact the work of teachers in early education programs. Moreover, this association works with other agencies to advocate for best practices. To illustrate, they worked with the International Reading Association to create a position statement on learning to read and write, and they have an ongoing working relationship with the National Council for Accreditation of Teacher Education (NCATE) to create and monitor teacher preparation programs to ensure they achieve high standards for educating future professionals.

Being an advocate yourself might seem like an overwhelming task. However, each time you interact with family members, colleagues, and community members, you are a teacher-leader. Your dedication to engaging in and sharing professional knowledge and practices makes you an advocate for young children, families, and the early childhood profession.

Other social policies also are affected by the availability, affordability, and quality of care for very young children. The following current issues in development and care are discussed in depth in later chapters:

- child abuse and neglect
- homelessness
- divorce and its impact on the family
- children with special needs
- the impact of AIDS on the community
- adverse environmental factors
- education of early childhood educators

Next we turn to trends within the macrosystem, the most general level of Bronfenbrenner's ecological systems theory. The child is ultimately affected by decisions made at this level because the macrosystem consists of the laws, customs, and general policies of the social system (government). This is where the availability of resources (money in particular) is determined. The macrosystem structure of the United States went through a remarkable change in the late 1990s. This can be understood best by explaining the changes in welfare reform legislation.

In the late 1980s and early 1990s child care needs increased significantly in the United States. In response to this need, providers expanded existing centers and opened new ones. This expansion increased the need for new curricula, materials, teachers, and directors. Training programs centered their efforts on the quality of services offered to families and children and continued to raise the standard of child care with federal and state investments. Laws were later passed to emphasize moving people from welfare into the workforce.

By 2003, the federal budget for Early Head Start was $653.7 million for over 700 programs, serving more than 62,000 children under the age of three (Mann, Bogle, & Parlakian, 2004). The money is used to provide a variety of services to low income families with children under the age of three and to poor pregnant women. While those figures may sound impressive, Early Head Services reach only about 3 percent of the infants and toddlers who are eligible for its services (Mann, et al, 2004). Even though far too few children are served by this important program, the children who are enrolled have documented positive outcomes in cognitive development, greater vocabularies, and social-emotional development (National Head Start Association [NHSA], 2007).

Because of the emphasis on work, welfare reform placed significant stress on the existing system of early childhood services and caused broad ramifications for the quality, accessibility, and affordability of services for poor and working families. Given the economic crisis of 2008 and 2009 in the United States, advocates for young children are working to find creative solutions to ease the effects of job loss and provide additional access to Early Head Start programs. On January 8, 2009, President Obama was asked to allocate 4.3 billion dollars as part of the economic recovery package to Early Head Start and Head Start (NHSA, 2009). This money would be used to expand high quality programs, alleviating stress on families. While those requests for funds were not met, in February 2009, the House and Senate did approve 1.0 billion dollars for Head Start with an additional 1.1 billion dollars for expanding Early Head Start (Grabell & Weaver, 2009).

This expansion adds to current concerns about methods of monitoring quality in child care; the ability to compensate teachers and directors; and the ability of programs to support and respond to the family's changing roles. Professionals have been working diligently to improve the minimal educational requirements for child care teachers by demanding that their local governments raise training and care standards. NAEYC, for example, has raised standards for teacher qualifications while maintaining their high standards for teacher-child ratios (NAEYC, 2005b). Taken together, these requirements demonstrate that good, affordable child care is not a luxury or fringe benefit for working families but essential brain food for the next generation.

VALUING CULTURAL DIVERSITY

As mentioned previously, child care settings are becoming increasingly diverse. We cannot ignore these differences, but rather need to respect, embrace, and value them. It is important for the early childhood educator to accept the challenge to develop a multicultural curriculum that involves both parents and children, because many young families are beginning to explore their own cultural backgrounds.

Multicultural curriculum development fits into Vygotsky's theory of the dissemination of culture. He viewed "cognitive development as a socially mediated process . . . as dependent on the support that adults and more mature peers provide as children try new tasks" (Berk, 1997). A culturally rich curriculum encourages the recognition of cultural differences and helps young families connect with the traditions of their own heritage and culture.

Each person employed in early childhood education draws upon his or her own cultural model for behavior that is both relevant and meaningful within his or her particular social and cultural group. The knowledge and understanding that caregivers use with families is drawn primarily from two sources: their educational knowledge base and their personal experiences as family members and educators. Therefore, we need to recognize and continually re-examine the way we put our knowledge into practice. We need to develop **scripts** that allow us to learn more about the families' cultural beliefs and values regarding the various aspects of child rearing. In other words, we must create a method or sequence of events for getting to know each family. That way we can understand the family's actions, attitudes, and behavior, as well as their dreams and hopes for their child.

Consideration of cultural models can help us bring coherence to the various pieces of information that we are gathering about families and organize our interpretation of that information. Organizing and ongoing reflection upon what parents tell us about their strategies can help us discover their cultural model for caregiving, and then compare it with the cultural models that guide our own practice (Finn, 2003).

We caregivers must recognize the richness and opportunity available to us in our work with families of diverse ethnic, racial, and cultural groups. We can learn the different ways that families provide care for their children when they are all striving toward similar goals—happy and healthy children who can function successfully within the family culture and the greater community. We can use that knowledge to construct a cultural model of culturally responsive practice, designed to support families in their caregiving and assist them in meeting their goals for their children (Finn, 2003).

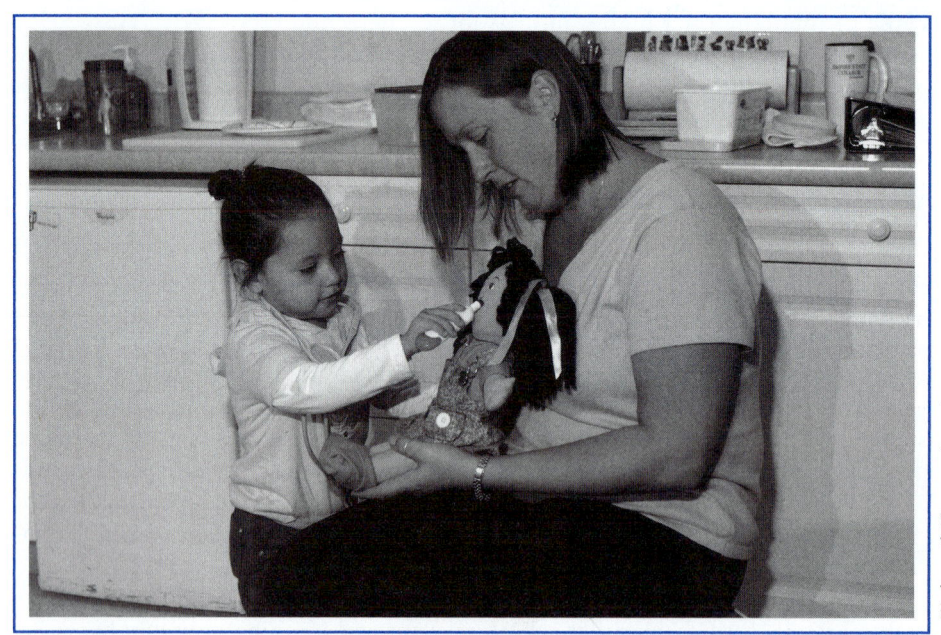

More children with a wide diversity of backgrounds are in early childhood education programs.

Bronfenbrenner's ecological systems theory assumes the interconnectedness of each person to others and examines the ways in which one system affects another. It recognizes the importance of respecting each individual's uniqueness and considers carefully the decisions made at every level that affect us all.

Transactional theories, such as Bronfenbrenner's, view care from the perspective of how the child interacts with and affects the environment (Sameroff, Seifer, Baldwin, & Baldwin, 1993). These theories help us understand that children are not passive recipients of whatever happens in their environment, but are very involved in influencing their environment and aiding their own development. It is important for the primary caregiver to understand that even newborns have a part in their own growth and development. Infants' wants, needs, and desires must be respected.

To summarize, current trends in child care involve the bidirectional and reciprocal relationship between the child and his or her environment. Early childhood education programs serve children from a wide diversity of backgrounds. As a result, there is an increased need for teacher education; parent education, including proper selection of care settings; innovative and child-centered practices such as continuity of care; effective use of resources; social and political advocacy for high-quality, affordable, and accessible care; and use of culturally diverse materials in child care curricula.

✓ reading checkpoint

Before moving on with your reading, make sure that you can answer the following questions about the material discussed so far.

1. Explain at least four of the current trends in early care and development.

2. How does the diversity of families in today's society influence early education programs and teachers?

Take it as your individual responsibility to be aware of the power of your actions and their immediate and future impact on children. When you see that the early childhood educator also directly influences the family, community, and culture, you can truly understand the old African saying, "It takes a village to raise a child." This often quoted saying is a simple way to understand that Bronfenbrenner's term *bidirectional* describes the relationships that influence a child, occurring between child and mother, child and father, child and teacher, and explains that the influences go both ways.

SUMMARY

Educators must come to understand universal and unique patterns of development within the four major areas: physical, emotional, social, and cognitive/language. When teachers working with infants and toddlers adopt a developmental perspective, they are more apt to address the capabilities of the children in their care. Therefore, this chapter provided an overview of major developmental theorists and theories that impact teacher behaviors and classroom practices. Bronfenbrenner's theory was utilized as a framework for understanding contextual variables which directly and indirectly impact children's development.

key terms

behaviorism	maturational perspective	positive reinforcers
classical conditioning	mesosystem	primary caregiving system
cognitive developmental theory	microsystem	psychoanalytic theory
continuity of care	milestones	psychosocial theory
developmental perspective	modeling	scripts
ecological systems theory	natural selection	social learning theories
ethological	negative reinforcers	sociocultural theory
exosystem	noble savages	stages
family grouping	normative approach	survival of the fittest
imitation	observational learning	tabula rasa
macrosystem	original sin	

case study

Trisha

Trisha works at the Little Folks Child Care Center as an assistant teacher while she attends classes at a local community college to earn her associate degree in early childhood education. She was surprised to learn that her center was using family grouping with continuity of care. Although she always knew that she had the same children from the time they enrolled until they were around three years of age, she did not know it was associated with a particular term or of such great educational value. Currently she assists the head teacher with caring for eight children who range in age from eight weeks to 17 months. Like those in the rest of the program, this group of children is culturally diverse. Trisha has worked with parents, staff, and the children on multicultural issues; she always attempts to learn more about each culture represented in her room. As part of a course, she organized a tool for gathering information about child-rearing practices and used the results to individualize routine care times.

As she has learned new ideas, such as the primary caregiving system, accreditation standards, and Bronfenbrenner's ecological systems theory, she has assumed a more active role in the microsystem. She has repeatedly discussed with her director and lead teacher the need to reduce the number of infants and toddlers per classroom to six and to adopt a primary caregiving system. While they are enthusiastic about learning more about the primary caregiving system, they have not yet seriously considered cutting the class size by two children per room, due to financial concerns.

1. Provide two examples of how Trisha has, in her words, "assumed a more active role in the microsystem."
2. In what other systems does Trisha work? Provide examples for each system you identify.
3. What might be the added benefits of the center adopting a primary caregiving system even if it is not possible for them to reduce the number of children in each room?

QUESTIONS AND EXPERIENCES FOR REFLECTION

1. Observe two children and take notes on the behaviors they exhibit during the period of one hour. Use the Developmental Prescriptions in Appendix A to analyze their skills.

2. Which developmental theory do you think would most influence your behavior as a professional educator? Why?

3. Think about two or three experiences you had as a student in a high school or college setting. Explain those experiences by using as many of the four systems of Bronfenbrenner's ecological theory as possible. Consider bidirectional influences in your analysis as well.

4. Talk with a teacher who is currently working with infants and/or toddlers. What does she see as the most important issue she faces in her job? How does she address that issue? What additional support or information could she use to be more effective in addressing that issue?

5. What experiences did you have growing up with people who were different from yourself? Consider all of the ways in which people differ including, but not limited to, race or ethnicity, religion, ability, or sexual orientation. How did you react to those differences?

REFERENCES

Acredolo, L. P., & Goodwyn, S. (2000). *Baby minds: Brain-building games your baby will love.* New York: Bantam Books.

Beilin, H. (1992). Piaget's enduring contribution to developmental psychology. *Developmental Psychology, 28,* 191–204.

Berk, L. E. (1997). *Child development* (4th ed.). Boston: Allyn and Bacon.

Berk, L. E., & Winsler, A. (1995). *NAEYC Research into Practice Series: Vol. 7. Scaffolding children's learning: Vygotsky and early childhood education.* Washington, DC: National Association for the Education of Young Children.

Bernhardt, J. L. (2000). A primary caregiving system for infants and toddlers: Best for everyone involved. *Young Children, 55*(2), 74–80.

Bodrova, E., & Leong, D. J. (2007). *Tools of the mind: The Vygotskian approach to early childhood education* (2nd ed.). Upper Saddle River, NJ: Prentice Hall.

Bowlby, J. (1958). The nature of the child's tie to its mother. *International Journal of Psychoanalysis, 39,* 350–373.

Bowlby, J. (2000). *Attachment and loss: Vol. 1. Attachment.* New York: Basic Books. (Original work published 1969).

Bronfenbrenner, U. (1995). The bioecological model from a life course perspective: Reflections of a participant observer. In P. Moen, G. H. Elder, Jr., & K. Luscher (Eds.), *Examining lives in context* (pp. 599–618). Washington, DC: American Psychological Association.

Darwin, C. (1936). *On the origin of species by means of natural selection.* New York: Modern Library. (Original work published 1859)

Diaz Soto, L., & Swadener, B. B. (2002). Towards liberatory early childhood theory, research, and praxis: Decolonizing a field. *Contemporary Issues in Early Childhood, 3* (1), 38-66.

Erikson, E. H. (1950). *Childhood and society.* New York: Norton.

Essa, E. L., Favre, K., Thweatt, G., & Waugh, S. (1999). Continuity of care for infants and toddlers. *Early Child Development and Care, 148,* 11–19.

Finn, C. D. (2003). *Cultural Models for Early Caregiving.* Washington, DC: Zero to Three.

Freud, S. (1973). *An outline of psychoanalysis.* London: Hogarth Press. (Original work published 1938)

Gerber, M., & Weaver, J. (Ed.). (1998). *Dear parent: Caring for infants with respect.* Los Angeles: Resources for Infant Educarers (RIE).

Gesell, A. (1928). *Infancy and human growth*. NY: Macmillan.

Grabell, M., & Weaver, C. (2009). The stimulus plan: A detailed list of spending. Retrieved August 10, 2009 from http://www.propublica.org/special/the-stimulus-plan-a-detailed-list-of-spending

Grusec, J. E. (1992). Social learning theory and developmental psychology: The legacies of Robert Sears and Albert Bandura. *Developmental Psychology, 28*, 776–786.

Gunnar, M. G., & Cheatham, C. L. (2003). Brain and behavior interface: Stress and the developing brain. *Infant Mental Health Journal, 24*(3), 195–211.

Gunnar, M. (2006). Stress, nurture, and the young brain. In J. R. Lally, P. L. Mangione, & D. Greenwald (Eds.), *Concepts for care: 20 essays on infant/toddler development and learning.* Sausalito, CA: WestEd. pp. 41-44.

Honig, A. S. (2002). *Secure relationships: Nurturing infant/toddler attachment in early care settings.* Washington, DC: National Association for the Education of Young Children.

Hyson, M. (Ed.). (2003). *Preparing early childhood professionals: NAEYC's standards for programs.* Washington, DC: National Association for the Education of Young Children.

Johnson, M. H. (2003). Neuroscience perspectives: Development of human brain functions. *Biological Psychiatry, 54*, 1312–1316.

Kovach, B. A., & De Ros, D. A. (1998). Respectful, individual, and responsive caregiving for infants: The key to successful care in group settings. *Young Children, 53*(3), 61–64.

Legendre, A. (2003). Environmental features influencing toddlers' bioemotional reactions in day care centers. *Environment and Behavior, 35*, 523–549.

Locke, J. (1892). Some thoughts concerning education. In R. J. Quick, (Ed.), *Locke on education* (pp. 1–236). Cambridge, London: Cambridge University Press. (Original work published 1690)

Mann, T. L., Bogle, M. M., & Parlakian, R. (2004). Early Head Start: An overview. In J. Lombardi and M. M. Bogle (Eds.). *Beacon of hope: The promise of Early Head Start for America's youngest children.* Washington, DC: Zero to Three. pp. 1-19.

Matusov, E., DePalma, R., & Drye, S. (2007). Whose development? Salvaging the concept of development within a sociocultural approach to education. *Educational Theory, 57* (4), 403-421.

McDevitt, T. M., & Ormrod, J. E. (2010). *Child development: Educating and working with children and adolescents* (4th ed.). Upper Saddle River, NJ: Pearson Prentice Hall.

Miller, K. (1999, September). Caring for the little ones: Continuity of care. *Child Care Information Exchange,* 94–97.

Morgan, B., Finan, A., Yarnold, R., Petersen, S., Rickett, A., & Wailoo, M. (2002). Assessment of infant physiology and neuronal development using magnetic resonance imaging. *Child: Care, Health & Development, 28*, Suppl. 1, 7–10.

National Association for the Education of Young Children. (2001). ACT (Adults and Children Together) Against Violence. *Young Children, 5*, 55.

National Association for the Education of Young Children. (2005a, April). Position Statement. Code of ethical conduct and statement of commitment. Retrieved October 31, 2006, from http://www.naeyc.org/about/positions/pdf/PSETH05.PDF

National Association for the Education of Young Children. (2005b, April). *NAEYC Early Childhood Program Standards and Accreditation Criteria.* Retrieved January 2, 2009 from http://www.naeyc.org/academy/standards/

National Head Start Association (2007). Research bites. Retrieved January 14, 2009 from http://www.nhsa.org/research/research_re_bites.htm

National Head Start Association (2009, January). Press Release. Up to 120,000 new jobs in worst-off U.S. communities possible from $4.3 billion boost for Head Start in Economic Recovery Package. Retrieved January 14, 2009 from http://www.nhsa.org/press/News_Archived/index_news_010809.htm

Oppenheim, D., & Koren-Karie, N. (2002). Mothers' insightfulness regarding their children's internal worlds: The capacity underlying secure child-mother relationships. *Infant Mental Health Journal, 23*, 593–605.

Rousseau, J. J. (1955). *Emile*. New York: Dutton. (Original work published 1762)

Sameroff, A. J., Seifer, R., Baldwin, A., & Baldwin, C. (1993). Stability of intelligence from preschool to adolescence: The influence of social and family risk factors. *Child Development, 64*, 80–97.

Shahar, S. (1990). *Childhood in the Middle Ages* (C. Galai, Trans.). London: Routledge.

Shore, R. (2003). *Rethinking the brain: New insights into early development* (rev. ed.). New York: Families and Work Institute.

Skinner, E. A., & Belmont, M. J. (1993). Motivation in the classroom: Reciprocal effects of teacher behavior and student engagement across the school year. *Journal of Educational Psychology, 85*, 571–581.

Thompson, R. (2000). The legacy of early attachment. *Child Development, 71*, 145–152.

U.S. Department of Education. (2006). Initial results from the 2005 NHES Early Childhood Program Participation Survey. Retrieved from http://nces.ed.gov/pubs2006/earlychild/tables/table_1.asp?referrer=report on December 29, 2008.

Vygotsky, L. S. (1986). *Thought and language* (A. Kozulin, Trans.). Cambridge, MA: MIT Press. (Original work published 1934)

Wink, J., & Putney, L. (2002). *A vision of Vygotsky*. Boston: Allyn & Bacon.

ADDITIONAL RESOURCES

Dunn, M., Mutuku, M., & Wolfe, R. (2004). Developmentally and culturally appropriate practice in the global village: The Kenya Literacy Project. *Young Children, 59*(5), 50–55.

Edwards, C. P., & Raikes, H. (2002). Extending the dance: Relationship-based approaches to infant/toddler care and education. *Young Children, 57*(4), 10–17.

Eliot, L. (2000). *What is going on in there? How the brain and mind develop in the first five years of life*. New York: Bantam Books.

Gallagher, K. C. (2005). Brain research and early childhood development: A primer for developmentally appropriate practice. *Young Children, 60*(4), 12–18, 20.

Gerber, M. (1989). *Educaring: Resources for infant educarers*. Los Angeles: Resources for Infant Educarers.

Grolnich, W. S., & Slowiacvek, M. L. (1994). Parents' involvement in children's schooling: A multi-dimensional conceptualization and motivational model. *Child Development, 65*, 237–252.

Hyun, E. (1998). *Rethinking childhood: Vol. 3. Making sense of developmentally and culturally appropriate practice (DCAP) in early childhood education*. New York: P. Lang.

Lynch, E. W., & Hanson, M. J. (2004). *Developing cross-cultural competence: A guide for working with children and their families* (3rd ed.). Baltimore: Paul H. Brookes.

For additional activities, web links, and other resources, please visit our website at www.cengage.com/education/swim

chapter 2

BIRTH TO THIRTY-SIX MONTHS: PHYSICAL AND COGNITIVE/LANGUAGE DEVELOPMENTAL PATTERNS

learning objectives

After reading this chapter, you should be able to:
- Define the differences between development and learning.
- Identify typical patterns of physical and cognitive/language development between birth and thirty-six months of age.
- Understand the characteristics and care of children with special rights related to physical and cognitive development.

chapter outline

- Differences between Development and Learning
- Patterns of Physical Development
- Patterns of Cognitive and Language Development
- Children with Special Rights
- Case Study: Sasha

DIFFERENCES BETWEEN DEVELOPMENT AND LEARNING

As mentioned in Chapter 1, developmental theories differ on a number of controversies. That chapter discussed universal versus unique patterns of development. In this chapter, we will investigate briefly the nature versus nurture controversy. Some theorists contend that child development is the result of heredity and natural biological processes, largely independent of learning and experience (nature), whereas others argue that development mostly depends on learning (nurture) (McDevitt & Ormrod, 2010). The best conclusion to date is that child development is a very complex process occurring through natural sequences and patterns that depend on learning and experience, among other processes (McDevitt & Ormrod, 2010).

Based on the nature-nurture complexity, this book defines **development** as cumulative sequences and patterns that represent progressive, refined changes that move a child from simple to more complex physical, cognitive, language, social, and emotional growth and maturity. It is recognized that while children grow in the developmental areas in the same general sequences and patterns, each child is affected differently by social, cultural, and environmental influences. Children move through these developmental sequences at widely varying rates.

In contrast, **learning** is operationally defined as the acquisition of knowledge and skills through systematic study, instruction, practice, and/or experience. This definition takes into consideration both overt behavioral changes in responses and more internal changes in perceptions resulting from practice or conscious awareness, or both. In other words, changes in a response to a stimulus can either be observable to another person (overt) or can occur internally without obvious change in observable behavior (internal). Both overt and internal learning occurs during the first three years of life. Therefore, caregivers must consistently observe the child very closely to understand how changes in responses create the perceptions, thoughts, beliefs, attitudes, feelings, and behaviors that constitute the young child's evolving map of the world. The biggest challenge for early childhood specialists is to understand each child's individual map for development and learning, since no two individuals can have the same one.

Figure 2-1 represents three different ways to conceptualize the relationship between development and learning. Given the definitions provided of each, which representation do you think fits best and why?

PATTERNS OF PHYSICAL DEVELOPMENT

Physical development includes neurological, gross physical, sensory, teething, motor, sleep, and elimination development. Each of these is discussed below.

Neurological Development
The nervous system is responsible for communication among all body parts and ultimately with the environment. This section defines and familiarizes the reader

A Separate concepts

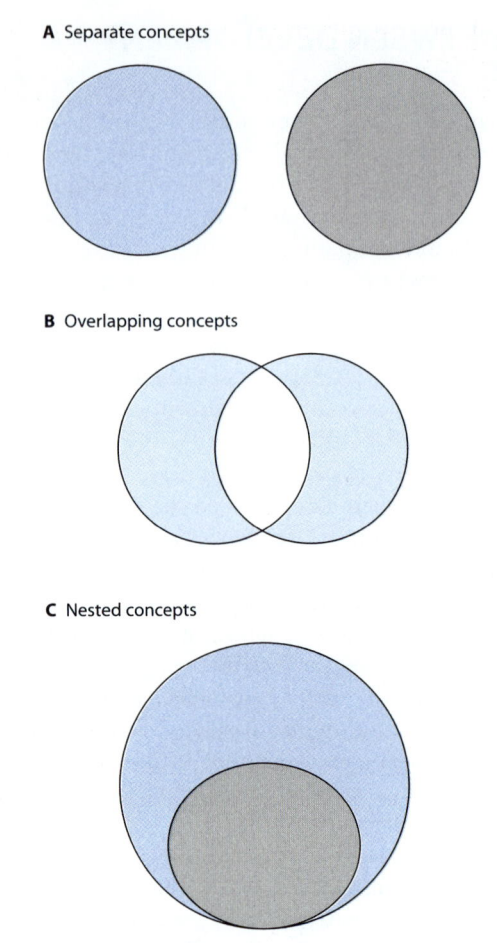

B Overlapping concepts

C Nested concepts

FIGURE 2-1 Possible conceptualizations of the relationship between development and learning

with the major nervous system functions. Newborns are complex beings whose growth and development are closely related to the health and integrity of the nervous system, which is made up of the brain, the spinal cord, and nerve cells (neurons).

At birth, the brain weighs 25 percent of an adult's, and by 24 months it has tripled its weight, being 75 percent of an adult's. This increased weight is due to specific brain cells, called glia, which consist of a fatty sheathing called myelin. Myelin is a substance that protects, coats, and insulates neurons, helping connect impulses from one neuron to another. These impulses are coded information lines that function like insulated electrical wires, carrying vital current to where it is needed in the body and brain. The myelin coating promotes the transfer of information from one neuron to another. This process, however, is not entirely under the control of genetic codes or biologically-driven factors.

As mentioned in Chapter 1, new technologies have led to a better understanding of how brain development results from complex interactions between nature (i.e., genetic makeup) and nurture (i.e., environmental factors). Genes are initially responsible for the basic wiring of the human brain. By the end of the eighth week of pregnancy the foundation for all body structures, including the brain and nervous system, is evident in the growing fetus. The electrical activity of brain cells while still in the womb changes the physical structure of the brain, just as it will facilitate learning after birth.

The growth and strength of the brain are directly influenced by which neurological circuits are activated and the number of times they are used (Johnson, 1999). At birth the brain is packed with an estimated 100 billion neurons, whose job is to store and transmit information. The newborn's brain is constantly taking in information available in the environment, utilizing all existing senses. The brain records these pieces of information, whether they are emotional, physical (sensory), social, or cognitive in origin. This information influences the shape and circuitry of the neurons, or brain cells. The more data taken in, the stronger the neuron connections and pathways become. A repeated behavior or the consistency of a behavior increases the chance of the pathway becoming strong. Each surviving neuron can make over 10,000 different connections to other cells over time (Beatty, 1995).

The brain has two specific yet different modes for responding to environmental inputs. First, if there is not a consistent pattern of stimulation introduced to the brain, the brain's job is to cut off the circuitry to that area, and the potential growth for a skill is significantly minimized. Many neurons will die due to lack of stimulation. In fact, through competition the brain eliminates, or *prunes*, synapses that are seldom used and leaves a pattern of emotion and thought (Nash, 1997). The second mode is called *brain plasticity*. This concept refers to the process of adaptation; when one part of the brain is damaged, another part of the brain takes over the functions of the damaged area. It also means that if there is a major change in the environment, infants can form new neural pathways to adapt to the change. However, the human brain does not have infinite capacity to change; not all damage can be compensated for, and not all neural pathways can be replaced. What this means for us as caregivers is that infants and toddlers are in the process of forming nerve pathways, and by providing them with the proper nutrition and experiences, we can influence the quality of their brain development.

Pathways and networks of neurons must be organized to carry coded information from all body parts to the brain. Thus, the brain is a complex system which is divided into three main parts; each part is further divided into specialized regions with specific functions (McDevitt & Ormrod, 2010). The hindbrain is responsible for regulating automatic functions, such as breathing, digestion, alertness, balance, and movement. This is also the site for storing emotional knowledge. Another part of the brain, called the midbrain, connects the hindbrain to the forebrain.

Like an old-time telephone operator's switchboard, this part of the brain tells the forebrain what messages from the hindbrain to respond to. The forebrain is what distinguishes our species as human; it contains the cerebral cortex which produces all of our complex thoughts, emotional responses, decision-making, reasoning, and communicating.

Considered the most important part of the brain, the cerebral cortex is the slowest-growing and largest part. The cerebral cortex begins at around 12 months to organize and specify functions for neuron activity. Other parts of the brain continue to grow rapidly only through the second year, whereas the cerebral cortex continues to grow until the fourth decade of life. The nervous system is the "command center" for all the vital functions of the body.

The cerebral cortex receives stimuli in the form of sensory information. Associations are formed between the thought processes and physical actions or experiences. Specific areas of the cerebral cortex control special functions, such as planning, vision, hearing, and production of language. Neurological development of these specialized areas follows predictable patterns as the overall development of the child progresses due to related brain development.

Brain development during infancy is best promoted when caregivers provide tasks that challenge children's emerging skills and abilities. For example, when infants are able to push up, adults can lay them on their bellies with an interesting toy or mirror at their sight level. During such interactions, adults need to provide support and guidance that is nurturing, responsive, and reassuring. When they act in this manner, it helps to build attachments between infants and adults (discussed in greater detail later in this section) which help very young children to develop not only emotionally but also physically and intellectually. Responsive adults tend to provide infants proper nutrition, protect them from harm, soothe them when they are distressed, and talk about objects, patterns, or people who have attracted their attention (Eliot, 1999; Shore, 2003). Immersion in a language-rich environment that includes sign language can stimulate brain development. Using sign language designed specifically for infants (see Acredolo, Goodwyn, & Abrams, 2009, for example) can promote language, memory, and concept development. Signaling needs and desires through simple gestures enables very young children to take an active part in interactions and helps to diminish frustration. Signing has been used successfully with children of diverse abilities, including those with autism and Down syndrome.

On the other hand, unresponsive, harmful, stressful, or neglectful caregiving behaviors affect the development of the brain negatively. For example, children who experience unresponsive and stressful conditions, either in a home or child care setting, were found to have elevated cortisol levels (see Gunnar & Cheatham, 2003, for a review). Monitoring cortisol levels in children may help in creating interventions and prevent negative outcomes associated with high levels of cortisol in adults, such as anxiety disorders and cognitive disturbances (for reviews, see Gunnar, 2001, and Lupien & McEwen, 1997, respectively).

Thus, responsive caregiving by parents, teachers, and others is a major factor in brain development. Competent caregivers for infants and toddlers recognize the impact they have on the children's neurological growth; they initiate activities that reinforce the natural sequences of behaviors supporting healthy growth in all areas. The adult role is critical because early experiences significantly affect how each child's brain is wired (Herr & Swim, 2002). Positive social, emotional, cognitive, language, and physical experiences all influence the development of a healthy brain (Acredolo & Goodwyn, 2000; Herr & Swim, 2002).

Physical Growth

The brain grows from the inside out. The size of the head doesn't change as drastically as the weight of the head (i.e., the head weighs three times more at age two than at birth). This weight is caused by the growing density of the brain, due to developing neuron pathways. Motor neuron pathways apparently expect specific stimuli at birth. These pathways are called experience-expectant. The environment provides expected stimuli; for example, reflex sucking during breastfeeding is experience-expectant. Infant survival obviously depends on experience-expectant pathways. Another set of neuron pathways, called experience-dependent, seems to wait for new experience before activation. Specific experience-dependent cells form synapses for stable motor patterns only after environmental stimuli are repeated several times. When stimulation from the environment occurs in a consistent way, a stable pathway is created and physical changes occur in the nervous system. One of the human brain's greatest assets is this ability to change neurologically and behaviorally from experience, allowing us our unique flexibility and adaptability to the environment.

Human babies are different from those of any other species because they cannot stand immediately after birth and so cannot get themselves out of harm's way. However, the gestation process results in a complete person because if it took any longer, the head would be too big to complete delivery safely. The newborn's head is the largest part of the body and is usually born first. The circumference of the head increases by about three inches during the first eight months, and by two years of age the head is 90 percent of adult size (Lamb & Campos, 1982). At birth, the baby's head is not fused but has "soft spots" in the front and back. The back soft spot closes after a few months, but the front spot stays soft for almost two years.

Reflexes are the beginnings of more complex behavior. As the cerebral cortex develops rapidly in the first weeks of life, reflexes quickly change from involuntary reactions to purposeful, intentional actions that support the growing child over time.

Children usually gain body weight at an astounding rate during the first 12 months of life as long as they are physically nurtured and active; however, children who are restrained from physical movement often gain weight at a slower rate. Height usually parallels weight, so children who gain weight slowly in the first three years also tend to grow in height slowly. The caregiver should be aware that there are large variations in the rate of physical growth in children under three years of age. Growth spurts and plateaus are normal for development of height, weight, activity levels, and so on; therefore, the caregiver should keep careful records of physical milestones and consult with parents and health professionals on body development.

Hearing and Vision Development

Newborns respond to a range of sounds. They startle easily with sudden loud noises and become agitated at high-pitched noises. They turn their heads to locate sound and show interest in their caregivers' voices. Infants explore their own utterings and use their bodies and toys to play with sound. Infants who are later discovered to be deaf or have impaired hearing coo and babble according to expected developmental patterns for the first few months. As hearing children increase their quantity and variability of babbling, deaf or hard-of-hearing children actually decrease (Marschark, 2007). This is why hearing problems can be difficult to detect until seven or eight months of age. For children who underwent routine screening (e.g., at the hospital after birth or at well-baby checkups), the diagnosis for severe to profound hearing loss was 6.8 months, while children who did not have such screening were not diagnosed, on average, until 20.5 months (Canale et al, 2006). Late diagnosis has implications for the impact of early intervention strategies on outcomes regarding speech, language, and the quality of parent and infant life (Canale et al., 2006; Storbeck & Calvert-Evers, 2008).

Talk with infants about what interests them. Discuss, for example, what they are looking at or what they are hearing.

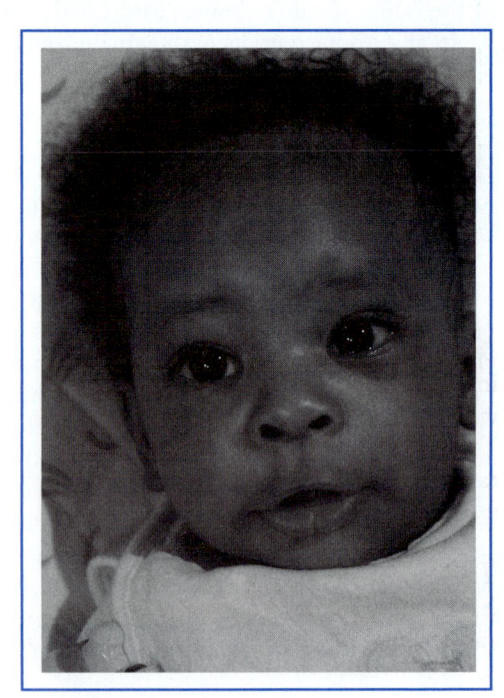

spotlight on research

Cleft Lip/Palate and Socio-Emotional Development

Cleft deformities of the palate are among the most common congenital malformations and can be diagnosed as early as the 17th week of gestation by means of ultrasonography (Biavati & Rocha-Worley, 2006). Yet, this technology is not 100 percent accurate, resulting in many children not being identified until birth. Given the value placed on physical appearances, it has been long assumed that children with cleft deformities would suffer from a variety of social and emotional outcomes. Collett and Speltz (2006) and Murray et al. (2008) set out to test this hypothesis with longitudinal studies. Both studies compared infants with cleft lip/palate to matched samples of children without cleft deformities.

Children with cleft lip/palate were found to have significantly lower scores in cognitive functioning at 18 months of age, but only for those children whose cleft deformity was not repaired until three to four months of age (Murray et al., 2008). Collett and Speltz (2006) had a similar result when they found that children with cleft lip/palate lagged significantly behind the comparison group in cognitive and motor development. However, their study followed children for a longer period of time and discovered that by age five and seven, those differences had disappeared.

There were no differences found in infant-mother attachment classifications or interactions and behavioral problems after two months of age (Collett & Speltz, 2006; Murray et al., 2008). At the two-month assessment, however, mothers whose infant had not yet received surgery to repair the cleft lip/palate "... were less positively involved and sensitive, and they looked less at their infants. In turn, infants in this group were more distressed, and they similarly looked less at their mothers" (Murray et al., 2008, p. 119).

Collett & Speltz (2006) gathered ratings of behavioral and social adjustment at age five, six, and seven. By age seven, "...children with and without clefts showed nearly equivalent levels of adjustment, as indicated by group means as well as percentages of children in each group exceeding conventional clinical thresholds" (Collett & Speltz, 2006, p. 283). Their last measure was an emotional regulation task where a situation was created to create disappointment in the children. Children with cleft lip/palate expressed less disappointment, through verbalization, facial expression, and mild tantrum behavior, than did the children in the control group.

Taken together, the results demonstrate that "Despite the many stressors associated with having a stigmatizing and chronic medical condition, the majority of young children with ... clefts appear to show normal social-emotional development, at least in early childhood" (Collett & Speltz, 2006, p. 286). However, the importance of early intervention is also evident for children with cleft lip/palate. Interventions to facilitate positive mother-child social interactions are particularly vital because "less sensitive maternal interactions accounted for the group differences in infant cognitive outcome" for those children who did not have surgery to repair their cleft deformity at birth (Murray et al., 2008, p. 121).

Infants use their eyes from birth, although their vision develops relatively slowly. By the fourth month, coordination of both eyes can be observed. Four-month-old infants demonstrated looking preferences that were similar to adult preferences when given simple visual, black and white displays (Chien, Palmer, & Teller, 2005). They focus well with both eyes at a distance of 12 inches, which is the normal distance for breastfeeding. By age two, vision is around 20/80; full 20/20 acuity is not expected until they reach school age.

Teething

Infants usually begin growing teeth between four and eight months, but individuals vary widely in teething. New teeth erupt every month or so after the first one. Sometimes an emerging tooth causes an infant to be very fussy and irritable, while at other times a new tooth just seems to appear with no discomfort at all. Many parents report their child having diarrhea, fever, and other symptoms like decreased appetite while teething. Research suggests that high fevers (104 degrees and above) are not associated with teething. The family should be alerted immediately if these symptoms occur (Macknin, Piedmonte, Jacobs, & Skibinski, 2000; Wake, Hesketh, & Lucas, 2000). Teething infants often drool profusely and like to bite things, using teething rings and anything else they can put in their mouths. When an infant seems to be in pain from teething, a cold teething ring provides both coolness and hardness for the child's gums. Gums should never be rubbed with an alcohol substance to relieve discomfort. A dentist or medical specialist should be consulted if pain persists.

Infants need assistance in caring for their newly erupting teeth. The average age for having all 20 baby teeth is around 33 months. Figure 2-2 shows the order and age at which teeth typically erupt. The American Dental Association (ADA) recommends that a dentist examine a child within six months of the eruption of the first tooth and no later than the first birthday (ADA, 2009). A dental visit at an early age is a "well baby checkup" for the teeth. Besides checking for tooth decay and other problems, the dentist can demonstrate how to clean the child's teeth properly and how to evaluate any adverse habits such as thumbsucking. Access to dental care, while improving, is not uniform within our society. Children who are black or multiracial relative to white, lower income, and lack a personal dentist were

FIGURE 2-2 Dental Eruption Chart

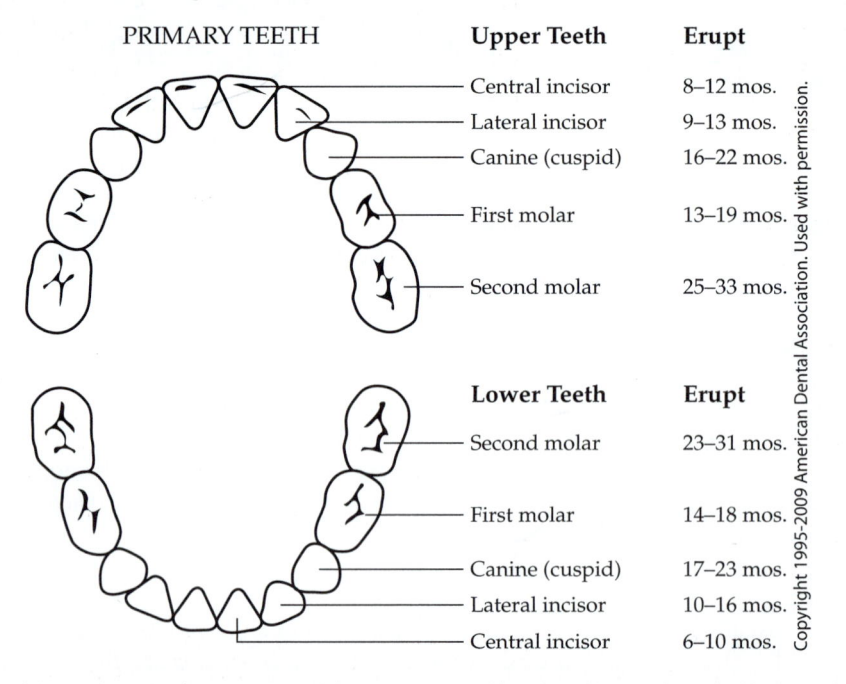

PRIMARY TEETH

Upper Teeth	Erupt
Central incisor	8–12 mos.
Lateral incisor	9–13 mos.
Canine (cuspid)	16–22 mos.
First molar	13–19 mos.
Second molar	25–33 mos.

Lower Teeth	Erupt
Second molar	23–31 mos.
First molar	14–18 mos.
Canine (cuspid)	17–23 mos.
Lateral incisor	10–16 mos.
Central incisor	6–10 mos.

Copyright 1995-2009 American Dental Association. Used with permission.

Source: Adapted from the American Dental Association, available at http://www.ada.org/public/topics/tooth_eruption.asp

significantly less likely to have a preventive dental visit within the previous year (Lewis, Johnston, Linsenmeyar, Williams, & Mouradian, 2007). Advising caregivers to brush infants' and toddlers' teeth after each meal and providing information to family members about the importance of regular dental checkups will support the development of lifelong, healthy dental habits.

Motor Development

One theory of motor development, called the dynamic systems theory, predicts that individual behaviors and skills of the growing infant combine and work together to create a more efficient and effective system. "Kicking, rocking on all fours, and reaching gradually are put together in crawling. Then, crawling, standing, and stepping are united into walking alone" (Hofsten, 1989). Each new skill is acquired by practicing, revising, and combining earlier accomplishments to fit a new goal. Consequently, infants typically achieve motor milestones around the same time but in unique ways.

Physical development occurs in a predictable order, starting from the head and chest and moving to the trunk and lower extremities. This directional growth is readily observable as the infant gains control of head, chest, trunk, and then legs to turn over. To crawl, the infant gains control of lower back and leg muscles; to walk, the infant gains control of neck, shoulders, back, legs, feet, and toes. Infants develop control of their arm movements from erratic waving to accurate reaching. Hand control develops from accidentally bumping and hitting to purposefully touching. Reaching occurs first, with an open hand grip. Then the fingers develop, from reflexive pinching, grasping, and reflexive releasing to controlled opening and closing.

Physical development involves both large movements, or **gross motor control**, and small muscle activity, **fine motor control**. Gross motor development involves large movements through milestone achievements, such as crawling, standing, walking, and throwing. Fine motor development milestones involve smaller, more refined movements, like grasping and pointing. Three areas of movement that develop over the first three years are (1) stability, (2) locomotion, and (3) manipulation. *Stability* refers to sitting and standing upright; *locomotion* refers to crawling, walking, and running; *manipulation* includes reaching, grasping, releasing, and throwing.

Milestones of development are essential for teachers to know because while the progression of motor development is fairly uniform, individual children vary within and between cultures in the age at which they develop both gross and fine motor skills. Appendix A provides a somewhat detailed Developmental Prescription of motor skill milestones for infants through three years of age. At around six weeks, infants begin to hold their heads steady and erect. By two months, they lift their upper bodies by their arms and can roll from side to back. From three to four months, babies begin grasping palm-size objects and can roll from back to side. From six to eight months, they can sit alone and begin to crawl. Between eight and ten months, babies pull up to stand and perhaps play patty cake. At this time they begin to stand alone, and then begin to walk. From 13 to 16 months, children can build a tower of

Walking is a milestone of physical development.

two cubes, vigorously scribble with a large crayon, and begin to walk up stairs with help. At around 20 to 24 months, toddlers begin to jump in place and kick objects. By 26 to 30 months, children begin to climb, stand on one foot, and have some interest in toilet learning. Usually at around 36 months, the child can jump and independently use the toilet.

As this general outline indicates, motor development does support the dynamic systems theory described earlier. Children progress from one milestone behavior to the next, based on successful integration of the previous behaviors and neurological maturity resulting from environmental experiences. Children who develop within the average range do not necessarily proceed through all of the developmental milestones or move in the exact sequence outlined in a specific Developmental Prescription. The challenge for the caregiver is to observe behavioral milestones and determine where individual children fall on the general scale of motor development. The caregiver should use a Developmental Prescription, perform careful observations of behavioral milestones, and clearly determine where each child is compared to the normal expectations for the age range. By performing evaluations on a regular basis, caregivers can determine a child's areas of motor development that require specific tasks and experiences to enhance development and areas in which he or she shows advanced development in motor skills.

Sleep Patterns

The stages of sleep and wakefulness are described as states. A *state* is an organized pattern of physical responses that relates to arousal levels. A state can last minutes, many hours, or even years. Changing a young child's state from crying or sleeping to being calm or fully alert can be difficult at times because states are relatively stable in young children. The following states of arousal have been defined and carefully studied in young children (Wolff, 1993; Zeskind & Marshall, 1991):

Quiet sleep. Respirations are regular, eyes are closed and not moving, and the child is relatively motionless.

Active sleep. Muscles are more tense than in quiet sleep, the eyes may be still or display rapid eye movements (REM), breathing is irregular, and there are spontaneous startles, sucks, and rhythmic bursts of movement.

Drowsiness. Eyes open and close and there is increased activity, more rapid and regular breathing, and occasional smiling.

Quiet alert. Eyes are open, scanning the environment; the body is still, and respiration is more rapid than in sleep.

Active alert. The child is awake and has body and limb movements, although the child is less likely to attend to external stimulation and focuses eyes less often than in the quiet alert state.

Crying. Activity and respiration rate are elevated, and the child exhibits cry vocalization and a facial expression of distress.

Newborns sleep an average of 16 to 17 hours per day. Sleep periods range from two to ten hours. By three to four months, infants regularly sleep more at night than during the day, but night awakenings are common throughout infancy and early childhood (Anders, Goodlin-Jones, & Zelenko, 1998; Kleitman, 1963). Assist very young children with transitioning from waking to sleeping. Do so by providing dimmed light and quiet, soft voice tones. Hold and rock the child before she goes to sleep and make every effort to reduce stimulation. Then, because of the risk of **sudden infant death syndrome**, place the baby on her back on a firm mattress. *Do not* let the child sleep with a bottle as that is a significant factor in dental caries.

A condition in which breathing momentarily stops is called sleep apnea (Hofsten, 1989). Short periods of apnea are normal during active (i.e., REM) sleep, but with some children these episodes are prolonged and more frequent. Infrequently, sleep apnea can become dangerous to a person's health because the period of not breathing becomes too long. Some research suggests that sudden infant death syndrome (SIDS) may be related to sleep apnea. SIDS is a tragic event in which a young child dies after going to sleep for a nap or at bedtime with no indication of having discomfort. Research on apnea in infants indicates that the baby's brain is not mature and therefore periods of instability occur. Since young children spend extensive periods in REM sleep, the instability of the nervous system may cause such extended apnea that the child stops breathing completely (Beatty, 1995). The incidence of SIDS is very low (two infants per 1000 births between one week and one year of age), but the American Academy of Pediatrics has found that infants who are placed on their backs to sleep have a lower incidence of SIDS (Stokes, 2001). As long as the child is awake and closely supervised, however, belly lying should be encouraged to develop chest muscles, which are important for normal development.

As children become more mobile and begin to crawl and walk, their sleep patterns change and they require less sleep. Children should still be encouraged to rest every day, and a well-planned child care program provides nap times that meet the individual needs for children who are under three years of age. A balance of structured physical activity and rest is essential for optimal physical and emotional development and growth.

Toilet Learning

Some babies accomplish toilet learning as early as six months of age, but there appears to be a moderate correlation between early forced bowel and bladder training and later emotional problems (Berk, 2000). The muscles that control bowel and bladder, called sphincter muscles, are usually not mature until after 18 months of age. Toilet learning requires the child to become aware of the sensations of the sphincter muscles and to control them until the appropriate time, when he or she relaxes the muscles to eliminate. This awareness first happens with larger muscles; control usually occurs first with bowel movements at around 24 months of age. However, children frequently do not learn to use the toilet independently until after three years of age. In fact, a child must be over four years old to be diagnosed as having encopresis, which is lack of bowel control, and must be over five years old to be diagnosed with enuresis, which is the inability to control urination (American Psychiatric Association, 1994).

When children are ready to start toilet learning, they practically teach themselves, with a little guidance and encouragement. The best approach to toilet learning is to provide specific feedback on success and avoid punishing or shaming for mistakes. The child should participate as much as possible for his or her age in cleaning up when mistakes are made. When you act as if a simple mistake was made, the child realizes that he or she can come to you for assistance.

Diapers should always be changed when wet. With young children, it is common to have seven or eight changes within a 12-hour period. Some children may have several bowel movements per day, while others may have only one. If a child does not have a bowel movement each day, the family should be notified because constipation can be a problem in some cases. Diarrhea can also be a problem because of the possibility of rapid dehydration. As with other areas of physical development,

Hard rattles are good for chewing on! According to Piaget, she learned this through the processes of assimilation and accommodation while exploring her environment.

accurate daily records should be kept on elimination and shared with family members. It is important to recognize that the child's family members are your partners in toilet learning.

All human relationships are bound to involve conflicts and disagreements. Toilet learning is an area ripe for such conflicts because it is accompanied by such a great deal of variability in cultural beliefs (Gonzalez-Mena, 2001; Gonzalez-Mena & Eyer, 2007). Cultural groups and individual families within those groups often have strong beliefs about when and how to assist with toilet learning. One family will start toilet learning at one year of age and another will wait until the child is "ready," while still another may not provide any formal assistance until the child is four years of age. None of these perspectives on timing is definitively correct or incorrect; they just reflect different belief systems. As a parent, member of a cultural group, and/or a teacher, you have beliefs about toileting also. Open communication and respectful listening are the beginning steps in addressing cultural conflicts, but they are not enough. You must be clear about your own views and the philosophy of the program so that you can truly listen and work toward solutions with the families. Issues like toilet learning will not be resolved in one conversation. Sustained dialogue is necessary for resolving the conflict (Gonzalez-Mena, 2001).

reading checkpoint

Before moving on with your reading, make sure that you can answer the following questions about the material discussed so far.

1. Explain how the growth of the brain demonstrates the complex interaction between nature (i.e., genetics or biology) and nurture (i.e., environmental factors).
2. Name the major milestones for motor development from birth to three years of age.
3. How is toilet learning a complex developmental accomplishment?
4. Why do infant and toddler teachers need to be aware of developmental patterns in such areas as seeing (vision), sleeping, and teething?

PATTERNS OF COGNITIVE AND LANGUAGE DEVELOPMENT

As mentioned in Chapter 1, the most widely applied theories of higher cognition are Piaget's cognitive developmental theory (Beilin, 1992) and Vygotsky's sociocultural theory (Rogoff & Chavajay, 1995). Later chapters detail several applications of these theories in child care settings, but major principles from each theory are discussed here before we move into language development.

Cognitive Development—Piaget's theory of reasoning

Newborns use all their senses—listening, seeing, tasting, touching, and smelling—to learn about their world. This leads to young children thinking differently from adults. Adults are logical thinkers; they consider facts, analyze relationships, and draw conclusions. Young children are *prelogical* thinkers; their conclusions are based on their interactions with materials and people in their environment and perhaps on an incomplete or inaccurate understanding of their experiences. For example, two-and-a-half-year-old Ivan has made a tilting stack of blocks. When he places a small car on top of the blocks, the stack tumbles down. Ivan tells Mrs. Young that the car broke the blocks. Ivan does not understand gravity, the need to stack blocks straight up rather than at a tilt, and why the car's rolling wheels may have started the car's movement downhill. The object Ivan put on the stack just before it fell was the car, so as far as Ivan is concerned, the car broke the blocks.

Jean Piaget's research contributed significantly to the knowledge of cognitive development in young children. A brilliant young scientist, Piaget began his studies as a biologist. Later, listening to children respond to questions on an intelligence test, he became intrigued by their incorrect responses and the patterns of their verbal reasoning. Combining his scientific orientation, his knowledge of biology, and his experiences with the children's incorrect response patterns, Piaget began to study children's cognitive development. Piaget's clinical observation method included close observations of his own three young children as well as many other children in his extensive subsequent research. He observed what children did and wrote narrative descriptions, including the date, the participants, and the actions. Later, analyzing these detailed observations, he developed his theories of cognitive development. Piaget's (1952) approach is central to the school of cognitive theory known as *cognitive constructivism;* other researchers, known as *social constructivists,* such as Vygotsky and Bruner, have placed more emphasis on the part played by language and other people in enabling children to learn (Wood, 1998; Atherton, 2005).

According to Piaget, children construct knowledge through their interactions with materials in their environment. As a stage theorist, Piaget believed that children developed higher cognitive skills in a systematic manner through four stages: (1) sensorimotor, (2) preoperational, (3) concrete operational, and (4) formal operational. Children use schemes, or patterns of actions, to learn at each of these stages through the intellectual functions of adaptation and organization.

Adaptation involves using schemes that have direct interaction with the environment; for example, grasping and dropping an object over and over. Accommodation involves changing schemes to better fit the requirements of a task or new information. Thus, a child will change or alter his or her strategies to fit the requirements of a task. For example, banging on a hard toy will produce a noise. Yet, when faced with a soft toy, the child finds that banging is insufficient to produce a response. Squeezing might be tried instead. When children are in a familiar situation, they function by means of assimilation, which involves dealing with an object or event in a way that is consistent with their existing schemes (McDevitt & Ormrod, 2010). When children are in such situations, they are considered to be in the internal state called equilibrium. Their current cognitive schemes work to explain their environment. However, when faced with information that is contrary to their current schemes and understanding or placed in an unfamiliar situation, they experience disequilibrium. This internal mental state provides a motivation for learning because the children are uncomfortable and seek to make sense of what they have observed or experienced. The movement from equilibrium to disequilibrium and back to equilibrium again is known as equilibration. Equilibration and children's intrinsic desire to achieve equilibrium move development toward greater complexity of thought and knowledge (McDevitt & Ormrod, 2010).

Another cognitive function through which schemes are changed is called organization, which takes place internally. Organization is a process of rearranging new schemes and linking them with other schemes to form a cognitive system. For example, a baby will eventually relate schemes for sucking, dropping, and throwing with new, more complex schemes of near and far.

Central to Piaget's theory is that there are stages of cognitive development; that is, four-month-olds are cognitively different from 24-month-olds. Piaget contended that the sequence of development is the same for all children. However, the age and rate at which it occurs differs from child to child. Although many of the hypotheses of Piaget's theory have come into question after the advent of research demonstrating that infants and toddlers have many more cognitive skills than Piaget theorized (Rast & Meltzoff, 1995), the principles and stages defined by Piaget have functional value for the caregiver in supporting children in their cognitive development. We turn our discussion to his stages of cognitive development next.

Piaget's first two stages of cognitive development involve children between birth and three years of age. These stages, the sensorimotor stage and the beginning of the preoperational stage, are the aspects of cognitive development relevant to an infant and toddler curriculum. The sensorimotor stage starts at birth, when the baby explores self and the environment. Sensorimotor development involves the infant understanding his or her body and how it relates to other things in the environment (Piaget & Inhelder, 1969). The earliest form of thinking occurs during this stage, at approximately 18 months, and involves assimilation of sensorimotor cause and effect, called interiorized actions. There are three key aspects of this early age: (1) infants play an assertive role in their own development, (2) their knowledge base is acquired by means of their own actions in the environment, and (3) infants need moderate challenges to master the environment. For caregivers, tasks should be provided that challenge babies but are not beyond their ability to succeed.

Sensorimotor Stage. The sensorimotor stage of cognitive development occurs from birth to about age two. Piaget identified six substages.

Substage 1 (birth to approximately 1 month)	*Reflex* Reflex actions become more organized. Directed behavior emerges.
Substage 2 (approximately 1–4 months)	*Differentiation* Repeats own actions. Begins to coordinate actions, such as hearing and looking.
Substage 3 (approximately 4–8 months)	*Reproduction* Intentionally repeats interesting actions.
Substage 4 (approximately 8–12 months)	*Coordination* Intentionally acts as a means to an end. Develops concept of object permanence (an object exists even when the infant cannot see it).
Substage 5 (approximately 12–18 months)	*Experimentation* Experiments through trial and error. Searches for new experiences.
Substage 6 (approximately 18–24 months)	*Representation* Carries out mental trial and error. Develops symbols.

Preoperational Stage. The early part of the preoperational stage is called the preconceptual substage and occurs from about two to four years of age. At this time, the child can now mentally sort events and objects. With the development of object permanence, the child is moving toward representing objects and actions in his or her thinking without having to have actual sensorimotor experiences. Development and structuring of these mental representations is the task undertaken during the preoperational stage of cognitive development. Cowan (1978) outlined the preoperational stage as follows:

Preconceptual substage
    Mentally sorts objects and actions.
    Mental symbols are partly detached from experience.

Nonverbal classification
    Organizes objects graphically.
    Focuses on figurative properties.
    Forms own interpretations.

Verbal preconcepts
    Meanings of words fluctuate, are not always the same for the child.
    Meanings of words are private, based on own experience.
    Word names and labels are tied to one class.
    Words focus on one attribute at a time.

Verbal reasoning
    Reasons tranductively—from particular to particular.
    If one action is in some way like another action, both actions are alike in all ways.
    Generalizes one situation to all situations.
    Reasoning is sometimes backward—from effects to causes.
    Reasoning focuses on one dimension.

Quantity
    How much?
    Some, more, gone, big.

Number
    How many?
    More, less.

Space
    Where?
    Uses guess and visual comparison.
    Up, down, behind, under, over.

Time
    Remembers sequence of life events.
    Now, soon, before, after.

Cognitive Functions. Piaget identified processes and functions in thinking. When you solve a problem, you feel that you understand it. As discussed previously in this chapter, Piaget's theory included concepts such as equilibrium, disequilibrium, equilibration, assimilation, and accommodation. For Piaget, an infant who reaches or touches an object quickly develops *knowing,* an active process of co-construction between what there is to know and the child's motivation and actions. More complex forms of knowing develop out of simple behaviors such as sucking, mouthing, and touching, according to Piaget.

All people use these processes and functions—assimilation, accommodation, and equilibration—continually through life. For example, Shane is looking around and notices a ball on the floor. As he crawls to it, he bumps the ball so the ball rolls. He crawls to it again, picks up the ball, looks at it, licks it, and puts it down on the floor. Shane started out in seeming equilibrium; that is, he seemed settled and quiet. Something caused disequilibrium; that is, something stimulated him. Shane responded to seeing the ball. What he saw may match in some way what he has seen before in previous play with a ball. He may have assimilated some idea about the ball. When he bumped the ball and it rolled, he was presented with additional information about the ball that did not fit into his present concept. Therefore, through accommodation, he makes adjustments in his concept of "ball" to include the rolling movement. His disequilibrium is over, and he once again for an instant has attained equilibration, a sense of balance, of understanding his world.

Cognitive Structures. Shane's actions also show one of the structures of intelligence. Shane constructs concepts or schemas as his mind organizes or structures its experiences. The schema or concept of ball is constructed as Shane sees, touches, holds, and tastes a ball. When he sees the ball roll, that does not fit into his schema or structure of ball-ness. He continues to construct his knowledge of ball-ness by reorganizing his schema so that now rolling is included in ball-ness. Shane's schema of ball today is different from his schema yesterday, when he had not noticed a rolling ball. Individual experiences and behavior bring about changes in schemas.

Knowledge Construction. Young children construct knowledge about themselves and their world. They cannot copy knowledge, but rather must act on their own and construct their own meaning. Each of their actions and interpretations is unique to them. They see an object and construct thoughts about that object. Young children's thinking organizes information about their experiences so they can construct their own understanding.

Types of Knowledge. Piaget identified three types of knowledge: physical knowledge, logico-mathematical knowledge, and social-arbitrary knowledge.

Physical knowledge is knowledge children discover in the world around them. Twenty-five-month-old Tommy kicks a pine needle as he walks in the play yard. He picks up the pine needle, throws it, and picks it up again. He drops it in the water tray, picks it up, and pulls it through the water. Tommy has discovered something about pine needles from the needle itself. Tommy uses actions and observations of the effects of his actions on the pine needle to construct his physical knowledge of pine needles.

Kamii and DeVries (1978) have identified two kinds of activities involving physical knowledge: movement of objects and changes in objects. Actions to move objects include "pulling, pushing, rolling, kicking, jumping, blowing, sucking, throwing, swinging, twirling, balancing, and dropping" (p. 6). The child causes the object to move and observes it rolling, bouncing, cracking, and so on. Kamii and DeVries (1978) suggest four criteria for selecting activities to move objects.

1. The child must be able to produce the movement by his or her own action.
2. The child must be able to vary his or her action.
3. The reaction of the object must be observable.
4. The reaction of the object must be immediate (p. 9).

A second kind of activity involves changes in objects. Compared to a ball, which when kicked, will move but still remain a ball, some objects change. When Kool-Aid® is put in water, it changes. Ann sees the dry Kool-Aid and observes that something happens when it is added to water. She can no longer see anything that looks like the dry Kool-Aid. She sees the water change color and can taste the difference between water without Kool-Aid and water with Kool-Aid in it. Her observation skills (seeing and tasting) are most important to provide her with feedback on the changes that occur.

Logico-mathematical knowledge is constructed by the child and involves identifying relationships between objects. Andrea is in the sandbox playing with two spoons: a teaspoon and a serving spoon. She notices the spoons are different. Although they fit into her schema of *spoon*, she notices some difference in size. Thus, in relationship to size, they are different. At some time someone will label these differences for her as different or bigger or smaller than the other, but these words are not necessary for her to construct her concepts of sizes.

Social-arbitrary knowledge is knowledge a child cannot learn by him- or herself. It has been constructed and agreed upon by groups of people (Branscombe, Castle, Dorsey, Surbeck, & Taylor, 2003). This type of knowledge is passed on or transmitted from one person to another through social interaction. "Language, values, rules, morality, and symbol systems are examples of social-arbitrary knowledge" (Wadsworth, 1978, p. 52).

Chad is eating a banana. He bites it, sucks on it, swallows it, looks at the remaining banana, and squeezes it. All of these are concrete actions which help him construct his physical knowledge of this object. Then someone tells him this object is a banana. The name *banana* is social-arbitrary knowledge. It could have been called *ningina* or *lalisa*, but everyone using the English language uses *banana* to name that object.

In another example of social-arbitrary knowledge, Kurt follows Mrs. Wesley into the storage room. She sees him and says, "Kurt, go back into our room right now. You are not supposed to be in this room." Kurt did not make the decision that it is not permissible for him to be in the storage room; someone else decided and told him the rule.

Children who feel secure are free to explore.

Play. Play is the child's laboratory for cognitive trial and error and rehearsal for real-life problem solving. Children begin active pretend play between 18 and 24 months. As they rapidly develop symbols and interpretations and start to reason verbally, complex sequences of play are executed. For example, two-year-olds might play "cooking," using blocks and sticks for food and utensils. From basic themes, children develop more complex strategies, perhaps using water and sand to explore measurement while learning about textures, temperatures, smells, and liquidity. Table 2–1 presents levels of exploratory and pretend play. Play develops from simple mouthing and touching objects to extremely abstract activity, in which materials are substituted and transformed to make up a complete story with beginning, middle, and end.

Cognitive Development—Vygotsky's sociocultural theory

Vygotsky viewed cognitive development as an interaction between children and their social environment. For Vygotsky, knowledge is co-constructed through social interactions. Cultural tools mediate and facilitate this construction of knowledge; the most important tool for humans is language because "Language is thought; language is culture; language is identity. . . . Denying language is denying access to thought" (Wink & Putney, 2002, p. 54). In Vygotsky's own words:

> Thought is not merely expressed in words; it comes into existence through them. Every thought tends to connect something with something else, to establish a relationship between things. Every thought moves, grows and develops, fulfills a function, solves a problem. (1934/1986, p. 218)

TABLE 2-1 LEVELS OF EXPLORATORY AND PRETEND PLAY

1. **Mouthing:** Indiscriminate mouthing of materials

2. **Simple manipulation:** Visually guided manipulation (excluding indiscriminate banging and shaking) at least 5 seconds in duration that cannot be coded in any other category (e.g., turn over an object, touch and look at an object)

3. **Functional:** Visually guided manipulation that is particularly appropriate for a certain object and involves the intentional extraction of some unique piece of information (e.g., turn dial on toy phone, squeeze piece of foam rubber, flip antenna of toy, spin wheels on cart, roll cart on wheels)

4. **Relational:** Bringing together and integrating two or more materials in an inappropriate manner, that is, in a manner not initially intended by the manufacturer (e.g., set cradle on phone, touch spoon to stick)

5. **Functional-relational:** Bringing together and integrating two objects in an appropriate manner, that is, in a manner intended by the manufacturer (e.g., set cup on saucer, place peg in hole of pegboard, mount spool on shaft of cart)

6. **Enactive naming:** Approximate pretense activity but without confirming evidence of actual pretense behavior (e.g., touch cup to lip without making talking sounds, touch brush to doll's hair without making combing motions)

7. **Pretend self:** Pretense behavior directed toward self in which pretense is apparent (e.g., raise cup to lip; tip cup, make drinking sounds, or tilt head; stroke own hair with miniature brush; raise phone receiver to ear and vocalize)

8. **Pretend other:** Pretense behavior directed away from child toward other (e.g., feed doll with spoon, bottle, or cup; brush doll's hair; push car on floor and make car noise)

9. **Substitution:** Using a "meaningless" object in a creative or imaginative manner (e.g., drink from seashell; feed baby with stick as "bottle") or using an object in a pretense act in a way that differs from how it has previously been used by the child (e.g., use hairbrush to brush teeth after already using it as a hairbrush on self or other)

10. **Sequence pretend:** Repetition of a single pretense act with minor variation (e.g., drink from bottle, give doll drink, pour into cup, pour into plate) or linking together different pretense schemes (e.g., stir in cup, then drink; put doll in cradle, then kiss good night)

11. **Sequence pretend substitution:** Same as sequence pretend except using an object substitution within sequence (e.g., put doll in cradle, cover with green felt piece as "blanket"; feed self with spoon, then with stick)

12. **Double substitution:** Pretense play in which two materials are transformed, within a single act, into something they are not in reality (e.g., treat peg as doll and a piece of green felt as a blanket and cover peg with felt and say "night-night"; treat stick as person and seashell as cup and give stick a drink)

Source: J. Belsky & R. K. Most. (1981). From exploration to play: A cross-sectional study of infant free play behavior. *Developmental psychology, 17,* 630–639.

Vygotsky believed that, once language is developed, children engage in **private speech**; in other words, they talk to themselves as a means of self-guidance and direction (1934/1986). Recent research supports this view with findings that young children who use more private speech show more improvement on difficult tasks (Berk & Spuhl, 1995; Winsler, Naglieri, & Manfra, 2006) and were more creative (Daugherty & White, 2008) than children who do not use much private speech. In addition, children use more private speech as tasks become more difficult (Berk, 1994; Winsler, Abar, Feder, Schunn, & Rubio, 2007), and when children with learning/behavioral problems use private speech, they are more likely to complete the task successfully (Winsler, Abar et al., 2007; Winsler, Manfra, & Diaz, 2007).

Vygotsky hypothesized that higher cognitive processes develop from verbal and nonverbal social interactions. This is accomplished when more mature individuals instruct less mature individuals within their **zone of proximal development** (Wink & Putney, 2002). This term refers to a range of tasks that a child is able to learn with the help of more knowledgeable others (e.g., peers or adults). The zone of proximal development is established by assessing the child's individual level of performance and the child's assisted level of performance. The gap between these two levels is considered the "zone" (Wink & Putney, 2002). As a child is able to accomplish skills at the assisted level independently, the zone shifts upwards to the next skill to be addressed. Children adopt the language and actions of dialogues and demonstrations of the more knowledgeable other into their private speech and then use those to guide and regulate their own actions. At least two other aspects of this process have found research support: intersubjectivity and scaffolding.

Intersubjectivity refers to how children and adults come to understand each other by adjusting their views and perspectives to fit the other person. Adults must invest energy in figuring out how the child is approaching or thinking about a particular task in order to be most effective in helping the child to acquire a new skill or understanding. **Scaffolding** involves changing the support given a learner in the course of teaching a skill or concept (Berk & Winsler, 1995; Bodrova & Leong, 1996; Wink & Putney, 2002). The more knowledgeable other can utilize a number of instructional strategies to scaffold learning during a new, challenging, or complex task. Verbal encouragement; physical assistance; coaching; providing hints, clues, or cues; asking questions; and breaking the task into manageable steps (without losing the wholeness of the task) are all strategies to assist in accomplishing the given task. As the learner starts mastering the new skills, the more knowledgeable other withdraws instruction and encouragement in direct response to the learner's ability to perform successfully. Caregivers who effectively learn to use intersubjectivity and scaffolding help promote development, because children learn to use positive private speech and succeed more easily (Behrend, Rosengran, & Perlmutter, 1992).

A final aspect of Vygotsky's theory involves the use of **make-believe play** in higher cognitive development. Vygotsky believed that children who engage in make-believe play use imagination to act out internal ideas about how the world operates and to set rules by which play is conducted, which helps them learn to think before they act (Berk & Winsler, 1995). Language, therefore, becomes critical for the development of

"I've been looking for a spoon to stir my cake." Make-believe play can occur in almost any learning area—inside and outside.

organized make-believe play because metacognitive self-control and self-monitoring behaviors are largely developed through language (Berk, Mann, & Ogan, 2006). The ability to organize or plan make-believe play at advanced levels appears to be dependent on a child's ability to use language for three distinct, yet interrelated purposes: 1) to reflect on past experiences, 2) to predict future experiences, and 3) to reason about the relationships between past and future events (Westby & Wilson, 2007). Lillard (1993) found that children who engage in make-believe and pretend play are more flexible and advanced in their problem-solving and thought processes.

Language Development

As is evident from the above discussion, language plays a critical role in cognitive development from a Vygotskian perspective. Language is a tool for thinking (Bodrova & Leong, 1996; McDevitt & Ormrod, 2010). How do children come to acquire language skills for thinking and communicating? The easiest answer, of course, is through engaging in conversations with others. When adults and children talk with infants and toddlers, they provide examples of the four basic components of language: **phonology**, the basic sounds of the language and how they are combined to make words; **semantics**, what words mean; **syntax**, how to combine words into understandable phrases and sentences; and **pragmatics**, how to engage in communication with others that is socially acceptable and effective (McDevitt & Ormrod, 2010).

Yet, the easy answer is not always the best answer. Complex and somewhat controversial theories have been developed about language and word acquisition. Booth and Waxman (2008) theorize that "As infants and young children establish word meanings, they draw upon their linguistic, conceptual, and perceptual capacities and on the relations among these" (p. 189). Language acquisition from this perspective is not merely the adding on of new vocabulary words but involves the cognitive functions of organizing words by grammatical function (e.g., noun) or conceptual dimensions (e.g., shape, size, real, or pretend). In their study, toddlers extended the use of novel nouns systematically based on the conceptual information provided to them in vignettes (Booth and Waxman, 2008).

Newman (2008), in contrast, suggests that language acquisition is about learning what information to store for later retrieval. She suggests that infants must store enough information so that new words can be distinguished from old words and that initially infants store too much information. Infants may store, for example, information on what words were spoken, who said them, and how they were spoken (e.g., tone).

To fully comprehend language, infants must learn to ignore perceptible but irrelevant information such as tone of voice and to recognize words spoken by a variety of talkers. Variability in the input helps infants recognize which acoustic properties are important and which can be ignored. When an infant is familiar with a word spoken by only a particular talker, or in a particular tone of voice, the word's representation is tied to that talker/tone of voice. However, if the infant hears the same word spoken by multiple talkers, in multiple tones of voice, the child learns that these other factors are irrelevant, and the representation becomes less tied to those details. . . . Across a range of language domains, when exposure is more varied, infants focus less attention on the specific details of the input and instead begin to abstract across exemplars, focusing on areas of commonality (Newman, 2008, p. 231).

Thus, from this perspective, providing infants with a language-rich environment involves exposing infants to a number of different speakers so that commonalities can be uncovered. As you can see, learning to communicate is a complex task that involves several different, yet related, skills.

Infants must learn strategies for sending verbal and nonverbal messages to others. Newborns initiate interaction by making eye contact, and by four months they gaze in the same direction as the caregiver (Tomasello, 1999). Around the same time, they also begin to engage in verbal communication when they **coo** (or make repetitive vowel sounds). Babies are able to screen out many sounds that are not useful in understanding their native language by the age of six months (Polka & Werker, 1994). Between six and twelve months of age, babies are usually able to recognize familiar words in spoken passages (Jusczyk & Hohne, 1997). These findings suggest that infants begin to discriminate, associate, and analyze the structure of words and sentences before nine months of age! This skill is vital to acquiring productive language skills within their native language.

Around six or seven months of age, infants begin to **babble** (or produce speech-like syllables such as *ba, ra*) using sounds from their native language. The first "real" word is typically spoken around the first birthday. For a while, toddlers will blend babble with a real word in what is called jargon. To illustrate, an infant says "tatata car bebe" while playing. The teacher might respond with elaboration by saying "You moved the car. You pushed it. It went bye-bye." In this case, the adult supplies words that help to explain what the child is experiencing; thus, encouraging the acquisition of other new words and facilitating the linking of two or three "real" words into sentences or telegraphic speech. Just as a telegraphic message omits words, telegraphic speech includes only the words vital to the meaning the toddler is trying to convey. By 36 months, most toddlers are able to clearly and effectively communicate their wants, needs, and ideas (see Baron, 1992; Herr & Swim, 2002; and Snow, 1998, for more information on communicating with infants.)

Gestural communication begins between nine and twelve months as the infant shows us what she wants. Babies touch or hold objects while making sure the caregiver notices and gives attention, and they direct the caregiver to do something by pointing or gesturing (Fenson et al., 1994). By the beginning of the second year, verbalization of words and phrases is associated with gestures to communicate accurately. As vocabulary increases and becomes more descriptive, gestures decrease toward the end of the second year (Namy & Waxman, 1998).

Like other developmental skills discussed in this and future chapters, optimal language development requires interactions with teachers, peers, and family members.

When the caregiver labels and describes what the baby is holding or gesturing at, language development is enhanced. Engaging in conversations about events as they happen supports and facilitates language development. Yet, that has been found to not be enough. When adults engage in what is called child-directed speech with babies, they unconsciously adjust their tone, volume, and speech patterns to capture and sustain focal attention from the baby (Moore, Spence, & Katz, 1997). It is also important for caregivers to label and describe things that the baby visually attends to because this significantly enhances language development. Dominey and Dodane (2004) theorized that when adults use both child-directed speech and joint attention (i.e., attend to what the child is looking at), infants are better able to use general learning mechanisms to acquire knowledge of grammatical constructions. To illustrate, when a caregiver copies or mimics the baby's vocalization, the child can attend to the sounds that the caregiver makes as well as engage in turn-taking: the baby vocalizes, the caregiver vocalizes in return and waits for a response, and the "conversation" continues. Games such as patty cake help babies to interact actively and even initiate turn-taking interactions.

These interactions are indicative of the relationships between the caregiver and a specific infant. Child-directed speech has been found to be different depending upon whether the adult is speaking with a boy or a girl, yet those differences do not seem to appear in children's productions before the age of three (Foulkes, Docherty, & Watt, 2005). If one person within the relationship is not functioning optimally, the relationship and the developmental outcomes for the children can be drastically altered. For example, caregivers who interrupt or restrict the baby's focal attention and activities impede language development (Carpenter, Nagell, &

Tomasello, 1998). In another example, babies who cry for long periods of time or who are frequently distressed may elicit fewer positive vocal interactions from the parent or caregiver, thus impeding the typical pattern of language development (Locke, 2006). The language relationship does not stay static over time but rather responds to the growing capabilities of the infant. Almost as soon as the baby starts to use "real" words, caregiver speech changes to more information, directions, and questions rather than child-directed speech (Murray, Johnson, & Peters, 1990).

You read about baby signing in the previous chapter. This technique has proven to be a wonderful way to prepare youngsters to conquer the challenges of communication and is considered by many to be a method that enhances learning. A follow-up study of children who learned Baby Sign demonstrated that those children outperformed their non-baby signing peers by a very impressive margin on the WISC III, a universal test to measure language (Acredolo, Goodwyn, & Abrams, 2009).

As you now understand, learning to receive and produce verbal and nonverbal communication is a very complex process on which theorists and researchers do not always agree. It is beyond the scope of this text to fully investigate all aspects of language development. It must suffice to say that young children quickly learn the rules of speech governing their native language and most are proficient language users by around six years of age. Teachers and parents enhance children's language development by labeling, describing, mirroring, and actively engaging the child in conversations.

✓ reading checkpoint

Before moving on with your reading, make sure that you can answer the following questions about the material discussed so far.

1. Discuss Piaget's stages of cognitive development in terms of learning experiences for two-year-olds. Include concepts such as assimilation, accommodation, and disequilibrium in your answer.

2. Provide a specific example of each of Piaget's types of knowledge.

3. Use Vygotsky's theory to explain how you would scaffold a toddler with the skill of dressing, including the concept of private speech.

4. Explain the typical pattern of language development and the role adults play in the process.

CHILDREN WITH SPECIAL RIGHTS

Taking a developmental perspective means valuing all of the individual characteristics for each infant and toddler in your care. In addition, it means being able to identify strengths and areas of growth for each child in order to support optimal growth, development, and learning. In the current context within the United States, educators tend to think about providing services to meet a child's identified special needs. This perspective is most likely an outgrowth of the federal law, the Individuals with Disabilities Education Act, which stipulates that children birth through 21 years of age who are identified with special development and learning needs are entitled to appropriate public education. The law provides that children should have the "least restrictive environment," which means that whenever possible children will be served in the environment (e.g., home, child care center, family child care center) that best fits their needs. We would like you to reframe this issue from a "deficit model" approach (i.e., focusing on what children lack) to a special rights approach.

When considering the rights that each child has, we might construct a list which includes the right to control her own learning, be silent, be alone, be only herself, and make mistakes (Arth & Lawton, 1973). Rathbone (2005) expands that list to include the right to follow through, take action, remain engaged, wallow, concentrate, take learning personally, collaborate, and be respected. If we recognized that all children have these rights and created educational contexts to respond to these rights, then what do we mean by special rights?

Educators in Reggio Emilia, Italy, expand on our basic value of individual rights to include the concept of **special rights** (Vakil, Freeman, & Swim, 2003). In that educational context, children with special needs have "immediate precedence" for admission into programs (Gandini, 2001, p. 55). This practice reflects "Our basic theoretical approach . . . to value differences and to bring out as much potential as we can. Each of us is different; this is considered positive. We acknowledge that a handicap brings with it a difference, but that is just one of many differences" for each child (Smith, 1998, p. 205). We add to this understanding of special rights the idea that teachers must start their work focusing on what each child can do independently and adding on what she is entitled to learn with assistance. When teachers, children, and family members discuss differences and come to terms with conflicting ideas, then everyone synthesizes a new identity (Smith, 1998). Thus, giving some children the status of special rights is seen as a way to improve everyone within the community.

In virtually every community in the United States, early interventions for at-risk infants and toddlers are currently available (Guralnick & Bennett, 1987; Odom, Teferra & Kaul, 2004). Children who are considered at risk sometimes require specialized equipment, care, and curricula, and the child care specialist must learn how to care for children with specific special rights. Because it is impossible to cover all the special conditions and procedures necessary to care for at-risk children in one text, an overview of categories and characteristics is provided here as related to physical and cognitive/language development (social and emotional special needs will be addressed in Chapter 3). However, you should recognize that the first source of information should be the child and family. Observe carefully and closely to understand the child. The partnerships you create should encourage the family members to freely exchange information with you. When you know the child well and need additional information about the disability in general, contact the appropriate local and national associations and organizations for information on how to care for an individual child with that specific special right. In other words, you should become an expert on each individual child first, then familiarize yourself with the disability (Brekken, 2004).

focus on terminology

The following terms are often used to describe children with special needs or services that they might receive:

disorder A disturbance in normal functioning (mental, physical, or psychological).

disability A condition resulting from a loss of physical functioning, or difficulties in learning and social adjustment that significantly interfere with normal growth and development.

exceptional A term describing any individual whose physical, mental, or behavioral performances deviate so substantially from the average (higher or lower) that additional support is required to meet the individual's needs.

special education Specially designed instruction provided to children, at no cost to the parents, in all settings (such as the classroom, physical education facilities, the home, and hospitals or institutions).

early intervention Comprehensive services for infants and toddlers who are disabled or at risk of acquiring a disability. Services may include education, health care, and/or social and psychological assistance.

(*See* Hardman, Drew, & Egan, 2005)

Some children require early intervention to promote physical development and coordination.

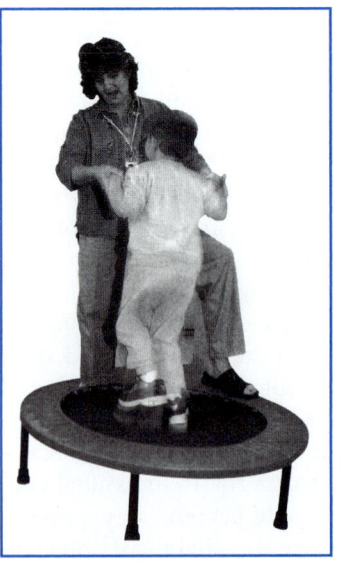

Approximately 13 percent of all children enrolled in Early Head Start and Head Start have been diagnosed with a disability and receive special education and/or related services to address their development or learning issues (Ewen & Neas, 2005). The following categories help to explain several of the common special rights infants and toddlers may have regarding physical and cognitive/language development.

1. Children with Motor Disabilities. Infants and toddlers with motor disabilities exhibit delayed motor development, retention of primitive reflexes, and abnormal muscle tone as the result of central nervous system (CNS) damage or malformation. The three major disabilities that are accompanied by motor handicaps are cerebral palsy, myelomeningocele, and Down syndrome. Infants and toddlers with motor disabilities usually exhibit delays in other developmental areas as well because learning occurs through active exploration of the world. Research on interventions involving systematic exercise and sensory stimulation and integration indicates that early intervention can improve motor and sensory development and encourage parent support and acceptance. For more information contact the American Medical Association, American Academy of Pediatrics, and local chapters of specific organizations such as the United Cerebral Palsy Foundation.

2. Biologically At-Risk Infants and Toddlers. Some children experience CNS damage, for example, from CNS infections, trauma, ingestion of toxins, and sustained hypoxia (lack of oxygen). Research results on interventions ranging from special nursery settings and free nursing and medical care, to infant stimulation by parents yield mixed results, with very short-term, positive effects. Interventions for this population appear to be more effective with parents than with children. For more information, contact the American Medical Association, the county health department, the American Academy of Pediatrics, or local pediatricians.

3. Children with Visual Disabilities. Infants and toddlers who are blind or have low vision are found in approximately one out of 3,000 births, with a wide range of severity and etiology. The most important consideration is visual efficiency, which includes acuity, visual fields, ocular motility, binocular vision, adaptations to light and dark, color vision, and accommodation. Research findings indicate that early intervention helps visually impaired infants and toddlers perform closer to typical developmental expectations. Interventions using a team approach, including parents, child care specialists, and other professionals, are more effective than individual treatment approaches. For more information, contact the National Society for the Prevention of Blindness, the National Council for Exceptional Children, the local health department, and agencies for the blind or those with low vision.

4. Children with Hearing Disabilities. Hearing disabilities are classified by type (sensorineural, conductive, or mixed), time of onset (at birth or after), severity (mild to profound), and etiology. Research indicates that early intervention programs should include parent counseling, staff with training in audiology, speech and language training, sign language as a normal program component, the flexibility to help each family, and the involvement of deaf adults as resources for children. For more information, contact the Council for Exceptional Children, the local health department, and the National Association of the Deaf.

5. Children Who Are Medically Fragile. A new subgroup of health disorders, referred to as medically fragile, has emerged in recent years (Hardman, Drew, & Egan, 2006). These individuals are at risk for medical emergencies and often require specialized support. For example, children with feeding tubes need highly trained individuals to provide necessary nutritional supplements. Other times medically fragile children have progressive diseases (e.g., AIDS or cancer) or episodic conditions (e.g., severe asthma or sickle cell anemia; Hardman, Drew, & Egan, 2006). Such disorders have an impact not only on the way the infant or toddler forms his or her own identity, but also on how others see and treat him or her. Seeking information from families or community agencies/organizations can help to alleviate your concerns and educate the child's peers about the specific disorder, improving peer relationships (McDevitt & Ormrod, 2010).

6. Children with Cognitive and General Developmental Disorders. Some infants and toddlers exhibit delays in several facets of cognition, such as information processing, problem solving, and the ability to apply information to new situations. These issues many have environmental or genetic sources such as Down syndrome or teratogenic damage. Global delays in motor, cognitive, language, and socioemotional areas are common. Children with cognitive and general developmental disorders tend to reach milestones but at a much slower rate, with lower final levels of development. Research strongly indicates that early intervention programs prevent the decline in intellectual functioning found in mildly retarded children without intervention. Programs for moderately and profoundly retarded children are more effective with active parental participation and training, but overall they appear to be less effective than with mildly retarded infants and toddlers. For more information, contact the American Association on Intellectual and Developmental Disabilities, formerly the American Association on Mental Retardation, the local special education administration, or local chapters of specific associations such as the Down Syndrome Association.

7. Children with Language and Communication Disorders. Infants and toddlers who exhibit problems with the mechanics of speech (phonation, moving air from the lungs through the mouth, and articulation) have speech disorders, and children with problems using the rules of language (labeling or forming sentences) have language disorders. Results of studies on various kinds of interventions suggest that the course of communication disorders can be modified through early intervention. For more information, contact the American Association for Speech and Language, the Association for Speech and Hearing, and local chapters of associations for speech and language disorders.

It is essential that early childhood educators do not work in isolation when caring for children with special rights. When any of the conditions described here is suspected, the teacher must consult professionals who are trained to evaluate, prescribe for, and intervene with these children. In fact, every child care program should have medical and psychological services as a regular part of the evaluation and care of children. It is also important for each caregiver to network with other child development professionals in the area, such as psychologists, pediatricians, and speech and language therapists. Caregivers must be aware of community resources for children with special rights, since many families lack funding sources. Sometimes community groups or generous, qualified professionals donate their time and energy to ensure proper treatment for children with special rights.

The research on interventions with children with all types of disabilities strongly indicates that a team approach that includes parents, all caregiving staff, and specialized professionals, is necessary to promote optimal growth and development for children with special rights. But when early interventions are delivered by strong partnerships, they can result in significant, positive changes in the child that is a direct result of everyone's combined actions.

✓ reading checkpoint

Before moving on with your reading, make sure that you can answer the following questions about the material discussed so far.

1. Why should infant and toddler educators think about a child having special rights rather than special needs?

2. Explain three special rights very young children might have in relationship to physical and cognitive/language development.

SUMMARY

Development and learning are not synonymous terms. They have precise definitions that need to be understood and applied to your observations of very young children. To build upon the foundation provided in the previous chapter, we explored in depth typical patterns of physical and cognitive/language development for children birth to age three. All children have individual rights such as the right to be alone, be herself, and to respected. High-quality care and education recognizes and values these rights for every child, even for those with identified special educational needs. We have asked that you specifically reframe your thinking about children with such needs: they have a right to have their capabilities honored and expanded.

key terms

- accommodation
- adaptation
- assimilation
- babble
- brain plasticity
- child-directed speech
- coo
- development
- disequilibrium
- equilibration
- equilibrium
- experience-dependent
- experience-expectant
- fine motor control
- gross motor control
- intersubjectivity
- jargon
- learning
- make-believe play
- organization
- phonology
- pragmatics
- private speech
- prunes
- scaffolding
- schemes
- semantics
- sensorimotor stage
- special rights
- Sudden Infant Death Syndrome (SIDS)
- syntax
- telegraphic speech
- zone of proximal development

case study

Sasha

Angelica, just over two years of age, is relatively new to Sasha's class of mixed-age infants and toddlers. She joined the class for part-time care (three days a week) about three months ago after she was formally adopted by her aunt (her biological mother's sister) and uncle. Angelica is now the youngest of three children. She is obviously adored by her parents and siblings. Sasha is concerned because she is having difficulty forming a close attachment with Angelica in the child care setting.

Angelica has missed more than two-thirds of the days that she was scheduled to be at child care due to her illness, sickle cell anemia or SCA. This is an inherited disorder that profoundly affects the structure and functioning of red blood cells for African Americans (Hardman, Drew, & Egan, 2005). Angelica's disorder was identified at birth, yet is progressing at a rapid rate; she seems to be experiencing frequent and serious complications. Angelica misses school when she has to get partial-exchange blood transfusions. These treatments tend to cause her to throw up. In the last three months, she has needed eight such transfusions. After the last treatment, she had to be admitted to the hospital overnight because of dehydration. Angelica had experienced only three partial-exchange transfusions before being adopted.

When Angelica enrolled in her class, Sasha began to find out more about SCA and how she could best meet the toddler's needs. Her first source of information was Angelica's parents, of course, but they are just learning about this disorder as well. Next, she searched the World Wide Web, but found conflicting information and not much about partial-exchange blood transfusions and their side effects. She did discover that minimizing stress, fatigue, and exposure to cold temperatures can assist those with a history of SCA crises. So, while she has gained some information, Sasha is still nervous about working with Angelica.

1. What else can Sasha do to learn more about SCA? What other sources would you suggest?
2. Do you think that knowing more about SCA will help Sasha form a close attachment with Angelica? Why or why not? Given Angelica's family history, should Sasha be concerned about forming such an attachment with her? Why or why not?
3. What strategies would you suggest that Sasha use to help develop a strong attachment when Angelica is able to come to school?

QUESTIONS AND EXPERIENCES FOR REFLECTION

1. Copy the Developmental Profile Form in Appendix B and assess one infant and one toddler by establishing a complete profile for each child's physical and cognitive/language development using the Developmental Prescriptions in Appendix A.

2. During the children's alert play time observe two children of different ages between birth and three years, focusing on one area (physical, emotional, social, or cognitive). Write down everything each child does and says for five minutes.

Make a chart to compare the behaviors, using the following as a guide:

Child: Age:	Child: Age:
Area:	Area:
Behaviors	Behaviors

3. Observe one child between birth and 12 months of age interacting with one adult. List the behaviors each uses to get and maintain the other's visual attention.

	Initial Behavior	Response
Child		
Adult		
Child		
Adult		
Child		
Adult		

4. Observe an infant and a toddler. Record all of their vocalizations. Analyze their speech using the research presented in this chapter. Then, classify any vocalizations that reflect private speech. How did the children use private speech to guide their actions?

REFERENCES

Acredolo, L. P., Goodwyn, S., & Abrams, D. (2009). *Baby signs: How to talk with your baby before your baby can talk* (3rd ed.). Chicago: Contemporary Books.

Acredolo, L. P., & Goodwyn, S. (2000). *Baby minds: Brain-building games your baby will love.* New York: Bantam Books.

American Dental Association (ADA). (2009). Oral health topics A-Z: Baby teeth. Retrieved from http://www.ada.org/public/topics/baby.asp on January 28, 2009.

American Psychiatric Association. (1994). *Diagnostic and statistical manual of mental disorders* (4th ed.). Washington, DC: Author.

Anders, T. F., Goodlin-Jones, B. L., & Zelenko, M. (1998). Infants' regularity and sleep-wake state development. *Zero to Three, 19*(2), 5–8.

Arth, A. A., & Lawton, E. J. (1973). Building a Bill of Rights for the Elementary-School Child. *The Elementary School Journal, 73* (4), 200–203.

Atherton, J. (2005). Piaget's developmental theory. Retrieved March 12, 2005, from http://www.learningandteaching.info/learning/piaget.htm

Baron, N. S. (1992). Growing up with language: How children learn to talk. Reading, MA: Addison-Wesley.

Beatty, J. (1995). *Principles of behavioral neuroscience.* London: Brown and Benchmark.

Behrend, D. A., Rosengran, K. S., & Perlmutter, M. (1992). The relation between private speech and parental interactive style. In R. M. Diaz & L. E. Berk (Eds.), *Private speech: From social interaction to self-regulation* (pp. 85–100). Hillsdale, NJ: Erlbaum.

Beilin, H. (1992). Piaget's enduring contribution to developmental psychology. *Developmental Psychology, 28*, 191–204.

Berk, L. E. (1994). Why children talk to themselves. *Scientific American, 271*(5), 78–83.

Berk, L. E. (2000). *Child development* (5th ed.). Boston: Allyn and Bacon.

Berk, L. E., Mann, T. D., & Ogan, A. T. (2006). Make-believe play: Wellspring for development of self-regulation. In D. G. Singer, R. M. Golinkoff, & K. Hirsh-Pasek *Play=learning* (pp. 74–100). New York: Oxford University Press.

Berk, L. E., & Spuhl, S. T. (1995). Maternal interaction, private speech, and task performance in preschool children. *Early Childhood Research Quarterly, 10*, 145–169.

Berk, L. E., & Winsler, A. (1995). NAEYC Research into Practice Series: Vol. 7. Scaffolding children's learning: Vygotsky and early childhood education. Washington, DC: National Association for the Education of Young Children.

Biavati, M. J., & Rocha-Worley, G. (2006). Cleft palate. Retrieved from http://emedicine.medscape.com/article/878062-overview on February 2, 2009.

Bodrova, E., & Leong, D. J. (1996). *Tools of the mind: The Vygotskian approach to early childhood education*. Upper Saddle River, NJ: Merrill Prentice Hall.

Booth, A. E., & Waxman, S. R. (2008). Taking stock as theories of word learning take shape. *Developmental Science, 11* (2), 185–194.

Branscombe, N. A., Castle, K., Dorsey, A. G., Surbeck, E., & Taylor, J. B. (2003). *Early childhood curriculum: A constructivist perspective*. Boston: Houghton Mifflin.

Brekken, L. (2004). Supporting children's possibilities: Infants and toddlers with disabilities and their families in Early Head Start. In J. Lombardi and M. M. Bogle (Eds.). *Beacon of hope: The promise of Early Head Start for America's youngest children*. Washington, DC: Zero to Three. pp. 148–167.

Canale, A. Favero, E, Lacilla, M., Recchia, E., Schindler, A., Roggero, N., & Albera, R. (2006). Age at diagnosis of deaf babies: A retrospective analysis highlighting the advantage of newborn hearing screening. *International Journal of Pediatric Otorhinolaryngology, 70* (7), 1283–1289.

Carpenter, M., Nagell, K., & Tomasello, M. (1998). Social cognition, joint attention, and communicative competence. *Monographs of the Society for Research in Child Development, 63*(4), 1–174.

Chien, S. H., Palmer, J., & Teller, D. Y. (2005). Achromatic contrast effects in infants: Adults and 4-month-old infants show similar deviations from Wallach's ratio rule. *Vision Research 45*(22), 2854–2861.

Collett, B. R., & Speltz, M. L. (2006). Social-emotional development in infants and young children with orofacial clefts. *Infants and Young Children, 19* (4), 262–291.

Cowan, P. A. (1978). Piaget with feeling: Cognitive, social, and emotional dimensions. New York: Holt, Rinehart and Winston.

Daugherty, M., & White, C. S. (2008). Relationships among private speech and creativity in Head Start and low—socioeconomic status preschool children. *Gifted Child Quarterly, 52* (1), 30–39.

Dominey, P. F., & Dodane, C. (2004). Indeterminacy in language acquisition: The role of child directed speech and joint attention. *Journal of Neurolinguistics, 17*, 121–145.

Eliot, L. (1999). What's going on in there? How the brain and mind develop in the first five years of life. New York: Bantam Books.

Ewen, D., & Neas, K. B. (2005). Preparing for Success: How Head Start Helps Children with Disabilities and Their Families. Retrieved from CLASP (Center for Law and Social Policy) website http://www.clasp.org/publications/hs_disabilities_updated.pdf on February 7, 2009.

Fenson, L., Dale, P. S., Reznick, J. S., Bates, E., Thal, D. J., & Pethick, S. J. (1994). Variability in early communicative development. *Monographs of the Society for Research in Child Development, 59*(5), 1–189.

Foulkes, P., Docherty, G., & Watt, D. (2005). Phonological variation in child-directed speech. *Language, 81* (1), 177–206.

Gandini, L. (2001). Reggio Emilia: Experiencing life in an infant-toddler center. Interview with Cristina Bondavalli. In L. Gandini & C. P. Edwards (Eds.). Bambini: The Italian approach to infant/toddler care. NY: Teachers College Press. pp. 55–66.

Gonzalez-Mena, J. (2001). *Multicultural issues in child care* (3rd ed.). Mountain View, CA: Mayfield.

Gonzalez-Mena, J., & Eyer, D. W. (2007). *Infants, toddlers, and caregivers* (7th ed.). New York: McGraw-Hill.

Gunnar, M. R. (2001). The role of glucocorticoids in anxiety disorders: A critical analysis. In M. W. Vasey & M. R. Dadds (Eds.), *The developmental psychopathology of anxiety* (pp. 143–159). New York: Oxford University Press.

Gunnar, M. G., & Cheatham, C. L. (2003). Brain and behavior interface: Stress and the developing brain. *Infant Mental Health Journal, 24*(3), 195–211.

Guralnick, M. J., & Bennett, F. C. (Eds.). (1987). *The effectiveness of early intervention for at-risk and handicapped children.* San Diego: Academic Press.

Hardman, M. L., Drew, C. J., & Egan, M. W. (2006). *Human exceptionality: School, community, and family* (9th ed.). Boston: Allyn and Bacon.

Herr, J., & Swim, T. J. (2002). *Creative resources for infants and toddlers* (2nd ed.). Clifton Park, NY: Thomson Delmar Learning.

Hofsten, C. Von. (1989). Motor development as the development of systems. *Developmental Psychology, 25*, 950–953.

Johnson, M. H. (1999). Developmental neuroscience. In M. H. Bornstein & M. E. Lamb (Eds.), *Developmental psychology: An advanced textbook* (4th ed.). Mahwah, NJ: Erlbaum.

Jusczyk, P. W., & Hohne, E. A. (1997). Infants' memory for spoken words. *Science, 277*, 1984–1986.

Kamii, C., & DeVries, R. (1978). Physical knowledge in preschool education: Implications of Piaget's theory. Englewood Cliffs, NJ: Prentice Hall.

Kleitman, N. (1963). *Sleep and wakefulness.* Chicago: University of Chicago Press.

Lamb, M. E., & Campos, J. J. (1982). *Development in infancy.* New York: Random House.

Lewis, C. W., Johnston, B. D., Linsenmeyar, K. A., Williams, A., & Mouradian, W. (2007). Preventive dental care for children in the United States: A national perspective. *Pediatrics, 119* (3), 544–553.

Lillard, A. S. (1993). Pretend play skills and the child's theory of mind. *Child Development, 64*, 348–371.

Locke, J. L. (2006). Parental selection of vocal behavior: Crying, cooing, babbling, and the evolution of language. *Human Nature, 17* (2), 155–168.

Lupien, S. J., & McEwen, B. S. (1997). The acute effects of corticosteroids on cognition: Integration of animal and human model studies. *Brain Research Review, 24*, 1–27.

Macknin, M., Piedmonte, M., Jacobs, J., & Skibinski, C. (2000, April). Symptoms associated with infant teething: A prospective study. *Pediatrics, 105*(4), 747.

Marschark, M. (2007). *Raising and educating a deaf child.* Oxford: Oxford University Press, Inc.

McDevitt, T. M., & Ormrod, J. E. (2010). *Child development: Educating and working with children and adolescents* (4th ed.). Upper Saddle River, NJ: Pearson Prentice Hall.

Moore, D. S., Spence, M. J., & Katz, G. S. (1997). Six-month-olds' categorization of natural infant-directed utterances. *Developmental Psychology, 33*, 980–989.

Murray, A. D., Johnson, J., & Peters, J. (1990). Fine-tuning of utterance length to preverbal infants: Effects on later language development. *Journal of Child Language, 17*, 511–525.

Murray, L., Hentges, F., Hill, J., Karpf, J., Mistry, B., Kruetz, M., Woodall, P. et al. (2008). The effect of cleft lip and palate, and the timing of lip repair on mother-infant interactions and infant development. *The Journal of Child Psychology and Psychiatry, 49* (2), 115–123.

Namy, L. L., & Waxman, S. R. (1998). Words and gestures: Infants' interpretations of different forms of symbolic reference. *Child Development, 69*, 295–308.

Nash, J. (1997, February 3). Fertile minds: How a child's brain develops and what it means for child care and welfare reform [Special report]. *Time, 149*(5), 48–56.

Newman, R. (2008). The level of detail in infants' word learning. *Current directions in psychological science: A journal of the American Psychological Society, 17* (3), 229–232.

Odom, S.L., Teferra, T., & Kaul, S. (2004). An overview of international approaches to early intervention for young children with special needs and their families. *Young Children, 59*(5), 38–43.

Piaget, J. (1952). *The origins of intelligence in children* (M. Cook, trans.). New York: International University Press.

Piaget, J., & Inhelder, B. (1969). *The psychology of the child*. London: Routledge and Kegan Paul.

Polka, L., & Werker, J. F. (1994). Developmental changes in perception of non-native vowel contrasts. *Journal of Experimental Psychology: Human Perception and Performance, 20*, 421–435.

Rast, M., & Meltzoff, A. N. (1995). Memory and representation in young children with Down syndrome: Exploring deferred imitation and object permanence. *Development and Psychopathology, 7*, 393–407.

Rathbone, C. H. (2005). A learner's bill of rights. *Phi Delta Kappan, 86* (6), 471–473.

Rogoff, B., & Chavajay, P. (1995). What's become of research on the cultural basis of cognitive development? *American Psychologist, 50*, 859–877.

Shore, R. (2003). *Rethinking the brain: New insights into early development* (2nd ed.). New York: Families and Work Institute.

Smith, C. (1998). Children with "special rights" in the preprimary schools and infant-toddler centers of Reggio Emilia. In C. Edwards, L. Gandini, & G. Forman, *The hundred languages of children* (2nd ed.). (pp. 199–214). Norwood, NJ: Ablex.

Snow, C. W. (1998). *Infant development* (2nd ed.). Upper Saddle River, NJ: Prentice Hall.

Stokes, I. (2001). The role of inheritance in behavior. *Science, 248*, 183–188.

Storbeck, C., & Calvert-Evers, J. (2008). Towards integrated practices in early detection and intervention for deaf and hard of hearing children. *American Annals of the Deaf, 153* (3), 314–321.

Tomasello, M. (1999). Understanding intentions and learning words in the second year of life. In M. Bowerman & S. Levinson (Eds.), *Language acquisition and conceptual development*. Cambridge, UK: Cambridge University Press.

Vakil, S., Freeman, R., & Swim, T. J. (2003). The Reggio Emilia approach and inclusive early childhood programs. *Early Childhood Education Journal, 30* (3), 187–192.

Vygotsky, L. S. (1986). *Thought and language* (A. Kozulin, Trans.). Cambridge, MA: MIT Press. (Original work published 1934).

Wadsworth, B. J. (1978). *Piaget for the classroom teacher*. New York: Longman.

Wake, M., Hesketh, K., & Lucas, J. (2000). Teething and tooth eruption in infants: A cohort study. *Pediatrics, 106* (6), 1374.

Westby, C., & Wilson, D. (2007, August). Children's play: The roots of language and literacy development. Paper presented at the 27th World Congress of the International Association of Logopedics and Phoniatrics, Copenhagen, Denmark. Retrieved from http://proceedings.ialp.info/FC23/FC23.1%20Final%20Paper.pdf on February 7, 2009.

Wink, J., & Putney, L. (2002). *A vision of Vygotsky*. Boston: Allyn & Bacon.

Winsler, A., Abar, B., Feder, M., Schunn, C., & Rubio, D. (2007). Private speech and executive functioning among high-functioning children with Autistic Spectrum Disorder. *Journal of Autism & Developmental Disorders, 37* (9), 1617–1635.

Winsler, A., Manfra, L., & Diaz, R. M. (2007). "Should I let them talk?": Private speech and task performance among preschool children with and without behavior problems. *Early Childhood Research Quarterly, 22* (2), 215–231.

Winsler, A., Naglieri, J., & Manfra, L. (2006). Children's search strategies and accompanying verbal and motor strategic behavior: Developmental trends and relations with task performance among children age 5 to 17. *Cognitive Development, 21* (3), 232–248.

Wolff, P. H. (1993). Behavioral and emotional states in infancy: A dynamic perspective. Cambridge, MA: MIT Press.

Wood, D. (1998). How children think and learn: The social contexts of cognitive development (2nd ed.). Oxford: Blackwell Publishing.

Zeskind, P. S., & Marshall, T. R. (1991). Temporal organization in neonatal arousal: Systems, oscillations, and development. In M. Weiss, & P. Zelago (Eds.), *Newborn attention: Biological constraints and the influence of experience* (pp. 22–62). Norwood, NJ: Ablex.

ADDITIONAL RESOURCES

Cowden, J. E., & Torrey, C. C. (2007). *Motor development and movement activities for preschoolers and infants with delays: A multisensory approach for professionals and families.* Springfield, IL: Charles C. Thomas Publisher, LTD.

Justice, L. M. (2010). *Communication Sciences and Disorders: A Contemporary Perspective* (2nd ed.). Upper Saddle River, NJ: Pearson Allyn & Bacon.

Nelson, C. A., de Haan, M., & Thomas, K. M. (2006). Neuroscience of cognitive development: The role of experience and the developing brain. Hoboken, NJ: John Wiley & Sons, Inc.

Skallerup, S. J. (2008). (Ed.) *Babies with Down syndrome: A new parents' guide* (3rd ed.). Bethesda, MA: Woodbine House.

For additional activities, web links, and other resources, please visit our website at www.cengage.com/education/swim

chapter 3

BIRTH TO THIRTY-SIX MONTHS: SOCIAL AND EMOTIONAL DEVELOPMENTAL PATTERNS

learning objectives

After reading this chapter, you should be able to:

- Identify typical patterns of emotional and social development between birth and thirty-six months of age.
- Understand the characteristics and care of children with special rights related to emotional and social development.

chapter outline

- Patterns of Emotional Development
- Patterns of Social Development
- Children with Special Rights
- Case Study: Marcus

PATTERNS OF EMOTIONAL DEVELOPMENT

Unlike most other warm-blooded species, human infants are totally dependent on the environment to supply their most basic needs. For independent physical survival, children are born nine months too soon because they require assistance for that amount of time before they can crawl and move independently within the environment. Therefore, a caregiver needs to create a safe and secure space for the physical and emotional survival of the child. A child should be provided with conscious care; be kept warm, fed, and exposed to minimal stress; and should have his needs responded to in a respectful manner. Very young children should be touched, kept close to the chest, talked to, exposed to soft music, and rocked. Babies should be provided with appropriate transportation to move from one place to another safely; an ideal device is a carrier in which the infant is carried next to the chest.

A safe and secure child care center creates a positive learning atmosphere in which children feel secure in initiating responses to their environment based on interest and curiosity. Children should not be judged because they are learning socially acceptable emotional responses; this takes a great deal of time—many, many years to accomplish. When the child's emotional needs are met, he experiences a world that invites his participation.

Evolution of Feelings

The most basic feelings on a physical level are pleasure and pain. It was once thought that newborns experience only these two general feeling states. However, anyone who has extensively cared for a young infant understands that they experience and express the full range of human emotion from ecstasy to deep sorrow. Through active experience with their environment, babies quickly learn to repeat behaviors that result in pleasurable experiences and avoid, as much as they can, those that result in pain. Yet, this desire to repeat or avoid outcomes goes way beyond a behavior-response pattern; it reflects how the brain is being wired (see Chapter 2). "What wires a child's brain, say neuroscientists—or rewires it after physical trauma—is repeated experience.... When the brain does not receive the right information—or shuts it out—the result can be devastating.... Emotional deprivation early in life has a similar effect" (Nash, 1997).

It is impossible to protect infants and toddlers from experiencing physical and emotional pain, no matter how sensitive and caring we are. Pain is a natural and normal life experience and is extremely valuable for our ability to stay alive and learn from experience. Just as athletes understand the saying "No pain: no gain" because muscles don't grow stronger unless they are taxed, most changes that produce growth cause some pain along with pleasure. A goal of a competent caregiver should be to help children remain at ease through their life experiences. Caregivers who try to protect children from all pain and keep them in a state of pleasure establish very unrealistic expectations for themselves and the children in their care.

However, it should be noted that infants and toddlers are especially vulnerable to painful experiences because of their lack of defenses. When a young child cannot escape a situation of persistent emotional pain, such as consistent abandonment, rejection, or adult anger, or a situation of chronic physical pain, such as physical or sexual abuse, **emotional detachment** can become severe and long lasting. Emotional or physical trauma can also cause pathological detachment. Under these conditions, detachment from one's own feelings or the feelings of other people, or both, can cause permanent lack of self-awareness and insensitivity to others.

It may seem that infants are selfish because they only attend to their own needs, but that is not possible because infants are limited in their ability to understand the impact of their behaviors on others. For example, when a baby wakes up hungry in the middle of the night, she does not have the experience or awareness that her hunger is an inconvenience to her sleeping caregiver. However, when the child's basic needs are filled, she is able to be extremely curious, sensitive, and aware of other people. From this basic level, children progress to balancing their own feelings and needs with the feelings and needs of other people and become capable of intimate relationships with equal give and take.

It sometimes appears that young children move through emotions rapidly. One minute a young toddler may scream, and the next moment jump into your arms and give you a hug. As cognitive and language skills develop with age, the child can use words better to specify and describe many different feeling states. By the age of five or six, children who have experienced quality caregiving are capable of sophisticated, conscious discrimination of self from others in terms of thoughts, feelings, and behaviors.

During the first three years of life, the combination of traits present at birth, including physical size, health, and temperament, interact with pleasurable and painful experiences in the environment to form the growing child's identity (e.g., the child's perceptions of self, others, and the world). The next sections describe two theories of identity development as they pertain to infants and toddlers. Both of the theories discussed here show how children create models of the world through a complex process whereby the characteristics they bring with them (e.g., temperament) impact and are shaped through interactions with adults and other children. These models of the world become the basis for the enduring reactions and patterns people have throughout life—what we call personality.

Erikson's Psychosocial theory
Erikson's lifespan theory (1950) adds to our understanding of how children develop emotionally by responding to life's challenges. He labeled his theory psychosocial "because the various challenges refer to qualitatively different concerns about oneself (*psycho-*) and relationships with other people (*-social*)" (McDevitt & Ormrod, 2010, p. 404). He believed that children must resolve eight crises or stages as they progress from infancy through old age. Each crisis is seen as a turning point where development can move forward successfully or take a turn in a more negative direction.

While he believed that the resolution of prior stages impact the outcomes of future stages, he also thought that people could revisit crises that were unresolved (or resolved toward a negative outcome) during later development. Of the eight stages, the first three are extremely important in the development of infants and toddlers.

1. *Basic trust versus mistrust*—Children learn to trust or mistrust themselves and the world during infancy depending on the warmth and sensitivity they are given. Trust is developed through consistent, responsive, and appropriate behavior from the caregiver. In those situations, infants learn that their needs are important and that they can trust others will respond to their signals with helpful solutions. When infants are required to wait too long for comfort, when they are handled harshly and insensitively, or when they are responded to in an inconsistent manner, they develop basic mistrust of themselves and others. While the responsibility for appropriate response rests solely on the shoulders of the adult, the child also plays an active part in the interaction. When infants are difficult to sooth, it is discouraging and levels of frustration rise. Hence, even if the adult starts out calm and responsive, when the issue is not easily resolved, negative emotions may become part of the interaction.
2. *Autonomy versus shame and doubt*—Once infants become mobile, a process of separation and individuation begins, eventually resulting in autonomy. Children need to choose and decide things for themselves. When caregivers permit reasonable free choices and do not force or shame children, autonomy and self-confidence are fostered. If caregivers place too many limits on behavior or constantly restrict choices, children learn dependency and lack confidence in their ability to make decisions.
3. *Initiative versus guilt*—When caregivers support a child's sense of purpose and direction, initiative in the form of ambition and responsibility is developed. When caregivers demand too much self-control or responsibilities that are not age appropriate, children respond by feeling over-controlled or guilty, or both.

Erikson's stages reveal how children develop the qualities that result in a happy, meaningful life. As the first stage suggests, developing a sense of trust during the first year of life, can result in positive, lasting personal assets that impact the resolutions of future stages. As caregivers, the impact of our day-in and day-out responses to children's basic needs cannot be overestimated.

Some ways to ensure consistent and appropriate caregiver behavior with children are to establish consistent routines and supply generous amounts of the three *A*s of child care: Attention, Approval, and Attunement (see Chapter 4). Consistently responding to the needs of the child with warmth and respect will help her to develop security and trust. Reading the infant's or toddler's cues as well as being able to look at things from her perspective are necessary components in responsive caregiving (Oppenheim & Koren-Karie, 2002). Security develops largely from consistent responses to specific behaviors, and trust develops largely from acceptance and appreciation of the child (Greenspan & Pollock, 1989). This is reflected in policies that ensure a low infant-caregiver ratio. Early childhood educators need to be available to respond to the many needs of each dependent infant or toddler.

According to Erikson, children also need reasonable freedom and expectations as they move beyond the infancy stage. To provide such freedoms and expectations you need to know (1) normal patterns of development and (2) each child's individual pattern of development. Because the sequence of development is similar among children, you have some guidelines for your expectations. A caregiver needs to know where each child fits within the range of development. If you expect children to accomplish things that are below or above them developmentally, you produce undue stress. For example, you can expect 30-month-old Mark to want to feed himself lunch because he possesses the skills to hold a spoon in his hand, fill it with food, and usually get it up to his mouth. It is unreasonable to expect nine-month-old Naomi to have that level of muscular coordination or the desire to show such initiative. Use of Developmental

Children need help from adults when learning to regulate their emotions.

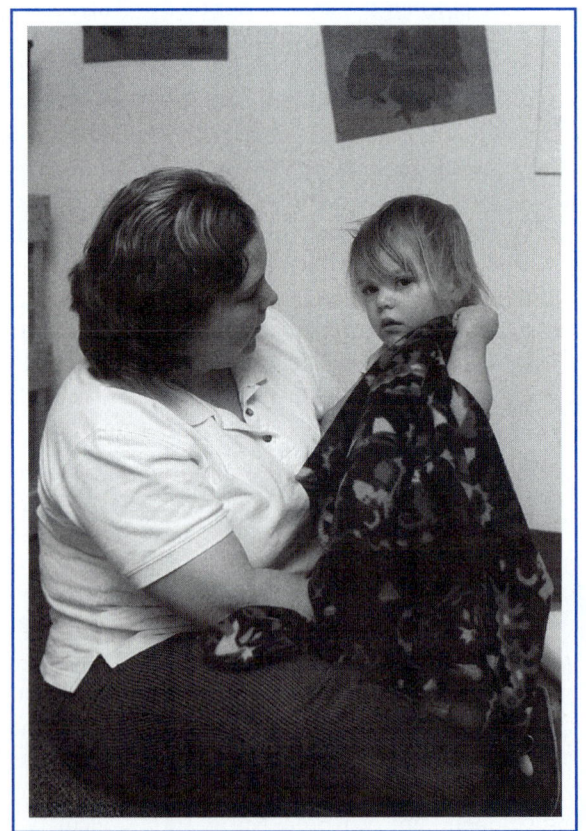

Prescriptions and Profiles is important. Consistent updating of developmental steps helps children establish security and trust, because they meet with success, mastery, and the three *A*s rather than stress, frustration, and rejection.

Mahler's Bonding and Separation-Individuation Theory

A pediatrician from Vienna named Margaret Mahler wrote extensively about the importance of bonding between parent and child and the process called separation-individuation (Greenberg & Mitchell, 1983). Personality development, security, trust, and self-concept are all related to the attachment between infant and caregivers and to how separation-individuation from caregivers is conducted and experienced by the child. Mahler's phases of the individuation process are valuable guidelines for caregivers of infants and toddlers to understand identity development. Mahler's four subphases of separation-individuation are as follows:

Subphase	Age
1. differentiation	four months to ten months
2. practicing	10 months to 15 months
3. rapprochement	15 months to 36 months
4. libidinal object constancy	36 months throughout childhood

The *normal autistic phase* occurs during the first few weeks of life, when time spent asleep exceeds time awake (Mahler, Pine, & Bergman, 1975). At three to four weeks, a maturational crisis occurs, in which the infant shows increased sensitivity to the external world and has a beginning awareness that the primary caregiver is an external object. During this normal symbiotic phase, the baby organizes experiences into good (pleasurable) and bad (painful) memories, which form the basis for identity.

At about four months, the separation-individuation phase begins, with some variations among individuals. From four to ten months, the *differentiation* subphase occurs, in which the baby begins to act in more self-determined ways and explores the caregiver (e.g., pulls hair, clothes). The baby also scans the world and checks back to the caregiver to discriminate "caregiver" from "other." The baby develops skill in discriminating external from internal sensations as well. This discrimination forms the basis for self-awareness (self-concept) as opposed to awareness of object (anything other than self, including other people).

Once the baby becomes mobile at around 10 months, the *practicing* subphase begins. Because the baby can now move away from the caregiver, increased body discrimination and awareness of separateness from others manifest themselves. The child begins using the caregiver as an emotional and physical "refueling station"—moving short distances away and then returning for refilling. Think of yourself as a recharging station, a physically and emotionally rewarding place where children feel a sense of security and return again and again for emotional nourishment.

The child becomes excited by the world, the caregiver, and his own body and capacities to function. During this phase, the child concentrates on her own abilities separate from the caregiver and becomes **omnipotent** (not aware of any physical limitations). According to Mahler and colleagues (1975), the caregiver must be able to allow physical and psychological separation during this phase if the child is to establish a strong identity.

Between 15 and 18 months, the toddler enters the *rapprochement* subphase, where the sense of omnipotence (having no limits) is broken. What is wanted is not always immediately available, so the child experiences frustration, separation anxiety, and the realization that caregivers are separate people who don't always say yes. Often, children will alternate between clinging neediness and intense battling with caregivers at this stage because of these conflicting dependence and independence needs. Because of rapid language development during this period, the child struggles with gender identity, accepting "no," and the development of beliefs, attitudes, and values to add to the already formed self-concept.

Mahler's final subphase of *libidinal object constancy* starts around 36 months and involves developing a stable concept of the self (one that does not change), and a stable concept of other people, places, and things. Self-constancy and object constancy are comparable to Piaget's **object permanence**, the stage at which people and things continue to exist in the child's mind even when they aren't in sight. During this phase, it is crucial that the caregiver be available as a buffer between the child and the world while supporting and respecting the competencies of the growing child to separate and individuate without anxiety or fear. Three-year-olds truly believe that their make-believe is real. Playing with them using toys and puppets can elicit information on how they are doing emotionally.

The two theoretical perspectives just presented demonstrate, albeit in different ways, the importance of adults in the formation of identity and personality during the first three years of life. Because of the significance of individual child characteristics in both of these theories, the discussion will now turn to three other factors integral to emotional development: temperament, emotional intelligence, and self-esteem.

Temperament

Temperament has been defined as "the basic style which characterizes a person's behavior" (Chess, Thomas, & Birch, 1976). All children are born with particular temperaments. Temperament will influence what they do, what they learn, what they feel about themselves and others, and what kinds of interactions they have with people and objects.

Early research suggested that temperament is stable and not very changeable by environmental influences (Caspi & Silva, 1995; Kagan, Reznick, & Gibbons, 1989). However, a growing body of research strongly suggests that child-rearing practices and other environmental factors can dramatically influence temperament during the first three years (Gunnar, 1998; Rubin, Hastings, Stewart, Henderson, & Chen, 1997; Worobey, & Islas-Lopez, 2009). More specifically, Jansen and colleagues found that infants in lower income families were more likely to have been rated as having a difficult temperament and that the association was partially explained by level of family stress and maternal psychological well-being (Jansen, Raat, Mackenbach, Jaddoe, Hofman, Verhulst, et al., 2009). This raises the question of whether child temperament is a cause or a consequence of particular contextual impacts because other research discovered that as aspects of infant temperament become more negative, parenting becomes more negative (Bridgett, Gartstein, Putnam, McKay, Iddins, Robertson, et al., 2009; Davis, Schoppe-Sullivan, Mangelsdorf, & Brown, 2009). These results suggest that infants play a significant role in shaping their own development.

Chess, Thomas, and Birch (1977) worked with hundreds of children and their parents to investigate how babies differ in their styles of behavior. The analysis of observations and interviews revealed nine patterns of behavior. Within each pattern they found a range of behaviors. Table 3–1 lists the nine categories and extremes of behaviors observed in each category. The behavior of most people falls somewhere between these extremes. Chess and her colleagues further collapsed the nine patterns into three basic types of temperament: flexible and easy, slow to warm up, and difficult.

TABLE 3–1 BEHAVIORAL CATEGORIES OF TEMPERAMENT

BEHAVIORAL CATEGORY	EXTREMES	
	MORE	LESS
(1) Activity Level	Hyperactive—can't sit still	Lethargic—sedate, passive
(2) Regularity	Rigid and inflexible patterns	Unpredictable and inconsistent patterns
(3) Response to New Situations	Outgoing, aggressive, approaching	Withdrawing, timid, highly cautious
(4) Adaptability	Likes surprises, fights routine, dislikes structure	Dislikes change, likes routine, needs structure
(5) Sensory Threshold	Unaware of changes in light, sound, smell	Highly sensitive to changes in light, sound, smell
(6) Positive or Negative Mood	Feels optimistic	Feels negative; denies positive
(7) Response Intensity	Highly loud and animated, high energy	Very quiet and soft; low energy
(8) Distractibility	Insensitive to visual and auditory stimuli outside self	Unable to focus attention, highly sensitive to visual and auditory stimuli
(9) Persistence	Persists until task completed	Gives up easily, doesn't try new things

The following descriptions illustrate the extremes of some of these patterns.

Activity level. Ryan runs into the room, yells "Hi," and goes to the blocks. He stacks them quickly, they fall down, and he stacks them again and leaves them as they tumble down. He walks over to stand by Melba, the caregiver, who is reading a picture book to another child. Ryan listens a few minutes and then moves on to another activity. Ryan has a high activity level. He has always been very active. He kicked and waved and rolled a lot when he was a baby. His body needs to move. He becomes very distressed when he is physically confined with a seat belt in the car or must sit quietly.

Bernadette sits quietly on the floor playing with nesting cans. She stacks the cans and then fits them inside each other. She accomplishes this task with few movements: her legs remain outstretched; her body is leaning forward slightly but remains mostly still; she has the cans close to her so her arms and hands need to move only slightly. Bernadette has a low activity level. She was a quiet baby, not kicking her blankets off or twisting and turning often. She becomes distressed when she has to rush around to put away toys or quickly get ready to go somewhere.

Approach or withdrawal as a characteristic response to a new situation. Jamol hides behind his mother as he enters the room each morning. He hides behind the caregiver whenever someone strange walks in the door. When others play with a new ball, he stands by the wall and watches. He leaves food he does not recognize on his plate, refusing to take a bite. Jamol is slow to warm up. He needs time to get used to new situations. Jamol is distressed when he is pushed into new activities. Telling him that a new ball will not hurt him or that the strange food is good for him does not convince him. When he feels comfortable, he will play with the new ball. He needs time and space for himself while he becomes familiar with a situation. It may take several offering before he eventually tries the new food.

Paulo arrives in the morning with a big smile. She looks around the room and notices a new puzzle set out on the table. She rushes over to it, asking the caregiver about it and giggling at the picture. She takes the puzzle pieces out, puts some of the pieces back in and then seeks assistance from the caregiver. Paulo warms up quickly. She is excited about new situations and eager to try new experiences.

Persistence and attention span. Jasmine takes the three puzzle pieces out of the puzzle. She successfully puts in the banana. She picks up the apple piece and tries to fit it into a space. When it does not fit, she drops the piece and leaves the table. Jasmine moves on to a new experience when she is not immediately successful.

Clayton takes the three puzzle pieces out of the puzzle. He then turns and pushes each piece until he has returned all three pieces to their proper places. Clayton persists with an activity even when it may be challenging or frustrating or takes a long time. When he completes his task, he expresses his pleasure with smiles and words.

Identifying each child's temperament as well as your own will help you to be an effective caregiver. Thomas and Chess (1977) suggest that the type of temperament a child has is less important to her overall functioning and development than the temperamental match she has with her caregiver. The adult-child **goodness-of-fit** model has been supported by research with families (Mangelsdorf, Gunnar, Kestenbaum, Lang, & Andreas, 1990; Paterson & Sanson, 1999; Schoppe-Sullivan, Mangelsdorf, Brown, & Szewczyk Sokolowski, 2007; Van Aken, Junger, Verhoeven, Van Aken, & Deković, 2007) and early childhood educators (Churchill, 2003; De Schipper, Tavecchio, Van IJzendoorn, & Van Zeijl, 2004).

Consider the following example: Olaf is playing with blocks. The tall stack he built falls over, one block hitting hard on his hand. He yells loudly. Ray is playing nearby and also is hit by a falling block. He looks up in surprise but does not say anything. What will you as a caregiver do? What will you say? What is *loud* to you? What is acceptable to you? Why is a behavior acceptable or not to you? Do you think Ray is *better* than Olaf because he did not react loudly? What you do and

I did it! I finally made it to the top of the "mountain."

what you say to Olaf reflects your acceptance or rejection of him as a person, reflects whether you are able to help him adapt to his environment, and reflects your ability to adapt to the child.

Franyo & Hyson (1999) found that temperament workshops designed especially for early childhood teachers resulted in their gaining important knowledge about temperament concepts. However, there was no evidence that these workshops effectively increased the caregivers' acceptance of children's behaviors and feelings. Carefully reflecting about your own and the children's temperament can assist you with identifying strategies to meet the needs of the children who are different from yourself responsively and respectfully, and helping each child have "goodness of fit" with you.

Emotional Intelligence

Emotional competence is the demonstration of self-efficacy in emotion-provoking social interactions. In other words, infants and toddlers must learn to know, for example, not only when they need to regulate their emotions but how they need to be regulated in a given situation. The application of emotional intelligence through the demonstration of emotional competence is a lifelong task that begins early.

Healthy emotional development involves more than helping young children recognize their feelings, experience security and trust in others, enhance their positive temperament traits, and establish a healthy balance between attachment and separation-individuation. It requires gaining specific skills and self-efficacy in "emotion-eliciting social transactions" (Saarni, Campos, Camras, & Witherington, 2006, p. 250). Researchers refer to these skills as emotional competence or emotional intelligence; this textbook will utilize the latter term. Daniel Goleman has provided a concise and comprehensive view of the skills necessary for healthy social and emotional development in his books entitled *Emotional Intelligence* (1996) and *Social Intelligence* (2006). In these books, Goleman reports that the usual way of looking at intelligence as consisting only of cognitive abilities is incomplete. Eighty percent of the skills necessary for success in life are determined by what he calls **emotional intelligence (Goleman, 1996)**.

From an extensive research review, Goleman defined five *domains* that are learned early in life and are necessary for high emotional intelligence and healthy identity development. Consistent with all five domains, families and caregivers need to trust their basic instincts and use the three *A*s (Attention, Approval, and Attunement) to promote the growth of emotional intelligence. Goleman's (1996) five domains are the following:

1. **Knowing one's emotions.** Recognizing a feeling as it happens, or **self-awareness**, is the keystone of emotional intelligence. The caregiver should start helping children at birth to recognize, experience, label, and express their feelings in healthy ways. Moreover, caregivers should also help young children develop the skills needed to observe their own thoughts, feelings, and behaviors. This self-observation is called **metacognition** by cognitive psychologists. Caregivers who give a lot of feedback and

ask a lot of questions about children's thoughts, feelings, and behaviors help children develop metacognition skills in relationship to emotions.

2. Managing emotions. Handling feelings in a way that is appropriate to the situation is a skill that builds on self-awareness. Skills in soothing oneself and maintaining a balance between thoughts, feelings, and behavior are necessary to manage emotions. Caregivers need to help children with this process of self-regulation by providing a model of balance between rational behavior and expression of emotions. Toddlers, while not being expected to control their emotions all of the time, should be assisted in gaining "effortful control." Toddlers who demonstrated high levels of effortful control were lower in externalizing behaviors and higher in social competence (Spinrad, Eisenberg, Gaertner, Popp, Smith, Kupfer, et al., 2007). Thus, it appears that toddlers who can manage their emotions are better able to get along with other age-mates.

As caregivers help infants regulate their emotions, they contribute to the child's style of emotional self-regulation. For example, a parent who waits to intervene until an infant has become extremely agitated reinforces the baby's rapid rise to intense stress (Thompson, 1988) This makes it harder for the parent to soothe the baby in the future and for the baby to learn self-soothing (Berk, 2000). Parents who expressed negative emotionality when their toddler was completing a task were associated with toddlers who were less attentive to the task (Gaertner, Spinrad, & Eisenberg, 2008). Thus, adult negativity might actually decrease a child's ability to attend when negative emotions are expressed. On the other hand, when caregivers validate children's wants and needs by supporting and helping the child fulfill the need expressed by a feeling, children internalize a positive approach to managing emotions, regulating negative behaviors, and interacting with others (Gaertner, Spinrad, & Eisenberg, 2008; Spinrad, et al., 2007).

3. Motivating oneself. Channeling emotions in the service of a goal is essential for paying attention, mastery, and creativity. Goleman refers to research on getting into the flow to illustrate how children can learn to balance thought and feeling and to behave in extremely competent ways (Nakamura, 1988). A basic attitude of optimism (the belief that success is possible) and self-responsibility appear to underlie the skill of getting into the flow (Csikszentmihalyi, 1990). Caregivers of young children and infants can observe flow in infants and toddlers. For example, when an infant becomes totally engrossed in exploring her hand or the caregiver's face, you can see that her cognition, perceptions, emotions, and behaviors are all intensely focused and coordinated in her joyful exploration. When a toddler is engrossed in exploring how a toy works, you can observe the coordination of thought, feeling, and behavior that reflect being in the flow.

Many researchers of motivation consider curiosity the primary human motivator. Infants and toddlers are naturally brimming with curiosity and the desire to explore. When caregivers help fulfill basic needs at appropriate physical and safety levels and respect the children as separate individuals with the ability to take some responsibility for their own experiences, children feel secure and are able to get into the wonderful flow of exploring both internal and external worlds.

4. Recognizing emotions in others. **Empathy** (sensitivity to what others need or want) is the fundamental relationship skill. Recent research in infant development has demonstrated that newborns exhibit empathy within the first two months of life. When an infant is in the same environment with another living being in pain, the infant will do whatever possible to comfort the other (Dondi, Simion, & Caltran, 1999; Zahn-Waxler, 1991). If it is true that empathy is present at birth, then insensitivity is learned from the environment. Styles of caregiving have a profound impact on emotional self-regulation and empathy as children grow; children who see adults model empathy and frustration tolerance are more likely to develop those qualities themselves (Eisenberg, Fabes, & Spinrad, 2006). On the other hand, care that is critical, negative, punitive, or aggressive results in children who rarely show signs of concern for others. Instead, they respond with fear, anger, and physical attacks (Klimes-Dougan & Kistner, 1990). In addition, it appears that a lack of appropriate care (i.e., neglect) during the early years negatively impacts emotional intelligence. Sullivan and colleagues found that four-year-old children who were neglected were rated more poorly on measures of emotional knowledge than age-mates who were not neglected. Teachers must take great care to create a positive learning environment that promotes stability and fosters compassion for children who have not had such experiences.

Implications of this research for caregivers of young children should be obvious: insensitivity, negativity, or aggression directed at infants and toddlers results in children exhibiting those qualities toward themselves and others. Child care that is sensitive, positive, and nurturing results in children who exhibit those qualities as they grow up. Although many skills need to be encouraged and modeled more than taught, teachers should intentionally implement an "emotion-centered curriculum" that facilitates the children's development of appropriate emotional responses, regulation, and styles of expression (Hyson, 2004).

5. Handling relationships. The last domain of emotional intelligence involves interacting smoothly and demonstrating skills necessary to get along well with others. It may seem odd at first to suggest that infants and toddlers manage their relationships with others, but research indicates that infants as young as four weeks detect others' emotions through crying contagion; research provides strong evidence for a valenced response to crying (Saarni, Campos, Camras, & Witherington, 2006). Infants clearly respond to the crying of other newborns by crying. Goleman (2006) explains that through a process called **emotional contagion** infants and other humans "catch" emotions from those they are around. "We 'catch' strong emotions much as we do a rhinovirus—and so can come down the emotional equivalent of a cold" (p. 22). This process of catching emotions is unconscious, occurring in the amygdala, an almond-shaped area in the midbrain that triggers responses to signs of danger.

Infants also imitate others' behaviors and expressions within the first three months. There is no question that the behavior of a baby elicits responses from caregivers. Many families even mark their child's first smile, step, word, and so forth with great celebration. Therefore, children learn very early in life that their behavior affects others, even though the conscious awareness that "When I do A, Mommy does B" doesn't come about until between 12 and 18 months. Specific skills in working with others are spelled out later in this textbook, but it is important to understand here that development of these people skills occurs during the first years of life as a part of the relationships with primary caregivers.

Very little research has been reported on how young children develop skills to manage emotions in others. Studies of the baby's contributions to their primary relationships involve the temperament research discussed previously and studies on **interactional synchrony** (Isabella & Belsky, 1991). This term is best described as a sensitively tuned "emotional dance" in which interactions are mutually rewarding to the caregiver and the infant. The two share a positive emotional state, and the caregiver usually "follows" while the infant "leads" in the dance. One study indicated that interactional synchrony occurs only about 30 percent of the time between mothers and babies (Tronick & Cohn, 1989). Caregivers need to learn how to establish rapport in this type of interaction with infants and toddlers, to enhance their emotional development and help them learn to manage their relationships.

Interactional synchrony is the basis for healthy relationships.

To summarize, healthy self-concepts develop from young children being helped to recognize their feelings and those of other people, establishing trusting relationships with their caregivers, having their temperament traits supported, and having a healthy balance between bonding and separation-individuation. In addition, caregivers should understand the five domains of emotional intelligence and use strategies that enhance them. McLaughlin (2008) argues in her critical reflection of emotional intelligence that while skills reside within a particular individual, they must be taught through emphasizing specific relationships and community building. In other words, while emotional intelligence can be boiled down to a set of skills to be learned, to be meaningful and useful, these skills must be intentionally taught during authentic, curricular experiences.

Self-Esteem

Self-esteem can be defined as follows: the evaluation which the individual makes and customarily maintains with regard to himself: it expresses an attitude of approval or disapproval, and indicates the extent to which the individual believes himself to be capable, significant, successful, and worthy. In short, self-esteem is a personal judgment of worthiness that is expressed in the attitudes the individual holds toward himself. (Coopersmith, 1967, pp. 4–5).

Summarizing his data on childhood experiences that contribute to the development of self-esteem, Coopersmith wrote, "The most general statement about the antecedent of self-esteem can be given in terms of three conditions: total or near total acceptance of the children by their parents; clearly defined and enforced limits; and the respect and latitude for individual actions that exist within the defined limits" (1967, p. 236). It is important that children think they are worthy people. Coopersmith's three conditions for fostering self-esteem—acceptance, limits, respect—provide guidelines for caregivers and will be discussed in more depth in Chapter 6.

In general, research in the area of self-esteem has found that people who develop good self-esteem have learned and exhibit three specific skills: self-responsibility, enlightened self-interest, and a positive attitude.

1. People with good self-esteem assume responsibility for their own thoughts, feelings, and behaviors. Self-responsibility is the keystone to independence. It is accurate to state that the most important task of child care is to prepare children to function as healthy, autonomous individuals capable of providing for their needs in ways acceptable to society. Caregivers should help children take responsibility for their own wants and needs as is appropriate for their developmental level, while allowing dependency in areas in which they are not yet capable of providing for themselves. For example, learning to manage one's emotions and respond using nonaggressive strategies when a want cannot be immediately fulfilled is a developmental challenge that children face early in life (Fuller, 2001). Helping a child take as much responsibility as is age appropriate provides the child with a sense of mastery and overall successful emotional development. More information will be provided regarding self-responsibility in this chapter in the section on social development.

2. People with good self-esteem are *sensitive* and kind toward other people while addressing their own desires. In a research study, toddlers were observed interacting with familiar peers in their own homes. The focus children in the study were found to respond more positively to distress they had caused in their playmate than to distress they merely witnessed (Demetriou & Hay, 2004). Hence, the toddlers were more sensitive and responsive when they were responsible for the source of their playmate's distress.

Learning to balance one's own needs with the needs of others is not a trivial task. It is interesting that a review of the English language reveals no single word that describes a healthy self-interest in having one's needs and desires fulfilled. On the other hand, many words are available to describe a lack of self-interest (*selfless*), too much self-interest (*selfish*), and a lack of interest in other people (e.g., *insensitive, egocentric, narcissistic, aloof*). Since the skills necessary for positive self-esteem and emotional intelligence require balance between awareness of one's own needs and sensitivity to the feelings of other people, a term is required that accurately denotes a healthy amount of self-interest in fulfilling one's own needs, combined with awareness of the needs of other people.

We use the term enlightened self-interest to describe the skill of balancing awareness of one's own needs and feelings with the needs and feelings of other people. A child who learns to make other people's feelings important to the exclusion of his own feelings becomes a selfless victim living a life burdened with inappropriate responsibilities for other people. On the other hand, a child who learns to make his or her own feelings important to the exclusion of other people becomes a selfish manipulator who is insensitive and therefore alienated from intimacy with other people.

Although there are individual differences at birth, the sensitivity that children exhibit toward others later in life is clearly related to the quality of sensitivity, kindness, and respect they are shown by caregivers in the first few years of life (see Lawrence, 2006). Yet, accounting for the impact of contextual variables is not always straight-forward. Demetrious and Hay (2004) found that toddlers who had older siblings were more likely than other target children to respond negatively to their playmate's distress. Thus, adults and siblings might provide conflicting models of how to respond sensitively to another person's distress and, therefore, impact the development of positive self-esteem in different ways.

3. People with good self-esteem have a **positive attitude** about themselves. In other words, they make *conscious positive statements* to themselves about their own value and self-worth (Kocovski & Endler, 2000). Infants and toddlers internalize the moral values, beliefs, and attitudes of the people in their environment. This becomes part of their personality. The infants and young toddlers adopt the attitudes, statements, and

feelings that their caregivers direct toward them. When caregivers consistently direct affection, positive attention, approval, and respect toward young children, they feel valuable, worthy, and proud. However, when caregivers are critical, angry, demanding, or judgmental toward children, they learn guilt, anxiety, shame, and self-doubt.

✓ reading checkpoint

Before moving on with your reading, make sure that you can answer the following questions about the material discussed so far.

1. How can you apply Margaret Mahler's separation-individuation substages to your work with very young children?
2. What factors influence how teachers use the concept of goodness-of-fit with children in their care? Why is it important to realize this concept with each child?
3. How does a child's emotional IQ influence her relationships with others?
4. Explain why caregivers should establish interactional synchrony with children.

PATTERNS OF SOCIAL DEVELOPMENT

Normal patterns for social development are the result of our all-important relationships with our primary caregivers. The word *relationship* implies two entities: one person *relates* with another.

Relationship Development

During infancy and toddlerhood, respect for the child's physical and psychological boundaries is crucial to healthy social development. Because infants begin life unable to care for their physical being, it is necessary for caregivers to intrude on their physical boundaries to provide care. *Intrude* is used here because the baby has no choice in how the caregiver handles his or her body. When the caregiver respects the baby's body, the baby feels secure and loved. However, when the caregiver doesn't respect the baby's body and is rough or insensitive, he or she causes feelings of insecurity and physical pain (Freed, 1991).

The same principle of respect holds true for emotional boundaries. When the caregiver respects the baby's feelings and provides a positive emotional connection, the baby feels secure. In contrast, anger, criticism, or ignoring the baby is disrespectful and results in insecurity and emotional pain. In the previous section on emotional development, handling relationships was discussed as one of the five domains of emotional intelligence. The skill of handling relationships requires that the caregiver manage her own emotions, demonstrate sensitivity to the child's feelings, and communicate in a way that creates interactional synchrony. To maintain this finely tuned emotional dance, the caregiver must be aware of and respect the

Healthy relationships develop from positive attention, approval, and attunement.

physical and emotional boundaries of the child and be aware of her own thoughts, feelings, and behaviors.

Children who have their physical and psychological boundaries respected learn to respect other people's feelings as well. As a result of being able to value their own wants and needs while being sensitive to other people, these children are able to establish, manage, and maintain healthy relationships with other people.

Once relationships are established with adults, the children use the acquired knowledge of how to treat others in their relationships with peers (Bowlby, 1969/2000). Infants demonstrate an increased desire to interact socially with peers over the first year of life. Research reveals "that during the second year of life, toddlers do display social skills of modest complexity" as they develop friendships and begin to negotiate conflicts (Rubin, Bukowski, & Parker, 2006, p. 587). The complexity can be shown in the quality and depth of their relationships with peers as toddlers. For example, toddlers have been found to have reciprocal relationships based "not only on their mutual exchange of positive overtures, but also by agonistic interactions" (Rubin, Bukowski, & Parker, 2006, p. 588). In other words, their relationships can be characterized by great warmth, aggression, and argumentative interactions as they learn to work closely with peers. As this research shows, there is rapid development in the acquisition of social skills during the first two years of life as infants move from not knowing they are separate individuals to developing reciprocal relationships with others.

spotlight on research

Father-Child Interactions and Developmental Outcomes

Much research has been conducted on the impact of mother-child interactions on developmental outcomes for young children. In the past couple of decades, researchers have shifted their focus to include the important and differential roles that fathers play in developmental outcomes. A meta-analysis of 24 publications discovered that 22 of the publications showed father engagement (i.e., direct interaction with the child) to be associated with a range of positive outcomes, although no specific form of engagement was shown to yield better outcomes than another (Sarkadi, Kristiansson, Oberklaid, & Bremberg, 2008). For example, there was "evidence to indicate that father *engagement* positively affects the social, behavioral, psychological and cognitive outcomes of children" (Sarkadi, et al., 2008, p. 155, emphasis in original).

Fathers seem to provide an important context as children are learning to regulate their emotions. The data suggest that fathers in low-income families are particularly important for helping very young children gain control over intense emotions. Children who live with their biological fathers or children who have involved nonresidential biological fathers had higher levels of self-regulation and lower levels of aggression when compared with children with unstable father connections (Vogel, Bradley, Raikes, Boller, & Shears, 2006). The researchers concluded that "to some degree, children living with their biological fathers seem developmentally better off, primarily in the self-regulatory and behavioral domains" (Vogel, et al., 2006, p. 204). When children are better able to manage their emotions, they should engage in aggressive or harmful behaviors less frequently. The meta-analysis described above also found that father involvement was associated with decreased aggressive behaviors for boys (Sarkadi, et al., 2008). While these positive behaviors are most important developmental outcomes, the origin of the pathway is still unclear. It is possible that the outcome of reduced aggression is linked to the increase in emotional regulation skills. More research is needed to discern the complex relationships between father involvement and child developmental trajectories.

Other research has shown the positive impact of father-child interactions on cognitive development. Feldman (2007) discovered that father-child synchrony at five months was related to complex symbol use and the sequences of symbolic play at three years of age. In addition, Bronte-Tinkew, Carano, Horowitz, & Kinukawa (2008), found that various aspects of father involvement (cognitively stimulating activities, physical care, paternal warmth, and caregiving activities) were associated with greater babbling and exploring objects with a purpose as well as a lower likelihood of infant cognitive delay. Another research study compared father-toddler social toy play for families involved in an Early Head Start (EHS) program to dads not involved in that program. These researchers found that fathers who had been in an EHS program showed more complexity in their play with their children (Roggman, Boyce, Cook, Christiansen, & Jones, 2004). For children, this complex play was associated with better cognitive and social outcomes; specifically, the children scored better on tests of cognitive competence, language acquisition, and emotional regulation.

This body of research makes it clear that educators need to create policies and engage in practices that actively involve fathers in the care and education of their infants and toddlers because doing so is related to better developmental outcomes (i.e., cognitive, social, and emotional) for the children. We need to (1) help families understand the "... the potential value of active father involvement in children's lives during these critical early years" (Roggman, et al., 2004, 103); and (2) involve fathers in the daily care and educational decisions as much as we do mothers. Many educators, like the population in general, continue to view mothers as the primary caregiver. This means that we tend to direct more communication toward them rather than the fathers. As the expectations of fathers change, many are often unsure of how to carry out these new responsibilities. Educators can provide information to families about the important role fathers play in promoting child development and coach fathers as they acquire the skills necessary for positive engagement and/or complex play with toys.

Other developmental milestones facilitate peer interactions and relationships as well. For example, between 24 and 36 months the rapid language development of the toddler provides the basis for understanding the feelings of other people, using more words to express feelings, and actively participating in managing relationships. As language increases, so does the toddler's more complete model of the social world. Active **self-talk** dialogues, make-believe play, and beliefs about the self, the world (including other people), and the self in relation to others are exhibited during this period (Gopnik & Wellman, 1994). By the time children reach school age, they have established a model of the world that includes self-concept, beliefs about the world (including other people), and a style of communication that influences how they will manage relationships with others.

Contributions by numerous social learning theorists help us to understand how infants and toddlers develop relationships. The first relationships we have in the world with our parent(s) and caregivers result in the formation of the self, which forms the basis for future relationships. Through these relationships, very young children come to understand how they are part of and separate from others (e.g., self-recognition) as well as how they produce reactions and react to other's behavior (e.g., sense of agency). Infants as young as nine months demonstrate the emergence of **self-recognition**; the majority of 15-month-olds have it (Bullock & Lutkenhaus, 1990).

Self-recognition is measured by putting a mark on an infant's face (typically the nose) and having him look in the mirror. If he demonstrates self-recognition, he wipes his nose to remove the mark; if he laughs at the reflection or touches the mirror to wipe away the mark, he has not yet demonstrated self-recognition. While it may seem like a simple concept to grasp, self-recognition is a complex developmental task which represents not only social development but also the brain's ability to represent the concept symbolically and mentally (Bard, Todd, Bernier, Love, & Leavens, 2006; Sugiura, Sassa, Jeong, Horie, Sato, & Kawashima, 2008).

Many theorists hypothesize that the development of self is also rooted in a **sense of agency**; for example, awareness that our actions cause other objects and people to react in predictable ways (Pipp, Easterbrooks, & Brown, 1993). By two years of age, a sense of self is well established and toddlers express possession of objects with *me* and *mine* (Levine, 1983).

The opposite side of the coin from separation-individuation is presented in the widely accepted view of infant emotional ties to the caregiver in Bowlby's ethological theory of attachment (Bowlby, 1969/2000). According to this theory, the infant's relationship to the parent starts as a set of innate signals that keep the caregiver close to the baby and proceeds through four phases, as follows:

1. *The preattachment phase* (birth to six weeks) occurs when the baby grasps, cries, smiles, and gazes to keep the caregiver engaged.
2. *The "attachment-in-the-making" phase* (six weeks to eight months) consists of the baby responding differently to familiar caregivers than to strangers. Face-to-face interactions relieve distress, and the baby expects that the caregiver will respond when signaled.

3. *The clear-cut attachment phase* (eight months to two years) is when the baby exhibits separation anxiety, protests caregiver departure, and acts deliberately to maintain caregiver attention.
4. Formation of a *reciprocal relationship phase* (18 months onward) occurs when children negotiate with the caregiver and are willing to give and take in relationships.

Researchers measure attachment history for young toddlers using an experimental design called the Strange Situation. This experiment involves a series of separations and reunions. Four categories have been used to classify attachment patterns: secure, ambivalent/insecure, avoidant/insecure (Ainsworth, 1967, 1973) and disoriented/insecure (Hesse & Main, 2000; Main & Solomon, 1990). These attachment patterns have been found to be influenced by the type of caregiving provided and to result in different social outcomes for toddlers, preschoolers, and school-age children.

Infants' attachment styles have been found to correlate to sets of caregivers' behaviors. Regarding secure attachments, infants and caregivers engage in finely tuned, synchronous dances where the adults carefully read the infants' cues, see events from the infants' perspectives, and respond accordingly (Isabella & Belsky, 1991; NICHD Early Child Care Research Network, 1997; Oppenheim & Koren-Karie, 2002). More specifically, infants classified as securely attached tend to have caregivers who

- consistently respond to infants' needs.
- interpret infants' emotional signals sensitively.
- regularly express affection.
- permit babies to influence the pace and direction of their mutual interactions (for reviews see Honig, 2002 and McDevitt & Ormrod, 2010).

In contrast, caregivers of insecurely attached infants tend to have difficulty caring for the infants (e.g., dislike physical contact, are inconsistent, unpredictable, insensitive, and intrusive) or are unwilling to invest energy in the relationship (Belsky, Rovine, & Taylor, 1984; Isabella, 1993; Thompson, 1998). In some instances the caregivers act on their own wishes rather than the infants' needs, while at other times, they respond to the infants' needs with irritability or anger. For children in the severest category of insecurity—disoriented—the caregivers can be addicted to drugs or alcohol or be severely depressed or otherwise mentally ill; they are unable to care for their own needs, let alone their children's. In several studies, these caregivers were found to have experienced their own attachment-related traumas when they were children (Behrens, Hesse, & Main, 2007; Hesse & Main, 2000; Madigan, Moran, Schuengel, Pederson, & Otten, 2007).

The Importance of Attachment

Attachment histories are important to early childhood educators because these childhood relationships set the foundation for later close relationships, especially those with peers. Securely attached children tend to be more independent, empathic, and socially competent preschoolers, especially in comparison to insecurely attached children (DeMulder, Denham, Schmidt, Mitchell, 2000; LaFreniere, & Sroufe, 1985; Rydell, Bohlin, & Thorell, 2005). The impact of infant attachment classification has also been associated with various aspects of social competence for school-age children and adolescents (Booth-LaForce, & Oxford, 2008; Feeney, Cassidy, & Ramos-Marcuse, 2008; Yoon, Ang, Fung, Wong, & Yiming, 2006). Thus, supporting and complementing strong, positive parent-child attachment can have long-term developmental consequences (Puckett & Black, 2002).

Fourteen-month-old Louise is walking in the yard carrying a small truck in her hand. She sees Randy, the caregiver, and squeals and giggles. She walks rapidly to Randy with arms up and a big smile on her face. The relationships families and caregivers form with very young children help to determine what relationships children will develop later in life. Strong, sensitive attachment can have a positive influence on a child's confidence, self-concept, and patterns of social interactions for the remainder of his or her life. While most research on caregiver-child relationships has examined infants with their parents, the findings from this research apply equally well to infant-caregiver relationships.

1. Infants need to establish emotional attachment with their caregivers. This attachment develops through regular activities that address the infants' basic needs such as feeding and changing diapers. Yet, caregivers should use sensitive physical contact such as cuddling and touching to comfort and stimulate interactions. When caregivers learn the child's needs, schedules, likes, dislikes, and temperament, and then respond to the child's preferences, they teach the infant that he or she is an important person.

As discussed in Chapter 1, when more than one caregiver is responsible for a group of children, a primary caregiving system can be used to divide the work and best meet the needs of the children. The primary caregiver works closely with family members to establish consistent routines and strategies for meeting the infant's needs. She can share her knowledge about the child's needs and preferences so that other caregivers can match their care to the child. Alternate caregivers should report observations about the child's behaviors to the primary caregiver. Thus, the primary caregiver has two main responsibilities: (1) to establish a special attachment with the child and (2) to gather, coordinate, and share information about the child with other caregivers and the family.

2. Each child needs to have a caregiver respond sensitively and consistently to cries and cues of distress. The child then learns to trust the caregiver. When crying infants are left alone for several minutes before a caregiver responds, or when the caregiver responds quickly sometimes and leaves them alone sometimes, children are confused and have difficulty establishing a strong attachment because they cannot develop a strong sense of trust in the caregiver. Responding quickly to infant and toddler needs does not spoil children. It conveys that you hear their communication and that they are important enough for you to respond to it. Your response should be quick but not hurried. To illustrate, Nancy is rocking Alvero when Karola wakes from her nap. Nancy greets Karola by saying, "Look who is awake. I am rocking Alvero. He is almost asleep. I'll put him in his crib and then get you up." As this example shows, Nancy talked to Karola, the crying infant, in a soothing voice before she was able to physically address her need to get out of her crib. While some readers may question the amount of language provided to Karola, they should recall that receptive language develops before productive language and that language serves not only a communication function but also as a tool for regulating strong emotions. Remember, the most important task for an infant or toddler is to develop trust and a secure attachment to the caregiver. For this to occur, the caregiver must respond consistently and sensitively to the child's needs.

3. Each child and his or her primary caregiver need special time together. This "getting to know you" and "let's enjoy each other" time should be a calm, playful time to relax, look, touch, smile, giggle, cuddle, stroke, talk, whisper, sing, make faces, and establish the wonderful dance of interactional synchrony. Sometimes this can be active time, including holding an infant up in the air at arm's length while you talk and giggle and then bringing the infant up close for a hug. Other times, this can mean very quiet activities, such as rocking, cuddling, and softly stroking in a loving way.

4. The caregiver must treat each child as a special, important person. Infants and toddlers are not objects to be controlled but individuals of worth with whom you establish a respectful, positive emotional relationship while providing for their physical, cognitive, and learning needs.

In conclusion, caregivers should be very aware of factors that affect attachment security in young children. Sensitive caregiving that responds appropriately to the child's signals and needs is the most important factor in supporting children's development. The findings from many studies clearly reveal that securely attached infants have primary caregivers who respond quickly to signals, express positive feelings, and handle babies with tenderness and sensitivity. The best principle for infant and toddler social development is probably that adults cannot be too "in tune" or give too much approval and affection; young children can't be spoiled. Your sensitive caring sets the basis for future relationships that they will have throughout their lives.

Locus of Control Development: Self-Control and Self-Responsibility
Our culture expects individuals to behave in ways that are not harmful to themselves, other people, or the environment. These expectations are taught to infants and toddlers by their families, caregivers, and society. To live successfully with other people, children must learn to control their desires and impulses (self-control), and to take responsibility for themselves appropriately for their age and developmental

abilities. The extent to which people perceive their lives as within their own control determines what is called **locus of control**. The word *locus* in this context means perceived location, so children who learn to take responsibility for themselves have an *internal* locus of control. Conversely, people who perceive their lives to be controlled by others have an *external* locus of control.

Throughout our discussions of emotional and social development, the cited research has repeatedly indicated that healthy emotional and social development are closely related to self-control and self-responsibility. For example, two domains of emotional intelligence are self-motivation and self-control, and good self-esteem requires self-responsibility. Therefore, understanding development of a healthy internal locus of control is essential for caregivers of young children.

Much research has been conducted on how young children develop morality, which is the basis for self-control. Current thinking is that children need to move beyond their family's perspectives and internalize from their own perspective that certain behaviors are right and wrong (Grusec & Goodnow, 1994). For infants and toddlers to internalize that certain behaviors are acceptable and others are not for *them*, they must feel that they have the power to choose their own actions. Unfortunately, many adults believe that they must control children's behavior in order to care for children and keep them safe. The fact that many families and other caregivers think that *they* control children's behavior may be largely responsible for many social problems created by people not taking responsibility for their own thoughts, feelings, and behavior. It is important to understand that it is the *perception* of control that adults have, and not actual control, that causes children to develop an external locus of control.

Many parents and caregivers perceive themselves to be responsible for children's behavior when, in fact, they are neglectful in caring for and providing proper guidance for children. The consistent emotional message communicated to children by adults who feel that they are responsible for the child's behavior is "You have no choice but to do what I tell you." Research on the effects of punishment reveals that children of highly punitive parents are especially aggressive and defiant outside the home (Strassberg, Dodge, Petitt, & Bates, 1994; Straus, 2001).

Child psychologists and counselors observe external locus of control in many young children referred for behavior problems. In two recent studies conducted with older children, researchers found that the more parents espoused an external locus of control (i.e., attempted to control their children's behavior) the higher the likelihood their children had externalizing behavior problems (e.g., increased aggression with peers, lack of frustration tolerance) as they got older (McCabe, Goehrigh, Yeh, & Lau, 2008; McElroy & Rodriguez, 2008). In another research study, staff in an agency for troubled children altered their practices to shift children from an external to a more internal locus of control by making the children responsible for setting and achieving therapeutic goals (Boldt, Witzel, Russell, & Jones, 2007). What early childhood educators should take away from this research is that (1) all children, regardless of their ages, need to feel a sense of power over their lives; and

Providing choices of what to clean up helps to develop responsibility and an internal locus of control.

(2) building an internal locus of control during the infant-toddler period is easier than attempting to replace an external locus of control in the future.

Development of an internal locus of control requires that caregivers respect the right of young children to make many choices within their environment, including choosing their behavior. Many strategies exist that are effective in developing an internal locus of control such as redirection, problem-solving, a warm caregiver-child relationship, and explanations of consequences, including expectations for future behavior (Larzelere, Schneider, Larson, & Pike, 1996; Marion, 2007). While these strategies will be discussed in more depth in Chapter 6, we will address child choice in the next section.

The question teachers face is how to respect children's choices and still provide the guidance and care the young children require to remain safe and healthy. In addition, since children choose their behavior, they must experience the positive consequences that follow when they choose to behave positively and the negative consequences that follow for choosing to behave negatively (within safety guidelines, of course).

More important than potential consequences for actions to this discussion, is the effect of the power to choose on the development of an internal locus of control.

Much research has been conducted investigating the impact of choice on internal control and motivation. In a meta-analysis of 41 research studies, Patall, Cooper, & Robinson (2008) found that choice does have a positive impact on internal motivation as well as effort, performance, and perceived competence. In addition, choices that allowed for the expression of individuality (e.g., what color of paper or pens to use) were particularly powerful motivators. Moreover, "the largest positive effect of choice on intrinsic motivation was found when participants made two to four choices in a single experimental manipulation" (Patall, et al., 2008, p. 295). Thus, it seems that having too few choices does not allow children to feel a sense of control over their environment, while having too many may result in cognitive overload. While none of the research studies included in the meta-analyses specifically studied infants and toddlers, the results are nonetheless instructional for teachers of very young children. Early childhood educators need to consider when they are providing choices throughout their day and how many choices are being provided at any one given time. In addition, the choices need to teach the children a sense of self-control and self-responsibility while encouraging self-expression.

A final word of caution regarding self-control is important here. Many children develop an internal locus of control that is too strict and limiting of their thoughts, feelings, and behavior. Over-controlled children are likely to become obsessive-compulsive, overly anxious, fearful of making mistakes, or rigid and judgmental toward other people. To avoid development of over-control with children, the definition of misbehavior should be limited to behaviors that are clearly harmful to the child, another person, pet, or the environment. Thoughts or feelings should not be defined as misbehavior. These are *never* wrong, but how we express them may be harmful. These distinctions are essential for helping infants and toddlers develop a healthy internal locus of control.

Prosocial behaviors

Children who possess a healthy internal locus of control know that their actions impact those around them. Yet, that is not a sufficient condition for insuring that the young children use their personal power to benefit others. It has been found that when parents adopt particular guidance strategies (e.g., induction, which is a type of verbal discipline in which the adult gives explanations or reasons for why the child should change her behavior), they tend to have children who exhibit more prosocial behaviors (see Eisenberg, et al., 2006 for a review). Thus, adults who provide feedback about appropriate, helpful behaviors, emphasizing the impact of the child's actions on another person, tend to be associated with children who engage in more prosocial behavior.

In this context, the difference between providing feedback and external rewards cannot be accentuated enough. Research shows that the application of verbal praise for prosocial behaviors actually undermines their development (Grusec, 1991).

Likewise, providing concrete rewards may increase prosocial behaviors in a given context, but the "long-term effect of concrete rewards may be negative" (Eisenberg, et al., 2006, p. 672). It appears that external rewards (verbal or concrete) decrease the internal drive to do a good deed because the adult places emphasis on getting something. In other words, such adult behaviors undo the child's natural tendencies toward prosocial behaviors by teaching him that he should engage in a prosocial behavior only if it benefits himself (Warneken & Tomasello, 2008).

In conclusion, it appears that healthy social development is related to secure attachment and trust in our primary caregivers, healthy identity development, and caregiver respect and sensitivity to children's physical and psychological boundaries. Healthy social development involves children being aware of their own needs and desires and those of other people, as well as communicating verbally and nonverbally in ways that establish interactional synchrony with others. Infants and toddlers need help in developing an internal locus of control, self-control, and self-responsibility. Table 3–2 presents some of the major milestones for social development from birth through thirty-six months.

TABLE 3–2   MILESTONES FOR SOCIAL DEVELOPMENT: BIRTH TO 36 MONTHS

AGE	ACTIVITIES
Birth to 6 months	Fusing with mother evolves into basic self-discriminations Matches feelings and tones of caregiver Demonstrates empathy Exhibits interactional synchrony Exhibits social smile Shows happiness at familiar faces Gains caregiver attention intentionally
7–12 months	Exhibits self-recognition and discrimination from others Seeks independence in actions Keeps family members or caregiver in sight Starts imitative play
12–24 months	Exhibits possessiveness Acts differently toward different people Commonly shows stranger anxiety Engages in parallel play Shows strong ownership
24–36 months	Shares, but not consistently Recognized differences between *mine* and *yours* Understands perspective of other people Helps others Begins to play cooperatively

chapter 3 BIRTH TO THIRTY-SIX MONTHS: SOCIAL AND EMOTIONAL DEVELOPMENTAL PATTERNS 93

✓ reading checkpoint

Before moving on with your reading, make sure that you can answer the following questions about the material discussed so far.

1. What does it mean for a child to be securely attached? Insecurely attached? Why is it important for caregivers to establish secure relationships with the infants and toddlers in their care?

2. What are the pros and cons of a child developing an internal locus of control? An external locus of control?

3. Provide and explain an example of a teacher facilitating the development of prosocial skills in a toddler.

CHILDREN WITH SPECIAL RIGHTS

As discussed in previous chapters, teachers must be aware of both universal and unique patterns of development for infants and toddlers. This section will outline just a few of the ways in which infants and toddlers might exhibit special rights in regards to emotional and social development.

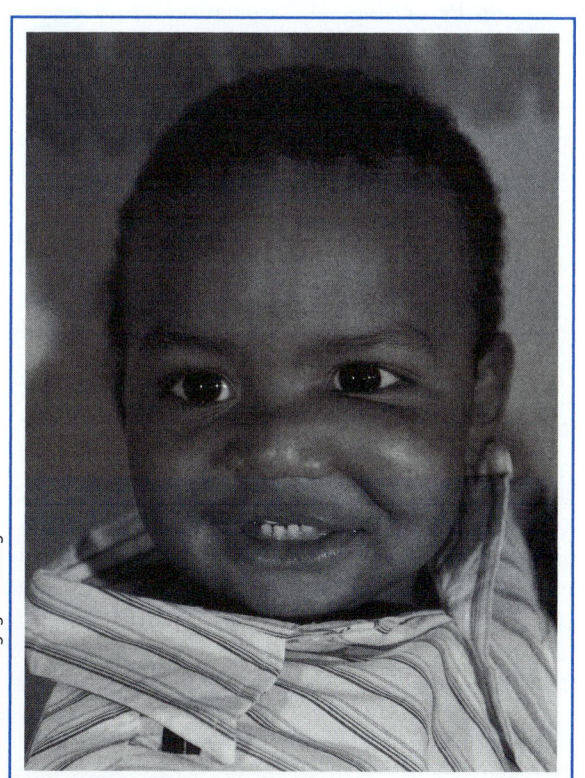

Children have different social and emotional abilities and needs.

1. **Children with Autism.** Infants and toddlers with autism exhibit disturbances in developmental rates and sequences, social interactions (i.e., extremely withdrawn), responses to sensory stimuli, communication, and the capacity to relate appropriately to people, events, and objects. The incidence of autism in the general population is very low: four to five in every 10,000 births, but males substantially outnumber females (American Psychiatric Association, 2000; Hardman, Drew & Egan, 2006). More recent data from the Centers for Disease Control and Prevention (CDC, 2008) suggests that the prevalence could range as high as seven to twelve in every 10,000 births because 1 in 150 eight-year olds in the six participating states were diagnosed with Autism Spectrum Disorders. Data on early assessment suggest that children as young as 18 months can be reliably diagnosed with autism, but that the tools fail to recognize the disorder in many toddlers who will later show clear symptoms of the disorder (Watson, Baranek, & DiLavore, 2003). Much research has continued to create tools and increase the reliability of diagnosing autism for infants and toddlers (see, for example, Brian, Bryson, Garon, Roberts, Smith, Szatmari, et al., 2008; Wetherby, Brosnan-Maddox, Peace, & Newton, 2008). Research on structured early intervention programs, which include parents, has yielded highly encouraging results. For more information, contact the National Society for Children and Adults with Autism, the American Psychological Association, or your local psychological association.

2. **Attachment Disorder** is a term intended to describe children who have experienced severe problems or disruptions in their early relationships. Children with an attachment disorder fail to form normal attachments to primary caregivers. Attachment disorders appear to be the result of "grossly inadequate care" during infancy and toddlerhood (Hardman, Drew & Egan, 2006, p. 239). This disorder results in noticeably abnormal and developmentally inept social relatedness (Cain, 2006). For more information, contact your state Infant Mental Health Organization, local mental health providers, and community-specific organizations, such as an Early Head Start program. In addition, the website of the American Academy of Child and Adolescent Psychiatry (AACAP) provides useful information as well as resources for families and teachers.

3. **Mental Health Disorders** describe a wide range of unique child characteristics that can begin during the infant-toddler developmental period. While the prevalence of such disorders is very, very low for this age group, serious disorders such as depression, childhood schizophrenia, and anxiety disorders have been known to occur. However, some research suggests that the interaction of particular parent characteristics (e.g., depression symptoms) and infant traits (e.g., components of temperament) predict higher levels of depression-like symptoms in toddlers (Gartstein & Bateman, 2008).

4. **Children with Multiple Disabilities.** As defined by the Individuals with Disabilities Education Act (IDEA) federal regulations, many children experience

multiple disabilities or concomitant impairments, meaning that they have more than one identified exceptionality. The particular combination causes such severe educational issues that the individual cannot be accommodated in special education programs designed solely for one of the special needs [34 Code of Federal Regulations 300.7(c)(7) (1999), as cited in Hardman, Drew, & Egan, 2006].

5. Children with Fetal Alcohol Syndrome or Fetal Alcohol Effect (FAS/FAE). Children with FAS/FAE were exposed to an adverse environmental agent, alcohol, during the periods of prenatal development. Children with FAS typically have growth delays, facial abnormalities, mental retardation, impulsivity, and behavioral problems (McDevitt & Ormrod, 2010). The difference between FAS and FAE seems to be the amount, frequency, and duration of alcohol consumed by the mother during the pregnancy. However, researchers and medical professionals do not know how much alcohol needs to be ingested to produce FAS instead of FAE. Because of the diversity of characteristics for these children, intervention programs tend to focus on specific aspects of the disability, i.e., cognitive disabilities.

6. Environmentally Promoted Problems for Infants and Toddlers. Children who experience abuse or neglect by their families are included in this category. Results from several studies reveal that the most effective interventions involve the whole family with specific focus being placed on coping with the effects of the maltreatment for the children (Hardman, Drew, & Egan, 2006). When the children attend day care, teachers can focus on providing adequate and nutritious food and assisting the children with acquiring specific skills such as impulse control and anger management. For more information, contact your local health department, department of social/ human services, or community-specific organizations, such as an Early Head Start program.

We would like to be very clear that teachers have particular responsibilities regarding the identification of special rights. Teachers should carefully observe, report those observations to family members, and, in partnership with the family members, enlist the assistance of experts trained in clinical diagnoses. Only such experts can diagnose a child. As a teacher you should never tell a family member that you think their child has a particular disorder or delay. In fact, doing so oversteps your areas of expertise and opens yourself to specific legal liabilities. Your job is to explain what you have observed and allow them to draw their own conclusions. You can note, however, if any of the behaviors "raise a red flag" (i.e., item of concern) or "raise a yellow flag" (i.e., item to be watched further) and why. First Steps (a federally funded intervention program), Early Head Start, and public schools should all have qualified personnel on staff to assess, evaluate, and provide diagnoses as appropriate. When an Individualized Family Service Plan has been constructed, it is your responsibility as a professional educator to carry out the aspects of the early intervention plan that are assigned or designated to you.

✓ reading checkpoint

Before moving on with your reading, make sure that you can answer the following questions about the material discussed so far.

1. Explain three special rights very young children might have in relationship to emotional and social development.
2. What is your role as a professional educator regarding children with special rights?

SUMMARY

Gaining emotional and social competence is a complex endeavor that results from the interplay between child characteristics and environmental influences. Adults must assume the responsibility for supporting and facilitating very young children's social and emotional development. One of the primary vehicles through which such competencies develop is the adult-child relationship. Responsive, attuned care that is delivered in synchrony with the child provides a strong foundation for concepts such as emotional intelligence, self-esteem, and prosocial behaviors. When children possess specific social and emotional rights, they benefit from individualized care plans that support their developing skills.

key terms

- **emotional intelligence**
- **empathy**
- **enlightened self-interest**
- **goodness of fit**
- **interactional synchrony**
- **locus of control**
- **metacognition**
- **omnipotent**
- **positive attitude**
- **self-awareness**
- **self-esteem**
- **self-recognition**
- **self-responsibility**
- **sense of agency**
- **separation-individuation**
- **temperament**

case study

Marcus

You should now have a working knowledge of normal patterns of development in each of the four areas for children under the age of 36 months. To test your understanding of information in Chapters 2 and 3, decide if Marcus is advanced, behind, or at age level in the following evaluation summary.

Marcus, who is 24 months old, is in child care from 7:30 A.M. to 4:00 P.M. five days a week. An evaluation of his development in each of the four major areas revealed the following observations:

Physical Factors. Marcus is 36 inches tall, weighs 35 pounds, has 20/20 vision, and can focus and track across a line of letters fluidly. He has all 20 baby teeth, can stand on one foot and hop, and is interested in toilet learning. He can throw a ball with each hand and use a fork to eat.

Emotional Factors. Marcus clings to his caregiver much of the time and shows anxiety at the presence of strangers. He is compliant and follows directions when he feels secure, but he can become whiny when he does not receive enough individual attention. He has difficulty understanding his feelings or soothing himself. When not involved with his caregiver or other children, Marcus has difficulty being at ease.

Social Factors. Marcus has some difficulty determining what things are his, and he cooperates with other children only when he has the full attention of his caregiver. He is easily emotionally hurt by other children and cannot defend himself when they take advantage of him. He is seldom able to be sensitive to the feelings of other children. Although his language skills are sufficient, Marcus screams rather than uses words when his peers bother him.

Cognitive Factors. When he feels secure, Marcus is curious, explores his environment, and gains a lot of physical knowledge. Although he has some difficulty interacting with peers, he participates in active, creative pretend play and exhibits a logical sequence in the stories he makes up. He uses double substitution in play and understands four- and five-direction sequences.

1. Determine if you think Marcus is advanced for his age level, at age level, or below age level for each area of development. Explain how you drew each conclusion.
2. In which of the four areas is it most difficult for you to make an assessment of Marcus? What additional information do you need? Why?
3. If you decided that Marcus is (1) advanced in physical development, (2) below age expectations for emotional and social development, and (3) at age level in cognitive development, then you have a good working understanding of typical, or universal, patterns of development. If not, explain how your answers were different. What information did you attend to and why?

QUESTIONS AND EXPERIENCES FOR REFLECTION

1. During the children's alert play time, observe two children of different ages between birth and three years, focusing on one area (emotional or social). Write down everything each child does and says for five minutes.

Make a chart to compare the behaviors, using the following as a guide:

Child:	Age:	Child:	Age:
Area:		Area:	
Behaviors		Behaviors	

2. Observe one child between birth and three years of age interacting with one adult. List the behaviors each uses to get and maintain the other's attention.

	Initial Behavior	Response
Child		
Adult		
Child		
Adult		
Child		
Adult		

3. Define emotional intelligence.

4. How do children learn from relationships? What role will you as caregiver play in this process?

REFERENCES

Ainsworth, M. D. S. (1967). *Infancy in Uganda: Infant care and the growth of love.* Baltimore: Johns Hopkins University Press.

Ainsworth, M. D. S. (1973). The development of infant-mother attachment. In B. M. Caldwell & H. N. Ricciuti (Eds.), *Review of child development research: Vol. 3. Child development and social policy.* Chicago: University of Chicago Press.

American Psychiatric Association. (2000). *Diagnostic and statistical manual of mental disorders* (4th ed., text revision). Washington, DC: Author.

Bard, K. A., Todd, B. K., Bernier, C., Love, J., & Leavens, D. A. (2006). Self-Awareness in Human and Chimpanzee Infants: What Is Measured and What Is Meant by the Mark and Mirror Test? *Infancy, 9* (2), 191–219.

Behrens, K. Y., Hesse, E., & Main, M. (2007). Mothers' attachment status as determined by the Adult Attachment Interview predicts their 6-year-olds' reunion responses: A study conducted in Japan. *Developmental Psychology,* 43 (6) 1553–1567.

Belsky, J., Rovine, M., & Taylor, D. G. (1984). The Pennsylvania Infant and Family Development Project, part 3. The origins of individual differences in infant-mother attachments: Maternal and infant contributions. *Child Development,* 55, 718–728.

Berk, L. E. (2000). *Child development* (5th ed.). Needham Heights, MA: Allyn and Bacon.

Bowlby, J. (2000). *Attachment and loss: Vol. 1. Attachment.* New York: Basic Books. (Original work published 1969).

Boldt, R. W., Witzel, M., Russell, C., Jones, V. (2007). Replacing Coercive Power with Relationship Power. *Reclaiming Children & Youth,* 15 (4), 243–248.

Booth-LaForce, C. & Oxford, M. L. (2008). Trajectories of social withdrawal from grades 1 to 6: Prediction from early parenting, attachment, and temperament. *Developmental Psychology,* 44 (5), 1298–1313.

Brian, J., Bryson, S. E., Garon, N., Roberts, W., Smith, I. M., Szatmari, P., & Zwaigenbaum, L. (2008). Clinical assessment of autism in high-risk 18-month-olds. Autism: The International Journal of Research & Practice, 12 (5), 433–456.

Bridgett, D., Gartstein, M., Putnam, S., McKay, T., Iddins, E., Robertson, C., Ramsey, K., & Rittmueller, A. (2009). Maternal and contextual influences and the effect of temperament development during infancy on parenting in toddlerhood. *Infant Behavior & Development, 32*(1), 103–116.

Bronte-Tinkew, J., Carano, J., Horowitz, A., & Kinukawa, A. (2008). Involvement among resident fathers and links to infant cognitive outcomes. *Journal of Family Issues,* 29 (9), 1211–1244.

Bullock, M., & Lutkenhaus, P. (1990). Who am I? The development of self-understanding in toddlers. *Merrill-Palmer Quarterly, 36,* 217–238.

Cain, C. S. (2006). *Attachment disorders: treatment strategies for traumatized children*. Lanham, MD: Jason Aronson.

Caspi, A., & Silva, P. A. (1995). Temperamental qualities at age three predict personality traits in young adulthood: Longitudinal evidence from a birth cohort. *Child Development, 66,* 486–498.

Centers for Disease Control and Prevention (CDC) (2008). Autism Information Center. Frequently Asked Questions: Prevalence. Retrieved on August 12, 2009 from http://www.cdc.gov/ncbddd/Autism/faq_prevalence.htm.

Chess, S., Thomas, A., & Birch, H. G. (1977). *Your child is a person: A psychological approach to parenthood without guilt.* New York: Penguin Books.

Churchill, S. L. (2003). Goodness-of-fit in early childhood settings. *Early Childhood Education Journal, 31,* 113–118.

Coopersmith, S. (1967). *The antecedents of self-esteem.* San Francisco: W. H. Freeman.

Csikszentmihalyi, M. (1990). *The psychology of optimal experience* (1st ed.). New York: Harper & Row.

Davis, E., Schoppe-Sullivan, S., Mangelsdorf, S., & Brown, G. (2009). The Role of Infant Temperament in Stability and Change in Coparenting Across the First Year of Life. *Parenting: Science & Practice*, 9(1/2), 143–159.

Demetriou, H., & Hay, D. F. (2004). Toddlers' Reactions to the Distress of Familiar Peers: The Importance of Context. *Infancy*, 6 (2), 299–318.

DeMulder, E. K., Denham, S., Schmidt, M., Mitchell, J. (2000). Q-sort assessment of attachment security during the preschool years: Links from home to school. *Developmental Psychology*, 36 (2), 274–282.

De Schipper, J. C., Tavecchio, L. W. C., Van IJzendoorn, M.H., & Van Zeijl, J. (2004). Goodness-of-fit in center day care: Relations of temperament, stability, and quality of care with the child's adjustment. *Early Childhood Research Quarterly*, 19, 257–272.

Dondi, M., Simion, F., & Caltran, G. (1999). Can newborns discriminate between their own cry and the cry of another newborn infant? *Developmental Psychology*, 35, 418–426.

Eisenberg, N., Fabes, R., & Spinrad, T. L. (2006). Prosocial development. In N. Eisenberg (Ed.), *Handbook of child psychology: Vol. 3. Social, emotional, and personality development* (6th ed., pp. 646-718). New York: Wiley.

Erikson, E. H. (1950). *Childhood and society*. New York: Norton.

Feeney, B. C., Cassidy, J., & Ramos-Marcuse, F. (2008). The generalization of attachment representations to new social situations: Predicting behavior during initial interactions with strangers. *Journal of Personality and Social Psychology*, 95 (6), 1481–1498.

Feldman, R. (2007). Parent-infant synchrony and the construction of shared timing; physiological precursors, developmental outcomes, and risk conditions. *Journal of Child Psychology and Psychiatry*, 48 (3/4), 329–354.

Franyo, G. A., & Hyson, M. C. (1999). Temperament training for early childhood caregivers: A study of the effectiveness of training. *Child & Youth Forum*, 28, 329–349.

Freed, A. M. (1991). *T. A. (transactional analysis) for tots*. Torrance, CA: Jalmar Press.

Fuller, A. (2001). A blueprint for building social competencies in children and adolescents. *Australian Journal of Middle Schooling*, 1(1), 40–49.

Gaertner, B. M., Spinrad, T. L., & Eisenberg, N. (2008). Focused attention in toddlers: Measurement, stability, and relations to negative emotion and parenting. *Infant & Child Development*, 17 (4), 339–363.

Gartstein, M. A., & Bateman, A. E. (2008). Early manifestations of childhood depression: influences of infant temperament and parental depressive symptoms. *Infant & Child Development*, 17 (3), 223–248.

Goleman, D. (2006). *Social intelligence: The new science of human relationships*. New York: Random House, Inc.

Goleman, D. (1996). *Emotional intelligence: Why it can matter more than IQ*. New York: Bantam Books.

Gopnik, A., & Wellman, H. M. (1994). The "theory" theory. In L. A. Hirschfeld & S. A. Gelman (Eds.), *Mapping the mind: Domain specificity in cognition and culture*. Cambridge, UK: Cambridge University Press.

Greenberg, J. R., & Mitchell, S. A. (1983). *Object relations in psychoanalytic theory*. Cambridge, MA: Harvard University Press.

Greenspan, G., & Pollock, G. (1989). *The course of life*. Madison, CT: International University Press.

Grusec, J. E. (1991). Socializing concerns for others in the home. *Developmental Psychology*, 27 (2), 338–342.

Grusec, J. E., & Goodnow, J. J. (1994). Impact of parental discipline methods on the child's internalization of values: A reconceptualization of current points of view. *Developmental Psychology*, 30, 4–19.

Gunnar, M. R. (1998). Quality of early care and buffering of neuroendocrine stress reactions: Potential effects on the developing human brain. *Preventive Medicine*, 27, 208–211.

Hardman, M. L., Drew, C. J., & Egan, M. W. (2006). *Human exceptionality: School, community, and family* (9th ed.). Boston: Allyn and Bacon.

Hesse, E., & Main, M. (2000). Disorganized infant, child, and adult attachment: Collapse in behavior and attachment strategies. *Journal of Psychoanalytic Association*, 48(4).

Honig, A. S. (2002). *Secure relationships: Nurturing infant/toddler attachment in early care settings*. Washington,

DC: National Association for the Education of Young Children.

Hyson, M. (2004). *The emotional development of young children: Building an emotion-centered curriculum* (2nd ed.). NY: Teachers College Press.

Isabella, R. A. (1993). Origins of attachment: Maternal interactive behavior across the first year. *Child Development, 64*, 605–621.

Isabella, R. A., & Belsky, J. (1991). Interactional synchrony and the origins of infant-mother attachment: A replication study. *Child Development, 62*, 373–384.

Jansen, P., Raat, H., Mackenbach, J., Jaddoe, V., Hofman, A., Verhulst, F., Tiemeier, A. (2009). Socioeconomic inequalities in infant temperament. *Social Psychiatry & Psychiatric Epidemiology, 44*(2), 87–95.

Kagan, J., Reznick, J. S., & Gibbons, J. (1989). Inhibited and uninhibited types of children. *Child Development, 60*, 838–845.

Klimes-Dougan, B., & Kistner, J. (1990). Physically abused preschoolers' responses to peers' distress. *Developmental Psychology, 67*, 599–602.

Kocovski, N. L., & Endler, N. S. (2000). Self-regulation: Social anxiety and depression. *Journal of Applied Biobehavioral Research, 5*(1), 80–91.

LaFreniere, P. J., & Sroufe, L. A. (1985). Profiles of peer competence in the preschool: Interrelations between measures, influence of social ecology, and relation to attachment history. *Developmental Psychology, 21*(1), 56–69.

Larzelere, R. E., Schneider, W. N., Larson, D. B., & Pike, P. L. (1996). The effects of discipline responses in delaying toddler misbehavior recurrences. *Child & Family Behavior Therapy, 18*, 35–37.

Lawrence, D. (2006). *Enhancing self-esteem in the classroom* (3rd ed.). London: Paul Chapman Educational Publishing.

Levine, L. E. (1983). Mine: Self-definition in 2-year-old boys. *Developmental Psychology, 19*, 544–549.

Madigan, S., Moran, G., Schuengel, C., Pederson, D. R., & Otten, R. (2007). Unresolved maternal attachment representations, disrupted maternal behavior and disorganized attachment in infancy: links to toddler behavior problems. *Journal of Child Psychology & Psychiatry, 48*(10), 1042–1050.

Mahler, M. S., Pine, F., & Bergman, F. (1975). *The psychological birth of the human infant: Symbiosis and individuation*. New York: Basic Books.

Main, M., & Solomon, J. (1990). Procedures for identifying infants as disorganized/disoriented during the Ainsworth Strange Situation. In M. T. Greenberg, D. Cicchetti, & E. M. Cummings (Eds.), *Attachment in the preschool years*. Chicago: University of Chicago Press.

Mangelsdorf, S., Gunnar, M., Kestenbaum, R., Lang, S., & Andreas, D. (1990). Infant proneness-to-distress temperament, maternal personality, and mother-infant attachment: Associations and goodness of fit. *Child Development, 61*, 820–832.

Marion, M. (2007). *Guidance of young children* (7th ed.). Upper Saddle River, NJ: Pearson Prentice Hall.

McCabe, K. M., Goehring, K., Yeh, M., & Lau, A. S. (2008). Parental Locus of Control and Externalizing Behavior Problems Among Mexican American Preschoolers. *Journal of Emotional & Behavioral Disorders, 16*(2), p118–126.

McDevitt, T. M., & Ormrod, J. E. (2010). *Child development: Educating and working with children and adolescents* (4th ed.). Upper Saddle River, NJ: Pearson Prentice Hall.

McElroy, E. M., & Rodriguez, C. M. (2008). Mothers of children with externalizing behavior problems: Cognitive risk factors for abuse potential and discipline style and practices. *Child Abuse & Neglect, 32*(8), 774-784.

McLaughlin, C. (2008). *Emotional* well-being and its relationship to schools and classrooms: a critical reflection. British Journal of Guidance & Counselling, 36(4), 353–366.

Nakamura, J. (1988). Optimal experience and the uses of talent. In M. Csikszentmihalyi, & I. S. Csikszentmihalyi (Eds.), *Optimal experience: Psychological studies of flow in consciousness* (pp. 150–171). Cambridge, UK: Cambridge University Press.

Nash, J. (1997, February 3). Fertile minds: How a child's brain develops and what it means for child care and welfare reform [Special report]. *Time, 149*(5), 48–56.

NICHD Early Child Care Research Network. (1997). The effects of infant child care on infant-mother attachment security: Results of the NICHD study of early child care. *Child Development, 68,* 860–879. Patall, E. A., Cooper, H., & Robinson, J. C. (2008). The effects of choice on intrinsic motivation and related outcomes: A meta-analysis of research findings. *Psychological Bulletin, 134* (2), 270–300.

Oppenheim, D., & Koren-Karie, N. (2002). Mothers' insightfulness regarding their children's internal worlds: The capacity underlying secure child-mother relationships. *Infant Mental Health Journal, 23,* 593–605.

Patall, E. A., Cooper, H., & Robinson, J. C. (2008). The effects of choice on intrinsic motivation and related outcomes: A meta-analysis of research findings. *Psychological Bulletin, 134* (2), 270–300.

Paterson, G., & Sanson, A. (1999). The association of behavioural adjustment to temperament, parenting and family characteristics among 5-year-old children. *Social Development, 8,* 293–309.

Pipp, S., Easterbrooks, M. A., & Brown, S. R. (1993). Attachment status and complexity of infants' self- and other-knowledge when tested with mother and father. *Social Development, 2,* 1–14.

Puckett, M. B., & Black, J. K. (2002). *Student enrichment series: Infant development.* Upper Saddle River, NJ: Pearson Prentice Hall.

Roggman, L. A., Boyce, L. K., Cook, G. A., Christiansen, K., & Jones, D. (2004). Playing With Daddy: Social Toy Play, Early Head Start, and Developmental Outcomes. *Fathering, 2* (1), 83–108.

Rubin, K. H., Bukowski, W. M., & Parker, J. G. (2006). Peer interactions, relationships, and groups. In N. Eisenberg (Ed.), *Handbook of child psychology: Vol. 3. Social, emotional, and personality development* (6th ed., pp. 571–645). New York: Wiley.

Rubin, K. H., Hastings, P. D., Stewart, S. L., Henderson, H. A., & Chen, X. (1997). The consistency and concomitants of inhibition: Some of the children, all of the time. *Child Development, 68,* 467–483.

Rydell, A., Bohlin, G., & Thorell, L. B. (2005). Representations of attachment to parents and shyness as predictors of children's relationships with teachers and peer competence in preschool. *Attachment & Human Development,* 7 (2), 187–204.

Saarni, C., Campos, J. J., Camras, L. A., & Witherington, D. (2006). Emotional development: Action, communication, and understanding. In N. Eisenberg (Ed.), *Handbook of child psychology: Vol. 3. Social, emotional, and personality development* (6th ed., pp. 646–718). New York: Wiley.

Sarkadi, A., Kristiansson, R., Oberklaid, F., & Bremberg, S. (2008). Fathers' involvement and children's developmental outcomes: A systematic review of longitudinal studies. *Acta Paediatrica, 97,* 153–158.

Schoppe-Sullivan, S., Mangelsdorf, S., Brown, G., & Szewczyk Sokolowski, M. (2007). Goodness-of-fit in family context: Infant temperament, marital quality, and early coparenting behavior. *Infant Behavior & Development, 30* (1), 82–96.

Spinrad, T. L., Eisenberg, N., Gaertner, B., Popp, T., Smith, C. L., Kupfer, A., Greving, K., Liew, J., & Hofer, C. (2007). Relations of maternal socialization and toddlers' effortful control to children's adjustment and social competence. *Developmental Psychology, 43* (5), 1170–1186.

Strassberg, A., Dodge, K., Petitt, G. S., & Bates, J. E. (1994). Spanking in the home and children's subsequent aggression toward kindergarten peers. *Developmental Psychopathology, 6,* 445–461.

Straus, M. A. (2001). New evidence for the benefits of never spanking. *Society, 38*(6), 52–60.

Sugiura, M., Sassa, Y., Jeong, H., Horie, K., Sato, S., & Kawashima, R. (2008). Face-specific and domain-general characteristics of cortical responses during self-recognition. *NeuroImage, 42* (1), 414–422.

Sullivan, M. W., Bennett, D. S., Carpenter, K., & Lewis, M. (2008). Emotional knowledge of young neglected children. *Child Maltreatment, 13* (3), 301–306.

Thomas, A., & Chess, S. (1977). *Temperament and development.* New York: Brunner/Mazel.

Thompson, R. A. (1988). On emotion and self-regulation. In R. A. Thompson (Ed.), *Nebraska Symposium on Motivation: Vol. 36. Socioemotional development* (pp. 367–468). Lincoln: University of Nebraska Press.

Thompson, R. A. (1998). Early sociopersonality development. In W. Damon (Editor-in-Chief) & N. Eisenberg (Vol. Ed.), *Handbook of child psychology: Vol. 3. Social, emotional, and personality development* (5th ed.). New York: Wiley.

Tronick, E. Z., & Cohn, J. F. (1989). Infant-mother face-to-face interaction: Age and gender differences in coordination and the occurrence of miscoordination. *Child Development, 60,* 85–92.

Van Aken, C., Junger, M., Verhoeven, M., Van Aken, M., & Deković, M. (2007, September). The interactive effects of temperament and maternal parenting on toddlers' externalizing behaviours. *Infant & Child Development, 16*(5), 553–572.

Vogel, C. A., Bradley, R. H., Raikes, H. H., Boller, K., & Shears, J. K. (2006). Relation between father connectedness and child outcomes. *Parenting: Science and Practice, 6* (2/3), 189–209.

Warneken, F., & Tomasello, M. (2008). Extrinsic rewards undermine altruistic tendencies in 20-month-olds. *Developmental Psychology,* 44 (6), 1785–1788.

Watson, L. R., Baranek, G. T., & DiLavore, P. C. (2003). Toddlers with autism: Developmental perspectives. *Infants and Young Children, 16*(3), 201–214.

Wetherby, A. M., Brosnan-Maddox, S., Peace, V., Newton, L. (2008). Validation of the Infant—Toddler Checklist as a broadband screener for autism spectrum disorders from 9 to 24 months of age. *Autism: The International Journal of Research & Practice,* 12 (5), 487–511.

Worobey, J., & Islas-Lopez, M. (2009). Temperament measures of African-American infants: change and convergence with age. *Early Child Development & Care, 179*(1), 107–112.

Yoon, P. O., Ang, R. P., Fung, D. S. S., Wong, G., & Yiming, C. (2006). The Impact of Parent-Child Attachment on Aggression, Social Stress and Self-Esteem. *School Psychology International,* 27 (5), 552–566.

Zahn-Waxler, C. (1991). The case for empathy: A developmental review. *Psychological Inquiry, 2,* 155–158.

ADDITIONAL RESOURCES

Chawarska, K., Klin, A. & Volkmar, F. R. (Eds.). (2008). *Autism Spectrum Disorders in Infants and Toddlers: Diagnosis, Assessment, and Treatment.* NY: The Guilford Press.

Kemple, K. M. (2003). *Let's be friends: Peer competence and social inclusion in early childhood programs.* NY: Teachers College Press.

Howes, C., & Ritchie, S. (2002). *A matter of trust: Connecting teachers and learners in the early childhood classroom.* NY: Teachers College Press.

Koplow, L. (2008). *Bears, bears everywhere! Supporting children's emotional health in the classroom.* NY: Teachers College Press.

Nelson, K. (2007). *Young minds in social worlds: Experience, meaning, and memory.* Cambridge, MA: Harvard University Press.

For additional activities, web links, and other resources, please visit our website at www.cengage.com/education/swim

chapter 4

THE THREE As: THE MASTER TOOLS FOR QUALITY CARE AND EDUCATION

learning objectives

After reading this chapter, you should be able to:

- Understand the purposes of using the three *A*s in daily child care.
- Explain the changing roles concerning attachment for early childhood educators.
- Articulate the relationship between theory and practice for the three *A*s.

chapter outline

- Introduction
- The Three *A*s: Attention, Approval, and Attunement as Tools
- The Attachment Debate and the Roles of Caregivers
- Understanding the Three *A*s
- Using the Three *A*s Successfully with Infants and Toddlers
- Case Study: Rangina

INTRODUCTION

Have you ever heard the cry of a troubled newborn that sends ripples down your spine? Ask any new parents in the first few nights of adjusting to family life what their baby's cry feels like to them. Instinctively, humans feel the distress almost as if the cry reaches the very fiber of their being. The response is almost universal: do whatever is necessary to soothe, calm, and reassure the infant. Once the goal of comforting is achieved, the experience is a sense of triumph like no other. How do we respond so quickly? Could it be that we re-experience our own sense of utter aloneness, a vibration so familiar and so foreboding that every cell wishes to quiet the call?

Teaching the concepts of the three *A*s—Attention, Approval, and Attunement—has been a passion for the authors for many, many years. The lifelong effects of positive, consistent, and conscious infant and toddler care have been understood by child development and early childhood experts for a long time. A working premise of this book is that what you do with children matters. Positive intention coupled with responsiveness to developmental characteristics makes a profound difference in the lives of children.

Children give back what they are given during early childhood. They return kindness, stability, consistency, and caring as they grow up and relate to other people in their schools, their workplace, and in their own families. As previously discussed, the quality of your caring, including actions, verbal messages, voice tone and tempo, and secure handling, helps create the neural pathways that determine each child's perceptions and models of the world. Your interactions with young children help determine how each child will eventually perceive himself or herself—as worthy or unworthy, capable or incapable, hopeful or hopeless.

Caregivers have a mission that is monumental in nature. Your daily movements, efforts, and attitudes affect the very fiber of each child; no position in society is more important. The three *A*s are the master tools that ensure that your effect on children is positive and productive. There is no better way to provide quality care than a wonderfully soothing dose of consciously administered attention, approval, and attunement.

The abilities to understand and fulfill academic requirements and to master specific skills, such as feeding babies and building appropriate curricula for toddlers, are necessary to your work and may even extend into your personal life. These immensely important aspects of child care, however, are not enough.

Students studying child care must also integrate their *selves* into their work because in no other field is the professional in need of self-integration more than in this most humanistic endeavor. Taking charge of tomorrow's leaders on a daily basis demands human investment, since it supports future human relationships. Just how valuable are these first relationships to future development? Let's look at what other experts have to say about the importance of human connections:

> "The child's self is constructed in the interpersonal relationships that bind her to others, she is known in the experience of connection and is defined by the responsiveness of human engagement" (Gilligan, 1988).

In the context of relationships, the needs and wishes of very young children are met, or not (Pawl, 1990). Once a child understands that adults have minds, "the child can now have the intention to affect someone's mind and to be a reader of minds.... The powerful wish to know and be known becomes more possible. This is a complex achievement that emerged from the child's experiences. All along this child has felt noticed, responded to, and has been aware of her impact in the moment and over time" (Pawl, 2006, p. 2).

Mothers who responded to their child's cues with insightfulness (e.g., seeing the problem from the child's perspective) had children who were significantly more likely to have secure attachment (Koren-Karie, Oppenheim, Dolev, & Sher, 2002).

John Dewey wrote that ". . . every experience lives on in further experiences" (1938, p. 28). In this way, "the experiences and feelings of childhood endure" (Bowman, 1989, p. 450); "they become part of children's biographies, providing the emotional foundation for future interactions and relationships" (Hatch, 1995).

As we acknowledge our responsibility as caregivers, we must also readily accept that involving "the child as an active, thinking participant" is the best way to support the developing brain (Thompson, 2006, p. 50). "More than any toy, CD, or video, a sensitive social partner can respond appropriately to what has captured the child's interest (and is thus the stimulus of brain activity), provoke new interests and exploration, calibrate shared experiences to the child's readiness for new learning, and accommodate the child's unique temperamental qualities (which may, for some, require gradual rather than fast-paced stimulation (Thompson, 2006, p. 49).

The importance of warm, loving, verbal interactions between parent or caregiver and child, particularly in the first two years should not be underestimated. Conversations, prompt attention, and immediate feedback about objects in the environment lead to better vocabulary and higher scores on later intelligence tests (Healy, 2004). In fact, early (i.e., two years of age) and later (i.e., four years of age) language skills were found to be related to young children's theory of mind. Specifically, those children with larger vocabularies were found to have more advanced false-belief understanding, possibly because the more advanced language skills underpin "the capacity to mark aspects of mind such as perspective, intention, obligation, and degree of certainty . . ." (Watson, Painter, & Bornstein, 2001, p. 454).

So, what do you need to learn that will allow you to be available, fresh, interested, involved, and ready to take on this awesome task?

THE THREE *A*s: ATTENTION, APPROVAL, AND ATTUNEMENT AS TOOLS

The three *A*s of child care are the master tools for promoting a positive environment and maintaining a positive emotional connection between the young child and the caregiver. The three *A*s of child care—Attention, Approval, and Attunement—are extremely powerful tools available to any person in just about any situation, yet they are *essential* in the care and education of very young children. The three *A*s are called master tools because they apply to everything we do all day long. Attention, Approval, and Attunement are necessary to function well, have good self-esteem, remain at ease, and interact with other people in a positive and productive manner.

The concepts of Attention, Approval, and Attunement are meant to empower the caregiver and help facilitate an attitude change toward yourself, which emphasizes that early childhood educators' feelings have a profound effect on children. The three *A*s are derived directly from the current perspectives on development and care (discussed previously): brain research and ecological systems, sociocultural, and attachment theories. In addition, they are supported by our understanding of the guidelines for developmentally appropriate practice (addressed in later chapters; Copple & Bredekamp, 2009). This theoretical knowledge helps a teacher appropriately care for and educate children; when that same caregiver uses this knowledge for personal development, he or she can enjoy benefits as well.

THE ATTACHMENT DEBATE AND THE ROLES OF CAREGIVERS

Discussion of the three *A*s begins with the scientific fact that infants and toddlers require secure attachments, or enduring emotional ties, to their caregivers for normal, healthy development. Further, a large body of research supports positive Attention, Approval, and Attunement between caregivers and children as the foundation for secure attachment.

An ongoing debate in the research literature concerns whether infants exhibit less secure attachment when they experience child care as opposed to being home-reared. This debate cannot be discussed without considering the changing roles of mothers and fathers in the care of infants. One historical view was that *only* the mother could bond with the infant sufficiently to ensure healthy development. In contrast, one current perspective suggests that non-familial persons can meet the needs of the infants equally well. Because a great number of infants and toddlers are spending the majority of their day in child care, the question of what quality of attachment to one consistent person the infant may require in order to develop security and trust is being studied more intensely.

Researchers have identified a secure pattern of attachment and three insecure patterns (Ainsworth, 1967, 1973; Ainsworth, Blehar, Waters, & Wall, 1978; Hesse & Main, 2000; Main & Soloman, 1990).

1. Secure attachment. The infant uses a parent or other family member as a secure base, strongly prefers the parent over a stranger, actively seeks contact with the parent, and is easily comforted by the parent after being absent.

2. Avoidant attachment. The infant is usually not distressed by parental separation and may avoid the parent or prefer a stranger when the parent returns.

3. **Resistant attachment**. The infant seeks closeness to the parent and resists exploring the environment, usually displays angry behavior after the parent returns, and is difficult to comfort.

4. **Disoriented attachment**. The infant shows inconsistent attachment and reacts to the parent returning with confused or contradictory behavior (looking away when held or showing a dazed facial expression).

A phenomenon related to attachment is **separation anxiety**, which appears to be a normal developmental experience, since children from every culture exhibit it. Infants from various cultures all over the world have been found to exhibit separation anxiety starting around six months and increasing in intensity until approximately 15 months (Kagan, Kearsley, & Zelazo, 1978). Separation anxiety is exhibited by securely attached infants, as well as different types of insecurely attached infants.

A summary of the research on infant attachment suggests that infants are actively involved in the attachment bond. Babies are normally capable of attaching securely to more than one adult or parent. Contemporary researchers have examined how children create attachments with caregivers, including fathers (Feinberg & Kan, 2008; Figueiredo, Costa, Pacheco, & Pais, 2007; Kazura, 2000), grandparents (Poehlmann, 2003), brothers and sisters (Volling, Herrera, & Poris, 2004), adoptive and foster families (Dyer, 2004; Oosterman & Schuengel, 2008; Stams, Juffer, & van IJzendoorn, 2002; Stovall-McClough & Dozier, 2004) and professional early childhood educators (Caldera & Hart, 2004; Howes, 1999; O'Connor & McCartney, 2006; Ritchie & Howes, 2003).

While infants can form multiple attachments, the quality of those attachments are not static; they can change over time in response to changing environmental conditions. Drastic changes in family circumstances, such as divorce, death, or job loss, detrimentally affect infant attachment (Egeland & Sroufe, 1981; Vaugh, Egeland, Sroufe, & Waters, 1979). Changes can also be in a positive direction. In other words, as stressors are reduced or parenting skills increase, the attachment relationship can become more secure (Egeland & Farber, 1984).

Caregiving that is supportive and sensitive to the child's needs using the three *A*s promotes secure attachment, while insensitive or inconsistent care results in insecure attachment. Finally, secure infant attachment and continuity of caregiving is related to later cognitive, emotional, and social competence. The research on adoptive families, for example, illustrates two of these patterns. Infants adopted at younger ages showed higher levels of secure behavior and more coherent attachment strategies than those adopted when they were older (Stovall-McClough & Dozier, 2004) and these positive attachment relationships predicted later socioemotional and cognitive development (Stams, Juffer, & van IJzendoorn, 2002).

From these findings we can draw several important implications for caregiving and parenting as well as changes in early childhood educators' roles. Research on

The type of attachment a child forms with her caregivers impacts how she relates to other adults and children.

attachment security of infants with full-time working mothers suggests that most infants of employed mothers are securely attached, and that this relationship is more influential on early social and emotional growth than the relationships a child has with other caregivers, both inside and outside the home (NICHD Early Child Care Research Network, 1997, 1998a, 1998b, 1999, 2005). However, when a child has an insecure relationship to her mother, early childhood educators can establish a secure relationship with the child, providing a buffer against some of the negative developmental outcomes (see Shonkoff & Phillips, 2000, especially Chapter 9). Hence, as more and more mothers of infants enter the workplace, the responsibility for forming secure attachments must be shared with fathers, other family members, and teachers. Everyone must work together to provide secure and consistent attachment and bonding with infants.

Forming reciprocal relationships or partnerships with families will assist in this process. Our responsibilities as teachers are twofold: we must not only help children to develop trust and secure attachments with us, but also assist family members to form strong, secure relationships with the infant. As discussed previously, employing particular strategies such as a primary caregiving system, family grouping, and continuity of care can ensure that each infant and toddler has as few caregivers as possible, each providing consistency and predictability over time. Pawl (2006) suggests that caregivers need to help the parent exist for the child and help the child know that she also exists for the parents when they are separated during the day. For example, reminding the child that his foster parent is "leaving work to come and get him because she misses him" is important both to providing quality care and supporting the development of strong relationships. The second prong of our approach must be to provide family support and education to help family members form and maintain secure attachments with their children. Family education should include the importance of mothers, fathers, and other family members providing direct nurture and care of the children so that they can experience consistent, loving, and healthy relationships.

Caregiver behaviors that ensure consistent, secure bonding and attachment with infants and toddlers are the three *A*s of child care. Early childhood educators who fully understand the three *A*s, use them effectively with children, and systematically model and teach parents to use them with their sons and daughters, do more than any other current force in society to ensure emotional security for infants and toddlers.

✓ reading checkpoint

Before moving on with your reading, make sure that you can answer the following questions about the material discussed so far.

1. Why are early relationships important to later development?

2. How does knowing about and understanding the attachment relationships that the children in your care have with their family members help you as an early childhood educator?

UNDERSTANDING THE THREE *A*s

Attention

"Smile and the whole world smiles with you." We've often been put at ease when greeted by a stranger's smile or felt instant rapport with someone who returns our smile. So much is communicated without words; often the unspoken message conveys exactly how a person is feeling. When we realize that 70 percent of our total communication is nonverbal, it is easy to understand why a smile says so much.

In the simplest way, a smile is a way to attend to yourself and to someone else. When you bring attention to a behavior in another person, you are sending a message about the importance of that behavior. Using the words of Vygotsky, you are helping children to construct an understanding of the meaning behind a smile. For example, the child may construct the notion that people smile when they are happy or see a behavior that they like. In this way, young children begin to associate a smile response with engaging in an appropriate behavior. A neural pathway is then built to remember this association; in this way, what we attend to helps the brain to grow. The opposite is also true. If we attend to negative behaviors displayed by children, then the children may construct an understanding that these behaviors are appropriate ways to interact with others; those neural pathways are strengthened and used to guide future behavior.

Of course, attending is much more complicated than just producing a smile or reacting to a negative behavior. Attention, for early childhood educators, also involves higher mental functions (Bodrova & Leong, 2007) or "cognitive processes acquired through learning and teaching ... [that] ... are *deliberate, mediated, internalized* behaviors" (pp. 19, 20, emphasis in original). Teachers, then, must learn to engage in focused attention to observe the behavior, skills, and needs of the children in their care. Observing closely, or attending, facilitates your analysis of the child's behaviors and appropriate responses to those behaviors. In other words, attending makes possible the identification of each child's **zone of proximal development (ZPD)**, "the distance between the actual developmental level as determined by independent problem solving and the level of potential development as determined through problem solving under adult guidance or in collaboration with more capable peers" (Vygotsky, 1978, p. 86).

Classifying the ZPD is vital for teachers because it determines where to place educational emphasis. Scaffolding, or assistance from a more-skilled other, facilitates learning at the "higher" end of the zone. In other words, behaviors by the more skilled partner contribute to acquiring skills that were outside of the child's independent level of functioning. Scaffolding behaviors will be addressed more comprehensively in future chapters.

Another component of attending entails recognizing ecological factors from other systems that impact the development and learning of the children (Bronfenbrenner, 1979, 1989). As discussed previously, these factors both affect the child and are influenced by the child. Such bidirectional influences must continually be considered by early childhood educators, in order to recognize the active role children play in their own development. For example, teachers must be culturally sensitive and responsive to the way families want to raise their children. Families hold particular beliefs that may or may not be shared by the caregiver; this should affect how you do your work. Altering your routines and behaviors to support family practices assists with more continuous care for very young children (Gonzalez-Mena, 2001).

In general, what we attend to matters. It communicates to us and others ideas regarding the meaning or value of particular behaviors while influencing the very behavior we are examining. Matusov, DePalma, and Drye (2007) suggest that, from a sociocultural perspective, the observer directly and indirectly influences the development of the observed by how the behavior is thought and talked about. To illustrate, Kemit takes a while each morning to join the group. He likes to watch the fish before selecting an independent activity. After he has played alone for

10–12 minutes, he usually selects a work with one of his friends. When the caregiver, Trace, speaks with Kemit's grandmother at pickup time, he often expresses concern about Kemit being "shy." Kemit's grandmother, who initially felt this behavior was acceptable and reflective of Kemit's way of doing things, becomes worried and she works with Trace to create a plan for helping Kemit transition to school "more smoothly." In this example, Trace has altered Kemit's grandmother's view of Kemit and her expectations for his behavior. By setting up this transition plan, they are directly changing Kemit's development. They are communicating to Kemit that working alone is not acceptable and are working to make him more interactive with peers. While these are not detrimental outcomes by any means, it does seem to be disrespectful of who Kemit is as a person.

Thus, we must continually remember that what we attend to matters. It matters because it alters the course of development for children—positively or negatively.

Approval

Approval from others teaches us to approve of ourselves. The best type of attention is approval. Approval of another person is a clear message that you have respect and positive regard for that person. According to the *American Heritage Dictionary of the English Language* (2000) respect is all of the following:

- to feel or show differential regard for
- to avoid violation or interference with
- the state of being regarded with honor or esteem
- willingness to show consideration or appreciation

How do early childhood educators translate this multifaceted definition into their daily practice? Swim (2003) suggests that both allowing children time to try or complete tasks and helping them to make choices reflect respect for the children because these behaviors demonstrate refraining from interfering with them. In addition, valuing individual children's ways of doing and being shows that they are held in high esteem by the caregiver.

Educational leaders in the municipal infant/toddler and preschool programs of Reggio Emilia, Italy, take the understanding of respect to another level. They have declared respect an educational value (Rinaldi, 2001) and devised the concept of the rights of children. This concept reflects their image of the child as "rich in resources, strong, and competent. The emphasis is placed on seeing the children as unique individuals with rights rather than simply needs. They have potential, plasticity, openness, the desire to grow, curiosity, a sense of wonder, and the desire to relate to other people and to communicate" (Rinaldi, 1998, p. 114). Teachers use their image of the child to guide their instructional decisions, curricular planning, and interactions with children (see, for example, Edwards, Gandini, & Forman, 1998).

To children, approval says they have done something right, and it helps them feel worthwhile. Approval builds trust and self-confidence, which in turn encourage children to try new things without fear. The most important concept a caregiver must learn is always to approve of the child as a person, even when you disapprove of his or her behavior. For example, it must be made clear to the child that you like who he is, but not what he is doing right now.

Appropriate and consistent approval develops trust in the child. Once a sense of trust is developed, children can readily approve of themselves. According to Erikson's eight stages of man, the general state of trust suggests that one has learned not only to "rely on the sameness and continuity of the other providers, but also that one may trust oneself" (Erikson, 1963).

Trust depends not only on the quantity (e.g., number of interactions), but also on the quality of the caregiver's interactions and relationships with children. Positive approval creates a sense of trust as a result of the sensitive way in which the caregiver takes time to care for the child's individual needs. Adults must convey to each child an honest concern for that child's welfare and a deep conviction that there is meaning in what he or she is doing. Trust based on consistent, positive caring allows children to grow up with a sense of meaningful belonging and trust.

According to ethological theory, parental responsiveness is adaptive in that it ensures that the basic needs of the infant are met and provides protection from danger. It brings the baby into close contact with the caregiver, who can respond sensitively to a wide range of infant behaviors (Bell & Ainsworth, 1972).

Some caution should be exercised regarding when to give approval. Caregivers who approve of every little behavior and shower children with unconditional approval lose respect with them. Genuine approval for meaningful accomplishments serves to encourage children to try harder and helps them value their own efforts. Make sure the children have made a genuine effort or have accomplished something of value, and your approval will help them become the best that they can be.

Attunement

Attunement involves being aware of someone, along with her moods, needs, and interests, and responding to all of these. In other words, when you are "in tune," you are providing high-quality care and education that meet the individual needs, interests, and abilities of each child.

Attuned caregivers often look natural in their interactions with infants and toddlers. However, being attuned is not instinctual for all persons. Often, our beliefs about child rearing or parenting interfere with providing such care. For example, a strongly held belief by many parents, teachers, and physicians is that responding to the cries of infants too quickly will spoil them. Of course, as we have stated previously, you cannot spoil a young child. All of the research on attachment reviewed in this chapter and the previous chapters discounts this belief. Responding sensitively to a child's communication strategies helps the child to develop trust in his or her caregiver, form strong, secure attachments, and grow socially and emotionally.

Attuned caregivers devote a great deal of time to observing and recording the infants' behaviors carefully. Having this knowledge affords the educator a strong foundation on which to base interactional, instructional, and caregiving strategies. For example, Nicole knows that Tiffany, 27 months, has a very regular routine for eating and sleeping. Today, however, she was not hungry right after playing outdoors and had difficulty relaxing for a nap. Upon closer observation and questioning, Nicole came to understand that Tiffany's throat hurt. Nicole was able to use her knowledge of Tiffany to "tune into" this change of routine and uncover the beginning of an illness.

When caregivers engage in respectful and responsive interpersonal interactions with infants and toddlers, they are attuned in the way researchers use the word. They are in synchrony with the child (Isabella & Belsky, 1991). Reading and responding to the child's cues is crucial to engaging in this "interactional dance." For example, picture caregiver Carlos feeding Judd his lunch. Judd is hungry and eating quickly. Carlos talks about how good the food must be for an empty stomach. He is smiling and laughing between bites. All of a sudden, Judd begins to slow the pace. Carlos reads this behavior and slows down his offering of food and pattern of speech. Judd smiles and turns his head away from Carlos. Carlos pauses and waits

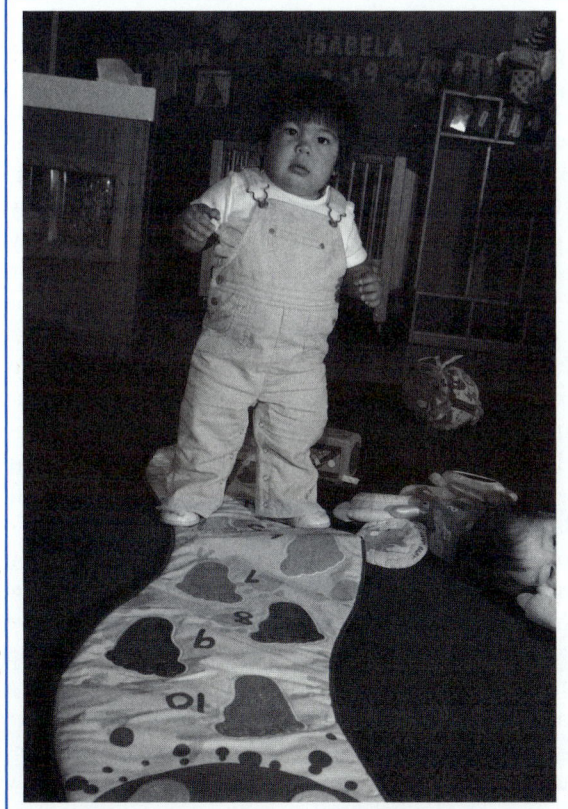

Caregivers are attuned to reactions when a stranger (e.g., parent of another child) enters the room.

for Judd to turn back around. He does turn back and opens his mouth. Carlos provides another bite of vegetables.

Perceptions, however, can get in the way of a person's ability to be attuned. Ghera, Hane, Malesa, and Fox (2006) found that maternal perceptions of infant soothability influenced the degree of maternal sensitivity. When mothers viewed their infants as more soothable, they were able to provide sensitive care even when the baby was displaying negative reactivity. On the other hand, when mothers viewed their infants as less soothable, they provided less sensitive care when their infants were displaying negative reactivity. As caregivers, we must reflect on our own views of children to insure that we identify and remedy beliefs that could interfere with our ability to be attuned.

Our positive, focused attention toward children's behavior directs our energy and intention. We provide genuine approval for real success and effort. Attunement communicates our feelings of respect, approval, and appreciation of children. When we, as early childhood educators, combine all three of these, children cannot help but respond positively to us, their world, and themselves. That is why the three *A*s are the master tools for child development and care.

USING THE THREE *A*s SUCCESSFULLY WITH INFANTS AND TODDLERS

The three *A*s of child care are a work in progress. In all likelihood, you use the three *A*s already without much thought about them. Consider how you approach an unknown infant. You get down to her level (floor, blanket, or chair). You act calmly, move slowly, make eye contact, enter her space, get even closer to her physically, smile, and gently begin soft speech to engage her. If you believe you have permission from her to stay close, you keep eye contact and slowly begin to inquire what she is doing, such as playing or eating. When she gestures, you follow the gesture with a similar response, this time making a sound that seems to identify her movement and keep pace. This usually elicits a smile or giggle. Once again you smile and make noise. You may try gently touching a shoulder or finger, and before long, you are accepted into the child's space. This slow progression of rapport-building is also the slow progression of the use of the three *A*s. First you give Attention, then Approval, and then Attunement. When this is done consciously, all involved feel worthy.

While many of these behaviors may come naturally to you, we would like you to spend a great deal of time thinking about them, reflecting on how you use them, and analyzing their impact on children. How, for example, can you use them more effectively? Only through conscious decision-making can you use these tools to help children develop to their fullest extent.

The three *A*s are powerful and rejuvenating for you as well. They elicit responses in children that will sustain you in your vocation. One of the most positive assurances of worthiness a caregiver can receive is the full-body hug given unconditionally as a gift from a gleeful toddler who sweeps down upon you when you are playing on the floor. This hug, which is often accompanied by a loud and joyful sound, enters

Infants and toddlers who feel safe can relax and rest peacefully.

your space with such focused positive energy that each of you feels the impact. The result of this positive energy is felt by the two of you, and brings smiles to the faces of all who observe it.

When caregivers take responsibility to care for themselves, they are ready to deal with the needs of children. Teachers are a recharging station—a physically and emotionally rewarding place where children feel a sense of security. The fact is you cannot give what you do not have. The personal resources of the caregiver are vital for successful outcomes with children. When you are strong in mind, body, and spirit, you can be a positive model for the children in your care.

reading checkpoint

Before moving on with your reading, make sure that you can answer the following questions about the material discussed so far.

1. List, define, describe, and provide a specific example for each of the three *A*s of child care.

2. How are the three *A*s grounded in the theoretical perspectives described in Chapters 1 and 2?

3. Why is using all of the three *A*s together a powerful tool for motivating children?

SUMMARY

When the three *A*s are focused on children, they promote appropriate behaviors and enhance a positive learning environment for children. The caregiver structures a safe place in which the young child explores and masters all of his or her growing abilities by solving problems that naturally occur within the environment. A stable, positive environment promotes trust and confidence and allows the growing infant to express all of his or her needs.

When the three *A*s are focused on you as a caregiver, they promote self-health and professional development. These skills help you to be more aware of your impact on children and revitalize you, so that you can sustain a high quality of care throughout the day. Attending to your own well-being promotes trust and ultimately teaches children, by your example, to be self-confident and have trust in themselves.

key terms

approval
attention
attunement
avoidant attachment
disoriented attachment
resistant attachment
respect
rights of children
secure attachment
separation anxiety
zone of proximal development (ZPD)

case study   Rangina

Rangina has been in Abebi's class for seven months now. Rangina's family immigrated from Afghanistan right before she was born. She started coming to the child care center when she was one year old. The transition was difficult at first, but Rangina quickly settled into a routine. Naptime was a particular challenge as Rangina cried herself to sleep nearly every afternoon. After many conversations between Abebi and Rangina's father, they decided that his wife would tape record her nightly singing and playing of the Waj instrument. When Abebi played this during naptime, the music and singing were so soothing that they helped not only Rangina to fall asleep but also some of the other children.

This particular morning Rangina came dressed in a new embroidered kuchi-style dress with a matching chador (head scarf). Her mother explained that they were observing Eid Al-Fitr which celebrates the first day after the Ramadan fast. Rangina was clearly excited about her new clothing. Abebi commented, "Your new dress must be soft. Can I feel it?" Rangina exclaimed, "Yes" and hugged her. Then, Rangina danced to another area of the classroom. Abebi noticed that she danced from one area to another during the first half of free choice time, and she seemed to have trouble finding experiences to engage her. For example, she declined to paint at the easel or draw with markers, some of her favorite things to do. When Abebi asked about these decisions, she would only say "No dirty." Abebi moved to her eye level and asked if she was afraid to get her new clothes messy. When Rangina replied yes, Abebi found other attractive, non-messy art materials for her to use. When it was story time, Rangina began to run around the room. Abebi decided that a game of follow the leader might be best, and she invited Rangina to be the first leader.

1. From the case study, what do you think is the most important tool a caregiver can use with a young toddler? Why?

2. How did Abebi's relationship with Rangina's parents help her to be more responsive to Rangina?

3. How does interactional synchrony apply to this case study?

QUESTIONS AND EXPERIENCES FOR REFLECTION

1. Apply all three *A*s to two separate children, and write down their reactions. How did these interactions feel to you? Why?

2. What is the difference between giving children attention and spoiling them?

3. Write a scenario using examples of the ways in which the three *A*s might calm children and promote a positive learning environment.

4. What is the most important aspect of this chapter for you? Why?

REFERENCES

Ainsworth, M. D. S. (1967). *Infancy in Uganda: Infant care and the growth of love.* Baltimore: Johns Hopkins University Press.

Ainsworth, M. D. S. (1973). The development of infant-mother attachment. In B. M. Caldwell & H. N. Ricciuti (Eds.), *Review of child development research: Vol. 3. Child development and social policy.* Chicago: University of Chicago Press.

Ainsworth, M. D. S., Blehar, M., Waters, E., & Wall, S. (1978). *Patterns of attachment.* Hillsdale, NJ: Lawrence Erlbaum Associates.

Bell, S. M., & Ainsworth, M. D. S. (1972). Infant crying and maternal responsiveness. *Child Development, 43,* 117–119.

Bodrova, E., & Leong, D. (2007). *Tools of the mind: The Vygotskian approach to early childhood education.* (2nd ed.). Upper Saddle River, NJ: Pearson Merrill Prentice Hall.

Bowman, B. (1989). Self-reflection as an element of professionalism. *Teachers College Records, 90*(3), 444–451.

Bronfenbrenner, U. (1979). *The ecology of human development: Experiments by nature and design.* Cambridge, MA: Harvard University Press.

Bronfenbrenner, U. (1989). Ecological systems theory. In R. Vasta (Ed.), *Annals of child development* (Vol. 6, pp. 187–251). Greenwich, CT: JAI Press.

Caldera, Y. M., & Hart, S. (2004). Exposure to child care, parenting style and attachment security. *Infant & Child Development, 13*(1), 21–33.

Copple, C., & Bredekamp, S., (Eds.). (2009). *Developmentally appropriate practice in early childhood programs* (3rd ed.). Washington, DC: National Association for the Education of Young Children.

Dewey, J. (1938). *Experience and education.* New York: Macmillan.

Dyer, F. J. (2004). Termination of parental rights in light of attachment theory: The case of Kaylee. *Psychology, Public Policy, & Law, 10*(1–2), 5–30.

Edwards, C., Gandini, L., & Forman, G. (Eds.). (1998). *The hundred languages of children: The Reggio Emilia approach—Advanced reflections* (2nd ed.). Westport, CT: Ablex.

Egeland, B., & Farber, E. A. (1984). Infant-mother attachment: Factors related to its development and changes over time. *Child Development, 55*(3), 753–771.

Egeland, B., & Sroufe, L. A. (1981). Attachment and early maltreatment. *Child Development, 52*(1), 44–52.

Erikson, E. H. (1963). The eight stages of man. In *Childhood & society.* New York: W. W. Norton.

Feinberg, M. E., & Kan, M. L. (2008). Establishing Family Foundations: Intervention Effects on Coparenting, Parent/Infant Well-Being, and Parent-Child Relations. *Journal of Family Psychology, 22* (2), pp. 253–263.

Figueiredo, B., Costa, R., Pacheco, A., & Pais, A. (2007). Mother-to-infant and father-to-infant initial emotional involvement. *Early Child Development & Care, 177* (5), pp. 521–532.

Ghera, M. M., Hane, A. A., Malesa, E. E., & Fox, N. A. (2006). The role of infant soothability in the relation between infant negativity and maternal sensitivity. *Infant Behavior & Development, 29,* 289–293.

Gilligan, C. (1988). Remapping the moral domain: New images of self in relationship. In C. Gilligan, J. Ward, J. Taylor, & B. B. Bardige (Eds.), *Mapping the moral domain* (pp. 3–19). Cambridge, MA: Harvard University Press.

Gonzalez-Mena, J. (2001). *Multicultural issues in child care* (3rd ed.). Mountain View, CA: Mayfield.

Hatch, J. A. (1995). *Qualitative research in early childhood settings*. Stamford, CT: Praeger Publishers.

Healy, J. (2004). *Your child's growing mind: A guide to learning and brain development from birth to adolescence.* (3rd ed.). New York: Broadway Books.

Hesse, E., & Main, M. (2000). Disorganized infant, child, and adult attachment: Collapse in behavior and attachment strategies. *Journal of Psychoanalytic Association, 48*(4).

Howes, C. (1999). Attachment relationships in the context of multiple caregivers. In J. Cassidy & P. R. Shaver (Eds.), *Handbook of attachment: Theory, research, and clinical applications* (pp. 671–687). New York: Guilford Press.

Isabella, R. A., & Belsky, J. (1991). Interactional synchrony and the origins of infant-mother attachment: A replication study. *Child Development, 62*, 373–384.

Kagan, J., Kearsley, R. B., & Zelazo, P. R. (1978). *Infancy: Its place in human development*. Cambridge, MA: Harvard University Press.

Kazura, K. (2000). Father's qualitative and quantitative involvement: An investigation of attachment, play, and social interactions. *Journal of Men's Studies, 9*(1), 41–57.

Koren-Karie, N., Oppenheim, D., Dolev, S., & Sher, S. (2002). Mothers' insightfulness regarding their infants' internal experience: Relations with maternal sensitivity and infant attachment. *Developmental Psychology, 38*, 534–542.

Main, M., & Soloman, J. (1990). Procedures for identifying infants as disorganized/disoriented during the Ainsworth Strange Situation. In M. Greenberg, D. Cicchetti, & M. Cummings (Eds.), *Attachment in the preschool years: Theory, research, and intervention* (pp. 121–160). Chicago: University of Chicago Press.

Matusov, E., DePalma, R., & Drye, S. (2007). Whose development? Salvaging the concept of development within a sociocultural approach to education. *Educational Theory, 57* (4), 403–421.

NICHD Early Child Care Research Network. (1997). The effects of infant child care on infant-mother attachment security: Results of the NICDH study of early child care. *Child Development, 68*, 860–879.

NICHD Early Child Care Research Network. (1998a). *Chronicity of maternal depressive symptoms, maternal behavior, and child functioning at 36 months: Results from the NICHD study of early child care.* Washington, DC: Author.

NICHD Early Child Care Research Network. (1998b). Relations between family predictors and child outcomes: Are they weaker for children in child care? *Developmental Psychology, 34*, 1119–1128.

NICHD Early Child Care Research Network. (1999). Child care and mother-child interaction in the first three years of life. *Developmental Psychology, 35*, 1399–1413.

NICHD Early Child Care Research Network. (2005). *Child care and child development: Results from the NICHD study of early child care and youth development.* NY: Guilford Press.

O'Connor, E., & McCartney, K. (2006). Testing associations between young children's relationships with mothers and *teachers*. *Journal of Educational Psychology, 98* (1), pp. 87–98.

Oosterman, M., & Schuengel, C. (2008). Attachment in foster children associated with caregivers' sensitivity and behavioral problems. *Infant Mental Health Journal, 29* (6), pp. 609–623.

Pawl, J. (2006). Being held in another's mind. In J. R. Lally, P. L. Mangione, & D. Greenwald (Eds.). *Concepts for care: 20 essays on infant/toddler development and learning.* Sausalito, CA: WestEd. pp. 1–4.

Pawl, J. (1990). Infants in day care: Reflections on experience, expectation and relationships. *Zero to Three, 10*(3):1–6.

Pickett, J. P. et al. (Eds.). (2000). *American Heritage Dictionary of the English Language.* Boston: Houghton Mifflin.

Poehlmann, J. (2003). An attachment perspective on grandparents raising their very young grandchildren: Implications for intervention and research. *Infant Mental Health Journal, 24*(2), 149–173.

Rinaldi, C. (2001). Infant-toddler centers and preschools as places of culture. In Project Zero and Reggio Children, *Making learning visible: Children as individual and group learners.* (pp. 38–46). Reggio Emilia, Italy: Reggio Children srl.

Rinaldi, C. (1998). Projected curriculum constructed through documentation—*Progettazione:* An interview with Lella Gandini. In C. Edwards, L. Gandini, & G. Forman (Eds.), *The hundred languages of children: The Reggio Emilia approach—Advanced reflections* (2nd ed.). (pp. 113–125). Norwood, NJ: Ablex.

Ritchie, S., & Howes, C. (2003). Program practices, caregiver stability, and child-caregiver relationships. *Journal of Applied Developmental Psychology, 24,* 497–516.

Shonkoff, J. P., & Phillips, D. A. (Eds.). (2000). *From neurons to neighborhoods: The science of early childhood development.* Washington, DC: National Academy Press.

Stams, G.-J. J. M., Juffer, F., & van IJzendoorn, M. H. (2002). Maternal sensitivity, infant attachment, and temperament in early childhood predict adjustment in middle childhood: The case of adopted children and their biologically unrelated parents. *Developmental Psychology, 38,* 806–821.

Stovall-McClough, K. C., & Dozier, M. (2004). Forming attachments in foster care: Infant attachment behaviors during the first two months of placement. *Development & Psychopathology, 16,* 253–271.

Swim, T. J. (2003). Respecting infants and toddlers: Strategies for best practice. *Earlychildhood NEWS, 15*(5), 16–17, 20–23.

Thompson, R. A. (2006). Nurturing developing brains, minds, and hearts. In J. R. Lally, P. L. Mangione, & D. Greenwald (Eds.). *Concepts for care: 20 essays on infant/toddler development and learning.* Sausalito, CA: WestEd. pp. 47–52.

Vaugh, B., Egeland, B., Sroufe, L. A., & Waters, E. (1979). Individual differences in infant-mother attachment at twelve and eighteen months: Stability and change in families under stress. *Child Development, 50*(4), 971–975.

Volling, B. L., Herrera, C., & Poris, M. P. (2004). Situational affect and temperament: Implications for sibling caregiving. *Infant and Child Development, 13,* 173–183.

Vygotsky, L. S. (1978). *Mind in society: The development of higher psychological processes* (M. Cole, V. John-Steiner, S. Scribner, E. Souberman, Trans.). Cambridge, MA: Harvard University Press.

Watson, A. C., Painter, K. M., & Bornstein, M. H. (2001). Longitudinal relations between 2-year-olds' language and 4-year-olds' theory of mind. *Journal of Cognition and Development, 2,* 449–457.

ADDITIONAL RESOURCES

Crouter, A. C., & Booth, A. (2003). (Eds.). *Children's influences on family dynamics: The neglected side of family relationships.* Mahwah, NJ: Lawrence Erlbaum Associates.

Grossmann, K. E., Grossmann, K., & Waters, E. (2005). (Eds.). *Attachment from infancy to adulthood: The major longitudinal studies.* NY: Guilford Press.

Raikes, H. H., & Edwards, C. P. (2009). *Extending the dance in infant and toddler caregiving.* Baltimore, MD: Paul H. Brookes Publishing Co.

For additional activities, web links, and other resources, please visit our website at www.cengage.com/education/swim

chapter 5

EFFECTIVE PREPARATION AND TOOLS FOR PROFESSIONAL EDUCATORS

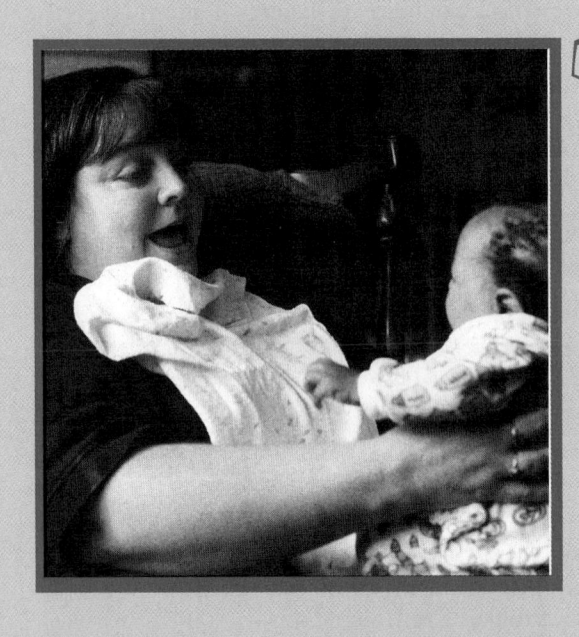

learning objectives

After reading this chapter, you should be able to:

- Describe the characteristics necessary to become a competent caregiver.
- Explain the various types of knowledge professional educators possess.
- Articulate the relationship between formal education experiences and child outcomes.
- Determine how to match observational tools with your data needs.

chapter outline

- Introduction
- Characteristics of a Competent Early Childhood Educator
- Acquiring Knowledge
- Professional Preparation of the Early Childhood Educator
- Impact of Teacher Education on Quality of Care and Education
- Observing Young Children to Make Educational Decisions
- Summary
- Case Study: Audrey

INTRODUCTION

The heart and soul of excellent care and education are people and the tools they use in supporting the development of young children. This chapter provides specific, effective tools that enhance development. The early childhood educator should practice using each of the tools in this chapter from the developmental perspective that was described previously. The authors subscribe to the idea that careful assessment of infants and toddlers is an essential starting point for professional child care. Recording specific, descriptive observations on an ongoing basis and then using that information to inform your educational decisions ensures optimal growth and development for the infants and toddlers in your care.

As you learned in Chapter 4, it is essential for caregivers to take good care of themselves in order to provide competent care for young children. Therefore, the first tools we will examine are those related to your professional preparation as a caregiver.

CHARACTERISTICS OF A COMPETENT EARLY CHILDHOOD EDUCATOR

Early Childhood Educators Are Physically and Mentally Healthy

Physical health is necessary to provide the high energy level needed in caregiving. Good health is also necessary to resist the variety of illnesses to which you are exposed. The importance of a healthy staff is reflected in state child care regulations. From Alabama to Indiana to Delaware to Wyoming, prospective teachers must provide evidence of being in good physical health and free from active tuberculosis in order to gain and remain employed in a child care setting. These policies were created to protect adults as well as the children. The American Academy of Pediatrics (1996) also recommends that the health record for each employee contains:

- an annual report of a negative tuberculosis Mantoux test.
- evidence of recovery after specified communicable diseases.
- reports of periodic evaluations.
- evidence of a Hepatitis B vaccine injection.

In your daily relationships, you must provide physical closeness and nurture for an extended time, give emotionally more than you receive, be patient and resolve conflicts caused by someone else, and calm one child right after you have been frustrated with another. Emotionally stable teachers have learned how to handle a variety of emotional demands in their daily experiences and how to encourage greater mental health in others.

Early Childhood Educators Have a Positive Self-Image

Your feelings of self-confidence and positive self-worth show that you believe in yourself. This gives you the strength to take risks, solve problems, consider alternatives, and make decisions in situations where there may be no obvious correct

The caregiver develops skill in working with children and gains satisfaction from interacting with them.

answer. Your perceptions, knowledge base, and opinions are all sources of information you can use in evaluating situations and making decisions. Awareness of your expectations and those of children help you remain open minded. Your decisions may not always be accurate or appropriate, because they are based on incomplete information. Admit this, reevaluate the data or gather more information and make a new decision. Doing so helps you to continue professional growth and enhances your self-image as a competent caregiver.

Early Childhood Educators Are Caring and Respectful

There is pleasure, enjoyment, and satisfaction in providing effective, high-quality care. Although some tasks may be difficult, unpleasant, or repetitious, your accepting behavior and considerate treatment shows that you value meeting the children's needs. They are worthy of your time and effort because they are important people. When early childhood educators reflect caring feelings to the children, families, and other staff members, they can build better partnerships, but it is more than that. According to Noddings (2002, 2005), human-to-human caring relationships for self, others, and community are the core that can bring social justice and caring together for world survival.

Early Childhood Educators Are Professionals

Caregiving is an essential profession which should receive more respect. You provide a very important service to children, families, and the community. The care you provide directly affects children at critical times in their lives. You have great influence and importance in the child's life and must be rational and objective in your decisions and actions.

Striving to do your best is essential for high-quality caregiving. Read, study, visit, observe, and talk with other early childhood educators. Professional knowledge is not static; it is not possible to finish learning everything you need to know to be an effective caregiver. New information and experiences lead to new insights, understanding, and skills. Openness to learning helps you seek new ideas and take advantage of new opportunities to expand your knowledge and skills.

ACQUIRING KNOWLEDGE

About Yourself

Why do you want to be an early childhood educator? What are your strengths? What are your weaknesses? What are your interests? What are your values? What are your expectations of yourself and others? Are you willing to put forth effort to satisfy yourself and others? How much time and effort do you think is appropriate to put into caregiving? Professional educators value and therefore set aside time for frequent and systematic reflection on their work. What plans do you have to learn about yourself, others, and your program?

About Children

Child development research continues to provide new information about children. The information helps identify each child's individual characteristics and levels of development. Your knowledge of the patterns of physical, emotional, social, and cognitive development influences how you plan for and act with children.

About Families

Each family situation is unique and affects your caregiving. As a caregiver you can expect families to represent a great deal of diversity: single parent, grandparent as head of household, gay/lesbian parents, adoptive families with Caucasian parents and Asian children. You will also work with families that reflect your own culture and those that are different from it. You should continually seek information from and maintain communication with family members. Families have special needs, desires, and expectations of themselves, their children, and you.

About Early Child Care and Education

Developmentally appropriate practice (Copple & Bredekamp, 2009) encompasses emotional interaction, instructional planning, and various types of teaching and learning techniques involving children, families, colleagues, and the community. How do we create experiences that are responsive to the needs of toddlers? How do we identify which materials are appropriate for the various development levels of infants? Answers to these questions, while not always straightforward, can be found in a number of sources, including licensing laws and accreditation standards. State or county agencies design licensing regulations to standardize the care and education of young children in group settings in both home- and center-based programs. These regulations govern such things as teacher-child ratios, space, safety and health requirements, fire codes, and zoning ordinances. Licensing identifies a set of minimum standards that the program meets; it does not guarantee quality of care. However, many states, like Indiana, are working to include important characteristics of quality programming in their licensing regulations. Professional organizations have well-established accreditation programs for family child care programs and center-based care, the National Association for Family Child Care (NAFCC) and the National Association for the Education of Young Children (NAEYC), respectively. Accreditation standards are significantly more stringent than licensing regulations and serve to recognize high-quality programs that meet the physical, social, emotional, and cognitive development of the children and families being served.

Becoming familiar with both licensing regulations and accreditation standards is a must for professional early childhood educators. Doing so will clarify the various roles that teachers of infants and toddlers play on a daily basis. You will need to balance these many roles to provide high quality care and education. Understanding the responsibilities of the various hats you wear will help determine your strengths and how to increase knowledge and personal growth.

One way to understand the various responsibilities is to read and discuss with colleagues NAEYC's Code of Ethical Conduct (NAEYC, 2005a). This document, created with significant input from teachers working directly with young children, provides guidance on balancing and resolving any conflicts among your professional responsibilities.

About Program Implementation

There are many successful ways to apply our knowledge of developmentally appropriate practice to nurturing, providing care, and teaching. Knowledge of these can help you adjust and individualize caregiving procedures to meet the specific needs of the environment and the children you serve.

About Partnerships

Early childhood educators cannot work in isolation and provide high-quality care (Bove, 2001; Colombo, 2006; Copple & Bredekamp, 2009). Partnerships with families, colleagues, and community agencies are a must. Family members possess knowledge about the child that you often do not have access to, unless you ask. When reciprocal or bidirectional relationships have been established between teachers and families, information flows freely, benefiting everyone involved.

Colleagues are invaluable resources whether you have worked in the early childhood profession five minutes, five months, or five years. Sharing professional knowledge, skills, and dispositions promotes growth for all parties (see, for example, Buell, Pfister, & Gamel-McCormick, 2002).

Partnerships with community agencies and organizations will add value and resources to your program (see, for example, Friedman, 2007). The number and type

Attending conferences renews your enthusiasm as a professional and provides opportunities for meeting other infant/toddler educators.

of agencies you form partnerships with will be determined by the characteristics of your community. A great place to start is your public library. Introduce yourself to the children's and adult librarians. They can offer assistance with books, websites, magazines, and journals to help you stay on top of the dynamic field of early childhood education. They can also apprise you of state and federal funding sources. Many communities have city- or county-wide consortiums of early childhood educators from public, private, center-based, and family child care settings that can offer services such as mentoring or helping to locate educational opportunities. Moreover, do not forget to participate in your local and state Association for the Education of Young Children. Networking through those organizations can provide additional avenues for partnerships.

About Advocacy

Professionals employ informal advocacy strategies in their daily work with children and families. As mentioned previously, every time you interact with family members, colleagues, and community members, you are a teacher-leader. Careful consideration must be given to your practices, as others look to you for examples of how to treat infants and toddlers. Engaging in developmentally appropriate practice, for example, demonstrates your beliefs about the capabilities of children and your positive influence on their development and learning. Your dedication to engaging in

TABLE 5-1 BRIEF LIST OF ORGANIZATIONS THAT PROVIDE ADVOCACY RESOURCES AND SUPPORT

National Association for the Education of Young Children	The National Children's Advocacy Center
Association for Childhood Education International	Child Welfare League of America
The Child Advocate	Voices for America's Children
National Association of Child Care Resource and Referral Agencies	The Immigrant Child Advocacy Center

and sharing professional knowledge and practices makes you an advocate for young children, families, and the early childhood profession as a whole.

Formal advocacy involves working with community members, other professional organizations, and even policy makers to improve the lives of children and families and the early childhood profession. Learning to be an effective advocate takes time, dedication, and the acquisition of skills (NAEYC, 2005b; Robinson & Stark, 2005). But don't worry because many organizations provide resources to assist you in acquiring or honing advocacy skills. Table 5–1 provides a sample of such resources.

✓ reading checkpoint

Before moving on with your reading, make sure that you can answer the following questions about the material discussed so far.

1. What important knowledge bases should professional educators have? Why?

2. How do partnerships with families and community agencies help to promote the development and well-being of very young children?

3. Discuss with someone your understanding of the concept "developmentally appropriate practice." How can you learn more about this idea?

PROFESSIONAL PREPARATION OF THE EARLY CHILDHOOD EDUCATOR

Both informal and formal educational opportunities are available to teachers of infants and toddlers. Informal experiences may be spontaneous or planned. A magazine article may stimulate your thinking by providing new information and raising questions. You may take time to do further thinking and discuss your ideas with colleagues, or you may think of the ideas periodically and begin changing your caregiving practices to incorporate what you have learned.

Formal educational opportunities are those that are planned to meet specific goals. You choose experiences to help you gain desired knowledge and skills.

The following types of learning opportunities contribute to your education either by using your experiences with children, through independent study, or a combination of both:

- A mentor or a more-experienced caregiver. Having such a person available gives you opportunities to observe, participate, and discuss techniques. Mentoring is organized, supervised, and evaluated.
- Workshops, seminars, or speakers. These may be sponsored by libraries, colleges, universities, hospitals, and community or professional organizations. They usually focus on a single topic or skill.
- Continuing education courses sponsored by local schools and colleges.
- Vocational school courses and programs in child care.
- Community college and university courses in early childhood education and/or child development.
- Child Development Associate Certificate. The Child Development Associate, or CDA, is a person who is able to meet the specific needs of children and who, with parents and other adults, works to nurture children's physical, social, emotional, and intellectual growth in a child development framework. "Becoming a CDA is a process that you work at, learn, and nurture until it grows from within. It is a process by which you grow as an individual and as a professional" (Council for Professional Recognition, 2006).
- Early childhood education degrees. Associate, bachelor's, master's, and doctorate degrees can be completed at colleges or universities. Hyson (2003) created guidelines for the educational preparation of teachers based on five core standards and a common set of professional knowledge, skills, and dispositions. Table 5–2 demonstrates the overlap of the CDA and NAEYC core standards. While there is a great deal of similarity of content between the credentials, the expectations of the professional increase with each higher level of education (Hyson, 2003).

spotlight *on organizations*

The Infant-Toddler Specialists of Indiana (ITSI) is a professional organization whose mission is to address the increased need for high-quality child care, education, and early intervention services for children birth to three years. This organization provides professional development and networking opportunities, and resources to enhance the professional identity of infant-toddler specialists.

This organization represents the collaborative efforts of Indiana University, Purdue University, the State of Indiana, and the Indiana Association for the Education of Young Children.

You can learn more about this organization by visiting their Web site.

TABLE 5–2 OVERLAP OF THE CDA AND NAEYC STANDARDS

CDA COMPETENCY AREAS PROFESSIONAL	NAEYC TEACHER PREPARATION STANDARDS					
	1. PROMOTING CHILD DEVELOPMENT AND LEARNING	2. BUILDING FAMILY AND COMMUNITY RELATIONSHIPS	3. OBSERVING, DOCUMENTING, AND ASSESSING	4. TEACHING AND LEARNING	5. BECOMING A PROFESSIONAL
I. Safe, healthy Learning environment	X			X	
II. Advance physical and intellectual competence	X			X	
III. Support social and emotional development; positive guidance	X			X	
IV. Positive and productive relationships with families		X			
V. Well-run, purposeful program			X		
VI. Commitment to professionalism					X

IMPACT OF TEACHER EDUCATION ON QUALITY OF CARE AND EDUCATION

Does teacher preparation make a difference in the quality of care and education provided and child outcomes? Evidence is mounting that it does; however, differences in variables studied and research methodologies makes this answer far from definitive (NICHD Early Child Care Research Network, 2005; Washington, 2008). Teachers who receive training on developmentally appropriate practices use these practices with greater frequency than teachers without it (Lee, Baik, & Charlesworth, 2006; Sherman & Mueller, 1996, as cited in Dunn & Kontos, 1997). In other samples, teachers with the greatest knowledge of developmentally appropriate practice had academic training in early childhood education and/or child development as well as supervised practical experience with young children (Buchanan, Burts, Bidner, White, & Charlesworth, 1998; McMullen, 1999; Snider & Fu, 1990). These results suggest that higher levels of specialized (i.e., early childhood) education influence practices employed with young children.

Do particular practices have a positive effect on child outcomes? Again, investigations have shown the positive impact of teachers' engaging in developmentally appropriate practices. For example, students whose teachers used approaches which fit their level of development had significantly higher social skills scores (Jones & Gullo, 1999) and letter-word identification and applied problem solving (Huffman & Speer, 2000) than those children whose teachers used developmentally inappropriate practices. Moreover, children who experienced preschool programs that were characterized by more active, child-initiated learning experiences (i.e., developmentally appropriate) had more success in their sixth year of school (Marcon, 2002). While these results are for older children, research on Early Head Start has discovered great variability in program quality (Love, Raikes, Paulsell, & Kisker, 2004) and child outcomes (Raikes, Love, Kisker, Chazan-Cohen, & Brooks-Gunn, 2004) because of the complex influence of participant characteristics (e.g., race, income, mental health) and program characteristics (e.g., home- or center-based) (Jung & Stone, 2008; Robinson & Emde, 2004). Taken together, this research indicates that higher levels of education for the caregiver are associated with more appropriate practices with young children, and those are related to better child outcomes.

Because teachers of infants and toddlers are more likely to have lower levels of education than teachers of older children (Berthelsen, Brownlee, & Boulton-Lewis, 2002) and the early years are critical to brain development (see, for example, Shore, 2003), we can no longer ignore the links among education, developmentally appropriate practice, and child outcomes. While this may seem obvious, learning to be a teacher of infants and toddlers poses particular challenges not found with teaching other ages. Infants and toddlers have special developmental needs. Here are four reasons to support that claim.

1. As discussed in earlier chapters, this period of growth and development is rapid—noticeable changes occur monthly, weekly, and, in some cases, daily (Swim & Muza, 1999).
2. Physical, social, emotional, and cognitive development are more interrelated for infants than for older children.
3. Infants are more dependent upon a consistent relationship with a caregiver to meet all of their needs.
4. Infants have no effective skills for coping with discomfort and stress, so they are more open to harm (Gunnar, 2006; Shonkoff & Phillips, 2000).

Many of these issues were highlighted by beginning teachers as challenges. Recchia & Loizou (2002) found that for teachers in their sample, adjusting to the physical and emotional intensity of nurturing very young children, setting limits and guiding the behavior of toddlers, and collaborating with others to ensure continuity of care were particular issues. This line of research, then, highlights the need for infant and toddler caregivers to receive specialized education, mentoring, and ongoing support during the early years of teaching.

✓ reading checkpoint

Before moving on with your reading, make sure that you can answer the following questions about the material discussed so far.

1. Name at least five different experiences that early childhood professionals can have that result in the growth of their professional knowledge and skills.

2. How do formal and informal education help early childhood teachers to be more effective in their various roles?

OBSERVING YOUNG CHILDREN TO MAKE EDUCATIONAL DECISIONS

The previous chapters have laid the groundwork for taking a scholarly approach to your work with infants and toddlers. You cannot, for example, plan appropriate curriculum or be attuned to a toddler if you have not observed what the child is trying to accomplish. Yet, early childhood educators are not in the business of testing children (NAEYC, 2003). Care should be taken to act prudently in this age of testing and judging children. You should pay close attention to why you are gathering the data, how you gathered it, and how to analyze it. Then, careful attention must be placed on how you use the data. This approach can be referred to as scholarly.

Scholars or researchers—like young children—are curious and inquisitive; they think, wonder, and ask lots of questions. They also gather data to answer their questions. What do you wonder about infants and toddlers? Use your curiosity to drive, inspire, and sustain your work because, according to Maguire-Fong (2006), "Curious infants do best when matched with curious adults who are just as intent in their desire to learn about the infants in their care as the infants are to learn about the world before them" (p. 118). This section will provide you with knowledge, skills, and tools for gathering data about infants and toddlers.

Observe and Record

Why Observe?

Observations provide important information needed for decision-making and communicating with others. Planning a responsive, developmentally appropriate curriculum requires specific, detailed knowledge about each child in your care. Observation must precede teaching, yet it is an ongoing process. As such, it occurs before, during, and after your experiences with young children. This creates a continuous loop of observing, planning, implementing, observing, and so on (see Chapter 9 for more details).

Observations that include details of your own behavior, the curriculum, the materials, and physical environment can provide particularly important information which is often overlooked. You may have observed that on Tuesday Jessica cried for ten minutes after being separated from her father. Including the fact that her father and primary caregiver were unable to locate her transitional object (a stuffed elephant) that day would help to explain her sudden, intense reaction to being separated.

In addition, effective communication with families, colleagues, and other professionals requires that you provide thorough reports (written and verbal) of what you observed. Making global or general statements without specific examples can break down communication rather than support it.

Who to Observe?

Each child in the child care home or center needs to be observed. All program plans and implementation start with what the teacher knows about each child and family. Setting aside time each day to observe each child provides you with a wealth of information. Observing how families interact with children and adults helps teachers to plan responsive curriculum. However, because family members participate to varying degrees in a child care program, you might have more information on one or two members rather than all who have significant impact on the child. Do not forget that each caregiver contributes unique ideas and behaviors to the child care setting; others can identify these by observing.

What to Observe?

Children's behavior helps us learn about them. Infants and toddlers often cannot use words to tell about themselves. Each child is unique. Early childhood educators must identify the characteristics and needs of each child, because the child is the focal point of decisions and plans regarding time, space, and curriculum. Each one is continuously changing. This growth and development produces expected and sometimes unexpected changes. Living with someone every day, you may not notice some important, emerging developments. Therefore, it is important to make periodic informal and formal observations (e.g., Developmental Prescriptions and Profiles) and to record them so that the changes in the child can be noted and shared. This information will affect your plans for, and interactions with, the child.

A caregiver's behavior provides needed information to analyze the child's behavior as well as her own behavior. You should record how you assisted the children with accomplishing a new skill or task. Vygtosky's theory (discussed in previous chapters) necessitates that data be gathered on both the independent level of performance and the assisted level of performance. Teachers also need to gather data to improve their own practices and effectiveness as caregivers. For example, Ms. Sheila knew that she needed to improve her organization and planning, because every day she would forget some supplies for snack time. She started making a checklist of snack items so she could make sure she had prepared everything. After snack time she noted whether she had all the supplies or whether she should add something else.

Her co-teacher provided feedback also. By focusing and recording in this way, Ms. Sheila was able to improve herself. Every early childhood professional is learning and continually developing skills. One caregiver may observe another one in order to learn new strategies or to reinforce those she already uses. Other people's observations can let caregivers know whether their actual practice matches the behavior intended. On-going evaluation and reflection, along with feedback, can help caregivers increase their effectiveness.

Ms. Josephine wanted to involve Monroe more when she shared a book with him. She selected a book she thought he would like and wrote down three questions to ask Monroe that would focus his thinking and questioning on objects from the book. She set up a small cassette tape recorder where she and Monroe would be sitting and invited Monroe over to share the book with him. Later, when Ms. Josephine listened to the tape recording of her time with Monroe, she discovered that she had talked all the time and told everything to Monroe rather than allowing him to talk, share, and question. Observations of interactions provide information about the kind of responses one person has to another person or to material, showing you how you have stimulated or inhibited the desired interaction.

The entire child care setting, including children, equipment, materials, and arrangement of space, should be examined to determine safe and unsafe conditions. Look at who is using what space and how it is being used to determine if the space is being used effectively. Do toddlers, for example, cause disruptions to others reading because they have to walk through the area to get to the bathroom? Or, is the addition of musical instruments near the art area having a positive influence on the work being accomplished by the older infants? Once you gather data to answer your question, respond to what you find by making necessary adjustments. The goal of this type of scholarship is to inquire into the impact of the learning environment on the children's needs. More information about creating and evaluating learning environments will be provided later in this text.

Why Record?

Making observations without having a method for recording your data is inviting trouble. Infant and toddler teachers may work with between 6 and 12 different children throughout the course of a day and make hundreds of observations. If you do not write down the important ones, you run the risk of incorrectly remembering what you saw or attributing skills or development to the wrong child. In addition, infants and toddlers change quickly. They add skills on a daily basis so failing to record them might mean missing this accomplishment altogether. Moreover, teachers, like young children, elaborate—add additional information based on previous knowledge and assumptions—to fill in any gaps (McDevitt & Ormrod, 2007). Thus, we may "see" something that really did not happen but fits with what we already know about the child. These examples should help

chapter 5 EFFECTIVE PREPARATION AND TOOLS FOR PROFESSIONAL EDUCATORS

Talking, listening, and recording your observations are important caregiver behaviors.

you to understand the importance of recording what you observed as quickly as you can. The following section provides guidance on methods of observing and recording.

How to Observe and Record

Observations may be spontaneous or planned, but they must be ongoing and regular. You may glance across the room and see Sammy roll over. This the first time you have seen that happen. You record this example in his portfolio and/or home-school journal. Sometimes a staff member will arrange to spend a few minutes specifically observing a child, a teacher, materials, or space. These observations can provide valuable information. Since infants and many toddlers cannot tell us in words what they have learned, we must attend carefully to their behaviors for clues. Writing what you observe gives you and other people access to that information later on.

Descriptions may be brief or very detailed and extensive. In either case, the focus is on reporting the exact behavior or situation in narrative form. You will need to learn the difference between descriptive and interpretative phrasing. Descriptive phrasing, the preferred type for reporting observations, involves using words or phrases to describe observable behaviors, behavior that another observer (or reader) could easily verify; interpretative phrasing, on the other hand, makes a judgment or evaluation but gives little or no observable data to justify the conclusions (Marion, 2004). An example of interpretative phrasing is "Eva refused to eat her cereal at breakfast." The reader has no way to verify the word "refused" in this description of this meal. Compare that to: "Eva sat in her chair with her eyes squinted, mouth pursed, and her arms crossed. She stated, 'No, oatmeal' and pushed her bowl away from her. I offered her a banana and she smiled and nodded 'yes.' She ate the entire banana and drank her milk." The difference in language is important because evaluative or interpretative phrasing is "emotionally loaded" and often leads to misunderstandings, whereas factual, descriptive statements can rarely be disputed.

There are three main categories of tools that early childhood teachers can use to observe and record the behaviors of young children: narratives (i.e., running and anecdotal records), checklists and rating scales, and authentic documentation. The first two methods are narrative because you observe an interesting incident and record essential details to tell a story.

Narrative. Running records are long narratives. They tell a story as it unfolds over a significant period of time for a child, a group, or an activity (Marion, 2004). This tool is useful for learning about child development. When you focus your attention on a child for a specific time period, say an hour, you can gather valuable information that might otherwise go unnoticed. Due to time considerations, running records are rarely used spontaneously. Teachers create schedules to routinely observe the development and behavior of every infant and toddler. Running records are closely related to an ethnographic report because they describe a total situation. An *ethnographic report* describes a total situation: the time, place, people, and how the people behave. Description of the total situation lets the reader know about things that may not be evident in just one part of a specific incident.

Adults unfamiliar with infants and toddlers may think that a young child does not do anything. An early education student observed the following behaviors during outdoor play in a family child care home one summer afternoon (see Table 5–3). She was to focus on one child and write down everything she saw and heard that child do and say. The purpose of this assignment was to identify and categorize the various experiences initiated by a 13-month-old child. The observer was not to interject her own interpretations into the narrative.

An anecdotal record is a brief narrative of one event. As the definition implies, you look for or notice one event and then write a short story about it. Anecdotal records are great for understanding individual child characteristics and how contextual variables impact the learning, development, and behavior of a child. With spontaneous anecdotal records, something happens that you did not anticipate, but that you want to record for possible use later. For example, you have planned to watch Julio's interactions with peers today, but he is sick. You then notice how Thomas John and Erika were sharing the space and materials while in the block area. You record the anecdotal record shown in Table 5–4.

TABLE 5–3 RUNNING RECORD WITH OBSERVATIONAL DATA

CONTEXT	OBSERVATIONS (BEHAVIORAL DESCRIPTIONS OF WHAT YOU SEE AND HEAR)	ANALYSIS/ INTERPRETATIONS/QUESTIONS
The play yard contained the caregiver Lynn, the observer, and six children ranging from seven months to six years of age.	2:20 • Lynn puts mat out and stands Leslie up in yard. • Leslie looks around (slowly rocking to keep balance). • Reaches hand to Lynn and baby-talks • Looks at me and reaches for me • Takes two steps, trips and falls on mat, remains sitting on it • Turns around to face me • Cries a little • Reaches for Lynn, then to me • Looks around and watches Jason (four-year-old who is riding trike) • Reaches hand toward Lynn • Watches Jason and sucks middle two fingers on right hand • Looks around • Swings right arm 2:45 • Takes Lynn's fingers and stands • Walks two steps onto grass • Swings right arm and brushes lips with hand to make sound—baby talk • Turns toward Lynn and babbles • Lane arrives. Leslie watches and rubs left eye with left hand. • "Do you remember Leslie?" Lynn asks Lane. • Leslie reaches out arms to Lynn and walks to her. Hugs her • Listens and watches Lynn. Holds onto her for support • Turns around and steps on mulch and lifts foot to see what it is • Watches Lynn tie Jason's shoe • Lynn lifts her in air, then sets her on her knee. • She lies back in Lynn's lap and laughs.	Leslie initiates a variety of interactions with people and materials. She is physically, emotionally, socially, and cognitively involving herself in her world. Teacher planning and facilitating can stimulate and build on Leslie's self-initiated behaviors. Wants to be picked up?

TABLE 5-4 ANECDOTAL RECORD

Child's Name: Thomas John
Observer's Name: Rachel
Setting: Block area

Age: 22 months
Date: October 1

WHAT ACTUALLY HAPPENED/WHAT I SAW:

Thomas John is building a block tower using the square blocks. Erika toddled into the area and picked up a rectangle block. She held it out to Thomas John. He took it from her hand and placed it on top of the tower. They both smiled as if to say, "It didn't fall." Thomas John then picked up another rectangle block and placed it on top. The structure wobbled but did not fall. He looked at Erika, smiled and knocked over the structure. They each began to build their own tower. They worked in the same area for 12 more minutes. Occasionally, they would hand blocks to one another and, like before, they did not verbalize.

REFLECTION/INTERPRETATION/QUESTIONS:

Thomas John is new to the class and he has not yet spoken. His parents have reported that he tells them all about his day on the ride home. Erika tends to verbalize frequently. She seemed to respect the fact that he was working in silence. I wonder if they will continue to work together and form a friendship.

Checklists and Rating Scales. Checklists and ratings scales are quick, efficient tools for gathering data. They bypass details and merely check or rate development and progress (Marion, 2004). They can be used to gather data on specific behaviors that you value (e.g., self-help skills) or might be concerned about (e.g., aggressive behaviors). In addition, many commercially designed tools for analyzing a child's progress on developmental milestones are checklists or rating scales. In fact, the Developmental Prescriptions discussed earlier and found in Appendix A are a combination of a checklist and a rating scale, so learning more about each will help you understand how to utilize this important tool.

A **checklist** is a record of behaviors that a child can perform at a given point in time. When you observe a child or group of children, you note whether each child does or does not show that characteristic or behavior. Placing a check beside an item indicates that you observed the child perform that behavior during the observation. Leaving the item blank tells others either that the child cannot execute the behavior or that you did not observe the execution of it at that particular time. Suppose you are particularly interested in the children acquiring self-help skills. Thus, you create a checklist to monitor progress in this area. Table 5–5 shows just part of your checklist for infants.

TABLE 5-5 SAMPLE CHECKLIST WITH DATA

	DAKOTA	TRAVIS	COLBY	RAJI	SARAH	LAKINTA	JOSE
Holds bottle	X		X			X	X
Holds spoon		X	X			X	
Lifts bottle to mouth				X	X		
Lifts spoon to mouth				X	X		

TABLE 5-6 EXAMPLE OF A RATING SCALE FOR BRUSHING TEETH

Name of Child: _____   Age: _____

Date of Observation: _____

	NEVER	SOMETIMES	FREQUENTLY	ALWAYS
Squeezes toothpaste on brush				
Brushes teeth independently				
Rinses mouth after brushing				
Rinses toothbrush				
Returns toothbrush to proper location				

Rating scales share many characteristics with checklists, but they are a listing of qualities of characteristics or activities (Marion, 2004). For example, instead of just knowing that Raji can lift the spoon to his mouth, you can rate the frequency (i.e., never, seldom, sometimes, often, always) of this behavior or the quality (i.e., all food on spoon placed in mouth, some of food on spoon placed in mouth, none of food on spoon placed in mouth) of it. Table 5–6 is an example of a rating scale.

Returning to the Developmental Prescriptions in Appendix A, you should now recognize which part of the tool is a checklist and which part is a rating scale. When you note the date of the first observation, the tool serves a checklist. When you evaluate the performance level at a later time (i.e., practicing or proficient), you are using the tool as a rating scale.

Authentic Documentation. "Documentation refers to any activity that renders a performance record with sufficient detail to help others understand the behavior recorded.... The intent of documentation is to explain, not merely display" (Forman & Fife, 1998, p. 241). This form of assessment involves gathering work samples, taking

Labeling this artwork as "a car" provides evidence of the child's language and representation skills. This artifact can be used as an entry in the child's portfolio.

photographs or videotapes of the children, and organizing the data using methods such as portfolios or documentation panels.

A **portfolio** is a tool for collecting, storing, and documenting what you know about a child and her development and learning (Marion, 2004). All of the information gathered using the methods described previously can be added to the photographs and work samples to create a more complete picture of the child's capabilities. Storing all of the data in one location allows for easy access and reflection. While originally designed for use with older children, portfolios can and should be used with very young children because they serve a number of purposes including but not limited to

1. Show the quality of the children's thinking and work.
2. Document children's development over time (one year or more).
3. Assist when communicating with families and other professionals.
4. Support developmentally appropriate practice by giving teachers "a strong child development foundation on which to build age- and individually appropriate programs" (Marion, 2004, p. 112).

5. Provide a tool for teacher reflection (e.g., expectations, quality of planned experiences).
6. Make available information for evaluating program quality and effectiveness (Helm, Beneke, & Steinheimer, 2007; Marion, 2004).

A **documentation panel** includes visual images and, whenever possible, narratives of dialogue that occurred during the experiences that were documented. The goal of creating documentation panels is to make visible to you, the children, and family members the development and learning that has been occurring in the classroom. As such, documentation panels include not only the objective record of your observations but also your reflections and interpretations of those events (Rinaldi, 2001). As you make visible your reflections and interpretations through the panels, they, too, become part of the data that can be read, reread, and analyzed (Rinaldi, 2001). The sharing of documentation panels with children, families, colleagues, and community members "moves learning from the private to the public realm" (Turner & Krechevsky, 2003, p. 42), something that traditional forms of observing and recording did not accomplish. In addition, documentation advocates seeing children as rich, capable learners who actively participate in their own development and learning (Swim & Merz, 2008). Like portfolios, this method can be used for children of all ages and ability levels (Cooney & Buchanan, 2001; Edmiaston & Fitzgerald, 2000).

Other Observation Tools. **Time and event sampling techniques** can be used to record quickly events or behaviors that you are interested in tracking. Use time sampling, for example, if you want to know what a group of toddlers does after waking from their naps. Create a chart of the areas of your classroom and, then, for two weeks, record the first area selected by each child after waking. Doing this over a number of days would provide insight into the children's interests. Event sampling is very similar to time sampling in that you are recording specific behaviors that occur. With event sampling, however, you typically watch one child and record every time a particular behavior occurs. To illustrate, Lela is interested in understanding how Savannah responds when angry. Lela made a chart of the behaviors that Savannah typically engages in when angry. Then, whenever Lela sees that she is getting angry, she charts the behaviors she observes. To better understand the possible causes of Savannah's anger, Lela also notes what she sees as triggers to Savannah's anger (Marion, 2004). Together, this information can provide Lela with insights into how to assist Savannah with gaining anger management skills.

Home-school journals can also be used to record useful information for both families and teachers. The journals are used to record daily or weekly information about key happenings, like developmental milestones, that might be of interest to family members and teachers. Teachers write in the journal and then the family members take the journal home to read it. They are strongly encouraged to write back responses or questions, or to explain behaviors or events happening at home.

These journals can be a fabulous tool for creating partnerships between teachers and families. Of course, teachers must pay close attention to how events and behaviors are described; descriptive language is a must.

Other records kept on a daily basis serve particular purposes, e.g., communication with families, but often yield little data for use in evaluating development or learning. The daily message center of your classroom, for example, contains a clipboard for each child. The clipboard contains a Daily Communication Log that covers routine care events such as eating, sleeping, toileting, and other. For consistency of care between family life and school, families and teachers have designated locations for recording information (see Table 5–7). Use the chart by writing down each time you perform a routine care event (e.g., change a diaper) and details about that event (e.g., record whether the diaper was wet or soiled). This can often be a useful place for noting supplies that are needed at school (e.g., diapers, dry formula).

TABLE 5–7   SAMPLE DAILY COMMUNICATION LOG

Routine Care for _____ on _____.

	HOME EVENTS	SCHOOL EVENTS
Eating		
Sleeping		
Toileting		
Other routine care		
Important information to know		

Set aside time on a regular basis to share information with colleagues who work with the same children.

Assess and Evaluate

Once you gather your data, the next component of a scholarly approach is reviewing, reflecting on, and analyzing the data. Set aside time on a regular basis, preferably each day, to assess and evaluate the data. When assessing, in general, your attention should be placed on coming to understand what the child can currently do. You can approach this aspect of your work by asking, "What is she capable of doing alone and with assistance?"

Assessment means comparing the data gathered with what we know about child development and learning. Compare the data also to what you currently know about the child's context, especially family characteristics and circumstances. You may focus your analysis on one area of development, such as cognition and language, or the whole child: for example, physical, emotional, social, and cognitive/language. Compare the child's level of development and behaviors to developmental milestones or expected patterns of development based on chronological age. Yet, be cautious with this approach. The age when children accomplish developmental norms varies greatly because of the influence of variables ranging from genetic predispositions to access to resources, to family beliefs and practices. Nevertheless, knowing the expected age range for a milestone will help you to determine how to use the data gathered. For example, infants typically produce their first word at 12 months of age; however, this can occur as early as 9 or as late as 16 months and still be considered normal development. Typically, there is a three- to six-month range on either side of the developmental milestone, but this will vary depending on the particular behavior. Knowing this information is vital because it provides you with a context for distinguishing warning signs from red flags. *Warning signs* are those behaviors that, although you and family members should monitor, are not of great concern yet. *Red flags* are those behaviors which deviate both from the developmental milestone and the expected range. When a number of behaviors within a particular area of development are found to be red flags, it is time to invite other professionals with specialized knowledge in observation, assessment, and early intervention, to join the conversations.

Few caregivers have received the specialized training required to use standardized assessment techniques. If your program wants to carry out specialized assessment, obtain the necessary training first. But note that these tools are often not as valuable as your careful, ongoing observations, records, and analysis of observational data from your specific classroom.

Using Data Gathered

A brief overview of various uses of the data that was gathered and analyzed will be provided because future chapters in this book describe them in more depth.

Care and Education Plans

The caregiver organizes care and educational plans on a daily and weekly basis to guide classroom experiences and selection of materials, as well as to promote continuity of development. The child's developmental profile provides information about the child's strengths and about areas where you can scaffold development. Planning specific experiences in advance for each child helps make sure you are considering the needs and development of the whole child, rather than focusing on one or two areas and shortchanging others. The results of your developmental assessments should be a strong influence on your planning.

Schedule

The caregiver organizes the schedule around the needs of the infants and toddlers based on data gathered during past and current observations of the children. You have to decide how to use the major blocks of time and how much flexibility you need in that schedule to meet each child's needs. Consistent patterns of events help children learn order in their lives. This develops feelings of security and trust, because they know that some parts of their world are predictable. This does not mean, though, that your schedule is bound by the clock. For example, it is 3:00 p.m., most children have awakened from their nap, and they are hungry for their afternoon snack. You would not wake the few sleeping toddlers just to stay on schedule. Your schedule is flexible in that snack comes after nap, whether that is 2:30 for three children, 3:00 for four children, or 3:20 for the last two children. Staggering snacks in this manner incidentally affords caregivers the chance to converse more easily with smaller groups of children. So, in this example, a flexible schedule also supports the children's verbal, social, and emotional development.

Environment and Materials

The caregiver organizes the environment—indoors and outdoors—and the materials within it to meet the developmental needs of the children. Effective infant and toddler programs need a variety of learning materials every day. Teachers rely on their knowledge of the individual children in their care as well as on their background in child development when selecting and arranging some materials and storing the rest. While each early childhood educator has to decide how and when to change the environment, all of them should follow principles of good environments (see Swim, 2004; 2005 and Chapter 8).

✓ reading checkpoint

Before moving on with your reading, make sure that you can answer the following questions about the material discussed so far.

1. Why must teachers observe and record the behavior of infants and toddlers? What observation tools will (or do) you use most often? Why? What are the benefits to you, the children, and families when using these tools?

2. List four available community resources and explain how each can be used to add value and resources to your child care program.

SUMMARY

Your work with children is different from custodial care. Custodial care is simply the physical maintenance of children. Being an early childhood educator requires a strong grounding in knowledge, skills, and dispositions. Not only should you know what to do in a given situation and have the skills to act in a particular way, but you should value acting in that manner.

Working independently and effectively with young children comes after receiving extensive instruction, investigating theories, writing papers, and getting mentoring. It comes after your positive intentions and caring have been transformed into a firm educational base of understanding. You will continue to grow professionally as you see the impact of your behavior, curriculum, and relationships on the children's development and learning. Your work is vital to the lives of very young children, their families, and the community: it is your way of making the world a better place, one child at a time.

key terms

- accreditation
- anecdotal record
- assessment
- checklist
- CDA
- descriptive phrasing
- developmentally appropriate practice
- documentation panel
- home-school journal
- interpretative phrasing
- licensing regulations
- NAEYC
- NAFCC
- partnerships
- portfolio
- rating scale
- running record

case study — Audrey

Eric, a four-and-a-half-month-old, is lying on the floor when he starts to cry. His teacher, Audrey, looks at the clock and picks him up. She "eats" his tummy and he laughs. She holds him up in the air and he smiles. She says, "Are you getting hungry?" Eric swings his arms as if to say, "Not right now, I want to play." Audrey "eats" his tummy again. Ria toddles over and looks at Eric. Audrey tells Eric what Ria is doing, to provide a language-rich environment. Ria toddles away and Eric begins to fuss. Audrey asks again if he is hungry. This time he continues to fuss, so she gets his bottle, sits in a chair, and feeds him. Eric gazes at Audrey and smiles between sips.

Grasping her finger, Eric looks around the room. Audrey notices he is looking towards Ria. She comments, "Ria is painting. She is making large circles." Audrey stands him in her lap facing Ria. "Can you see better now?" He laughs. She holds him while he dances and laughs. Audrey turns him around so that he is facing her. She holds his hands to pull him to and fro, and kisses him. He watches Audrey's mouth and responds as she talks to him. He leans on her shoulder and burps as he fingers the afghan on the back of the chair.

1. Use the information provided about Eric to assess his social and emotional development.
2. What suggestions would you give to Audrey for organizing the environment to support Eric's social and emotional development? Why?
3. What characteristics about Eric should she consider as she interacts with and designs educational experiences for him?

QUESTIONS AND EXPERIENCES FOR REFLECTION

1. Identify your own strengths and weaknesses as a professional. Create a growth plan for yourself. In other words, list two goals you have for professional growth and explain the steps you will take to meet those goals.

2. Observe one infant and one toddler for 30 minutes each. Use narrative running records to describe what you see and hear. Analyze the behaviors of each child.

3. Using the record of Leslie in the play yard (Table 5–3), list her behaviors using the following categories: (a) physical, (b) emotional, (c) social, (d) cognitive and language.

4. Observe two caregivers, each for 10 minutes. Tally a mark in the appropriate category in the chart (shown at right) each time you observe the caregiver assuming that role.

5. How can you be an advocate of the information presented in this chapter? In other words, how can you teach what you have learned to others?

	Caregiver 1	Caregiver 2
Observer 　of children 　of self		
Recorder 　routine care events chart 　other observation tools		
Assessor/Evaluator 　of children 　of self		
User of data to organize 　care and education 　　plans 　schedules 　environment and 　　materials		

REFERENCES

American Academy of Pediatrics. (1996). *Recommendations for day care centers for infants and children.* Evanston, IL: Author.

Berthelsen, D., Brownlee, J., & Boulton-Lewis, G. (2002). Caregivers' epistemological beliefs in toddler programs. *Early Child Development and Care, 172*(5), 503–516.

Bove, C. (2001). *Inserimento:* A strategy of delicately beginning relationships and communications. In L. Gandini and C. P. Edwards (Eds.), *Bambini: The Italian approach to infant/toddler care* (pp. 109–123). New York: Teachers College Press.

Buchanan, T. K., Burts, D. C., Bidner, J., White, V. F., & Charlesworth, R. (1998). Predictors of the developmental appropriateness of the beliefs and practices of first, second, and third grade teachers. *Early Childhood Research Quarterly, 13*(3), 459–483.

Buell, M. A., Pfister, I., & Gamel-McCormick, M. (2002). Caring for the caregiver: Early Head Start/family child care partnerships. *Infant Mental Health Journal, 23*(1–2), 213–230.

Colombo, M. (2006). Building school partnerships with culturally and linguistically diverse families. *Phi Delta Kappan, 88*(4), 314–318.

Cooney, M. H., & Buchanan, M. (2001). Documentation: Making assessment visible. *Young Exceptional Children, 4*(3), 10–16.

Copple, C., & Bredekamp, S., (Eds.). (2009). *Developmentally appropriate practice in early childhood programs* (3rd ed.). Washington, DC: National Association for the Education of Young Children.

Council for Professional Recognition. (2006). *Assessment system and competency standards for infant/toddler caregivers* (2nd ed.). Washington, DC: Author.

Dunn, L., & Kontos, S. (1997). Research in review. What have we learned about developmentally appropriate practice? *Young Children, 52*(5), 4–13.

Edmiaston, R. K., & Fitzgerald, L. M. (2000). How Reggio Emilia encourages inclusion. *Educational Leadership, 58*(1), 66–69.

Forman, G., & Fife, B. (1998). Negotiated learning through design, documentation, and discourse. In C. Edwards, L. Gandini, & G. Forman, *The hundred languages of children* (2nd ed., pp. 239–260). Westport, CT: Ablex.

Friedman, S. (2007). Coming together for children: Six community partnerships make a big difference. Beyond the Journal *Young Children* on the Web. Retrieved on October 13, 2008 from http://www.journal.naeyc.org/btj/200703/pdf/BTJFriedman.pdf.

Gunnar, M. (2006). Stress, nurture, and the young brain. In J. R. Lally, P. L. Mangione, & D. Greenwald (Eds.). *Concepts for care: 20 essays on infant/toddler development and learning.* Sausalito, CA: WestEd. pp. 41–44.

Helm, J. H., Beneke, S., & Steinheimer, K. (2007). *Windows on learning: Documenting young children's work* (2nd edition). New York: Teachers College Press.

Huffman, L. R., & Speer, P. W. (2000). Academic performance among at-risk children: The role of developmentally appropriate practices. *Early Childhood Research Quarterly, 15*(2), 167–184.

Hyson, M. (Ed.). (2003). *Preparing early childhood professionals: NAEYC's standards for programs.* Washington, DC: National Association for the Education of Young Children.

Jones, I., & Gullo, D. F. (1999). Differential social and academic effects of developmentally appropriate practices and beliefs. *Journal of Research in Childhood Education, 14*, 26–35.

Jung, S., & Stone, S. (2008). Sociodemographic and Programmatic Moderators of Early Head Start: Evidence from the National Early Head Start Research and Evaluation Project. *Children & Schools, 30*(3), 149–157.

Lee, Y. S., Baik, J., & Charlesworth, R. (2006). Differential effects of kindergarten teacher's beliefs about developmentally appropriate practices on their use of scaffolding following inservice training. *Teaching and Teacher Education, 22*(7), 935–945.

Love, J. M., Raikes, H. H., Paulsell, D., & Kisker, E. E. (2004). Early Head Start's role in promoting good-quality child care for low-income families. In J. Lombardi and M. M. Bogle (Eds.). *Beacon of hope: The promise of Early Head Start for America's youngest children.* Washington, DC: Zero to Three. pp. 44–62.

Maguire-Fong, M. J. (2006). Respectful teaching with infants and toddlers. In J. R. Lally, P. L. Mangione, & D. Greenwald (Eds.). *Concepts for care: 20 essays on infant/toddler development and learning.* Sausalito, CA: WestEd. pp. 117–122.

Marcon, R. A. (2002, Spring). Moving up the grades: Relationships between preschool model and later school success. *Early Childhood Research and Practice, 4*(1). Retrieved December 12, 2006, from http://ecrp.uiuc.edu/v4n1/marcon.html

Marion, M. (2004). *Using observation in early childhood education.* Upper Saddle River, NJ: Pearson Prentice Hall.

McDevitt, T. M., & Ormrod, J. E. (2007). *Child development: Educating and working with children and adolescents* (3rd ed.). Upper Saddle River, NJ: Pearson Prentice Hall.

McMullen, M. B. (1999). Characteristics of teachers who talk the DAP talk and walk the DAP walk. *Journal of Research in Childhood Education, 13*(2), 216–230.

NAEYC. (2005a). Position statement: Code of ethical conduct and statement of commitment. Washington, DC: Author. Retrieved December 12, 2006, from http://www.naeyc.org/about/positions/pdf/PSETH05.PDF

NAEYC. (2005b). Advocates in action. Building your advocacy capacity. *Young Children, 60*(3), 79.

NAEYC. (2003). Early childhood curriculum, assessment, and program evaluation: Building an effective, accountable system in programs for children birth through age 8. Joint Position Statement of NAEYC and National Association of Early Childhood Specialists in State Departments of Education (NAECS/SDE). Washington, DC: Author.

NICHD Early Child Care Research Network. (2005). *Child care and child development: Results from the NICHD study of early child care and youth development.* NY: Guilford Press.

Noddings, N. (2005). *The challenge to care in schools: An alternative approach to education* (2nd ed). NY: Teachers College Press.

Noddings, N. (2002). *Starting at home: Care and social policy.* Berkeley: University of California Press.

Raikes, H. H., Love, J. M., Kisker, E. E., Chazan-Cohen, R., & Brooks-Gunn, J. (2004). What works: Improving the odds for infants and toddlers in low-income families. In J. Lombardi and M. M. Bogle (Eds.). *Beacon of hope: The promise of Early Head Start for America's youngest children.* Washington, DC: Zero to Three. pp. 20–43.

Recchia, S. L., & Loizou, E. (2002). Becoming an infant caregiver: Three profiles of personal and professional growth. *Journal of Research in Childhood Education, 16*(2), 133–147.

Rinaldi, C. (2001). Documentation and assessment: What is the relationship? In Project Zero and Reggio Children (Eds.), *Making learning visible: Children as individual and small group learners.* Reggio Emilia, Italy: Reggio Children srl.

Robinson, A., & Stark, D. R. (2005). *Advocates in action: Making a difference for young children* (Rev. ed.). Washington, DC: National Association for the Education of Young Children.

Robinson, J. L., & Emde, R. N. (2004). Mental health moderators of Early Head Start on parenting and child development: Maternal depression and relationship attitudes. *Parenting: Science and Practice, 4.* 73–97.

Sherman, C. W., & Mueller, D. P. (1996, June). Developmentally appropriate practice and student achievement in inner-city elementary schools. Paper presented at Head Start's Third National Research Conference, Washington, DC.

Shonkoff, J. P., & Phillips, D. A. (Eds.). (2000). *From neurons to neighborhoods: The science of early childhood development.* Washington, DC: National Academy Press.

Shore, R. (2003). *Rethinking the brain: New insights into early development* (Rev. ed.). New York: Families and Work Institute.

Snider, M. H., & Fu, V. R. (1990). The effects of specialized education and job experience on early childhood teachers' knowledge of developmentally appropriate practice. *Early Childhood Research Quarterly, 5*(1), 69–78.

Swim, T. J. (2005). Advance reflection on principles of classroom design: Considering the child's perspective. *Early Childhood NEWS, 17*(1), 34–39.

Swim, T. J. (2004). Basic premises of classroom design: The teacher's perspective. *Early Childhood NEWS, 16*(6), 34–42.

Swim, T. J., & Merz, A. H. (2008). Deconstructing policy and practices through rich images of children and teachers. Manuscript submitted for publication.

Swim, T. J., & Muza, R. (1999, Spring). Planning curriculum for infants. *Texas Child Care, 22*(4), 2–7.

Turner, T., & Krechevsky, M. (2003). Who are the teachers? Who are the learners? *Educational Leadership, 60*(7), 40–43.

Washington, V. (2008). Role, relevance, reinvention: Higher education in the field of early care and education. Boston: Wheelock College.

ADDITIONAL RESOURCES

Atkins-Burnett, S., & Meisels, S. (2005). *Developmental screening in early childhood: A guide.* (5th ed.). Washington, DC: National Association for the Education of Young Children.

Boylan, J., & Dalrymple, J. (2008). *Advocacy for children and young adults.* Philadelphia, PA: Open University Press.

Campbell, E. (2003). *The ethical teacher.* Philadelphia, PA: Open University Press.

Coopersmith, S. (1967). *The antecedents of self-esteem.* San Francisco: W. H. Freeman.

Copple, C., & Bredekamp, S. (2005). Basics of developmentally appropriate practices: An introduction to teachers of children 3 to 6. Washington, DC: National Association for the Education of Young Children.

Jones, M., & Shelton, M. (2005). Developing your portfolio—enhancing your learning and showing your stuff: A guide for the early childhood student or professional. Washington, DC: National Association for the Education of Young Children.

For additional activities, web links, and other resources, please visit our website at www.cengage.com/education/swim

PART 2
Establishing a Positive Learning Environment

The four chapters in this section integrate the skills, principles, and theories learned in Part I into practical applications for care. These strategies include communicating with children, families, and colleagues; guiding the behavior of young children; preparing positive indoor and outdoor environments; and designing and implementing curricula for infants and toddlers.

This section provides the professional early childhood educator with the tools necessary to assess individual children using Developmental Profiles, establish goals for growth using Developmental Prescriptions, as well as design and structure specific experiences and activities for each child and the group as a whole. In addition, you will learn positive communication strategies to use when creating partnerships with family members. Only through collaboration with families can you promote the optimal growth and development of very young children.

Infants and toddlers help to develop their own curriculum by engaging energetically in activities that contribute to their growth. Through sensitivity to each child's unique characteristics, family strengths, cultural traditions, and community resources, a positive learning environment for individual children can be established and maintained.

chapter 6

BUILDING RELATIONSHIPS WITH AND GUIDING THE BEHAVIORS OF INFANTS AND TODDLERS

learning objectives

After reading this chapter, you should be able to:

- Describe reasons for creating a caring community of learners.
- Reflect on your own image of the child.
- Apply strategies for communicating with very young children about emotions.
- Understand methods for helping children gain self-regulation skills.

chapter outline

- Introduction
- Reggio Emilia Approach to Infant-Toddler Education
- Strategies for Respectfully Guiding Children's Behavior
- Case Study: Enrique

INTRODUCTION

As this book emphasizes, children need strong, positive relationships with adults in order to thrive in all areas of development. While these relationships are supported through family grouping, continuity of care, and primary caregiving, these are not enough. The ways in which you interact with very young children need to become a focus of your attention. The first guideline for developmentally appropriate practice, creating a **caring community of learners**, speaks directly to the type of relationships adults need to establish with and among children (Copple & Bredekamp, 2009). In a caring community, each learner is valued, and teachers help children learn to respect and acknowledge differences in abilities and to value each other as individuals (Copple & Bredekamp, 2009). Teachers need to select a variety of strategies for helping children acquire the skills for interacting with others, such as emotional management and perspective-taking. How a teacher guides the behavior of the children sends a clear message about what actions are socially acceptable: we demonstrate through our interactions how to treat one another.

Another aspect of creating a positive environment involves what psychologists have labeled as **mastery climate**. This term is used to describe how adults create a context that focuses on self-improvement, effort, persistence, and task mastery through providing challenging tasks (see, for example, Smith, Smoll, & Cumming, 2007). In this context, mistakes are seen as opportunities for learning because of the valuable feedback they provide to the learner. In other words, there is an intentional emphasis on internal motivation rather than external motivation. The impact of focusing on internal motivation via choice was reviewed in Chapter 3. As way of review here, we would like to stress the finding that choice had a positive impact on internal motivation as well as effort, performance, and perceived competence (Patall, Cooper, and Robinson, 2008). When investigating the impact of coaching behaviors within a mastery climate, Smith, Smoll, and Cumming (2007) found that athletes in such an atmosphere reported lower levels of anxiety. Applying the mastery climate concept to an educational setting should result in teachers focusing more on performance and movement towards achieving goals (rather than just the product or end point reached). It would also be a logical assumption that reduced levels of anxiety might result in more focused, risk-taking behaviors and thus greater levels of learning.

Creating positive learning environments and providing conscious, purposeful caregiving to individual children has been a leading premise of this book since its inception. One of the finest child care programs in the world operates in Reggio Emilia, Italy. While that program existed long before this text, they clearly share a common focus on promoting the highest quality care for our youngest citizens.

REGGIO EMILIA APPROACH TO INFANT-TODDLER EDUCATION

History

After World War II, the women of a village in Europe decided to build and run a school for young children. They funded the project with salvaged, washed bricks from destroyed buildings and money from the sale of a tank, trucks, and horses left behind by the retreating Germans (Malaguzzi, 1998). They desired "to bring change and create a new, more just world, free from oppression . . ." (Gandini, 2004). This school formed the foundation for the later development of the municipal infant/toddler and preschool programs in Reggio Emilia, Italy (Malaguzzi, 1998). A series of national laws related to women's rights, workers' rights, and children's rights created a context that supported the establishment of nationally funded infant/toddler and preschool programs (see, for example, Gandini, 2004; Ghedini, 2001). While creating nationally funded programs for preschoolers was a challenge, it was less of a battle than they faced with infant-toddler care. The Italian public feared potential damage to children or to the mother-child relationship (Mantovani, 2001). However, with time these attitudes changed and now infant-toddler centers are "viewed as daily-life contexts with the potential to facilitate the growth and development of all children" (Mantovani, 2001, p. 25). As recently as 1997, laws were passed to establish local projects and services that address the needs of all children and youth (0–18 years old; Ghedini, 2001) These advancements continued the view that care and education of very young children is the responsibility of the broader community (New, 1993, 1998).

Philosophy

The programs of Reggio Emilia are built on educational experiences consisting of reflection, practice, and further careful reflection leading to continual renewal and readjustments (Gandini, 2004). Similar to the theoretical grounding of this book, several theorists influenced their philosophy, including but not limited to Dewey, Decroly, Vygotsky, Erikson, Bronfenbrenner, Piaget, and more contemporary people such as Shaffer, Kagan, Morris, Gardner, Von Foerster, and Heinz (Malaguzzi, 1998). Reading and discussing the writings of these educational leaders assisted them in forming their views about the route they wanted to take when working with young children.

The educators in Reggio Emilia strive to reflect on and recognize in their practices the following 14 principles (see Gandini, 2004, for an explanation of each principle):

1. The image of the child
2. Children's relationships and interactions within a system
3. The three subjects of education: Children, parents, and teachers
4. The role of parents
5. The role of space: An amiable school
6. The value of relationships and interaction of children in small groups

7. The role of time and the importance of continuity
8. Cooperation and collaboration as the backbone of the system
9. The interdependence of cooperation and organization
10. Teachers and children as partners in learning
11. Flexible planning vs. curriculum (*Progettazione*)
12. The power of documentation
13. The many languages of children
14. Projects

Some of these principles have been discussed in previous chapters (e.g., Chapter 5), some will be addressed later (e.g., Chapters 8 and 9), and some are covered in this chapter because they relate to how we build relationships with very young children.

Image of the Child

The educators in Reggio Emilia first and foremost speak about the image they hold of the child and how this affects their interactions, management of the environment,

How do you describe the characteristics and capabilities of very young children?

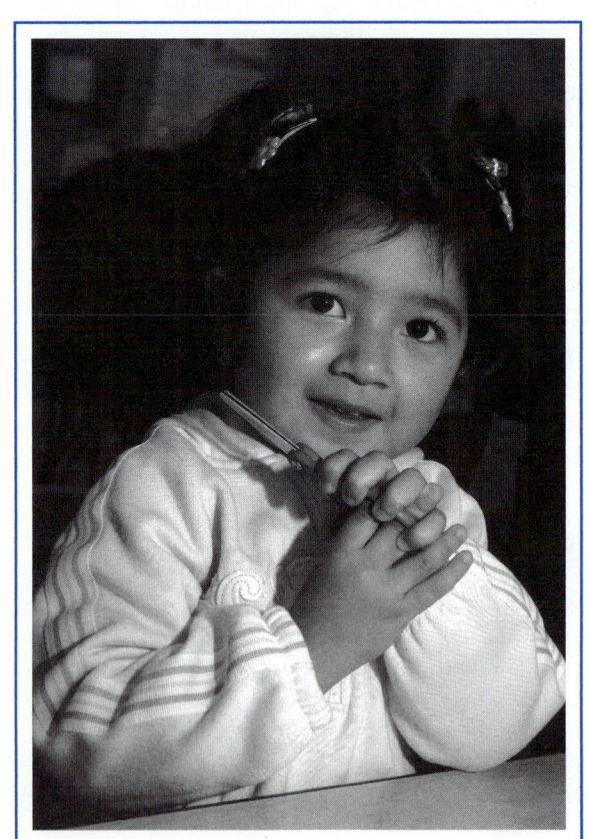

and selection of teaching strategies (Edwards, Gandini, & Forman, 1998; Gandini, 2004; Wien, 2008; Wurm, 2005).

Take a moment and think about three words or phrases that you would use to describe the characteristics, abilities, or expectations you hold of infants and toddlers. While looking over the list, ask yourself, "What do these words say regarding my beliefs about young children?" Does your list include words such as active, possessing potential, independent, curious, full of desire, competent, capable, problem-solvers, communicative, social? The teachers in Reggio believe that all children are unique in their own ways and their job is to recognize and support these differences. More specifically, according to Rinaldi (2001), their "image is of a child who is competent, active, and critical; therefore, a child who may be seen as a challenge and, sometimes, as troublesome" (p. 51). Children need adults that assist in the acquisition of skills that support an active construction of their own worlds (White, Swim, Freeman, & Norton-Smith, 2007). Young children must come to understand how they receive as well as produce change in all systems with which they interact (Rinaldi, 2001). This image, then, is a social and political statement about active participation in a democratic society, not just an educational one (Malaguzzi, 1998; Swim & Merz, 2008).

According to Rinaldi (2001), their creation of the image of the child ". . . was developed by the pedagogy that inspires the infant-toddler centers . . ." (p. 50). For educators in Reggio Emilia, there is a constant back and forth between theory (i.e., the image) and practice. Knowledge and meaning are never static, but rather generate other meanings (Malaguzzi, 1998). Hence, you should not despair if your **image of the child** is not quite fully developed. Reading, reflecting, reading some more, interacting with children, reflecting, and so on will facilitate this development.

Inserimento

Educators in these programs have deeply respectful ways in which they relate to children and parents. *Inserimento*, which can be roughly translated as "settling in" or "period of transition and adjustment," is used to describe the strategy for building relationships and community among adults and children when the child is first entering an infant-toddler center (Bove, 2001). While this period is individualized for each family, there is a general model to support educators' decision-making: parent interviews and home visits before the child starts at the center; parent-teacher meetings before, during, and after the initial transition process; documentation; large or small group discussions with families; and daily communication between families and teachers (Bove, 2001). The model is an attempt "to meet each family's needs, to sustain parental involvement, and to respond to the parents' requests for emotional support in caring for their young children" (Bove, 2001, p. 112). This process is flexible in order to respond to the cultural variations found in families. Some families transition to school quickly as the need to return to work becomes pressing, while other families may make several visits to the school over a number of weeks before actually leaving the child with the teachers. Only careful observation of the family members and the child will indicate the best way to proceed with each family (Bove, 2001; Kaminsky, 2005).

part 2 ESTABLISHING A POSITIVE LEARNING ENVIRONMENT

Dominique's parents drop in to the university child care center to see him before their next class.

As this model demonstrates, parents are viewed as integral partners in caring for and educating the youngest citizens. It is part of our responsibility as professional educators to devise routines that help infants and toddlers simultaneously separate from and form strong bonds with family members (Balaban, 2006). In other words, we must do all we can to assist in building and maintaining strong, healthy attachments at home and school. Helping parents, other relatives, siblings, and children become full participants of the program community is viewed as vital because this supports the well-being and development of not just the infant or toddler but the entire family. Which of the Reggio Emilia principles discussed previously support the practices of *inserimento*?

✓ reading checkpoint

Before moving on with your reading, make sure that you can answer the following questions about the material discussed so far.

1. Why should infant-toddler teachers focus their attention on creating a caring community of learners?

2. What are some principles of the Reggio Emilia approach to early education? How might knowing these influence your behavior with very young children?

A DEVELOPMENTAL VIEW OF DISCIPLINE

Newborns do not arrive in this world knowing how to behave. Yet, they immediately begin to understand the world around them and their role in it. Infants and toddlers work minute by minute to construct their understanding of socially acceptable behaviors. It is your responsibility to help them learn to be socially competent with peers and other adults. The primary avenue adults have to assist very young children with this is to carefully plan their indoor and outdoor learning environments (see Chapter 8) and use positive strategies for guiding their behavior.

Many experts on infant and toddler development avoid discussing discipline out of fear that their comments will be used inappropriately with children. While we clearly understand this, it is essential that teachers use developmentally appropriate guidance strategies to help children learn to follow rules that keep themselves, other people, and property secure and safe (Marion, 2007). Therefore, discipline is an indispensable aspect of helping children develop. The term *discipline* is used here to mean teaching appropriate behavior and setting limits on inappropriate behavior. It *does not* mean punishing children or controlling their behavior. The purpose of guidance or discipline is to help young children learn about themselves (e.g., emotions, feelings) and to teach them ways to interact successfully with others (Keyser, 2006).

Everyone holds implicit, unexamined theories and beliefs regarding discipline (Marion & Swim, 2007). These have developed over time as the result of how we were treated as members of our own families and how we have treated others in our care. Some teachers were punished harshly as a child and remember the negative emotions that accompanied such treatment. As a result, they do not treat children in the same manner. However, some teachers have not acknowledged their emotional response to inappropriate care and continue to utilize those strategies (or aspects of them, such as sarcastic remarks) in their interactions with children. As a professional, it is time to take stock of your personal experiences and how they have shaped your beliefs.

Do so by remembering a time when you were "in trouble" as a child. Write down all that you can remember about this event: the setting, who was involved, how people acted and reacted, what the outcomes were for you and others. Then, answer the following questions as a strategy for reflecting on and evaluating the impact of the experience. What discipline or punishment strategies did the adults use? Did you think the outcome was fair or appropriate? Why or why not? How do you think that event impacted you as a child? As an adult? What did you learn from this event? How does that learning impact your behaviors with children today? Provide at least one example.

Sometimes reflecting on past experiences can be painful. However, it is intended to assist you in acknowledging and uncovering your hidden, implicit theories about how to guide the behavior of young children. Doing so should highlight aspects of your theories that are useful to you as a professional educator and aspects that you should consciously address to improve. In any case, without reflecting to bring hidden theories to light, new information is often openly discarded because it doesn't fit with an existing worldview (Pintrich, Marx, & Boyle, 1993). We would prefer that the following information in this chapter be helpful in changing your beliefs and practices as you strive to adopt a developmental perspective on child guidance.

Mental Models

Different mental models help teachers to understand their role when guiding the behavior of young children. The two mental models presented here share some fundamental commonalities which will be discussed after a brief description. Resources and Instruction for Staff Excellence (RISE; 2000) created a videoconference series about guiding the behavior of young children. This series promoted the mental model of Self, Environment, Child. When a situation arises, a teacher must first evaluate her responses and determine who owns the problem. If the child owns the problem, the adult should continue to the next level of the mental model. If, however, the adult owns the problem, then she must determine how to solve it by examining the situation more carefully. The adult can ask, for example, if the child's behavior is annoying or is it really harmful? Or, do I just want to control a child? One of the most common errors beginning teachers make is to assume responsibility for controlling children's behavior. When you feel responsible for a child's behavior, you set up a no-win situation, wherein you must try to control the child, which is impossible. It is essential to accept the fact that even young children largely control their own behavior, and that you can only control your own behavior. If control is an issue, then this is your problem, and you need to find other ways to view and respond to the way the child behaves.

The next level involves an evaluation of the environment to reveal whether or not something should be changed to result in more positive behaviors. For example, is the child tired? If so, getting out a cot or offering a quiet activity might solve the problem. In another example, is the block area too small, or do too many children want to use that area at one time? If so, then how can the physical arrangement of the room be altered to accommodate the children's interest in building? If no clear environmental cause can be found, then specific strategies can be used to assist the child in acquiring a missing skill. To illustrate, if an infant is biting others, then your intervention might be talking for the infant, thus providing a language-rich context so that additional vocabulary and communication skills can be gained.

The second mental model is offered by Powell, Dunlap, & Fox (2006). The first level of this model (see Figure 6-1) focuses on building positive relationships among children, families, and caregivers. Thus, all that we have described in previous chapters about the importance of building relationships with young children forms the foundation for the prevention of challenging behaviors. Recall also how those chapters linked the building of quality, secure relationships with the acquisition of positive social skills. The second level of this mental model is the building of high quality environments. "Classroom schedules, routines, and activities also provide valuable tools for preventing the development and occurrence of problem behaviors" (Powell, et al. 2006, p. 29). Every day should be carefully planned to minimize transitions as

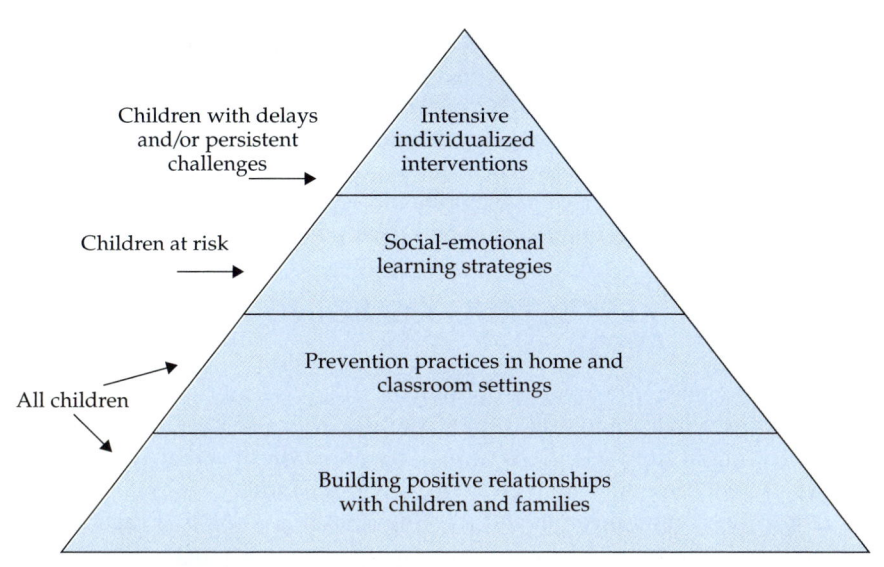

```
                    Intensive
Children with delays    individualized
   and/or persistent     interventions
     challenges

                      Social-emotional
   Children at risk   learning strategies

                   Prevention practices in home and
                         classroom settings
   All children
                     Building positive relationships
                        with children and families
```

FIGURE 6-1 A Model for promoting young children's special competence and addressing challenging behavior.

From: Powell, Dunlap, & Fox (2006). Prevention and Intervention for the Challenging Behaviors of Toddlers and Preschoolers. *Infants and Young Children, 19*(1), 25–35. (page 27). Used with permission.

"[c]hallenging behavior is more likely to occur when there are too many transitions, when all the children transition at the same time in the same way, when transitions are too long and children spend too much time waiting with nothing to do, and when there are not clear instructions" (Hemmeter, Ostrosky, Artman, & Kinder, 2008, p. 1). In other words, when teachers carefully plan transitions, and the rest of their day, they decrease opportunities for disruptive behavior.

You may have noticed that levels one and two of this model are intended to address behaviors that may be considered challenging when displayed by any child. The next two levels address behaviors that are unresolved by positive, stable relationships and a carefully planned learning environment. These remaining behaviors need specific interventions to assist children in acquiring more positive social interaction or emotional regulation skills. The next section will describe some specific strategies teachers can use when faced with challenging behaviors. But first, important links between the two mental models will be discussed.

Both mental models begin by highlighting the important roles adults play in guidance encounters, albeit in different ways. For example, Powell, Dunlap, and Fox's (2006) mental model begins with the adults' responsibility to build relationships with each child. NAEYC's model asks that teachers carefully examine their reactions and beliefs before moving on to the next level: the environment. At that level, both models ask that teachers reflect on and make necessary adjustments to the environment before applying specific guidance strategies to particular children. In this way, both models acknowledge the vital roles that environments play as the "third teacher" (see Chapter 8 for a full explanation of this concept). Suffice it to say that children and adults receive many cues of how to behave from the physical environment. When teachers intentionally manage learning environments, they assist young children in acquiring important skills. It is only when the first levels of each mental model do not resolve the guidance issues that teachers should seek more specific strategies for assisting children with acquiring missing knowledge and/or skills.

STRATEGIES FOR RESPECTFULLY GUIDING CHILDREN'S BEHAVIOR

Creating a caring community involves not only learning to read the children's cues but also helping them to learn to read yours (Gonzalez-Mena & Eyer, 2007). Infants and toddlers communicate their needs using a combination of verbal and nonverbal strategies. As we communicate with them, we do the same. The strategies used to facilitate positive communication and learning are an outgrowth of the theories presented earlier as well as the three *A*s. The purpose of your acquiring these strategies is to make strong relationships between you and the children possible and to promote optimal development and learning.

We have already discussed how using the three *A*s helps children to learn appropriate behavior and to self-regulate their behavior. When caring for children under 36 months, the approach required is to assess their needs and help fulfill them. It is *never* appropriate to completely remove attention, approval, or attunement from infants, nor is shaking, hitting, or being physically or emotionally "rough" in any way acceptable. Problems usually arise when we have done everything we can think of, and the baby still screams and cries or the toddler still pinches. This is the time to stop, gather as much information as possible, reflect on it, and decide what strategies to implement.

This section provides an explanation of several different guidance strategies that can be used to assist young children in acquiring various social, emotional, and behavioral skills that will help them to be more competent in their interactions with others.

Labeling Expressed Emotions

Caregivers should begin labeling feeling states from the time children are born. A good way to teach states is to verbalize your own feelings and your impressions of others' feelings. "I'm feeling rushed today," "Jaime seems sad," and "You really look excited!" are examples of labeling feeling states or emotional talk (Marion, 2007). Teachers should also model and mirror feeling states. Giving children feedback by repeating their words or mimicking their facial expressions helps to develop self-awareness and sensitivity to other people's feelings.

Feelings are inborn, but emotional reactions are learned. It is important to teach young children to identify their feeling states accurately and express them in healthy ways. It is often easy to determine the emotions of even young infants. For example, young babies often "beam" when happy, have a "tantrum" when frustrated or

FIGURE 6–2 Feelings Chart

angry, and "coo and smile" when happy and at ease. Caregivers should label feeling states for nonverbal infants, and as young children develop language, they should be taught to label and express their emotions accurately. One effective tool for helping young children pay attention to and identify feelings is to use a chart such as the one shown in Figure 6–2. This chart illustrates five primary emotions: At Ease, Happy, Sad, Angry, and Afraid, and can be used to help children accurately label their internal feelings. All human emotions are normal and are therefore healthy; a feeling state is neither bad nor good. The main goal is to help children be consciously aware of their feelings and to express them in ways that are helpful to them and not harmful to others.

Affective education starts with bringing attention to the child's internal state and labeling the child's feeling. Often the physical meter for children's feeling states are their whole bodies as they respond to different situations. The trained observer can easily identify children who are upset by their body language. Before they are able to discuss or label feelings, children must learn to recognize their at-ease state. This is most recognizable while having fun and feeling happy.

Early childhood educators use their power of observation to assist children with being aware of good feelings when they are in a state of ease. Ask children how their bodies feel when at ease or while playing and having fun. Often, children will simply smile. State the feeling you sense with nonverbal children and infants and connect it to the nonverbal cues the child is displaying. To illustrate, you can state, "I think you are at ease because you are concentrating hard on putting the puzzle together. Your body is relaxed."

At other times, you want them to learn to connect their feelings with symbols of those feelings. When you see a child expressing an emotion, show him or her the five faces (At Ease, Happy, Sad, Angry, and Afraid). Identify Happy, and point to it, saying, "You're happy." If the child indicates agreement, say "Yes, that's right; you feel happy." Showing the children a picture of the happy face and saying, "You look like this picture" assists them with associating their internal state with the happy face symbol over time. Children will eventually be able to point to the picture and identify this state for themselves.

Give children feedback when they appear to be in a particular feeling state. Tell them that they look At Ease, Happy, or Afraid. Show them the pictures and ask how they feel. If the child says, "I feel bad," quickly respond with, "You are good, but I think that you are feeling afraid now." You could continue the conversation by saying, "Your body looks like you feel afraid," and point to the picture that fits your interpretation of her body language. Then ask, "Is that right?"

As children learn to identify their own body responses, discuss when they started to feel unhappy or afraid. After listening, the early childhood educator can use the specific information about the children's conflicts to address problems. It is important to understand that there are no judgments placed on emotional reactions, because all emotions are normal. When adults do not judge or blame feeling states, children learn to identify and express emotion and develop the potential to be healthy adults.

As the previous paragraphs indicate, good caregiving is **emotion-centered**, meaning that children's emotions are viewed as natural, valid, and important (Hyson, 2004). Children need adult assistance to express their feelings in positive ways. To facilitate expression of emotions in a positive way, *accept all emotions and the need to express them as normal.* Toddlers are filled with energy, extremely curious, and very busy exploring their world. This often leads to frustration and all the unbridled emotions that go with learning how to handle new experiences. Conflicts arise from not getting what they want immediately.

A primary caregiver who knows a child well has learned through observation how that child expresses emotions in certain situations; she is emotionally available to pick up signals of frustration and alleviate a potential problem by identifying the emotions as they occur and working with the child to find appropriate ways to express and manage those emotions. Distracting the child, involving him or her in a special project, or giving the child special attention may be effective strategies to alleviate emotions in the short run, but they do not assist with acquiring important skills associated with emotional intelligence. Therefore, you need to consider carefully which strategies to employ in a given situation in order to balance immediate needs with more long-term learning and development.

An excellent example of needing to be careful when selecting instructional strategies occurs when a toddler has a temper tantrum. Toddlers are known for expressing strong emotions such as frustration and anger through tantrums. These episodes are very scary for a young child. Using emotional talk at the first sign of the emotion can often alleviate the child's feeling of being emotionally overwhelmed and prevent a tantrum in the first place. However, when a child does have a temper tantrum, make sure all furniture and harmful objects are out of the way. Remove undue attention from her until she is through, ask her privately to tell you what she felt if she can verbalize, and then welcome her into the group again. Articulate your observations of the child's emotional state and how it changed over the episode. For example, you could say, "You were very angry with me. I wouldn't let you paint. You like to paint. It must've been frightening when you were so out of control. Now you are calm." This is the most appropriate way to deal with tantrum behavior once it has started because it doesn't cause further emotional harm to the child. This calm approach communicates that the child is still important to the teacher and the group. It is important that adults never hold a grudge against a child. This only demonstrates their lack of emotional skills. If they become overwhelmed by the intensity of the situation, then they should find a way to regain their emotional balance and return to a state of at ease.

Teaching Emotional Regulation

Teaching infants and toddlers to soothe themselves and manage their emotions, known as **emotional regulation**, may be the single most challenging task a caregiver faces. Infants and toddlers, like all other humans, are unique in the ways in which they express their emotions. As discussed previously, this can be related to their temperament (see Chapter 3), family, community, and culture. Professional early childhood educators honor this individuality when they modify their curriculum to build on each child's preferences and strengths (Hyson, 2004).

Infants rely almost exclusively on other people for their need fulfillment, so they are not developmentally prepared at birth to soothe themselves. They must gradually learn that they can calm and soothe themselves through the feedback provided by their caregivers. Professional early childhood educators who sensitively administer the three *A*s and systematically teach children to use the three *A*s for themselves promote and develop **self-soothing**.

You should encourage children's actions and help them to manage emotions as they progress toward set goals. For example, when a child indicates the desire to hold an object and finally succeeds after trying several times with your help, the work is validated in a sense of achievement by your attention, approval, and attunement. This builds a feeling of confidence and a willingness to try the next time when the child reaches for the same object. The child may attempt the task on his own, or he may look for your encouragement or help, but eventually he will feel confident enough to succeed without your help.

Appropriate words of encouragement help children of all ages. Timing of when to give approval depends on the needs of the child. The child may start out wanting something, but becomes too tired to finish. If the child is too tired, the primary need must be cared for first (holding the child until he or she goes to sleep). After the

TABLE 6–1 APPROVAL VALIDATES MASTERY

CHILD BEHAVIOR	CAREGIVER RESPONSE	OUTCOME
1. eyes an object	observes child	caregiver attention
2. reaches for object	encourages with words like "You can do it."	approval for mastery attempt; increased child motivation
3. looks at caregiver; tries to grasps objects again	continues to encourage, softly saying "Try again; you can do it!" models success	approval for mastery attempt; increased child motivation
4. successfully grasps object	compliments effort, makes eye contact, gentle hug	approval and affection for mastery of task
5. smiles and shows excitement—brings object to mouth	says "Nice job! I knew you could do it!" Give three As.	validation of mastery; observable self-approval

primary needs have been met, children will once again bring their attention to other activities.

Early childhood educators can help build strong self-images for the toddlers in their care. By being good role models, and by using reinforcing, positive self-talk, they can build language for the child to adopt. Positive self-talk is the internalization of messages we hear about ourselves from others. These messages represent how children feel about themselves, and what they are capable of over time. If the messages are positive and encouraging, the child will become confident, but if they are negative, the child feels limited in the ability to succeed. These messages become the belief system of the child and the foundation for self-concept and future success or failure.

Scaffolding, or building sets of ideas and demonstrating how to use them, can be used to promote positive self-talk. Table 6–1 illustrates how scaffolding works when approval sustains the infant's attention. This approval validates children's mastery of their environment. Children internalize the validation they hear and make it their own as you reduce feedback.

BUILDING THE FOUNDATIONS FOR PERSPECTIVE-TAKING

Successful relationships and social acceptance depend on developing an awareness of other people's perspectives. Children must learn to act without harming themselves, others, or the environment, because internal controls are not innate. Children

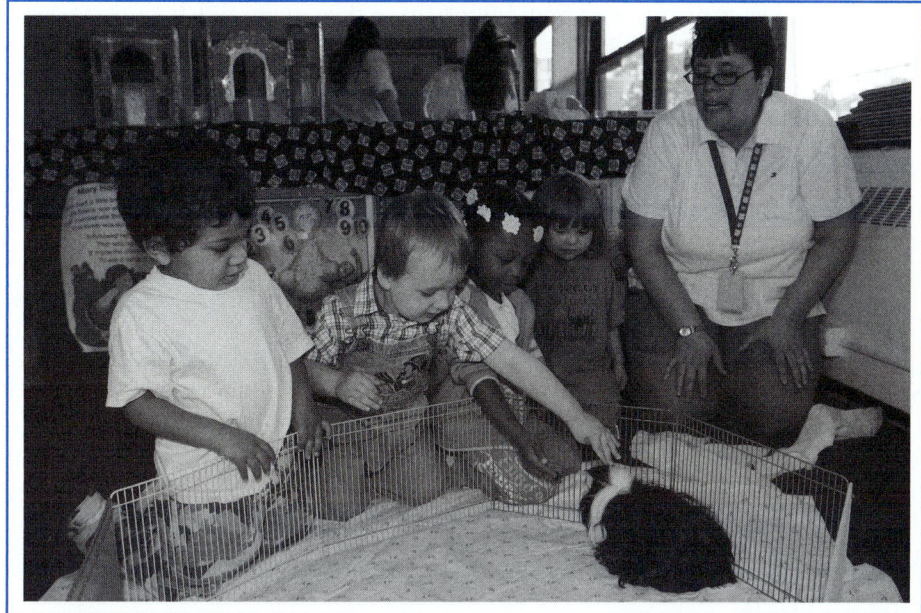

Class pets help toddlers learn perspective-taking skills and responsibility.

need to be taught the foundations of **perspective-taking** skills to have successful, positive relationships.

One way of helping children is to explain how their behavior may make others feel. By announcing out loud how others are reacting to a given behavior, you help all of the children involved to begin to understand the others' perspectives. For instance, say Ms. Barbara works in a licensed family child care center. She waits for three-year-old Eroj to come home from the Head Start center at the bus stop with his two-year old sister Inara. She greets Eroj with a smile and hug. His sister is happy to see him too. He has his art projects in both hands, but drops them when he goes to hug Ms. Barbara. His sister grabs the papers and, in the excitement of the moment, she crumples one of them. Eroj becomes angry and begins to yell at his sister, who starts to cry. As Ms. Barbara helps him gather up his work, she places Inara on her hip and places her hand firmly on Eroj's shoulder. She says to him, "I'm so sorry you dropped your papers. I can tell that you worked so hard on them (looking at papers he is showing her while walking). You should be proud of them. When we get back, you can show everyone your work and then put them on the wall if you like."

To show Inara's perspective, Ms. Barbara continues by saying in Inara's presence, "You know, Eroj, Inara did not mean to crumple your papers. I know she would not do anything to hurt you. I know she misses you when you go to school because several times during the day she stands by the door and says your name. I know she loves you and wants to be with you. I don't think that she meant to crumple your paper. She just got so excited to see you."

This example has a very specific theme. The teacher provided Eroj and Inara information they would not have had and dealt with them in a very careful way. She greeted Eroj warmly, validated his feelings of anger and self-worth, soothed his sister by picking her up, and discussed the situation openly and honestly with both children. She expressed positive observations about their relationship. In addition, the teacher was acting as Inara's advocate.

The same theme can be used with very young children. Caregivers can offer similar comfort to children by using statements like "Oh, I know Michael didn't mean to knock down your block pile, Dori; he just lost his balance." The key to successful use of this strategy is to know the child, know the facts of the situation, and communicate, as best as possible, the intentions and actions of the people involved.

While very young children may be able to consider another child's perspective with assistance, it is inappropriate to expect them to do so independently. The goal of your behaviors is not to teach them how to take someone's perspective but rather to lay a foundation for it, because acquiring perspective-taking skills is a long, arduous task that lasts from birth through adulthood.

Setting Limits

Once children become mobile and enter late infancy and toddlerhood, they must learn to accept "no" about certain behaviors. Adults must help very young children learn that some behaviors are not acceptable, while recognizing ourselves that many of their behaviors are the result of acting on their natural instinct to explore their world (Walsh, 2007). For example, a mobile infant should be firmly, but kindly told, "No. Leave the trash in the can" if she were reaching for an item that had been disposed of. *However, the number of behaviors they must accept "no" to is much smaller than many adults demand.* The main principle to use in selecting which behaviors children must accept "no" to is to start with only those behaviors that are directly harmful to themselves, other people, or property. For example, hitting another child with a toy and calling another child "stupid" are directly harmful; one is physically harmful and the other is emotionally so.

Limits and rules, while they help children to accept "no" about certain behaviors, are best received if stated positively. Let the children know what to do in as specific language as possible (Marion, 2007). Telling the crawling infant, "No touch" as she is pulling on the lamp to stand is less than helpful. The child will not learn where to pull to reach a standing position, because you have not told her the desired behavior. When you establish rules for children that are phrased in what *not* to do, you are actually increasing attention to the behaviors that you do not want to see. Returning to the example, saying instead "Couches are for pulling up on" and moving the child to the couch will help the child to construct an understanding of safe furniture for pulling on. Limits, then, are for stopping inappropriate behaviors and replacing them with more appropriate ones.

Not enough can be said about the importance of stating limits positively. Both of the authors have spent time in classrooms where all limits started with the word *no*. Not only is it a negative place to be (who wants to be told no all of the time?) but also the children do not know what to do to be successful. They are told not to run, so they hop. They are told not to hop, so they crawl. It seems as if they are playing a guessing game with the adult. When adults want children to do something, it is best for them to state their expectations for a desired behavior positively and directly. For example, if you want toddlers to park their tricycles on the cement slab beside the toy shed, then tell them: "It is time to put the tricycles up. Park them at the sign beside the toy shed."

While each classroom and early childhood program needs rules or limits, these should be few in number. Infants and toddlers typically lack the cognitive skills to recall more than a few limits (Marion, 2007). Even with a few rules, however, teachers should not expect the toddlers to remember them. Pure recall is the most challenging type of memory skill to develop, taking several years. Therefore, educators

Classroom limits help children and treasured possessions remain safe.

should make the effort to remind the children of the rules gently as preventative measures. For example, if you notice that Kennedy is looking out the window and getting excited because she sees her grandmother coming to pick her up, you could say, "Let's walk to the door to greet her." This gentle reminder assists Kennedy in both walking and in expressing her love towards her grandmother.

Establishing Consequences

Once limits have been defined, discussed, and modeled, consequences for each limit need to be established. The most effective consequences for learning appropriate behaviors are natural and logical (Marion, 2007). Natural consequences are those outcomes that occur without teacher intervention. Elisabetta runs through the block area of the classroom, trips over a wooden truck, and falls on the carpet. She is surprised but unhurt. Elisabetta has experienced a natural consequence of running in the classroom. Early childhood educators cannot allow all natural consequences to occur because they are too dangerous. Permitting a toddler to fall (i.e., experiencing a natural consequence) because he climbed over the top railing of the climbing structure is obviously not acceptable.

Logical consequences are outcomes that are related to the limit but would not occur on their own. For example, your rule is for the children to put their toys back on the shelf when they are done. If a child does not put her puzzle back on the shelf after being reminded, she will not be able to choose another activity until the first one is cleaned up.

Establishing consequences helps young child become autonomous, self-regulated individuals. Toddlers should be allowed and even encouraged to voice their own opinions and have a say in what happens to them. Unfortunately, this developmental phase is often referred to as the "terrible twos." This important period of personality and self-development is mislabeled as "terrible" by controlling adults who have difficulty accepting children saying "no" to them. It is vital that children be allowed to say "no" to teachers and other adults in order to develop a healthy sense of self. Caregivers who do not accept "no" from a child when he is not harming himself, others, or property do great harm to the child's sense of self-responsibility. Young children must learn to make decisions and establish boundaries with other people. Two additional guidance strategies to use with children who say "no" to practically everything are giving choices and redirection.

Providing Choices

People learn to make wise choices by being able to choose. Caregivers who give children choices that they can handle for their age avoid many confrontations and teach children to choose wisely (Marion, 2007). Yes-no questions are often problematic, as is a statement that commands the child. For example, "Do you want lunch?" is likely to result in "no," as is the statement "You're going to eat your lunch now." A much more effective approach is to give a choice, such as "Do you want a banana or apple slices with your grilled cheese sandwich? You choose." As discussed previously, providing choices increases peoples' internal motivation to complete a task because they feel they are more in control of their destiny (Patall, et al. 2008).

This is the exact outcome we are seeking for young children: we want them to learn that they are powerful people with opinions that should and will be heard. In other words, providing choices fosters the development of young children's self-efficacy.

Redirecting Actions

There are two different types of redirection strategies (Marion, 2007). First, you can divert and distract a young child's attention to safe and acceptable activities to prevent confrontations. This strategy is useful for very young children with under-developed object permanence because for them out-of-sight is equivalent to out-of-mind. Older toddlers are not always so easy to distract because they can continue to think about the desired object even if they cannot see it. For example, if you take a young child into a setting with many breakable objects, diverting the child's attention to objects and activities in the setting that are not breakable can avoid problems. Your attention and interest most often evokes interest on the child's part, so rather than attending to all the breakable things, pay attention and draw the child into activities that are safe and appropriate.

The second type of redirection involves finding a substitute activity based on the child's underlying desire. If a toddler is chewing on a wooden block, find her a teething ring to chew on. If a child wants to climb and jump from the shelf, take him outside to jump. Redirecting attention to the appropriate location recognizes children's underlying needs and can help them learn to monitor and regulate their expression of emotions (Hyson, 2004).

Solving Problems

Infants and toddlers encounter problems frequently throughout their day. These can originate from physical objects, their abilities or lack thereof, and interactions with others. While some adults may not recognize all of these situations as problems to be solved, it can be helpful to reframe their issues in this way. Doing so often makes adults and young children feel more powerful and directly in control of outcomes.

Consider this example. Susanna, 7 months, awakes from her morning nap. Her teacher, Yu-Wen, picks her up while saying soothing words. Susanna begins to cry in earnest. Yu-Wen shifts positions and decides to check her diaper even though it was a short nap, but she is dry. Yu-Wen offers Susanna a bottle, but she refuses it. Then she holds her while gently swaying back and forth, a motion that Susanna typically likes, but not right now. Her crying intensifies. After twenty minutes of trying to solve the problem and strained emotions, Yu-Wen asks her co-teacher if she will take Susanna for a few minutes while she goes to get a drink of cold water. Yu-Wen uses that time to regain her composure and decides to try a strategy that she recently read about in a teacher journal. She prepares a soft blanket on the floor with two soft toys on it. She takes Susanna from her co-teacher and places her tummy up on the blanket. Susanna continues to cry, but the intensity lessens. Within a few moments she is staring at her feet; a small smile plays on the corner of her lips. Yu-Wen is pleased that the strategy of giving children the freedom to move in order to solve their own problem worked (Gonzalez-Mena, 2007).

Toddlers are moving from being dependent to being independent; from wanting to play along to playing parallel or even cooperatively with others; and from thinking simplistically to thinking in more complex ways. All of these developmental advances provide them many opportunities to problem-solve. Because toddlers are more skilled than infants, they should be more involved in the problem-solving process. The following are guidelines for how to solve a problem (Epstein, 2007; Marion, 2007; Swim & Marion, 2006).

1. Describe what you saw; have children verify if you are accurate.
2. Ask Yes/No questions to engage children in the process of identifying and labeling the problem to be solved.
3. Volunteer an idea, choice, or solution to the problem.
4. Help the children select one solution.
5. Help the children implement the solution.
6. Ask Yes/No question to reflect on whether or not the solution worked for everyone.

As with the other guidance strategies described in this chapter, teachers are always the "more knowledgeable others," to use Vygotsky's term, and thus must assume the responsibility for providing children with necessary language and processes for solving problems.

Not all problems can be solved quickly. Change takes time for everyone. You should not try to solve all problems independently; seek guidance from colleagues or your director. As part of creating positive, reciprocal relationships with families, you should also seek their input and guidance. For example, if an infant or toddler shows signs of discomfort for more than two hours, family members should be consulted. The goal of this conversation is to obtain more information and to seek advice on additional strategies that have worked for them in the past. As demonstrated earlier, professional teacher journals are another source of information on ways to solve problems.

As you are guiding the behavior of young children, remember that achieving social and emotional competence is a long journey. Do not expect perfection from yourself, the families, or the children. Observe what the children can do on their own and what they can do with assistance (i.e., identify their zones of proximal development). Then, use teaching strategies to scaffold them to the next level of development. Persistent, small gains add up to big changes over time.

✓ reading checkpoint

Before moving on with your reading, make sure that you can answer the following questions about the material discussed so far.

1. Why is taking a developmental approach to guidance beneficial for children and teachers?
2. List and explain three strategies for positively guiding and supporting the development of very young children's self-regulation skills.

SUMMARY

Creating a caring community of learners is an important aspect of the work that teachers of infants and toddlers do. This involves building positive relationships with each child. Those relationships should start from a strong foundation of respect for the "richness" that each child possesses. Creating a caring community also requires that teachers reflect on their personal and professional experiences. A key component of such a community is the many positive guidance strategies that teachers can use to facilitate the development of self-regulation and socially acceptable behaviors.

key terms

caring community of learners
consequences
discipline
emotion-centered
emotional regulation

emotional talk
image of the child
inserimento
limits
mastery climate

perspective-taking
positive self-talk
self-regulate
self-soothing

case study

Enrique

"Should I call her mother again?" Enrique, a toddler teacher, asks his co-teacher as Regina struggles to free herself from his gentle hold. Regina has just bit the same peer for the second time today.

"Yes, I think you should. We could use some information." While Regina is 27 months old, this is her first time attending child care.

Enrique calls to share how happy he is to have to Regina in his classroom. He asks Ms. Gonzalez what strategies they use when she is upset. She provides him several things to try.

Ms. Gonzalez arrives about 30 minutes earlier than normal for pickup looking frazzled and upset. Enrique greets her and tells her that her suggestion to sing quietly worked wonders. He also asks if she came early because of the phone call. They discuss how the call was not intended to upset her but rather was to gather more information to help Regina.

They move closer to Regina who is working by herself at a table lining up clowns. Enrique and Ms. Gonzalez take a few moments to watch her work. Regina methodically lines the clowns around the perimeter of a piece of construction paper. She seems not to notice the other activities around her. The other children have divided themselves into two groups, working with blocks and pouring water through waterwheels.

Enrique asks Ms. Gonzalez what she is noticing. She replies by asking, "Does she usually play alone?"

"No. She typically works in the same area as other children. This is expected because as children get older, they usually begin to play in small groups. Regina's interactions with the other children sometimes result in her biting them, like today. I am wondering if you can tell me how she interacts with you and your husband at home."

"We usually interact with her. If we ask her a question, she will nod yes or no. She is very quiet and does not seem to have many wants. But, if she does want something, she will point at the object."

(Box continues)

"I'm wondering if she is biting because she does not have the language to tell her classmates what she wants. I'm also wondering what I can do to best help her. Can we both take some time to think about Regina and meet early next week to talk further?"

"That would be nice. Is it okay if my husband comes also?" inquires Ms. Gonzalez.

"Of course. Let me know what times work best for your schedules. And, thank you so much for coming to get Regina early and taking the extra time to speak with me today. The more we work together, the better we can support Regina's needs."

1. How did Enrique's approach serve to value the relationships among Mr. and Ms. Gonzalez, Regina, and himself?
2. Describe what you believe is Enrique's image of the child. What information from the case did you use when drawing this conclusion?
3. What strategies would you suggest Enrique use to support Regina's acquisition of socially accepted behaviors? Why?

QUESTIONS AND EXPERIENCES FOR REFLECTION

1. Read one of the chapters cited about the Reggio Emilia approach to infant-toddler care and education. Report what you find to your colleagues.

2. Julianne Wurm (2005) asks us to consider other questions about our image of the child. Record your responses to these questions in your journal. Then, compare your responses with a colleague.

- Who is a child?
- What is childhood?
- How do children learn?
- What is the meaning of *to educate*?
- What is the relationship between teaching and learning?
- What is the relationship between theory and practice?
- What is the role of school in society?

3. Observe an adult interacting with a mobile infant or toddler. Collect four anecdotal records on the communication strategies used by the adult and how the child responded to them.

4. Interact with a child that you know well. Try out one new guidance strategy and explain how you felt doing it, how the child responded, and how others around you responded. How might your past interactions with this child have influenced the effectiveness of this strategy?

5. Return to the fussy baby example provided in the Solving Problems section. What would you have done next if giving Susanna the freedom to move had not worked? Why?

REFERENCES

Balaban, N. (2006). Easing the separation process for infants, toddlers, and families. *Beyond the Journal: Young Children on the Web*. Retrieved March 12, 2009, http://journal.naeyc.org/btj/200611/pdf/BTJBalaban.pdf

Bove, C. (2001). *Inserimento*: A strategy of delicately beginning relationships and communications. In L. Gandini & C. P. Edwards (Eds.), *Bambini: The Italian approach to infant/toddler care* (pp. 109–123). New York: Teachers College Press.

Copple, C., & Bredekamp, S. (Eds.). (2009). *Developmentally appropriate practice in early childhood programs* (3rd ed.). Washington, DC: National Association for the Education of Young Children.

Douville-Watson, L. (1997). *Conscious caregiving.* Bayville, NY: Instructional Press.

Edwards, C., Gandini, L., & Forman, G. (Eds.). (1998). *The hundred languages of children: The Reggio Emilia approach—Advanced reflections* (2nd ed.). Westport, CT: Ablex.

Epstein, A. S. (2007). Essentials of active learning in preschool: Getting to know the High/Scope curriculum. Ypsilanti, MI: High/Scope Press.

Gandini, L. (2004). Foundations of the Reggio Emilia approach. In J. Hendrick (Ed.), *Next steps toward teaching the Reggio way: Accepting the challenge to change* (2nd ed., pp. 13–26). Upper Saddle River, NJ: Prentice Hall.

Ghedini, P. (2001). Change in Italian national policy for children 0–3 years old and their families: Advocacy and responsibility. In L. Gandini & C. P. Edwards (Eds.), *Bambini: The Italian approach to infant/toddler care* (pp. 38–45). New York: Teachers College Press.

Gonzalez-Mena, J. (2007). What to do for a fussy baby: A problem-solving approach. *Beyond the Journal: Young Children on the Web.* Retrieved March 14, 2009, http://journal.naeyc.org/btj/200709/pdf/Gonzalez-Mena.pdf

Gonzalez-Mena, J., & Eyer, D. W. (2007). *Infants, toddlers, and caregivers: A curriculum of respectful, responsive care and education* (7th ed.). New York: McGraw-Hill.

Hyson, M. (2004). *The emotional development of young children: Building an emotion-centered curriculum* (2nd ed.). New York: Teachers College Press.

Kaminsky, J. A. (2005). Reflections on *inserimento*, the process of welcoming children and parents into the infant-toddler center: An interview with Lella Gandini. *Innovations in early education: The international Reggio exchange, 12*(2), 1–8.

Keyser, J. (2006). Socialization and guidance with infants and toddlers. In J. R. Lally, P. L. Mangione, & D. Greenwald (Eds.), *Concepts for care: 20 essays on infant/toddler development and learning.* Sausalito, CA: WestEd. pp. 101–104.

MacLean, P. D. (1990). *The triune brain in evolution, role in paleocerebral functions.* New York: Plenum Press.

Malaguzzi, L. (1998). History, ideas, and basic philosophy: An interview with Lella Gandini. In C. Edwards, L. Gandini, & G. Forman (Eds.), *The hundred languages of children: The Reggio Emilia approach—Advanced reflections* (2nd ed., pp. 49–97). Westport, CT: Ablex.

Mantovani, S. (2001). Infant-toddler centers in Italy today: Tradition and innovation. In L. Gandini & C. P. Edwards (Eds.), *Bambini: The Italian approach to infant/toddler care* (pp. 23–37). New York: Teachers College Press.

Marion, M. (2007). *Guidance of young children* (7th ed.). Upper Saddle River, NJ: Prentice Hall.

Marion, M., & Swim, T. J. (2007). Intentionality in Child Guidance: Helping ECE Pre-service Students Understand the Concept. Paper presented at the National Association for the Education of Young Children's Professional Development Institute, Pittsburg, PA.

New, R. (1993). Italy. In M. Cochran (Ed.), *International handbook on child policy and programs* (pp. 291–311). Westport, CT: Greenwood Press.

New, R. (1998). Social competence in Italian early childhood education. In D. Sharma, & K. W. Fisher (Eds.), *Socioemotional development across cultures* (New Directions for Child Development No. 81, pp. 87–104). San Francisco: Jossey-Bass.

Patall, E. A., Cooper, H., & Robinson, J. C. (2008). The effects of choice on intrinsic motivation and related outcomes: A meta-analysis of research findings. *Psychological Bulletin, 134* (2), 270–300.

Pintrich, P. R., Marx, R. W., & Boyle, R. A. (1993). Beyond cold conceptual change: The role of motivational beliefs and classroom contextual factors on the process of conceptual change. *Review of Educational Research, 63* (2), 167–199.

Powell, D., Dunlap, G., and Fox, L. (2006). Prevention and intervention for the challenging behaviors of toddlers and preschoolers. *Infants and Young Children, 19* (1), 25–35.

Resources and Instruction for Staff Excellence (2000). *Winning teams: Guiding behavior for young children videoconference series.* Cincinnati, OH: Author.

Rinaldi, C. (2001). Reggio Emilia: The image of the child and the child's environment as a fundamental principle. In L. Gandini & C. P. Edwards (Eds.), *Bambini: The Italian approach to infant/toddler care* (pp. 49–54). New York: Teachers College Press.

Smith, R. E., Smoll, F. L., & Cumming, S. P. (2007). Effects of a motivational climate intervention for coaches on young athletes' sport performance anxiety. *Journal of Sport & Exercise Psychology, 29* (1), 39–59.

Swim, T. J., & Merz, A. H. (2008). Deconstructing policy and practices through rich images of children and teachers. Paper submitted for publication.

Walsh, D. (2007). *No: Why kids–of all ages–need to hear it and ways parents can say it.* NY: Free Press.

White, B., Swim, T. J., Freeman, R., & Norton-Smith, L. (2007). *Powerful infants and toddlers: Provocations and dialogue with preverbal children.* Paper presented at the National Association for the Education of Young Children Annual Conference, Chicago, IL.

Wien, C.A. (Ed.). (2008). *Emergent curriculum in the primary classroom: Interpreting the Reggio Emilia approach in schools.* NY: Teachers College Press.

Wurm, J. (2005). *Working in the Reggio way: A beginner's guide for American teachers.* St. Paul, MN: Redleaf Press.

ADDITIONAL RESOURCES

Adams, S. K., & Baronberg, J. (2005). *Promoting positive behavior: Guidance strategies for early childhood settings.* Upper Saddle River, NJ: Pearson Merrill Prentice Hall.

Fox, L., & Lentini, R. H. (2006). Teaching children a vocabulary for emotions. *Beyond the Journal: Young Children on the Web*. Retrieved March 14, 2009, http://journal.naeyc.org/btj/200611/pdf/BTJFoxSupplementalActivities.pdf

Lewin-Behham, A. (2006). *Possible schools: The Reggio approach to urban education.* New York: Teachers College Press.

Noddings, N. (2002). *Educating moral people: A caring alternative to character education.* New York: Teachers College Press.

For additional activities, web links, and other resources, please visit our website at www.cengage.com/education/swim

chapter 7

SUPPORTIVE COMMUNICATION WITH FAMILIES AND COLLEAGUES

learning objectives

After reading this chapter, you should be able to:

- Develop procedures for informal and formal communication with families.
- Analyze the working relationships and responsibilities of the staff with whom the caregiver is working.
- Analyze your own skills when communicating with family members and colleagues.
- Understand the active listening process and how it differs from mirroring.

chapter outline

- Introduction
- Skills for Effective Communication
- Communicating with Families
- Family Situations Requiring Additional Support
- Communicating with Colleagues
- Case Study: Sheila

INTRODUCTION

Caregivers and family members* have a common goal: to provide high-quality experiences for children. When children are being cared for by someone other than an immediate family member, all persons involved must join in partnership to achieve this goal. The fifth guideline for developmentally appropriate practice as outlined by NAEYC is "Establishing reciprocal relationships with families" (Copple & Bredekamp, 2009). Recognizing the complexity of this guideline is necessary for beginning teachers. Oversimplifying and regarding the objective as just parent education on the one hand, or total parent control on the other, minimizes the role of the teacher in joining with parents to provide the best care and education for their very young children. The primary components of this guideline are highlighted here.

- Reciprocal relationships require mutual respect, cooperation, shared responsibility, and negotiation of conflicts to achieve shared goals.
- Frequent two-way communication must be established and maintained between early childhood teachers and families.
- Families are welcomed into the program and invited to participate in decisions about their children's care and education as well as program decisions.
- Family members' choices and goals are responded to with sensitivity and respect, without abdicating professional responsibility.
- Teachers and families share their knowledge of the child, including assessment information, to maximize everyone's decision-making abilities.
- Families are linked with community resources based on identified priorities and concerns.
- Professionals having educational responsibility for a child should, with family participation, share information (Copple & Bredekamp, 2009).

Our experiences with pre-service teachers and beginning educators demonstrate that building relationships with families can provoke fear. "I'm comfortable with children, not adults" is a common statement. Thus, this chapter is devoted to assisting you in considering this topic more in depth and developing the skills to be successful.

Effective communication between caregivers and families and among the early childhood program staff is a must. Communication is a two-way process. It requires both active listening and effective expression of thoughts and feelings.

The attitudes caregivers and families have toward each other are reflected through their communication process. The nonverbal, emotional messages that are sent in

---

*In this chapter, the terms *family, families, family member*, and *family members* will be used interchangeably to refer to people who interact with and impact the learning and development of infants and toddlers in their home settings. These terms should be understood to include mother(s), father(s), legal guardians, grandparent(s), siblings, aunt(s), uncle(s), etc. The term *parent* or *parents* is used to refer specifically to a mother and/or a father.

the questions asked and the statements made will either help or hinder successful communication. We must also give attention to cultural diversity; families differ in how they communicate (Christian, 2006). The goal of coming to understand our own and the families' cultures is to communicate effectively about children's strengths and needs, not to change the children or the families (Im, Parlakian, & Sanchez, 2007).

In order to be an effective caregiver, it is necessary to communicate well with children, families, staff, other professionals, and community members. This chapter teaches you important communication skills such as rapport building, "I statements," active listening, and mirroring. These skills will assist you in communicating successfully with other people in a sensitive and accepting style. Practicing these skills will help you listen to and understand others and be able to express yourself so that other people will understand and accept what you say.

SKILLS FOR EFFECTIVE COMMUNICATION

In Chapter 4 we discussed the three *A*s of child care and how they affect communication between caregiver and child.

Figure 7–1 shows the general communication process. A *sender* (A) sends a message verbally and nonverbally to a *receiver* (B), who interprets the message and gives the sender feedback as to what the message means to the receiver.

Rapport Building

Rapport is an agreement between two people that establishes a sense of harmony. This harmonious agreement with infants and toddlers has been discussed in previous chapters as interactional synchrony. When you learn to build rapport with an adult, just as you've done with an infant or toddler, you must follow the person's lead while you carefully observe his or her movements. Think of this as learning to dance well with another person. Rapport building involves two components: calibrating and pacing. Calibrating means carefully observing the specific steps and pacing means carefully moving in harmonious synchrony. There are three specific sets of behaviors that must be calibrated and paced for you to build rapport and dance well with another person.

1. Posture. Align yourself in a complementary physical posture with the adult. If he is sitting, sit also. Change your posture to "dance" with the person face to face.

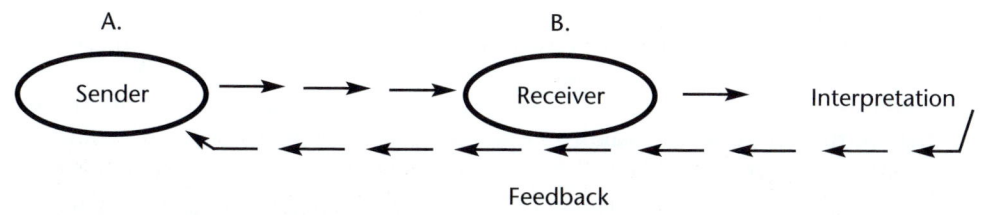

FIGURE 7–1 The communication process.

2. Nonverbal communication. Listen carefully to the tone of voice, tempo of speech, and the intensity of the physical and emotional undertones of the gestures. What is the adult trying to tell you? Do the nonverbal communication strategies match the verbal ones?
3. Representational systems. This set of behaviors is hardest to learn to calibrate and pace because it includes all ways that the adult represents his or her beliefs, perceptions, and understanding of the world. Representational systems are culturally based, so it is imperative that you spend considerable time learning how culture influences communication for the families with whom you are working.

You should observe calibrating and pacing with the families in your classroom. Ask yourself questions such as "How does the adult let the child lead?" "How is the adult sensitive to the three sets of behaviors?" and "How does the adult pace the child?" Once you have practiced observing the calibrating and pacing that others use, try them in your own relationships with adults and children. You'll find out quickly that it is well worth the effort; you can establish rapport effectively when you become proficient at using this strategy.

I Statements versus You Statements

We also communicate to other people from the perspective of expressing our own thoughts and feelings through **I statements**, or giving advice or judgments about the other person by making **you statements**.

I statements usually start with the word *I* and express responsibility for our own perceptions without judging the other person. For example, "I am angry" is an I statement because it expresses a feeling without blaming another person. You statements are often disrespectful and tell the other person how he or she is thinking, feeling, or behaving. You statements often start with the word *you* and offer advice or an opinion about the other person. For example, "You make me angry" is a you statement because it offers an opinion about the other person (he or she is doing or saying something wrong), and it makes the other person responsible for the speaker's feeling (anger).

When you want the other person to feel accepted and understood, make I statements rather than you statements. I statements are respectful and take responsibility for the speaker's thoughts, feelings, and behaviors. You statements, on the other hand, offer opinions, advice, and judgments about the other person and often close off further communication.

We can also make *disguised* I and you statements. Active listening responses, which are discussed below, are an example of disguised I statements. When we give feedback to a sender that clearly takes responsibility for our own perceptions and map of the world, we are making I statements. For example, if a person sends the message, "I can't stand Mary, she is always complaining," a good active listening response might be, "It sounds like Mary's complaining is making you feel angry."

Notice that, although neither *I* nor *you* were used, the feedback takes responsibility for the receiver's perception by using the words "It sounds (to me) like ..." without blaming or criticizing the sender. Active listening and I statements keep communication open by giving nonjudgmental feedback, which allows the sender to confirm that the message was understood ("That's right, I really get angry with her") or correct the message ("Well, I don't really get angry, just a little annoyed").

Disguised you statements sometimes sound like I statements and may even start with the word *I*, but they always end up judging or giving advice to the sender. For example, "I'm angry because you did that" is a disguised you statement because, even though it starts with *I*, it blames and judges the other person.

Caregivers need to practice daily using I statements with children, family members, and colleagues. Once you master making I statements and giving active listening feedback, other people will respond by feeling open, relaxed, and understood in their interactions with you. Caregivers who communicate using you statements cause other people to feel disrespected, uncomfortable, and unwilling to continue interactions with the person.

Active Listening: The "How" in Communication

Most common communication errors can be avoided by applying a technique called **active listening**. The most important skill in active listening is very simply to "feed back" the deeper feeling message (not the words) of the sender in the words of the receiver. This simple definition of active listening requires further explanation because, although it may sound simple, it takes practice to learn to give deeper feedback effectively.

Active listening differs from most common types of communication in the kind of feedback given to the sender. The type of feedback most commonly given is a *reaction* to the words in the message. When we give reactionary feedback, we most often close off the communication process because we become emotionally involved in the words of the message. Common reactionary feedback messages are "You shouldn't say that!" "I don't agree with you!" "You're wrong!" and "I don't want to hear that kind of talk!"

Active listening, on the other hand, involves objectively listening, in a nondefensive way, for the deeper message of the sender and then giving *reiterating* feedback. Rather than reacting to the words of the sender, the active listener interprets the entire message of the sender and gives it back to the sender.

Active listening feedback allows the sender to affirm, reject, or clarify his message. By continuing to feed back the total message of the sender, the receiver can help the sender clarify the problem and, in most cases, arrive at his or her own solution.

An active listener also looks at body language. The look on a person's face, the position of the body, and what the person does with his or her hands and arms can help you to understand the full message on the deepest level. Nonverbal behavior, as well as words, feelings, and attitudes, combine to transmit the complete, deep message.

Although active listening may sound simple enough to learn, it requires practice because most of us have learned to give reactionary feedback, particularly to children. With practice, however, caregivers will find the rewards of active listening worth the effort it takes to master the technique.

Here are some ways to test how well you are communicating with others.

1. Listen to the way you now respond to people. If you catch yourself reacting to the words of messages instead of the deeper meaning, you are "just talking." An active listener listens for the whole, deep message, including the words, feelings, attitudes, and behaviors.
2. An active listener never judges, criticizes, or blames another. Listen for deeper feelings, because feelings can never be wrong! Since the active listener looks for the deeper message, most feedback starts with words such as "It sounds like . . . ," "You seem to feel . . . ," "I hear you saying . . . ," and other phrases that reflect the sender's feelings.
3. An active listener never responds to a message with advice or personal feelings. The idea of communication is to understand completely what the other person thinks and feels. This skill may be more difficult for caregivers to learn in their relationships with children in their charge because adults have so much more experience than children; it is hard to accept the fact that children can arrive at their own solutions to problems. Adults tend to want to teach and advise children before they have completely understood the whole message that children are trying to communicate. Doing so, however, would contradict the image of the child as capable and competent. These behaviors would actually reflect an image of the child as incapable of problem solving about important matters. Which image do you hold? Which image do you want to display to families and colleagues? Reflecting on your behaviors in light of the image you hold will assist you with keeping your theory (i.e., image) and your practice consistent. One of the causes of the well-known generation gap is that children learn that adults don't understand them and don't "know where they're at." Even young children will furnish good solutions to problems if adults have the patience to hear them out and give back the meaning of the messages they hear and experience without teaching or advising.
4. An active listener only adds information to a message when the other person directly asks for it and after that person has completely expressed the entire message. You will know you have received the entire message when you hear real feelings and concern about what to do. At this point, feedback such as "Have you thought about what you can do?" or "How would you solve this?" will give the child a chance to ask for advice or begin problem solving on his or her own.

Mirroring

A simple but very effective technique for establishing rapport and making sure your messages are understandable and that you understand theirs, is **mirroring**. Mirroring simply means repeating exactly what is said without adding or interpreting any of the speaker's words. You may notice a parallel between mirroring and being attuned to infants; that is not a coincidence. When you communicate with staff, families, or children, it can be very helpful to ask the person to repeat exactly what you say before he or she responds. When the other person mirrors you before responding, and you mirror him or her before responding, a sense of trust and understanding quickly develops that is very hard to obtain any other way. By mirroring each other, mutual respect and understanding is quickly developed. Mirroring is especially effective when communicating with others from cultural and/or language backgrounds different from your own.

Try mirroring with your family or friends first so you get the idea of how it works. The only words you are allowed to change in mirroring are personal pronouns, so if the other person says "I am happy," your mirroring response is "You are happy." One final rule in mirroring is that each speaker uses I statements rather than you statements, as discussed previously. By using I statements when speaking and mirroring each other before you respond, you can prevent many conflicts and misunderstanding. As discussed in the previous chapter, mirroring by mothers was found to have positive impact on the infants' behaviors such that mothers who were good at mirroring had babies who maintained their social engagement longer than infants whose mothers displayed fewer mirroring behaviors (Legerstee & Varghese, 2001).

✓ reading checkpoint

Before moving on with your reading, make sure that you can answer the following question about the material discussed so far.

1. What are effective communication skills and why?

COMMUNICATING WITH FAMILIES

Teacher Beliefs

Teachers hold different beliefs about the responsibilities of those involved in the educational process. Korkmaz (2007) surveyed 148 teachers concerning their beliefs about the responsibilities teachers, parents, and schools have in facilitating learning. A theme running through the responses was the importance of communication for all involved parties. More specifically, she discovered that two-thirds of the teachers believed that parents should have good communication with teachers. They also thought that parents should be willing to participate in meetings held at school. When asked about the responsibilities of the school, 56 percent of the teachers expressed the importance of the school keeping parents informed about the progress of their child as well as the curriculum being implemented. Interestingly enough, only 44 percent of the teachers reported their responsibilities to "… communicate clearly with students and have positive dialogue and interactions with them inside and outside the classroom… [listening] attentively to students' questions, comments, and views" (Korkmaz, 2007, p. 397). There were no examples provided of teachers saying that they held responsibility for communicating well with family members.

As you can see, this text deviates from those research results as it places particular emphasis on the decisive role teachers play in creating a positive context that supports open and ongoing communication with family members and children. Yet, our text does not differ from other research on "instructional communication competence" (Worley, Titsworth, Worley, & Cornett-DeVito, 2007) with award-winning teachers who explained and demonstrated that use of active listening with students was extremely important to develop productive relationships. It is our premise that good teaching, at any level, relies on the skilled use of active listening.

Using Active Listening with Families

Active listening helps caregivers understand families as they express their concerns and raise questions about parenting. Family members are often isolated from other support systems and need the caregiver to listen to them and help them come up with solutions. Active listening and mirroring helps overcome language and cultural barriers as well (Lally, 1992).

Family members may want the caregiver to agree with them or reassure them, to confirm or reject ideas, and to respond to pressures from family and friends. For example, Mabel rushed in one morning with her son and said, "I called my mother

Parent and caregiver assist the child in making the transition between home and the early childhood program.

last night and told her I went back to work this week. She had a fit. She said it was too soon and that right now my place was at home." Listen to Mabel's words, her tone of voice; read her nonverbal cues, her facial expressions and degree of tenseness. She may be telling you that she is feeling frustrated and guilty, or she may be stating her mother's view while feeling fairly comfortable with her own choice of going back to work. You must listen to the whole story (words, tone, cues) to interpret accurately what Mabel is telling you.

Families express their desires for their children. One parent might say, "I want Velma to be happy. It bothers me to see her cry when I leave." A mother, Arlene, may tell you, "I want Pearl to get used to babies because my baby is due next month." Listen to what the parent is saying about the child and about his or her own needs.

Actively listen to family members so that you will fully understand what care they expect you to provide. Some family members have very definite ideas and will tell you about them. Others do not say anything until they disagree with something, and then they may express frustration or be angry with you. If this happens, give feedback that takes into account the family members' emotions, as well as the words they say to you.

Families tell you much information about their children and themselves. Details about what the child does at home are needed by the caregiver each morning. Listen carefully and record the information as soon as possible.

Gathering Information

Families have a wealth of information about their children. For continuity between home and school, teachers need to know how the family typically responds to the child's needs. Many states require that licensed infant/toddler programs have families complete and regularly update questionnaires that ask about child characteristics, habits, and preferences as well as family routines, goals, and expectations for the child. For example, knowing that Oliver has difficulty relaxing for a nap if he does not have his favorite blankie with him and his back patted will help the early childhood educator to meet his body's needs for sleep.

While questionnaires are effective means for gathering information, going beyond the minimal requirements will help you to form effective partnerships, meeting the guidelines for developmentally appropriate practice. Talking informally during drop-off and pick-up about the child's experiences at home and school help all of the caregivers to have updated information that will shape their reactions to the child's behavior. When face-to-face interactions are not possible, home-school journals, mentioned in Chapter 5, are valuable tools for sharing and gathering information. This two-way communication strategy involves family members writing a few notes about the child's day(s) when at home and then the caregiver responds with information about the child's experience while at the early childhood program. Of course, it is overly optimistic to think that caregivers and families will write in the journal every day. Yet those who do this on a regular basis develop a strong sense of partnership (Gandini, 2001).

Sharing Information

Families need information about the daily experiences their child has in your care. Many tools are available (see Chapter 5) to help organize and record important things the child has done and share them with family members. Special experiences, such as the child's excitement about a visiting rabbit, may go into the written record or the caregiver may tell a family member.

The child's rate and pattern of development should be shared with family members. Refer to the child's Developmental Profile (see Appendix B) to focus on recent developments and identify developmental tasks the child may soon be mastering. However, as Clements and Kuperberg (2008) remind us, to communicate effectively, this information should not be delivered using professional jargon, slang, or fad expressions; any of these can lead to misunderstanding rather than a common understanding. When we share common knowledge about the child and set goals together, then everyone can do things in their environments that support or enhance the child's development. However, when working with families you should be clear in emphasizing the difference between facilitating and pushing the child. Families are often very interested in ideas for age-appropriate activities and homemade toys (see Chapters 10–16; Herr & Swim, 2002).

When you share your observations with the family members, seek their observations as well. Mabel may have noticed that her two-month-old child isn't distressed at all by being left at child care, and she wants more information relating to the effect of child care on young infants. Phyllis may be ready for information about separation anxiety because Branson is starting to show distress. Arlene may need information to help her understand that Pearl's sharing Mommy with the new baby involves much more than practice in getting used to babies. Changing sleeping and eating patterns and toilet learning are other areas families frequently raise questions about. Of course, if your assessments reveal that a child is ahead of or behind age-expected levels, special emphasis should be placed on communicating with families. As discussed in previous chapters (e.g., Chapters 2 and 3), deciding together when and how to proceed with involving other professionals is vital.

Families need information about the child care program. Before the child is admitted, the program director shares with them program goals, policies, a description of the daily program and the practical use of Developmental Prescriptions. Many programs will include a developmental screening as part of the initial evaluation of the incoming child. This will help guide caregivers as they make their decisions about program implementation. Many situations occur that family members need to clarify and discuss with caregivers. For example, Sal wants his 23-month-old daughter Gabriele to stop using her fingers when she eats. The caregivers can help Sal by sharing development information with him, assuring him that eating with fingers is perfectly normal at this age and use of utensils will come later when fine motor control is further developed.

Feelings

Caregiving involves feelings and emotions. Family members want to know that you are knowledgeable and concerned about their child and about them (Huber, 2003). In a variety of ways, let families know that you like and respect their child. Families look for caregivers who accept and like their child and who provide emotional security.

Share the excitement of the child's new developments with family members. The first time you see children pulling themselves up on the table leg, teetering on two steps, holding utensils, riding a tricycle, turning book pages, hugging a friend, asking to go to the toilet, or catching a ball, you should be excited and pleased with their accomplishments. When you share these experiences with families, let them know how elated you are. Yet much caution must be exerted in this type of communication. Many family members, especially mothers, feel guilty about needing or even wanting to return to work. They may feel that they are missing the most important moments of their children's lives. Sharing "firsts" with them would only serve to reinforce these feelings. An alternative approach would be to alert families for behaviors to look for at home without explicitly stating that you saw the accomplishment first. While some readers might interpret this as lying by omission, the news should be reframed so that you help family members to see and share an important event for their child.

Uncovering Families' Expectations and Setting Goals

All families have expectations for their children; some will be explicitly stated, while others may not be fully articulated (Christian, 2006). Engage families in ongoing conversations to uncover these expectations and support them in achieving their goals. Not all families will have realistic or developmentally appropriate expectations for their child. Some families, especially first-time parents, set goals that are too high, while other families set their expectations too low. Either case can lead to poor child outcomes. It is your responsibility as a professional early childhood educator to work with them to realign their expectations. The communication skills discussed earlier are very important in these situations. You want to establish rapport, use active listening and I statements, and mirror their words. When asked your opinion, you can be ready to guide them toward more developmentally appropriate expectations. This approach reflects the guidelines for establishing reciprocal relationships with families, especially that parents' choices and goals are responded to with sensitivity and respect without abdicating professional responsibility (Copple & Bredekamp, 2009).

Work together with family members to create goals that are acceptable to both of you. Sometimes that means taking baby steps towards meeting your personal goals for the child. In an educational context, that is far more acceptable than ignoring the family members' goals. Expect to devote considerable time in negotiating the goals that you will work toward together. Partnering means working until a common ground is found. This should be a win-win situation, not a hostile takeover of the families' goals in favor of your own or vice versa (see, for example, Gonzalez-Mena, 2001). Given that children grow and change rapidly during the infant-toddler period, you should also expect to engage in such negotiations two to three times a year.

Sharing Expectations

After working to uncover the families' expectations and create goals together, explain what those goals might look like in practice. Your casual statements may take on more meaning than formal, written goal statements. When explaining how to encourage a toddler's independence, you might say: "We want to help children become as independent as they can, so when Louella resists my helping her take off her bib, I will let her try to take it off by herself. If she gets stuck, I will help her lift one arm out, and then encourage her to do the rest by herself."

Families are interested in what you expect of yourself as a caregiver. What kinds of things do you do? How committed are you? How friendly are you? Do you think you are more important than they are? Do you extend and supplement the roles of families or do you expect to supplant them? You communicate these expectations through your words, attitudes, mannerisms, and interactions with children and family members.

What do you expect of the children in your care? A child care program utilizing a developmental perspective emphasizes the development of the whole child and of individuality among children. Assure families that development does not follow a rigid schedule and is not identical among children. Adults often compare their child's development with another child's and gloat or fret at what they see. Caregivers who show that they believe children behave differently within a broad range of normal activity communicate to families that adults can challenge children without putting harmful pressure on them.

Caregivers expect many things of family members. Some expectations you may express; others you should keep to yourself. You might expect them to

- love and like their child.
- want to hear about special occurrences in their child's day.
- want to learn more about their developing child.
- be observant of the child's health or illness.
- be willing to share information about the child with you.
- use respect as a basis for forming relationships.

Some families will not meet your expectations. Because caregiving occurs in the family as well as in the child care program, you will need to resolve your differences with important people in the child's life. In some cases, you may need to change your expectations of family members. We speak of accepting children as they are, so we need to take the same attitude toward family members. They come to the child care program because they need love and care for their child outside the home. While they often need and want additional information about parenting and a sense of community, they usually are not looking for situations that place additional demands and expectations on them as parents (Mantovani, 2001). Creating systems to serve families and build a stronger community is an important advocacy function that early childhood programs can easily provide (Galardini & Giovannini, 2001). Information to help family members grow can be offered but not forced upon them. You may increase your awareness of the unique situation each family faces simply by actively listening to them without making judgments.

Partnering with Families

Family members should have an active relationship with their caregivers. This partnership exists in order to facilitate the learning and well-being of children.

In Decision-Making

Some programs involve family members in decision-making. Many not-for-profit child care centers have policy boards that include family representatives. These boards may make recommendations and decisions about center policy. Sometimes family members even serve on boards that make administrative decisions about hiring and firing staff and selecting curricula. However, few family child care homes and for-profit child care centers involve families in decision-making about policy, staff, or curricula.

Families of infants and toddlers must be involved in some decisions relating to their child's care. The family or pediatrician selects the infant's milk or formula; the caregiver does not make that decision. Families and caregivers must share information about the child's eating and sleeping schedules. The length of time from afternoon pick-up to mealtime and to bedtime varies among families. Since late afternoon naps or snacks may improve or disrupt evening family time, early childhood educators should set aside time to discuss what schedule is best for the child and family. Toilet learning must be coordinated between families and caregivers. Both parties share information about the appropriateness of timing, the failures and successes of the child, and the decision to discontinue or continue toilet learning. If a family member insists that toilet learning start or continue when you think the child is not ready, share with that person information about the necessary development of the child before learning can occur. Tell him, for example, about actions children take when they are showing an interest in or a readiness for toilet learning. Communicate also the harmful effects on children of consistent failures and too much pressure. When the child is ready for toilet learning, the procedures at home and in child care must be the same so that the child does not become confused. Reassure the family members that you do not mind changing their child's diapers. Emphasize that this is another time for you to spend relating positively one on one.

About Children

Most adult family members of infants and toddlers in child care are employed. Therefore, family involvement during the child care day is often limited to arrival and pick-up time. They can help the child take off a coat or unpack supplies when leaving the child in the morning, and can share with the caregiver information about the child's night, health, or special experiences. At pick-up time the caregiver initiates conversations about the child's experiences and projects during the day, while the family member helps the infant or toddler make the transition back to home life by hugging the child or helping to put on outdoor clothes. Sharing written notes and photographs taken of work that occurred during the day is always a good way to start conversations.

Family Education

Knowing the strengths and areas the family members may want to improve on can help you communicate effectively and plan ways to extend the care program into the home to enhance the development of each child. You can conduct a brief survey at the beginning of the year that asks parents if they would like more information on particular parenting topics. The survey should also ask them how they might like that content delivered (e.g., newsletter articles, guest speakers, videos). You may discover, for example, that half of the families in your toddler room want more information on choosing and creating safe, developmentally appropriate, and growth-producing environments for their children. The next step should be deciding how to disseminate the information to the families. Keep in mind that such information should be delivered by someone the families trust and whose competence and experience will meaningfully affect the decisions they make. Your decisions about how to communicate this information should also reflect how adults learn. Making resources available that they can read, listen to, and view will help them to construct their ideas about rearing young children. As part of this education, they may also want a designated time and place to discuss ongoing concerns, such as balancing work and family commitments, with other families with similarly aged children. Having a monthly coffee klatch might be just the thing for the parents in your classroom.

The child care facility, regardless of the type of setting, can fill these types of family education needs. All the measures are suggested with the goal of building strong partnerships between families and caregivers so that optimal child growth and learning results. In addition, such educational efforts should raise the family members' awareness of related state and national concerns. How might their problem-solving on the local level help others to solve the related larger-scale problem? Informing families of whom to communicate with at local, regional, and national levels to share their solutions or lobby for other solutions will empower them and can benefit everyone involved in early childhood education.

Family-Caregiver Conferences

When a primary caregiving system is used in conjunction with regular conferences, the teacher is able to be a well-informed advocate for each child in her care.

Having specific knowledge about a child that can be shared with family members strengthens relationships between teachers and families (Huber, 2003).

It is important that **family-caregiver conferences** have structure and occur at least twice per year. Preparing and sharing in advance an agenda and checklist, being a good listener, and keeping confidences are some of the important factors to consider (Orstein & Chapman, 1988). Consideration of differences in education, language, and culture is also important (Bauette & Peterson, 1993).

Busy families often have difficulty scheduling formal conferences. To make the most efficient use of time, plan what will be discussed thoroughly. Identify the major purpose of the conference. If a family member requests a meeting, ask what concerns need to be discussed so you can prepare ahead of time. If the teacher requests the conference, tell the family members why, so they have time to think about it beforehand. Gather background information to discuss the topic. Caregiver records of observations, both formal and informal, should be consulted. Outside sources such as articles, books, pamphlets, tapes, and videos may provide information for the caregiver and can be shared with the family members. You may also need information on community agencies or organizations in your region.

Providing an agenda, checklist, and feedback sheet at least three days in advance helps to prepare everyone involved in the meeting. This will give them time to look over what you want to accomplish and to understand what their role in the conference will be. A sample agenda for a teacher-initiated conference might resemble the following:

1. Welcome
2. How do you see _____ (Rodney) _____ developing at home?
3. Do you have any questions or concerns about his development?
4. Review checklist sent home to discuss what behaviors and skills have been noticed at school.
5. What developmental and learning goals should we set for _____ (Rodney) _____?
    a. Discuss: Family's goals
    b. Discuss: Teachers' goals
    c. Create list of our goals together.
6. Brainstorm: How can we work on these goals together?
7. Do you have any feedback to share about the program or our (family-teacher and teacher-child) relationships?

The format of the agenda highlights many important aspects of good conferences. First, they start with engaging the family members in reporting their observations and evaluations of the child. Then, the teacher shares some of her observations. In this way, two-way communication is used as an essential tool for developing a positive family-caregiver relationship as everyone should feel free to bring up concerns, problems or issues as well as joys and accomplishments (Davis & Keyser, 1997). Step 4 serves the purpose of interpreting each child's progress to family members from a developmental approach to help them understand and appreciate developmentally appropriate early childhood programs (NAEYC, 2005). The most important part of the conference is the negotiation of developmental and learning goals. Allow plenty of time to engage in this aspect of the conference because it typically has a large influence on whether or not the family members feel that the teacher has listened to them.

When a family initiates a conference, you can provide them with a sample agenda and ask them to modify it for their needs, or you can ask them if they prefer that you create one. In any case, the goal is the same as a teacher-initiated conference: to support listening of family members and work together to find solutions to the issues being raised. The sample agenda might include:

1. Welcome and thank you for calling this meeting.
2. What are your concerns? (*Then, be sure to listen actively.*)
3. Respond with information or observations if it is appropriate and helpful to the discussion.
4. How can we deal with these concerns?
5. Create a plan of action together.
6. Set a follow-up meeting to monitor progress.

While conducting any conference, it is vital that you minimize power differences between you and family members. One way to do so is to arrange the physical environment so that all adults are sitting next to one another with no barriers. Placing chairs in a circle with no desk or table between you accomplishes this. Physical comfort should also be considered. Early childhood educators are accustomed to sitting in child-size chairs on a regular basis. However, family members rarely are. Providing adult-size chairs can help everyone feel more at ease and be physically comfortable. Having water, coffee, or juice and a box of tissues nearby may also add to everyone's comfort.

Home Visits

Home visits are a regular part of Early Head Start and Head Start programs, but few other child care programs make them. Home visits can be valuable opportunities for the family and the caregiver to learn more about each other. The teacher can see how the family members and child relate to each other in their own home. Home visits must be planned carefully to respect the family's time and space.

1. Identify and discuss with the family members the purpose for the visit: to get acquainted? to gather information? to work with the parents, child, or both?
2. Negotiate a time that is convenient for all family members and yourself. It can often be helpful to have a couple of dates in mind when you call to schedule the home visit.
3. Gather background information the visit requires. Do you need to take along any forms to be filled out? Will you be sharing your program goals?

If so, do you have a flyer or pamphlet or will you just tell them? Are there specific problems or concerns you want to discuss? Do you have written documentation of the child's behavior to share, such as daily reports or notes, or resource and referral information?

4. Conduct the home visit as you would a family-teacher conference. For example, ask questions to elicit information from family members, work together to create solutions for any issues of concern, and ask for feedback.

When you make a home visit, you are a guest in the family's home. You are there to listen and learn. While you want to be friendly, this is not a social call; families have busy lives and you do too. Therefore, when you have finished talking about the issues, thank them for their interest, time, and hospitality, and then leave.

✓ reading checkpoint

Before moving on with your reading, make sure that you can answer the following questions about the material discussed so far.
1. Why is effective communication with families important?
2. Write an agenda for a family-teacher conference initiated by you to discuss a child's toilet learning.

FAMILY SITUATIONS REQUIRING ADDITIONAL SUPPORT

This section discusses four types of families that may need additional support from early childhood educators: grandparents as parents, families who have children who are at risk for later difficulties, families where abuse or neglect is present, and teenage parents. For all of these families, it is imperative that you utilize the positive communication skills discussed earlier.

Grandparents as Parents

Statistics indicate that grandparents are taking care of children more than ever before. According to the Children's Defense Fund, more than 2.5 million grandparents were solely responsible for raising their own grandchildren in 2007 (Children's Defense Fund, 2008). Of these grandparent-headed homes, 60 percent of the head-of-households were employed in the labor force, and 1 in 5 of the families (19 percent) were poor.

You should extend a special invitation to grandparents who are now facing the challenge of raising grandchildren as primary caregivers, since this family situation is not always obvious. Some grandparents are frustrated, and some are isolated. As the statistics above show, they are often balancing the demands of working full time and the pressures of being impoverished with being in the role of primary caregiver. All of these factors increase the grandparents' stress. They need encouragement, support, and someone to confide in. The Children's Defense Fund has created fact sheets which provide important data regarding the prevalence of grandparent-headed households in each state as well as lists of useful resources. These fact sheets are free and easy to download, print, and share with families as they might need them.

At-Risk Families and Children

As discussed in Chapter 2 and 3, children can be *at risk* for a number of reasons, including genetic or chromosomal disorders and environmentally produced problems. Significant contributors to being at risk are living in a poverty-stricken home, having one or more caregivers who have low levels of education, experiencing malnutrition or being undernourished, and lacking positive environmental stimulation (for reviews, see Duncan & Brooks-Gunn, 1997; Shonkoff & Phillips, 2000). Many families, especially single-parent households, struggle financially to meet the basic needs of their infants and toddlers, so they may focus their attention on survival rather than on strategies for promoting optimal development and learning. Families who are

Early childhood educators are often the child's first line of defense for preventing and identifying abuse and neglect.

poverty-stricken care deeply for their children. They may work two or three jobs to provide shelter, food, and clothing, and even these may not be completely adequate.

Supporting families in these situations involve not only listening actively but also having contact information for community resources readily available. Including these resources regularly as part of your communication with families (such as in a section of your newsletter) is relatively simple for you but can have a significant impact on them. Knowing when and where to receive free immunizations, for example, can be key to promoting the physical well-being of infants and toddlers. In addition, providing strategies for interacting with the child during the car or bus ride home can facilitate the development of language and cognition skills and has the advantage of being free (Herr & Swim, 2002).

spotlight *on research*

Prolonged Separations for Young Children: Parental Incarceration and Military Deployment

In 2009, the Bureau of Justice Statistics reported that over 800,000 prisoners or 53 percent of those being held in U.S. prisons were parents of children under the age of 18; a rate which represents a 113 percent increase for mothers since 1991 (Glaze & Maruschak, 2009). Mothers in state prisons reported that 18 percent of the children were four years old or younger, while that percentage was 14 percent for those in federal prisons (Glaze & Maruschak, 2009).

In January 2008, there were 160,000 U.S. troops deployed in Iraq (Global Security, 2008). Thousands of more troops and reservists have been deployed around the world in the "Global War on Terrorism." Approximately 1.2 million children live in U.S. military families (Kelly, 2003), and at least 700,000 of them have had at least one parent deployed (Johnson et al. 2007, both cited in Lincoln, Swift, & Shorteno-Fraser, 2008). In addition, approximately six percent of active duty and eight percent of Reserve and National Guard military personnel are single-parents (Yeary, 2007). Thus, young children whose parents are incarcerated or in the military often experience serious, prolonged separations and disruptions in their lives.

The literature reveals mixed results when measuring the impact of having a prolonged separation due to incarceration or military deployment on child outcomes such as social-emotional and intellectual development. For example, children who already had a secure attachment to their incarcerated mother and received more stable continuous care in her absence were able to create secure emotional attachments with another adult (Poehlmann, 2005a). This strong, new relationship seemed to provide a protective factor against negative developmental outcomes. Similarly, infants and toddlers who experienced separation due to military deployment tended to respond to the remaining parent's or caregiver's reaction (Lincoln, et al. 2008). In other words, when the caregiver expressed high levels of sadness or anxiety, infants were more likely to be irritable or unresponsive, and toddlers were more likely to experience sleep disruption or increased periods of crying. In contrast, when child had a positive relationship with the parent at home, higher levels of psychological well-being were noted (Lincoln, et al. 2008). Another study also underscored the impact of the current family environment on mediating intellectual outcomes for children of incarcerated mothers. Poehlmann (2005b) discovered that the children's intellectual outcomes were compromised by their high risk status at multiple contextual levels and that their intellectual outcomes were also mediated by the quality of their current family environment (Poehlmann, 2005). In other words, even if a child experienced several risk factors, if she was being currently cared for in a positive, supportive environment, she was more likely to have better intellectual outcomes.

(Box continues)

spotlight (continued)

Some children appear to be more vulnerable before the separation and demonstrate this continued vulnerability during it. For example, children with disorganized attachments (see Chapter 3) were more likely to continue the pattern of disorganization during their mothers' incarceration, which placed them at further risk for social and emotional difficulties (Dallaire, 2007). Likewise, children who had a history of needing psychological counseling were more likely to need it again during the deployment of a parent (Lincoln, et al. 2008).

As just discussed, separation from family members can be very stressful as the loss is felt deeply. However, Faber, Willerton, Clymer, MacDermid, & Weiss, (2008) and Williams & Rose (2007) found that reuniting with family members after a deployment can be equally stressful as new roles and responsibilities have been negotiated and assumed in the parent's absence. Parents who were once incarcerated have to rebuild a relationship with their child and assume their parental responsibilities. As this can be an overwhelming task, researchers have become interested in determining if programs can be developed to assist incarcerated mothers with being better parents once they are released. According to the Bureau of Justice Statistics, "Mothers (27 percent) were about two and a half times more likely than fathers (11 percent) to attend parenting or childrearing classes" (Glaze & Maruschak, 2009, p. 9). A recent review of literature on parent education and child-visitation programs for incarcerated parents demonstrated positive changes for mothers who participated (Bruns, 2006). It was noted, however, that more funding is needed to continue such programs as well as to extend the research to include an evaluation of the long-term outcomes for the children (Bruns, 2006).

As educators, we must assume a supportive role for family members and children when they experience a prolonged separation. In this situation, using the positive communication techniques described previously is vital to determining how to talk with the young children. The children will experience a period of sadness (Poehlmann, 2005a) that should be discussed openly, honestly, and sensitively. Yet, you must collaborate with the family members to know what words to use during the conversations. In addition, specific activities can be planned at school and home to encourage open communication such as drawing or reading picture books on the topic.

Families Experiencing Child Abuse or Neglect

Child abuse and neglect, while often closely linked in discussions, are two distinct constructs. Abuse is an action that causes harm to another and comes in three forms: physical, sexual, and emotional/psychological; neglect is failing to provide for the basic needs or affection of a child or not adequately supervising children's activities (McDevitt & Ormrod, 2010). Abuse and neglect can and do occur in families of any racial and ethnic background, socioeconomic status, and community. Early childhood educators are often the child's first line of defense for preventing and identifying abuse and neglect.

Continually communicating about and modeling strategies for implementing the three *A*s can foster family members' thinking about capabilities and appropriate expectations for children from birth to age three. Oftentimes, children are abused because family members do not know what is reasonable to expect of children at a certain age (English, 1998; McElroy & Rodriguez, 2008). For example, not knowing that it is unreasonable to expect a toddler to sit quietly in a restaurant and not interrupt the after-dinner conversation can result in stress and anger for the adult and abuse for the child. In addition, understanding that infants cry to communicate needs and that crying can oftentimes be frequent or of long duration can help parents to cope in those situations.

Identifying children who are being abused or neglected is part of your professional and ethical responsibilities. Use your observation skills to inspect the child's body during routine care times to notice physical or sexual abuse. For example, while diapering, look at the child's arms, body, and legs. Any suspicious marking should cause you to inquire politely and discreetly of family members as to how the marks occurred. Immediately after your conversation, write down in the child's file exactly what you asked and what you were told. The use of descriptive language (see Chapter 5) cannot be overemphasized in this situation. Interpretative language will make the record of little use to other professionals who may need to investigate the case. Reread your entry and reflect on the conversation. Ask yourself: Does this seem like a reasonable event to have happened to a child of this age and mobility? If your answer is yes, then do nothing. However, if your answer is no, you need to involve the appropriate authorities.

Each early childhood program should have a stated policy on how to handle suspected cases of child abuse. In some programs the director or staff social worker must be informed of the situation and be the one to report the incident to the appropriate community agency. This policy is often set in place to protect the teacher-family relationship. However, it is not that staff member's job to decide whether or not the incident needs reporting. If you, the teacher, believe that an incident should be reported, then it must be reported to protect you and your colleagues from being accused of neglect (i.e., failure to report a crime).

Deciding whether or not to report an incident can be emotionally difficult. The ethical dilemma stems from the fact that you are responsible for safeguarding the health and well-being of the children and maintaining relationships with families (NAEYC, 2005). To ease your mind, the determination of whether intentional abuse has occurred has nothing to do with your obligation under the law to report it. Your responsibility is to report your suspicions. Therefore, you are not to launch a full investigation to verify or disprove your suspicions; this is the responsibility of the community agency. If you report an incident in good faith, you are not legally liable if it is not substantiated by other professionals.

Supporting families who are experiencing abuse or neglect is essential for them to acquire more positive ways of interacting and meeting each others' needs. Reporting child abuse to the appropriate community agency can be the first step in intervention. Contrary to popular belief, these agencies do all they can to assist parents in making good parenting choices. Linking families to other community resources, such as support groups or agencies that can provide education, is a way to facilitate the acquisition of positive parenting strategies.

Teenage Parents

According to the Annie E. Casey Foundation (2008), the teenage birth rate in 2005 was 40 births per 1,000 women aged 15–19. These figures represent a 17 percent decrease from the 2000 rate. While the occurrence of U.S. teenage pregnancy is still the highest among economically advantaged nations, this figure continues to represent a record low birth rate for U.S. teens (Annie E. Casey Foundation, 2008; Martin, Hamilton, Sutton, Ventura, Menacker, & Munson, 2005).

The consequences of teenage pregnancy can be severe for both the teens and the infants. Teenage mothers are more likely to experience poverty, as evidenced by the fact that 80 percent of teen mothers receive public assistance, while teen fathers are more likely to engage in delinquent behaviors such as alcohol abuse or drug dealing (Planned Parenthood Federation of America, 2006). Both teen mothers and teen fathers complete fewer years of schooling than their childless peers (Planned Parenthood Federation of America, 2006). Thus, the results of teenage pregnancy should be seen for what they are: a consequence for society through the perpetuation of the increasing inequalities in health and social opportunities (Paranjothy, 2009).

Researchers have long been interested in public norms about nonmarital pregnancy. When surveyed, teenagers reported levels of embarrassment that were

TABLE 7-1 COMPARISON OF TEEN PREGNANCY RATES (PER 1,000)

HIGHEST RATES OF TEENAGE PREGNANCIES

15–17 year olds	RATE	18–19 year olds	RATE
District of Columbia	40	Arkansas	104
New Mexico	37	Mississippi	102
Texas	36	Texas	101
Arizona	34	District of Columbia	100
Mississippi	33	Arizona New Mexico	97

LOWEST RATES OF TEENAGE PREGNANCIES

New Hampshire	7	Vermont	34
Vermont	8	New Hampshire	35
Maine Massachusetts	11	Massachusetts	38
Connecticut New Jersey	12	Connecticut	41
Minnesota	13	New Jersey	42

Source: Kids Count Census Data (2008, December). Teen births, by age group: Rate per 1,000: 2005. Retrieved March 2, 2009, from http://www.kidscount.org/datacenter/compare_results.jsp?i=10 <http://www.kidscount.org/datacenter/compare_results.jsp?i=10

stronger than those of adults (Mollborn, 2009). In addition, for teens, perceived levels of embarrassment predicted their reports of possible sanctions in their family through the withholding of needed material resources (Mollborn, 2009). While this research study used hypothetical situations to assess embarrassment and sanctions, it is reasonable to assume that such outcomes are realistic for many teens.

The stress of limited financial resources coupled with a lack of life experiences can impact a teen parent's ability to interact with his or her infant or toddler. As any family member knows, raising children can be trying and very difficult even under the best of circumstances. Possessing sound coping mechanisms and the ability to make informed decisions is vital. These skills develop over time with life experiences and emotional maturity. Thus, parenting can be very challenging for teen parents, especially those who do not have family support. Add to this the necessity to set aside dreams and aspirations and place a baby's needs before their own, and it is no wonder that a large majority of teenage parents have emotional conflicts that decrease their ability to provide good parenting.

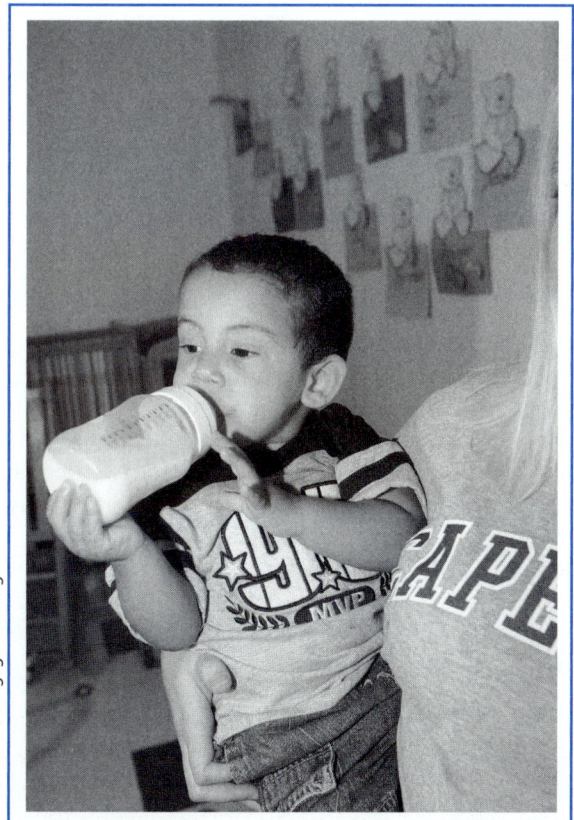

Children experience many different family situations that can cause joy and stress.

The role of the early childhood educator cannot be underestimated in these situations. Teenage parents (both mothers and fathers) need you to encourage their positive parenting abilities and acknowledge their efforts, successes, and challenges. This requires you to set aside additional time to empathize with, actively listen to, and mirror the teen parent. In addition, providing contact information for community services (e.g., parenting courses, financial management, and social service agencies) as part of your regular communication with families can be invaluable for both the teen parents and their offspring.

Teenage parents need vital information, support, and role models that teach, through example, the daily competent care of infants and toddlers. This modeling should include the conscious application of attention, approval, and attunement in addition to the mechanics of care. A competent child care professional will help the teenage parents to develop by appropriately extending positive attention, approval, and attunement to them. Teenage parents are not yet adults and need to be accepted, not judged or labeled, for who they are as individuals.

✓ reading checkpoint

Before moving on with your reading, make sure that you can answer the following questions about the material discussed so far.

1. List two family situations that would require extra support from you. What can you do to minimize stress for a family in those situations?

2. Explain why many of these situations such as the ones you described in your answer to question one raise ethical dilemmas for educators.

COMMUNICATING WITH COLLEAGUES

When a child care program has more than one staff member, effective communication among staff is essential. Arranging to meet with staff members regularly enhances communication. Although family child care providers often work alone in their own homes, they can contact licensing staff and other family child care providers for support. Group family child care arrangements employ at least two people who work with a larger group of children in the home. Child care centers usually have a staff that includes a director and one or more caregivers. The size of enrollment determines the number and kind of additional staff; these may be caregivers, cooks, custodians, bus drivers, early childhood educators, social workers, and health personnel. No matter if the staff is two or 22, regular, uninterrupted time to communicate, solve problems, and make decisions is necessary.

Listening to Colleagues

Each caregiver needs to be a listener. Staff can exchange information and discuss program issues in a reasonable way only if all are active listeners. How you listen to one another reflects how you respect one another.

Collaborating with Colleagues

Share Information and Areas of Expertise

Your educational and professional experiences give you information, insights, and perspectives that will help others understand issues and deal with problems. Each person has special talents and unique insights to share with colleagues, children, and families. Nobody appreciates know-it-alls, but we all benefit from people who are willing to share ideas that can be discussed, accepted, modified, or rejected.

Share Your Feelings and Actively Listen While Expressing Your Excitement and Joy about Working with Your Colleagues

As a part of a team, you all benefit from sharing pleasurable experiences. Tactfully express frustrations, disappointments, and anger. Keeping those feelings bottled up can harm all of you. Determine what is distressing you and discuss the issue. By staying within your active listening guidelines you can focus on how staff activities are affecting program goals. You will be more likely to clear up misunderstandings and misperceptions if you focus your discussion on issues rather than on personalities.

Share Feedback

Both informal and formal observations provide you with feedback to share with your colleagues. Noting how other caregivers behave with people and materials in various settings, schedules, and routines can help the entire staff evaluate the current program and make necessary adjustments. Feedback can highlight caregiver actions that are helpful and effective, but you should use tact when commenting on a situation in which you believe your colleagues might act differently. Focus on what is best for the children and what changes can improve the situation, not on what a caregiver did wrong. Actions are more often *inappropriate* than wrong. Since all caregivers are developing their skills, comments that make colleagues feel incompetent are not helpful; however, focusing on appropriate alternative actions is productive.

Share Responsibilities

Your colleagues will notice whether you are willing to carry your load. Not all of your responsibilities are explicit in your job description. Martha is responsible for getting snacks ready, but today she is rocking Natalie, who after crying and fussing has finally settled down but does not seem quite ready to be put down to play. If another caregiver volunteers to set up snacks, Natalie will not become distressed again and so will not disturb the other children.

Supporting Colleagues

Caregiving is physically and emotionally draining. Remember and put into practice the three *A*s of caregiving presented in Chapter 4 to help yourself and your

Supportive relationships are necessary among caregivers who work together in a child care program.

colleagues cope with stress. For example, assisting a colleague when extra help is needed reduces stress. You can provide positive emotional support by listening, using honest compliments, giving credit, and reassuring colleagues about ideas or actions of theirs that you think are appropriate. Knowing that you are working together rather than against each other is in itself powerful emotional support.

Making Decisions

Early childhood educators need information to make intelligent staff decisions. Meet with other staff members regularly. Study issues and learn to identify relevant factors so that you will be able to discuss subjects intelligently and make wise decisions. Raise questions with colleagues; listen, think, and take an active part in making decisions related to delivering professional care and education for very young children.

✓ reading checkpoint

Before moving on with your reading, make sure that you can answer the following questions about the material discussed so far.
1. Why is effective communication with colleagues important?
2. How can you contribute to effective, positive staff relationships?

SUMMARY

While most of us enter the early childhood profession because of our desire to work with children, we are also responsible for interacting positively with family members and colleagues. Developing communication strategies that assist in the building of strong partnerships is another key component of developmentally appropriate practices. Many factors such as incarceration, child abuse, and teenage pregnancy, provide challenges to us and families. Learning to work as a member of a team can alleviate some negative outcomes and stress for us, families, and most importantly, the children.

key terms

active listening
calibrating
family-caregiver conferences
home visits
I statements
mirroring
pacing
rapport
you statements

case study

Sheila

Amanda Hasha is a nine-month-old girl who has been in child care for the past three months. Lately, Sheila, her primary caregiver, notices that Amanda is not gaining weight, looks tired but does not sleep well, and cries often. Sheila meets with the director and other caregivers to share her concerns and actively listens as they all confirm her observations and suggest a family conference. Sheila then sets up a conference with Mrs. Hasha to discuss Amanda's problems.

Sheila starts the conference by describing her observations using I statements. She informs Mrs. Hasha that the other caregivers have observed the same behaviors and tells her the steps that have been taken to comfort Amanda. Sheila then asks Mrs. Hasha what she sees at home, and actively listens to her.

MRS. HASHA: "I've had a lot of problems lately that I'm sure have affected Amanda. Her father had an accident and is in the hospital, so I go to see him every chance I can."

SHEILA: "My! It sounds like you have been under a lot of stress and worry lately."

MRS. HASHA: "I just don't know what to do. No one else is around to help, so I sometimes have Amanda's sister watch her even though she's only eight."

SHEILA: "So, you've had no help except for your older daughter. It sounds overwhelming."

MRS. HASHA: "Yes, it certainly is! I wish I knew how to get the kids cared for so I could be at the hospital more often."

SHEILA: "It sounds like you really need help with the children so you can help your husband more."

MRS. HASHA: "That's right. Do you have any idea who might help me?"

SHEILA: "I know there are many sources for help in the community. Have you thought to ask at the hospital, your church, or at school?"

MRS. HASHA: "That's a very good idea. Our church has a volunteer program, but I'm embarrassed to ask our minister."

SHEILA: "Would you like me to ask around at some of the programs the county offers? I'm sure help is available for this kind of situation."

MRS. HASHA: "Yes. Thank you so much. I will ask at church also. I know that Amanda will be better if she has an adult to care for her when I can't be there."

(Box continues)

Within a week, Mrs. Hasha has volunteers from her church helping to care for the children. Amanda's disposition has changed from stressed and insecure to calm and happy. She has begun to eat better at school and minimal weight gain has been noted. Through the use of a family conference, Sheila was able to help Mrs. Hasha share her problems and arrive at solutions to improve Amanda's health and development.

1. Discuss what communication tools Sheila used and their effectiveness in producing outcomes.
2. How did Sheila use her colleagues to support and enhance her work with Amanda's family?
3. Imagine that Sheila used the following you statements in her conversation with Mrs. Hasha: "You leave Amanda with your eight-year-old daughter. Do you know how dangerous that is?" How might the outcome of the conversation been affected? Why?

QUESTIONS AND EXPERIENCES FOR REFLECTION

1. Actively listen to a dialogue between a family member and the caregiver when a child arrives in the morning. Write down the statements and then categorize them in the chart below.

	Family Member	Caregiver
Information		
Questions		
Affirmation		
Other		

2. Conduct one simulated family-caregiver conference initiated by the caregiver and another initiated by a family member.

3. Interview a teacher in an Early Head Start or a Head Start program about a home visit they have completed. Determine this teacher's purposes and procedures for the visit.

4. Role-play a child care center staff meeting about the problems of sharing play yard space.

5. Identify the responsibilities of a caregiver in a setting with which you are familiar. Categorize the activities according to whether the caregiver attends to them independently or in cooperation with other staff members, using a chart like the following.

Task	Accomplishes Independently	Needs Cooperation of Other Staff

6. Describe two situations in which caregivers interact with each other to solve a conflict of working together. Identify the interpersonal skills needed.

Situation	Skills Needed: Caregiver 1	Skills Needed: Caregiver 2

7. List your perceived strengths in interpersonal relationships with families and staff. List areas where you need to set growth goals.

REFERENCES

Annie E. Casey Foundation. (2008). *2008 Kids Count Data Book*. Baltimore, MD: Author. Retrieved March 9, 2009, from http://www.aecf.org/~/media/Pubs/Topics/Juvenile%20Justice/Detention%20Reform/2008KIDSCOUNTDataBookStateProfilesofChildWell/AEC178%202008KCDB.pdf

Bauette, G., & Peterson, E. (1993). Beginning to create a multicultural classroom. *Dimensions of Early Childhood, 21*(2), 11–12.

Bruns, D. A. (2006). Promoting mother-child relationships for incarcerated women and their children. *Infants and Young Children, 19*(4), 308–322.

Children's Defense Fund. (2008). *The state of America's children 2008*. Washington, DC: Author.

Christian, L. G. (2006, January). Understanding families: Applying family systems theory to early childhood practice. *Beyond the Journal: Young Children on the Web*. Retrieved December 14, 2006, from http://www.journal.naeyc.org/btj/200601/ChristianBTJ.pdf

Clements, R., & Kuperberg, M. (2008). Viewpoint: Reaching our goals through effective communication. *Journal of Physical Education, Recreation, and Dance, 79*(3), 4–6, 11.

Copple, C., & Bredekamp, S., (Eds.). (2009). *Developmentally appropriate practice in early childhood programs* (3rd ed.). Washington, DC: National Association for the Education of Young Children.

Dallaire, D. H. (2007). Children with incarcerated mothers: Developmental outcomes, special challenges and recommendations. *Journal of Applied Developmental Psychology, 28*, 15–24.

Davis, L., & Keyser, J. (1997). *Becoming the parent you want to be*. New York: Broadway Books.

Duncan, G. J., & Brooks-Gunn, J. (1997). *Consequences of growing up poor*. New York: Russell Sage Foundation.

English, (1998). The extent and consequences of child maltreatment. Protecting Children from Abuse and Neglect [Issue]. *The Future of Children, 8*(1), 39–53.

Faber, A. J., Willerton, E., Clymer, S. R., MacDermid, S. M., & Weiss, H. M. (2008). Ambiguous absence, ambiguous presence: A qualitative study of military reserve families in wartime. *Journal of Family Psychology, 22*(2), 222–230.

Galardini, A., & Giovannini, D. (2001). Pistoia: Creating a dynamic, open system to serve children, families, and community. In L. Gandini & C. P. Edwards (Eds.), *Bambini: The Italian approach to infant/toddler care* (pp. 89–105). New York: Teachers College Press.

Gandini, L. (2001). Reggio Emilia: Experiencing life in an infant-toddler center, An interview with Cristina Bondavalli. In L. Gandini & C. P. Edwards (Eds.) *Bambini: The Italian approach to infant/toddler care* (pp. 55–66). New York: Teachers College Press.

Glaze, L. E., & Maruschak, L. M. (2009). Parents in prison and their minor children. U. S. Department of Justice, Office of Justice Programs, Bureau of Justice Statistics. Retrieved March 10, 2009, from http://www.ojp.usdoj.gov/bjs/pub/pdf/pptmc.pdf

Global Security (2008). Military: US ground forces end strength. Retrieved on March 10, 2009 from http://www.globalsecurity.org/military/ops/iraq_orbat_es.htm

Gonzalez-Mena, J. (2001). *Multicultural issues in child care* (3rd ed.). Mountain View, CA: Mayfield.

Herr, J., & Swim, T. (2002). *Creative resources for infants and toddlers* (2nd ed.). Clifton Park, NY: Thomson Delmar Learning.

Huber, L. K. (2003). Knowing children and building relationships with families: A strategy for improving conferences. *Early Childhood Education Journal, 31*(1), 75–77.

Im, J., Parlakian, R., and Sánchez, S. (2007). Understanding the Influence of Culture on Caregiving Practices . . . From the Inside Out. *Beyond the Journal: Young Children on the Web*. Retrieved March 2, 2009, from http://journal.naeyc.org/btj/200709/pdf/RockingRolling.pdf

Korkmaz, I. (2007). Teachers' opinions about the responsibilities of parents, schools, and teachers in enhancing student learning. *Education, 127*(3), 389-399.

Lally, J. R. (Ed.). (1992). *Language development & communication: A guide, infant/toddler caregiving series.* San Francisco: Far West Lab.

Legerstee, M., & Varghese, J. (2001). The role of maternal affect mirroring on social expectancies in three-month-old infants. *Child Development, 72*(5), 1301–1313.

Lincoln, A., Swift, E., & Shorteno-Fraser, M. (2008). Psychological adjustment and treatment of children and families with parents deployed in military combat. *Journal of Clinical Psychology, 64*(8), 984–992.

Mantovani, S. (2001). Infant-toddler centers in Italy today: Tradition and innovation. In L. Gandini & C. P. Edwards (Eds.), *Bambini: The Italian approach to infant/toddler care* (pp. 23–37). New York: Teachers College Press.

Martin, J. A., Hamilton, B. E., Sutton, P. D., Ventura, S. J., Menacker, F., & Munson, M. L. (2005). Births: Final data for 2003. *National Vital Statistics Reports, 54*(2). Hyattsville, MD: National Center for Health Statistics.

McDevitt, T. M., & Ormrod, J. E. (2010). *Child development: Educating and working with children and adolescents* (4th ed.). Upper Saddle River, NJ: Pearson Merrill Prentice Hall.

McElroy, E. M., & Rodriguez, C. M. (2008). Mothers of children with externalizing behavior problems: Cognitive risk factors for abuse potential and discipline style and practices. *Child Abuse & Neglect, 32*(8), 774–784.

Mollborn, S. (2009). Norms About Nonmarital Pregnancy and Willingness to Provide Resources to Unwed Parents. *Journal of Marriage & Family, 71*(1), 122–134.

National Association for the Education of Young Children (NAYC). (2005). Position statement: Code of ethical conduct and statement of commitment. Washington, DC: Author. Retrieved December 14, 2006, from http://www.naeyc.org/about/positions/pdf/PSETH05.PDF

Orstein, A. C., & Chapman, J. K. (1988). The parent-teacher conference. *PTA Today, 14*(1), 8–10.

Paranjothy, S. (2009). Teenage pregnancy: Who suffers? *Archives of Disease in Childhood, 94*(3), 239–245.

Planned Parenthood Federation of America (2006). Pregnancy & childbearing among U.S. teens. Washington DC: Author. Retrieved March 9, 2009, from http://www.plannedparenthood.org/issues-action/abortion/roe-v-wade/reports/teen-pregnancy-6239.htm

Poehlmann, J. (2005a). Representations of Attachment Relationships in Children of Incarcerated Mothers. *Child Development, 76*(3), 679–696.

Poehlmann, J. (2005b). Children's family environments and intellectual outcomes during maternal incarceration. *Journal of Marriage and Family, 67,* 1275–1285.

Shonkoff, J. P., & Phillips, D. A. (Eds.). (2000). *From neurons to neighborhoods: The science of early childhood development.* Washington, DC: National Academy Press.

Williams, D. S., & Rose, T. (2007). I say hello; You say good-bye: When babies are born while fathers are away. *Zero to Three, 27*(6), 13–19.

Worley, D., Titsworth, S., Worley, D. W., & Cornett-DeVito, M. (2007). Instructional Communication Competence: Lessons Learned from Award-Winning Teachers. *Communication Studies 58*(2), 207–222.

Yeary, J. (2007). Operation parenting edge: Promoting resiliency through prevention. *Zero to Three, 27*(6), 7–12.

ADDITIONAL RESOURCES

Fontes, L. A. (2005). *Child abuse and culture: Working with diverse families.* NY: Guilford Press.

Holden, G. W. (2009). *Parenting: A dynamic perspective.* Thousand Oaks, CA: Sage Publications, Inc.

Lamb, M. E. (Ed.). (2003). *The role of the father in child development* (4th ed.). NY: Wiley.

Lindsay, J. W. (2008). *Teen dads: Rights, responsibilities, and joys* (3rd ed.). Buena Park, CA: Morning Glory Press.

NAEYC (2008). Resources for children, teachers, & families affected by military deployment. *Beyond the Journal: Young Children on the Web.* Retrieved March 10, 2009, from http://journal.naeyc.org/btj/200803/pdf/BTJ_Military_Deploy_Resources.pdf

Pavlicin, K. M. (2007). *Life after deployment: Military families share reunion stories and advice.* St. Paul, MN: Elva Resa Publishing.

For additional activities, web links, and other resources, please visit our website at www.cengage.com/education/swim

chapter 8

THE INDOOR AND OUTDOOR LEARNING ENVIRONMENTS

learning objectives

After reading this chapter, you should be able to:
- Identify components of high-quality and developmentally appropriate indoor and outdoor learning environments from the teacher's perspective.
- Identify components of high-quality and developmentally appropriate indoor and outdoor learning environments from the child's perspective.
- Understand criteria for selecting materials.
- Evaluate policies and procedures for protecting the health and safety of very young children.

chapter outline

- Introduction to Principles of Environmental Design
- The Teacher's Perspective
- The Child's Perspective
- Society's Perspective
- Ongoing Reflection on the Physical Environment
- Selecting Equipment and Materials
- Protecting the Children's Health and Safety
- Case Study: Ena

205

INTRODUCTION TO PRINCIPLES OF ENVIRONMENTAL DESIGN

"... the issue is not having space but how it is used"
V. Vecchi, quoted in Gandini, 1998, p. 165

Reflecting on the role of space is imperative, as has been demonstrated as a principle of the schools in Reggio Emilia, Italy (Chapter 6). The classroom environment is considered the "third teacher" (e.g., Edwards, Gandini, & Forman, 1998), a concept that acknowledges the role of adults in carefully preparing and selecting materials for indoor and outdoor learning environments. In other words, the environment is planned to provide guidance to the children and adults about appropriate behavior.

Consider for a moment how your actions are influenced differently by being in a place of worship, a library, a shopping mall, or a family restaurant. All of these environments reflect messages of appropriate behavior. For example, a library may have special sections designated for quiet reading, small groups to gather and enjoy stories, computer work, and playing with puppets. The way space and materials are arranged provides clues for appropriate behavior. The adults responsible for managing the space seldom have to remind others of their expectations; the environment does it for them. Similar to the designer of the library, a teacher's careful classroom environment planning will help children meet expectations for the use of the space and promote optimal development and learning.

We must design learning environments so that they facilitate the best care and education of young children. "The drive to protect our children is profound and easily can lead to cleansing their lives of challenge and depth. Early childhood is a time when children begin to live in the world and hopefully learn to love the world. They can't do this when fenced off from the messy richness of life to live in a world of fluorescent lights and plastic toys, two-dimensional glowing screens, and narrow teaching instruction" (Greenman, 2005, p. 7). Think about what the classroom environment you help create says about your educational values, your beliefs about the capabilities of young children, and the role of families. The focus of this chapter is on answering: *How do teachers create meaningful learning environments that facilitate optimal development for children?*

THE TEACHER'S PERSPECTIVE

Many teachers prepare their indoor and outdoor areas for learning, but do they prepare them to promote optimal learning?* When making educational decisions such as the arrangement and selection of materials, you should begin by reflecting on the

---

*This section was originally published in a slightly different form as T. J. Swim, "Basic premises of classroom design: The teacher's perspective," *Early Childhood NEWS, 16*(6), (2004), 34–42. Article commissioned by Jonti-Craft. Copyright © 2004 by Excellence Learning Corporation. Reprinted by permission.

age of children in your classroom; their needs, interests, and abilities; your program's philosophy; licensing and accreditation standards; and guidelines for developmentally appropriate practice (to be discussed further in Chapter 9). Each of these factors helps you to shape the various areas in which the children will grow and learn.

Learning Centers

Learning centers organize the space and materials and encourage specific types of behaviors in one location. For infants and toddlers you can organize centers in several ways. A popular approach for toddlers involves dividing the indoor and outdoor space into use areas. A quiet zone or private space, a construction center, a wet center, a project area, a reading and listening center, or a dramatic play center can be created by using tables, short shelves, transparent dividers, and flooring to indicate an area inside. For infants, these areas may be less well defined. For example, a manipulation area will allow for exploring toys with the hands, while a more open space becomes a gross motor area. The rest of the room might be subdivided

A library center with developmentally appropriate materials can foster a love of reading.

into areas for specific types of routine care times such as diapering or napping. The outdoor space should also be divided into learning centers. Any experience done inside can be done outside; teachers should not overlook the importance of the outdoor learning environment (DeBord, Hestenes, Moore, Cosco, & McGinnis, 2002; Stephenson, 2002). Painting, riding trikes, climbing and jumping, playing in sand and water, growing vegetables or flowers in a garden, dramatic play, and storytelling are all centers that should be outside (DeBord et al., 2002; Torquati & Barber, 2005). Sutterby and Frost (2002) also suggest the use of outdoor cooking experiences for promoting healthy eating. Given the importance of learning centers for promoting development, it is assumed that your child care setting will be flexibly organized into them.

When planning your learning environment, base the number and type of learning centers on the size of the space and the age of the children. In general, to maximize choice and minimize conflict over possessions, a rule of thumb to follow for toddlers and older children is to provide one-third more work spaces than the number of children in your classroom. To illustrate, if you have 12 older toddlers in your group, you will need at least (12 × 1/3) + 12 or 16 spaces for working. This might mean including two or three spaces at the sensory table, two at the easel, two or three at the art center, three or four in blocks/construction, three or four in dramatic play, two in the listening/library area, and two private spots. The same rule of thumb can apply to outdoor space, but having more play spaces available maximizes the amount of time children are moving and exercising and thus remaining physically fit and healthy (Sutterby & Frost, 2002).

Real Objects versus Open-Ended Materials

Children need a balance of novel and familiar materials to attract and maintain their attention (see the next section for a more in-depth discussion). When children are engaged with materials and ideas, they have less opportunity to create mischief or misbehave, thus enabling teachers to change their supervision from guidance of behavior to guidance of learning. Developmentally, throughout the early childhood period, young children are learning to use objects as tools for representing their thoughts and theories about how the world works. Therefore, providing a balance of real and open-ended materials promotes cognitive development. Making available real objects such as child-size shovels for digging in the garden, Navajo pottery for storing paintbrushes, or child-size glass tumblers for drinks during meals (for older toddlers) serves two further purposes: (1) it demonstrates trust in the children's ability to care for objects and (2) it connects home and school environments. Real objects, when provided in response to the children's expressed interests, can also facilitate thinking about a particular topic or concept.

Open-ended materials, on the other hand, can be used by the children to expand their understanding of concepts and demonstrate creative uses of materials. Open-ended materials include collected items such as fabric, cardboard, plastics, pebbles, shells, pinecones or egg cartons, as well as commercially produced objects

Open-ended materials can provide extensive opportunity for play and representation of ideas.

such as wooden blocks, animal and people figurines, or connecting manipulatives. Open-ended materials can spark, support, and enhance learning and development in any learning environment. Neatly arranging them in baskets or clear containers and displaying them on a shelf at the children's height will make them easily accessible to the children whether they are working indoors or outdoors. Of course, some open-ended materials might pose a choking hazard for infants and toddlers, so never leave the child unattended during the experience.

Independence versus Dependence
A primary goal for adults is that children become independent, self-regulated learners. In order for this to occur, teachers must carefully plan the physical environment with this in mind. As mentioned above, providing easily accessible open-ended materials promotes cognitive development. This practice also promotes social and emotional development, since the children can independently select the materials they need for their work and can more easily help with cleanup before they leave the

learning area. Moreover, modifying the bathroom so that all necessary hand-washing supplies can be reached fosters the children's independence. Outside faucets that have an attachment allowing children to serve themselves encourage the toddlers to get water whenever they need it for their work.

Use of Space

An important question to begin your work is "How do I want the children to use this space?" Teachers create environments to promote learning in all areas of development as well as in particular content areas, such as mathematics or social studies. Therefore, a thorough understanding of child development and learning theories will guide you in planning how to use your classroom space.

Messy versus Dry

Designing space for daily opportunities to explore messy materials is a must. In fact, Bredekamp and Copple (1997) suggest that toddlers should have daily experiences with sand and water because of their educational value. Messy experiences are particularly significant for young children because they build cognitive structures or schemas (i.e., tightly organized sets of ideas about specific objects or situations) through sensorimotor and hands-on, minds-on experiences. Some typical messy

Messy experiences for young children build cognitive structures through sensorimotor and hands-on, minds-on experiences.

centers include water and/or sensory tables, painting easels, and art. Water play, for example, provides opportunities for learning about quantity, building vocabulary, and negotiating the sharing of materials.

What does a teacher need to consider when managing messy experiences in a classroom setting? First, setting up messy experiences in an area with vinyl or linoleum flooring allows for ease of cleanup when spills occur. Second, placing these experiences near a water source can aid in cleaning up and refilling containers or even adding a new element to an experience. For example, if a sensory table is filled with dry sand, children can transfer water from the source using pitchers, thus transforming the properties of the sand. Third, placing a hand broom and dustpan nearby prompts children to keep the area clean.

If you do not have an area with flooring that allows for easy cleanup, you will need to be creative in order to provide such valuable learning experiences. Placing newspaper, towels, or a shower curtain under a sensory table or easel can resolve this issue. Another way to address this challenge is to plan daily experiences with messy materials outside.

Noisy versus Quiet

Some classroom experiences are noisier than others. Cooperating and negotiating requires children to interact with one another. Although sometimes interactions can become heated, a caregiver's goal should be to enable such interactions so that the children gain necessary perspective-taking and problem-solving skills, not to stop the interactions or prevent them in the first place. To manage the environment and facilitate learning, teachers can place noisy areas close together. Noisy centers include blocks and construction, dramatic play, music and movement, and project work space. Placing these centers adjacent to one another serves two purposes. First, the higher noise levels will be located in a particular section of the room. This allows children to concentrate better in the quiet areas, with fewer distractions close by. Second, placing areas that require more supervision and support together permits the teacher to engage in these interactions (e.g., assisting children with problem solving) without having to travel between different parts of the room.

Quiet centers consist of the library, listening centers, and private spaces. For your mental health and that of the children you must provide both indoor and outdoor areas for children to be alone. These private spaces allow the children to regroup and gather their thoughts before rejoining others. A note of caution is needed here. You should never send a child to the quiet or private areas as a consequence for misbehavior. Children should freely choose these areas to help them relax. If you use the areas for punishment or the children perceive them as such, they will not serve their purpose of helping them to relax and regroup.

Play in some other centers, such as with manipulatives or science/discovery, fluctuates between quiet and noisy, depending on the type of materials provided and the children's levels of engagement. These areas can be used to transition between the noisy and quiet centers.

When deciding where to place learning centers, teachers also need to consider the needs of the different types of centers. To illustrate, the music and movement center needs an electrical outlet for a tape or CD player, shelves for musical instruments, baskets for scarves or strips of fabric, mirrors for observing motions, and space for creative movement and dance. Teachers often have limited resources and need to maximize the use of equipment and materials they do have. Locating the music and movement center near the dramatic play area is one way to do this: these two centers can share materials such as a mirror or basket of fabric.

Calm, Safe Learning Environment

Another question that you will encounter is "How can I create a calm, safe environment that provides stimulating learning experiences for the children?" In this section, we will focus attention on the last part of this question: "stimulating learning experiences."

Novel versus Familiar

Teachers and children deserve to be surrounded by beautiful objects and materials that are displayed in an aesthetically pleasing fashion. A well-planned environment should offer a mix of novel and familiar experiences and objects that each infant can explore at her own pace (Copple & Bredekamp, 2009). In other words, some of these objects should be part of the environment on a regular basis, while others can be included occasionally to spark interest. For example, hanging a framed print of Monet's sunflowers on the wall near the easel will create a beautiful environment for toddler children. Surprising the children with a display of Pueblo Indian pottery one day will create a different motivation to use the easel.

Learning spaces should be varied so that children have the opportunity to explore different perspectives. To illustrate, having the ability to change one's physical location by climbing up the stairs to a loft or playscape and looking down on a teacher provides a child with a new view of the world. Another way that teachers can vary the space and provoke thinking is by providing a new display or object to explore and discuss. A ground covering with two or more variations can naturally demonstrate hard versus soft and warm versus cold. Sitting on soft, lush grass on a hot summer day will feel cool to an infant's touch, thus providing him an opportunity to experience his environment in a different way.

Another way to conceptualize the familiar is to create spaces that parallel those found in home environments. For example, placing a couch, rocking chair, and end table with a lamp in the entryway mimics a living room in a home. A cozy nook like this not only adds warmth and comfort to the learning environment but also helps to create a sense of security at school: a home away from home. Having a hanging swing, the kind families might have on their front porch, gives the adults and children a place to snuggle and relax on a warm springtime afternoon.

Pathways versus Boundaries

As you are planning your layout, you need to consider how you will define your learning centers. Having visible boundaries for centers provides children with a clear message about the use of materials in a particular area. Use a variety of dividers, such as short shelving units, bookcases, transparent fabrics, and sheets of decorated acrylic. Flower beds, raised gardens, or cobbled pathways make great dividers for outdoor learning centers. Transparency, or the ability to see between centers, both allows teachers to supervise and facilitates children's play, because they can make connections between materials in different centers in each environment. Even though materials are organized into learning centers, we should be flexible in allowing the children to move materials that they need from one center to another. When planning the boundaries for a learning center, you must carefully consider how much space to devote to that area. As described above, the noisier areas often require more space than quieter areas. This is because these areas tend to elicit more associative and cooperative play, requiring two or more children at a time.

A teacher also needs to consider how to utilize open space. Because we need gathering spaces for toddlers that can easily accommodate most of the children and caregivers in the room at one time, we often set aside this space for that one purpose. Then, when no one is using the space, children may convert it to a place for "rough and tumble" play. Using the gathering space for movement and gross motor activities as well may be logical, given the space needs of a particular center.

Pathways into and out of the room as well as between centers need to be carefully considered. When children arrive for the day, they should be able to complete a gradual transition from home to school. Having to walk to the opposite side of the classroom to store their belongings in their cubbies can be stressful, especially if they must pass by noisy centers. When considering movement between centers, remember that walking through one center to get to another can cause children to become distracted. Do you want the children to walk through a center such as the block/construction area to get to the music center? It would quickly become evident from the children's behavior that such an arrangement does not work well.

Basic Needs

As you are considering the educational needs of the children, you must also dedicate space for meeting the children's basic needs for eating, toileting, resting, and playing. The question here is: "How do I plan the environment to meet these basic requirements?"

Eating versus Toileting

Some infant and toddler classrooms separate the changing table and food preparation counter with a small sink. This practice may seem to be an efficient use of counter space, but it could jeopardize both the early childhood educators' and the children's health. For hygienic purposes, then, it is imperative that the eating and toileting areas be separated. Although this is relatively simple in a preschool classroom, it may be more difficult in an infant and toddler classroom, because the typical restroom just does not have enough space for toilets, sinks, and a changing table. Since infant and toddler teachers must both continually supervise the children and also spend a significant amount of time diapering, changing tables are often placed in the classroom. Where should a changing table be located? Placing it next to a water source assists with good hand-washing practices. You should also position it away from a wall, so that your back is not to the rest of the children when you are changing a diaper.

The food area can require a number of small appliances such as a mini-refrigerator or microwave (per licensing regulations); therefore, cabinet space near electrical outlets is very important. For toddlers and older children, space for eating can be shared with other areas of the classroom. For example, the tables that are used for art can be cleaned and sanitized when it is snack or meal time. Infant teachers must address other issues when planning the environment. Depending upon your state regulations, you may or may not need a separate high chair for each infant. Finding storage space for mealtime equipment must be given careful consideration.

Teachers must plan the environment and adopt practices to protect their own and the children's health.

Sleep and comfort versus Play

Children and adults need locations to store special items and belongings from home. This not only reaffirms the importance of both environments but it also teaches respect for one's own and others' belongings. Switching between environments can be stressful for people of all ages, so plan for comfortable places for children to make the transition from home to school, snuggle, relax, and enjoy reunions with family members. Couches and rocking chairs located in a variety of classroom areas provide an excellent avenue for this.

All children need time throughout the day to rest and rejuvenate. Teachers should create a calm, relaxing environment during nap or rest time. Closing blinds on the windows, plugging in a night light, playing soft instrumental music, and providing comfort items for each child (e.g., blankets, favorite stuffed animals) might assist with shifting from play to sleep. You should also organize the environment to address the needs of children who require less sleep during the day, by creating baskets with books, paper and pencils, and other quiet toys that can be used by a child lying on a cot or sitting at a table.

At times children may prefer to nap outdoors after exerting themselves during activities and play. A shady and easily supervised space made soft with quilts or blankets should be readily available for resting.

We have now considered the learning environment from the teacher's perspective, but it is time to consider the child's perspective. While presenting the material in this manner may create paradoxes (seemingly contradictory messages), keep in mind that these are different sides of the same coin. In other words, consider and prepare to articulate the common focus of each perspective.

✓ reading checkpoint

Before moving on with your reading, make sure that you can answer the following question about the material discussed so far.

1. When planning classroom environments, why do we need to balance opposites such as real objects versus open-ended materials, noisy versus quiet, and novel versus familiar?

THE CHILD'S PERSPECTIVE

First and foremost, the educational space has to guarantee the well-being of each child and of the group of children.[†] Children have the right to educational environments that facilitate their social, emotional, moral, physical, linguistic, and cognitive

---

[†] This section was originally published in a slightly different form as T. J. Swim, "Advance reflection on principles of classroom design: Considering the child's perspective," *Early Childhood NEWS, 17*(1), (2005), 34–39. Article commissioned by Jonti-Craft. Copyright © 2005 by Excelligence Learning Corporation. Reprinted by permission.

development; they also have the right to environments that are free of excessive stress, noise, and physical and psychological harm (Malaguzzi, 1998). The following section explains ten principles that are important to consider when creating your educational environment from the child's perspective. You may notice that these principles are not restricted to a particular learning center, but rather apply across educational spaces.

Consider each of the general principles in relationship to the specific children in your care. The environment must reflect and be responsive to the unique developmental characteristics of children of specific ages as well as the individual children within that age group (Copple & Bredekamp, 2009). Although the general principles are relevant to all environments for young children, they may manifest themselves differently for the various age groups. One or two principles may be more relevant for a particular age group or setting. To briefly illustrate, continuity of care between home and school environments is vital for the appropriate care of infants (see, for example, Bergen, Reid, & Torelli, 2001; Bove, 2000; Essa, Favre, Thweatt, & Waugh, 1999). Thus, plenty of space needs to be devoted to areas where family members and teachers can comfortably communicate and ease each infant's transition. Less space may be required for this purpose with preschoolers.

Before providing detailed explanations of each principle, a general overview of each will be provided, highlighting questions that a child might want to ask:

Transparency—Can I see my friends, teachers, and family members from almost any place in the room? Is there a place I can have some time alone? Can I quickly find the materials I want to use?

Flexibility—Can I find areas that support my interests in the classroom?

Relationships—Can I build relationships with other people in my classroom?

Identity—Am I an important person in this environment?

Movement—Can I move my body freely?

Documentation—Do the important adults in my life communicate about me frequently?

Senses—Is the environment warm and welcoming and a place that I want to spend four to ten hours of my day?

Representation—Can I tell you in multiple ways about my understanding of and theories about the world?

Independence—Can I do things myself?

Discovery—Can I find interesting things to examine closely and learn about?

Transparency

Can I see my friends, teachers, and family members from almost any place in the room? To support connections and relationships, children need to be able to see materials and one another. From the adult's viewpoint, transparency adds to the ease of supervision. You should be able to see from one side of the room to the other. This should not remove all privacy, however. Children and adults need secluded spaces to be alone and gather their thoughts (Marion, 2007). To achieve this principle, you can use translucent fabrics, shelves with the backing removed, or sheets of decorated acrylic to divide areas (Curtis & Carter, 2003).

A second concern a child might have is, "Can I quickly find the materials I want to use?" Another aspect of transparency considers the amount and the presentation of materials in the environment. In general, you want the room to be as uncluttered as possible. You should regularly analyze your environment to identify unused toys or materials and then locate places to store those items to minimize clutter (Cutler, 2000).

For those items that are being used regularly, carefully observe the quantity of material being used by the children; have you provided too many objects or not enough? You should strive to provide a sufficient amount of material. The definition of *sufficient* is guided by your professional interpretation; realize that it differs for each group of children. The aim is to provide materials to spark older toddlers' interests, yet not totally satisfy them; thus provoking them to use their emerging skills of imagining, pretending, and transforming objects for use. The phrase "less is more" is key to this principle. Try to display the materials and supplies in baskets or clear containers on shelves that are low and open, because displaying materials in this

"Hiding" behind the transparent barrier.

manner permits children to see what is available and to select and clean up materials independently (Isbell & Exelby, 2001; Marion, 2007; Topal & Gandini, 1999).

Flexibility

Can I find areas that support my interests in the classroom? The environment should change in response to individual children and each group of children living in it (Copple & Bredekamp, 2009). To illustrate, an infant-toddler teacher modified her classroom as the children got older and she noticed particular interests. For example, to support and further enhance the children's interests in building, she designed her room with two separate construction areas. This seemed to work well for this group because they could spread out to work in the distinct spaces. As one of the children's projects grew, she altered another area of the classroom to support their representation of a city surrounded by train tracks. For a short period of time, this teacher had three classroom areas devoted to construction! She flexed her environment to best meet the needs of the children.

To many teachers' dismay, child care programs often lack adequate space for all that the children and teachers want to do. Combining or rotating learning centers is one way to maximize learning opportunities without overloading the setting (Isbell & Exelby, 2001). For example, a toddler teacher in a church-based program had to combine the writing and art center, while her colleague decided to carefully select materials to merge science exploration and reading/library into one center. In contrast, another of their colleagues provided space in the outdoor environment for daily experiences at the sensory table and easel and to better utilize classroom space.

Related to that idea of combining centers is the notion of providing open-ended materials that can be used in many areas of the classroom (Curtis & Carter, 2003). Encouraging the children to borrow or move material among the learning centers is another way to demonstrate the flexibility of the environment. Hence, another question a child might wonder is, "Can I move the materials and supplies around the room to do my work?"

Relationships

Can I build relationships with other people in my classroom? The environment needs to support and facilitate the development of strong, enduring relationships among children, families, and staff members (Honig, 2002; Galardini & Giovannini, 2001; New, 1998). As discussed in previous chapters, continuity of care should be a priority to support optimal social and emotional development. Space needs to be allocated and arranged so that adults and children have soft, warm areas for gathering, snuggling, communicating, or just being together. This space also serves to create an "at home" feeling, which is important because it helps high-quality child care programs avoid an institutional feel.

To illustrate this principle, consider the infant teacher who reorganized the entry to his classroom to include two rocking chairs and a small table. This provided space for him to speak with families at the beginning of the day, gathering information about family events and sharing anecdotes from the previous day. He also noticed

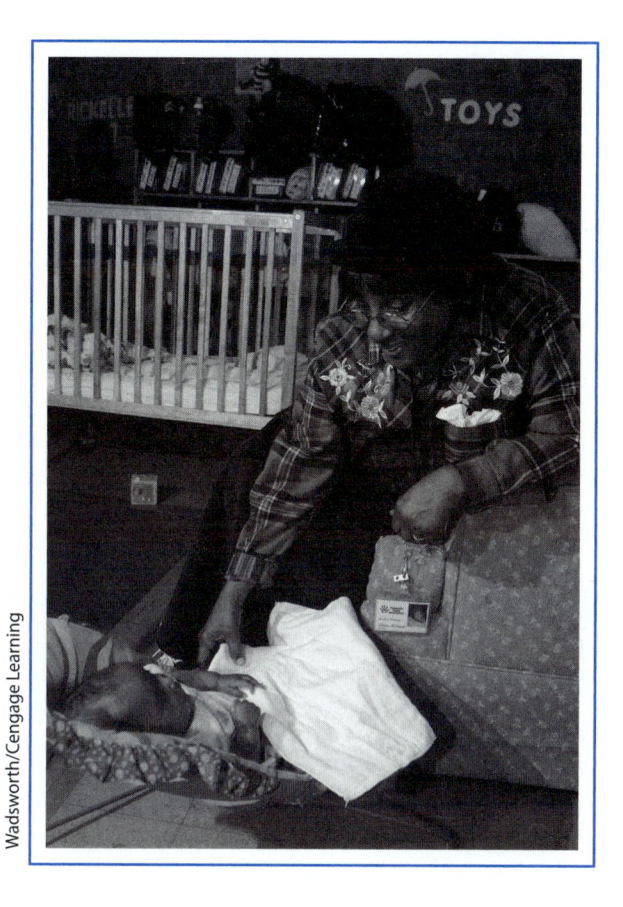

Space needs to be allocated so that adults and children have soft, warm areas for gathering, snuggling, or just being together.

that some families would linger in this area to say their goodbyes. Moreover, he used the same chairs to read to and snuggle with individual children before naptime.

Identity

Am I an important person in this environment? Your learning space should provide traces of those who live in it. Providing special spots for belongings is also a must, because it tells children that items of value from home are welcomed and respected in the classroom. Photographs of children working and playing, as well as family members and staff members both at work and at home should be displayed in prominent locations around the classroom. Panels documenting the work of the children and teachers provide clear explanation and evidence of the persons living and learning in the space (Turner & Krechevsky, 2003; Brown-DuPaul, Keyes, & Segatti, 2001; Forman & Fyfe, 1998). Such documentation also communicates that it is important to understand the children and their work and adds to their sense of self (Project Zero & Reggio Children, 2001; Malaguzzi, 1998).

Mirrors also provide valuable information that contributes to the development of children's identity.

Do not restrict yourself to displaying traces of the children, families, and staff on classroom walls. No space should be considered marginal (Gandini, 1998). Using the door of the playground shed, a shelf in the entryway, bathroom walls or stall doors to display photographs or works of art, for example, demonstrates to children the importance of that space and can provide additional information to help them build their identities (see Wien, Coates, Keating, & Bigelow, 2005). For example, a toddler teacher created a hand-washing chart using photographs of the children engaged in the various steps of the process. This chart not only provided the necessary information required to be posted by the state regulatory agency, but also assisted the children with independently completing this self-help task. An additional idea is to place mirrors around the classroom in strategic places.so that children notice their work or actions from another perspective (Smith, 1998).

Another way to conceptualize identity is to consider the ways in which individual children think about and engage with the world. Some children are persistent when faced with a challenging task, while other children are incredibly inventive and use materials in ways others would never consider. Good environments assist young children with developing a variety of important dispositions, or "frequent and voluntary habits of thinking and doing" (Da Ros-Voseles & Fowler-Haughey, 2007). Teachers must plan environments to support social dispositions such as being cooperative, empathetic, and accepting as well as intellectual dispositions such as being creative and curious, asking questions, solving problems, investigating, and communicating (Da Ros-Voseles & Fowler-Haughey, 2007).

Movement

Can I move my body freely? The environment needs to provide plenty of opportunities for children to move around and explore their bodies in space. Rather than trying to suppress children's bodies and their energy, teachers should find ways to include them in the learning process (Curtis & Carter, 2003). Large areas can be devoted to smaller spaces for climbers, obstacle courses, dancing, or acting out stories. The materials in this section of the classroom should be easily transportable so that they can be moved when the space is needed for other purposes, such as a classroom gathering (Isbell & Exelby, 2001).

High-quality spaces for infants and toddlers minimize, or eliminate entirely, equipment that confines children. A playpen, for example, not only physically limits a child but creates a barrier that socially and emotionally isolates the child from others. Holding a child offers more safety and security than the most expensive playpen. In addition, wheeled walkers do not enhance upright mobility development of infants; they can actually promote the acquisition of bad habits such as walking on tiptoes. Before using equipment that confines children (indoors or out), check with your state and local licensing regulations.

Creating multilevel spaces inside and outside provides additional ways for the children to explore their bodies in space. Playscapes, platforms, and lofts, for example, not only provide a quiet space for reading or writing but also offer a different viewpoint of the room and the objects within it (Curtis & Carter, 2003). When standing in a loft, many toddlers are larger than their caregivers for the first time, thus filling them with a new sensation: power!

Another aspect of this principle involves the ability to move easily from one area to another. Learning areas should be well defined but have clear traffic paths between them. These paths afford the children spaces to engage deeply in their work with minimal interruptions from those seeking new experiences (Marion, 2007).

Documentation

Do the important adults in my life communicate about me frequently? Some classroom space should be dedicated to communicating and record keeping, because reciprocal relationships are built on open, ongoing communication among the adults in the children's lives (Copple & Bredekamp, 2009). Adults require comfortable places to read and send messages, record observations, and store or display documentation about each child, such as portfolios or panels. Returning to the example provided in the "Relationship" section above, the teacher also used his entryway as a place for providing written communication with families. Beside one chair, he placed a basket that held the home-school journals (see Chapter 5). In addition, he had a bookshelf where all of the children's portfolios were stored. The table provided space for him to spread out artifacts collected over the week and make decisions about what to add to the portfolio.

Senses

Is the environment warm and welcoming—a place that I want to spend four to ten hours of my day? The environment should be pleasing to the senses. There needs to be a balance of hard and soft, rough and smooth, novel and familiar, simple and complex, quiet and noisy (Bergen, Reid, & Torelli, 2001). Neutral or natural tones are preferable for both furniture and walls. Young children bring plenty of color to the environment; their natural beauty should be a focal point rather than having it compete with "loud background noise."

The principle of the senses also includes the use of natural light. As often as possible, rely on natural sunlight to supply lighting for the classroom, since it

A developmentally appropriate environment supports young children in making decisions and in doing things alone.

is less harsh on the senses for you and the children. However, when this is not possible, you can provide additional lighting in the form of lamps. Place them on shelves, end tables, or on the floor to create smaller areas for work and gatherings. Avoid relying on overhead, fluorescent lighting, which tends to be less warm and welcoming.

To provide complexity and aesthetic pleasure, you can include paintings, sculptures, or photographs in the environment (Curtis & Carter, 2003). Pillows, nontoxic potted plants, and fabrics can also be used to soften the environment and lower the height of the ceiling. Moreover, scented potpourri, oils, or plug-ins (kept out of the reach of the children, of course) can be used to provide a pleasant aroma.

You also need to provide opportunities for infants and toddlers to explore and learn using their senses. You can't be afraid to get dirty or to let the children get dirty. For example, imagine that an older infant is crawling outside on a small mound of dirt. She repeatedly pats the dry dirt flat. If you pour a bit of water in one area to see how she responds, she is likely to squish the mud between her fingers and giggle in delight. Adding water may make the child dirtier, but enhances the experience for her.

Representation

Can I tell you in multiple ways about my understanding of and theories about the world? Children need multiple opportunities to express their current understanding of the world. Representation of ideas can occur through painting, drawing, dramatic play, music, writing, sculpting, or any of the other "hundred languages" (New, 2003; Edwards, Gandini, & Forman, 1998). The environment, then, needs to provide space and open-ended materials for these purposes.

Independence

Can I do things myself? Children desire independence. This is a natural and healthy aspect of social-emotional development. A developmentally appropriate environment supports young children in making decisions, doing things alone, solving problems, and regulating their own behavior (Marion, 2007; Copple & Bredekamp, 2009). Use care in selecting where to place materials, supplies, and learning areas, since this is one way to foster independence. As mentioned previously, displaying materials and supplies in baskets or clear containers on low shelves allows children to select and clean up materials, with assistance from others (Isbell & Exelby, 2001; Marion, 2007).

Careful placement of learning centers adds to this sense of independence. One toddler teacher placed her easel on the tile floor closest to the sink. Not only was this more convenient for her, but it also encouraged the children to take responsibility for cleaning up spills or splatters. In the beginning of the year, she discussed with children where paper towels and sponges were kept, while assisting them in cleaning up the paint. In no time at all, many of the children were cleaning up after themselves, oftentimes without even notifying her.

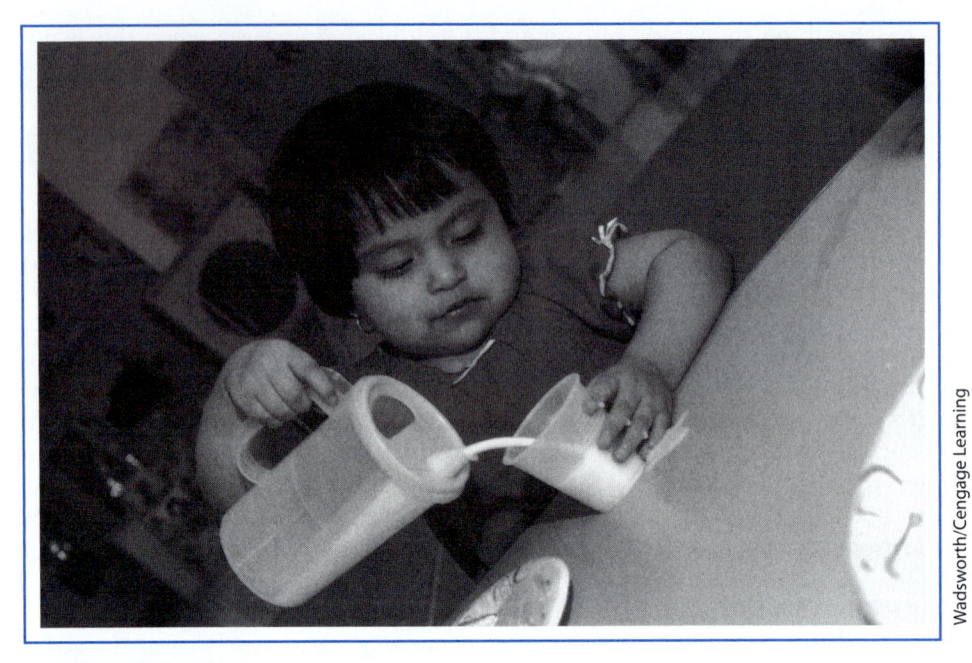

Plan for independence.

Discovery

Can I find interesting things to examine closely and learn about? As mentioned in the "Senses" section, the environment needs to provide a balance of novel and familiar materials, permitting new discoveries that keep the learners engaged. Providing unique things to explore, examine, and learn about does not have to be expensive. Arranging familiar materials in a new location or display is one technique for renewing interest. Another method to cultivate interest in infants and toddlers is to offer treasures or items from nature that they can explore and investigate (McHenry & Buerk, 2008). Rocks, feathers, flowers, tree branches, and things that sparkle or shine are all worthy of investigation (Curtis & Carter, 2003). In addition, providing recycled or found materials in aesthetically pleasing arrangements or containers provokes children to think about them in new ways (Topal & Gandini, 1999). The intention is to help the children with "finding the extraordinary in the ordinary" (L. Gandini, personal communication, January 26, 2001). Of course, remember to examine each item or material carefully for sharp edges and the like to ensure that it is safe for the infants and toddlers.

Before moving on to the last perspective on environmental design, we want to recap using Table 8-1, the major components from the first two perspectives: teacher and child.

chapter 8 THE INDOOR AND OUTDOOR LEARNING ENVIRONMENTS

TABLE 8–1	KEY ASPECTS OF ENVIRONMENTAL DESIGN BY PERSPECTIVE
Teacher's Perspective	Learning Centers
	Real Objects vs. Open-ended materials
	Independence vs. Dependence
	Use of Space
	Messy vs. Dry
	Noisy vs. Quiet
	Calm, Safe Learning Environment
	Novel vs. Familiar
	Pathways vs. Boundaries
	Basic Needs
	Eating vs. Toileting
	Sleep and Comfort vs. Play
Child's Perspective	Transparency
	Flexibility
	Relationships
	Identity
	Movement
	Documentation
	Senses
	Representation
	Independence
	Discovery

reading checkpoint

Before moving on with your reading, make sure that you can answer the following questions about the material discussed so far.

1. Why is it important to consider the child's perspective when designing a learning environment?

2. What can teachers do to make sure that a given environment addresses a given child's development and learning?

SOCIETY'S PERSPECTIVE

This section focuses on making decisions about the environment that are good for the greater society. In other words, we are asking you to consider ways in which you can "go green" or "reduce your carbon footprint" when working with infants and toddlers in educational settings. Some changes to consider might seem very small and others more than a teacher can do alone. That is okay. Each teacher has to make changes at her own pace. However, each of us should consider what we can do to make long-term differences in the future world of the infants and toddlers that we work with today. If we don't think big and do our part, we run the risk of permanently changing the earth's climate in negative directions (Sivertsen & Sivertsen, 2008).

Environmental Changes

Teachers can take many steps to build an earth-friendly environment in their learning environments (i.e., indoors and outdoors). One suggestion for reducing energy use in a classroom is to plug appliances such as a CD player, microwave, and computers into one or two plug strips. Turn the strips off at the end of the day. Another idea is to use natural sunlight to light the classroom during the day. This was mentioned earlier as being good for the children, not just the environment. Taylor (2008) provided evidence that older children are able to concentrate better when they are in a green school that utilizes natural light. A logical extension of this finding would be that the infants and toddlers also learn and grow better in natural light. When additional light sources are needed, use lamps with compact fluorescent lightbulbs (CFLs). As CFLs now come in a variety of color spectra, try out a few different types until you find one that you prefer. Some CFLs give off a warm light similar to the old incandescent light bulbs, so they are more pleasing in the environment. In addition, you can consider using light-emitting diodes (LEDs) such as rope lights to provide a small amount of light in specific areas of the classroom. Stringing rope lights around the book corner provides additional light on overcast days and makes the area feel warm and cozy.

Plants were discussed earlier as a way to soften the environment. They should also be included in the environment as a way to improve air quality. Plants naturally clean the air that we breathe. In addition, if you select flowering plants or herbs, they can emit pleasant aromas.

Teachers can also make decisions about how to create recycling areas in their learning environments. In an infant classroom, create the space based on how you use items. For example, it might be most convenient for you to have three containers side by side: one for trash, one for plastic (e.g., baby wipes or baby food containers), and one for glass (e.g., baby food jars). Have small containers near the phone and documentation area to hold recycled paper for writing notes. In a toddler classroom, make an area for recycling containers that the toddlers can access independently or with supervision. For example, you could put a box in the art center to collect paper that can be reused. Help the toddlers to learn to distinguish paper that is reusable from that which should be recycled in another area. At other times, guide the toddlers to place items to be recycled in the proper areas.

Curricular Changes

Many young children grow up in homes where food is purchased entirely from grocery stores and where the outdoors is viewed as a dangerous place. It is our responsibility as educators to help them feel safe and to connect appropriately with nature. Yet, there is so much more to be learned by engaging with nature. Nimmo and Hallet (2008) argue that planting and tending to a garden teach young children about "play and inquiry, safe risk taking, the building of relationships, and deeper understandings of diversity" in nature and society (p. 1). Thus, teachers must intentionally incorporate into their curriculum (to be discussed in the next chapter) opportunities for engaging with nature.

Infants and toddlers explore their world and work hard to understand it and their role within it. As discussed previously, one way to address their interest in the natural world is to create spaces both inside and outside for exploring nature. We would like to suggest here that teaching about the environment goes beyond providing selected items from nature; young children need ongoing, meaningful experiences. To illustrate, you could plant a garden to attract butterflies in your outdoor learning space. You could place magnifying glasses outside for the children to use along with paper and pencils for recording their observations. These experiences over time would afford the children the opportunity to talk about what they see, create hypotheses, and search for answers. For example, if the toddlers notice that the butterflies fly back to the garden each morning, you could ask, "Where do the butterflies go at night?" Together, you could search for answers through observations or in books.

Toddlers are also very interested in how things grow. They cognitively link their own personal experiences to explain their observations of changes in other living things. Growing a vegetable garden is a particularly engaging experience for toddlers because of this interest. You could enlist the assistance of the toddlers to plant fruits and vegetables that the children are familiar with as well as novel ones. Encourage them to assist in tending to the crops, harvesting them, cooking and preparing them, and, of course, eating them. Toddlers understand, albeit in a primitive way, that they eat food in order to grow. You can assist them in discovering that plants need food also. To extend this thinking and further help the environment, you can compost their uneaten food from snack and lunch to enrich the soil. Thus, the toddlers will come to see that they can play an active role in helping to sustain their environment. More importantly, however, learning to care for plants and the environment is part of developing a more disposition to care (Noddings, 2005), and, as the following quote reminds us:

> "The human heart and the environment are inseparably linked together. If you think only of yourself, ultimately you will lose" (Dalai Lama XIV, 2002).

Partnerships and Advocacy

Teachers cannot tackle some of the bigger environmental issues without creating partnerships with family members, colleagues, directors, and/or licensing agents. For example, instead of needing to recycle individual baby food jars, it may be possible to make the baby food in the kitchen at the center or family child care home. Whenever possible, you should shop locally at farmers' markets or directly from farmers to obtain fresh fruits and vegetables in addition to those available at your local supermarket (Marriott, 2008; Taylor, 2008). Clean, cook, and mash the food as necessary before serving it to the children. Involving children in the process also tends to increase their desire to eat the "fruits of their labor," which can be a real benefit if you are introducing new vegetables to a group of toddlers. When you need to begin with frozen vegetables, you can quickly thaw a serving of peas, for example, from the larger package, cook, and then mash them for an infant. Not only would this practice be better nutritionally for the infant, but it would also eliminate the need to recycle jars.

Another option is for child care centers to reduce their reliance on disposable napkins, paper towels, and baby wipes. Much waste is created each day in an infant/toddler classroom. Teachers can rethink their practices to eliminate some of the waste. To illustrate, just imagine how much paper would be saved if you switched to cloth napkins at lunchtime. In addition, instead of cleaning up children with paper products, consider the warmth and softness of a warm, wet washcloth on the skin after snack or lunch. This may also start the soothing, calming process before naptime. When paper products cannot be eliminated entirely, purchase those manufactured with recycled materials, such as office paper products, toilet paper, and paper towels.

Consider all of the waste with each diaper change. Given the yet-unresolved-controversies regarding cloth versus disposable diapers, we just suggest that if a family wants to use cloth diapers, you should make every attempt to support this decision. Consult your local licensing representative for specific procedures that should be followed. Beyond that issue, there are other ways to reduce the use of diaper wipes. When an infant is just wet, it is better for the child's skin to be cleaned with a washcloth that has been dampened with warm water. You could place a lidded clothes basket next to the diaper pail and dispose of the cloth much as you would the soiled diaper. Then, the clothes are washed at the end of each day so that they can be reused.

Child care center and family child care homes should consider speaking with their licensing representatives to find ways to reduce the use of harsh chemicals. According to Taylor (2008), research shows that when hospitals use green cleaning products, patients recover faster and they spend less time in the hospital. It would seem logical that subjecting infants and toddlers to harsh cleaning products, in order to disinfect surfaces, may not be the best option. (Taylor, 2008, also provides a list of cleaning products that are considered environmentally friendly.) In addition,

chapter 8 THE INDOOR AND OUTDOOR LEARNING ENVIRONMENTS

> **TABLE 8-2 CHANGES FOR "GOING GREEN": MAKING A POSITIVE ENVIRONMENTAL IMPACT**
>
> Utilize solar or wind power to provide part of your electricity needs. Research available rebates and incentives at the state and federal levels.
>
> Order an energy audit from your local utility company. Follow as many of the suggestions as you can. For example, install a programmable thermostat to minimize heating/cooling the building at night.
>
> Join a purchasing group with other child care centers/family providers to purchase paper and food items as well as bulk equipment.
>
> Create partnerships with families and local businesses to recycle nonhazardous "beautiful stuff" that can be used in unique ways by the children.
>
> Obtain permission to adopt a section of a local park or community area. With the help of the children and families, plant and maintain flowers, shrubs, and trees.

it is important to remember that washing children's hands with soap and warm water is the best defense against spreading germs. We would suggest avoiding the use of hand sanitizers with very young children.

This section has provided just a few ways to start thinking about how teachers and programs can "go green" to build a more sustainable society for the next generations. Table 8-2 provides a list of suggestions that have the potential to have a greater positive impact on the environment.

✓ reading checkpoint

Before moving on with your reading, make sure that you can answer the following questions about the material discussed so far.

1. What are three things that teachers could do to "go green" in their classrooms?

2. Compare the teacher's perspective, the child's perspective, and society's perspective on environmental design. How are they alike, and how are they different?

ONGOING REFLECTION ON THE PHYSICAL ENVIRONMENT

We hope we have made it clear that an environment should never be considered "finished" or "complete." You should frequently (i.e., at least once a month) consider the primary question of this chapter, "How do teachers create meaningful learning environments that facilitate optimal development for the children?" Regularly review all the ways that the physical environment impacts the children's development and learning and vice versa, because the answer is constantly evolving. Teachers must continually assess and respond to the changing developmental needs and interests of young children.

SELECTING EQUIPMENT AND MATERIALS

Early childhood educators must carefully select the equipment and materials they make available to the children, based on the children's needs and abilities (Table 8–1). For example, with young infants you should have a high chair available for feeding; infants who can sit unassisted skillfully can sit on a low chair at a table. Materials include nesting toys, balls, books, rattles, paper, paint, clay, sand, glue, tricycles, water, boxes, tires, and other items that children use indoors or outdoors.

The following table provides a brief list of materials to use in a child care setting depending on the children's needs (Table 8–2). Kate, for example, may need a toy that puts her into contact with others, such as a beach ball. Another time she may need a soft, cuddly toy that encourages seclusion, such as a teddy bear.

When selecting materials from catalogs, be aware that the age classifications provided will not accurately fit each child. This brings up the crucial distinction between age and individual appropriateness. Caregivers must determine when an item is appropriate for a particular child. Materials may have merit for some children but not others, or for some experiences and not others.

Classical music is a great educational resource because you can select some slow and some fast music. For example, for children 18 to 21 months a great contact activity is to form a circle with classical music playing in the background. Dance with all of the children or use "The Flight of the Bumblebee" (Rimsky-Korsakov) to pretend everyone is a bumblebee buzzing around the room. However, playing this music right before naptime would not serve to assist children with relaxing and transitioning to sleep.

Materials and equipment must be selected with special care because very young children put everything they touch to a hard test: they bite, pinch, hit, fling, bang, pound, and tear at whatever they can. In their exploration, they focus on actions and do not think in terms of cause and effect, so far as use is concerned. Therefore, caregivers must take care to provide only materials and equipment that can safely withstand use by multiple children.

Age-Appropriate Materials

Selection of appropriate equipment and materials involves the caregiver's knowledge of the program goals, the children's needs and interests, the time and space for use, and the budget. With program goals emphasizing holistic development, a variety of items facilitating physical, emotional, social, and cognitive development are needed. Use Table 8–3 to help you visualize which items match a particular category. Some materials attract interest at particular ages. The age groupings in the guide are approximations; an 11-month-old and a 13-month-old may use the same item. The guide will help you see which items a wide age range can use and which ones only a limited age range can use. Each age group needs a variety of items.

TABLE 8–3 BASIC EQUIPMENT FOR INFANTS AND TODDLERS

CHILD CARE CENTER CLASSROOM	CHILD CARE HOME
	Indoor
EATING	
high chairs	low chairs and tables
	booster seats for kitchen and dining room chairs
low chairs and tables	kitchen and dining room table
SLEEPING	
rocking chair	rocking chair
cribs	cribs
cots	family beds and sofa covered with the child's sheet and blanket for naps
TOILETING	
changing table	changing table or counter space in the bathroom for changing
sink and hand-washing supplies	
free-standing potties	diapers, hand washing and storing supplies
supply storage	
toilet seat adapter	toilet seat adapter
steps (if needed at sink)	steps (if needed at sink)
STORAGE	
coat rack	coat rack near door
cubbies	especially designated shelves in the family room, living room, and/or bedroom where books and toys are kept for the child care children
shelves: toys, books	
RECORD KEEPING	
bulletin boards	corked wall and refrigerator door space to exhibit art treasures
record-keeping table, counter	table, counter, drawer
	Outdoor
CLIMBING STRUCTURES	
wood, tile, rubber tires, steps, tied ropes	rubber tires, steps, tied ropes
CONTAINERS	
sand table or box	large plastic trays, pools for sand and water
water table or pool	

Since infants and toddlers interact with their environment through their senses, they need items that stimulate the senses. Remember that children of different ages make use of their senses in different ways. In the first few months of life, infants see many things and need items that stimulate their interest in seeing. They do not have much control of their hands and fingers, so touching is limited to bumping, banging, and finally grasping. A limited number and kind of items are needed to stimulate touching. However, two-year-olds actively use all their senses, so they need a wider range of items to stimulate each of their senses.

Some equipment and materials can be used in only one way; others have flexible uses (refer to the discussion of open-ended materials versus real objects in previous sections). Children and caregivers can adjust and adapt open-ended materials in a variety of ways to facilitate development. Single-use materials are in themselves neither good nor bad, but may be costly.

When initially purchasing equipment for all child care settings, consider buying a **choke tube** (see photo on this page); many states require its use. Toy pieces

Many states require a choke tube in all child care settings.

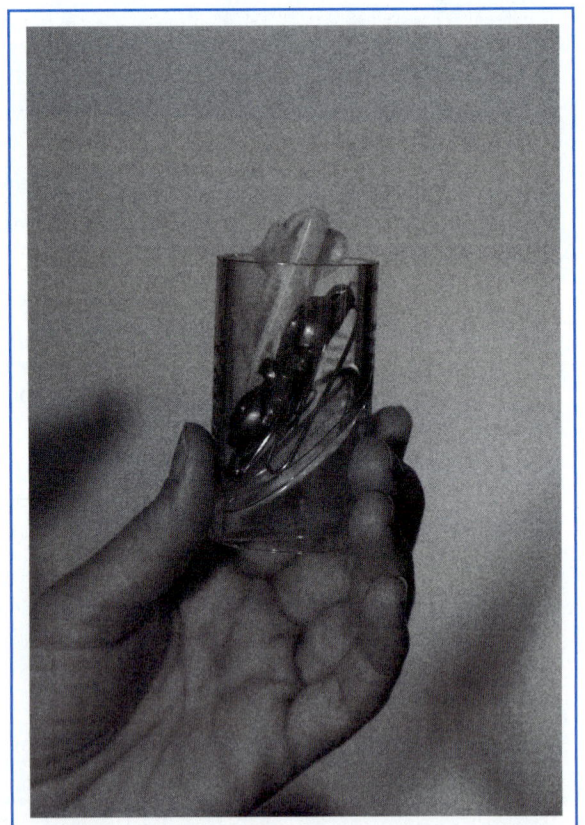

are dropped through an opening in the device; if the pieces go through the tube they are considered a swallowable hazard and are discarded or used only when toddlers are under constant supervision. Toys with pieces larger than the opening are presented to the child as part of the regular learning environment. In other words, items that are not a choking hazard can be put on a shelf for a child to select independently.

It is important to analyze how materials and equipment are constructed. What they are made of and how they are put together will determine their durability when used by the children. This in turn will determine whether the item can serve the purposes for which it is intended in the program. Poorly constructed items that fall apart are frustrating, often unsafe for children, and costly.

All child care programs must consider costs. To determine whether an item is cost effective, analyze the following factors for each item:

- the importance for program goal attainment
- the areas of development facilitated
- the durability of construction
- the number of ways it can be used
- the number of children who can use it
- the ages of children who can use it

A $45 wooden truck that is well constructed may be used for years and years by hundreds of children. In contrast, five $9 plastic trucks will probably be damaged and have to be thrown away within a year or so. Thus, for the same amount of money, the wooden truck would be more cost effective.

The cost of equipment and materials can become astronomical. Therefore, most programs must decide which commercially made items they can purchase and which items they can make themselves. Some maintain that only commercially made equipment and materials have the quality young children require. No child care program can afford to purchase all items, so quality must be built into their homemade items or the program must get along without some things.

Homemade Materials

Homemade items should meet high standards for construction, durability, and safety. Some things we make can be more individualized than commercially prepared items, which stimulates the interest and development of children in the program. For example, a cardboard-mounted color photograph of each child in your room or home is an individual homemade item that will appeal to the children.

Diligent scrounging of free and inexpensive materials from parents, friends, and community businesses and industries can greatly reduce the cost of homemade items. One group that has developed a very creative and beneficial support system to help child care programs locate and use scrounged materials is the Maryland Committee

The refrigerator door becomes a bulletin board in a family child care home.

for Children. In Baltimore, Maryland, it operates reSTORE, a recycling center for discarded or excess industrial materials that can be used by child care providers and parents to provide learning activities for children at a fraction of the usual cost.

Some books and articles are available that specify appropriate homemade materials. Burtt and Kalkstein (1981), Herr and Swim (2002), and Zeller and McFarland (1981) are but a few resources that will help you to match homemade materials, ages, and skill development levels. In addition, Part III of this text includes ideas for homemade materials.

✓ reading checkpoint

Before moving on with your reading, make sure that you can answer the following questions about the material discussed so far.

1. How can caregivers determine whether a piece of equipment or material is useful in the program?

2. List four safety factors caregivers must consider in selecting toys and equipment for infants and toddlers.

3. Describe how a toy or piece of equipment may be safe for one child and unsafe for another.

PROTECTING THE CHILDREN'S HEALTH AND SAFETY

All early childhood education programs must have clearly defined policies and procedures for protecting the children's health and safety. The child care program should be a model for families to duplicate. These policies should be well thought out and designed from the viewpoint of the child and with prevention as the underlying tenet for health and safety.

Policies will need to be determined on such issues as:

- respectful care and treatment of children, families, and staff
- confidentiality of children's records
- detection and prevention of child abuse
- emergency care and training for staff
- communicable diseases
- keeping medical records and files for children and staff (including performance evaluations) up to date

A policy similar to the Back To Sleep Campaign should be in place to protect the safety of infants. This national campaign involves placing babies on their backs to sleep, refraining from smoking around them, laying them on flat, firm mattresses, washing all bedding before using it, removing all articles (including pillows) from cribs, and arranging regular health checkups.

Emergency Procedures

Each program should have policies and procedures in place and practice them regularly to insure that the needs of the children can be immediately and effectively met in the event of natural disasters that are common to the area (e.g., hurricane, tornado) as well as fire. Emergency numbers, evacuation routes, and established meeting places should be up to date and posted in a convenient place for staff to see.

Materials or supplies needed during an emergency, such as fire extinguishers, need to be organized in an accessible location and tested periodically to ensure they are in proper working condition.

Fire drills should be performed, timed, and recorded on a monthly basis. In fact, many state licensing regulations require this. Talk with the children about times when all of you might need to get out of the building quickly; be careful, however, not to scare them. Discuss how the sirens or signals might be loud and hurt their ears. When practicing a fire drill, warn the children in advance to minimize feelings of fright. If you have nonwalkers, select one crib that can fit through doorways, put heavy-duty wheels on it, and put a special symbol on it. In case of fire or during a drill, put the nonwalking children in this special crib and wheel the crib outside. If you have toddlers, hold hands, talk calmly, and walk the toddlers as quickly as possible out of the building to the designated spot.

Immunization Schedule

All children must be immunized before attending a child care program in a center or home. Center policies should reflect the requirements set forth by the appropriate state licensing agency. However, the immunization schedule in Table 8–4, from the American Academy of Pediatrics, provides a general guide of immunizations for very young children.

Signs and Symptoms of Possible Severe Illness

Each center or family home program that provides care to young children must have policies and procedures in place to recognize and respond to illnesses and communicable diseases. Severe illness may be indicated by the following signs and symptoms:

- temperature
- change in typical behavior (e.g., uncontrolled crying)
- unusual lack of movement
- uncontrolled crying
- coughing
- different breathing or wheezing
- uncontrolled diarrhea
- vomiting
- rash
- sores in the mouth
- red conjunctivitis
- head lice

Children who exhibit any of the above symptoms or who demonstrate unusual behavior in relation to any of the above symptoms should be removed to a predetermined place of isolation, where they should be supervised until a parent takes them home. For additional information, contact The American Red Cross, National Headquarters, Health and Safety, 2025 E Street NW, Washington, DC 2006.

Another publication available for health and safety is the *Child Care Health Handbook* published by the King County Department of Public Health in Washington (see "Additional Resources"). You can also contact your local Health Department, or a local registered nurse or pediatrician, who will be happy to help you with additional library source information.

First Aid

First aid refers to treatment administered for injuries and illnesses that are not considered life threatening. While states vary in their laws, the authors believe that all staff members (including cooks and cleaning staff) should be trained in first

TABLE 8–4 TYPES OF EQUIPMENT AND MATERIALS

SOFT	HARD
cloth puppets	blocks
cloth and soft plastic dolls	hard plastic dolls
dress-up clothes	cars, trucks
fur	sand
pillows	paper
mats	cardboard
rugs	books
water	posters
paint	wood
cloth wall hangings	linoleum
cushions	baseballs
ribbon or yarn	plastic bottles
cloth mobile	magazines
rubber balls	buttons
sponge balls	metal cans
cloth or foam scraps	sandpaper

OPEN-ENDED	CLOSED/REAL OBJECTS
clay	puzzle
doll	zipper
water	button/buttonhole
sand	snaps
blocks	stacking rings

SIMPLE	COMPLEX
one-piece puzzle	four-piece puzzle
doll	doll clothes
clay	clothes fasteners

HIGH MOBILITY	LOW MOBILITY
bike	water
toy cars, trucks	slide
stroller, buggy	books
balls	blocks

TABLE 8-5 GUIDE FOR ANALYZING EQUIPMENT OR MATERIALS

ANALYSIS	ITEMS
FACILITATED DEVELOPMENT	**TELEPHONE (EXAMPLE)**
physical	
emotional	
social	X
cognitive	X
AGE GROUP	
0–6 months	
6–12 months	
12–18 months	X
18–24 months	X
24–30 months	X
30–36 months	X
SENSES APPEALED TO	
seeing	
hearing	X
touching	X
tasting	
smelling	
NUMBER OF USES	
single	X
flexible	
SAFETY FACTORS	
nontoxic	X
sturdy	X
no sharp edges	X
CONSTRUCTION	
MATERIAL	
fabric	
paper	
cardboard	
rubber	
plastic	
wood	X
metal	
QUALITY	
fair	
good	
excellent	X
DURABILITY	
fair	
good	
excellent	X
COST—$	
commercial	$15.00
homemade	
COMMENTS:	

TABLE 8-6 RECOMMENDED IMMUNIZATION SCHEDULE

Recommended Immunization Schedule for Persons Aged 0 Through 6 Years—United States • 2009
For those who fall behind or start late, see the catch-up schedule

Vaccine ▼ Age ▶	Birth	1 month	2 months	4 months	6 months	12 months	15 months	18 months	19–23 months	2–3 years	4–6 years
Hepatitis B[1]	HepB	HepB	see footnote 1		HepB						
Rotavirus[2]			RV	RV	RV[2]						
Diphtheria, Tetanus, Pertussis[3]			DTaP	DTaP	DTaP	see footnote 3	DTaP				DTaP
Haemophilus influenzae type b[4]			Hib	Hib	Hib[4]	Hib					
Pneumococcal[5]			PCV	PCV	PCV	PCV				PPSV	
Inactivated Poliovirus			IPV	IPV		IPV					IPV
Influenza[6]						Influenza (Yearly)					
Measles, Mumps, Rubella[7]						MMR		see footnote 7			MMR
Varicella[8]						Varicella		see footnote 8			Varicella
Hepatitis A[9]						HepA (2 doses)				HepA Series	
Meningococcal[10]										MCV	

Range of recommended ages

Certain high-risk groups

This schedule indicates the recommended ages for routine administration of currently licensed vaccines, as of December 1, 2008, for children aged 0 through 6 years. Any dose not administered at the recommended age should be administered at a subsequent visit, when indicated and feasible. Licensed combination vaccines may be used whenever any component of the combination is indicated and other components are not contraindicated and if approved by the Food and Drug Administration for that dose of the series. Providers should consult the relevant Advisory Committee on Immunization Practices statement for detailed recommendations, including high-risk conditions: http://www.cdc.gov/vaccines/pubs/acip-list.htm. Clinically significant adverse events that follow immunization should be reported to the Vaccine Adverse Event Reporting System (VAERS). Guidance about how to obtain and complete a VAERS form is available at http://www.vaers.hhs.gov or by telephone, 800-822-7967.

1. **Hepatitis B vaccine (HepB).** *(Minimum age: birth)*
   At birth:
   - Administer monovalent HepB to all newborns before hospital discharge.
   - If mother is hepatitis B surface antigen (HBsAg)-positive, administer HepB and 0.5 mL of hepatitis B immune globulin (HBIG) within 12 hours of birth.
   - If mother's HBsAg status is unknown, administer HepB within 12 hours of birth. Determine mother's HBsAg status as soon as possible and, if HBsAg-positive, administer HBIG (no later than age 1 week).

   After the birth dose:
   - The HepB series should be completed with either monovalent HepB or a combination vaccine containing HepB. The second dose should be administered at age 1 or 2 months. The final dose should be administered no earlier than age 24 weeks.
   - Infants born to HBsAg-positive mothers should be tested for HBsAg and antibody to HBsAg (anti-HBs) after completion of at least 3 doses of the HepB series, at age 9 through 18 months (generally at the next well-child visit).

   4-month dose:
   - Administration of 4 doses of HepB to infants is permissible when combination vaccines containing HepB are administered after the birth dose.

2. **Rotavirus vaccine (RV).** *(Minimum age: 6 weeks)*
   - Administer the first dose at age 6 through 14 weeks (maximum age: 14 weeks 6 days). Vaccination should not be initiated for infants aged 15 weeks or older (i.e., 15 weeks 0 days or older).
   - Administer the final dose in the series by age 8 months 0 days.
   - If Rotarix® is administered at ages 2 and 4 months, a dose at 6 months is not indicated.

3. **Diphtheria and tetanus toxoids and acellular pertussis vaccine (DTaP).** *(Minimum age: 6 weeks)*
   - The fourth dose may be administered as early as age 12 months, provided at least 6 months have elapsed since the third dose.
   - Administer the final dose in the series at age 4 through 6 years.

4. ***Haemophilus influenzae* type b conjugate vaccine (Hib).** *(Minimum age: 6 weeks)*
   - If PRP-OMP (PedvaxHIB® or Comvax® [HepB-Hib]) is administered at ages 2 and 4 months, a dose at 6 months is not indicated.
   - TriHiBit® (DTaP/Hib) should not be used for doses at ages 2, 4, or 6 months but can be used as the final dose in children aged 12 months or older.

5. **Pneumococcal vaccine.** *(Minimum age: 6 weeks for pneumococcal conjugate vaccine [PCV]; 2 years for pneumococcal polysaccharide vaccine [PPSV])*
   - PCV is recommended for all children aged younger than 5 years. Administer 1 dose of PCV to all healthy children aged 24 through 59 months who are not completely vaccinated for their age.
   - Administer PPSV to children aged 2 years or older with certain underlying medical conditions (see *MMWR* 2000;49[No. RR-9]), including a cochlear implant.

6. **Influenza vaccine.** *(Minimum age: 6 months for trivalent inactivated influenza vaccine [TIV]; 2 years for live, attenuated influenza vaccine [LAIV])*
   - Administer annually to children aged 6 months through 18 years.
   - For healthy nonpregnant persons (i.e., those who do not have underlying medical conditions that predispose them to influenza complications) aged 2 through 49 years, either LAIV or TIV may be used.
   - Children receiving TIV should receive 0.25 mL if aged 6 through 35 months or 0.5 mL if aged 3 years or older.
   - Administer 2 doses (separated by at least 4 weeks) to children aged younger than 9 years who are receiving influenza vaccine for the first time or who were vaccinated for the first time during the previous influenza season but only received 1 dose.

7. **Measles, mumps, and rubella vaccine (MMR).** *(Minimum age: 12 months)*
   - Administer the second dose at age 4 through 6 years. However, the second dose may be administered before age 4, provided at least 28 days have elapsed since the first dose.

8. **Varicella vaccine.** *(Minimum age: 12 months)*
   - Administer the second dose at age 4 through 6 years. However, the second dose may be administered before age 4, provided at least 3 months have elapsed since the first dose.
   - For children aged 12 months through 12 years the minimum interval between doses is 3 months. However, if the second dose was administered at least 28 days after the first dose, it can be accepted as valid.

9. **Hepatitis A vaccine (HepA).** *(Minimum age: 12 months)*
   - Administer to all children aged 1 year (i.e., aged 12 through 23 months). Administer 2 doses at least 6 months apart.
   - Children not fully vaccinated by age 2 years can be vaccinated at subsequent visits.
   - HepA also is recommended for children older than 1 year who live in areas where vaccination programs target older children or who are at increased risk of infection. See *MMWR* 2006;55(No. RR-7).

10. **Meningococcal vaccine.** *(Minimum age: 2 years for meningococcal conjugate vaccine [MCV] and for meningococcal polysaccharide vaccine [MPSV])*
    - Administer MCV to children aged 2 through 10 years with terminal complement component deficiency, anatomic or functional asplenia, and certain other high-risk groups. See *MMWR* 2005;54(No. RR-7).
    - Persons who received MPSV 3 or more years previously and who remain at increased risk for meningococcal disease should be revaccinated with MCV.

The Recommended Immunization Schedules for Persons Aged 0 Through 18 Years are approved by the Advisory Committee on Immunization Practices (www.cdc.gov/vaccines/recs/acip), the American Academy of Pediatrics (http://www.aap.org), and the American Academy of Family Physicians (http://www.aafp.org).

DEPARTMENT OF HEALTH AND HUMAN SERVICES • CENTERS FOR DISEASE CONTROL AND PREVENTION

aid, universal precautions, and cardiopulmonary resuscitation (CPR). Thus, first aid procedures should be based on principles that are familiar to everyone involved in the care setting. Take the following steps in the event of an emergency:

1. Summon emergency medical assistance (call 911 in most areas) for any injury or illness that requires more than simple first aid.
2. Stay calm and in control of the situation.
3. Always remain with the child. If necessary, send another adult or child for help.
4. Keep the child still until the extent of injuries or illness can be determined. If in doubt, have the child stay in the same position and await emergency medical help.
5. Quickly evaluate the child's condition, paying special attention to an open airway, breathing, and circulation.
6. Carefully plan and administer appropriate emergency care. Improper treatment can lead to other injuries.
7. Do not give any medications unless they are prescribed to save a life in certain life-threatening conditions.
8. Do not offer diagnosis or medical advice. Refer the child's parents to health professionals.
9. Always inform the child's parents of the injury and first aid care that has been administered.
10. Record all the facts concerning the accident and treatment administered; file in the child's permanent folder.

As stated above, all early childhood educators should be educated in first aid and keep their certification up to date. Most states grant legal protection to individuals who administer emergency care unless their actions are judged grossly negligent or harmful. This protection is commonly known as the Good Samaritan Law. Many states require a signed Emergency Care Permission form from the parent.

First aid kits should be open, visible, and easily accessible to teachers, but out of the reach of children. Kits should be available in all indoor classrooms and outdoor environments. If the playground is large, you should consider having two kits so they are more easily reached. The contents of first aid kits should reflect your particular state's licensing regulations, but might include:

- adhesive tape
- bandages of assorted sizes
- blanket
- cotton balls
- flashlight
- gauze pads, sterile, 2″ × 2″s, 4″ × 4″s
- hot water bottle

- instant ice pack or plastic bags
- needle, sewing
- roller gauze, 1- and 2-inch widths
- latex gloves
- safety pins
- scissors, blunt tipped
- soap, preferably liquid
- spirits of ammonia
- splints
- thermometers
- tongue blades
- towels, large and small
- tweezers
- vaseline
- first aid book

Universal Precautions

Universal precautions must be understood and used by every person in the care setting who is around body fluids. Medical gloves must be worn every time bodily fluids are present, such as when changing diapers and wiping up spills. Universal precautions are a set of procedures to prevent coming into contact with bodily fluids. It is the responsibility of each caregiver to receive the training and updates necessary to be aware of current policies.

Blood contaminants such as hepatitis B pose a real health threat. Blood fluid (watery discharge from lacerations and cuts) poses a risk of the greatest concern. In addition, hepatitis B can survive in a dried state in the environment for at least a week or even longer. Other fluids, such as saliva contaminated with blood, may contain the live virus. Procedures for handling spills of bodily fluids—urine, feces, blood, saliva, nasal discharge, eye discharge, and tissue discharges—*after putting on the medical gloves*, are as follows:

1. For spills of vomit, urine, and feces: The floors, wall, bathrooms, tabletops, toys, kitchen countertops, and diaper-changing tables should be cleaned and disinfected.
2. For spills of blood or blood-containing bodily fluids, as well as injury and tissue discharges: The area should be cleaned and disinfected.
3. Persons involved in cleaning contaminated surfaces are to avoid exposure of open skin sores or mucous membranes to blood or blood-containing bodily fluids by using gloves to protect hands. Illnesses may be spread in varying ways, such as coughing, sneezing, direct skin-to-skin contact, or touching

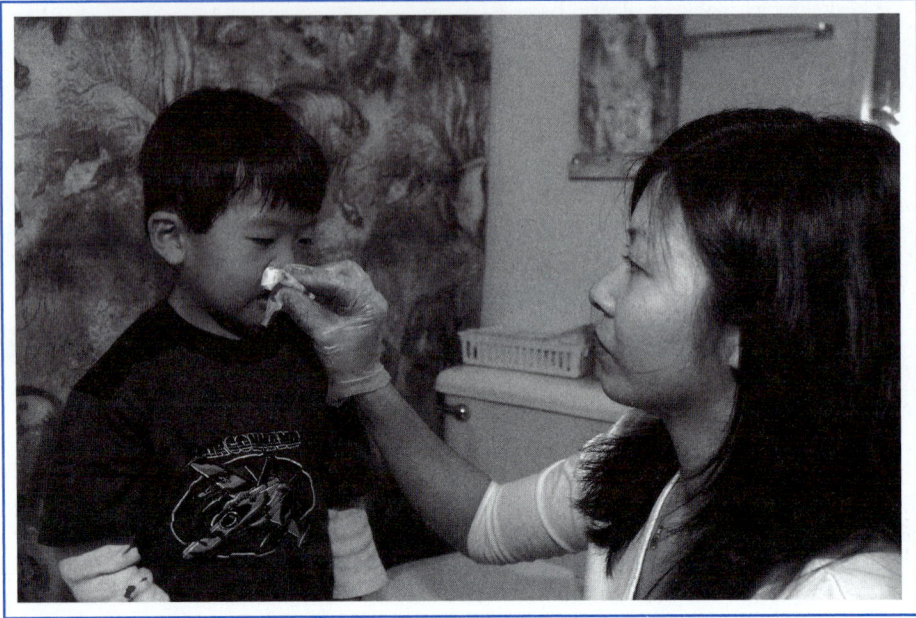

Medical gloves must be worn every time bodily fluids are present.

an object or surface with germs on it. Infectious germs may be contained in human waste (urine, feces and body fluids, saliva, nasal discharge, tissue and injury discharges, eye discharges, and blood). Because many infected people carry communicable diseases without symptoms, and many are contagious before they experience symptoms, staff need to protect themselves and the children they serve by routinely carrying out sanitation and disinfection procedures that prevent every potential illness-spreading condition.

Education of staff regarding cleaning procedures can reduce the occurrence of illness in the entire group of children. Use a solution of 1/4 cup liquid chlorine bleach to one gallon tap water when cleaning contaminated surfaces.

4. Mops should be cleaned, rinsed in sanitizing solution, wrung as dry as possible, and hung to dry.
5. Blood-contaminated material and diapers should be disposed of in a plastic bag with a secure tie, and labeled with a tag.
6. Toys and all equipment should be sanitized, disinfected, and well-maintained. Ensure that frequently used rooms and items are disinfected regularly. Rooms with nondiapered children should be cleaned weekly. Thermometers, pacifiers, and the like should be disinfected between uses.

Individual children's items and travel items for personal hygiene should be sent home with parents to be cleaned weekly, or after each use if more than one child uses a crib. Crib mattresses should be cleaned at least weekly. Each child should have his or her own bed, not to be shared with other children. Regular cleaning of the entire facility should be done weekly.

Hand-washing instructions (see Chapter 9) involve modeling and assisting children in adjusting water temperature and pressure, cleaning palms and backs of hands and wrists, using liquid soap properly, cleaning nails and between fingers, drying hands properly, and disposing of paper towels.

Human Immunodeficiency Virus (HIV) Infection
This infection attacks and destroys white blood cells making the person more susceptible to illnesses. Acquired Immune Deficiency Syndrome (AIDS) is the final stage of the HIV infection. "On the basis of available data, there is no reason to believe H. I. V.-infected adults will transmit HIV. in the course of their normal child duties" (American Academy of Pediatrics, 1996). HIV cannot be transmitted as long as there are no open sores or other blood sources existing. HIV-positive adults may care for children. However, the HIV caregiver is at great risk due to the highly contagious environment that child care settings represent.

Parents of HIV-infected children should be alerted to exposure to such agents as measles and chicken pox. Their pediatrician will probably inject them with an immune booster such as immunoglobulin. Universal precautions are used in every incident of spilled blood or possible blood exposure.

If an HIV-infected child leaves the center due to exposure, the decision to return will be made by the child's pediatrician or nurse practitioner, the parents, and the director of the center. This is also a procedure for a known HIV-infected caregiver. Laws from federal, state, and local authorities are designed to protect families, and confidentiality is a legal right. All information, medical records, and personal information is set aside and kept confidential. No one shall have access to this information unless the parents give written releases. Only staff who have a need to know will be informed. They also must sign a disclosure form that is kept in the child's record.

Injuries
Kennedy (2006) reports that an estimated 205,860 preschool- and elementary-age children receive emergency care for injuries sustained on playground equipment each year. In 2001, the number specifically for preschool children in child care programs was estimated to be 64,000 (Mack, Sacks, Hudson, & Thompson, 2001). Using data available online through the U.S. Consumer Product Safety Commission (2009) in conjunction with those statistics revealed that swings, climbing apparatus (such as monkey bars and gyms), and slides account for many of the injuries (see Table 8-7). The elimination of seesaws and merry-go-rounds from the list is important as it

TABLE 8-7 POPULATION ESTIMATES FOR INJURIES ASSOCIATED WITH PLAYGROUND EQUIPMENT FOR PRESCHOOL CHILDREN (2–5 YEARS OF AGE) BY TYPE OF EQUIPMENT AND BY LOCATION

	SCHOOL NUMBER OF ER VISITS*	POPULATION ESTIMATE	HOME NUMBER OF ER VISITS*	POPULATION ESTIMATES
Climbing Apparatus	292	9,548	62	2,112
Slide	141	4,004	93	2,959
Swings	46	1,489	217	8,403
Playground equipment, not specified	73	2,007	14	n/a
Seesaw	12	n/a	10	n/a
Other playground equipment**	30	n/a	26	n/a

* It is not reliable to attend solely to the raw number of Emergency Room (ER) visits. Rather, the population estimates should be your focus because those estimates, when viewed as reliable, could be extrapolated with confidence from the raw data. When the extrapolation could not be done with confidence, the national estimate is listed as n/a (not applicable).

** Includes figures for merry-go-rounds.

Source: National Electronic Injury Surveillance System (NEISS) On-Line, 1/1/07–12/31/07, U.S. Consumer Product Safety Commission (2009).

reflects concerned effort on the part of playground specialists who petitioned for increased supervision and the elimination of such unsafe equipment. While that is good news, it should still be concluded that the consistency of annual playground equipment-related injuries to children means that we must continue our efforts to prevent such injuries (Vollman, Witsaman, Comstock, & Smith, 2009).

The National Program for Playground Safety (NPPS) provides resources to child care teachers as they work to keep playgrounds safe for children. This organization suggests that when teachers use S.A.F.E., they uphold their responsibility for keeping children safe (NPPS, 2006). S.A.F.E. stands for:

1. SUPERVISION: does not mean standing back and watching. Actively engage in learning experiences with the infants and toddlers to support their play and provide necessary redirection to prevent injuries.
2. AGE-APPROPRIATE: All equipment should be designed for the age of children who are using it. The steps on a slide or a climber, for example, should be spaced at the appropriate distance depending on how long the children's legs are. Of course, just because it is age-appropriate does not always insure that it is individually appropriate. Extra supervision will be necessary in those situations.
3. FALL SURFACE: The American Academy of Pediatrics, American Public Health Association, and the National Resource Center for Health and

Only sterilized sand should be used in sandboxes for children.

Safety in Child Care (2002) suggests these modifications to make safer playgrounds: place climbing structures closer to the ground (i.e., one foot per year of age for intended users); mount them over 9–12 inches of uncompressed, shock-absorbing material such as pea gravel, tree bark, or shredded tires; have enough space (33–75 square feet of space for each child using the playground at any one time, depending on the child's age) to place all equipment far enough away from other structures and child traffic patterns to prevent collisions; cover sharp edges and exposed bolts; and teach children to play safely. Mack et al. (2001) found that child care centers with indoor equipment were using mats designed for exercising or tumbling as fall surfaces. When tested, those mats were found to be insufficient for preventing injuries. Thus, attention to selecting the correct type of fall surface is just as important indoors as out.

4. EQUIPMENT MAINTENANCE: Unsafe climbers, slides, and other playground equipment should be modified or eliminated. All equipment, indoors and outdoors, should be examined daily to insure it is functioning properly and pose no hazards to the children. The Massachusetts Department of Public Health has developed a Site Safety Checklist and a Playground Safety Checklist that can be used or adapted for assessing and providing safe and healthy indoor and outdoor environments for infants and toddlers (see Appendix A).

In addition to the guidelines just mentioned, all staff should be trained in recognizing and locating resources to change hazardous conditions. As a part of this safety training, everyone should also know how to complete an injury reports properly. Then, the reports should be routinely examined to identify and correct trouble spots. A regular, systematic study of injury in child care centers and in home child care is needed to assist adults in making provision for the safe care of children (Aronson, 1983).

✓ reading checkpoint

Before moving on with your reading, make sure that you can answer the following question about the material discussed so far.

1. Explain how universal precautions serve to protect everyone's safety, but especially the caregivers'.

SUMMARY

Teachers must consciously plan to support the physical, social, emotional, and intellectual needs of children. That is why preparing high-quality indoor and outdoor learning environments and selecting appropriate equipment and materials take planning and reflecting. This chapter approached planning environments from three different perspectives: child, adult, and society. These perspectives often work in concert, but at time conflict. You should be able to explain to another person how and why you came to your decisions. Teachers also have to create policies and procedures to protect the health and safety of themselves and very young children.

key terms

choke tube
HIV infection
identity
learning centers
universal precautions

case study   *Ena*

Ena Robson, who was seven-and-a-half months old, had an unusual first day in the group family child care center. One of the helpers got sick in the middle of the day, and another provider was called on to take her place. The first provider had been ready to begin an assessment of Ena, but her replacement was not told of this, so she did not conduct one.

Ena was small, frail, and odd-looking. Her skull was box-shaped, her eyes were set far apart, and her mouth seemed to be in an unusual position when you looked straight at her. She had only a wisp of hair, she was mostly inactive, and her eyes appeared to be slow in reacting to visual changes. On her first day Ena was dressed in a tattered but clean outfit with strawberry patches and a hat.

(Box continues)

case study (continued)

Ena

Since the regular provider was sick again the next day, the director took care of Ena and noted her appearance after checking her medical records. She performed a developmental assessment with the following results.

Physical, cognitive, and language skills were at the four-month level. Her social and emotional skills were at the six-month level. Since there was a significant delay in three areas (two months with a seven-and-a-half-month-old), the director decided that a conference was needed soon so that appropriate referrals for further evaluation could be made.

A conference was arranged with Ena's mother to obtain permission in writing for the referrals. Mrs. Robson arrived with Ena's grandmother, who was a trained nurse's aide, early in the morning for the conference. The director had reviewed the medical and family records in advance and found no unusual medical or family history. Della, Ena's mother, was tall but appeared to have been sick because she needed help walking, had deep circles under her eyes, and had a rather gray color to her skin. Della explained that Ena had experienced many fevers off and on but that she was well at present. The director began asking questions from an interview form, and after a short time Della became visibly stressed. Her voice changed, her arms and hands waved when she spoke, and she refused to answer questions about the pregnancy and Ena's birth. When the director rephrased the question to ask if Ena was a full-term baby, Mrs. Robson became agitated and Ena's grandmother answered in a calm voice that it would probably be best if they stopped the conference but that she would like to set up an evening appointment. A home visit was scheduled for that evening in Ena's home, and her grandmother said she would speak to Della in the meantime.

The apartment where Della and Ena lived was small and sparsely furnished. The grandmother and a registered nurse were administering an intravenous injection to Mrs. Robson when the director arrived. When Mrs. Robson saw the director, she began to cry, and Ena's grandmother sadly explained that both Della and Ena had AIDS. The director maintained a professional demeanor and actively listened to the grandmother as she discussed her sadness, anger, and disappointment. It was obvious that both Della and her mother were very fearful that the director would not allow Ena to stay in the child care setting. The director learned that Della's disease was progressing rapidly in spite of medications, and that Ena would start on medication the next day. Both Della and her mother asked the director to please keep Ena.

The director assured them that they would keep Ena in the child care center as long as she was not running a fever or showing other disease complications. She assured the family that all of her staff used universal precaution techniques, and they were all aware that blood was the only transmitter of the disease. She reassured the family that her staff would hold, feed, and play with Ena in both the indoor and outdoor environments. They discussed the importance of administering the medication on a regular basis at the same time of day. As long as Ena was without disease symptoms, the director assured them that Ena was welcome to attend the center. Both Della and her mother were relieved to hear that the staff would keep the illness confidential, since that was permitted by law.

The result of the home visit was that no further referrals were made at that time. The director and teacher decided that Ena might need more time to adjust to her new routine before another assessment could be made. In the meantime, Ena was cared for in both indoor and outdoor environments at the child care center, just like the other children. The staff provided her with more rest and activities to enhance her physical, cognitive, and language skill areas, and Ena showed improvement in her growth and development.

1. Discuss your feelings about working with a child like Ena, who has AIDS. How do you feel you would handle such a responsibility?
2. What tools did the director use to deal with this situation? List them.
3. What information should the caregivers use when selecting equipment or materials for Ena?
4. What other steps or help might the director have provided to this family?

QUESTIONS AND EXPERIENCES FOR REFLECTION

1. Use the Guide for Analyzing Equipment and Materials, Table 8–5, to analyze five pieces of equipment and five materials used indoors, along with five pieces of equipment and five materials used outdoors in a child care setting.

2. Observe two children playing with materials. Write down the actions of each child as he or she manipulates the objects. Are the objects age appropriate?

3. Observe and sketch the basic layout of an infant-toddler classroom, including all attached spaces that are used throughout the day, such as a child bathroom or covered patio area. Also, indicate on your sketch the location of electrical outlets, partitions, and other permanent structures or furniture that cannot be moved (e.g., a classroom sink with surrounding cabinets), as well as the type of floor covering. After leaving the classroom, evaluate the layout from both the teacher's and the children's perspectives.

4. How are the teacher's and child's perspectives in agreement about planning learning environments? Discuss your responses with a colleague.

5. Draw a diagram of the playground arrangement. Identify activity areas. List equipment and materials in each area. Evaluate their appropriateness.

6. Interview a caregiver at a child care program in which age groups share the outdoor space. Describe how that program facilitates playground use and ensures safety.

7. Research grants available for equipment for both indoor and outdoor use.

8. "Go shopping" and "buy" all the fine motor equipment and materials a group of 24-month-olds will need (use supply catalogs from companies such as Child Craft and Community Playthings) and give yourself a realistic budget to work with.

REFERENCES

American Academy of Pediatrics, American Public Health Association, and National Resource Center for Health and Safety in Child Care. (2002). *Caring for our children: National health and safety performance standards: Guidelines for out-of-home child care programs (2nd ed.).* Elk Grove Village, IL: American Academy of Pediatrics and Washington, DC: American Public Health Association. Also available at http://nrc.uchsc.edu

Aronson, S. S. (1983). Injuries in child care. *Young Children, 38*(6), 19–20.

Bergen, D., Reid, R., & Torelli, L. (2001). *Educating and caring for very young children: The infant/toddler curriculum.* New York: Teachers College Press.

Bove, C. (2000). *Inserimento*: A strategy for delicately beginning relationships and communication. In L. Gandini & C. P. Edwards (Eds.), *Bambini: The Italian approach to infant/toddler care.* New York: Teachers College Press.

Brown-DuPaul, J., Keyes, T., & Segatti, L. (2001, Summer). Using documentation panels to communicate with families. *Childhood Education,* 209–213.

Burtt, K. G., & Kalkstein, K. (1981). *Smart toys.* New York: Harper & Row.

Consumer Product Safety Commission. (2001). Publication 35: *Playground equipment injury.*

Consumer Product Safety Commission. (2003). Publication 325: *Playground safety.* Available at http://www.cpsc.gov/CPSCPUB/PUBS/325.pdf

Copple, C., & Bredekamp, S. (Eds.). (2009). *Developmentally appropriate practice in early childhood programs (3rd ed.).* Washington, DC: National Association for the Education of Young Children.

Curtis, D., & Carter, M. (2003). *Designs for living and learning: Transforming early childhood environments.* St. Paul, MN: Redleaf Press.

Cutler, K. (2000). Organizing the curriculum storage in a preschool/child care environment. *Young Children, 55*(3), 88–92.

DeBord, K., Hestenes, L. L., Moore, R. C., Cosco, N., & McGinnis, J. R. (2002). Paying attention to the outdoor environment is as important as preparing the indoor environment. *Young Children, 57*(3), 32–34.

Dalai Lama (2002). *The heart of compassion.* Twin Lakes, WI: Lotus Press.

Da Ros-Voseles, D., & Fowler-Haughey, S. (2007). Why children's dispositions should matter to ALL teachers. *Beyond the Journal: Young Children on the Web.* Retrieved March 11, 2009, from http://journal.naeyc.org/btj/200709/pdf/DaRos-Voseles.pdf

Edwards, C., Gandini, L., & Forman, G. (Eds.). (1998). *The hundred languages of children: The Reggio Emilia approach—Advanced reflections* (2nd ed.). Westport, CT: Ablex.

Essa, E., Favre, K., Thweatt, G. & Waugh, S. (1999). Continuity of care for infants and toddlers. *Early Child Development and Care, 148,* 11–19.

Forman, G., & Fyfe, B. (1998). Negotiated learning through design, documentation, and discourse. In C. Edwards, L. Gandini, & G. Forman (Eds.), *The hundred languages of children: The Reggio Emilia approach—Advanced reflections* (2nd ed.). Westport, CT: Ablex.

Galardini, A., & Giovannini, D. (2001). Pistoia: Creating a dynamic, open system to serve children, families, and community. In L. Gandini & C. P. Edwards (Eds.), *Bambini: The Italian approach to infant/toddler care.* (pp. 89–105) New York: Teachers College Press.

Gandini, L. (1998). Educational and caring spaces. In C. Edwards, L. Gandini, & G. Forman, *The hundred languages of children: The Reggio Emilia approach—Advanced reflections* (2nd ed.). Westport, CT: Ablex.

Greenman, J. (2005, May). Places for childhood in the 21st century: A conceptual framework. *Beyond the Journal: Young Children on the Web.* Retrieved January 9, 2007, from http://www.journal.naeyc.org/btj/200505/01Greenman.pdf

Herr, J., & Swim, T. J. (2002). *Creative resources for infants and toddlers* (2nd ed.). Clifton Park, NY: Delmar Learning.

Honig, A. S. (2002). *Secure relationships: Nurturing infant/toddler attachment in early care settings.* Washington, DC: National Association for the Education of Young Children.

Isbell, R., & Exelby, B. (2001). *Early learning environments that work.* Beltsville, MD: Gryphon House.

Kennedy, (2006). Playgrounds: A commitment to safety can help schools prevent injuries. *American School & University, 78*(11), 16.

Mack, M., Sacks, J., Hudson, S., & Thompson, D. (2001). The impact of attenuation performance of materials under indoor equipment in child care centers. *Injury Control and Safety Promotion, 8*(1), 45–47.

Malaguzzi, L. (1998). History, ideas, and basic philosophy: An interview with Lella Gandini. In C. Edwards, L. Gandini, & G. Forman (Eds.), *The hundred languages of children: The Reggio Emilia approach—Advanced reflections* (2nd ed.). Westport, CT: Ablex.

Marion, M. (2007). *Guidance of young children* (7th ed.). Upper Saddle River, NJ: Prentice Hall.

Marriott, S. (2008). *Green baby.* NY: Dorling Kindersley.

McHenry, J. D., & Buerk, K. J. (2008). Infants and toddlers meet the natural world. *Beyond the Journal: Young Children on the Web.* Retrieved March 11, 2009, from http://journal.naeyc.org/btj/200801/pdf/BTJNatureMcHenry.pdf

New, R. (1998). Theory and praxis in Reggio Emilia: They know what they are doing, and why. In C. Edwards, L. Gandini, & G. Forman (Eds.), *The hundred languages of children: The Reggio Emilia approach—Advanced reflections* (2nd ed.). Westport, CT: Ablex.

New, R. (2003). Reggio Emilia: New ways to think about schooling. *Educational Leadership, 60*(7), 34–38.

Nimmo, J., & Hallet, B. (2008). Childhood in the garden: A place to encounter natural and social diversity *Beyond the Journal: Young Children on the Web.* Retrieved March 11, 2009, from http://journal.naeyc.org/btj/200801/pdf/BTJNatureNimmo.pdf

Noddings, N. (2005). *The challenge to care in schools: An alternative approach to education* (2nd ed). NY: Teachers College Press.

Project Zero and Reggio Children (2001). *Making learning visible: Children as individual and group learners.* Reggio Emilia, Italy: Reggio Children srl.

Sivertsen, L., & Sivertsen, J. (2008). *Generation green: The ultimate teen guide to living an eco-friendly life.* NY: Simon Pulse.

Smith, C. (1998). Children with "special rights" in the preprimary schools and the infant-toddler centers of Reggio Emilia. In C. Edwards, L. Gandini, & G. Forman (Eds.), *The hundred languages of children: The Reggio Emilia approach—Advanced reflections* (2nd ed.). Westport, CT: Ablex.

Swim, T. J. (2003). Respecting infants and toddlers: Strategies for best practice. *Early Childhood NEWS, 15*(3), 16–23.

Swim, T. J. (2004). Theories of child development: Building blocks of developmentally appropriate practices. *Early Childhood NEWS, 16*(2), 36–45.

Stephenson, A. (2002). Opening up the outdoors: Exploring the relationship between the indoor and outdoor environment of a centre. *European Early Childhood Education Research Journal, 10*(1), 29–38.

Sutterby, J. A., & Frost, J. L. (2002). Making playgrounds fit for children and children fit for playgrounds. *Young Children, 57*(3), 36–41.

Taylor, N. H. (2008). *Go green: How to build an earth-friendly community.* Layton, UT: Gibbs Smith.

Topal, C. W., & Gandini, L. (1999). *Beautiful stuff: Learning with found materials.* Worcester, MA: Davis.

Torquati, J., & Barber, J. (2005). Dancing with trees: Infants and toddlers in the garden. *Young Children, 60*(3), 40–46.

Turner, T., & Krechevsky, M. (2003). Who are the teachers? Who are the learners? *Educational Leadership, 60*(7), 40–43.

Vollman, D., Witsaman, R., Comstock, R. D., & Smith, G. A. (2009). Epidemiology of playground equipment-related injuries to children in the United States, 1996-2005. *Clinical Pediatrics, 48* (1), 66–71.

Wien, C. A., Coates, A., Keating, B., & Bigelow, B. C. (2005, May). Designing the environment to build connection to place. *Beyond the Journal: Young Children on the Web.* Retrieved January 9, 2007, from http://www.journal.naeyc.org/btj/200505/05Wien.pdf

Zeller, J. M., & McFarland, S. L. (1981). Selecting appropriate materials for very young children. *Day Care and Early Education, 8*(4), 7–13.

ADDITIONAL RESOURCES

Colker, L. J. (2005). *The cooking book: Fostering young children's learning and delight.* Washington, DC: National Association for the Education of Young Children.

Greenman, J. (2005, May). Print and online resources on environments that support exploring, learning, and living. *Beyond the Journal: Young Children on the Web.* Retrieved January 9, 2007, from http://www.journal.naeyc.org/btj/200505/06Resources.pdf

Johnson, J. E., Christie, J. F., & Wardle, F. (2005). *Play, development, and early education.* Boston: Pearson.

Sanders, S. W. (2002). *Active for life: Developmentally appropriate movement programs for young children.* Washington, DC: National Association for the Education of Young Children.

Van Hoorn, J., Nourot, P. M., Scales, B., & Alward, K. R. (2006). *Play at the center of the curriculum* (4th ed.). Upper Saddle River, NJ: Prentice Hall.

Wright, R. T. (2008). *Environmental science: Towards a sustainable future* (10th ed.). Upper Saddle River, NJ: Pearson Prentice Hall.

For additional activities, web links, and other resources, please visit our website at www.cengage.com/education/swim

chapter 9

DESIGNING THE CURRICULUM

learning objectives

After reading this chapter, you should be able to:

- Identify major influences on the curriculum.
- Examine the caregiver's role in curriculum development.
- Distinguish two components of curriculum for infants and toddlers.
- Create individualized curricula for a group of infants and toddlers.
- Write daily or weekly (integrated) lesson plans.

chapter outline

- Infant-Toddler Curriculum
- Influences on the Curriculum
- Routine Care Times
- Planned Learning Experiences
- Case Study: Lukaz

INFANT-TODDLER CURRICULUM

We have already discussed how teachers actively construct the physical and social environments for infants and toddlers. Now, we will turn our attention to the intentional design of the intellectual environment. **Curriculum** is everything that you do with a child or that a child experiences through her interactions with the environment from the time she enters the classroom until the time she leaves it (Greenman & Stonehouse, 1996). While this definition may seem simplistic, it is rather complicated because it causes you to consider all of your actions and reactions throughout the day.

You should plan curriculum based on what you know about each child's development; that is, what the child can do now independently and what he can do with assistance. Your teaching or caregiving strategies should scaffold or challenge the child to move toward the next level.

Infants and toddlers participate actively in selecting their curriculum and initiating their activities. When Jessie babbles sentence-like sounds and then pauses, Ms. Howard looks over at her, smiles, and answers, "Jessie, you sound happy today. That is a pretty red ring in your hand." Jessie is playing with a large, colored plastic ring that Ms. Howard has set near her. Jessie determines what she will do with the ring and what she will say. Her sounds stimulate Ms. Howard, who makes a conscious choice to respond, reinforcing the child's competence as a communicator (Figure 9–1). Daily experiences provide an integrated curriculum for children actively involved with themselves and the world around them. All are parts of the curriculum.

In Figure 9–1, Ms. Howard (caregiver) offers choices to the child. Then, Jessie (the child) chooses—makes a decision to play with the toy the way she wants to, is self-stimulated, and looks to the caregiver and vocalizes sounds. In response to Jessie's behaviors, Ms. Howard is stimulated and motivated to respond.

Since the infant and toddler curriculum involves the whole child, the child should have experiences that enhance his or her physical, emotional, social, and cognitive/language development. The caregiver is responsible for planning and facilitating this holistic curriculum.

Each child is a distinct being, differing from others in some ways, yet sharing many of the same basic needs. *There is no single curriculum for all infants.* Caregivers have a special responsibility to design each child's curriculum by observing, thinking, and planning. We must compile many different skills and information, using a developmental perspective as a framework and analyzing observational data as the method.

In order to meet the individual needs of infants and toddlers, early childhood educators need to gather observational data continually, analyze it, and use it when selecting materials and planning curricular experiences (see Chapter 5). Thus, careful, ongoing observation on the part of the adults (e.g., caregivers and family members) facilitates child contributions to the curriculum; it is responsive to the needs, abilities, and interests of each child. Daily curriculum should be designed with a purpose in mind. In other words, you should be scaffolding skill development in all areas with the goal of addressing development of the whole child.

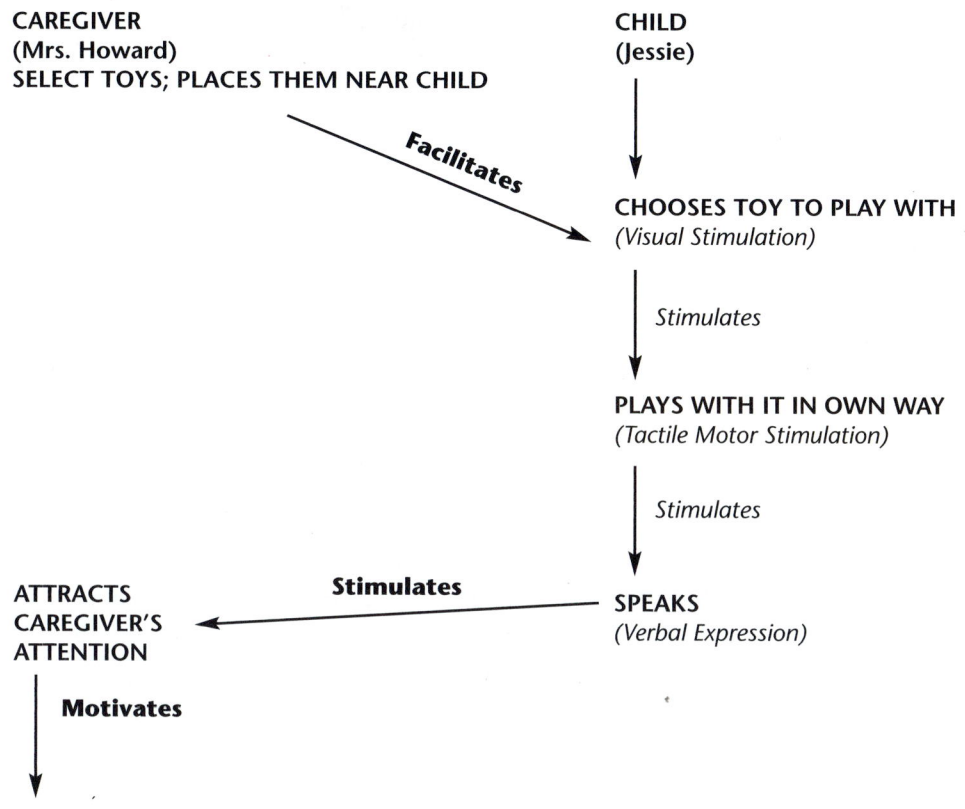

```
CAREGIVER                                    CHILD
(Mrs. Howard)                                (Jessie)
SELECT TOYS; PLACES THEM NEAR CHILD
                    │                          │
                    │    Facilitates           │
                    └──────────────▶  CHOOSES TOY TO PLAY WITH
                                     (Visual Stimulation)
                                              │
                                              │ Stimulates
                                              ▼
                                     PLAYS WITH IT IN OWN WAY
                                     (Tactile Motor Stimulation)
                                              │
                                              │ Stimulates
                                              ▼
ATTRACTS          Stimulates         SPEAKS
CAREGIVER'S   ◀─────────────────     (Verbal Expression)
ATTENTION
    │
    │ Motivates
    ▼
Responds verbally and with smile
```

FIGURE 9–1 An example of an interaction among caregiver, child, and material that individualizes the curriculum

INFLUENCES ON THE CURRICULUM

Society, the setting, the child, and the caregiver all influence the infant and toddler curriculum. Each of these influences on the child is discussed in detail in the following sections.

Influences of Society

Society

As discussed in earlier chapters, aspects of society beyond the family influence the functioning of that family. For example, as you learned in Chapter 6, citizens in Italy have made high-quality child care a priority by voting into law policies for funding such programs. The democratic process allowed the voices of families to be heard. However, this law was not viewed as beneficial only to children and families but rather to society as a whole. "The broad intention is to promote, within a new social welfare system, a relationship between citizens and institutions that allows for shared responsibility among local public and private institutions, nonprofit organizations, and families..." (Ghedini, 2001, p. 45).

In the United States, child care is seen as the responsibility of each individual family. The two exceptions to this trend are for very low-income families who cannot afford to pay for child care and work at the same time and for some corporate workers. Families with low incomes must rely on early childhood education programs to provide quality care at extremely reduced costs. Unfortunately, families often get what they pay for: the ratings of quality in both home- and center-based programs vary significantly based on costs (see, for example, Kontos, Howes, Shinn, & Galinsky, 1995).

Some larger corporations and institutions are beginning to recognize the need for the organization to help workers manage family- and work-life issues. One way in which they have assisted families with this balance is to provide on-site child care centers. Banks, manufacturers, the federal government, school districts, colleges, and hospitals lure new employees with this useful perk. Families particularly like having child care on site, because they can visit their children during their breaks or can be paged when their child is attempting or accomplishing a new task such as a first step or toilet learning. While the decision to offer corporate child care is up to each individual company or institution, a recent president of the United States supported such efforts when he said, "The private sector needs to make an increasing effort to support partnerships between themselves and their employees. Child care is a national concern.... The welfare of tomorrow's business depends on the services offered to today's children" (Clinton, 1997).

Families

Families place children in child care outside their own homes for a variety of reasons. The majority of families do so because the adults work. Since a family's primary goal is to make sure their children are safe in a stable situation they can trust, they are concerned about the physical environment and how it is used.

Family members may share their expectations with caregivers. One aspect of curriculum is to help families meet their needs as they relate to child-rearing and child care. Cultural variations will be evident during your meetings with them. Different family members have different ideas about child-rearing and parenting techniques. The following questions can stimulate varying responses from family members:

- Should a mother breast-feed or bottle-feed?
- How frequently should a family member hold and cuddle the infant?
- Should adults respond immediately to the crying infant?
- When and how should family members talk, sing, and play with the infant?
- What are appropriate mothering (grandmothering) behaviors?
- What are appropriate fathering (grandfathering) behaviors?

Family members also look to teachers to reinforce and extend their own child-rearing practices. They usually convey to the early childhood educator their expectations for their children and their attitudes concerning parenting roles and children's behaviors.

Family members view themselves in various ways. Some family members expect to be *perfect* parents. The realities of parenting often cause them to feel guilty when they fall short of perfection or when they turn the child over to the caregiver. Their frustrations may affect their attitudes about themselves and their interactions with their children and caregivers. Sometimes jealousies develop. Early childhood educators can help these adults establish more realistic expectations.

Some family members seem very casual. They move in a very offhand way from one parenting task to the next with seemingly little thought of goals or consequences. Some of these family members seem to place their children into child care with the attitude, "Do what you want to with them; just keep them out of my hair." The caregiver may need to emphasize the worth of the child and tell the family how important it is for them to demonstrate in multiple ways how they value the child. Between these two extremes are family members who want to engage in positive parenting behaviors and who look to caregivers to assist them and their children.

Family members will express positive and negative expectations about what the caregiver should do verbally and nonverbally, in direct and indirect ways. They expect caregivers to help their children learn their values and to reinforce behaviors the family approves of. Families expect caregivers to be professionally competent. They place their trust in the caregiver to provide safe, healthy, reliable, affectionate, concerned, and intellectually engaging care and education for their children. Family members have their own ways of judging caregiver competence. Some judgment is intuitive, based on listening to and watching the caregiver with their child, while some judgment is based on what they think is responsible behavior.

Influences from Cultural Expectations

Families feel pressure from their friends and relatives about their own child-rearing activities. They receive comments, praise, suggestions, scolding, and ridicule on a variety of topics. Sometimes they hear conflicting comments on the same topic, such as the following:

- The parent should stay home with the newborn and very young infant vs. It is acceptable for the parent of a child of any age to work outside the home.
- The parents are wasting their time when talking to and playing with a young baby vs. The parents should talk to and play with the infant.
- The infant should start solid foods at four months of age vs. The infant should start solid food at a later age.

Parents must reconcile their attitudes and expectations with those of people around them. This is a long and laborious task that often results in inconsistent

Each infant is a unique being who deserves positive support to remain unlimited and reach his or her full potential.

beliefs and practices. It may seem that parents are wishy-washy or flip-flopping about what they do versus what they want you to do. When you understand the various pressures on families and use active listening, you can help them to resolve these parenting conflicts. Like families, each caregiver brings unique cultural experiences and expectations to the caregiving role. Be aware of how these are similar to or different from those of the families and other staff in order to plan and provide a curriculum acceptable to all.

Cultural Diversity

Caregivers must be sensitive to **cultural diversity**, the cultural differences in the children and families with whom you have contact. If you are embarrassed about discussing differences or prejudices, you might actually help and encourage children to form biases. You could, through omission, perpetuate oppressive beliefs and behavior (Jones & Derman-Sparks, 1992).

Child care settings offer many opportunities to experience cultural diversity. In order not to limit young children's beliefs and perceptions, plan activities and experiences that directly include multiculturalism (Turkovich & Mueller, 1989).

Every culture has somewhat different customs, mores, beliefs, and attitudes toward child care. While the style and form may vary from one culture to the next, all cultures have healthy child care practices. An example of different forms is the use of unleavened bread to provide nourishment. In the Mexican culture corn flour is made into tortillas, in Sweden and Norway people eat a flat wheat bread, and in China and India, rice is used. An example of different styles are the bright, contrasting colors of some cultures and the more subdued hues of other cultures. Each style is important and valuable to the people who practice it.

Prejudging the style and forms of a culture is called having bias. To integrate style and form into a curriculum successfully, early childhood educators must be aware of and examine their bias for certain styles and forms. These biases may not be obvious until they are examined carefully, and only then can they be changed.

When working with young children, it is important to be able to relate to each of them without bias or prejudice. Each infant or toddler is a unique being who develops in the same way and deserves the same positive support to remain unlimited and reach his or her full potential.

Some cultures do not talk to young children as much as other cultures. Some do not smile at them or expect a response. Some carry their babies on their backs; other cultures carry them over their hearts. Father involvement is different from one culture to another, as is the way family members interact with each other. Families also differ on how they define independence for their child. Brainstorming and other problem-solving techniques, along with active listening, will help to address any misunderstandings that may occur. Moreover, valuing these differences and working to understand child-rearing practices within every culture is important for becoming a competent early childhood educator. Acceptance of these differences and the ability to perceive healthy child care practices within every culture is important for infant and toddler teachers.

It is crucial that the child care program honor each individual family's sociocultural milieu. Pacific Oaks College, in Southern California, has done exemplary work in their Anti-Bias Curriculum. Merrill Palmer Institute Child Development Lab in Detroit, Bank Street College in New York, and Thomson Delmar Learning in Clifton Park, New York, have also developed materials that focus on cultural diversity. Other resources available for young children and adults include:

Anti-Bias Curriculum: Tools for Empowering Young Children (1989), by Louise Derman-Sparks and the A. B. C. Task Force. Washington DC: National Association for the Education of Young Children.

Beyond the Whiteness of Whiteness: A White Mother of Black Sons (1996), by Jane Lazarre. Durham, NC: Duke University Press.

Creative Resources for the Anti-bias Classroom (1999), by Nadia Saderman Hall. Clifton Park, NY: Thomson Delmar Learning.

Diversity and the New Teacher: Learning from experience in urban schools (2008), by Catherine Cornbleth. NY: Teachers College Press.

Educating citizens in a multicultural society (2nd ed.) (2007), by James A. Banks. NY: Teachers College Press.

Everyday Acts Against Racism: Raising a Child in a Multicultural World (a collection) (1996), by Marian Reddy (Ed.). Seattle: Seal Press.

Roots and Wings: Affirming Culture in Early Childhood Programs (1991), by Stacey York. St. Paul, MN: Redleaf Press.

Teaching/Learning Anti-racism (1997), by Louise Derman-Sparks and Carol Brunson Phillips. New York: Teachers College Press.

What if All the Kids Are White? Anti-bias Multicultural Education with Young Children and Families (2006), by Louise Derman-Sparks and Patricia Ramsey. New York: Teachers College Press.

Child care programs represent stepping stones to the formal education system; therefore they need to create partnerships with families for progressive change. Some school systems have added programs into their curriculum that show great promise for bridging the cultural gap resulting from teacher biases. Early childhood educators need to work with the local school districts to ensure that anti-bias techniques and tools are consistent in the transition from child care to formal schooling. For example, the national **Seeking Educational Equity and Diversity (SEED)** Project on Inclusive Curriculum at Wellesley College prepares teachers to lead year-long seminars in their schools reflecting on local practices. The project, which is in its twenty-third year, helps teachers welcome and respond to all children in a class and deal with student sensitivity to complex identity matters, such as race and gender.

Andrea King, director of the Easter Seals California Child Development Center Network, discussed providing culturally consistent care (2001). She tells us that the 'Anti-Bias' movement asks us to acknowledge that each of us is biased toward what we have always known or our own experiences. We must find ways to be open to looking at other ways of doing things that might be equally valid. We are asked to tolerate each other by considering people who are different from us and ideas that are different from ours, and finding ways of living together.

In her discussion of cultural empowerment she presented six guidelines:

1. Culture is learned. Children learn rules both directly by being taught ("Hold your fork in your left hand and your knife in your right") and through observation. It can be a mistake to assume a person's culture from his or her appearance.
2. Culture is characteristic of groups. Cultural rules come from the group and are passed from generation to generation; they are not invented by the

individual. Do not mistake individual differences for cultural differences. We share some characteristics with our cultural group, but we are also defined by our individual identities.

3. Culture is a set of rules for behavior. Cultural rules influence people to act similarly, in ways that help them understand each other. For instance, how we greet and address each other is influenced by our cultural backgrounds. Culture is not the behavior, but the rules that shape the behavior.
4. Individual members of a culture are embedded to different degrees within their culture. Because culture is learned, people learn it to different degrees. Family emphasis, individual preferences, and other factors influence how deeply embedded one is in one's culture.
5. Cultures borrow and share rules. Every culture has a consistent core set of rules, but they are not necessarily unique. Two cultures may share rules about some things, but have very different rules about other things. This gets very confusing for a person operating within two cultures that have some similarities and some differences.
6. Members of culture groups may be proficient at cultural behavior but unable to describe the rules. Because acculturation happens gradually, as a natural process, a person may not even be aware of the consistent rules that govern his/her behavior. Just as a four-year-old who speaks very well may not know the technical rules of the language, people who are culturally competent may not know that they are behaving according to a set of cultural rules. They have simply absorbed the rules by living with them. However, teachers must do the extra work to reflect on and identify the cultural rules, beliefs, and practices that they bring to their work (Im, Parlakian, & Sanchez, 2007).

Influences from the Care Setting
Family Child Care Home

Influences of the setting on your curriculum are varied. Physical location, financial limitations, family work schedules, and other factors influence the schedule, environment, and curriculum in family child care homes. Establishing a positive learning environment is essential to quality care no matter which resources and limitations you find in your particular setting. Establishing a consistent, warm, friendly environment where large doses of the three *A*s (Attention, Approval, and Attunement) are administered is the way to create the most powerful positive influence in any physical setting.

Family child care homes provide a homelike situation for the infant or toddler. During the transition for a child to a new caregiver and a new situation, the caregiver should quickly establish a setting that is familiar to the child: crib, rooms, and routines of playing, eating, and sleeping. A warm one-on-one relationship between the teacher and the child provides security in this new setting.

part 2 ESTABLISHING A POSITIVE LEARNING ENVIRONMENT

Child Care Center

Some child care centers care for infants six weeks of age and older, and a few centers are even equipped to care for newborns. The very young infant must receive special care. One caregiver in each shift needs to be responsible for the same infant each day. The caregiver should adjust routines to the infant's body rhythm rather than trying to make the infant eat and sleep according to the center's schedule. The early childhood educator will need to work closely with family members to understand the infant's behavior and changing schedule of eating and sleeping. Consistently recording and sharing information with the family is necessary to meet infant needs and involve the family in their child's daily experiences.

Time

The number and age of children in a group will affect the amount of time the caregiver has to give each child. The needs of the other children also affect how the time is allocated. Schedules in the child care home or center should be adjusted to meet the children's needs and the family members' employment schedules. For instance, if the father works the 7 a.m. to 3 p.m. shift, special planning may be required for the infant who awakens from a nap at 2:45 p.m. to be ready when he arrives. Through the use of attunement, the quality of interaction can remain high, even when time for interaction is limited.

Educational Philosophy of Program and Teachers

The *philosophy* of the program needs to be clearly articulated to teachers and families. Educational decisions should be evaluated in light of the program's philosophy. However, philosophy statements are often broad leaving much room for interpretation. This is where your personal philosophy, or *image of the child*, comes into play. You must consider your beliefs and how they apply to daily interactions with children, family members, and colleagues. The authors have spent considerable time pondering the educational philosophies that serve as the basis for this book. They are as follows:

1. All people are viewed developmentally. From the moment of birth to the time of death every person is constantly growing in many ways. Focusing on the positive changes resulting from growth helps maintain a positive learning environment.
    a. Each infant and toddler is progressing through specific sequences or stages of development at his or her own rate.
    b. Parenting styles differ: some are new parents, some are experienced, some anxious, some relaxed, some informed, some nonchalant, and some eager.
    c. Each family member adds to his or her knowledge and skills. Each caregiver has his or her own level of competence too. Caregivers have knowledge obtained from talking, reading, and studying, as well as individual experiences with children and families. Their views and expectations of themselves as people and caregivers all contribute to their increasing competence as caregivers.

2. Development and growth occur through active interaction with one's environment and can be observed through the four major Developmental Areas. Each person
   a. is an active learner with rights and responsibilities.
   b. constructs knowledge through active interactions with people and materials.
   c. adapts previous experiences to current situations.
   d. builds on the knowledge and skills learned from previous experiences.
   e. initiates interactions with other people.
   f. initiates interactions with materials in the environment.
   g. uses multiple modes of representation to express understanding about the world.

Influences from the Child

Every child has an internal need to grow, develop, and learn. During the first years of life children's energies are directed toward those purposes both consciously and unconsciously. Though children cannot tell you this, observers can see that both random and purposeful behaviors help them.

The children look, touch, taste, listen, smell, reach, bite, push, kick, smile, and take any other action they can in order to involve themselves actively with the world. The fact that children are sometimes unsuccessful in what they try to do does not

The caregiver facilitates each child's development by making the child feel secure.

stop them from attempting new tasks. Sometimes they may turn away and begin a different task, but they will keep seeking something to do.

Infants learn from the responses they get to their actions. When the caregiver consistently answers cries of distress immediately, infants begin to build up feelings of security. Gradually these responses will help infants learn to exert control over their world. If caregivers let infants cry for long periods before going to them, the infants remain distressed longer, possibly causing them to have difficulty developing a sense of security and trust. Remember that the more immediately and completely needs are fulfilled, the more securely and happily children will develop. You can't love or fulfill an infant or toddler too much. Add large measures of the three *A*s to this principle, and the result will be happy and secure children.

Joey, age seven months, is crying hard. After checking to see if he is wet, tired, hungry, too hot, or too cold, Paulette picks him up and holds him close. She walks with him slowly around the room, rocking him gently in her arms. Joey soon calms down. We can see how Paulette's actions influenced Joey. A child can influence her caregiver in many ways as well. Eden, 30 months, has started to hide and make faces during her bowel movements. Mrs. Frank has noticed and recorded it in Eden's daily log. Mrs. Frank soon begins to introduce Eden to toilet learning as a result of the child's own influence.

As you will learn in your day-to-day work with children, influence runs in many directions. The family can influence your behavior just as society can, and all come into play within the four walls of your classroom.

✓ reading checkpoint

Before moving on with your reading, make sure that you can answer the following questions about the material discussed so far.

1. List and explain three influences on the curriculum. Make sure that your answer provides examples from three different types of influences.

2. Write a brief newsletter article for a child care center explaining their approach to cultural diversity.

ROUTINE CARE TIMES

Infants and toddlers have needs that must be met on a regular basis. Some needs, such as eating and eliminating, occur frequently throughout the day. Infant and toddler teachers often think that all they do is feed, rock, and diaper children. Our traditional notion of teaching seems—and is—inappropriate for very young children (Swim & Muza, 1999). That is why our definition of curriculum presented earlier is so important. You must come to understand that everything you do facilitates development and learning. As discussed in previous chapters, using the three *A*s, attention, approval, and attunement, while meeting the basic needs of infants and toddlers promotes optimal development and learning. The following provide examples of ways to organize and plan the routine care times of the curriculum. First, however, we need to discuss daily schedules.

Flexible Schedule

The schedule you create for the day should reflect each individual child's physical rhythms. Thus, your schedule depends on the infant or toddler you are caring for. The goal is not to coordinate the children's physical schedules but rather to have a flexible plan for meeting the needs of the children. During the first months the infant is in the process of setting a personal, internal schedule. Some infants do this easily; others seem to have more difficulty. So when a child is first entering your care, ask family members what the infant or toddler does at home. Write this down to serve as a guideline. Next, observe the child to see whether he or she follows the home schedule or develops a different one.

The daily schedule must be individualized in infant and toddler care. It focuses on the basic activities: sleeping, feeding, and playing. Andrea arrives at 7:45 a.m.; Kevin is ready for a bottle and nap at 8:00 a.m.; Myron is alert and will play until about 9:00 a.m., when he takes a bottle and a nap; and Audrey is alert and will play all morning and take a nap immediately after lunch. As their caregiver, noting these preferences will provide you with guidelines for your time.

Children's schedules and preferences for routines change over time. Each month infants sleep less. This affects when they eat and when they are alert. As infants change their sleeping schedules, they will adjust to allow more time for exploration and engagement with materials. Toddlers will also differ in how much time they spend asleep and awake. Morning and afternoon naps do not fit into a rigid schedule from 8:30 to 9:45 or from 12:00 to 2:00, respectively. You can identify blocks of time for specific types of activities but should keep in mind that no schedule can fit all children.

Arrival Time

During this special time the primary caregiver greets the parent and child and receives the infant or toddler. This is the time for the caregiver to listen to the family member tell about the child's night and about any joys, problems, or concerns. They should write down important details on the message board, for example, "exposed to measles last night."

Arrival time is also a time to help the infant or toddler make the transition from home to school. The caregiver's relationships with the child should provide a calming, comfortable, accepting situation so that the child will feel secure. Touching, holding, and talking with the child for a few minutes helps the child re-establish relations with the caregiver. When the child is settled, the caregiver may move on to whatever activity the child is ready to do.

Sleeping

Most of a newborn's time is spent sleeping, although the time awake gradually lengthens. If you are responsible for several infants or toddlers, plan your time carefully so you are available to help each child fall asleep by providing quiet time, holding, talking, singing, rubbing, and rocking. Make available open-ended materials for the other children who are awake so they will be productively occupied. You control many factors that determine how well a child will sleep, so consider how you separate the sleeping and playing areas of your classroom. Have you blocked sunlight during the afternoon? Do you play calming background music? Each child has preferences that you must learn in order to build your curriculum. Some infants like to be rocked to sleep; some enjoy back rubs. Some prefer to snuggle with a favorite blanket or stuffed animal. Ask family members how they put their child to sleep at home so that you can coordinate your routines at school.

Each child should have a separate crib for sleeping. If children share a crib on different days (e.g., Emily attends Monday and Friday, and Samantha attends Tuesday,

Even though they are the same age, Yolanda takes a morning and afternoon nap, while Simonyi takes only an afternoon nap.

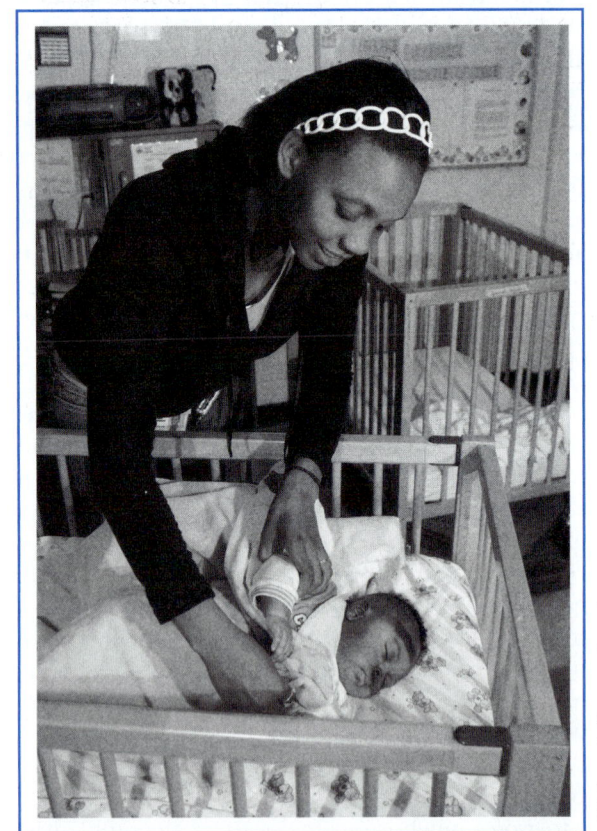

Wednesday, and Thursday), always remove sheets and personal belongings and disinfect the crib between children. Some infants and toddlers have difficulty relaxing and falling asleep. Schumann (1982) has described relaxation techniques she has used with children as young as 18 months old. After creating an environment conducive to sleep, she uses the following procedures. A quiet, steady voice along with stroking facilitates relaxation even when the child may not understand all the words being used.

> Use a quiet even voice to help the children relax each part of their bodies. Repeatedly (six to eight times) state that the body part is "heavy." For some children it may help to stroke firmly with two hands over the body part to be relaxed. Begin with the toes and work up the body in the following fashion: toes, feet, legs, back (or abdomen, depending on position), fingers, hands, arms, shoulders, neck, eyes, lips, and chin. After relaxing each body part, check it to see how successful each child has been. Tenseness is indicated by a raised bulging or rigid muscles or by movement of a muscle or body part. Using firm hands, strive for being able to move the body part yourself at the joint without the child's helping or keeping the area stiff. Give POSITIVE reinforcement for the way you want the body part to be. Explain to the children to let the feet stay "heavy" while you are checking that part. As you move from talking about one body part to the next, keep your voice a continuous monotone rather than pausing. After doing two or three body parts, repeat the idea that the previous ones are still "heavy" also.
>
> For example, "Your toes are heavy. Your toes are heavy. Your toes are heavy. Your toes are heavy." (Check for relaxation, insert positive comment) "Your feet are heavy. Your feet are relaxed. Your feet are heavy. Your feet are heavy." (Check for relaxation, insert positive comment) "Your toes are heavy. Your feet are heavy. Your legs are heavy." By the time each child is told his eyes are heavy, it is likely that he will either already have them closed or be willing to close them at your request.... If a child still seems fairly alert at the end of the toe-to-head release sequence, try repeating the sequence but eliminating touch and checking of the body for relaxation. Some children might require or seek more body contact than others (pp. 17–18).

Waking

Some infants and toddlers wake up alert and happy. Others awaken groggy and crying. You can help ease the infant or toddler into wakefulness. Some you can pick up and cuddle. Talk quietly to them, and move them around so they see things in the room that may be interesting. Usually infants and toddlers need to have their diapers changed or need to go to the bathroom when they wake up. Some infants will be hungry and need a bottle at this time.

Record the child's sleeping time. Family members need to know how long and at what time their child slept, and the caregiver needs to know when each infant or toddler can be expected to sleep. Each infant or toddler in your home or room may have a different nap time.

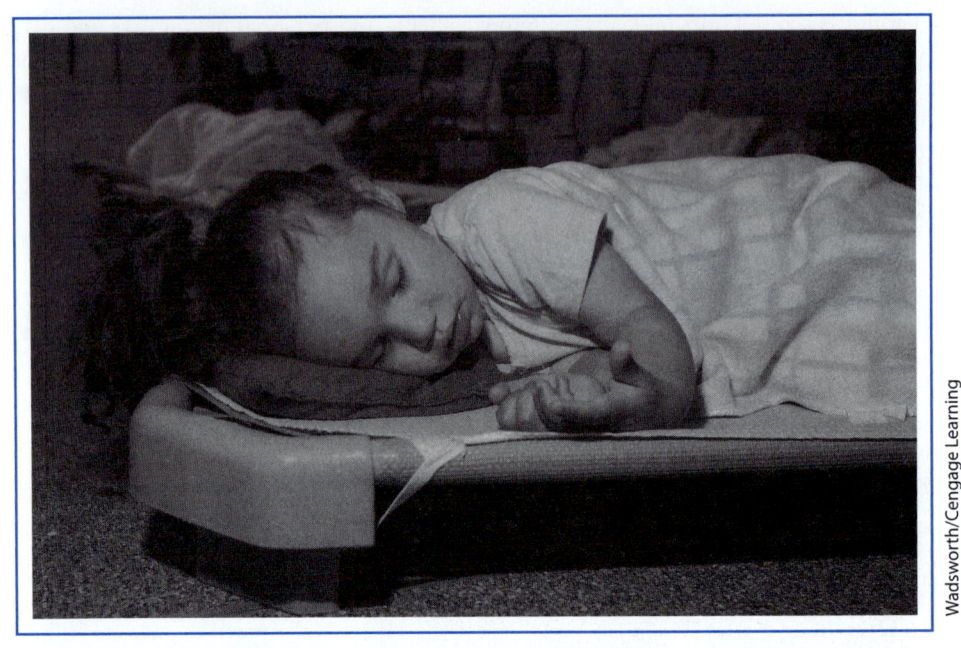

part 2 ESTABLISHING A POSITIVE LEARNING ENVIRONMENT

To help very young children learn that cribs and cots are for sleeping, remove them as soon as they wake.

Eating

The very young infant may eat every two to four hours. They should eat when they are hungry. This is called **demand feeding**. Demand feeding involves more flexibility for the caregiver and is one of the first steps to building a bond between that person and the children in his or her care. It is also the first step toward the child internalizing a sense of trust and security. Ask family members how often the baby eats at home. Infants will tell you when they are hungry by fussing and crying. Learn their individual schedules and their physical and oral signals, so you can feed them before they have to cry. Record the time of feedings and the amount of milk or formula the baby drank.

Hold the infant when you are giving a bottle. This curricular time is to meet the nutritional needs of the child. All food offered to the children should be nutritious. State licensing regulations often provide plenty of information on how to address the children's nutritional needs. (See the "Additional Resources" and "Helpful Web Sites" sections at the end of this chapter for more on nutrition.) But eating is also a curricular time for nurturing physical, emotional, social, cognitive, and language development. There are great advantages to caring for the child consciously. Holding, feeding, relating, maintaining eye contact, and ultimately building a secure foundation for the child are only possible through this type of care.

As children get older, they begin to exert independence while eating.

As children get older, they begin to exert independence while eating. They no longer want you to hold the bottle for them or feed them with a spoon. This is normal behavior and should be supported as much as possible. During this time, however, parents and caregivers often worry that the child is not getting enough to eat. You may find that a child in this situation wants to eat more often; providing additional opportunities to eat can ensure that the child's need for food is being met. Children may also want to exert their independence by skipping a meal or snack occasionally. Encourage community involvement by having the child stay in the area where the other children are eating, or allowing the child to sit on your lap.

All eating must be supervised, as the chance of choking is high for very young children who are learning to eat solid foods. Food for older infants should be cut into pieces no larger than a quarter of an inch. Older toddlers can have one-half-inch pieces. But the best way to supervise is to eat with the older infants and toddlers. Sit at the table and engage them in conversation.

Diapering and Toileting

Most infants and toddlers cannot communicate that they need a curricular experience involving a diaper change. You must be vigilant about checking. Often they need their diapers changed or to sit on the toilet after eating. The toddler who is engaged in toilet learning may also need special attention after nap and during play. Children who have learned to use the toilet may need to be reminded when they typically need to go to the bathroom (for example, after a nap).

Attending to this routine care time requires planning. Doing so will allow you to talk and sing and engage in positive experiences while you are providing for this basic need (see Herr & Swim, 2002, for example). Make this a pleasant time for both of you. The steps in the diapering process (Aronson, 2002; Swim, 1998) are as follows:

1. Gather all of the supplies (e.g., latex gloves, diaper wipes, clean diaper, and change of clothes) you will need and place them in the changing area within reach.
2. Put on latex gloves. Remove the infant's clothes or pull them up to the chest level. Remove the soiled diaper and place it on the edge of the area out of the infant's reach.
3. *Keep one hand on the infant at all times.*

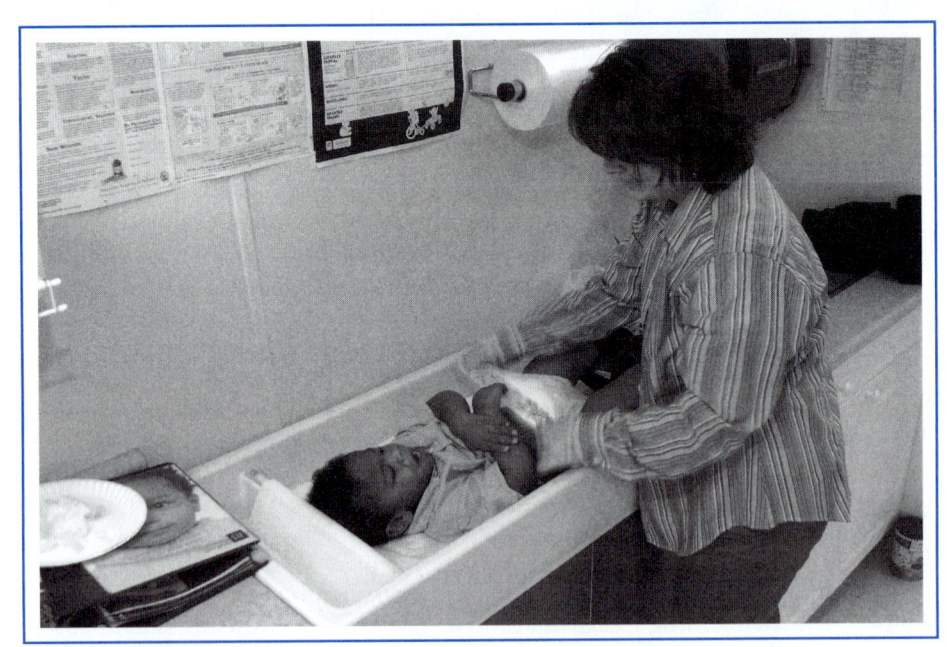

Make diapering a pleasant time for both of you.

4. Wipe off bowel movement with a diaper wipe or toilet tissue, going from front to back. Put this wipe on the soiled diaper. Continue until the child's bottom is clean.
5. Take off your gloves and wrap the soiled disposable diaper and wipes inside of them. Do this, for example, by holding the diaper in your right hand and using your left hand to pull the glove over and around the diaper. Then, put the diaper into your left hand and pull the glove over them again.
6. Throw away a soiled disposable diaper immediately in a foot-activated, covered, plastic-bag-lined container. Put a soiled cloth diaper in a plastic bag, which will be closed with a twist tie when you are finished. When using cloth diapers, throw away the soiled wipes separately in the trash container.
7. Wash your hands with a diaper wipe. If at any time from this point forward you notice bodily fluid, *put gloves on*.
8. Put a clean diaper on the child, fitting it snugly around the child's legs and waist. Dress the infant again or put on new clothes, as necessary.
9. Wash the child's hands in running water and carry the child to the next activity.
10. Return to the changing area to clean it. Spray the changing area with disinfectant. Wash your hands thoroughly with soap and running water before you do anything else.
11. Record the time and consistency of bowel movements. You and the child's family members need this information to determine patterns of normalcy and to look for causes of irregularities.

Toilet learning should begin when the toddler is ready. Toddlers will indicate when they are ready to begin this process. Their diapers may be dry for a few hours; they may tell you they have urinated or had a bowel movement after they have; they may watch other children use the big toilet—a motivation available when you have children who are already toilet-trained.

Discuss the timing with the toddler's parents. Both the home and the child care program need to begin at the same time and use the same procedures. Frequent, regular dialogue between parents and caregivers is needed to determine whether to continue toilet-learning or to stop and begin again a few months later.

It is often difficult for families to resist cultural pressures for early toilet learning even when they know the toddler is not ready and is unsuccessful in attempts. The caregiver can help family members understand the needs and development of their toddler.

The toddler needs two major functions for toilet learning—biofeedback and muscular control. Toddlers learn to recognize the feelings their bodies have before they urinate or have a bowel movement. They can use this biofeedback to decide what to do. At first they seem to just observe the feelings and afterward label what has happened.

Toddlers will learn to use the toilet when they are developmentally ready and motivated to do so.

When they decide to go into the bathroom *before* elimination, they need to use muscular control until they are safely on the toilet. Timing and control must be coordinated. At first toddlers may have some control but not enough to last as long as it takes to get into the bathroom, get clothes out of the way, and get seated or standing. Through trial and error, feedback and adjustments, toddlers learn what their bodies are doing and what they can control and plan.

When the child starts toilet learning, use training pants at home and at the child care program. Do *not* put diapers on the toddler during nap time. Outer clothes must be loose or easily removed to facilitate self-help.

Take the toddler to the bathroom and instruct how to pull down necessary clothes and how to get seated on the adapter seat or potty chair. For the boy who can reach while standing, determine where he should stand and where he should direct his penis. Put on your gloves before proceeding. Wait until the child goes to the toilet, or wait a few minutes. Teach how to get toilet paper and how to wipe from front to back. Then let the child try to do it alone. Check to see if assistance is needed in cleaning the child's bottom. Give help in getting clothes back up. Facilitate, as necessary, hand washing with soap and water.

Wipe off the toilet seat and spray with disinfectant if there is urine or feces on the seat or sides. *Remove gloves and wash your hands thoroughly before doing anything else.*

Occasionally during play time ask children whether they need to go to the bathroom. Ask them to go after lunch and before nap time. As soon as they get up from their naps, have them go to the bathroom.

Toilet learning should be a positive developmental experience and take a very short time. Problems in learning to use the toilet most often arise when adults do not notice the child's lack of readiness. They pressure the child through weeks of unsuccessful experiences, during which they blame the child for the failure rather than blaming themselves for wrong timing. Help family members and colleagues understand that timing for toilet learning is individual, as is learning to walk. There is no *right* age by which all children should be using the toilet independently. However, girls often can between 30 and 36 months of age and boys by 36–42 months (Carr, 1993).

Hand Washing

Frequent hand washing is a vital routine for caregivers and children to establish, since failure to do it is directly related to the occurrence of illness. Hand-washing procedures should be thorough: A quick rinse with clear water does not remove microorganisms.

The caregiver must wash hands before

- working with children at the beginning of the day.
- handling bottles, food, or feeding utensils.
- assisting child with face and hand washing.
- assisting child with brushing teeth.

The caregiver must wash hands after

- feeding.
- cleaning up.
- diapering (after rubber gloves are removed).
- assisting with toileting (remove gloves first).
- wiping or assisting with a runny nose (remove gloves first).
- working with wet, sticky, dirty items (remove gloves first).

The child must wash hands before

- handling food and food utensils.
- brushing teeth.

The child must wash hands after

- eating.
- diapering or toileting.
- playing with wet, sticky, and/or dirty items (e.g., sand, mud).

Proper procedures for hand washing include wetting the whole hand with warm water, applying soap, and rubbing the whole hand—palm, back, between fingers, and around fingernails. Rinse with clean water, rubbing the skin to help remove the microorganisms and soap. Dry hands on a disposable paper towel that has no colored dyes in it. Throw away the towel so others do not have to handle it. You can also use small washcloths as towels, with each child using his own once and then putting it in the laundry basket.

Toddlers who can stand on a stepstool at the sink can be assisted in washing their own hands. You can turn on the water, push the soap dispenser, verbally encourage them to rub their hands together, turn off the water for them, and if necessary hand them a towel.

Toothbrushing
Help toddlers climb up on the stepstool at the sink if they need assistance. Turn on the faucet so a small stream of water is running. Wash your hands. Assist in the child's hand washing. Then, allow the toddler to wet her own toothbrush. Shut off the water. Put a small amount of toothpaste on the toothbrush and then encourage the toddler to brush all of her teeth (not just the front ones).

Fill a small paper or plastic cup half full with water. Encourage the toddlers to rinse their mouths well. Give them more water if needed. Turn on the faucet and allow the toddlers to rinse their own toothbrushes and rinse out their cups. Have the

Help children to establish healthy habits early.

children wipe off their mouths with a tissue. Return the toothbrush and plastic cup to their proper place or throw away the paper cup.

End of the Day

At the end of each child's day, collect your thoughts and decide what to share with family members. To help you remember, or to gather information for other caregivers who work with the child, review the notes in the child's portfolio or on the report sheet. This sharing time includes the family members in the child's day and provides a transition for the child from the school to home.

✓ reading checkpoint

Before moving on with your reading, make sure that you can answer the following questions about the material discussed so far.

1. Write a statement that could be included in a policy handbook describing why flexibility in schedules is important in an infant and toddler program.

2. List three routine care times. Explain how each event can be used to promote the development of the child.

Routine	Development
1. _____	_____
2. _____	_____
3. _____	_____

PLANNED LEARNING EXPERIENCES

In between sleeping and eating, infants and toddlers have **alert times** when they are very aware and attracted to the world around them. This is the time when the caregiver does special activities with them (see Part III for suggestions). The infant or toddler discovers him- or herself, plays, and talks and interacts with you and others. Children have fun when in an alert state, as they actively involve themselves in the world.

Determine the times when the infants and toddlers in your care are alert. Decide which times each individual child will spend alone with appropriate materials you have selected and which times you will spend together one-on-one or in a small group. Each infant or toddler needs some time during each day to play with his or her primary caregiver. This play time is in addition to the time you spend changing diapers, feeding the child, and helping the child get to sleep.

As you play with the infant or toddler, you will discover how long that child remains interested. Stop before the child gets tired. The child is just learning how to interact with others and needs rest times and unpressured times in between highly attentive times. With an infant you might play a reaching-grasping game for a

Plan time throughout the day to interact one on one with each infant or toddler.

couple of minutes, a visual focusing activity for about a minute, and a standing-bouncing-singing game for a minute. Watch the infant's reactions to determine when to extend the activity to two minutes, five minutes, and so on. Alternate interactive times with times playing alone. Infants will stay awake and alert longer if they have some times of stimulation and interaction.

Toddlers spend increasing amounts of time in play. There should be opportunities for self-directed play as well as challenge and interaction with the caregiver. Toddlers also need quiet, uninterrupted time during their day. Constant activity is emotionally and physically wearing on them.

NAEYC's guidelines for developmentally appropriate practices support our understanding of how to create learning experiences. They include:

1. providing experiences for all areas of development: physical, cognitive, social, emotional, and verbal
2. including a broad range of content across disciplines that reflects the children's interest and is meaningful to them

3. building on what the children already know and are able to do to foster the acquisition of new concepts and skills
4. integrating content across subject matter or developmental areas
5. promoting the development of knowledge and understanding, processes and skills, as well as a disposition toward learning
6. supporting home cultures and languages while developing a shared culture of the learning community
7. setting goals that are realistic and attainable for each child (Copple & Bredekamp, 2009).

In addition, Freeman and Swim (in press) challenge teachers to evaluate the intellectual integrity of their work. Examining educational rituals and classroom practices often uncovers instructional strategies that are more about the teacher than for an individual or a group of children. Giving infants dittos or pages from a coloring book, for example, focuses on the perceptions of the teachers and other adults (e.g., family members) rather than the learning needs of infants. When infants are able to hold a spoon, they are able to hold a chunky crayon. Yet, they should be encouraged to make their own marks on blank paper.

The following sections discuss the specifics of how to create curriculum for infants and toddlers.

Daily Plans

For infants and young toddlers, you should plan experiences daily for each child. Assess the four areas of development for children using the Developmental Prescriptions (Appendix A). Next, copy the Developmental Profile form in Appendix B. Use the sample profile to plot a profile for each child in your care. Finally, analyze your data and determine the skills that the child can do independently and with assistance. Translate these skills into **daily plans**.

After implementing some **planned experiences**, you can use the data observed and recorded to plan new experiences for the next day. You can see how curriculum planning becomes a circular process that builds on itself (see Table 9–1).

When planning experiences you should not only consider the children's developmental needs and abilities but also their interests. If you want an infant to practice finding hidden objects, for example, hide a rattle that the child likes. Curricular experiences should balance practicing or reinforcing skills with introducing new ones. Introducing too many new experiences can overstimulate the infant or make him overtired. Carefully read the child's nonverbal communication to know when to stop the experience.

Weekly Plans

For older toddlers, you can plan experiences by the week, but you must modify the **weekly plans** throughout the week to respond to the children's needs. Planning for the entire week affords you the ability to carefully plan the learning environment

part 2 ESTABLISHING A POSITIVE LEARNING ENVIRONMENT

This child might be thinking, "I pushed them together. Now do they come apart?"

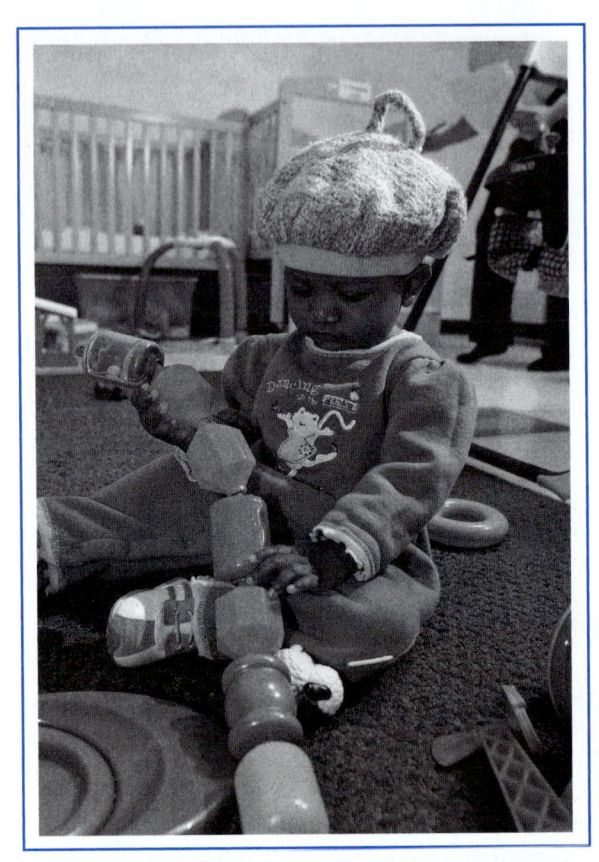

TABLE 9–1   SAMPLE SECTION OF A WEEKLY PLAN FOR TWO INDIVIDUAL CHILDREN

EXAMPLE: CHILD'S NAME:		WEEK:
AREA OF DEVELOPMENT	**MATERIALS**	**CAREGIVER STRATEGIES AND COMMENTS**
Physical: (Seeing) Roberto: Visual tracking	Red ribbon bow	Hold bow where infant can focus. Slowly move bow to side, to front, to other side. Observe eyes holding focus. Stop. Talk to infant, and repeat moving bow.
Naomi: Changing focus	Red and blue ribbon bow	Hold red bow where infant can focus. Lift up blue bow and hold a few inches to side of red bow. Observe eyes changing focus. Continue changing positions with both bows.

(see Chapter 8) and make available appropriate materials, equipment, and supplies. Materials are a vital part of the curriculum; they should be carefully selected to provoke the children's thinking and learning (White, Swim, Freeman, & Norton-Smith, 2007). The infants and toddlers learn by interacting with materials; the construction of knowledge comes from holding, tasting, shaking, hitting, throwing, taking apart, and listening to objects. Select open-ended materials such as wooden unit blocks, clay, and sand, because they provide a variety of experiences and can be used by each child to meet his or her needs and ideas (Curtis & Carter, 2003).

Learning Centers

As discussed in Chapter 8, learning centers organize the room and materials and encourage specific use of a particular space. Select materials for each learning center by matching them with the needs, interests, and abilities of the children. Do so carefully, because a poor selection of materials can actually impede the children's development. Materials that are too easy can be boring, while those that are too difficult can be frustrating. Using currently popular materials or those labeled "educational" may or may not be appropriate or effective for promoting development for your group of toddlers or a particular toddler. On the other hand, selecting developmentally appropriate materials for each child can facilitate growth and skill advancement (see Part 3).

For example, you notice that José seems to attend carefully to the wind chime outdoors. You want to promote his reaching and grabbing of objects, so you secure a wind chime in the manipulative area just within his reach. In Elizabeth's case, however, you want her to practice transferring objects from hand to hand, so you put out attractive clear blocks with interesting materials inside. You anticipate that when she picks one up to examine it, the material inside will shift locations, encouraging her to switch hands for a better view.

Projects

Once you know the children's interests and abilities, it is time to plan a week's worth of engaging curriculum. Instead of selecting themes, you should identify *moments* that can be developed into an ongoing project. Many *projects* have no clear beginning; they emerge (with much teacher observation and reflection) slowly over time from the documentation (see Chapter 5) that the teacher has collected or her experiences interacting with the children. Small moments encountered by one or two children can become projects in their own ways (May, Kantor, & Sanderson, 2004). Following our approach about the daily plans, projects should be individualized for each child or a small group of children.

You can outline experiences and questions to support the project or line of thinking and integrate the areas of development. In the infant-toddler centers of Reggio Emilia, teachers have constructed a particular approach to curricular planning referred to as *progettazione* or flexible planning (Rinaldi, 1998). Teachers there plan open-ended experiences to facilitate the co-construction of knowledge for children and themselves. They view the teacher's role as that of a resource who does

To plan engaging and challenging experiences, create curriculum based on your prior observations of each individual child.

not simply satisfy needs or answer questions, but instead helps children discover their own answers and, more importantly, helps them learn to ask good questions (Rinaldi, 1998). Therefore, this "... is a dynamic process based on communication that generates documentation and is regenerated by documentation" (Gandini & Goldhaber, 2001, p. 128).

As discussed earlier, a key principle of the educational approach used in Reggio Emilia, Italy, involves the many languages of children. Children are provided with multiple opportunities and avenues for expressing their understanding of the world. Thus, children use their "one hundred languages" to tell adults and peers what they know. Some avenues for expression include, but are not limited to, sculpting with clay or wire, painting, building with found materials, sketching, acting out stories, and dancing with scarves. These types of curricular experiences serve to cultivate and elaborate on the image of the child as a competent, capable, active learner who is constantly creating and re-creating theories about the world.

Sample Project. This section provides two examples of projects that can be done with a group of children. The number and types of projects appropriate for children this age are only limited by teachers' thinking. The first example extends from the butterfly garden discussed in the previous chapter. The toddlers were curious about the butterflies that come and go in their garden, asking many questions about how they fly. You notice that the children have discovered that they can see the butterfly garden from a window in the classroom. You decide to extend their interest by placing a small table near the window. On this table, you place a book about butterflies, two pairs of binoculars, and two clipboards with blank paper/pencils for drawing and writing. This proves to be a popular area, with many children visiting it for 10-15 minutes at a time. You decide to post a large piece of easel paper on the wall and record all of the questions you hear being asked. After reviewing the list, you decide to provide a new provocation and add a bird feeder to the garden. The children immediately notice it and wonder who else might visit the garden. When the yellow finches come to feed, the opportunity to discuss and compare how the butterflies and birds fly arises.

The other example is a project about wheeled vehicles that was created for a group of older toddlers. Joan and Derek displayed interest when the wheels fell off a vehicle in the block area. They immediately noticed that the car didn't move as easily without the wheels and after about five minutes of "hard" pushing, left it lying on the edge of the carpet.

Picking up on the children's frustration about the car, Sue decided to provoke the children's thinking about wheels further. She placed a full-size car tire (that had been cleaned) in the center of the room and waited to see what the children would do. Derek ran right to it and began to climb on it. Sue stood back and watched as other children began to join in the excitement. After about seven minutes, she sat on the floor near the children and asked questions such as "What is this?" "What is this for?" "How does it help a car move?" "Can a wheel help you move?" "What helps you move?" and recorded their answers. Later that day when the children were napping, she took a few moments to review her notes. She began to *web* what the children knew about the movement of wheels and people (Figure 9–2).

Sue decided to build on the children's interest in the wheels and planned the curricular experiences for the following week. To "kick off" the project, she planned to take the children on a walking field trip in their neighborhood to look for wheels. She mapped out the route to take so they would pass by the used car dealership and the playground with the tire swings. She prepared a clipboard (e.g., a piece of cardboard cut to 9" × 12" with unlined paper held on by a binder clip) with a pencil for each child to sketch what he or she saw. Later in the week, they were going to work with clay to represent wheels and possibly cars. She would put books about transportation in the reading/listening center and in the art center for when they worked with paint or clay. She planned to add wheels to the construction area that fit on the unit blocks so children could build their own cars.

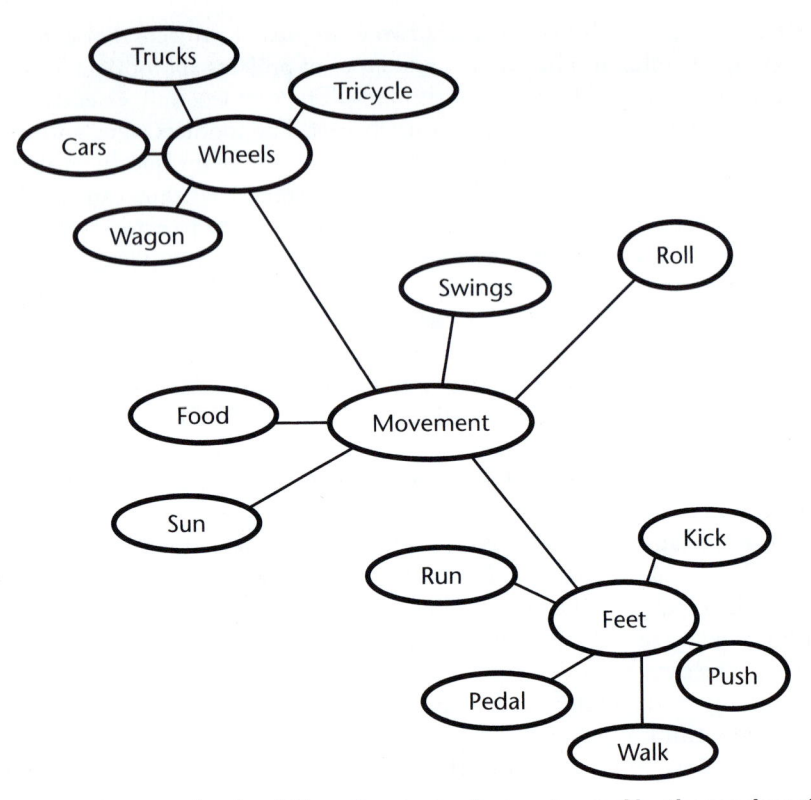

FIGURE 9–2 An example of webbing about wheels, constructed by the teacher after conversing with the children

Of course, Sue and her co-teacher, Joni, will document these classroom events using their digital video camera (which takes still photographs as well), running records of conversations, and work samples. These data will be reviewed daily during naptime and on Friday before planning experiences for the next week.

As mentioned in the previous chapter, the educators in Reggio Emilia speak of the importance of finding the "extraordinary in the ordinary" (L. Gandini, personal communication, January 26, 2001). In other words, early childhood educators should balance novel and familiar objects in the environment. Exploring flashlights on a dreary, rainy day meaningfully engages the children in investigating light, dark, and shadows. Wurm (2005) explains that there are four types of overlapping projects that teachers and children in Reggio engage in on a regular basis. The four types are intentional, daily life, self-managed, and environmental projects. The ones most important to infants and toddlers are daily life and environmental, which can both lead into intentional projects. Daily life projects are those events which occur repeatedly, or on an ongoing basis for very young children. Learning to eat and dress independently and to separate from family members, for example, are daily life projects. May, Kantor, and Sanderson (2004) provide additional examples of daily life projects about object permanence and identity development.

Environmental projects are inherently built into the classroom as part of the learning environment (Wurm, 2005). In other words, these projects emerge directly from the space and materials in which the children live and work. Children investigate methods of construction and principles of physical sciences (e.g., balance, force) due to the availability of different types of blocks (e.g., large, hollow, unit blocks or cardboard bricks). Returning to our example above, the children noticed the importance of wheels to make a vehicle move while pushing cars around on the carpet. When the teachers provided provocations to extend the children's thinking, they moved the work in the direction of an intentional project. Intentional projects result from the teachers' careful observation of and attention to the children's daily life and environmental projects and the teachers' planning and designing of flexible learning experiences (Wurm, 2005).

Good infant-toddler curriculum, then, should provide children with continuity from home to school and from day to day or even week to week. Children need time and support to construct and co-construct their knowledge of the world (see, for example, Cross & Swim, 2006).

Feedback

Feedback is a critical part of the curriculum cycle. You should solicit feedback from family members, colleagues, your own reflections, and the children themselves. Analyzing the documentation of the children's involvement, for example, ensures that the children have a balanced curriculum in the formal, planned times with you. Putting these data together with those collected during routine care times should provide evidence of a holistic, nurturing curriculum for each child in your care. If you find that any child is not receiving well-thought-out care, determine what changes are needed and make them to improve the quality of care and education provided for each child.

✓ reading checkpoint

Before moving on with your reading, make sure that you can answer the following questions about the material discussed so far.

1. List three reasons for creating daily plans for infants and young toddlers.
2. How can a project be used to involve a child physically?
    emotionally?
    socially?
    cognitively?

SUMMARY

Infant-toddler curriculum, or everything that happens with a child during the time in a classroom, must cover routine care times (e.g., eating and diapering) and planned learning experiences (e.g., daily plans or projects). Thus, teachers of very young children have jobs that are more complicated than those who work with older children and focus on just the latter component. In addition, the designed curriculum is influenced by several factors within and outside of the child care center.

key terms

- alert times
- bias
- cultural diversity
- curriculum
- daily plans
- demand feeding
- philosophy
- planned experiences
- *progettazione*
- projects
- routine care times
- Seeking Educational Equity and Diversity (SEED)
- toilet learning
- weekly plans

case study

Lukaz

April is a teacher in a birth to two year old, mixed-age classroom at a local university. Lukaz has been in her class since he was six weeks old, so she is very familiar with him and his family. He is a healthy 18-month-old child who has outstanding verbal skills. He speaks in full sentences and possesses an extensive vocabulary. He has a close friend in Tyler who is almost two. The two boys are almost inseparable: they both love to read books, build ramps, and play chase games. She has noticed lately that these two children seem bored in the classroom and have disrupted others who were working on two different occasions. For example, on Monday, Mackenzie was painting at the easel and Lukaz pushed her arm as he walked by. Tyler laughed when Mackenzie started to cry. As these behaviors are not typical for either boy, April decided to spend the next two days watching them closely and gathering some additional data.

Here are some data April gathered along with her wonderings.

1. Lukaz is in the book area. He picked up a board book, opened one page, and tossed it back towards the basket. He said "These are for babies." Tyler responded with, "Yeah, babies. Let's go." They left the area. [April's wonderings: When did I last add new books? and Are they ready for stories with more words or more complex art work?]

2. In the block area, Tyler has built a simple ramp using unit blocks. Lukaz helped him line up the plastic people at the end of the ramp. They have one car and are taking turns pushing it down the ramp to knock over the people. [April's wonderings: What else could challenge them with ramps? What questions should I ask? Should I be concerned about running over people—doesn't seem very caring?]

3. Mackenzie, Lukaz, and Tyler are sitting at the art table working with clay. Lukaz is making a car. He is challenged by the wheels not rolling. His voice is getting louder as he rolls a wheel between his palms. Mackenzie tells him to "Stop." He reaches over and pounds on her creation. She begins to cry.

1. Before addressing the specifics of the case, think about planning curriculum in general. What must be accomplished before an individualized curriculum can be developed for any child? Why?

(Box continues)

case study (continued)

2. Do you think that April's initial conclusion that Lukaz and Tyler are bored is accurate? Why or why not? Use the data she gathered to help provide evidence for your conclusion.

3. What curricular experiences would you plan if you were April? Provide examples of daily plans as well as plans for an ongoing project.

QUESTIONS AND EXPERIENCES FOR REFLECTION

1. Interview a teacher in a family child care program. Inquire how she responds to cultural diversity. For example, how does she use the home language of the children? How does she modify curriculum to respond to the cultural beliefs of families?

2. Diaper a child and reflect on your behavior. How well did you follow the guidelines as presented in the chapter? How did you interact with the child to promote security and development?

3. Observe a child in a child care center and record your observations using the Developmental Prescriptions (Appendix A). Transfer your data to the Developmental Profile (Appendix B). Create two daily plans in response to this data.

4. Observe toddlers on a playground. Use a narrative method for recording your observations (Appendix A). Think about the children's interests and create a flexible plan for a project.

REFERENCES

Aronson, S. S. (Ed.), compiled with P. M. Spahr. (2002). *Healthy young children: A manual for programs.* Washington, DC: National Association for the Education of Young Children.

Bredekamp, S., & Copple, C. (Eds.). (1997). *Developmentally appropriate practice in early childhood programs* (Rev. ed.). Washington, DC: National Association for the Education of Young Children.

Carr, L. (1993). *Toilet training toddlers.* Selden, NY: Lecture Series to Suffolk County "Mommy & Me Parent Trainers."

Cataldo, C. Z. (1983). *Infants and toddlers programs: A guide to very early childhood education.* Reading, MA: Addison-Wesley.

Clinton, W. J. (1997). *National Child Care Forum* [Television broadcast]. Washington, DC: National Broadcasting Corporation.

Cross, D. J., & Swim, T. J. (2006). A scholarly partnership for examining the pragmatics of Reggio-inspired practice in an early childhood classroom: Provocations, documentation, and time. *ScholarlyPartnerships.EDU, 1*(1), 47–68.

Curtis, D., & Carter, M. (2003). *Designs for living and learning: Transforming early childhood environments.* St. Paul, MN: Redleaf Press.

Freeman, R., & Swim, T. J. (in press). Intellectual Integrity: Examining Common Rituals in Early Childhood Curriculum. *Contemporary Issues in Early Childhood.*

Gandini, L., & Goldhaber, J. (2001). Two reflections about documentation. In L. Gandini & C. P. Edwards (Eds.), *Bambini: The Italian approach to infant/toddler care* (pp. 124–145). New York: Teachers College Press.

Ghedini, P. (2001). Change in Italian national policy for children 0–3 years old and their families: Advocacy and responsibility. In L. Gandini & C. P. Edwards (Eds.) *Bambini: The Italian approach to infant/toddler care* (pp. 38–45). New York: Teachers College Press.

Greenman, J., & Stonehouse, A. (1996). *Prime times: A handbook for excellence in infant and toddler programs.* St. Paul, MN: Redleaf Press.

Herr, J., & Swim, T. (2002). *Creative Resources for Infants and Toddlers* (2nd ed.). Clifton Park, NY: Thomson Delmar Learning.

Im, J., Parlakian, R., and Sánchez, S. (2007). Understanding the Influence of Culture on Caregiving Practices . . . From the Inside Out. *Beyond the Journal: Young Children on the Web.* Retrieved on March 2, 2009, from http://journal.naeyc.org/btj/200709/pdf/RockingRolling.pdf.

Jones, E., & Derman-Sparks, L. (1992). Meeting the challenge of diversity. *Young Children, 47*(2), 12–17.

King, A. (2001, November). Providing culturally consistent care for infants and toddlers—strategies from the Program for Infant/Toddler Caregivers. Paper presented at the National Association for the Education of Young Children Annual Conference, Anaheim, CA.

Kontos, S., Howes, C., Shinn, M., & Galinsky, E. (1995). *Quality in family child care and relative care.* New York: Teachers College Press.

May, N., Kantor, R., & Sanderson, M. (2004). There it is! Exploring the permanence of objects and the power of self with infants and toddlers. In J. Hendrick (Ed.), *Next steps towards teaching the Reggio way: Accepting the challenge to change* (2nd ed., pp. 164–174). Upper Saddle River, NJ: Pearson Merrill Prentice Hall.

Rinaldi, C. (1998). Projected curriculum constructed through documentation—*Progettazione:* An interview with Lella Gandini. In C. Edwards, L. Gandini, & G. Forman (Eds.), *The hundred languages of children: The Reggio Emilia approach—Advanced reflections* (2nd ed., pp. 113–125). Westport, CT: Ablex.

Schumann, M. J. (1982). Children in daycare: Settling them for sleep. *Day Care and Early Education, 9*(4), 14–18.

Swim, T. J. (1998). Proper procedures: Preventing the spread of disease in infant and toddler classrooms. *Early Childhood News, 10,* 45–47.

Swim, T. J., & Muza, R. (1999, Spring). Planning curriculum for infants. *Texas Child Care, 22*(4), 2–7.

Turkovich, M., & Mueller, P. (1989). The multicultural factor: A curriculum multiplier. *Social Studies and the Young Learner, 1*(4), 9–12.

White, B., Swim, T. J., Freeman, R., & Norton-Smith, L. (2007). *Powerful infants and toddlers: Provocations and dialogue with preverbal children.* Paper presented at the National Association for the Education of Young Children Annual Conference, Chicago, IL.

Wurm, J. (2005). *Working in the Reggio way: A beginner's guide for American teachers.* St. Paul, MN: Redleaf Press.

ADDITIONAL RESOURCES

Howard, G. R. (2006). *We can't teach what we don't know: White teachers, multiracial schools* (2nd ed.). New York: Teachers College Press.

Marotz, L. R., Cross, M. Z., & Rush, J. M. (2006). *Health, safety and nutrition for the young child.* Clifton Park, New York: Thomson Delmar Learning.

Ramsey, P. G. (2004). *Teaching and learning in a diverse world* (3rd ed.). New York: Teachers College Press.

Topal, C. W., & Gandini, L. (1999). *Beautiful Stuff! Learning with found materials.* Worcester, MA: Davis Publications.

For additional activities, web links, and other resources, please visit our website at www.cengage.com/education/swim

PART 3

Matching Caregiver Strategies, Materials, and Experiences to the Child's Development

The chapters in Part 3 describe how the caregiver works with infants and toddlers of different ages. Each chapter refers to the developmental profiles and characteristics of children in a specific age range, lists materials, and presents examples of caregiver strategies that can be used with individual children. Recall that this text applies a developmental perspective to the work of early childhood educators who care for and teach infants and toddlers. Thus, careful observation and analysis of patterns of development serve as a foundation for caring for each individual child.

As discussed earlier, the *sequence* of development presented is common to most infants and toddlers. The *age* at which behaviors occur or the *rate* of development frequently differ. Since two 11-month-olds may be at different levels of development, concentrate on each child as an individual. Accept the uniqueness of each child, and compare each one only to his or her developmental progression. Look at her individual records to see where she is making appropriate progress, gradually developing new, more complex skills and behaviors, or where she seems to be stuck at one level.

chapter 10

THE CHILD FROM BIRTH TO FOUR MONTHS OF AGE

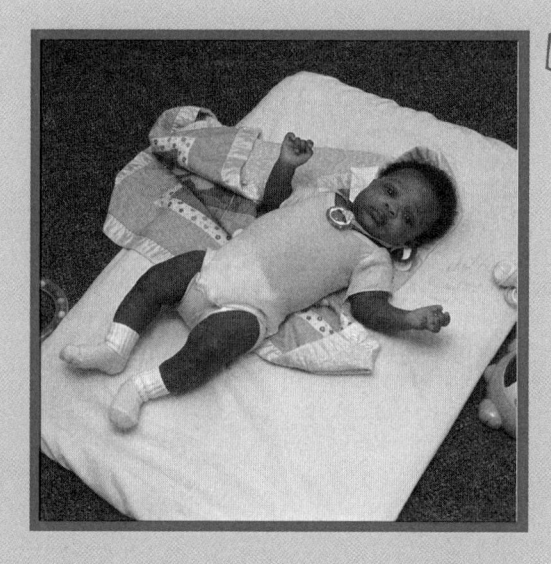

learning objectives

After reading this chapter, you should be able to:

- Identify and record sequences of change in the physical, cognitive/language, emotional, and social development of infants from birth to four months of age.
- Select materials appropriate to a particular infant's developmental level.
- Devise caregiving and teaching strategies for an infant appropriate to his or her developmental level.

chapter outline

- Materials
- Caregiver Strategies to Enhance Development
  Physical Development
  Cognitive and Language Development
  Emotional Development
  Social Development
- Case Study: Kierston

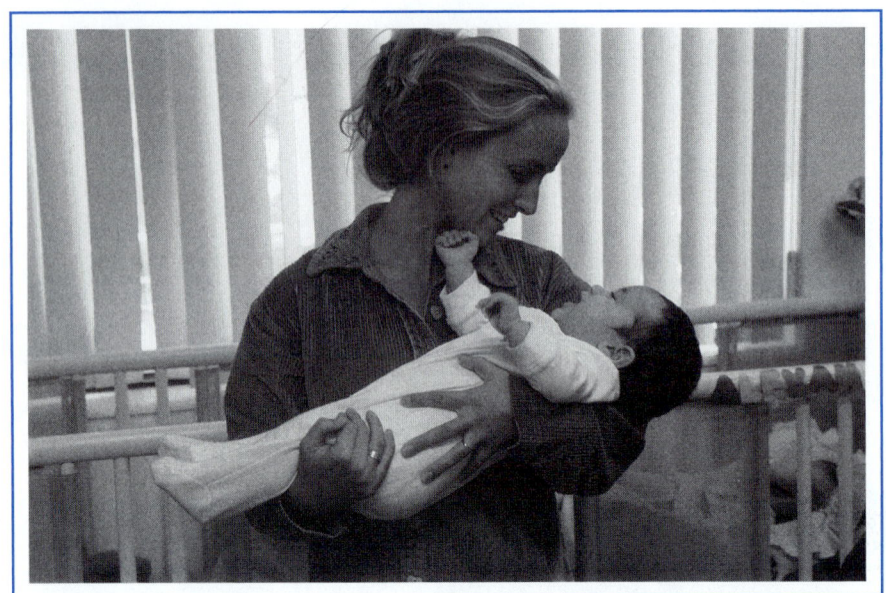

The caregiver anticipates and provides for the newborn's needs.

Kierston's Story

Kierston, two-and-a-half-months old, has just arrived at the child care home. She sits in her infant seat, which is on the floor by the sofa. Kierston's fists are closed and her arms and legs make jerky movements. As each of the other children arrive, they smile and "talk" to her, with the caregiver watching close by. Kierston does not make eye contact with any child, and after a few minutes she starts to whimper, then cry. Bill, the caregiver, picks her up and says, "Are you getting sleepy? Do you want a nap?" Bill takes Kierston into the bedroom and puts her in her crib, where she promptly falls asleep.

MATERIALS

Materials used with infants of this age must be both challenging and safe. Every object infants can grasp and lift will go into their mouths. *Before* you allow an infant to touch a toy, determine whether it is safe. Each toy should meet *all* the following criteria:

1. It is too big to swallow (use a choke tube to measure objects; see Chapter 8).
2. It has no sharp points or edges to cut the skin or eyes.
3. It can be cleaned.
4. It has no movable parts that can pinch.
5. Painted surfaces have nontoxic paint.
6. It is sturdy enough to withstand biting, banging, and throwing.

To be challenging for the young infant, each material should do the following:

1. It should catch the infant's attention so that she will want to interact with it in some way, such as reaching, pushing, grasping, tasting, or turning, and being able to practice these movements over and over again.
2. It should be movable enough to allow the infant to successfully manipulate the object and respond to it with arms, legs, hands, eyes, ears, or mouth.
3. It should be usable at several levels of complexity, so that the infant can use it with progressively more skill.

Look for toys and materials that the infant can use in several different ways. These provide greater opportunities for the infant to practice and develop new skills. Change the toys often so they seem new and interesting.

Types of Materials

Small toys to grasp   Mirrors
Mobiles   Sound toys
Rattles   Pictures, designs
Yarn or texture balls   Crib gym

Examples of Homemade Materials

Materials may be homemade or commercially made. Following are suggestions for making some of your own materials (Figure 10-1).

RATTLES

Film canister (plastic or metal): Put in one teaspoon uncooked cereal. Replace the cap and tape it on with colored tape.

Plastic measuring spoons: Tie together on a circle of strong yarn.

YARN BALLS

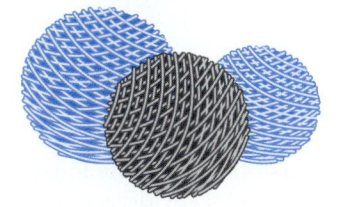

Roll up balls of washable yarn. Tuck the loose end inside. Make the balls different sizes and different colors.

FIGURE 10-1

(continued)

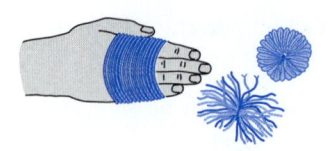

Wrap yarn around the palm of your hand until you have a thick mitt. Carefully slide it off your hand and tie a short piece of yarn tightly around the middle of the "mitt." Cut the ends apart. Pull the loose ends around to shape a pom–pom.

FABRIC TWIRLS

Cut out the center of a lid from a margarine tub. Cut carefully, leaving a clean, smooth edge. Use the remaining rim ring. Sew on three strips of printed washable fabric 3 inches long by 2 inches wide. Hang from the crib gym or put on the infant's wrist.

DESIGNS

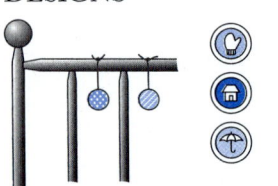

Cut faces, wallpaper, pictures, and contrasting colored fabric to fit inside the lids of margarine or yogurt tubs. Glue one piece in each lid. Give several to the infant to play with.

FIGURE 10–1 *(continued)*

✓ reading checkpoint

Before moving on with your reading, make sure that you can answer the following questions about the material discussed so far.

1. List three more toys or materials (not explicitly given as examples in previous section) that can be used with infants from birth to four months of age. List the area(s) of development that each can enhance.

	Toy/Material	Area(s) of Development
a.	_____	_____
b.	_____	_____
c.	_____	_____

CAREGIVER STRATEGIES TO ENHANCE DEVELOPMENT

Observations provide important information needed for decision-making, especially when planning a responsive, developmentally appropriate curriculum (see Chapters 5 & 9). This ongoing process or continuous loop of observing, planning, implementing, observing, and so on is vital to your being a professional educator.

Yet, assessing young children can be challenging. Because of the difficulties inherent in assessing what is expected of young children, some authorities advise caregivers not to assess children at all! Avoiding assessment is not only impossible but also results in care and education without any clear goals. The best approach, then, is to observe children formally and informally on a daily basis and make frequent adjustments in curriculum according to their progress in development, while honoring the uniqueness of each child. When teachers plan curriculum that balance experiences for supporting and challenging skills in all developmental areas, then they are meeting the core concept of "teaching to enhance development and learning" as outlined in the guidelines for developmentally appropriate practices (Copple & Bredekamp, 2009).

Physical Development

Infants from birth to four months of age show a very rapid rate of physical development, which varies widely from infant to infant. One baby may turn from stomach to back early while another may reach for objects early and turn over late. Starting at birth with reflexive movements, infants rapidly gain an increasing level of **muscular control** over much of their bodies. In general, development moves from the simple to the more complex movements.

The control begins with their heads and necks and continues to their shoulders, backs, waists, and legs. For example, they first lift their heads up before they have the muscular control to sit, and they sit before they can use their legs for standing.

Muscular control also develops from mid-body out to the hands and feet. Gradually infants are able to control their arm and leg movements to some degree, before they develop control of their hands, and to control their hands before they can grasp or pick up things with their fingers.

Infants also increase their ability to notice differences and experience their world through seeing, hearing, touching, smelling, and tasting. While these perceptual senses are listed in the Prescription in Appendix A as part of the Physical area, they also influence cognitive development (see Chapter 2).

Movements

Newborns' movements are reflexive; they occur without the infants' control or direction. Through growth and learning, infants begin to consciously control their movements.

In the first few months infants learn to perform many movements well, but they have not yet coordinated them. Bruner (1968) observed, recorded, and analyzed infant behavior. He found that infants learn to control their sucking in the first month of life and that sucking is used for relieving distress, holding attention, and exploration as well as for feeding. Infants require being held more than older children, which is why it is important to hold a baby while feeding.

Reflexive hand and arm movements develop into a grasping-groping action, which can be independent of vision. Within the first four months "this slow reaching has the mouth as its inevitable terminus. There is an invariant sequence: activation, reach, capture, retrieval to the mouth, and mouthing" (Bruner, 1968, p. 38).

Over the next several months hand and arm movements will become directed, voluntary activities that are visually controlled.

Stability

The newborn's head moves reflexively from side to side. When upright, the neck cannot yet support the head. Within the first month infants can lift their heads when lying on their stomachs. By the third month they are using their arms to push against the floor or bed to raise their heads and chests.

During these first three months infants are also busy with their legs. The legs have been kicking and pushing in the air and against anything within range. Infants roll and kick their legs from side to side. Their upper and lower back muscles are developing so that one day when they kick and roll to one side, they keep going right onto their backs or their stomachs. The baby has rolled over!

Many caregiving strategies at this time involve providing appropriate space so infants can move as they want to. Of course, the caregiver does not tell the infants to arch their backs, kick their legs, or wave their arms wildly. Infants do this naturally. The caregiver facilitates infant movement by making sure their clothes do not limit movement, by providing a circle of safety, and by offering the infant materials and toys that are safe and appropriate.

Sleep

Most newborns sleep between 14 and 17 hours a day. There will be times when they are actually awake, though their eyes are closed, and they will respond to stimulation. Newborns are relatively light sleepers, and deep sleep periods are only about 20 minutes long. The longest sleep period is usually four or five hours.

Marisol is sleeping for three- to four-hour stretches, befitting her age. She wakes at 11:30 a.m. from her morning nap each day. Bernice has recorded Marisol's sleep patterns and begins her caregiving for Marisol at 11:15 a.m. by preparing a bottle of formula and cleaning/arranging the changing table with her supplies. Bernice wants to be prepared so that the time to meet the infant's routine care needs is efficient and allows plenty of time for talking and singing. When Marisol stirs, Bernice greets her verbally but does not pick her up, to give her time to fully wake up. Due to Bernice's timing strategy, the process of changing and feeding proceeds without a hitch and she is able to engage meaningfully with her.

Infants' living patterns usually take on regularity in the first months of life. The infant who establishes a regular, though slowly changing, schedule for eating and sleeping creates a predictable world into which the caregiver can easily fit. Infants whose feeding and sleeping times remain erratic create stress for themselves and their caregivers. Gradually gaining stability in the sleep-wake cycle is not only important for growth and physical development but also for social development (Feldman, 2006). Infants who are more consistent in their sleep-wake cycles were associated with greater mother-infant synchrony at three months of age. When analyzed separately, high-risk premature infants displayed disorganized biological rhythms, lower thresholds for demonstrating negative emotions, and lower levels of mother-infant synchrony (Feldman, 2006). With increases in infants born prematurely, teachers and parents must find ways to assist these infants with organizing their sleep-wake patterns.

Suggestions for Implementing Curriculum
Physical development can be encouraged by providing opportunities for physical activity such as changing the baby's position, and motivating movement without instilling "pressure to perform" (Eisenberg, Murkoff, & Hathaway, 1989).

The caregiver can employ several strategies to enhance the infant's muscular control.

1. Place infants in positions where they can practice developing muscular control. For example, when you lay them on their stomachs, they can keep trying to lift their heads, shoulders, and trunks. Never place infants on their stomachs to sleep.
2. Until infants can roll over, sit up, and stand by themselves, they will need to be moved into those different positions several times each day during their waking hours.
3. Interact with the infant in order to stimulate her. Grasp the infant's hands and slowly lift the child upright. Hold your hands in different places so the infant will look around and reach for you. Gently snap your fingers behind, beside, and in front of the infant and watch the child turn her head to locate the sound.

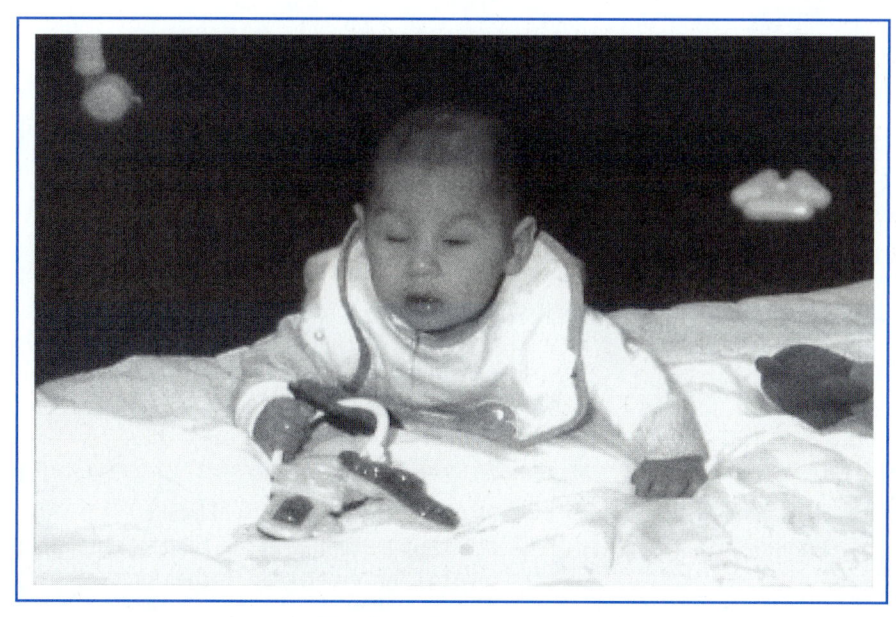

The caregiver moves a toy where the infant can see and touch it.

SUGGESTIONS FOR IMPLEMENTING CURRICULUM—PHYSICAL DEVELOPMENT

CHILD BEHAVIOR	MATERIALS	EXAMPLES OF CAREGIVER STRATEGIES
Reflex		
Grasp reflex (hand closes)	finger, rattle	Lift infant's body slightly. Place object in palm of infant's hand.
Startle reflex	mirror, mobile	Touch and hold infant to calm him.
Tonic neck reflex (head facing one side or other, not facing up)	toys, designs	Place objects at side of crib, not above middle of crib.
Muscular Control (develops from head to feet)		
Head and Neck		
Turns head	stuffed toy	Place infant on back or stomach. Place toy to one side.
Holds head upright with support		Support infant's head when holding infant upright.
Lifts head slightly when on stomach		Place infant on stomach.
Holds head to sides and middle		Place infant on stomach.
Holds up head when on back and on stomach		Place infant on stomach or back.
Holds head without support		Set and hold infant upright.
Trunk		
Holds up chest		Place infant on stomach.
Sits with support; may attempt to raise self; may fuss if left lying down with little chance to sit up		Place infant in sitting position. Support head and back with arm or pillow. Lengthen sitting time as infant is able.
Holds up chest and shoulders		Place infant on stomach.
Leg		
Rolls from stomach to back		Place infant on flat surface where infant cannot roll off.
Muscular Control (develops from mid-body to limbs)		
Arm		
Moves randomly	toys	Place objects within reach of infant.
Reaches	bright toys that make noise	Place objects slightly beyond reach of infant; give to infant when child reaches for it.

(continued)

CHILD BEHAVIOR	MATERIALS	EXAMPLES OF CAREGIVER STRATEGIES
Hand		
Opens and closes	toys with handles that fit in fist	Place handle in fist; help infant close fist around object.
Keeps hands open		
Plays with hands	colorful plastic bracelet	Place on infant's hands and fingers colorful, safe objects that attract infant's attention.
Uses hand to grasp object, whole hand, and fingers against thumb	toys with bumps to hold on to	Place object within reach of infant.
Thumb and forefinger	toys that can be grasped with one hand	Place object within reach of infant.
Holds and moves object	toys that can be pushed, pulled, or lifted with hands; toys that make noise	Place toy on flat surface free from obstructions.
Eye-Hand Coordination		
Moves arm toward object; may miss it	toy, bottle	Place within reach of infant.
Reaches hand to object; may grab or miss it	toy, bottle	Place within reach of infant.

4. Use toys and materials to play with the infant; offer some for the infant to use independently.

Place objects within the vision and reach of the infant. Select toys the infant can grasp. First there is a gross, grabbing movement. Later the infant is able to use a more refined finger-thumb or pincer grasp.

Sight. The teacher can use several strategies to enhance the infant's seeing.

1. Place the infant or objects at the correct distance so the infant can focus to see people or objects. The newborn focuses at about 8 to 14 inches. When infants are about four months old, they can adjust focal distance as adults do. The caregiver can place materials that attract the infant's attention at the proper focusing distance.
2. Select eye-catching materials. Contrasts seem to interest infants: designs, patterns, shapes, colors. Faces also attract their attention.

SUGGESTIONS FOR IMPLEMENTING CURRICULUM—SIGHT DEVELOPMENT

CHILD BEHAVIOR	MATERIALS	EXAMPLES OF CAREGIVER STRATEGIES
Seeing		
Focuses two inches from eyes	mirror, mobile, toys, pictures, designs (e.g., patterns, faces)	Place object eight inches from infant's face.
Follows with eyes	mobile, toys, hand	Move object slowly after infant focuses on object.
Sees objects beyond eight inches	people, pictures, toys	Attract attention by shape, color, movement.
Looks from object to object	toys, mobile, designs, pictures	Provide two or more objects of interest to infant.
Looks around; stops to focus on object that has caught attention, then looks at something else; continual visual searching		Provide eye-catching items in room: faces, patterned designs, contrasting colors in objects, and pictures.

The caregiver talks and listens to the infant.

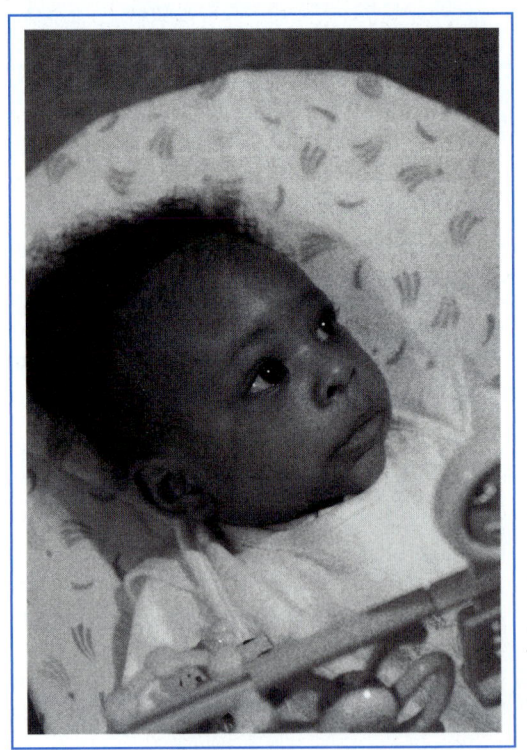

spotlight *on practice*

Voices from the Field

My co-teacher and I took a walk with our group of seven infants. Upon returning, I noticed that Everett (three months of age) was yawning while still buckled in the buggy. While we took out two other children, Everett continued to yawn. I took him out and asked, "Are you tired? You are yawning quite a lot. Let's sit down and I'll rock you to sleep."

I sat Everett upright, where his head rested on my shoulder. I spoke to him about being tired, and he just yawned again. I allowed his head to rest on my shoulder; he rested his head and seemed very relaxed. Everett didn't move except to get to a comfortable position and breathe very deeply. We sat down in a rocking chair, and I began to rock Everett while patting his back. After 10 minutes of rocking, Everett fell asleep.

In this example, I used each of the *three A's* as I demonstrated my respect for Everett's needs. Applying the *three A's* in this situation allowed him to develop trust and me to better understand how he likes to be held and rocked.

Sleep. The caregiver can use several strategies to enhance the infant's sleep. Anticipate when the infant will probably take a nap. Plan a very calming time and activities for the infant just before naptime so the baby can get in the mood to sleep. Sitting with the infant in a rocking chair and humming a lullaby often proves very effective.

Eating. The caregiver can use several strategies to enhance the infant's eating. Parents and pediatricians determine what and how much infants are fed during their first four months. The caregiver is responsible for making eating a happy, successful time for the infant. Organize your time so you can hold each infant when bottle-feeding. Eye focusing, eye-hand coordination, as well as emotional bonding, language, and communication all occur while holding the infant for feeding.

Cognitive and Language Development

Cognitive Development

Early childhood educators provide for the care *and* education of very young children. What we do matters immensely to the developing child, especially when considering brain development. Neuropsychologist Jane Healy discusses brain development of an infant in her book *Your Child's Growing Mind* (2004).

> Amazingly, although the number of cells actually decreases, brain weight can double during the first year of life. As neurons respond to stimuli seen, heard, felt or tasted, they fire off messages that build new physical connections to neighboring cells, linking them into efficient relay systems. . . . During the first six months after birth, they become extremely active as sensory messages bombard the infant brain, which must

spotlight on research

Breast-Feeding and Later Development

"You are what you eat" is a slogan many of us have heard quite frequently throughout our lives. This saying is the basis for the long-standing belief that, in order to be healthy, you have to eat well. Breast-feeding—a natural resource for mothers—is considered by many to be the best for meeting infants' nutritional needs. Recent research has examined whether or not this practice has benefits beyond physical development to other areas, such as cognitive and social, or emotional development. Extending the focus from nutrition to other areas of development highlights the **feeding relationship** or the dynamic interactions that parents and children establish around food that influences lifelong eating habits (Parlakian & Lerner, 2007; Satter, 1992).

Much research has supported the link between breast-feeding and later cognitive development (see Benton, 2007, for a review). The mechanisms for this link are not yet understood. Some researchers hypothesize that the high levels of fatty acids in breast milk impact later cognitive development because the fatty acids are incorporated into the brain during growth spurts and those fatty acids play an important structural role in cell membranes, helping cells to communicate more easily with each other (Benton, 2008). Tanaka, Kon, Ohkawa, Yoshikawa, and Shimizu (2009) investigated the relationship between levels of DHA (a type of fatty acid) in red blood cell membranes and the cognitive functioning of very-low-birth-weight infants at five years of age. The results showed that the levels of DHA at four weeks were significantly lower from formula-fed infants than breast-fed infants. At five years of age, breast-fed infants scored significantly higher on three different measures of cognitive functioning. In his review of research, Benton (2008) concluded that "in preterm babies the diet of the neonate can have lasting implications for brain development . . . and hence cognitive functioning" (p. 35).

The impact of breast-feeding on social and emotional development is also of interest to many researchers. In 2008, research was conducted on early determinants of mental health issues for young children (Robinson, Oddy, Jianghong, Kendall, de Klerk, Silburn, et al.). Of interest to this discussion is the result that shorter durations of breast-feeding were associated with greater mental health issues, specifically internalizing (withdrawn/depressed) and externalizing (aggressive/destructive) behavior problems. This study suggests that early childhood mental health is affected by a variety of prenatal, perinatal, and postnatal variables within a child's environment, including breast-feeding. Do maternal beliefs about breast-feeding matter?

Bai, Middlestadt, Joanne Peng, and Fly (2009) examined mothers' beliefs about exclusive breast-feeding for at least six months. They found that mothers in the study reported valuing the emotional benefits of breast-feeding for themselves and their infants. Thus, it may be that mothers who breast-feed are more attuned to their infants' emotional needs. It may also be that these beliefs are held very strongly within their social contexts because these mothers also reported receiving approval from family members to continue this practice, even though they felt disapproval from others within their community. Thus, this strong emphasis on caring for the nutritional and emotional needs of their infants overrode the negativity they perceived from others outside their family.

The difficulty in drawing conclusions from this line of research is that many women who breast-feed, especially in the United States, tend to be more economically well-off, have higher levels of education, and be of higher intelligence making it "difficult to distinguish the provision of mother's milk from a range of environmental benefits" (Benton, 2008, p. 28). However, Mortensen's (2007) commentary regarding recent articles on the impact of breast-feeding on social competency suggested that there are effects of breast-feeding on mental health that are independent of global measures of cognitive abilities and maternal intelligence. More research needs to be conducted to understand this complex relationship more clearly.

Nonetheless, practitioners need to evaluate their practices and policies so that they provide another source of support for families who want to breast-feed. Having quiet spaces where mothers can visit and breast-feed during the day would be one important type of support. In addition, following all guidelines for storing and preparing breast milk for feedings while the infant is at child care would be beneficial. Another example of support could be holding ongoing discussions with families about the benefits and challenges of breast-feeding. While this is the most "natural" way to feed an infant, it is by no means an easy process to start and maintain for today's busy families where a majority of mothers return to work within the first year.

learn to receive them and then pass them from one area to another.... Synaptic connections are strengthened by repeated use; if they fail to connect, they die off.... Every response to sights, sounds, feelings, smells, and tastes make more connections. (pp. 17–20)

This means that caregivers take every opportunity to teach, knowing that to increase an infant's stimulation is to increase ultimate human intelligence.

Piaget's theory of cognitive development categorizes the first four months of life as a part of the sensorimotor stage. Infants get information in this stage through their senses and motor activity. Infants use all their senses. With experience they refine their capacities for seeing, hearing, smelling, tasting, and touching. Moving themselves, moving others, and handling objects become coordinated with their senses. For example, when hearing a sound, infants turn their heads in the direction it comes from.

> Sensorimotor intelligence is primarily focused on action, not on classification and organization ... the knowledge that young infants have of objects is in terms of the sensorimotor impressions the objects leave on them and the sensory and motor adjustments the objects require. For young infants objects do not have an existence independent of their reactions to them. (Anisfeld, 1984, p. 15)

The sensorimotor stage has been divided into six substages; the first two are evident in the first four months. In each stage the infant develops new behaviors.

In Stage 1 the newborn's behavior is reflexive. Infants quickly start to change their behavior from passive reactions to active searching. Each of the senses operates independently.

During Stage 2 infants begin to coordinate their senses. They begin to develop hand-mouth coordination, eye coordination, and eye-ear coordination. One behavior can stimulate another; for example, a reflexively waving arm may attract the infant's attention so that he visually focuses on his own hand.

Newborns spend a great deal of time looking at the human face and demonstrate preferences for looking at faces which are upright with a straight head (Farroni, Menon, & Johnson, 2006). Infants also show a preference for looking at female faces (Ramsey, Langlois, & Marti, 2005). While the authors believe that their results have implications for how infants learn about males and females, teachers should make a habit of supporting fathers' interactions with their newborns, infants, and toddlers as these are equally important to the mental health (e.g., socio-emotional development) of very young children (see, for example, Collins, Mascia, Kendall, Golden, Schock, & Parlakian, 2003; Susman-Stillman, Appleyard, & Siebenbruner, 2003).

The sensitive caregiver uses several strategies to enhance cognitive development. Selecting items for and arranging an attention-catching environment stimulates the infant to respond in any way possible at his or her particular stage. Repeating and discussing the infant's behaviors provides them with a responsive and language-rich environment.

SUGGESTIONS FOR IMPLEMENTING CURRICULUM—COGNITIVE DEVELOPMENT

CHILD BEHAVIOR	MATERIALS	EXAMPLES OF CAREGIVER STRATEGIES
Piaget's Stages of Sensorimotor Development		
STAGE 1 (*Reflex*) Carries out reflexive actions—sucking, eye movements, hand and body movements		Provide nonrestricting clothes, uncluttered crib, which allow freedom of movement.
Moves from passive to active search	visually attractive crib, walls next to crib, objects; occasional music, singing, talking, chimes	Provide environment that commands attention during infant's periods of alertness.
STAGE 2 (*Differentiation*) Makes small, gradual changes that come from repetition		Provide change for infant; carry infant around, hold infant, place infant in crib. Observe, discuss, record changes.
Coordinates behaviors, e.g., a sound stimulates looking	face and voice, musical toy, musical mobile, rattle	Turn on musical toy; place where infant can see it.
Puts hand, object in mouth and sucks on it	objects infant can grasp and are safe to go in mouth	Place objects in hand or within reach. Infants attempt to put *everything* in their mouths. Make sure they get only safe objects.
Moves hand, object to where it is visible	objects which infant can grasp and lift	Provide clothes that allow freedom of movement. Place objects in hand or within reach.
Produces a pleasurable motor activity and repeats activity		Provide time, space for repetition.
Piaget's Concept of Object Permanence[a]		
SENSORIMOTOR STAGES 1 AND 2 Follows moving objects with eyes until object disappears; looks where object has disappeared; loses interest and turns away; does not search for it	toys and objects that attract visual attention	Place object in range of infant's vision. Allow time for infant to focus on object. Move object slowly back and forth within child's field of vision. Move object where infant cannot see it, e.g., roll ball behind infant.

[a] Object permanence means knowing that an object or person exists even when out of sight or touch.

Language Development

Language is a tool used to communicate with oneself and with others. Crying is one way infants communicate with others. Even newborns cry in different ways, depending on whether they are startled or uncomfortable.

"Prelinguistic vocalizations contribute to the infant's developing ability to speak. In the first eight weeks vocalizations are of two kinds: One category consists of vegetative sounds and includes burping, swallowing, spitting up, and the like. The other category consists of discomfort sounds and includes reflexive crying and fussing" (Anisfeld, 1984, p. 221). Infants produce sounds as they use their mouths and throats. These sounds are the infants' "talk." At first they seem unaware of their sounds, and then gradually they begin to repeat their own sounds. Infants talk to themselves for the pleasure of making the sounds and hearing themselves talk.

Infants use several kinds of sounds as part of their language. They produce sounds as they eat and as they play with their tongues and mouths. They use their throats, saliva, tongues, mouths, and lips to produce gurgling, squealing, smacking, and spitting noises. Gradually they produce repetitive, vowel-like sounds that can be classified as cooing. A second stage of vocalization occurs between 9 and 20 weeks. "It is characterized by cooing and laughter; sustained laughter occurs at 16 weeks" (Anisfeld, 1984, p. 222).

When infants hear someone talk to them, it stimulates them to make sounds (see the parental selection hypothesis in Locke, 2006). This dialogue is very important. Effective dialogue can occur when the caregiver looks at the infant while alternately listening to and answering the child's talk. The one-to-one dialogue is what stimulates the infant to engage in more positive vocalizing at later ages (Henning, Striano, & Lieven, 2005). Talking that is not directed to the infant personally is not as effective a stimulator. Adults conversing with each other in the presence of the child, or playing a radio or television broadcast, do not involve the child in language dialogue.

Suggestions for Implementing Curriculum. The caregiver can use several strategies to enhance the infant's language development.

1. Talk: Say words, sentences, and nursery rhymes; read stories aloud and show the baby pictures of different faces and designs.
2. Sing: Hum; sing words set to your own music, nursery rhymes, lullabies, and songs; play African drums or recorded bagpipe music.
3. Listen and respond: Infants will make sounds by themselves for a few months. This talk will decrease if the infants do not have someone to listen to them and to "answer" them.
4. Initiate conversation: Almost every encounter with an infant is an opportunity for conversation. Routine physical care like feeding, changing diapers, and rocking all present the necessary one-on-one situations where you and the infant are interacting. It is not necessary or helpful to talk all the time or to be quiet all the time. The infant needs times for language and conversation and times to be quiet.

SUGGESTIONS FOR IMPLEMENTING CURRICULUM—LANGUAGE DEVELOPMENT

CHILD BEHAVIOR	MATERIALS	EXAMPLES OF CAREGIVER STRATEGIES
Physical Components Involved in Language Communication		Observe and record infant's use of sound.
Back of throat		
Nose		Record repetitions, changes, and new sounds.
Mouth cavity		
Front of mouth		Record mood of infant when infant is making longer repetitions of sounds.
Tongue		
Lips		
Saliva		
Actions Involved in Language Communication		

Changes air flow:
   through nose
   through mouth		

Uses tongue to manipulate air flow, saliva		
Plays with tongue: twists, turns, sticks it out, sucks on it		
Uses saliva in various places and changes sounds: gurgling in back of throat, bubbling in center of mouth, hissing, spitting with partially closed lips and tongue		
Initiating-Responding	rattle, objects that make sounds or noises, music box, music, talking, singing	Talk, sing to infant while feeding, changing diapers and clothes, holding, carrying around, rocking. Carry on normal conversation with infant—talking, listening, silence.
		"Answer" infant with sounds or words.
Initiates making sounds		
Responds vocally to another person		Hold infant: look at infant eye to eye; make sounds, talk, sing to infant; listen to infant's response; talk, sing again; listen, and so on.

(continued)

CHILD BEHAVIOR	MATERIALS	EXAMPLES OF CAREGIVER STRATEGIES
Makes sound, repeats sound, practices the sound for a few minutes, and then lengthens the practice to longer blocks of time.		Talk with infant, show interest, look at infant.
Imitates sounds already known		Repeat sound infant has just made; listen to infant make sound; repeat it again; and so on.
Experiments with sounds		
Crying		
Cries apparently automatically in distress and frustration		Empathize with the infant. Respond to infant's crying immediately and consistently.
Cries differently to express hunger, discomfort, anger		Attend to the need infant expressed by crying.
Cries to gain attention		Find out what infant wants.
Cries less as vocalizing increases		
Cooing		
Repetitive vowel-like sounds		Imitate, respond, and talk to infant.
Adds pitch		

✓ reading checkpoint

Before moving on with your reading, make sure that you can answer the following question about the material discussed so far.

1. State two reasons why it is helpful to an infant's cognitive and language development to have a caregiver talk to him or her.

Emotional Development

During the first months of life infants develop their basic feelings of security. There seems to be little "catch-up" time for emotional security. If the infant does not develop these feelings of security at this time, it is difficult, but not impossible, to develop them as adequately later. Along with the parents, the caregiver plays a key role in providing the kinds of relationships and experiences that enable the infant to develop this basic security.

Feelings of security and trust develop out of relations with others, not by infants on their own. Infants develop these feelings from the way other people treat them.

Parents and the primary caregiver are probably the most influential people in the lives of young infants in child care. Therefore, the caregiver is very directly responsible and involved in helping the infant feel secure.

Two caregiver behaviors of special importance are responding immediately to the infant's distress signals and responding unfailingly to the infant's signals of stress, need, or pleasure.

Temperament, or the infant's basic style of behavior, gradually emerges in the first four months. Some styles are easily recognized, whereas others may be more difficult to observe.

The activity level of infants is obvious. They may kick, wriggle, and squirm a great deal, or they may lie quietly while either asleep or awake. Highly active infants may kick their covers off consistently and get tangled in their clothes. Their bodies get plenty of activity. They may need to be checked frequently to be sure they can move freely and aren't tangled in a bed sheet, blanket, or article of clothing. A blanket may be more of a bother than it is worth, since it seldom covers the infant. Infant suits or long smocks and socks may keep the active infant just as warm. Very quiet infants may seem easy to care for. They seldom kick off their covers or need their clothes adjusted. They may, however, need to be picked up and moved around to stimulate their physical movement.

Differing levels of **sensory threshold** are apparent in young infants. One infant will awake when a light is turned on or a person steps into the room. Another infant will sleep in a brightly lit room with the CD player on. When several children are in one room, special adjustments must be made for the sleeping infant who reacts negatively to light and sound.

Infants characteristically use differing levels of energy when responding to stimuli. One infant will cry loudly every time. Another infant will whimper and fuss and occasionally cry more loudly when very distressed. The caregiver, when responding to the infant's cries, will need to learn cues other than loudness to determine the type and severity of stress. The caregiver may need to check infants who fuss and cry quietly to make sure their needs are being met. While the link between temperament and attachment security is still empirically debated, Marshall and Fox (2005) found that infants who showed high levels of negative affect in response to stimulation at four months were more likely to be classified with an insecure attachment at 14 months than were infants who scored low on affective reactivity.

The caregiver can use several strategies to enhance the infant's emotional development. Whereas physical development can be enhanced by moving the infant, toys, and oneself around, emotional development demands more than manipulation; it requires consistent interactions. When relating to the infant, the three *A*s—Attention, Approval, and Attunement—play a most crucial part in the daily emotional development of the child. The following strategies will help the caregiver to be conscious of the three *A*s while performing tasks such as diapering and feeding:

- Use your relationship with the child.
- Focus your attention on the child's needs.

Gentle touching and cuddling comforts the infant.

- Engage the child—make eye-to-eye contact.
- Move slowly and with intention.
- Make meaningful physical contact.
- Actively listen to her whole body message.
- Reflect vocal expressions and sounds back to him or her.
- Try to sense how the child is feeling—is the child excited, happy, frustrated?
- Try to judge the amount of stimulation the child prefers.
- Try to get in rhythm with the child. Let him or her lead you vocally.
- Talk and sing, hum and smile.
- Place the child where she can observe room activity.
- Involve the child in activity.
- When leaving the infant, indicate where you'll be in the room if she needs you.

SUGGESTIONS FOR IMPLEMENTING CURRICULUM—EMOTIONAL DEVELOPMENT

CHILD BEHAVIOR	MATERIALS	EXAMPLES OF CAREGIVER STRATEGIES
Types of Emotions-Feelings		
Shows excitement	attention-catching objects	Use voice and facial expression to mirror excitement.
Shows stress	calming touch, talk, music, singing	Determine cause. Change situation to reduce stress, e.g., change diaper, change position, talk to infant (child may be bored).
Shows enjoyment	interesting, challenging toys, objects	Provide pleasant experiences, e.g., give infant a bath, snuggle, converse, smile.
Shows anger or frustration		Determine cause. Remove or reduce cause. Divert infant's attention, e.g., turn infant around to look at something else.
Shows fear		Hold, comfort infant. Remove fear-producing object or change situation, e.g., hold infant startled by sudden loud noise.
Protests		Determine what infant is protesting about. Eliminate activity or do it a different way, e.g., change how you wash infant's face. If behavior continues, ask another caregiver to take child for you.
Control of Emotions-Feelings (seems to occur automatically)		
Decreases crying	activities, toys that catch infant's attention and that infant likes	Involve infant in an activity.
Increases sounds (talking)		Initiate "conversations" and respond to infant's talking.
Reflects feelings in sounds		Respond to the feelings expressed, e.g., comfort (by talking) a whining child, change situation.
Feels comforted when held		Consistently hold, caress, cuddle, and comfort when infant needs it.
Temperament		
Observe the nine behavior categories (see Chapter 3)		List adjustments you need to make to result in better "goodness of fit."

Social Development

The caregiver must become emotionally involved with infants in order to provide for their social needs. According to **attachment theory**, just as infants develop a unique attachment to their mothers, they can develop an additional attachment to their primary caregivers in child care settings. Thus, many of the caregiver strategies previously discussed for building emotional relationships between infants and teachers involve frequent use of looking and touching, which serve a dual function of supporting attachment.

Attachment theory and research have identified phases in the development of attachment. Ainsworth (1982) identified infants' social behaviors during the first few months of life that relate to developing attachment.

Phase 1: Undiscriminating Social Responsiveness (first two to three months)

- orienting behaviors: visual fixation, visual tracking, listening, rooting, postural adjustment when held
- sucking and grasping to gain or maintain contact
- signaling behaviors: smiling, crying, and other vocalizations to bring caregiver into proximity or contact

Infants from birth to four months are egocentric; they have only their point of view. They use their senses to begin to develop a global concept of self. They need to see, hear, smell, touch, and taste for themselves. People and objects are familiar insofar as they interact with the infant's sense experiences. For infants at this level, people and objects do not exist as separate objects.

SUGGESTIONS FOR IMPLEMENTING CURRICULUM—SOCIAL DEVELOPMENT

CHILD BEHAVIOR	MATERIALS	EXAMPLES OF CAREGIVER STRATEGIES
Attachment		
Shows special closeness to parent; differentiates response to parent—voice, touch, presence, absence		Accept that the infant will respond differently to you than to parent. Closely observe the parent-infant interaction and then model some of the caregiving behaviors, sounds, and other characteristics of the parent.
Develops familiarity with one primary (significant other)		Same caregiver provides most of infant's care, although other caregivers may share responsibility occasionally.
Needs security		Provide consistent care of infant: feed; comfort; change diapers and clothes; talk, sing, and play with infant; rock and hold; put to bed; pick up when awake; respond to infant's special needs, likes, and dislikes. Touch, hold, caress, and cuddle the infant.

(continued)

CHILD BEHAVIOR	MATERIALS	EXAMPLES OF CAREGIVER STRATEGIES
Self		
Becomes aware of hands	bright clothes, materials for hands, feet; bare feet sometimes	Provide clothes that allow freedom of movement. Occasionally put on hands and feet to bright colors or dots on hands and feet to attract infant's attention.
Smiles spontaneously, sometimes immediately at birth		
Smiles at self in mirror	mirror	Smile with infant.
Others		
Establishes eye contact with another person		Hold infant so the caregiver is in infant's range of vision. Engage infant in eye contact.
Recognizes voice of parent		
Smiles at people (social smile)		Hold infant. Smile, talk with infant.
Watches people		Place infant where you can be seen moving about. Carry infant around to see others.
Talks (coos) to people		Respond and initiate talking, singing with infant.
Shows longer attentiveness when involved with people		Spend time during infant's alert times interacting with infant.
Recognizes parent visually		
Recognizes individual people		Provide daily care, interactions with a few persons other than parent.
Behaves differently with parent than with others		Accept different responses.
Interacts with people		Initiate interactions, respond; place or carry infant where infant can meet people.
Laughs		Play with infant, laugh with infant, respond to infant's laugh.
Differentiates self from parent		
Initiates talking to others		Answer infant's talk.
Plays with toys	toys that attract and challenge infant	Provide toys; change toys to renew interest.

Herr and Swim (2002) suggest that the most important plaything for infants is a responsive caregiver. The caregiver can use several strategies to enhance the social development of infants of this age. The caregiver can respond quickly to the infant's needs and can initiate interactions by looking, holding, stroking, talking, playing, carrying, and rocking the infant. While interacting, teachers should remember to use positive communication skills such as active listening and mirroring. In fact, the positive outcomes for mirroring have been established through research. High-affect-mirroring mothers were associated with infants (two- to three-month-olds) who ranked high on prosocial behavior and social expectancy—responded more frequently with smiles, vocalizations, and gazes (Legerstee & Varghese, 2001).

reading checkpoint

Before moving on with your reading, make sure that you can answer the following question about the material discussed so far.

1. Select one emotional and one social skill. Explain how a teacher would select caregiving strategies that demonstrate responsiveness and are appropriate for each skill.

SUMMARY

Very young infants can be unpredictable because they are just beginning to create organized responses or patterns in their actions. Because of this, caregivers face particular challenges in responding to their developmental capabilities. Observe frequently, formally and informally, to note changes or modifications in desires, needs, skills, interests, and so on. Then, build strategies that are responsive to their current levels.

key terms

| attachment theory | cooing | sensorimotor stage |
| cognitive development | muscular control | sensory threshold |

case study

Kierston

You were introduced to Kierston in the beginning of the chapter, but this section provides additional information to assist with understanding her behavior. She is the youngest of eight children, and the sibling she is closest to is 17 years her senior. Both of her parents are first-generation immigrants. Her mother is over 45 years old, and during the pregnancy her husband, who was 57 years old, suddenly died of a heart attack. Kierston was delivered by cesarean. Since her birth, her mother has cared for her only occasionally, while her siblings, aunts, and uncles provide most of her care. The grief of the family is obvious to anyone observing them. The well-meaning but numerous

(Box continues)

caregivers provide very inconsistent care for Kierston. The variety of different faces and personalities who care for her may help explain her lack of desire to interact with others.

The child care center is aiming to compensate for the lack of consistency in Kierston's environment by assigning one primary caregiver, Bill, to her. Bill will establish a consistent daily routine around her needs; he plans to handle and speak to her gently in order to enhance her sense of trust and security. As part of their Early Head Start program, home visitations will also occur. These regularly scheduled times should benefit Kierston because the home visitor will discuss the importance of using consistent caregiving techniques and creating similar schedules with the various family members.

1. What effect do you think a depressed family member has on the development of a two-month-old? Support your thoughts with evidence.
2. What suggestions do you have for Bill as he implements the three *As* with Kierston?
3. What should be Bill's next steps if Kierston's development does *not* improve after her home life becomes more consistent?

QUESTIONS AND EXPERIENCES FOR REFLECTION

1. Observe one infant under four months of age. Record the infant's behavior in two five-minute sequences. Transfer the descriptions to the Developmental Profile in Appendix B.

2. Select toys from catalogs and newspaper ads that are said to be appropriate for an infant under four months of age. Read the toy description. Do these toys match the level of development for the infant you observed (for the first question)? Why or why not?

3. Select one category of the Developmental Profiles (for example, physical development). Observe a caregiver and classify the strategies the caregiver used from that category (for example, physical support: holds hand behind infant's head and neck).

4. List five strategies that you use competently with infants from birth to four months. Then, list strategies you need to develop and ways you intend to develop them.

REFERENCES

Acredolo, L. P., & Goodwyn, S. (2000). *Baby minds: Brain-building games your baby will love.* New York: Bantam Books.

Ainsworth, M. D. (1982). The development of infant–mother attachment. In J. Belsky (Ed.), *In the beginning: Readings on infancy.* New York: Columbia University Press.

Anisfeld, M. (1984). *Language development from birth to three.* Hillsdale, NJ: Lawrence Erlbaum Associates.

Bai, Y. K., Middlestadt, S. E., Joanne Peng, C.-Y., & Fly, A. D. (2009). Psychosocial factors underlying the mother's decision to continue exclusive breastfeeding for 6 months: an elicitation study. *Journal of Human Nutrition and Dietetics, 22* (2), 134–140.

Benton, D. (2008). The influence of children's diet on their cognition and behavior. *European Journal of Nutrition, 47* (3), 25–37.

Bruner, J. S. (1968). *Processes of cognitive growth: Infancy.* Worcester, MA: Clark University Press.

Collins, R., Mascia, J., Kendall, R., Golden, O., Schock, L., & Parlakian, R. (2003). Promoting mental health in child care settings: Caring for the whole child. *Zero to Three, 23*(4), 39–45.

Eisenberg, A., Murkoff, H. E., & Hathaway, S. E. (1989). *What to expect the first year.* New York: Workman Publishing.

Farroni, T., Menon, E., & Johnson, M. H. (2006). Factors influencing newborns' preferences for faces with eye contact. *Journal of Experimental Child Psychology, 95*(4), 298–308.

Feldman, R. (2006). From biological rhythms to social rhythms: Physiological precursors of mother-infant synchrony. *Developmental Psychology, 42*(1), 175–188.

Healy, J. (2004). *Your child's growing mind: A guide to learning and brain development from birth to adolescence.* (3rd ed.). New York: Broadway Books.

Henning, A., Striano, T., & Lieven, E. V. M. (2005). Maternal speech to infants at 1 and 3 months of age. *Infant Behavior & Development, 28*(4), 519–536.

Herr, J., & Swim, T. J. (2002). *Creative resources for infants and toddlers* (2nd ed.). Clifton Park, NY: Thomson Delmar Learning.

Legerstee, M., & Varghese, J. (2001). The role of maternal affect mirroring on social expectancies in three-month-old infants. *Child Development, 72*(5), 1301–1313.

Locke, J. L. (2006). Parental selection of vocal behavior: Crying, cooing, babbling, and the evolution of language. *Human Nature, 17*(2), 155–168.

Marshall, P. J., & Fox, N. A. (2005). Relations between behavioral reactivity at 4 months and attachment classification at 14 months in a selected sample. *Infant Behavior & Development, 28*(4), 492–502.

Mortensen, E. L. (2007). Neuro-developmental effects of breastfeeding. *Acta Paediatrica, 96*(6), 796–797.

Parlakian, R., & Lerner, C. (2007). Promoting Healthy Eating Habits Right from the Start. *Beyond the Journal: Young Children on the Web.* Retrieved April 11, 2009, http://journal.naeyc.org/btj/200705/pdf/RockingandRolling.pdf

Ramsey, J. L., Langlois, J. H., & Marti, N. C. (2005). Infant categorization of faces: Ladies first. *Developmental Review, 25*(2), 212–246.

Robinson, M., Oddy, W. H., Jianghong, L., Kendall, G. E., de Klerk, N. H., Silburn, S. R., Zubrick, S. R., Newnham, J. P., Stanley, F. J., & Mattes, E. (2008). Pre- and postnatal influences on preschool mental health: a large-scale cohort study. *Journal of Child Psychology & Psychiatry, 49*(10), 1118–1128.

Satter, E. (1992). The feeding relationship. *Zero to Three, 12*(5): 1–9.

Susman-Stillman, A., Appleyard, K., & Siebenbruner, J. (2003). For better or worse: An ecological perspective on parents' relationships and parent-infant interaction. *Zero to Three, 23*(3), 4–12.

Tanaka, K., Kon, N., Ohkawa, N., Yoshikawa, N., & Shimizu, T. (2009). Does breastfeeding in the neonatal period influence the cognitive function of very-low-birth-weight infants at 5 years of age? *Brain and Development, 31*(4), 288–293.

For additional activities, web links, and other resources, please visit our website at www.cengage.com/education/swim

chapter 11

THE CHILD FROM FOUR TO EIGHT MONTHS OF AGE

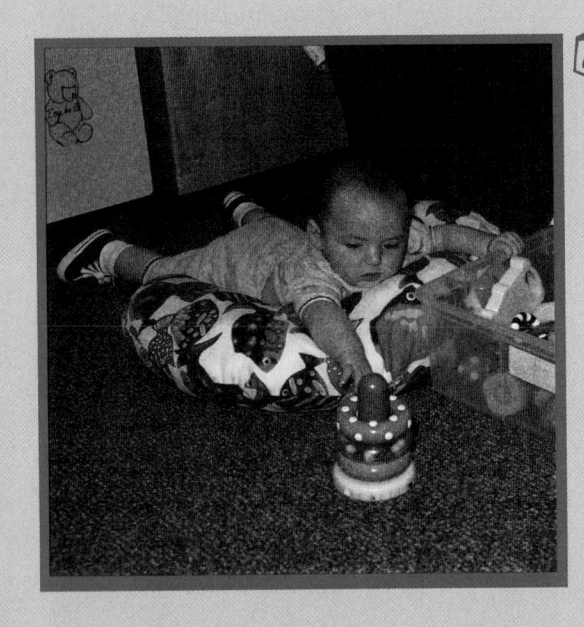

learning objectives

After reading this chapter, you should be able to:

- Identify and record sequences of change in the physical, cognitive/language, emotional, and social development of infants from four to eight months of age.
- Select materials appropriate to the development of infants at that age level.
- Devise strategies appropriate to infants of that developmental level.

chapter outline

- Materials and Activities
- Caregiver Strategies to Enhance Development
  Physical Development
  Cognitive and Language Development
  Emotional Development
  Social Development
- Case Study: Theresa

THERESA'S STORY

Theresa, six months old, is lying on her stomach on the floor, kicking her legs and waving her arms. She looks at a toy radio and drools. She fingers the toy radio, chews, and drools some more. She "sings" with the music. Ellie, the caregiver, winds up the toy radio. Theresa kicks her feet and smiles. She watches the radio and kicks her feet. Ellie smiles at Theresa, and Theresa smiles back. She kicks her feet rapidly. While Theresa looks at Wayne, another infant, Ellie speaks to her. Theresa tries to lift herself by pushing on the floor with her arms. She turns herself around, still on her tummy. She kicks her feet and keeps trying to lift herself up onto her knees to a crawling position. She presses her feet against furniture. During this time she has turned about 180 degrees.

MATERIALS AND ACTIVITIES

Materials for this age group must be safe for the infants to mouth and hit and bang on themselves. These infants have developed some manual skills, but their limited control of their arm and hand muscles causes them to be rather rough on their toys and themselves. Attention-catching toys stimulate the interest of these infants and lengthen their playtime.

Types of Materials

foam toys	toys safe to bang and hit
small toys and objects to grasp	low material and equipment to climb on and over
soft balls	
sound toys	mirror (unbreakable)
toys safe to throw	teething toys

Materials may be homemade or commercially made. Following are suggestions for making some of your own materials (Figure 11-1).

Examples of Homemade Materials

BLOCKS

Cut foam rubber into squares, circles, rectangles, triangles, and other shapes. Cover the foam with printed fabric sewn to fit the shapes. Large shapes can be stacked as blocks.

Cut 1-inch-thick sponges into shapes. Make sure the finished pieces are a good size to handle but too big to swallow.

FIGURE 11–1

(continued)

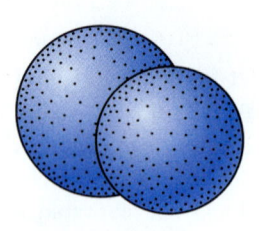

314 part 3 MATCHING CAREGIVER STRATEGIES, MATERIALS, AND EXPERIENCES TO THE CHILD'S DEVELOPMENT

Cover foam ball with washable pattern fabric.

RATTLES

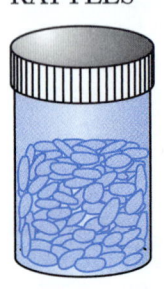

Empty and wash childproof clear plastic medicine bottles. Put in uncooked cereal—one teaspoon white, one teaspoon red (dyed in food coloring). Use sturdy glue to fasten cap tightly.

MUSIC, SOUND TOYS

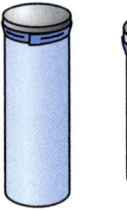

Use empty cardboard cans with lids (e.g., from oatmeal). Put jingle bells or loose items like blocks inside. Glue the lid on securely and tape around the edges. When the infant pushes and rolls it, the bells or blocks will make a noise.

FOIL PIE PANS

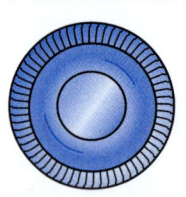

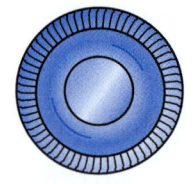

Place disposable pie pans near the infant to use for a mirror, for grasping, and for banging. Check frequently. If a sharp edge or tear develops, discard.

BEANBAG

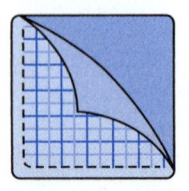

Sew together along three sides two double layers of 3-inch-square colorful terry cloth. Turn right side out. Fill the pouch half full with aquarium rocks that have been boiled to sanitize them. Sew the fourth side shut.

FIGURE 11–1

(continued)

BRACELET

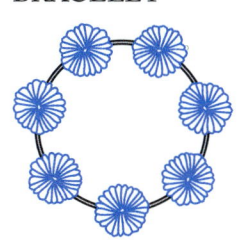

Sew a 4-inch length of elastic together to make a circle. Sew on several yarn pom-poms. Place on wrist or ankle for infant to watch while waving arms and kicking feet.

SOCK DOLL

Use a child's sock. Make eyes, nose, and mouth with permanent nontoxic marker or sew features with embroidery thread. Sew on short yarn hair. Stuff with foam or nylon scraps. Sew closed at bottom (top of sock). Caution: Make sure the "hair" is secured and cannot be pulled out.

FIGURE 11-1 *(continued)*

CAREGIVER STRATEGIES TO ENHANCE DEVELOPMENT

As mentioned numerous times already, teachers make educational decisions based on specific observations of an infant's development. Sometimes, however, they need to learn more about a particular development or contextual issue. Many resources are available at local universities, public libraries, or through professional organizations. The Spotlight on Organizations box provides information on one organization of great benefit to teachers.

spotlight *on organizations*

Zero to Three

This professional organization is dedicated to assisting professionals and parents learn more about (1) the development of infants and toddlers, (2) methods for providing appropriate care for infants and toddlers, and (3) current topics in public policy. In addition, this organization has many resources for individuals who want to advocate for infants, toddlers, and their families.

Zero to Three produces many high-quality resources for teachers, families, intervention specialists, and other professionals who might work with infants and toddlers, including books, videos, and the *Zero to Three* journal. Moreover, this organization provides many professional training opportunities. They have a train-the-trainer format for some of their programs such as *Cradling literacy: Building teachers' skills to nurture early language and literacy birth to five,* or you can schedule an on-site trainer at your center for topics such as reflective supervision or identifying developmental difficulties of infancy and toddlerhood.

Physical Development

Infants are highly motivated to master physical skills and explore their environments (McDevitt & Ormrod, 2010); as a result they develop rapidly during this four-month period. They are awake and alert longer. Their movements are becoming more coordinated: They can sit when propped or in a high chair, and are developing the ability to sit alone. They can roll over and may creep. They can grasp objects intentionally and move and bang them purposefully.

The head, neck, arm, chest, and back muscles are used to maintain a sitting position. These are developing from the pushing, pulling, kicking, and rolling the infant does. Even when the infant can sit when propped or alone, these muscles tire easily, so care must be taken to allow the infant to change positions.

By the middle of the first year, infants can stand on their legs. The muscles in their heads, necks, arms, chests, backs, and legs are all functioning but are not yet coordinated. With the aid of people and furniture, infants can stay standing and begin to take steps. Their ankle, foot, and toe muscles develop strength and coordination with the rest of their bodies.

Locomotion

While infants are developing some stability in relation to the force of gravity (sitting, standing), they are also attempting to move their bodies forward through space (locomotion).

At this age infants are often uncertain—sometimes fearful—of new experiences and people.

Between the fourth and fifth months, the infant will roll from stomach to back, and by the sixth month most infants can roll from back to stomach. Creeping is the first locomotor movement, starting around the sixth month (refer to Physical Development in the Developmental Prescriptions in Appendix A). Regan is lying on her stomach, reaching for a toy. She twists her body, pulls with her arms, and pushes with her legs. Slowly she moves forward to the toy. To accomplish this major task Regan used her head, neck, back, arm, and leg muscles to move and lift the top part of her body up and down without tipping over. She may even get up on her hands and knees and rock. Infants can be encouraged to move at this stage by placing toys just out of reach.

By the seventh month she may actually be able to crawl about on her hands and knees and may pull herself to a standing position. By the eighth month she may put one foot in front of the other when held in a standing position.

Manipulation

Manipulation involves reaching, grasping, and releasing. In the first year infants move from reflexive to voluntarily controlled manipulation. During the first six months arm movement develops from erratic waving to carefully controlled reaching. Infants use shoulder, elbow, wrist, and hand movements to coordinate with what they see in order to reach purposefully and successfully grasp an object. Control of reaching must accompany the task of grasping.

Newborns grasp reflexively. For the next few months their hands will close on anything that touches them. They will grasp objects with either hand. Gradually infants begin to open their hands and use the whole hand to "palm" a toy. Around the end of the fourth month, the child will be able to move toys from one hand to the other. By the end of the first year, an infant will be able to use thumb and forefinger to assist in grasping objects (see the "Hand" section in the Developmental Prescriptions).

Eating

Many pediatricians recommend that infants begin solid foods at about six months of age. Mouthing and swallowing solid foods involves a coordination of muscles different from those used for sucking. Begin solid foods when family members request it. Use the same kind of spoon they use so the infants do not have to adjust to different sizes and shapes of spoons while they learn to retrieve food from a spoon and swallow it without spitting it out or choking.

Feeding time presents an opportunity to socialize; the infant may be distracted from eating to coo and gurgle with his caregiver between eating spurts. This social exchange is very important to later social development.

By the sixth month, the infant may insist on holding the bottle or may try drinking from a cup, even without being ready to give up the bottle. By the seventh month, even though it is too early to use a spoon, the infant will want to feed himself or herself and will show resistance to being fed. It's time to let the child try it! At this time **finger foods** are developmentally appropriate. The experience of eating with fingers is an important one.

Teething

Infants usually begin **teething** at this age. Infants react differently to teething. Sometimes an emerging tooth causes an infant to be very fussy and irritable, while other times a new tooth just seems to appear with no change in the infant's behavior. Teething infants often like to bite on something. They use teething rings as well as anything else they can put into their mouths. If an infant seems to be hurting, a cold teething ring or crushed ice in a clean cloth provides coldness as well as hardness for the child's gums. Since teething infants may drool profusely, they may need to wear bibs all day, changed frequently to keep their clothes dry.

SUGGESTIONS FOR IMPLEMENTING CURRICULUM—PHYSICAL DEVELOPMENT

CHILD BEHAVIOR	MATERIALS	EXAMPLES OF CAREGIVER STRATEGIES
Muscular Control		
Head and Neck		
Holds head up independently		Allow infant to lift head. Keep hand near to provide support.
Holds head in midline position	mobiles, crib gyms	Put some objects above center of crib.
Holds head up when on back, stomach, and sitting		Place infant where child can safely look around.
Trunk		
Holds up chest, shoulders; arches back, hips		Provide clothes that allow freedom for pushing up, kicking, and wriggling. Check area for safety.
Sits with support; may attempt to raise self; may fuss if left lying down with little chance to sit up		Provide pillows and firm items to prop infant against. Hold infant in sitting position.
Leans back and forth	toys within reach	Keep area around infant free of sharp objects. Infant topples over easily.
Sits in a chair	chair with back	Use chair strap for safety. Let infant sit in chair, but for a short time, since the infant's muscles tire quickly.
Sits unsupported for short time	safe, flat sitting space	Place in safe area where infant can sit and play or watch. Infant will tire soon and lie down.
Pushes self to sitting position	flat sitting space	Provide uncluttered space where infant can roll around and push with arms and legs to sit up alone.

(continued)

CHILD BEHAVIOR	MATERIALS	EXAMPLES OF CAREGIVER STRATEGIES
Leg		
Lifts legs when on back and stomach		Provide clothes that allow free kicking.
Rolls from stomach to back		Place where infant can move freely and safely. Keep crib sides up. Keep hand on infant while changing diapers.
Straightens legs when standing		Hold infant in standing position for short periods. Hold infant's sides firmly when child bounces.
Stamps feet when standing		Firmly hold infant upright and provide flat surface for infant to push and move feet against.
Rolls from back to stomach		Place where infant can move freely and safely. Keep crib sides up. Keep hand on infant while changing diapers.
Raises to hands and knees		Place on flat, firm surface.
Stands with support		Hold infant's sides or hands while infant is standing on flat surface.
Pulls self to standing position		Hold infant's hands and allow infant to use his or her own muscles to pull self up. Check furniture and shelving to make sure neither will tip over when infant pulls on them to stand up.
Locomotion		
Kicks against surface to move	floor space, sturdy furniture	Provide area where there is safe resistance, e.g., carpeting that helps traction, bare feet on vinyl, furniture to push against.
Rocks on hands and knees	blanket on floor	Provide clear, safe area where infant can safely raise self up and rock, then lurch forward and fall on face. Praise infant for success in getting to hands and knees.
Creeps on stomach	blanket on floor	Provide clear safe area where infant can creep. Place a toy slightly out of reach to motivate creeping. Encourage and praise creeping.
Uses legs to pull, push self when sitting	floor space	Sit a short distance from infant. Call child's name. Encourage infant to come to you. Show excitement and give praise.
Arm		
Visually directs reaching, hitting	crib toys, movable toys	Provide toys that infant can reach and hit. Provide large toys infant can accurately hit against.
Throws objects	soft, light toys and objects	Select toys that are light and will not go far and hit other children. Place infant in an area where child can safely throw objects.

(continued)

CHILD BEHAVIOR	MATERIALS	EXAMPLES OF CAREGIVER STRATEGIES
HAND		
Grasps objects with whole hand and fingers against thumb	clutch ball	Provide toys that allow infant to wrap hand around some part. Flat surfaces slip out of grasp.
Uses thumb and forefinger	small toys of any shape	Make sure toys are too big to be swallowed. Infant will pick up anything and mouth it.
Picks up object with one hand; passes it to the other hand	small toys of any shape	Place toys around infant so child will use both hands. Ask for toy from one hand. Give toy to each hand.
Uses objects in both hands	banging toys	Play banging game with blocks, bells, balls.
Grasps and releases objects	toys that fit in one hand or have handles	Play game, "Put it here." You put toy in a pile. Infant picks up and puts down a toy in the same place.
Drops objects	unbreakable toys and objects, pail	Provide space for dropping. Play game, "Drop it." Stand up and drop toy into pail. Infant stands against chair and drops toys into pail.
Seeing		
Focuses on objects near and far	designs, pictures, wall space	Regularly change pictures, floor-to-ceiling projects, and bulletin boards to stimulate vision.
Distinguishes color, distance; depth perception	colorful objects	Provide colorful items. Put materials within reach so infant can succeed. Respect infant's resistance to moving where she or he does not feel safe.
Distinguishes visually attractive objects	faces, designs, shapes, color in room's materials and space	Note preferences for faces, designs, shapes. Make frequent changes.
Has visual preferences	favorite faces, pictures, objects	Observe infant's reactions to pictures, objects. Provide access to favorites by displaying them again later.
Hearing		
Listens to others' voices		Place near other infants and caregivers. Direct your talking to the infant.
Looks around to locate sound	sound toys, cans, bells	Play game: shake can beside infant. Wait for child to turn around and find you shaking the can. Shake bells beside you. Wait for infant to locate the ringing bells. Talk and sing with the infant.
Sleeping		
Takes a long morning nap and a long afternoon nap		Adjust routines to fit infant's changing sleep schedule.

(continued)

CHILD BEHAVIOR	MATERIALS	EXAMPLES OF CAREGIVER STRATEGIES
Eating		
At six months, begins solid foods		
Eats baby food (new tongue and swallowing technique)	mashed foods, baby spoon, heated dish, plastic-lined bib, washcloth	Clean up infant and self for feeding time. Check with the family about desired food. Feed patiently while infant learns to eat from a spoon. Talk calmly. Praise infant's accomplishments. Clean up.
Drinks from cup tongue and swallowing	Cup with cover to control flow of milk, juice	Hold cup for infant. Tilt up and back to give infant time to swallow before next drink. Allow infant to help hold cup.
Eats at "mealtimes" with solid foods, milk, juice	food grinder	Provide milk or juice in cup and solid foods at regular mealtimes to fit into the infant's sleep and play schedule.
Feeds self finger foods	bite-size food	Clean up infant, self, and eating area. Provide food and time to eat it. Minimize distractions. Talk with infant, encourage infant, label food and actions. Clean up.
Teeth		
First teeth emerge: two middle lower, two middle upper	hard teething rings: firm, safe objects to bite, cold objects to bite	Provide objects safe for infant to bite on hard.

✓ reading checkpoint

Before moving on with your reading, make sure that you can answer the following questions about the material discussed so far.

1. When an infant can roll from stomach to back and from back to stomach, what additional caregiver strategies are needed? Explain your rationale for at least three strategies.

2. Describe the development in eye-hand coordination of an infant between four and eight months old.

Cognitive and Language Development

Cognitive Development

Infants in Piaget's sensorimotor stage 3 are constructing the beginnings of the concept of objects separate from themselves. When the object an infant is watching disappears, she will visually search for it, but not manually. When the object she is holding disappears, she will search for it manually. Infants' senses still strongly control their actions; when the object is found, they will usually celebrate by mouthing it. As Jane Healy said in her book *Your Child's Growing Mind*,

> Each child must build individual networks for thinking; this development comes from within, using outside stimuli as materials for growth. Most babies give explicit clues about what kind of input is needed and let you know when it is overpowering or not interesting anymore.... Human brains come equipped with the "need to know"; our job is to give them love, acceptance, and the raw material of appropriate stimulation at each level of development. Your own common sense augmented by current knowledge is the best guide (Healy, 2004, p. 50).

SUGGESTIONS FOR IMPLEMENTING CURRICULUM—COGNITIVE DEVELOPMENT

CHILD BEHAVIOR	MATERIALS	EXAMPLES OF CAREGIVER STRATEGIES
Piaget's Substages of Sensorimotor Development		
SUBSTAGE 3 (Reproduction)		
Produces a motor activity, catches interest, and intentionally repeats the activity over and over	objects that attract attention: contrasting colors, changes in sounds, variety of textures, designs	Watch movements the infant repeats. Waving arm may hit the crib gym; the infant may wave arm more to hit the crib gym again. Watch which movements the infant repeats. Provide materials that facilitate, e.g., new items on the crib gym.
Repeats interesting action		The infant may pound fists on legs. Watch to see that child's actions are safe.
Develops hand-eye coordination further; looks for object, reaches for it, and accurately touches it	toys	Place blocks, dolls, balls, other toys near the infant where child can reach them.
Imitates behavior that is seen or heard	toy, food, body	Initiate action; wait for infant to imitate it; repeat action, e.g., smile, open mouth.
Piaget's Concept of Object Permanence		
Substage 4 (Coordination)		
Visually follows object	toys, bottle, or objects that attract visual attention	Show infant a toy. Play with it a minute and then hide the toy. Bring it out and play with it again. (You will not *teach* the infant to look for the toy. Enjoy playing with the infant and toy.)
Searches visually for short time when object disappears		
Does not search manually		
Sees part of object; looks for whole object when object disappears	familiar toy, bottle, rattle, teething ring, ball, doll	Cover up part of object with a blanket or paper. Infant will pull object out or push off blanket, i.e., play peekaboo.

A ball poses particular challenges, cognitive as well as physical, for a newly mobile child.

spotlight *on practice*

Voices from the Field

I work in a mixed-age classroom with children age six weeks to 18 months. Paul and Abraham are both eight months of age. They were sitting on a mat playing with toys from a nearby shelf. I took a small receiving blanket and joined them on the mat. As Paul sat down, I covered up the small stuffed dog he was playing with, using the blanket, and said, "Where did the dog go?" Paul looked at me with a nervous look on his face. I then replied, "Let's find the dog." as I slowly pulled the blanket off the stuffed animal. During this time, Abraham was sitting beside Paul, watching the dog being covered and uncovered by the blanket. When I covered up the dog again, Paul reached over and grabbed a different toy.

I then turned to Abraham and placed the blanket over his toy. Abraham immediately grabbed the blanket and pulled it off the toy. He began smiling and clapping his hands. We repeated this game several times. I then added a variation by placing the blanket over Abraham's face. He responded in a similar manner by pulling it off, smiling, laughing, and clapping his hands.

This experience was important for me because prior to this, I had been treating Paul and Abraham in very similar ways. If I planned an activity for one, I immediately invited the other to join. I learned that not all eight month olds are at the same developmental level for all skills. While I should've known this, I think I am more aware of this now.

Language Development

The crying, cooing, and babbling of the infant help develop the physical mechanisms that produce speech. Developmentally, the cooing period is followed by an extended period of babbling. Babbling continues the diversification of sounds begun in cooing yet with the addition of consonants (for example, g, t, k, b, r). According to Anisfeld (1984), the main difference between the two is in function: cooing has the function of expressing feelings of comfort, whereas babbling is primarily playing with sounds.

Infants seem to produce sounds first and then discover them to reproduce over and over again. They experiment with these sounds and begin to make changes in them. The difference may consist of the same sound made from a different part of the mouth. For instance, when infants play with a voiced sound and the tongue and saliva at the back of their mouths, they produce a gurgle. With the same sound, tongue, and saliva at the front of the mouth, they produce a hissing or spitting sound. Infants listen to themselves and seem to enjoy their vocal play.

Babbling is playing with speech sounds. It is spontaneously produced rather than planned. While babbling, infants use and learn to control their physical speech mechanisms. They babble different speech sounds and combine them into two- and three-syllable sounds. They control air flow to produce wordlike sounds and change the intensity, volume, pitch, and rhythm of their babbling sound play.

Babbling does not occur in social isolation. Infants listen to the sounds around them. When you repeat the sounds infants have just made, they may imitate your sound. Contingent (i.e., attuned), maternal behavior was found to facilitate more

The caregiver talks and listens to the infant's new sounds.

frequent, complex, and phonologically advanced vocal behavior by infants six to ten months in age (Goldstein, King, & West, 2003). Vocal stimulation that is relevant to the infant's behaviors and vocalizations seems to increase their babbling and, therefore, their control over their language. This stimulation also helps infants begin the two-way communication process of talking-listening-talking. They are finding that when they talk, you will listen; infants make you talk to them. Cooing and babbling sounds are used to provide pleasure as well as to convey feelings. Conversations include pitch and volume added to strings of sounds that seem like syllables or words. Infants imitate and initiate private and social talking.

Researchers have discovered that by six months, infants can distinguish **lexical words** or words that have a concrete or abstract connection to objects or events (e.g., nouns, verbs, and adverbs) from **grammatical words** or function words that have little meaning on their own yet affect the meaning of other words (e.g., articles, prepositions, or conjunctions; Shi & Werker, 2001). Moreover, infants demonstrate a distinct preference for lexical words (Shi & Werker, 2001, 2003) which may be related to the acoustic and phonological salience of these words (2003). In response to this developmental preference, teachers should label and describe objects and events in the environment using rich language. For example, when an infant is lying on her back looking at a sun catcher, you could say, "You are looking at the shimmering sun catcher. It sparkles in the sunlight."

SUGGESTIONS FOR IMPLEMENTING CURRICULUM—LANGUAGE DEVELOPMENT

CHILD BEHAVIOR	MATERIALS	EXAMPLES OF CAREGIVER STRATEGIES
Coos for many minutes		Respond with talk.
Babbles syllable-like sounds		Respond with talk.
Responds to talking by cooing, babbling, and smiling		Talk directly to infant.
Imitates sounds		Make sounds, talk, sing to infant.
Initiates sounds		Listen and respond.
Makes vowel sounds		
Looks for person speaking		Place yourself so that the infant can see you when you converse together.
Looks when name is called		Call the infant by name and talk with child.
Makes consonant sounds		
Babbles conversation with others		Respond with talking.
Reflects happiness or unhappiness in sounds made		Let your voice reflect response to mood.
Babbles two- and three-syllable sounds		Respond with talking.
Uses intensity, volume, pitch, and rhythm		Use normal speaking patterns and tones when talking to the infant.

reading checkpoint

Before moving on with your reading, make sure that you can answer the following questions about the material discussed so far.

1. When an infant can roll from stomach to back and from back to stomach, what additional caregiver strategies are needed? Explain your rationale for at least three strategies.

2. Describe language development for infants between four and eight months old. Match two developmental changes with caregiver strategies.

Emotional Development

Infants at this age now express a wider range of emotions. Pleasure, happiness, fear, and frustration are displayed in a variety of sounds, such as gurgles, coos, wails, and cries, along with physical movements like kicking rapidly, waving arms, bouncing, rocking oneself, and smiling.

Fear

Many infants experience what is called **stranger anxiety** in the latter half of the first year and well into the second year of life (McDevitt & Ormrod, 2010). People whom the infant doesn't know or does know but does not often see may find that the infant fears them. The infant may cry, cringe, hide, or move away. This very normal infant behavior occurs at a time when the infant is beginning to construct the idea of self as separate from others. It is important that "strangers" not feel something is wrong with them. A substitute teacher may experience this infant withdrawal because the infant has established familiarity and attachment to the primary caregiver, whereas he is different and unknown.

It is also during this period that the infant may demonstrate anxiety at being separated from his mother or other primary caregiver. The infant may become nervous or distraught if the caregiver is too far away or out of sight. Take every opportunity to tell the child that you will leave and will return. Introduce the other early childhood educator and explain that this person will take good care of him until you return. It is important to tell the infant when you have returned.

Temperament

As discussed previously, infants have different temperaments or characteristic ways of approaching their surroundings. You will need to know where a child falls in each of the nine behavioral categories (activity level, regularity, response to new situations, adaptability, sensory threshold, positive or negative mood, response intensity, distractibility, and persistence; for descriptions, see Chapter 3) so that you can adjust to the child's approach to the world and help him or her

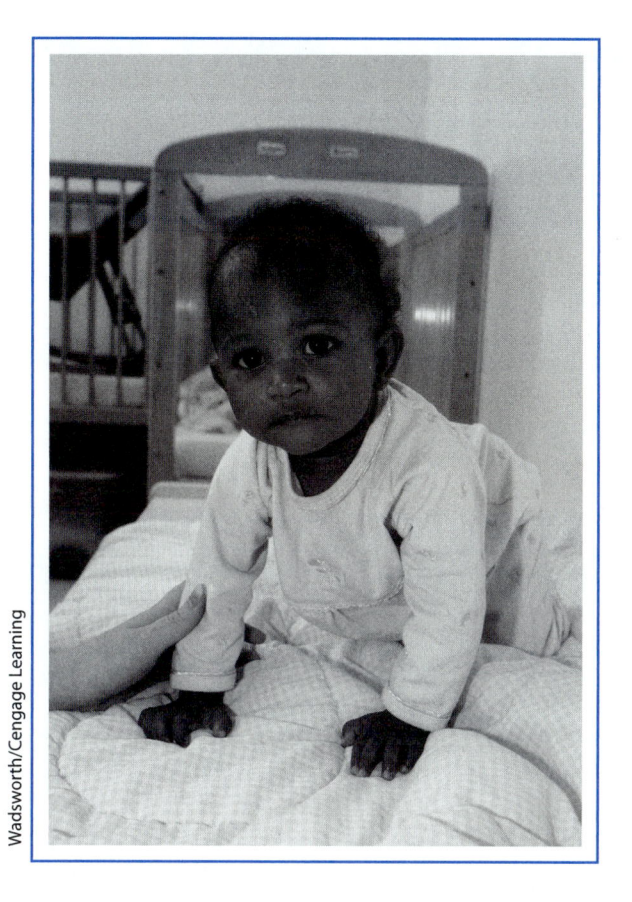

Special attention must be provided to children who hesitate to try new experiences.

cope with daily situations. As discussed previously, the important issue surrounding temperament is the teacher's ability to create a *goodness of fit* between the child and her environment (Marion, 2007). When family members provided responsive care despite infants' negative reactions, children were more willing and eager and less angry in interactions as they became toddlers (Kochanska, Aksan, & Carlson, 2005). It is logical to deduce that similar outcomes would result when teachers provide responsive care.

For example, the high active infant may kick, wriggle, and jerk, and therefore tip over when sitting propped up more often than the low active infant. High active infants need sitting times too, even though they need more caregiver assistance. On the other hand, low active children are easy to leave in a sitting position longer than may be good for their muscles because they may not fuss and move enough to tip over. These children need to be moved from sitting to lying on their stomachs,

SUGGESTIONS FOR IMPLEMENTING CURRICULUM—EMOTIONAL DEVELOPMENT

CHILD BEHAVIOR	MATERIALS	EXAMPLES OF CAREGIVER STRATEGIES
Types of Emotional Feelings		
Shows pleasure in watching others		Place infant where child can see others playing.
Shows pleasure in repetitive play	favorite toys	Provide favorite toys. Share pleasure in repetitive actions, e.g., clapping hands.
Shows fear of strangers		Introduce new people carefully. Do not let strangers hover closely. Give the infant time to become accustomed to the stranger at a distance.
Shows fear of falling down		When infant is standing and falling, keep area safe. Comfort when needed and then encourage infant and praise infant's standing.
Shows frustration with stimulation overload		Provide quiet space and time for the infant. Constant visual and auditory stimulation is nerve-racking. Comfort, hold, and talk softly to frustrated infant.
Shows happiness, delight, joy; humor expressed with laughs, giggles and grins		Share laughing, giggling. Play funny games, e.g., "Touch your nose"; hold your finger by your head and slowly move it to touch the infant's nose while you say excitedly, "I'm going to touch your nose."
Shows rage		Allow infant to kick legs, flail arms, scream, and cry for a short time. Determine the cause of the rage. Reduce or eliminate the cause if possible. Use touching, rocking, soothing talk to help the infant calm down.
		Verbally affirm and acknowledge the infant's anger and distress. Remain calm and present soothing support.
Control of Emotions-Feelings		
Sometimes stops crying when talked to, sung to		Talk calmly, soothingly to crying infant.

to holding, to sitting. The teacher must attend and be attuned as well as use her understanding of each child's temperament in order to create appropriate learning experiences.

Social Development

Infants are now developing definite and strong attachments to family members and primary caregivers. The primary caregiver's presence, consistent care, and emotional involvement with the infant all reinforce the attachment.

Infants are engaged in several new social experiences. Their developing physical skills of manipulating objects and moving themselves around contribute to the cognitive development of constructing a concept of self and not-self. During this time, from four to eight months of age, many infants interact more frequently with other children and adults. Their interest and mobility contribute to their initiating and responding to interactions with others.

Ainsworth (1982) identified several social behaviors during this age range.

Phase 2: Discriminating Social Responsiveness
(at six months or older)

> Discriminates between familiar and unfamiliar persons.
>
> Responds differently to them.
>
> Exhibits differential smiling, vocalizing, crying.

Phase 3: Actively Seeking Proximity and Contact
(around seven months)

> Signals intended to evoke response from mother or attachment figure.
>
> Locomotion which facilitates proximity seeking.
>
> Voluntary movements of hands and arms.
>
> Following, approaching, clinging—active contact behaviors.

Caregivers help children who can sit upright to explore materials and interact with each other.

SUGGESTIONS FOR IMPLEMENTING CURRICULUM—SOCIAL DEVELOPMENT

CHILD BEHAVIOR	MATERIALS	EXAMPLES OF CAREGIVER STRATEGIES
Attachment		
Shows strong attachment to family members		Reinforce attachment to family members.
Differentiates response to family members		
Shows familiarity with one specific caregiver		Assign a specific, primary caregiver to a specific infant. One caregiver can be a primary person (significant other) to four or fewer infants. Primary caregiver assumes responsibility for emotional involvement with the infant while providing care for the whole child.
Shows intense pleasure and frustration with person to whom attached		Accept and share pleasure; calm, soothe, stroke, and sing during infant's frustrated periods.
Self		
Recognizes self in mirror	foil, metal, or plastic shatterproof mirrors	Provide hand mirror for the infant to see self. Provide full-size mirror for infant to see self and others.
		Dots on bare feet and hands extend the infant's interest in his or her body.
Seeks independence in actions		Allow infant to accomplish tasks by self when possible, e.g., creeping to toy, pulling self up.
Plays self-designed games		Allow infant to play his or her own game. Do not distract infant or make infant change and play your game.
Others		
Observes others		Place the infant where child can observe others' activities.
Imitates others		Play games with the infant. Imitate each other, e.g., open mouth wide, stick out tongue.
Recognizes children		Allow infant to touch and "talk to" other children. Stay close so each is safe from pinching or hitting.
Plays with people		Let older children and other adults play games with the infant involving looking, hearing, and touching.
Seeks family's and caregiver's attention by movement, sounds, smiles, and cries		Respond immediately and consistently to happy, sad, or angry pleas for attention.
Follows adults		Arrange the room so the infant can see you from any place in the room.
Resists pressures from others regarding feeding and eating		Encourage but do not force the infant to eat. Adjust the time to stop and start according to the infant's rhythm.
Acts shy with some strangers		Hold and provide security to the infant when meeting a stranger. Allow the infant time to hear and see the stranger before the stranger touches the infant or even gets too close.

✓ reading checkpoint

Before moving on with your reading, make sure that you can answer the following questions about the material discussed so far.

1. Deborah, a five-month-old, is sitting up against a pillow on the floor. She is looking at the toy she has just thrown out of her reach. She leans forward, tips over, and cries. Describe what you would do next. Explain why you would do it.

2. List three caregiver strategies that facilitate the social development of the infant between four and eight months.

SUMMARY

Teachers make educational decisions based on specific observations of an infant's development. Many different developmental milestones are reached for infants between the age of four and eight months. For example, they become mobile, begin to babble, develop stranger anxiety, and express strong emotions. Careful use of the *three A*s: attention, approval, and attunement will help you to respond to the capabilities of the ever-changing infant.

key terms

babbling	**lexical words**	**stranger anxiety**
finger foods	**locomotion**	**teething**
grammatical words	**low active**	
high active	**manipulation**	

case study — Theresa

Theresa's parents both work at home. Her mother works late evenings and her father works early mornings. Theresa's mother is breast-feeding her on demand except for one day a week, when both parents are out of the house. During that day, she gets thawed, previously frozen breast milk from a bottle.

Both parents care for Theresa. They both manage to take breaks at the same time to give quality time to "Terry Bear," as she is affectionately called. Sometimes they all take walks together, taking turns carrying the baby. She enjoys the movement and facing her parents in her infant front carrier, but she is also curious about the sights and sounds around her. She has really begun to wiggle on these walks, so her parents are considering a new backpack where she can ride on their back and look around better.

While her parents really liked this schedule, work changes now require that Theresa attend child care two mornings a week. She has recently started going to a family child care and is learning to adjust and make the transition.

(Box continues)

She seems to be building a strong bond with Ellie, her caregiver. Ellie quickly discovered that Theresa is easily calmed by being given her satin blanket and talking in a soothing voice. Theresa really chews on her blanket when upset or trying to go to sleep.

1. Why is Theresa allowed to keep her blanket and chew on it?
2. What would happen to Theresa if you took away her blanket? Why do you think that would happen?
3. How old should a child be before she or he no longer needs "attachments" to favorite things?

QUESTIONS AND EXPERIENCES FOR REFLECTION

1. Listen to the talk of one infant between four and eight months of age. Write down the sounds you hear (they may be strings of vowels or syllables, e.g., *aaaa* or *babababa*).

2. Observe a caregiver talking to an infant of this age. Write down what the caregiver says and how the infant responds, both vocally and behaviorally.

3. Observe one infant from four to eight months of age. Record the infant's behavior in two five-minute sequences, using narrative description. Transfer the descriptions to the Developmental Profile.

4. Observe one infant who is creeping. Write a description of the infant's physical movements.

5. List strategies you need to develop and list ways you intend to develop them.

REFERENCES

Ainsworth, M. D. (1982). The development of infant-mother attachment. In J. Belsky (Ed.), *In the beginning: Readings on infancy*. New York: Columbia University Press.

Anisfeld, M. (1984). *Language development from birth to three*. Hillsdale, NJ: Lawrence Erlbaum Associates.

Douville-Watson, L., & Watson, M. (1995). *Improving learning development with games*. Glen Cove, NY: Instructional Press.

Goldstein, M. H., King, A. P., & West, M. J. (2003, June). Social interaction shapes babbling: Testing parallels between birdsong and speech [Electronic version]. *Proceedings of the National Academy of Sciences, USA, 100*(13), 8030–8035.

Healy, J. (2004). *Your child's growing mind: A guide to learning and brain development from birth to adolescence*. (3rd ed.). New York: Broadway Books.

Kochanska, G., Aksan, N., & Carlson, J. (2005). Temperament, relationships, and young children's receptive cooperation with their parents. *Developmental Psychology, 41*(4), 648–660.

Marion, M. (2007). *Guidance of young children* (7th ed.). Upper Saddle River, NJ: Pearson Prentice Hall.

McDevitt, T. M., & Ormrod, J. E. (2010). *Child development: Educating and working with children and adolescents* (4th ed.). Upper Saddle River, NJ: Pearson Prentice Hall.

Shi, R., & Werker, J. F. (2001). Six-month-old infants' preferences for lexical words. *Psychological Science, 12*(1), 70–75.

Shi, R., & Werker, J. F. (2003). The basis of preference for lexical words in 6-month-old infants. *Developmental Science, 6*(5), 484–488.

Solchany, J. (2007). Consequences of divorce in infancy: Three case studies of growth faltering. *Zero to Three, 27*(6), 34–41.

Swaminathan, S., Alexander, G. R., & Boulet, S. (2006). Delivering a very low birth weight infant and the subsequent risk of divorce or separation. *Maternal Child Health Journal, 10*, 473–479.

For additional activities, web links, and other resources, please visit our website at www.cengage.com/education/swim

chapter 12

THE CHILD FROM EIGHT TO TWELVE MONTHS OF AGE

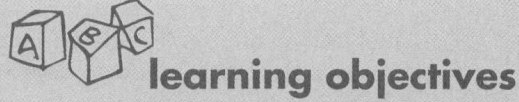

learning objectives

After reading this chapter, you should be able to:
- Identify and record sequences of change in the physical, cognitive/language, emotional, and social development of infants from eight to twelve months of age.
- Select materials appropriate to the development of infants at that age level.
- Devise strategies appropriate to infants of that developmental level.

chapter outline
- Materials and Activities
- Caregiver Strategies to Enhance Development
  Physical Development
  Cognitive and Language Development
  Emotional Development
  Social Development
- Case Study: Marcel

333

Marcel's Story

Marcel, nine months old, is sitting on the floor with several toys in front of him that Miss Virginia, the caregiver, has just placed there. He picks up a pink toy elephant, lifts it up and down with his right hand and says, "Ahh. Ah, Ah, Yah, Ahya." He picks up lock blocks, saying, "Eee, Ahh, Ahh." He throws down the blocks and then picks up blocks and twirls one in his left hand. He puts down the blocks and crawls away to another part of the room and sits up to watch a child run cars. He crawls to Miss Virginia and pulls himself to stand. He stares at her and says, "Ayy." He crawls to the toys, sits back, and then pulls on the train. He sits up on his knees and pats the ball. He starts to stand up and goes back to his knees. He pushes the train and it goes forward; his eyes get big. Miss Virginia says, "You are driving the train. Toot. Toot." Marcel stands and goes up on his toes as he reaches for her hands. Miss Virginia picks him up and holds him in her lap a minute before he climbs down and crawls back to the train.

MATERIALS AND ACTIVITIES

Most infants in this age range are mobile and will encounter an expanded world. All objects within reach must be safe to taste and touch and move. These infants need space as they continue to develop control of gross motor movements, such as crawling, standing, pulling, and throwing objects. Materials to manipulate must be small enough to grasp with the palm and fingers or with thumbs and forefingers, but not small enough for them to swallow. Attention-catching materials stimulate infants to select and use those materials.

Types of Materials

very low materials to climb over	stroking, textured objects
sturdy furniture to pull self up next to and walk around	sound toys
	mirrors
balls to clutch	crayons
stacking objects	puppets
nesting objects	pictures
pail and small objects to drop into it	one-piece puzzle

Examples of Homemade Materials

CLUTCH BALL

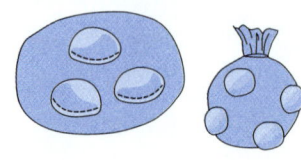

Cut a circle of colorful, washable fabric. Put polyester filling on one part of the fabric and sew around it, creating a lump. Repeat, making a second lump. Baste around the edge of the circle and pull the circle almost closed. Stuff in polyester filling to pad the ball. Sew through the fabric and wind thread around the gathered end, creating a tuft of fabric.

FIGURE 12–1

(continued)

chapter 12 THE CHILD FROM EIGHT TO TWELVE MONTHS OF AGE   **335**

Sounds and objects attract the infant's attention.

NESTING TOYS

Select three containers of different sizes, such as plastic margarine tubs or cardboard tubes.

PUZZLE

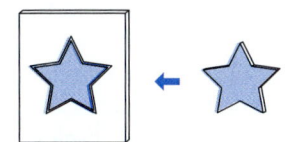

Glue a picture of one simple object on a piece of thick cardboard (use white glue and water mixture to cover the whole picture and cardboard). Cut out the object, making a simple shape. Place the object into the matching frame.

PUPPET

On a child-sized white sock, use a nontoxic waterproof marker to draw a face on one side, hair on the other side.

FIGURE 12-1 *(continued)*

CAREGIVER STRATEGIES TO ENHANCE DEVELOPMENT
Physical Development

Infants of this age are rapidly developing muscular control. They learn to sit alone. They crawl, stand with support, and walk with help. Creeping evolves into **crawling**, where the arms and legs are used in opposition. On hands and knees the infant first slowly moves one limb and then another. With increased control, crawling can become a very fast and efficient means of locomotion, providing the infant with a new world of possible experiences. Quickly after learning to crawl, infants begin to pull themselves up and stand with the assistance of objects and people. When infants have gained stability in standing upright, they can turn their efforts toward moving forward (walking). Many months of movement precede the actual accomplishment of walking. Shirley (1931) identified four stages.

1. An early period of stepping, in which slight forward progress is made (three to six months)
2. A period of standing with help (six to ten months)
3. A period of walking when led (nine to twelve months)
4. A period of walking alone (twelve to fifteen months)

All infants proceed through this sequence of locomotion, though the age varies among infants. A formerly low active baby may show a sudden spurt of activity during this time.

Ryan is standing next to a chair watching a bright toy on the floor sparkle in the sunshine. He leans toward it and reaches for it, but he cannot reach it. He takes one step away from the chair while still holding on to it. He still cannot reach the toy. He takes another step, and his hand slips off the chair. He is now on his own. He takes another step, stops, weaves, takes another step, and then falls down. Ryan is beginning to walk. His first attempts at locomotion are filled with standing, stepping, weaving, sitting or falling down, pushing himself back up to standing, and trying again.

A dynamic systems framework helps us to understand that multiple layers of child-environment interaction influence both the long-term and short-term changes that infants experience in their movements and actions (Newell, Liu, & Mayer-Kress, 2001). Ryan will repeat this cycle thousands of times, a process that strengthens his muscles and develops his coordination. Infants quickly, within the first month of walking, move from making short steps from a wide-base stance with feet pointed outward to longer steps made from a smaller base with feet pointed forward (Adolph, Vereijken, & Shrout, 2003). These authors believe that the experience of walking over and over again is what assists infants with developing the more adult-like walk. To accomplish this developmental task, Ryan needs open floor space, where he can walk without bumping into furniture or having to step on or over toys on the floor.

To promote the optimal development of gross motor skills, infants need adequate floor space where they can roll, crawl, climb, reach, stand, and walk. Caregivers should be cautious about the equipment they provide. Playpens can very easily become prisons that restrict movement. Wheeled walkers or stationary jumpers can put undue strain on the infant's back, restricting the development and coordination of head, neck, arm, chest, back, leg, and foot muscles, while putting too much emphasis on leg movement.

In the following paragraphs, we will turn our attention to fine motor control, where the development of capabilities is just as impressive between eight and twelve months.

> Although the baby starts practicing muscle control almost immediately, integrating reflex motor movements into controlled patterns takes a long time. The baby needs many things to see and to touch with body, mouth and hands. At first the infant's movements seem random, but as he gets the feel of his own body in space, connections build . . . to help the child organize his muscles around independent plans of action. (Healy, 2004, p. 43)

Infants of this age often hold a finger straight and poke at themselves and objects around them. They push and pull and may keep repeating their actions. In addition, they use their thumb and fingers to grasp objects, perfecting the **pincer grasp**. Using this skill often, they continue to develop their finger muscles and eye-hand coordination. Because they do not have good control of the strength of the pinch, they may sometimes pinch another child hard enough to hurt.

These infants are also developing control of their arms; now they can clap and bring both hands to mid-body repeatedly. Their hands can grasp some objects, so they may bang objects together. They can hold crayons and make marks with them (refer to Appendix A, Developmental Prescription: Muscle, Hand). By the end of this time period, infants are gaining enough control of their arm and hand movements to be able to touch lightly or stroke objects.

Infants eight months to one year old are also beginning to use each hand for different tasks. They may pick up a toy with one hand, transfer it to the other hand to hold, and then pick up another toy. They may reach out and stack one block, transfer the other toy to that hand, and stack the second block.

Advances in motor control, both fine and gross, assist infants with eating. They often use two fingers or a spoon to eat and may even use them at the same time. Infants want to get the food into their mouths, and they use every way they can to accomplish this task. So be prepared for spills, dropped food, and other messes by carefully planning the eating environment. Because infants use their new teeth to bite anything put into their mouths, caution should be used when selecting eating utensils. Plastic, disposable utensils often cannot withstand the infants' biting. Infants should be skilled at holding their own bottles and may be beginning to use a cup without a lid. Allow them to complete these skills independently or provide only the necessary amount of assistance.

Sleep patterns continue to change gradually. At this age infants take a morning and afternoon nap but have more time awake in which to be alert and play. Each infant has a personal sleep schedule that is affected by the child's own body needs for sleep, as well as by the sleep routines at home. If the infant is awakened at 5:00 a.m. to get ready to come to child care, that child may need a morning nap earlier than an infant who is able to sleep until 7:00 a.m.

part 3 MATCHING CAREGIVER STRATEGIES, MATERIALS, AND EXPERIENCES TO THE CHILD'S DEVELOPMENT

Crawling, indoors and outdoors, enables the infant to explore a wide new world.

SUGGESTIONS FOR IMPLEMENTING CURRICULUM—PHYSICAL DEVELOPMENT

CHILD BEHAVIOR	MATERIALS	EXAMPLES OF CAREGIVER STRATEGIES
Trunk, leg		
Raises self to sitting position	flat surface	Keep area clear of objects that would hurt the infant if child falls on them.
Sits alone		Provide a short time to sit. Infant may tire soon.
Stands holding on to furniture or hand	sturdy chair, bench, table	Remove furniture that could tip over on infant.
Stands without assistance	flat surface	Allow infant to stand alone.
Sits from standing		Keep area clear of objects that could hurt infant. Infant often falls down when trying to sit down from standing.
Squats and stands		Watch sharp-cornered furniture. Pad corners as needed. Infant often stands up underneath furniture (tables) and bumps head.

(continued)

CHILD BEHAVIOR	MATERIALS	EXAMPLES OF CAREGIVER STRATEGIES
Locomotion		
Crawls	obstacle-free space	Allow infant to crawl. Play with infant to stimulate crawling. Place toys slightly beyond reach to stimulate crawling.
Steps forward	obstacle-free space	Hold infant's hand; provide furniture to lean on for support when stepping forward.
Crawls up steps	low two- to four-step equipment	Allow infant to crawl up steps. Watch so you can assist infant in getting back down safely. Barricade any steps you do not want the infant to use.
Steps sideways	equipment, furniture	Allow infant to stand and step around to hold on to furniture. Keep chairs, toys away from path.
Walks with help	obstacle-free area	Hold infant's hand(s). Slowly walk around, allowing infant to step and balance as needed. Infant's swaying body will give you clues for stopping and starting.
Climbs on furniture	low, sturdy furniture	Infant can climb but has not learned how much space his or her body takes up so may climb into areas where he or she does not fit. Watch, caution, and assist when necessary.
Hand		
Uses thumb and forefinger	toys, dolls	Provide objects small enough to pinch and lift.
Uses thumb and two fingers	toys, dolls	Provide objects small enough to pinch and lift.
Brings both hands to middle of body	banging objects, foil pie pans, blocks	Play clapping, banging games with infant. Play patty cake.
Uses finger to poke	pillow, ball, small box	Provide soft objects to poke into. Watch carefully because infant may poke other children's face, eyes, and so on.
Carries objects in hands	attractive objects small enough to grasp but too big to swallow	Provide objects that can be carried.
Holds and uses pen, crayon	flat surface, fat felt marker, fat crayon, paper	Provide materials and space. Demonstrate where marks go (on paper, not floor or table). Remain with infant when child is using marker or crayon. Allow child to make the kind and number of marks he or she wants to. Praise child for the interest and effort. Put materials away when child decides he or she is finished.

(continued)

CHILD BEHAVIOR	MATERIALS	EXAMPLES OF CAREGIVER STRATEGIES
Reaches, touches, strokes object	textured objects	Provide objects of different textures. Infants can stroke, not just grasp and pinch. Demonstrate gentle stroking. Describe the texture, e.g., "the feather is soft." Allow infant to gently stroke many objects.
Uses one hand to hold object, one hand to reach and explore	objects small enough to grasp	Provide several objects at once that stimulate infant's interest.
Stacks blocks with dominant hand	blocks, small objects	Allow infant to choose which hand to use in stacking objects.
Takes off clothes	own clothes with big buttonholes, zippers	Infant's fingers are beginning to handle buttons, zippers. Allow infant to play with these. Infant does not understand when to undress and when to keep clothes on. Discourage undressing when you want infant to stay clothed.
Sleeping		
May have trouble sleeping	calming music, musical toy	Provide adequate time to spend with infant preparing for sleep. Rock, sing and talk to, and stroke infant. Respond immediately if infant awakens during regular sleep time. Rub child's back, talk quietly as you attempt to help infant go to sleep again.
Takes morning nap and afternoon nap	quiet, dim, clean sleeping space	Determine infant's preferences for going to sleep. Feed, hold and rock, rub infant's back, hum and sing to help get the infant to sleep.
Seeks parent or caregiver presence		Primary caregiver should prepare infant for sleep, put infant to bed, respond if sleep is interrupted, and get infant up from nap.
Eating		
Holds bottle	bottle	Allow infant to hold bottle while you hold infant.
Holds cup	cup with special cover	Allow infant to hold own cup. Assist when necessary; e.g., the spout is at infant's nose rather than mouth.
Holds and uses spoon	child-size spoon	Provide food that can fit on spoon. Allow infant to use spoon to feed self. Assist when necessary with difficult food. Praise infant's efforts and successes. Child will hold spoon in one hand and eat with fingers of other hand.
Uses fingers to eat most food	finger food	Wash hands and face *before* eating. Allow infant to use fingers to pick up food. Wash hands, face, chair, and whole area after eating time.
Starts establishing food preferences		Identify and record infant's food likes and dislikes. Plan a balanced diet for child, emphasizing foods child likes. Do not force foods child does not like.

(continued)

CHILD BEHAVIOR	MATERIALS	EXAMPLES OF CAREGIVER STRATEGIES
May eat less		Do not force eating. Infant's body may need less. Children make adjustments in the amount they eat. Be sure children have food available they like so they can make choices about *amount* rather than *kinds* of foods.
Teeth		
Begins to get teeth	teething ring; cold, hard objects to bite; bib	Provide objects safe to bite. Cold soothes the gums. Change bib as needed since drooling increases.

spotlight *on practice*

Voices from the Field

I am the owner/teacher of my family child care center. I planned a musical experience for the two infants (nine and eleven months of age) and the toddler in my care. It was one of the first I've done with children this young. I just recently read an article about the importance of music for very young children, so I decided to try it out. In the middle of the kitchen floor, I put out several different types and sizes of bowls as well as plastic tubes of different lengths. I then placed wooden and metal spoons on the floor.

I didn't take the children to the materials but rather waited for them to discover them. Ethan found them first. He squealed with joy as he picked up two metal bowls and banged them together. He squinted his eyes and dropped the pans. He had a scared look on his face as he gazed up at me. I said, "What a loud noise you made. Did that scare you? (pause) Maybe you should hit the bowl with your hand." He did just that and resumed smiling.

Kei crawled quickly into the room with a curious look on her face. She reached for a tube and a wooden spoon. She began banging the spoon on the tube.

Ethan and Kei passed materials back and forth between them on two separate occasions. I was impressed with their developing social skills and with how engaged they were with the materials. This was also an important cognitive experience for them as they produced music independently through their own actions. I will need to think about other ways to engage Maisy as she never joined in the experience.

Cognitive and Language Development

Cognitive Development

Assimilation and accommodation begin to operate independently (refer to Chapter 2 for definitions of these terms). Infants of this age are beginning to separate their thinking about what they want to accomplish from how they can accomplish it.

The establishment of **object permanence** is the major development during this age range. The infants remember events, people, and objects for increasingly longer periods. Awareness of object permanence forms the basis for rapid development of representations in play and language.

These infants are constructing a concept of self separate from all other entities, but have not completed it. People and toys are eventually perceived as real entities that continue to exist even when the infants cannot see them. With this concept, infants now actively search visually and manually for people or objects that are no longer visible. These infants are mentally constructing a representation of the person or object. This mental representation of the real entity forms the foundation for increasingly complex forms of representation.

Along with thinking about other people as separate from themselves, infants of this age also begin to determine that others can cause actions. They will incorporate others' actions into their own play.

At this stage infants imitate people and things that are not present. They have established *deferred imitation*, which requires sufficient cognitive skills to remember and reproduce things they have seen and heard: "... early imitation serves a learning function, that is, infants imitate to advance their comprehension and mastery of behaviors that interest them" (Anisfeld, 1984, p. 44).

SUGGESTIONS FOR IMPLEMENTING CURRICULUM—COGNITIVE DEVELOPMENT

CHILD BEHAVIOR	MATERIALS	EXAMPLES OF CAREGIVER STRATEGIES
Piaget's Substage of Sensorimotor Development		
Substage 4 (Coordination)		
Differentiates goals; can focus on reaching and on a particular toy	toys, visually attractive objects	Place objects near infant.
Piaget's Concept of Object Permanence		
Establishes object permanence, that object exists when it is no longer visible, e.g., child seeks toy that rolls behind box		Play hiding games, e.g., hide the doll under the blanket; place the block behind you.
Causality		
Learns that others cause actions		Verbalize caregiver's own actions, e.g., "I put the ball behind me."
Imitation and Play		
Imitates other's actions; uses actions as play		Introduce new copying games. Allow time and space for infant to play.

spotlight on research

Infant Persistence

Infants are born curious about the world and their place in it. This curiosity results in a great deal of internal motivation. It should be no surprise, then, that infants spend a great deal of time exploring the people and objects in their environment. Is being persistent a stable, individual quality that varies among individuals and, if so, how does more or less persistence impact later development?

Banerjee and Tamis-LeMonda (2007) set out to explore these questions with their sample of 65 low-income mother–infant dyads. These researchers videotaped infant-mother interactions in their home during a teaching task when the infants were six and fourteen months of age. The measure of infant persistence was coded from a three-minute interaction with a toy at six months of age. Infant cognition was measured after each session using the Mental Scale of the Bayley Scales of Infant Development.

The results showed that as early as six months of age, infants differ in their degree of persistence and that there was a significant correlation in persistence scores over the eight-month period. In other words, infants who were more persistent at six months tended to be more persistent at fourteen months. Additionally, "infants who persisted early on also ... had higher scores on the Bayley Mental Development Index" (Banerjee & Tamis-LeMonda, 2007, p. 487). Thus, persistence was associated with greater levels of cognitive development.

Next, the researchers investigated the impact of mothers' teaching on cognitive development. They found that "mothers' teaching at six but not fourteen months was associated with persistence at both ages and predicted cognitive development at fourteen months" (Banerjee & Tamis-LeMonda, 2007, p. 487). The researchers concluded from this result that mothers' early teaching had a dual function of helping infants to persistent at a challenging task as well as promoting cognitive development.

This research study has implications for early intervention specialists as well as early childhood educators. If teachers and intervention specialists work with infants and their families to support the development of persistence, we would also be supporting important cognitive skills. Wheeler and Stultz (2008) suggest that music therapy can be used to assist young infants with regulating their interest in and their interactions with environmental stimuli, especially people. For example, therapists can use their voice, face, and hands as tools for gaining the attention of an infant. Then, they attempt to gain eye contact, even if infrequent, and to be attuned to the infant's cues while working to extend periods of interactions. It would seem reasonable to conclude that "extending periods of interactions" (Wheeler & Stultz, 2008) is another way to describe the infant's ability to persist in an interaction with another person. Gaining and maintaining this balance is not easy as infants frequently change states of arousal and often have difficulty regulating their reactions to new stimuli. Wheeler and Stultz (2008) conclude that therapists support moderate arousal by soothing and containing the agitated child, enticing the withdrawn child, and inviting the child's attention to the social environment.

Language Development

Infants, around one year of age, typically speak their first recognizable words and use a combination of sounds, babbling, and single words to communicate with themselves and others (McDevitt & Ormrod, 2010). "Just as the sensorimotor exploration of objects lays the groundwork for object representation, so the sensorimotor exploration of speech lays the groundwork for speech representation" (Anisfeld, 1984, p. 224).

Newborns are born with the capacity for distinguishing frequency and pitch (Healy, 2004), and develop finer auditory discrimination during the first year.

Just as we provide infants with a well-balanced diet, we should also provide a well-balanced auditory environment, as "soothing, pleasant and interesting sounds inspire curiosity and a receptive attitude" toward language (p. 46). Sing and talk often with the infants. However, because too much noise, noises that are too loud, or nonstop noise can cause confusion and be detrimental to development (Healy, 2004), monitor background sounds and discuss this issue with family members.

Anisfeld identified levels of meaning, characterizing the first level as pre-symbolic use of words. "The early words have a sign character. . . . They are **context bound**" (1984, p. 67). Infants learn to associate a word with a particular object or action. They respond to the word in that context but cannot identify it in other contexts. For example, each day the caregiver says "Sit in your chair" as she gets the infants ready for lunch. When told, "Sit in your chair," Beverly looks at her chair. She does not look at other chairs around the room. *Chair* relates to a specific chair, not to a class of objects called *chairs*. ". . . [C]hildren's early words are nonsymbolic because they function primarily as responses to specific stimulus contexts" (p. 69). An infant says the word in association with the context in which it was learned: ". . . the context-boundness of the first level results from a conceptual limitation. The child does not automatically conceive of words as independent of the specific contexts of their use" (p. 70).

Reading aloud to infants facilitates their ability to visually focus, reinforces basic concepts, stimulates imagination, and develops and enhances language development and listening skills (Zeece & Churchill, 2001). As infants experience multiple readings of the same book, they begin to join in the reading, identifying objects in illustrations by either pointing to or verbally acknowledging an object (Zeece & Churchill, 2001). Adults should actively engage with infants when reading. The Allen County Public Library in Fort Wayne, Indiana, suggests that adults should, follow the children's lead by following the "CAR" or

Comment and wait*
Ask questions and wait*
Respond by adding a little more
*Waiting gives the child time to respond (Allen County Public Library, 2009).

Linda Lamme (1985) extends this idea when she states in *Growing Up Reading*:

Pointing to things in pictures and labeling them orally is especially important in the first year when your infant, though not yet talking, is acquiring so much language. Relate what is in the book to your infant's experience. "You have a ball just like that one!" Repetition is important also. After seeing a page several times, your infant will begin to recognize the pictures. You'll quickly come to realize your infant has distinct book preferences.

The last guideline is: The earlier you begin to read aloud, the better. If your child can become used to having stories read aloud before he or she starts walking, reading-aloud sessions can be sustained during those mobile, early walking times. Children who are learning to walk have a hard time sitting still to listen to a story if they have not previously become hooked on book reading (p. 51).

Makin (2006) researched shared book readings between ten mother-infant pairs. She discovered that they showed varying patterns of language use, conversation structure, and use of nonverbal communication strategies such as facial expressions, tempo, and gestures. This variation highlights how children acquire different types of knowledge in their homes. Some family cultures are more expressive, while others are more reserved in how they demonstrate emotions. Neither approach is inherently right or wrong. Teachers should not judge, but rather come to understand these differences so that bridges between home and school can be built; literature is a powerful tool for building bridges and routines for helping children transition from home to school (Lawhon & Cobb, 2002; Zeece, Harris, & Hayes, 2006).

Scribbling is related to the language/reading/writing processes the infant is developing. In her earlier work on infants, *Growing Up Writing*, Lamme (1984) wrote the following:

> Well before his first birthday, your child is ready to make marks on paper or chalkboard. Those first marks will be random scribbles. Your child won't even be watching as he is making the mark and will not see the connection between the mark on paper and the writing tool in his hand. The first stage of development is called "uncontrolled scribbling."
>
> The outstanding feature of these early writing attempts is that they are more than random marks; they represent your child's intentions to create something. Scribbling has been termed "gesturing with a pencil." The role of scribbling in writing development has been compared with babbling in oral language development. In each case, there is probably some random sound or scribble made but, in both cases, your child is intending to communicate (p. 38).

SUGGESTIONS FOR IMPLEMENTING CURRICULUM—LANGUAGE DEVELOPMENT

CHILD BEHAVIOR	MATERIALS	EXAMPLES OF CAREGIVER STRATEGIES
Babbles		Respond with talk.
Shouts		Respond to infant's feelings.
Labels sounds	bell, rattle	Name important objects with one word. Then use in a sentence, e.g., "Bell" (while pointing to it). "Ramon has a bell."
Uses names: Mama, Dada		Reinforce by talking about Mama and Dada.
Responds to familiar sounds		Provide familiar music, routine changes. Acknowledge infant's response, e.g., "Tasha heard the spoons being put on the table."

(continued)

CHILD BEHAVIOR	MATERIALS	EXAMPLES OF CAREGIVER STRATEGIES
Responds to familiar words		Frequently use names or labels that infant is learning, e.g., ball, shoe, coat.
Responds to own name		Use infant's name when you start talking with that child.
Makes sounds that reflect emotions		Respond to the infant's message about how he or she feels. Name the emotions, e.g., "Garrett is angry."
Repeats syllables, words, e.g., *bye-bye*		Label frequent behaviors and respond to infant's use, e.g., say "bye-bye" and wave; repeat occasionally.
Makes sounds like conversation		Respond verbally to infant's "conversation," e.g., "Holly is talking to her truck."
Repeats, practices word over and over		Allow infant to play with words. Respond and encourage.
Connects words with objects, e.g., says "kitty"—points to kitty	familiar toys, objects	Point or touch objects you verbally label.
Chooses books	picture books of familiar objects	Point to picture of object and say name of object. Repeat often.
Scribbles randomly	paper, markers	Provide writing space and materials.

✓ reading checkpoint

Before moving on with your reading, make sure that you can answer the following questions about the material discussed so far.

1. List five strategies you can use to facilitate the physical development of an infant in this age range, using the format below.

Caregiver Strategy	Specific Physical Development
a.	
b.	
c.	
d.	
e.	

2. An 11-month-old is responding to labels of objects. Describe a game you can play with this child to stimulate the child's understanding and use of language.

Emotional Development

Positive interactions with caregivers help infants develop good feelings about themselves. Infants express their happiness in many ways. Anger is expressed more often during this time period. Infants can now conceive of goals or desires and actively pursue them. For example, when Tomas does not want his father to leave at drop-off time, he might crawl over and cling to his leg. Or he might crawl to the door and bang on it once his father has left. Tomas is clearly communicating his desire to keep his dad near and sadness (most often expressed through anger) at not being able to do so. Teachers must help infants and family members create rituals for coping with the emotions that stem from being separated on a daily basis (Balaban, 2006). Infants will express their anxiety and fears in a multitude of ways, and teachers must learn to crack the message encoded in their behaviors (Marion, 2007).

Out of fear, uncertainty, and/or changes in family characteristics, an infant may regress temporarily to an earlier stage. Understanding this **regression** helps the caregiver to be aware that the child may need more reassurance than is given to a younger infant. The caregiver should be alert and notice when the child is feeling confident once more and able to function at the higher level again.

The caregiver smiles, talks, and encourages the infant's movements.

At this age infants are developing preferences and independence. Providing toys they like not only adds to their pleasure in playing with the toys but also enhances their feelings of asserting some control over their world. As discussed previously, developing physical skills also make infants more independent in feeding and dressing themselves. Allowing them to accomplish as many tasks as possible on their own helps them strengthen their identity or who they are as an individual.

External influences like a verbal "no" or a firm look may sometimes cause infants to change their behavior. Follow up your restrictive words or looks with an explanation. For example, when an infant throws food on the floor, the caregiver can say, "No. You need the carrots up here in your dish. Let's see you put a carrot in your mouth." Sometimes infants will stop their own negative action. You may see them pick up food or a toy, start to throw, and then stop their arm movement and put the object down carefully. This early self-restriction may be caused by distraction rather than self-control. Nevertheless, acknowledge such actions to help the child better understand the acceptable behavior.

As soon as the child has a modicum of verbal skills, promoting perspective-taking skills and applying the three *A*s will elicit positive emotions. Remember that the most powerful way to promote positive feelings is to *provide attention for appropriate behavior*. Redirecting negative behaviors to positive or desired behaviors works better than drawing attention to negative ones. Be sure to trust the child's motives. Children are doing the best they can at all times.

The temperaments of infants produce varying responses to experiences. Some infants approach new situations openly. When new solid foods and finger foods are introduced, they try them. They accept and eat many of the foods, and those they reject, they reject with minimal fussing. Other infants are hesitant or resist new situations. Each new food causes these infants to pull back and at first reject the new food. With encouragement, these infants may taste the new food and then determine whether they like it or not. Sometimes they so actively resist a new food that it is difficult to get them to eat enough of it to develop an acceptance of it.

Variation in intensity of response often shows up when infants are pulling themselves up and falling down. Falling down, whether toppling forward or sitting down hard on their bottoms, always surprises infants and can sometimes be painful. One infant will scream and cry loudly. Another may cry quietly or whimper or perhaps look surprised and upset but will not verbalize his or her discomfort.

Persistence at trying to stand upright and step forward leads toward walking. Very persistent infants will try again and again to stand or step. Falling down becomes a deterrent only after many tries. Other infants persist only a few times, then stop their efforts and change to some new task or interest.

SUGGESTIONS FOR IMPLEMENTING CURRICULUM—EMOTIONAL DEVELOPMENT

CHILD BEHAVIOR	MATERIALS	EXAMPLES OF CAREGIVER STRATEGIES
Types of Emotions and Feelings		
Shows happiness, joy, pleasure		Share infant's feelings. Return smile, use a positive tone of voice, hug and pat the child.
Shows anxiety		Use calm, quiet talking, singing. Cuddle and stroke the child. Remove from situation if necessary.
Shows fear		Determine and remove cause of fear if possible. Use calm, quiet talking to describe the feeling. Sing, cuddle, and stroke to calm.
Shows anger, frustration; has tantrums		Determine and remove cause if possible. Use calm talking about child's goal and other ways to pursue it. May sometimes hold and soothe infant. Help infant start a new activity. Keep child safe, but ignore a tantrum.
Rejects items, situations		Allow infant to make choices. Figure out alternative choices for situations he or she needs to experience, e.g., time or place choices.
Develops preferences with people		Identify and record infant's preferences. Make sure these toys are available frequently.
Shows independence—helps with feeding and dressing self	cup, spoon, clothes child can manipulate	Allow infant to help feed and dress self. This takes much time and patience. Lengthen eating time to adjust to self-feeding skills.
Shows affection		Accept and return affection with smile, hug, cuddle.
Begins developing self-esteem		Provide positive affirmation of infant through your tone of voice, looks, touch.
Control of Emotions and Feelings		
Begins to learn to obey "No"		Use "no" sparingly so infants can determine important situations when they must control their behavior. Use firm, not angry, voice. Use firm, not smiling, look on face.
Sometimes inhibits own behavior		Praise infant for self-control; e.g., infant raises arm to throw something, but puts it down on table.
Obeys commands: "No-no"; "Stop"		Use commands sparingly. Praise infants when they obey.

Social Development

Interactions with others are increasing. The mobility infants now have enables them to encounter different people or to move away from them. These infants initiate interactions with others and respond to others' interactions with them.

The infant's egocentric perspective is evident. Infants at this age do not clearly separate others' desires and needs from their own. Therefore, they are often fearful, uncertain, and occasionally clingy. They are very possessive of materials and people. Such materials and people still seem part of the infant, not completely separate, and thus they seem to belong to the infant.

Low teacher-child ratios and a primary caregiving system assist in meeting the social needs of infants (Gallagher & Mayer, 2008). When these characteristics are in place, teachers are more familiar to the infant and thus can better meet each infant's need for security and social interaction. You will see hints of the quality of the teacher-child relationship by watching the infants' behaviors. Securely attached mobile infants, for example, will stay "with a trusted caregiver, watching newcomers with a healthy suspicion" (Gallagher & Mayer, 2008, p. 82).

Trusted caregivers are used as a secure base for exploring. When the infant wanders too far or encounters someone new, he returns for comfort.

SUGGESTIONS FOR IMPLEMENTING CURRICULUM—SOCIAL DEVELOPMENT

CHILD BEHAVIOR	MATERIALS	EXAMPLES OF CAREGIVER STRATEGIES
Others		
Initiates interactions with others		Respond to infant's behavior. Talk, play with infant. Allow infant access to other children and adults.
Responds		Initiate talking and playing with infant.
May fear strangers		Keep strangers from forcing themselves on infant, who may not want to be held by stranger.
Keeps parent or caregiver in sight		Allow infant to follow you around. Arrange room so infant can see you from different areas of the room.
Initiates play		Respond and play infant's game, e.g., patty cake.
Becomes assertive; initiates action to fill needs		Encourage infant's assertiveness. Observe to determine whether infant is getting aggressive and will need cautions.
Wants own pleasure; may not consider others		Verbalize limits and help infant choose other activities, materials.
Initiates play		Play games with infant, e.g., "Can you do this?" Wave hand, clap hands, etc.
Is possessive of people		Verbally assure infant you will be here and will come back to talk and play with infant again.
Is possessive of materials	many toys	Provide enough toys and materials so infant does not need to share.
May become shy, clinging		Hold, hug, pat; allow infant to remain close; verbally assure infant you are there.
May demand attention		Provide positive verbal attention even though you may be busy with another child.

✓ reading checkpoint

Before moving on with your reading, make sure that you can answer the following questions about the material discussed so far.

1. Why is sharing difficult for the infant between eight and twelve months of age?
2. Identify four ways an infant in this age range asserts independence.
3. Explain the concept of *object permanence* and how it reflects and impacts both social and cognitive development.

SUMMARY

A major developmental task for infants between eight and twelve months of age is learning to walk independently. This skill has ramifications for not only their physical skills but also the other three areas of development. Watch how the infant uses her walking skills to explore materials in the environment, to make social connections with others, and to express her independence. As infants change, so do the strategies used by caregivers. You should notice how your interactions are different now that the infant is becoming more of a toddler.

key terms

context bound
crawling
deferred imitation
object permanence
pincer grasp
regression

case study — Marcel

Marcel, for being nine months, is advanced in both learning and motor skill development. He has learned to stand and crawl with balance and coordination. He has taken independent steps. No obstacle seems to stop him. This may be related to the fact that he has a three-and-a-half-year-old brother he plays with and tries to keep up with. Marcel's brother encourages and enjoys playing with Marcel.

Marcel enjoys the support and care of two grandmothers and one grandfather besides his father. All three grandparents stay at home, and both Marcel and his brother attend half-time child care. At the time of the first assessment, Marcel had no evidence of teeth emerging. When he spent one five-day period showing signs that four teeth were about to break through the gums, his happy disposition suddenly changed. It seemed that nothing pleased him, and he refused to stay in one position for any length of time. Marcel's grandmother wanted to put whiskey on his gums, but the family pediatrician convinced her that any product with alcohol was not good for children, recommending a cold washcloth and a hard teething ring instead. Marcel's father works nights, so he takes the afternoon shift caring for Marcel and his brother. Marcel is strong enough to squirm away and slip out of a holding grip when a wave of teething pain comes over him. Marcel tested the frustration limits of everyone in the household, including his brother. At one point a grandmother started to get angry, shouting at Marcel, and the other grandmother quickly declared that it was her turn to care for Marcel. With help from the child care staff, the family decided to move a large bed into the corner of Marcel's room, and an adult lay down with Marcel at night so he could move about as he needed to in safety as he tried to sleep. After a week of the ordeal, all four teeth broke through his gums, and Marcel quickly returned to his pleasant and active self. The bed was removed from the room and he easily returned to his crib to sleep.

1. Why would applying alcohol to his gums be bad for Marcel?
2. What might be the emotional effects of becoming angry with a child who is as agitated and in as much pain as Marcel was? Why?
3. What do you think the behavior of a less physically developed child with a similar teething problem would be?
4. What learning experiences would you plan during this time for Marcel? Why?

QUESTIONS AND EXPERIENCES FOR REFLECTION

1. Observe one infant who is walking with support. Identify the following:
   a. what infant holds onto for support
   b. where infant walks
   c. what you think causes the infant to sit or fall down
2. Use narrative description to record your observations of one caregiver for five minutes. Then categorize the caregiver's behaviors that relate to social development.
3. Observe one infant between eight and twelve months of age. Record the infant's behavior in two five-minute sequences using a narrative, running record (Appendix A). Transfer the descriptions to the Developmental Profile.
4. List five caregiving and teaching strategies that you use with infants between eight and twelve months of age.

REFERENCES

Adolph, K. E., Vereijken, B., & Shrout, P. E. (2003). What changes in infant walking and why. *Child Development, 74*(2), 475–497.

Allen County Public Library. (2009). Talking and reading to infants and toddlers: Follow the CAR. [Brochure]. Fort Wayne, IN: Author.

Anisfeld, M. (1984). *Language development from birth to three*. Hillsdale, NJ: Lawrence Erlbaum Associates.

Balaban, N. (2006, November). Easing the separation process for infants, toddlers, and families. *Beyond the Journal: Young Children on the Web*. Retrieved January 16, 2007, from http://www.journal.naeyc.org/btj/200611/pdf/BTJBalaban.pdf

Banerjee, P. N., & Tamis-LeMonda, C. S. (2007). Infants' persistence and mothers' teaching as predictors of toddlers' cognitive development. *Infant Behavior & Development, 30* (3), 479–491.

Gallagher, K. C., & Mayer, K. (2008). Research in review: Enhancing development and learning through teacher-child relationships. *Young Children, 63* (6), 80–87.

Healy, J. (2004). *Your child's growing mind: A guide to learning and brain development from birth to adolescence*. (3rd ed.). New York: Broadway Books.

Lamme, L. L. (1984). *Growing up writing*. Washington, DC: Acropolis Books.

Lamme, L. L. (1985). *Growing up reading*. Washington, DC: Acropolis Books.

Lawhon, T., & Cobb, J. B. (2002). Routines that build emergent literacy skills in infants, toddlers, and preschoolers. *Early Childhood Education Journal, 30*(2), 113–118.

Makin, L. (2006). Literacy 8–12 months: What are babies learning? *Early Years: Journal of International Research & Development, 26*(3), 267–277.

Marion, M. (2007). *Guidance of young children* (7th ed.). Upper Saddle River, NJ: Prentice Hall.

McDevitt, T. M., & Ormrod, J. E. (2010). *Child development: Educating and working with children and adolescents* (4th ed.). Upper Saddle River, NJ: Pearson Prentice Hall.

Newell, K. M., Liu, Y., & Mayer-Kress, G. (2001). Time scales in motor learning and development. *Psychological Review, 108*(1), 57–82.

Shirley, M. M. (1931). *The first two years: A study of twenty-five babies. Postural and Locomotor Development*: Vol. 1. Minneapolis: University of Minnesota Press.

Wheeler, B. L., & Stultz, S. (2008). Using Typical Infant Development to Inform Music Therapy with Children with Disabilities. *Early Childhood Education Journal, 35*, 585–591.

Zeece, P. D., & Churchill, S. L. (2001). First stories: Emergent literacy in infants and toddlers. *Early Childhood Education Journal, 29*(2), 101–104.

Zeece, P. D., Harris, B., & Hayes, N. (2006). Building literacy links for young children. *Early Childhood Education Journal, 34*(1), 61–65.

ADDITIONAL RESOURCES

Bremner, G., & Fogel, A. (Eds.). (2001) *Blackwell handbook of infant development*. Malden, MA: Blackwell.

Bremner, G., & Slater, A. (2004) (Eds.). *Theories of infant development*. Malden, MA: Blackwell.

Heritage Key (catalog containing information on multi-ethnic children's titles) 6102 East Mescal, Scotsdale, AZ 85254. Phone: (602) 483-3313.

Walsh, D. (2007). *No: Why kids—of all ages—need to hear it and ways parents can say it*. NY: Free Press.

Zigler, E., Finn-Stevenson, M., & Hall, N. W. (2002). *The first three years and beyond: Brain development and social policy*. New Haven: Yale University Press.

For additional activities, web links, and other resources, please visit our website at www.cengage.com/education/swim

chapter 13

THE CHILD FROM TWELVE TO EIGHTEEN MONTHS OF AGE

learning objectives

After reading this chapter, you should be able to

- Identify and record sequences of change in the physical, cognitive/language emotional, and social development of toddlers between 12 and 18 months of age.
- Select materials appropriate to the development of toddlers at that age level.
- Devise strategies appropriate to toddlers of that developmental level.

chapter outline

- Materials and Activities
- Caregiver Strategies to Enhance Development
  Physical Development
  Cognitive and Language Development
  Emotional Development
  Social Development
- Case Study: Andrea

CAREGIVERS OF TODDLERS

Caregivers or teachers who are in charge of toddler programs strive to be

- empowered facilitators who structure environments to minimize conflicts and maximize explorations.
- practiced in the three *A*s of child care—Attention, Approval, and Attunement.
- skillful, patient observers who help with problem solving and promote a positive perspective.
- organized and imaginative.
- knowledgeable in toddler development so that they may understand toddlers' daily struggles and enjoy their daily triumphs.
- consistent, gentle, yet firm.
- easily amused.
- genuinely fond of toddlers.

Andrea

Andrea, 15 months old, stands looking around. She walks over to two-year-old Jenny, who is sitting on the sofa. She stands between Jenny's legs and bounces up and down to Hokey Pokey music from the record player. Andrea and Jenny dance around. Jenny lies down on the floor and Andrea crawls on top of her. Jenny moves and Andrea follows. They both lie quietly for a minute. Andrea walks to a dramatic play shelf with toys. She picks up a toy plastic milk bottle and lifts it to her mouth to drink. She sits down and puts three lock blocks in the bottle. Allen, the caregiver, says, "What do you have?" Andrea shakes the bottle, and it makes a noise. She shakes it again. She puts a pail over her head and walks around peeking under the edge of the pail and "talking" to Allen. She toddles over the child's rocking chair beside Allen, climbs up, turns around to sit down, and starts rocking. Allen leaves to attend to another child who just woke from a nap. Andrea "talks" while rocking, then looks over to where Allen was sitting. She cries out and moves across the room to his side.

MATERIALS AND ACTIVITIES

Toddlers solve problems on a physical level. Watch toddlers at play for just five minutes and you will see them walk (which looks like wandering), climb, carry things around, drop things, and continually dump whatever they can find.

Walking is a major development for toddlers at this age. They are fascinated with toys to pull or push as they toddle around. They climb over objects. They may ride wheeled toys. They grasp and throw and drop objects again and again. These large-muscle activities are not done to irritate adults—they are the legitimate activity of

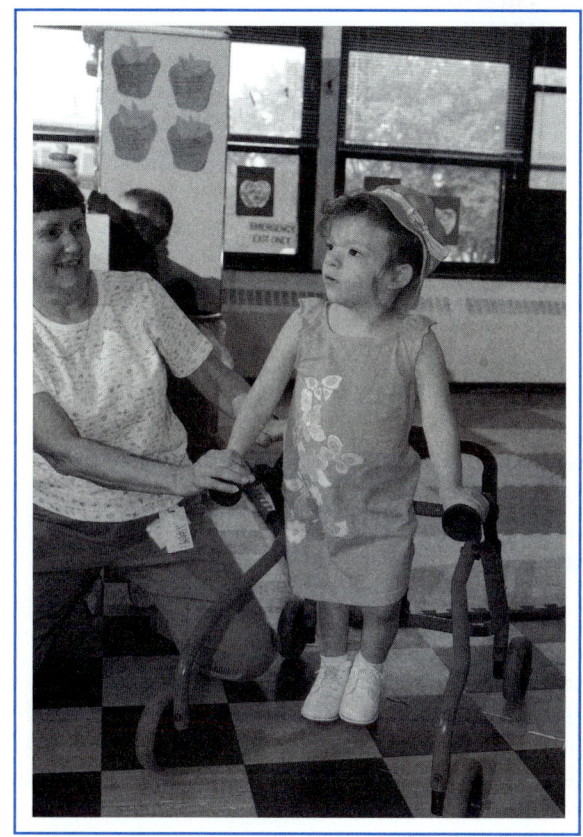

Toddlers need space and equipment that encourage walking, jumping, and other physical activities.

toddlers (Gonzalez-Mena & Eyers, 2007). Their play will change over the next few months as they begin to use toys for imaginative play. Teachers will need to provide materials that can facilitate this type of play.

Types of Materials

pull toys
push toys
trucks, cars
low, riding wheel toys
low, three-step stairs to climb
blocks
pail with objects to put in and take out
area with water and sand toys

soft objects to throw
mirrors
dolls
puppets
puzzles
picture books and cards
paper, nontoxic markers, crayons
audiotapes and CDs

part 3 MATCHING CAREGIVER STRATEGIES, MATERIALS, AND EXPERIENCES TO THE CHILD'S DEVELOPMENT

Examples of Homemade Materials

PULL TOY — *Use plain or painted empty spools. Thread and knot spools on a length of clothesline rope.*

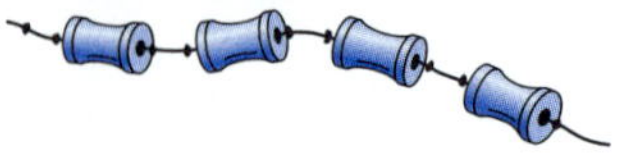

SOUND/SIGHT BOTTLE — *Use a clear plastic liter bottle (soft drink). Wash it thoroughly and allow to dry inside. Put in material or objects that will make noise (such as sand, wooden or plastic blocks, metal bottle caps). Add confetti for color interest. Screw on bottle cap and glue securely. Tape over rough edges of cap.*

TOSS BOX — *Collect several small, soft toys and place in a cardboard box. Show child how to take out objects, stand away from the box, and throw the objects into the box. Paint the inside of the box as a target to attract the child's attention.*

EXPLORING TUBS — *Place one solid object in a margarine tub. Put lid on. When children shake it, they hear a noise. Encourage the children to take off the lid to discover what is inside. Put lid back on. Have several tubs available with different objects inside, e.g., plastic clothespins, large wooden spools.*

PICTURE CARD — *Use a square of two- or three-ply cardboard. Place a photograph of a child on the cardboard and cover the whole square (front, back, and sides) with contact paper or laminating film. Also use colorful pictures cut from magazines. Select pictures that are simple and show one object, such as a car, cat, flower, or bird. Select pictures of objects the child is familiar with.*

CLOTHING FRAME BOARD — *Cover a piece of wood 12" × 12" × 2" with fabric. Glue one piece of fabric to each side of the wooden frame, with fabric opening at center of frame. Sew buttons on one side at center, buttonholes on other side. Or put on large snaps. Or sew in a large-toothed zipper.*

FIGURE 13–1

CAREGIVER STRATEGIES TO ENHANCE DEVELOPMENT

Physical Development

An expanding world opens up to toddlers as they become mobile. They walk, lurch, run, fall, bump into things, and persist in moving around in their world. They are unstable when they walk. They may topple over from stepping on an object, by leaning too far, or walking too fast. They are learning to make adjustments so that they can remain upright. The experience gained from walking results in their walking becoming more stable and adult-like (Adolph, Vereijken, & Shrout, 2003). Falling is a valuable learning experience as well (Joh & Adolph, 2006), so avoid rescuing the child too quickly; let her get back up and try again.

> They toddle about their own environment not necessarily to get from one part of it to another, but because they are up on their feet and it is satisfying to practice walking. Chairs become things to push and carry because pushing and carrying are also newly

Physical development promotes cognitive development.

obtained skills a toddler delights in practicing. Chairs can also be climbed into and later, if the chairs are an appropriate size, two-year-olds may discover they can back up to them and sit down, apparently an exciting achievement when you are just learning how to do it. (Brickmeyer, 1978)

Toddlers learn with their whole bodies—not just their heads. They learn more through their hands than they do through their ears. They learn by touching, mouthing, and trying out, not by being told. They learn by doing because it leads to thinking.

Toddlers can become absorbed in discovering the world around them. If you are convinced that toddlers have short attention spans, just watch them with running water and a piece of soap. Hand washing can become the main activity of the morning! Eating is another major activity, as many toddlers switch from very messy to neat in a short time. Filling and dumping are great activities for exercising fine and gross motor skills. Of course, toddlers do put things in containers as part of the process, but they are more likely to end with dumping (Gonzalez-Mena & Eyer, 2007).

Roberto, a fourteen-month-old in a family child care program, likes to combine emptying with transporting things. He finds favorite spots or hiding places: under the bed, in the wastebasket, or even in the sink and toilet bowl. Because he is so engaged with emptying, his teacher provides baskets that can be filled and emptied endlessly (Caplan & Caplan, 1980), rather than trying to limit his behavior.

Piaget's substages 5 and 6 explain the link between cognitive and physical development for toddlers between 12 and 18 months. This stage marks the onset of experimentation. The child deliberately begins to invent new actions she has never tried before and to explore the novel and unique features of objects. She tries to find out what will happen if she uses objects in new ways. She combines objects with other objects to create new ways of doing things and uses trial-and-error approaches to discover new solutions to problems. Newly acquired skills allow the toddler to explore objects in new ways and therefore construct new understandings of the world.

SUGGESTIONS FOR IMPLEMENTING CURRICULUM—PHYSICAL DEVELOPMENT

CHILD BEHAVIOR	MATERIALS	EXAMPLES OF CAREGIVER STRATEGIES
Muscular Control *TRUNK*		
Shows high energy, is active, moves from one activity to another		Provide a variety of materials and activities so the child can often change activities and play objects. These toddlers frequently do not make anything or complete an activity. Schedule cleanup and help put away toys at end of playtime.

(continued)

CHILD BEHAVIOR	MATERIALS	EXAMPLES OF CAREGIVER STRATEGIES
Raises self to standing	sturdy furniture to grasp; flat surface	Provide space where toddlers can stand up safely. Caution them about standing up under furniture.
LOCOMOTION		
May prefer crawling to walking		Allow toddler to crawl when desired. It is faster than walking when the child is just beginning to walk.
Walks alone		Allow toddler to walk alone when desired. Provide a hand to hold onto when child seeks help.
Climbs up stairs with help	stairs	Provide handrail or your hand to assist child with balance.
Climbs down stairs with help	stairs	Provide handrail *and* your hand. Balance is still poor when walking down stairs.
Climbs over objects	low, sturdy furniture, equipment, boxes	Provide low climbing equipment, furniture, e.g., ot toman, sturdy cardboard boxes, covered foam incline.
HAND		
Uses thumb against fingers	small toys, crayons, pens	Provide materials toddler can grasp.
Shows hand preference		Allow toddler to use whichever hand he or she chooses.
Points with finger	pictures, books, objects	Play pointing game, e.g., open picture book, "Point to the tree."
Throws objects	soft, small objects	Provide a place and target where toddler can throw objects.
Rolls and catches objects	large, small balls	Sit on floor with legs open and outstretched and roll ball back and forth with toddler.
EYE-HAND COORDINATION		
Scribbles	paper, nontoxic markers, crayons	Provide flat surface for toddler to use paper and marker or pen. Admire and describe the marks the toddler makes.
Helps in dressing and undressing	buttons, snaps, zipper, cards, books, clothing frame board, large dolls with clothes	Allow toddler to do as much as possible. Assist when toddler needs help.
Sleeping		
Begins to change from morning and afternoon nap to just afternoon nap. May fall asleep during lunch.		Adjust eating and nap schedule so toddler does not miss lunch.
Eating		
Eats three meals and regular snacks		Determine mealtime. Make adjustments for individual children as necessary.

(continued)

CHILD BEHAVIOR	MATERIALS	EXAMPLES OF CAREGIVER STRATEGIES
Eating (cont.)		
Feeds self: uses cup, spoon, and fingers	food, plate, cup, spoon	Allow toddler to feed self as much as possible. Assist when necessary.
Expresses food likes and dislikes		Record food preferences. Provide foods child likes. Introduce new foods gradually. Combine foods child does not like with ones child does like to provide needed nutrition.
May eat less food		Do not force eating. Make food as attractive as possible.

Cognitive and Language Development
Cognitive Development

This is a time for learning, so opportunities to learn should be provided, including learning how to learn. Too often adults give children answers to remember rather than problems to solve. This is a grave mistake. "Unless children develop the art of problem solving . . . their brains will remain underdeveloped" (Healy, 2004). Children construct their knowledge and understanding of the world through their experiences with the environment (Elkind, 2003). According to Piaget, however, people engage in individual constructivism, in which a single person individually creates new understandings, interpretations, and realities through interactions with materials, equipment, and people in their environment

spotlight *on organizations*

National Association for the Education of Young Children

This national organization began in the 1920s and was originally called the National Association for Nursery Education (NANE). This group of dedicated volunteers organized conferences, bulletins, and publications. In addition, they developed and implemented nursery school and child care programs through the Works Progress Administration (WPA) during World War II. In 1964, NANE was reorganized and renamed the National Association for the Education of Young Children (NAEYC). This year a great deal of attention was focused on early childhood education as the federal Head Start program was launched as part of the war on poverty. This organization currently has expanded to include a wide number of services for its 100,000 plus members. For example, this organization supports two annual conferences and four publications, *Young Children, Early Childhood Research Quarterly, Beyond the Journal,* and *Teaching Young Children.* The organization also supports the development of teachers by producing books, videos, and pamphlets that can be shared with families and community members. High-quality early childhood programs can be accredited through this organization (see Chapter 5). Another way that this organization impacts the field of early childhood education is through its national standards for teacher preparation. In other words, NAEYC works closely with faculty in universities and colleges to identify the knowledge, skills, and dispositions that teachers with associate, bachelors, and master's degrees should possess.

(McDevitt & Ormrod, 2010). Adults must provide developmentally appropriate learning experiences that challenge toddlers' current level of development but are achievable (Copple & Bredekamp, 2009), causing disequilibrium and influencing their development now and in the future. For example, as object permanence becomes more firmly established, toddlers may search for an object they have seen moved and hidden. So playing hiding games such as "Doggie, doggie, where's your bone?" engages and challenges the children.

Toddlers of this age are interested in observing the effects of their own and other's actions, learning about **cause and effect**. Exploration is done using **trial and error**. These little explorers try, probe, and practice activities and observe the results of their actions. A trial-and-error approach to the world can result in guidance encounters with adults as they experiment with new ways to do things. For example, what happens when sand is thrown? Can I go down the slide head first?

Now that toddlers are aware that others cause actions to occur, imitation of others' behaviors becomes a part of their play. They use some play behaviors repeatedly in the same pattern and develop their own ritual play. Researchers have found that stimulating playthings are more important for cognitive development after age one than in earlier months. According to Healy (2004), availability of interesting and challenging play materials in the child's environment after the first year "predict[s] later IQ and school achievement in reading and math" (p. 53).

SUGGESTIONS FOR IMPLEMENTING CURRICULUM—COGNITIVE DEVELOPMENT

CHILD BEHAVIOR	MATERIALS	EXAMPLES OF CAREGIVER STRATEGIES
Piaget's Substages of Sensorimotor Development *SUBSTAGE 5 (Experimentation)* Object Permanence Watches toy being hid and moved. Looks for it where it was moved.		Play game with child. Hide the object while child watches. Let the child watch you move the object to a different place under the blanket. Ask, "Where is it? Can you find it?" Observe and allow child to find the object. Describe their behaviors of watching and thinking.
Causality Investigates cause and effect		Allow and encourage child to search to identify the relationship between an action and the effect of it, e.g., "What made the ball go under the table?"
Sees self as causal agent		Verbally identify the child as cause of the action, e.g., "Laquata kicked the ball."

(continued)

CHILD BEHAVIOR	MATERIALS	EXAMPLES OF CAREGIVER STRATEGIES
Explores various ways things happen	water toys, water basin	Allow the child time to play with the water and toys to discover different actions of water and of objects in the water.
Employs active trial-and-error to solve problems	narrow-neck milk carton, different sizes and shapes of objects	Provide time and materials that stimulate child to think and try out ideas. Ask questions but do not tell answers or show child.
Experiments with objects		Provide open-ended toys and materials that encourage several uses. Encourage child to see how many ways he or she can use them. Ask questions and allow time for the child to experiment; ask "What happens?"
Imitation and Play		
Copies behaviors of others		Encourage child to pretend: to drink from a pretend bottle like baby Gwen, to march like Pearl, to pick up toys. Think about your own behaviors; child will copy what you do. Be sure your actions are the kind of actions you feel comfortable seeing the child copy.
Turns play with imitation into rituals		Allow child to repeat own play and develop own preferences. For example, a child may see you hug a child who comes in the morning and imitate your hugging. The child may repeat this imitation and develop the ritual of hugging the child who has just arrived.

✓ reading checkpoint

Before moving on with your reading, make sure that you can answer the following questions about the material discussed so far.

1. With the development of eye-hand coordination, what can toddlers do now that they could not do as well several months earlier?

2. Describe something a 16-month-old would do that shows she has mastered object permanence.

Language Development

Language in toddlers of this age expands, with less reliance on sounds and babbling and more use of recognizable words. A toddler uses many word approximations, which, when acknowledged, become a usable part of his or her expressive vocabulary.

Provide materials that create opportunities for children to talk or sing.

Toddlers may **overgeneralize** or use one word for many different things. *Wawa* may mean anything to drink. *Mama* may mean any woman. Word meaning is usually flexible. The toddler may call anything that is round a *ball*. This is the time the vocabulary of the toddler can be expanded by your use of words to label actions and objects. It is also a time to make them more aware of the world around them by pointing out sounds to listen to and naming what they are. By 18 months toddlers will be asking what things and sounds are as they categorize their world.

Reading and books can provide enjoyable experiences for toddlers as well as promote language and cognitive development. Several different kinds of children's literature interest toddlers.

> Point-and-say books have pictures of familiar objects and little text. The object of reading this type of literature is to increase each child's vocabulary, to compare pictures in a book with known items in the environment, to familiarize the child with books, and to show infants and toddlers that books have meaning.
>
> Nursery rhymes, chants, poems, and songs are best chanted or sung throughout the day rather than just presented at read-aloud sessions. Then, at a later time, it can be thrilling to watch infants and toddlers associate the rhymes that he or she already knows with the picture representing that rhyme in a book. Nursery rhymes help them become familiar with the sounds of language. They assist the transition from telegraphic speech, where one to three words represent a sentence, to mature language, where each word is pronounced. (Lamme, 1985, pp. 57–58)

The interrelationships among language, reading, and writing are evident at an early age. Writing can be encouraged by giving children paper and pens or pencils to draw or write on (Lamme, 1984). Toddlers want to represent objects in their world. This is a beginning stage of writing. When you support them as they talk about what they have drawn or written, they connect symbols (mental representations) with language. Furthermore, encouraging children to watch as you write names, labels, and notes models how cultures use written texts to communicate. These joint interactions assist toddlers in coming to understand the multifaceted dimensions of roles in literacy events: who does what, with whom, and for what purposes (Rowe, 2008).

SUGGESTIONS FOR IMPLEMENTING CURRICULUM—LANGUAGE DEVELOPMENT

CHILD BEHAVIOR	MATERIALS	EXAMPLES OF CAREGIVER STRATEGIES
Uses intonation		Use intonation when you talk to the toddler.
Babbles sentences		Respond to toddler's babbling.
Repeats, practices words		Repeat toddler's word. Occasionally expand it to a sentence, e.g., "gone-gone," "The milk is all gone."
Imitates sounds of other people, objects		Enjoy toddler's sounds. Play sounds game: point to objects and make sound of object, e.g., dog barking.
Responds to word and gesture conversation		Become very familiar with toddler's words and gestures. You often have to guess what the toddler is saying. Make a statement or ask a question to determine if you are interpreting correctly, e.g., "Taylor wants to go outside."
Responds to many questions and commands even if he or she cannot say them		Choose a few questions and commands you can use often and consistently. The toddler will learn what they mean through many experiences, e.g., "Go get your coat."
Uses word approximations for some words		Watch the toddler's behavior to help you experience what the child is experiencing. What do you see at the point where the child is looking, pointing, reaching? Say a word or sentence to test whether you are interpreting the word correctly.
Uses words in immediate context		Notice what the toddler is doing, saying, or needing right now. Toddler's talk is about immediate needs and desires, not past or future situations.
Identifies familiar pictures	pictures, picture book	Orally label objects. Ask toddler to point to or name familiar pictures.
Uses markers, chalk	markers, paper, chalk	Provide table space and materials. Write labels and sentences for child.

Emotional Development

Toddlers seek both dependence and independence. Erikson (1963) called this developmental crisis the need to resolve Autonomy versus Shame and Doubt, his second stage of development. For many tasks toddlers need help. The caregiver can provide toddlers with emotional strength and security, accepting their very real dependence (Wilson, 1987). Toddlers are also trying to become independent. Emotionally they need support that affirms their importance as individuals who can make some choices and accomplish certain tasks all by themselves. Their growing sense of achievement enhances their developing positive feelings of self-worth and demonstrates an understanding of cause and effect.

Toddlers experience a wide variety of emotions and sometimes seem to swing wildly between them. One moment they are happy, and the next they are fearful. Many fears at this age are learned from adults because our reactions influence the toddler's response. Research showed that higher levels of compliance to cleanup tasks by toddlers was related to both child characteristics (lower levels of anger proneness and social fearfulness) and maternal characteristics (sensitivity and structuring of

What part of tying his shoe can he do so that he feels independent?

the task) (Lehman, Steier, Guidash, & Wanna, 2002). Hence, adults help children learn to control strong emotions and comply to requests when they use the three *A*s of caregiving—Attention, Approval, and Attunement. Caregivers must take an inventory of themselves and recognize what emotional messages they are conveying to an impressionable toddler. It is the continued responsibility of the caregiver to promote a positive learning environment.

Because toddlers lack the skills to regulate their strong emotions, their anger and frustration may come out as temper tantrums. Adults should prevent temper tantrums whenever possible by attending to and changing the conditions that caused the child's frustrations. Of course, not all sources of frustration and anger can be modified or removed. In those cases, respond to frustration tantrums by quietly talking about the emotion being experienced, the cause of the tantrum, and how scary it feels to be out of control of one's body. Toddlers sometimes have tantrums in order to get their own way. These manipulation tantrums should be ignored, because giving attention during the tantrum may encourage toddlers to use this strategy routinely as a way to get what they want. Instead, the caregiver should make sure that the child is safe and then provide positive attention soon after the tantrum is over.

Toddlers may also express negativism by saying "No!" Their pursuit of independence may result in doing the opposite of what was requested or carrying out their own ideas (not the adult's). Rephrase command statements and refocus attention to something of interest to the toddler. For example, you might rephrase "Put the doll away" to "Mary Jane, do you want to the put the doll in the bed or on the blanket?" Providing choices in this way assists toddlers in complying with requests and learning to make appropriate choices (Marion, 2007). Children learn concepts of right and wrong from adults. Toddlers are just beginning to use words, and they respond to some labels and commands. But words alone will not control their behavior until they internalize the language and construct concepts of right and wrong.

These concepts are constantly being revised and expanded as the toddlers compare their behavior with adults' reaction to that behavior. At this age toddlers cannot separate themselves from their actions enough to understand the idea, "I like you, but I do not like what you are doing." Therefore, caregivers need to find ways to help toddlers discriminate between right and wrong while still accepting each child as a worthy person no matter how he or she behaves.

Use positive guidance strategies. Don't depend on words alone; utilize physical touch or intervention when necessary. For example, prevent a harmful behavior before it occurs by holding back a child's threatening arm before it has a chance to hit. Lead a child by the hand back to the table to clean up after a snack. Don't let children get in trouble and then yell or otherwise express anger toward them. Allowing the child to choose between two positive and equally desirable outcomes helps the child learn to make decisions as well as to have more control over his or her environment (Swim & Marion, 2006). In addition, consistently using the three *A*s of caregiving—Attention, Approval, and Attunement—when the child has behaved correctly will help the child know what is right. If you find yourself saying "I knew that was going to happen," ... next time, don't predict it, *prevent* it (Gonzalez-Mena & Eyer, 2007; Marion, 2007).

Children's responses to a change in routine during this developmental stage are influenced by their temperament. The toddler who is very adaptable may change routines easily or with a little fussing. For example, putting that toddler's chair in a different place in the room may create interest for the child. A toddler who has difficulty adapting to change may react negatively, resisting the moving of the chair by fussing or crying or even having a tantrum. This child may combine resistance to change with negativism.

SUGGESTIONS FOR IMPLEMENTING CURRICULUM—EMOTIONAL DEVELOPMENT

CHILD BEHAVIOR	MATERIALS	EXAMPLES OF CAREGIVER STRATEGIES
Types of Emotions-Feelings		
Expresses emotions in behavior and language		Determine and respond to toddler's emotions.
Recognizes emotions in others		Be consistent in showing emotions, e.g., happiness—smile and laugh; anger—firm voice, no smile.
May fear strangeness		Introduce new people, new experiences to toddler. Caution others not to rush the child. Allow child to approach or withdraw at his or her own rate.
Shows excitement, delight		Respond with similar excitement, e.g., touching a pretty flower, an animal.
Expresses sense of humor		Giggle and laugh with toddler.
Shows affection		Accept and return physical and verbal shows of affection.
Displays negativism		Provide honest, workable choices, e.g., "Do you want to eat at the red or the green table?"
Has tantrums		Determine and remove cause if possible. Sometimes ignore. Proceed calmly with involvement with other children, activities.
Uses play to express emotions, resolve conflicts	blocks, dolls, home objects, clothes, toy animals	Provide props for acting out fear, frustration, insecurity, joy.
Seeks dependency, security with parent and caregiver		Provide touching, holding, stroking interactions; respond quickly and consistently to toddler's needs.
Seeks to expand independence		Allow toddler to attempt activities by him- or herself. Do not take over if toddler can be successful without you.

(continued)

CHILD BEHAVIOR	MATERIALS	EXAMPLES OF CAREGIVER STRATEGIES
Control of Emotions-Feelings		
Begins to learn right and wrong		Verbalize which behavior is right and which behavior is wrong. Give reasons. Since toddlers are only just beginning to conceptualize right vs. wrong, only occasionally can they apply the concept to control their own behavior.
Reinforces desired behavior		Provide positive feedback when a toddler controls his own behavior.

spotlight on research

Peer Interactions of Young Toddlers

Many researchers are interested in how young children acquire complex social skills over the course of their first few years of life, examining this development from a wide variety of perspectives. Deynoot-Schaub and Riksen-Walraven conducted a research study where 70 toddlers were observed with their peers during 90-minute free play situations at their child care center. They found that the 15-and 23-month-old children were significantly more likely to have contact with a child care provider than with their peers (Deynoot-Schaub & Riksen-Walraven, 2006a) and that the rate of negative interactions with their caregivers, but not positive, decreased from 15- to 23-months-of-age (Deynoot-Schaub & Riksen-Walraven, 2006b). In addition, those interactions with caregivers were predominantly positive, whereas interactions with peers were balanced across positive and negative interactions (Deynoot-Schaub & Riksen-Walraven, 2006a; 2006b).

When examining the factors which might relate to peer-initiated peer contacts, these researchers discovered that more peer-initiated peer contacts occurred in classrooms with higher child-caregiver ratios (Deynoot-Schaub & Riksen-Walraven, 2006a). In addition, children directed more negative initiative towards peers in environments that were rated lower on the learning activities and social interactions subscales of the Infant Toddler Environmental Rating Scale (Deynoot-Schaub & Riksen-Walraven, 2006a). When examining the longitudinal data, the researchers also found that ratings of aggressive/disruptive behaviors at 23 months were predicted by higher rates of negative initiative towards peers at 15 months (Deynoot-Schaub & Riksen-Walraven, 2006b). In other words, when more children are present in a lower-quality classroom environment, children initiate negative interactions with peers more often, and the earlier negative behaviors are predictive of later aggressive behavior with peers. These authors concluded that "… the quality of childcare appears to affect children's contact with peers during childcare at a very early age. Early peer contacts can thus contribute to children's well-being and socio-emotional adjustment or maladjustment" (Deynoot-Schaub & Riksen-Walraven, 2006a, p. 725).

The research examined above evaluated children's interactions from a dyadic perspective. In other words, they carefully examined the interactions between two people: toddler-teacher or toddler-peer. Can toddlers successfully interact within a small group of three people? Ishikawa and Hay (2006) examined social behaviors when three toddlers, unknown to each other, interacted in a laboratory observation room. Of the 715 episodes identified, 193 (27 percent) were found to be triadic. This research demonstrated that toddlers can actively and successfully engage in triadic interactions of two- and three-move sequences (Ishikawa and Hay, 2006). Contrary to research with adults, toddlers were more likely to engage in triadic interactions when there was no conflict present. This research demonstrates that toddlers are able to engage in complex social interactions with peers. Further research which uncovers factors that explain changes in triadic interactions could be helpful in understanding the importance of early peer relations for children's later social development (Ishikawa and Hay, 2006).

Social Development

Toddlers are egocentric; they see the world from their own point of view or perspective. In the first year and a half of life, their bodies and the objects they play with are perceived to be part of *self*. Gradually, as the concept of object permanence develops, they differentiate *self* from other objects and people, which become *not self*. This major development provides the basis for lifelong expansion of their concept of self and their interactions with others and provides the child with one of his or her earliest experiences with self-image. Caregiver acceptance is extremely important at any stage of development. This acceptance is internalized and becomes part of the child's self.

Toddlers behave differently toward different people. They recognize differences in people and adjust their interactions with them. They may be eager and excited with a familiar caregiver but quiet and withdrawn with a substitute teacher.

Toddlers play with toys and materials and sing and talk usually by themselves in play. They may look at other children and play near them, but typically they do not interact with them in play. Toddlers now engage in solitary play (playing alone) and parallel play (playing near but not with other children); they decide what kind of

Toddlers use familiar games like peekaboo to initiate interactions with peers and teachers.

interaction they want with others. At this age the toddler is more adept at dealing with older children and adults than with peers.

SUGGESTIONS FOR IMPLEMENTING CURRICULUM—SOCIAL DEVELOPMENT	
CHILD BEHAVIOR	**EXAMPLES OF CAREGIVER STRATEGIES**
Self	
Has concept of self	Positively reinforce toddler as an individual.
Is egocentric: understands only his or her own viewpoint	Do not expect toddler to feel sorry for someone she has hurt. Toddler assumes everyone thinks and feels the way he or she does.
Others	
Seeks presence of family members or caregiver	Allow toddler to follow you around. Tell child when you are going out of sight.
Initiates and plays games	Play games with toddler. Respond and play child's games.
Occasionally shares	Provide enough materials and equipment so sharing can be encouraged but not required.
Acts differently toward different people	Expect different responses to different people. Accept toddler's choices.
Uses variety of behaviors to gain attention	Identify toddler's usual behaviors to gain attention. Respond to any of those behaviors as quickly as possible.
May be shy with some people	Do not force toddler to interact with all people. Allow child to keep his or her distance and watch.
Engages in parallel play	Provide materials and space so toddlers can play with own materials but near each other.

✓ reading checkpoint

Before moving on with your reading, make sure that you can answer the following questions about the material discussed so far.

1. Describe two situations in which a toddler interacts with others. Describe two situations in which a toddler plays alone.

With others

a.
b.

Alone

a.
b.

2. List four fears a toddler who is between 12 and 18 months of age might have. Explain how you would respond to these fears.

SUMMARY

Between the age of 12 and 18 months, toddlers spend most of their waking moments exploring their environment. They investigate objects with their hands, mouth, eyes, and ears. They are eager to discover how many objects fit into a given space as they constantly fill and spill containers. Responsive caregivers plan the learning environment carefully to encourage such explorative practices. In addition, toddlers are becoming more interested in interacting with adults and peers. They seek out people to "talk" with, show objects, and demonstrate affection. When adult-toddler ratios are in line with standards for high-quality care and education, the toddlers tend to be more positive in these interactions.

key terms

cause and effect
egocentric
individual constructivism
overgeneralize
parallel play
solitary play
trial and error

case study — Andrea

Andrea is a 15-month-old who comes from an upper-middle-class professional family. Both of her parents have successful professions and work full time, so Andrea is in full-time child care. Thorough observations by Allen, her primary caregiver, led him to conclude that Andrea has average to above average overall development but is weak in the development of self-interest. Allen hypothesizes that this may be because (1) a new co-teacher just joined the classroom and he was actually in charge of the entire group of children or (2) her parents are very busy and Andrea must seek their attention. Andrea seems anxious and seems to need the attention and approval of other people frequently in order to feel secure and happy. When Allen pays attention to other children, Andrea appears to get upset, withdrawing and crying.

Allen established a plan to help Andrea share attention and enjoy time by herself. First, the strategy of "labeling her feelings" was used to assist her with identifying her feelings and her need to be close to others. He also gave her attractive choices of favorite experiences to engage in alone. Second, the co-teachers divided the work more equitably as the new teacher was ready to assume her role as a primary caregiver. Third, a meeting was held with Andrea's parents to see if a "special time" could be established each day with each of them. Her parents did not realize how their busy work lives might be spilling over in the home and the potential consequences to Andrea. They worked together to create a new evening routine. Within a short time, Andrea was able to spend time by herself enjoyably and share the attention of Allen.

1. Describe how and why each of these strategies would help with Andrea's problem.
2. What other strategies could be used to help children play independently more often?
3. What would be the next steps to take if these strategies didn't help Andrea?

QUESTIONS AND EXPERIENCES FOR REFLECTION

1. Interview one caregiver. Ask the caregiver to select a toddler between the ages of 12 and 18 months and then to describe the following:
   a. the child's behaviors when angry
   b. your behaviors when responding to the toddler's angry behavior

Write the caregiver's descriptions and then put an X beside the descriptions of the behaviors of the toddler and the caregiver that represent *emotions* or *emotional talk*.

Behavior of Angry Toddler	Responding Behaviors of Caregiver

2. Listen to one toddler. Make a list of the child's words and "sentences." Watch the child's body language and nonverbal gestures. Then write down the complete sentences you think the child meant (you must think about the context in which the toddler was talking).

Word or Phrase	Meaning
Gone-gone	It is all gone; She went away.

3. Write one lesson plan to use with a toddler to help reinforce a word the toddler uses and to expand the use into sentences. Use the plan with the toddler. Evaluate the toddler's involvement. Evaluate the written lesson plan.

4. Observe one toddler between 12 and 18 months of age. Record the toddler's behavior in two five-minute sequences, using a narrative running record (see Appendix A). Transfer the descriptions to the Developmental Profile (Appendix B).

5. List guidance strategies you need to use more proficiently and ways you intend to acquire these skills.

REFERENCES

Adolph, K. E., Vereijken, B., & Shrout, P. E. (2003). What changes in infant walking and why. *Child Development, 74*(2), 475–497.

Brickmeyer, J. (1978). *Guidelines for day care programs for migrant infants and toddlers*. New York: Bankstreet College.

Caplan, F., & Caplan, T. (1980). *The second twelve months of life*. New York: Bantam/Grosset and Dunlap.

Copple, C., & Bredekamp, S. (Eds.). (2009). *Developmentally appropriate practice in early childhood programs* (3rd ed.). Washington, DC: National Association for the Education of Young Children.

Deynoot-Schaub, M. J. G., & Riksen-Walraven, J. M. (2006a). Peer contacts of 15-month-olds in childcare: Links with child temperament, parent-child interaction and quality of childcare. *Social Development, 15* (4), 709–729.

Deynoot-Schaub, M. J. G., & Riksen-Walraven, J. M. (2006b). Peer interaction in child care centres at 15 and 23 months: Stability and links with children's socioemotional adjustments. *Infant Behavior & Development, 29*, 276–288.

Elkind, D. (2003, Winter). Montessori and constructivism. *Montessori Life, 15*(1), 26–29.

Erikson, E. (1963). *Childhood and society* (2nd ed.). New York: Norton.

Gonzalez-Mena, J., & Eyer, D. W. (2007). *Infants, toddlers, and caregivers* (7th ed.). New York: McGraw-Hill.

Healy, J. (2004). *Your child's growing mind: A guide to learning and brain development from birth to adolescence.* (3rd ed.). New York: Broadway Books.

Ishikawa, F., & Hay, D. F. (2006). Triadic interaction among newly acquainted 2-year-olds. *Social Development, 15* (1), 145–168.

Joh, A. S., & Adolph, K. E. (2006). Learning from falling. *Child Development, 77*(1), 89–102.

Lamme, L. L. (1984). *Growing up writing.* Washington, DC: Acropolis Books.

Lamme, L. L. (1985). *Growing up reading.* Washington, DC: Acropolis Books.

Lehman, E. B., Steier, A. J., Guidash, K. M., & Wanna, S. Y. (2002). Predictors of compliance in toddlers: Child temperament, maternal personality, and emotional availability. *Early Child Development and Care, 172*(3), 301–310.

Marion, M. (2007). *Guidance of young children* (7th ed.). Upper Saddle River, NJ: Prentice Hall.

McDevitt, T. M., & Ormrod, J. E. (2010). *Child development: Educating and working with children and adolescents* (4th ed.). Upper Saddle River, NJ: Pearson Merrill Prentice Hall.

Rowe, D. W. (2008). Social Contracts for Writing: Negotiating Shared Understandings. About Text in the Preschool Years. *Reading Research Quarterly, 43*(1), 66–95.

Swim, T. J., & Marion, M. (2006, November). Terrific toddlers: Good relationships build autonomy, self-regulation, and emotional intelligence. Paper presented at the annual conference of the National Association for the Education of Young Children, Atlanta, GA.

Wilson, L. C. (1987). Mommy, don't go! *Pre-K Today, 2*(1), 38–40.

ADDITIONAL RESOURCES

Emde, R. N., & Hewitt, J. K. (Eds.). (2001). *Infancy to early childhood: Genetic and environmental influences on developmental change.* Oxford, UK: Oxford University Press.

Hyson, M. (2004). *The emotional development of young children: Building an emotion-centered curriculum* (2nd ed.). New York: Teachers College Press.

Meier, D. (2009). *Here's the story: Using narrative to promote young children's language and literacy learning.* New York: Teachers College Press.

Riley, D., San Juan, R. R., Klinkner, J., & Ramminger, A. (2008). *Social and emotional development: Connecting science and practice in early childhood settings.* St. Paul, MN: Redleaf Press.

For additional activities, web links, and other resources, please visit our website at www.cengage.com/education/swim

chapter 14

THE CHILD FROM EIGHTEEN TO TWENTY-FOUR MONTHS OF AGE

learning objectives

After reading this chapter, you should be able to:
- Identify and record sequences of change in the physical, cognitive/language emotional, and social development of children from 18 to 24 months of age.
- Select materials appropriate to the development of children at that age level.
- Devise strategies appropriate to children of that developmental level.

chapter outline

- Materials and Activities
- Caregiver Strategies to Enhance Development
  Physical Development
  Cognitive and Language Development
  Emotional Development
  Social Development
- Case Study: Lennie

Lennie's Story

Lennie, 23 months old, walks to a child-sized rocking chair, backs up to it and sits down. He rocks and watches the other children. He gets off the chair and sits on his legs to pick up blocks. He picks up a block wagon, stands up, and walks around. He holds the block wagon in his left hand, tries to put in another block with his right hand, and succeeds. He puts the wagon on the floor and pushes it. He takes off one block and then takes off five blocks; he puts them back on. Jasper walks past and Lennie says, "Noooo." Tracey takes the block wagon. Lennie reaches for it but does not get it. He bites Tracey on the arm; when she lets go of the wagon, he picks it up and begins putting blocks in it. He picks up the block wagon and a block bag, gets up and walks around, talking to himself.

MATERIALS AND ACTIVITIES

Walking, climbing, and riding materials and activities are enjoyable for children at this age. As they practice their gross motor skills, they develop increased competence in using them. Their finger and wrist muscles are developing so they can manipulate more complex objects. Their imaginations are expanding as they construct internal representations of their world. Figure 14-1 provides examples of homemade materials that support toddlers' development.

Types of Materials

textures	tunnel
snap toys	riding toys and cycles
large stringing beads	water play equipment
blocks	sand play equipment
toy people	soap paint
caps or lids to twist off containers	finger paint
toys to throw	tempera paint
tools: hammer, broom, shovel	puzzles
cars, trucks	books
zippers	telephones
hairbrush	dolls
toothbrush	stuffed animals
low, wide balance beam	puppets
slide	music: CDs, tapes
pull and push toys	modeling dough
balls	markers, crayons, chalk, pens
low stairs	containers to fill and empty

Examples of Homemade Materials

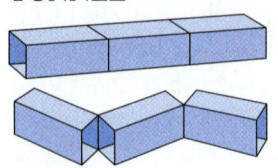

TUNNEL
Use a sturdy, long cardboard box large enough for child to crawl through. Cut out ends and tape edges to prevent scraping the child and tearing the box. Place several boxes end to end or in a square or zigzag pattern.

PUPPET
Use a paper plate. The child tears colored paper and yarn and pastes the pieces on the paper plate. These puppets are safer without a wooden stick handle.

TARGET
Use a plastic pail (empty ice cream or peanut butter container). Place tennis balls or yarn balls in the pail. Use a piece of yarn to mark where the child will stand to throw objects into the pail.

MODELING DOUGH RECIPE
2 cups flour
2 cups water
1 cup salt
3 teaspoons cream of tartar
2 tablespoons oil
food coloring

Combine flour, salt, and cream of tartar. Combine oil, food coloring, and water. Pour liquids into flour-salt mixture in a pot. Stir to get pie dough consistency. Cook, stirring over medium heat until ball forms. Store in a covered container. Shape into a ball, then dip into food coloring, rolling ball back and forth. Watch colors change. Keep manipulating dough to keep it soft. All sorts of shapes can be made, such as a vase (make paper flowers to go in it).

BOOK
Cut three pieces of sturdy cardboard. Select three magazine pictures that make a sequence or that have something in common (e.g., they are all red). Glue one picture on each piece of cardboard. Cover the pictures and cardboard with clear Con-Tact paper. Connect the pieces by punching holes in the side of the cardboard and tying together with yarn.

FIGURE 14–1

CAREGIVER STRATEGIES TO ENHANCE DEVELOPMENT
Physical Development

Children of this age are gaining much more stability and coordination. They can stand up, squat, reach over, and stand upright again without toppling. They climb on just about everything and, when they are around 18 months old, they try climbing out of their cribs. They will soon succeed. They climb up and down stairs by holding onto a rail or hand to maintain balance, but still do not alternate their feet. These children can now move rapidly, both walking and running, and jump with both feet. They become increasingly more adept at kicking balls. By around 22 months they can pedal cycles such as Big Wheels, and they love to push and pull toys and objects. They can throw objects at targets rather than randomly throwing and tossing, though they seldom hit the intended target.

These children's fine motor muscles are developing, so they have increased control of their fingers and wrists. They probe, twist, and turn objects. They can consciously tell their muscles to relax so they can more easily release the objects they have grasped, allowing them to drop or throw objects when they choose to. They also are more accurate in directing the objects dropped or thrown. These increased fine motor skills allow toddlers, around 18 months of age, to turn several pages of a book at a time; by 24 months, most will be able to turn pages one at a time.

Some children may favor one hand over the other. Determine each child's dominant hand and allow the child to use it. The child may occasionally use the other

Caregivers provide a variety of experiences and materials to promote fine motor development.

Determine each child's dominant hand and allow the child to use it.

hand when using a spoon, for example; if the child occasionally chooses to do so, this will not be harmful. The caregiver should allow the child to develop and maintain the handedness that is comfortable. Do not attempt to make a left-handed child use utensils and toys with the right hand. That child's neurological patterns have developed with his or her left-handedness. Attempting to change a child's handedness may cause both neurological and muscular stress.

SUGGESTIONS FOR IMPLEMENTING CURRICULUM—PHYSICAL DEVELOPMENT

CHILD BEHAVIOR	MATERIALS	EXAMPLES OF CAREGIVER STRATEGIES
Muscular Control		
LOCOMOTION		
Walks forward	flat floor, ground; clear of toys	Keep area clear of toys or caution child about obstacles.
Walks backward		
Walks sideways	area clear of toys	Play with child: walk sideways, forward, backward.
Runs with stops and starts	clear area	Provide *flat* running space. On incline child may run down too fast and fall on face.

(continued)

chapter 14 THE CHILD FROM EIGHTEEN TO TWENTY-FOUR MONTHS OF AGE

CHILD BEHAVIOR	MATERIALS	EXAMPLES OF CAREGIVER STRATEGIES
Jumps with both feet	low steps, box, block, plastic crate	Keep other children away from jumping spot when one child is jumping to the floor. Sometimes catch child as he or she jumps. Release and steady child so he or she can climb and jump again.
Kicks object	large ball: beach ball, Nerf ball, soccer ball, volleyball, rubber ball	Provide space where child can kick the ball and it will not go too far, e.g., into a big cardboard box or into a corner.
Walks up stairs holding railing; walks down stairs holding railing	steps and rail	Provide equipment and time for child to safely walk up and down.
Pushes and pulls objects while walking	small wagon, strollers, pull toys, push toys that make noise, attract visual attention	Provide clear space for walking where pushed and pulled toys have room to move without bumping and catching on equipment, furniture, rug.
Climbs	sturdy box, cubes, footstool, low climbing gym	Provide equipment. Remain close by to assist in getting down if needed.
Pedals cycle	low riding cycle; not high tricycle	Provide space for fast and slow riding, for turning curves and in circles. Keep away children on foot.
ARM		
Throws object at target	bean bag; ball, box, cardboard or wood shape with large holes cut in it	Place target at edge of play area so object is thrown away from children.
HAND		
Grasps and releases with developing finger muscles	small toys, objects, pail, box	Provide objects for game of pick-up-and-drop.
Pulls zippers	zipper board, book, clothes with large zipper with tab	Provide large zipper with tab large enough for small fingers to pinch and pull. Demonstrate where to hold fabric in other hand.
Helps dress and undress self		Allow child to do as much as possible. Plan ahead to provide enough time for child who dresses and undresses slowly.
Scribbles	paper, pens, crayons, markers, pencils, flat hard surface	Provide space and time to scribble.
Increases wrist flexibility; turns wrist to turn object	small objects to twist and turn; jars and screw-on lids	Provide toys that stimulate manipulating, e.g., attractive, textured on several sides. Demonstrate twisting jar lid on and off.
Establishes right- or left-handedness		Allow child to pick up objects and use them with hand child chooses. Do not change object into other hand.

(continued)

CHILD BEHAVIOR	MATERIALS	EXAMPLES OF CAREGIVER STRATEGIES
Turns book pages	sturdy pages in books	Read to child, carefully turning each page by grasping the upper right-hand corner and moving hand down to middle of page to gently turn the page.
Moves to music	play a CD or other recording	Move with child to the pace of the music.
Digs with tool	shovel, scoop, spoon; sand, dirt	Provide tools which are not sharp and will not bend. Provide space designated for digging. Demonstrate where sand or dirt may and may not go.
Makes individual marks with crayon or pen	paper, pen, crayon, marker	Listen if child talks about his or her marks. Provide feedback about what you see (e.g., colors, shapes) to child.
Sleeping		
May move from crib to bed or cot	firm cot, mattress	Talk about the change *before* it happens. Emphasize child is getting bigger and now can use a *bigger* bed. Demonstrate where shoes go, where blanket is. Provide quiet talk, music, touch familiar to child.
Eating		
Controls cup and spoon better		Emphasize how well child is using cup, spoon. Be patient with spills.
May eat anything, then change to picky eating		Allow child to change eating behavior. Don't fuss at or push child. Child usually will get adequate nutrition if variety of foods are provided.
Teeth		
Has most baby teeth; uses toothbrush	toothbrush, toothpaste, cup of water	Assist when necessary with applying toothpaste and cleaning face afterward.

Cognitive and Language Development

Cognitive Development

Children of this age are experiencing Piaget's substage 6 or even are transitioning to the preoperational stage of development. This means that they are gradually using mental trial and error. This is much faster than the sensorimotor trial and error, in which children had to manipulate objects. A toddler can now make decisions mentally about how something might work or how he or she might affect an object.

While object permanence is well established, toddlers of this age repeatedly engage in games such as peekaboo. They will explore the hiding locations of objects both on their own or when an adult prompts them. May, Kantor, and Sanderson (2004) described a curriculum project which grew from two children's ritualistic investigation of object permanence. In this project, teachers supported the children's interest by planning activities that provided new or novel opportunities for hiding and promoted development by scaffolding the toddler's learning.

Because of their ability to store and recall mental representations, toddlers are now able to follow one- and sometimes two-step oral directions. In addition, these memory skills help children of this age become skilled at imitating past events. Imitative behaviors often show up in the children's play. For example, the caregiver washing the child's face is imitated later by the child as the child washes a doll's face.

Play begins to move from imitative to symbolic during this time period. **Symbolic play** is children's representation of objects or feelings or ideas. They begin to connect past experiences into their current world as they take on simple roles. Infants and toddlers begin symbolic play by imitating actions associated with particular props, learning to substitute one thing for another, and acting as if they are someone else who is familiar to them (Isenberg & Jalongo, 2001; Van Hoorn, Nourot, Scales, & Alward, 2003). Simone might pretend to be a cook and make soup by stirring a spoon in a pot. You might hear Simone say "More salt" just as a cook might say after taste-testing. Symbolic play serves several functions: Children can express conflicts and work them out in the pretend world. They can pretend to be other people or objects, thereby reflecting their understanding of other people or objects as separate from themselves and trying behaviors similar to or different from their own. For those reasons, play is a window for adults to observe and tune into the children's emotional lives (i.e., their worries, fears, and joys; see Honig, 2005). Yet, caution must be exhibited when teachers observe a child's play. While toddlers often imitate a person's behavior, they also put their own spin on the situation by joining together reality and fantasy. For example, a toddler who has never been spanked or hit by a family member might hit a doll. So, for accuracy purposes, teachers should watch play behaviors over a period of time before making interpretations (Marion, 2004).

At around 22 to 24 months, a caregiver can determine what is going on with a child cognitively by **role playing** with puppets or dolls. Often the troubled child explains (verbally or nonverbally) very clearly to the caregiver a situation that might have been disturbing or upsetting. Role playing is also a good way for the child to get feedback in a positive way, a good place to use the three *A*s, and a good way to help them solve problems and continue to develop good *self-esteem*.

SUGGESTIONS FOR IMPLEMENTING CURRICULUM—COGNITIVE DEVELOPMENT	
CHILD BEHAVIOR	**EXAMPLES OF CAREGIVER STRATEGIES**
Piaget's Substages of Sensorimotor Development *SUBSTAGE 6 (Representation)* *Mental trial and error* Tries out ideas mentally, based on past concrete experiences	Allow child time to figure out solutions. If child seeks assistance, help child think about the problem, e.g., "What can you use to reach that block?"

(continued)

CHILD BEHAVIOR	EXAMPLES OF CAREGIVER STRATEGIES
Object permanence	
Sees object disappear, mentally remembers object, and figures out where it went	Allow the child to think and search for object. Give clues, ask questions only after the child has acted and still needs assistance.
Deferred imitation and symbolization	
Imitates past events	Observe the child's representations. Identify the ideas that seem very important to the child.
Symbolic play	
Resolves conflicts	Allow the child to act out conflict by playing with toys and materials. Observe how the child works out conflict so he or she feels better.
Compensates for unsatisfied needs	Observe child's play. Identify consistent themes in child's play, e.g., child's talk and actions about being a good or a naughty child.
Tries roles	Provide clothes and materials that help child pretend to be someone else.

Language Development

Language throughout life is clearly linked with positive relationships, and it is important to remember that children who get enough cuddling and unconditional love have a better chance at learning language—and everything else (Healy, 2004).

Caregivers must be careful not to criticize children's speech patterns. Good grammatical structure is learned by children when adults set good examples and repeatedly use words correctly. Remember to use the three *A*s when speech is used correctly as well as to encourage children when they have verbalized.

At this age children's vocabulary is expanding rapidly as they label objects that they now recognize as separate entities. Children construct the principle that

> words are labels for socially defined classes of objects and events. This achievement is reflected in more systematic and productive extension of words and in accelerated growth of vocabulary. . . . This is the time when children may tire their caregivers by constantly asking for the names of things (e.g., what's this?). They eagerly utter the words they hear and explore their uses. (Anisfeld, 1984, p. 86)

Children use their language to express needs and to direct others. They question as they seek to learn about their world (Wilson, 1988). Toddlers now use nouns, verbs, and pronouns as they combine their words into two- and three-word sentences. These children produce **telegraphic speech**, that is, a sequence of several words that conveys a thought or action but has omitted words. In general, telegraphic speech is almost exclusively made up of lexical words, rather than grammatical words (McDevitt & Ormrod, 2010; see Chapter 11 for the difference between lexical and grammatical words). For example, Cameron says, "Key go car" when he

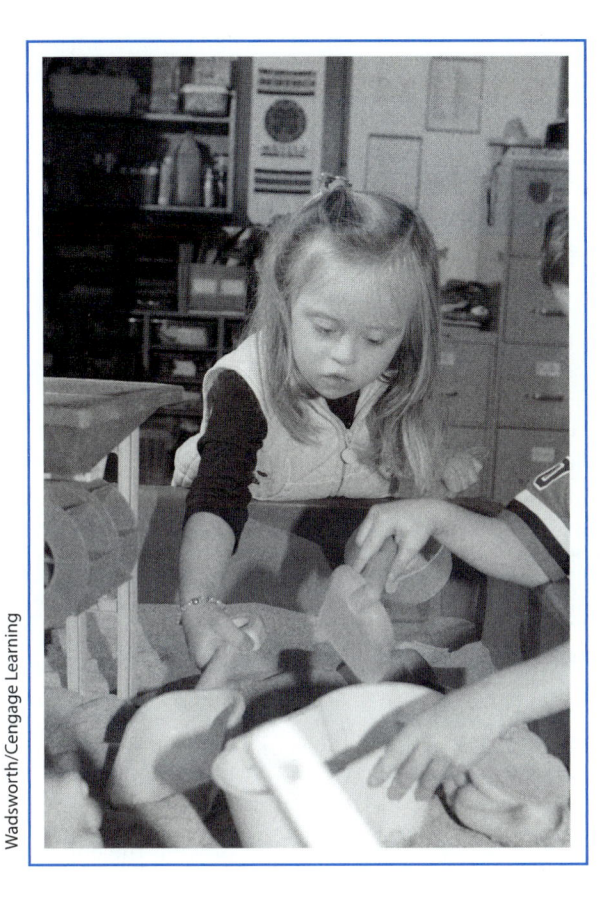

Indoor and outdoor activities provide many opportunities to observe, question, label, and describe the toddler's actions.

sees his mother take the key ring out of her purse. She responds, "Yes, I have the key. We're going in the car."

There are two broad classes of language functions: "the cognitive function—to name, indicate, describe, and comment; and the instrumental function—to request, reject, manipulate, and express desires.... [W]ords are used for cognitive purposes before they are used for instrumental purposes" (Anisfeld, 1984, p. 91). Caregivers and children use words to classify objects and actions. Words help children organize what they see and hear and do. Anisfeld (1984) reported that when adults do the following things they help young children develop proper language:

- The adult speaks to children in short sentences.
- The adult articulates more clearly to young children than to others.
- The adult talks about the situation in which the child is involved.
- The adult expands what the child says ("fills in the missing words as she echoes the child's utterance").

Toddlers do not share toys easily, so the early childhood teacher should provide enough toys of a similar nature for them to use.

- The adult extends what the child says ("continues a thought started by a child").
- The adult imitates what the child says ("repeats all or part of what the child has said").

Pictures, books, and storytelling stimulate language interactions among caregivers and children. Rosenkoetter & Barton (2002) explain how reading to infants and toddlers builds relationships between adults and children as well as between children and books.

> During the early years, reading together is more significant than targeting any specific content or skills. While sitting on a lap, rocking in a chair, or even sprawling side-by-side on the floor with a favorite adult, the toddler builds very positive associations and happy preverbal memories of "reading." . . . With young children, reading times can be very brief, but they must happen every day. Shared reading helps children explore new worlds, laugh across generations, and learn about amazing as well as ordinary things. (p. 34)

As just stated, teachers need to provide opportunities for shared reading frequently—several times during the day, because they tend to be of short duration. Refrain from only reading to a group of toddlers; each child needs time to snuggle up with a primary caregiver and a good book throughout the day. Choose reading materials for young children carefully. Stimulate the toddlers' interests in reading and hearing stories often. Providing a variety of reading materials, such as magazines, board books and picture books, small books and big books, nonfiction and storybooks, assists children with acquiring knowledge as well as a love of reading. In addition, making a flannel board or puppets with characters from familiar stories encourages toddlers to actively engage with the story (Lamme, 1985). Be prepared to read favorite stories again and again or to chant beloved nursery rhymes over and over.

Notice that toddlers differ in how they attend to the books. Some children are very engaged, pointing and vocalizing, while others are more passive. How toddlers demonstrated joint attention during book reading was associated with later language development (Fletcher, Perez, Hooper, & Claussen, 2005). While more research needs to be conducted, it would be logical to hypothesize that these and other child characteristics influence the quality of the adult-child reading interactions. Thus, teachers may need to demonstrate extra patience when interacting with children who are more passive.

Regarding written representations, toddlers experiment with markers, chalk, and crayons as their interest in scribbling continues. Encourage their scribbling by providing time and attention to their use and enjoyment of writing. Avoid asking the child what his scribbles are. The scribbles at this stage may not represent anything. Rather, comment on what you see—lines from top to bottom or across the page, dots, and colors. You might make descriptive comments such as, "I like your orange and brown picture" or "What bold blue lines!" While the focus should be on the process of scribbling rather than the end product, do not forget to display some of the children's work in prominent locations in the environment (Lamme, 1984). This type of documentation assists the toddlers in valuing their own work and models the need to value such developmental milestones to other adults (e.g., family members and colleagues).

spotlight *on practice*

Voices from the Field

I am a toddler teacher in a church ministry. I have the same five children each morning and a different group of five children each afternoon. The children in both of my groups love to look at books. I get new books every two weeks from the public library. I invite a librarian to read stories once a month. I've learned several skills from her such as how to ask open-ended questions throughout the book. It is amazing to me how the children's interests impact their reactions to the stories. For example, Selene is interested in books with a story line. She does not attend long to books with only one word on a page. Fiorenzo loves dinosaurs. I selected a book with different animals in it thinking that would attract his attention. He didn't show much interest until we got to the page with his favorite animal on it. When I pointed to the dinosaur and said its name, Fiorenzo smiled and began talking quickly using a combination of telegraphic speech and jargon.

SUGGESTIONS FOR IMPLEMENTING CURRICULUM—LANGUAGE DEVELOPMENT

CHILD BEHAVIOR	MATERIALS	EXAMPLES OF CAREGIVER STRATEGIES
Uses language to reflect own meaning; expects others to have same meaning		Recognize limited meaning of child's use of words. Be careful not to read extra meaning into what the child says.
Expands vocabulary rapidly, labeling objects		Verbally label objects and actions in child's world. Point to and touch the objects. Also expand the label into a sentence, e.g., "Ball. Michael has a ball."
Points to objects and pictures named by others		Play games, look at pictures, read books; say, "Point to the bird," or "Where is the car?"
Learns social words: *hello*, *please*, *thank you*		Consistently use social words in their correct context. Say "please" and "thank you" to the child.
Uses language to express needs, desires		Listen to child's expression of needs. Verbally respond so child knows that his or her words get your attention and you understand them. Use words and actions to meet child's needs or explain why you cannot meet them, e.g., "The milk is all gone."
Uses language to direct others		Listen to child's commands. Respond verbally and with action following child's directions or explain why you are not, e.g., "Here is a napkin" when child asks for one.
Questions; asks "What's that?"		Answer child's frequent and persistent questions. This is how the child learns labels and other information about the world. Provide simple answers, not complicated ones, e.g., "That is a flower" rather than a description of petals, leaves, stem, etc.
Uses nouns, verbs, pronouns		Speak normally with the child so child can hear complete sentence patterns.
Is learning prepositions		Use in natural contexts, e.g., "The ball rolled under the table," "Put the book on the shelf."
Calls self by name		Use the child's name when talking directly to child.
Follows one-step directions		Use simple directions and praise when the child follows them, e.g., "Please put the truck here."
Follows two-step directions		Make sure child is aware that you are giving directions. Use simple directions, e.g., "Please pick up this book and put it on the shelf."
Makes two- and three-word sentences		Use both short and long sentences with the child. Encourage child and respond to child's sentences with elaboration, e.g., Child: "Coat on?" Caregiver: "Yes, you need your coat on."
Looks at books	cloth or paper or cardboard picture books	Read books with child. Demonstrate proper care of books. Allow child to look at books alone.
Listens to stories and rhymes		Tell stories that the child can understand. Use rhymes, poems.
Scribbles	markers, chalk, crayons, paper	Provide writing space and materials. Show interest and approval of scribbling. Share scribbling with others.

✓ reading checkpoint

Before moving on with your reading, make sure that you can answer the following questions about the material discussed so far.

1. List three ways symbolic play helps a child develop cognitively.
2. Identify two possible developments in the child's language and state two strategies for each that a caregiver can use to facilitate that development.

Emotional Development

Children of this age are continuing to develop positive and negative feelings about themselves. They interpret responses from caregivers and other children as reflecting their self-worth. At this stage, children's feelings are hurt by criticism and they are afraid of disapproval or rejection. They become easily frustrated and are able to communicate some feelings and desires. It is important to consciously use the three *A*s to promote positive development.

Children's fantasies increase at this age. They are very real and may sometimes be frightening. Improvements in memory and other cognitive skills (e.g., object permanence) result in toddlers expressing more fears and experiencing increased levels of stress due to them. Toddlers may feel fearful of being separated or abandoned by family members, monsters, loud noises, being sucked down the toilet, or of losing control. Teachers can respond to their distress by creating new routines or maintaining existing routines (Simpson & McGuire, 2004). For example, Ms. Linda helps each family to create their own good-bye routines which include hugs, kisses, and waving good-bye from the good-bye window (Balaban, 2006; Herr & Swim, 2002). Because shared reading provides security and calms children's emotional agitation (Rosenkoetter & Barton, 2002), Ms. Linda uses books to calm children after they are separated from their family. She keeps in reach a few favorite books about emotions and being separated from favorite objects or possessions (see Zeece & Churchill, 2001, for book suggestions) that she reads individually to children after they have been dropped off at her family child care center. Ms. Linda also helps families to provide security objects (e.g., blankets, stuffed animals) when a child responds positively to their presence (see, for example, Steir & Lehman, 2000).

Emotions are reflected in intense behaviors. These children can swing between extremes, such as smiling or laughing, followed by screaming, or crying. Their basic pattern of intensity of response is affected by their swings into even more intense behaviors. Children who usually respond loudly may now scream and yell or laugh shrilly. Children who have a low intensity of response may use more energy and respond more loudly or actively than usual, or they may exhibit even more withdrawn behaviors in response to increased stress.

As toddlers approach their second birthdays, they become aware that they have a self and that they are separate from the world of other people and things. They now

Toddlers feel emotions, express emotions, but do not yet understand emotions. Feeling strong emotions can overwhelm and scare toddlers.

want to act like separate social beings. Becoming a separate psychological being is one of the most complicated tasks a toddler has to face. During the two years starting from birth, the child establishes a very strong attachment to family members and other primary caregivers. When dependence on others begins to diminish, separation follows. The more enjoyable and secure the relationships have been, the easier the separation process (Caplan & Caplan, 1980).

SUGGESTIONS FOR IMPLEMENTING CURRICULUM—EMOTIONAL DEVELOPMENT	
CHILD BEHAVIOR	**EXAMPLES OF CAREGIVER STRATEGIES**
Types of Emotions and Feelings	
Shows one or more emotions at same time	Identify the child's emotions. Respond to the child's needs.
Continues to develop feelings about self	Provide consistent behavior and feedback that helps the child feel good about self; help child know he or she is a worthy person.
Changes feelings about self	Tell child that he or she is still a loved person when child reflects negative or angry feelings about self.

(continued)

CHILD BEHAVIOR	EXAMPLES OF CAREGIVER STRATEGIES
Seeks approval	Provide verbal and nonverbal approval of child as a person and of child's behavior when it is positive.
May develop new fears	Listen to child's fears. Accept them as real. Comfort child. Reassure child of your concern and of your presence. You may demonstrate that the object, for example a siren toy, is harmless. If you cannot calm the child, remove the toy and introduce it again later.
Increases fantasy	Listen to child's fantasies. Accept them as real to the child. Enjoy funny, happy fantasies. Comfort and reassure child of his or her safety when child has scary fantasies, e.g., "There's a monster in the kitchen."
May increase aggressiveness	Remain nearby to caution, remind, and sometimes remove object or child from situation.
Seeks security in routines	Provide consistent routines that child can use by him- or herself as child increases competence and seeks independence.
May become shy again	Allow child to hold back or withdraw. Provide time for child to observe without having to enter into interactions with others.
Sometimes rejects family members or caregiver	Allow child to express rejection in words and behaviors. Continue to express your affection for the child.
Control of Emotions and Feelings	
Uses reactions of others as a controller of own behavior	Use words, facial expressions, gestures to indicate approval and disapproval of child's behavior.
May resist change	Explain change *before* it happens. Provide reason for the change. Motivate by emphasizing the specialness of the child who now is allowed to do something else. Remember that development is a process not a product. Give time for lessons to be learned.
Moves to extremes, from lovable to demanding and stubborn	Allow child to express swings in behavior. Show acceptance of child as a person. Help child work on his or her demands and stubbornness by suggesting alternatives in behavior.

Social Development

Children of this age are continuing to develop a sense of self. They use words that identify them as separate people, such as *I*, *mine*, *me*, *you*. These children are also expanding their relationships with others. They are beginning to recognize other people's feelings, and they are working slowly at understanding another person's intentions. Hay, Castle, and Davies (2000) discovered that when toddlers age 18 to 30 months attributed a hostile intent to familiar peers during interactions, they were more likely to use personal force. In other words, if a peer pointed toward or reached for an object that the toddler was using, she was likely to protest, withdraw the object, or physically harm the peer. This pattern of outcomes is particularly noteworthy because it suggests that some toddlers may be prone to attributing hostile intent, which may interfere with their ability to form positive relationships with new acquaintances, and that "social misunderstandings and processes of peer rejection might begin even before a child enters formal group care" (p. 465).

Caregivers should help the toddlers to interpret the behaviors of their peers by providing descriptive language. If a toddler reaches for the toy of another, the teacher should describe what he sees and provide an alternative perspective and possible strategies. For example, "Burke, you are watching Libby smash the play dough with the rolling pin. Do you want to roll? Here is another rolling pin for you." You should then involve Libby in the conversation to facilitate her interpretation of Burke's reaching behaviors by saying, "Burke likes the way you are flattening the dough. He was watching you work. He wants to use the rolling pin also. I found one for him." In Chapter 6, we discussed the importance of communicating the intentions and actions of the people involved to assist very young children with beginning to learn perspective taking.

Toddlers are still working on showing ownership and are not yet ready to share. Provide multiple supplies and equipment so that they can engage alongside each other in parallel play.

spotlight on research

Conflicts with Peers

Infants and toddlers have strong desires and they work to fulfill them. In group settings such as child care centers, these desires can often be in conflict with others want or need them to do. Responding with strong emotions or harmful behaviors when a desire cannot be fulfilled does not necessarily mean that children are aggressive or antisocial. When fighting over objects, the intention is rarely to harm another; the children act to protect their own desires. While it may seem counterintuitive, this can be a positive learning situation because it causes the children to begin to consider why others may be resisting them. In other words, "as their everyday social interactions increase in frequency and complexity, young children must learn how to engage in a process of responsible decision making as they negotiate their relationships with others" (Warren, Denham, & Bassett, 2008, p. 34).

While we know that infants and toddlers experience conflicts with their peers, minimal empirical data exist on the content of these conflicts. Licht, Simoni, and Perrig-Chiello (2008) conducted a longitudinal investigation with 28 infants. These infants were observed and videotaped during free play situations in their child care center at 8, 14, and 22 months of age. Then, the videotapes were coded for instances of conflict. These researchers defined conflict as needing at least three actions: 1) Child A does something that influences Child B, 2) Child B resists, and 3) Child A persists. Ninety-eight incidents of conflict were found (14 at Time 1; 26 at Time 2; and 58 at Time 3). Then, the behaviors of the target child and peer were analyzed for each conflict.

At Time 1, the eight month olds' motivations for conflict were characterized by "interruption of activity" and "exploration." In both cases, infants sought to continue their interactions with a given toy and either resisted their activity being interrupted by a peer or persisted with wanting to explore the toy that a peer possessed. At Time 1, the researchers concluded that infants at this age were too young to understand possessions or jealousy. Therefore, the infants focused on their desired interactions with a toy.

(Box continues)

spotlight (continued)

At Time 2 and 3, the most frequent displays of motivations for conflict continued to be those identified with the infants: interruption of activity and exploration. The toddlers also exhibited other motivations (e.g., Time 2: "awoken needs" and the "will to effect" and Time 3: "contact and sensation seeking" and "dominance") but at less than a 6 percent frequency each. At Time 3, however, another motivation was identified as occurring at 24 percent possession. This motivation was described as the display of the desire to control the object along with intense emotions. When experiencing these types of conflicts, the older toddlers' verbal and nonverbal expressions referred to the child's own self (e.g., "mine"; pointing to object and to herself).

Licht, Simoni, and Perrig-Chiello (2008) conclude from this research that " the role that the urge to explore plays in conflicts between peers in the first two years of life has been underestimated" (p. 245). Furthermore, "… ascribing conflicts among children in this age group solely to a motive such as possession is a reductive and misleading interpretation of children's capacities and their social life" (p. 245). Toddlers are working on being able to infer another's emotion, use emotional language, and solve social problems, all of which are crucial to positive peer relationships (Warren, Denham, & Bassett, 2008). To attribute all of their conflicts to possession minimizes their efforts.

SUGGESTIONS FOR IMPLEMENTING CURRICULUM—SOCIAL DEVELOPMENT

CHILD BEHAVIOR	EXAMPLES OF CAREGIVER STRATEGIES
Self	
Is egocentric, sees things from own point of view	Recognize that child thinks others think and feel the way he or she does. Help child identify own ideas and feelings.
May change identity of self from day to day	Provide feedback to child about self so child can identify consistency within self.
Identifies materials as belonging to self	Recognize and allow ownership of toys.
Uses *I*, *mine*, *me*, *you*	Verbally respond to child's use of pronouns, reinforcing distinction child makes between self and others.
Others	
Demands attention	Both initiate and respond to child to provide attention to child's needs. Share looks, touch, and words with child when you may be busy with another child.
Begins to be aware of others' feelings	Help child identify and verbalize the feelings he has that appear in his behavior, e.g., "Allen is crying; he is sad."
Believes that people have changes in identity—that a change in role changes a person	Identify yourself in your different tasks, e.g., as you sweep and clean, as you cook, as you rock a child.
Expands social relationships	Encourage child to interact with others. Be present and provide your support when child encounters a new child or adult.

(continued)

CHILD BEHAVIOR	EXAMPLES OF CAREGIVER STRATEGIES
Looks to others for help	Consistently provide assistance when needed. Praise child for seeking help with something child would not be able to do for self, e.g., putting on shoe and then seeking help for tying laces instead of fussing and crying.
Imitates tasks of others	Allow and enjoy child's watching you and others. Enjoy the imitations and don't be concerned that the imitation might be incomplete or inaccurate. The child will continue to watch and imitate.
Wants to help, assist with tasks, clean up	Encourage the child to help put toys away, clean up, etc. Work along with child. Child can be a very good helper if he or she sees how you do it.
May do opposite of what is requested	Carefully word your requests. The child's negativism comes out in a frequent "no." Think of different ways to produce desired behavior without saying, "Do this."
Has difficulty sharing	Provide enough toys and materials so child does not have to share. Suggest allowing another child to play with toy when child finishes. Provide alternative toys to the child who must wait for a desired toy.
Engages in parallel play	Provide toys, materials, and space for children to play near each other. Talk to each of them. Allow them to choose if they want to trade toys or do something else.

reading checkpoint

Before moving on with your reading, make sure that you can answer the following questions about the material discussed so far.

1. Provide three examples of how routines can be used to help children deal with emotional stress.
2. Chris and Marlin both pick up a car and start pulling on it. What can you do and say that shows appropriate understanding of each child's needs and desires?

SUMMARY

As toddlers transition from sensorimotor to preoperational thinking, their growing capabilities allow them to solve problems in new ways: mental trial and error. They also are experiencing a rapidly growing vocabulary. These new cognitive/language skills play a significant role in their ability to engage in symbolic play and deal with strong emotions. Adults can help toddlers develop emotional coping skills by creating flexible routines.

key terms

cognitive function
instrumental function
role-playing
symbolic play
telegraphic speech

case study
Lennie

Louise and her colleagues were very frustrated with Lennie's biting behavior. Not only had he broken the skin on several children's bodies, his daily tantrums caused damage to furniture and equipment. As Lennie's primary caregiver, Louise decided to invite Lennie's parents and the center's director to a conference after doing extensive observation, to discuss the biting and tantrum behaviors.

On the day of the meeting, Lennie's father was unable to attend the meeting due to a medical emergency with his father. Louise opened the conversation by expressing her concern for Lennie's grandfather and then by sharing some positive anecdotes about Lennie and his development. She then asked Lennie's mother about the types of behaviors they were seeing at home. Lennie's mother was very defensive and provided few details. When asked directly about biting behaviors, she spoke loudly saying, "No matter how many times we spank him, we can't get him to stop biting his older sister. It worked with his hitting." When probed, she stated, "We solved his hitting by spanking him each time. He doesn't hit us anymore."

Louise asked Lennie's mother about other strategies they use at home that she might be able to use at school, explaining that ethically and legally she would not hit a child because it might cause harm. Lennie's mother was unable to come up with any other strategies. Louise changed the subject slightly to ask about potential causes of his biting and tantrums. His mother was just as unclear as she was to the potential causes of his biting and angry outbursts. They seem to happen frequently with a wide variety of children in very different situations.

Louise and Lennie's mother agreed to do more observations to record the potential triggers or causes of his biting and tantrums. They set a follow-up meeting for the next week.

They collected the following data:

Bit two children at school who took his toys

Three tantrums at school when told it was time to stop playing and clean up

Two tantrums at school when stopped from riding trike in the grass

Two tantrums at home when sister wouldn't let him play with her toys

Three tantrums at home when he didn't want to go to bed

Bit sister two times when she took a toy of hers away from him

The data showed some clear patterns of behaviors for Lennie. It appeared to Louise and his mother that he doesn't deal well with frustration or not being able to carry out his ideas. They created a plan that involved using the following tools: labeling and expressing feelings, providing a toy for self-soothing, giving warnings, and setting clear, positive limits. The plan also involved talking weekly about how the strategies were working at home and at school.

After a month of implementing the plan, Lennie's behavior had improved significantly at school but not at home. Louise began to model, whenever she could, some of these techniques for his parents. She also invited them to spend more time in the classroom. They slowly improved in their use of the strategies and reported that the biting and tantrums had decreased at home.

1. How would you react emotionally to Lennie's behaviors at the start of the case? How would you deal with and express these feelings?
2. How did Louise's behavior during the first conference impact the outcomes? How else could you imagine it happening? What do you think made a difference?
3. Do you think it was a good idea for Louise to suggest using four new strategies at one time? Why or why not?
4. Neither Louise nor the parents described Lennie's language skills. What might be the relationship between language development and aggressive acts?

QUESTIONS AND EXPERIENCES FOR REFLECTION

1. Observe one caregiver for ten minutes. Use a narrative running record (Appendix A) to write down everything the caregiver does and says. Then categorize the behavior using a format like the following.

Caregiver Behavior (What Caregiver Did)	Caregiver Initiated	With Whom?	Caregiver Responded	To Whom?

2. Identify one child's characteristic temperament (by records, caregiver information, or your own observation). Observe how the caregiver makes adjustments in the routine or expectations of the child in response to the situation and how the caregiver helps the child make adjustments. For example, the caregiver may warn a low active child several times that a transition is going to occur.

3. Make one toy and allow two children who are 18–24 months old to use it. Observe and write down how they used it, what they said, and your judgment about whether they seemed interested, challenged, or bored with it. Also evaluate the toy's construction.

4. Observe one child between 18 and 24 months of age. Observe the child's behavior for two five-minute periods, and write two observations using an anecdotal record (Appendix A). Then transfer the descriptions to the Developmental Profile (Appendix B). Analyze the results and create a project by outlining three or four related learning experiences to support the child's development and interests.

5. List five strategies to use with children between 18 and 24 months of age.

Toy	How Used	Child's Comments	Interesting, Challenging, Boring?	Sturdy, Torn, Broken?
Child 1				
Child 2				

REFERENCES

Anisfeld, M. (1984). *Language development from birth to three*. Hillsdale, NJ: Lawrence Erlbaum Associates.

Balaban, N. (2006). Easing the separation process for infants, toddlers, and families. *Beyond the Journal: Young Children on the Web*. Retrieved January 16, 2007, from http://www.journal.naeyc.org/btj/200611/pdf/BTJBalaban.pdf

Caplan, F., & Caplan, T. (1980). *The second twelve months of life*. New York: Bantam/Grosset and Dunlap.

Fletcher, K. L., Perez, A., Hooper, C., & Claussen, A. H. (2005). Responsiveness and attention during picture-book reading in 18-month-old to 24-month-old toddlers at risk. *Early Child Development and Care*, 175(1), 63–83.

Hay, D. F., Castle, J., & Davies, L. (2000). Toddlers' use of force against familiar peers: A precursor of serious aggression? *Child Development, 71*(2), 457–467.

Healy, J. (2004). *Your child's growing mind: A guide to learning and brain development from birth to adolescence.* (3rd ed.). New York: Broadway Books.

Herr, J., & Swim, T. J. (2002). *Creative resources for infants and toddlers* (2nd ed.). Clifton Park, NY: Thomson Delmar Learning.

Honig, A. S. (2005, April). What infants, toddlers, and preschoolers learn from play: A dozen ideas. Paper presented at the American Montessori Society meeting, Chicago, IL.

Isenberg, J. P., & Jalongo, M. R. (2001). *Creative expression and play in early childhood* (3rd ed.). Upper Saddle River, NJ: Merrill Prentice Hall.

Lamme, L. L. (1984). *Growing up writing*. Washington, DC: Acropolis Books.

Lamme, L. L. (1985). *Growing up reading*. Washington, DC: Acropolis Books.

Licht, B., Simoni, H., & Perrig-Chiello, P. (2008). Conflict between peers in infancy and toddler age: What do they fight about? *Early Years, 28*(3), 235–249.

Marion, M. (2004). *Using observation in early childhood education.* Upper Saddle River, NJ: Pearson Prentice Hall.

May, N., Kantor, R., & Sanderson, M. (2004). There it is! Exploring the permanence of objects and the power of self with infants and toddlers. In J. Hendrick (Ed.), *Next steps toward teaching the Reggio way: Accepting the challenge to change* (2nd ed., pp. 164–174). Upper Saddle River, NJ: Prentice Hall.

McDevitt, T. M., & Ormrod, J. E. (2010). *Child development: Educating and working with children and adolescents* (4th ed.). Upper Saddle River, NJ: Pearson Prentice Hall.

Rosenkoetter, S., & Barton, L. R. (2002). Bridges to literacy: Early routines that promote later school success. *Zero to Three, 22*(4), 33–38.

Simpson, C. G., & McGuire, M. (2004). Are you ready? Supporting children in an uncertain world. *Dimensions of Early Childhood, 32*(3), 35–38.

Spinrad, T. L., Eisenberg, N., Gaertner, B., Popp, T., Smith, C. L., Kupfer, A., Greving, K., Liew, J., & Hofer, C. (2007). Relations of maternal socialization and toddlers' effortful control to children's adjustment and social competence. *Developmental Psychology, 43*(5), 1170–1186.

Steir, A. J., & Lehman, E. B. (2000). Attachment to transitional objects: Role of maternal personality and mother-toddler interaction. *American Journal of Orthopsychiatry, 70*(3), 340–350.

Van Hoorn, J., Nourot, P. M., Scales, B., & Alward, K. R. (2003). *Play at the center of the curriculum.* (3rd ed.). Upper Saddle River, NJ: Merrill Prentice Hall.

Warren, H. K., Denham, S. A., & Bassett, H. H. (2008). The emotional foundations of social understanding. *Zero to Three, 28*(5), 32–39.

Wilson, L. C. (1988). What's in the box? *Pre-K Today, 2*(4), 38–39.

Zeece, P. D., & Churchill, S. L. (2001). First stories: Emergent literacy in infants and toddlers. *Early Childhood Education Journal, 29*(2), 101–104.

For additional activities, web links, and other resources, please visit our website at www.cengage.com/education/swim

chapter 15

THE CHILD FROM TWENTY-FOUR TO THIRTY MONTHS OF AGE

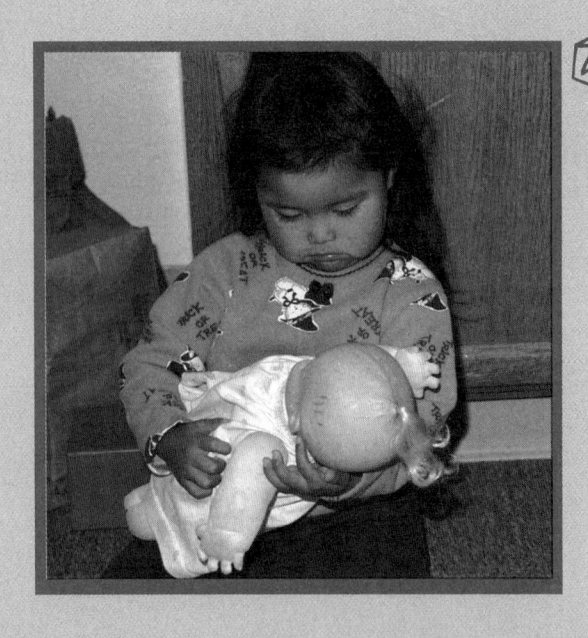

learning objectives

After reading this chapter, you should be able to:

- Identify and record sequences of change in the physical, cognitive/language emotional, and social development of children from 24 to 30 months of age.
- Select materials appropriate to the development of children at that age level.
- Devise strategies appropriate to children at that developmental level.

chapter outline

- Materials and Activities
- Caregiver Strategies to Enhance Development
  Physical Development
  Cognitive and Language Development
  Emotional Development
  Social Development
- Case Study: Ming

Ming's Story

Twenty-six-month-old Ming picks up a fire truck and walks up on the porch with it. She pushes it around on the floor, then picks it up and takes it out into the yard. Ms. Tao asks her what she has. Ming responds, "A truck," and smiles. Ms. Tao asks what kind of truck. Ming says, "Red," and smiles. Ming picks up a ball and says, "Watch me throw it." She moves the fire truck and tells Ms. Tao, "Can't find ladder." Ms. Tao finds the ladder and starts to put it on the fire truck. Ming requests, "Me do it." Ming puts a toy fire fighter in the truck and plays with it. She says to Ms. Tao, "See the truck," and then, "See if it goes?" As Ming plays with the fire truck, the ladder falls off again and she says, "Oh, no," and looks at Ms. Tao. She takes the truck to Ms. Tao to fix the ladder, saying "It fall off" and pointing to the ladder. She watches Ms. Tao fix the ladder and plays with it again. Another child gets the fire truck and begins to play with it. Ming tells the child, "I want the truck." Bill gives the fire truck back to Ming, who says, "Thank you, Bill."

MATERIALS AND ACTIVITIES

Riding toys are favorites at this age. The children also use climbing and jumping equipment frequently. Kicking and throwing, both more accurate than before, are enjoyed by the children. Finger, hand, and wrist movements, including grasping and

Trikes and other riding toys pose natural challenges for toddlers.

releasing, now coordinate with vision, enabling the children to string beads and to use crayons and other drawing and writing tools with greater accuracy. Children take pleasure in manipulating objects and materials. They focus on the process rather than on producing a product. They respond to and create music. They enjoy symbolic play. Children of this age can find meaning in pictures and books representing ideas with which they are familiar.

Most adults who work with toddlers wonder when and how children begin to be able to look at situations from another person's viewpoint. Some toddlers may seem to behave in an empathetic fashion occasionally or briefly. Such behavior is probably indicative of actions they have observed and reflects an emergent understanding of what someone else is feeling. A toddler may, for example, look concerned if another child cries, may rush over to pat the unhappy one, offer a cracker or toy, or may even burst into tears. Spinrad and Stifter (2006) found that when mothers were more responsive in their interactions with very young children, the toddlers displayed more concerned attention to a crying doll baby and to maternal distress. Logically, teachers who use the three *A*s consistently will assist toddlers in learning to be empathetic and to display empathy with peers.

Types of Materials

balance beam	large pegs and boards
climbing equipment	large beads and string
bouncing equipment	markers, crayons, pens, chalk
rocking boat	modeling dough
wagon	construction material: wood, Styrofoam, glue
cycles	
wheeled toys	rhythm instruments
items to throw	CDs
balls	audiotapes
blocks	puppets
trucks, cars	dress-up clothes
dolls, people, animals	pictures
jars with twist lids	books
items to put together or pull apart	puzzles
knobs	matching games

Examples of Homemade Materials

BALANCE BEAM

Put masking tape on the floor to indicate a line on which the child can walk.

In the yard partially bury a tree trunk so that several inches remain above ground. Place so that no branch stubs are on the top walking surface.

FIGURE 15–1

(continued)

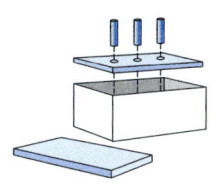

chapter 15 THE CHILD FROM TWENTY-FOUR TO THIRTY MONTHS OF AGE

PEG BOARD — *Cut a piece of heavy cardboard to fit in the bottom of a box (such as for shoes or gifts). Cut holes in the cardboard. Cut ½-inch dowel rod into roughly two-inch lengths. Paint if desired. Store cardboard and pegs in the box and use the lid.*

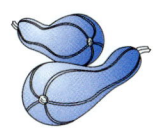

MARACAS — *Collect gourds in the fall. Allow to dry. The seeds will rattle when the gourd is shaken.*

DRUM — *Poke a hole in each end of an oatmeal box. Pull a strong string through the box and both ends and extend 12–24 inches (measure on one of your children). Tape the box lid onto one end of the box. Tie a knot or leave the ends loose and tie a bow each time you put it around a child's neck.*

SOAP PAINT — *Use one part soap flakes, one part water, and food coloring. Beat the mixture with a hand eggbeater. Skim off soap suds to paint on tabletop, shelf paper, or freezer paper.*

FINGER PAINT — *Use liquid starch, dry tempera paint, and soap flakes. Pour out about a tablespoon of liquid starch on shelf or freezer paper. Sprinkle dry paint on starch. Sprinkle soap flakes on starch. Children mix ingredients as they paint.*

TEMPERA PAINT — *Mix ½ cup dry tempera paint and ½ cup dry detergent. Add water until mixture is thick but not runny. Keep in covered jar.*

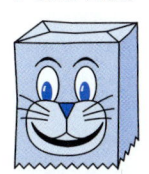

PUPPETS — *Use paper lunch bags. Child can use crayons or glue on paper to decorate puppet. Help child fit hand in bottom of sack.*

FIGURE 15–1

(continued)

CLOTH BOOK

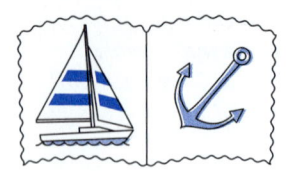

Use pinking shears to cut heavy cloth to make several pieces the same size. Stack the pieces and sew down the middle by machine or by hand. Cut out colored pictures from magazines or greeting cards. Glue one picture per page. Make a theme book, e.g., children riding, or use pictures of different objects or activities.

GROUP BOOK

Have children tear out magazine pictures of objects; the pictures may fit a theme. Glue to pieces of paper. Staple the pages together. Write the title page. Write what children dictate to you for the other pages.

PUZZLE

Cut out one uncluttered colored picture from a magazine. Gather two pieces of cardboard that are slightly larger than the picture.

a. Glue the picture to the center of one piece of cardboard.
b. Cover the picture and cardboard with clear adhesive. Outline three to five sections that are visually recognizable (head, legs, tail) with a pencil. Cut around the picture, being careful to cut cleanly through the cardboard.
c. Cut the remaining hole in the cardboard slightly larger.
d. Glue a backing onto the cardboard with a second piece of cardboard the same size. Fit the puzzle pieces into place. If necessary, trim so the pieces come out easily.

MATCHING GAME

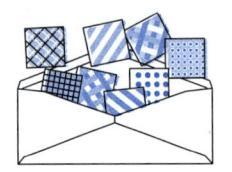

Cut two 2-inch squares from each page of a wallpaper sample book. Make about six pairs, using different pages. Store the pieces in an envelope. To play, mix up the pieces and then select squares that match.

MATCHING GAME

Select four picture pairs of objects that are alike, e.g., two cardinals, two mice, two daisies, two German shepherds. Glue one of each pair onto the bottom of a Styrofoam tray. Glue the other four pictures onto cardboard and cut into small squares. Glue part of an envelope in the tray to hold the loose cardboard pieces. Randomly pick pieces that match the pictures on the tray. Ask child to point to matching object.

FIGURE 15–1 (*continued*)

Activity Ideas

The following are examples of activities that help children construct knowledge, along with some of the items, concepts, and actions involved.

Exploration
Cooking

recipe chart	stir	see
oral language	beat	hear
measure	smell	taste
sift	feel	

Growing Plants

carrots	bean sprouts	observations
sweet potatoes	food	comparisons
beans	care	charting
lettuce	rate of growth	

Representations
Oral Language

conversation	poetry	singing and rhythms
information gathering	nursery rhymes	dramatic play
storytelling	fingerplays	

Objects
painting rocks, seeds, pine cones
creating prints with found objects or body parts such as feet, hands, fingers

Pictures
magazines, photographs
art media: crayons, painting, tear and paste

Books
wordless picture books
naming books
books with a story line to read or tell in your own words

CAREGIVER STRATEGIES TO ENHANCE DEVELOPMENT

Physical Development

The two-year-old can stand, bend, walk, run, and jump. While riding toys are still favorites at this age, these children also use climbing and jumping equipment frequently. Kicking and throwing are increasingly accurate and enjoyable for the children. Toddlers are more flexible and stable in their movements than before

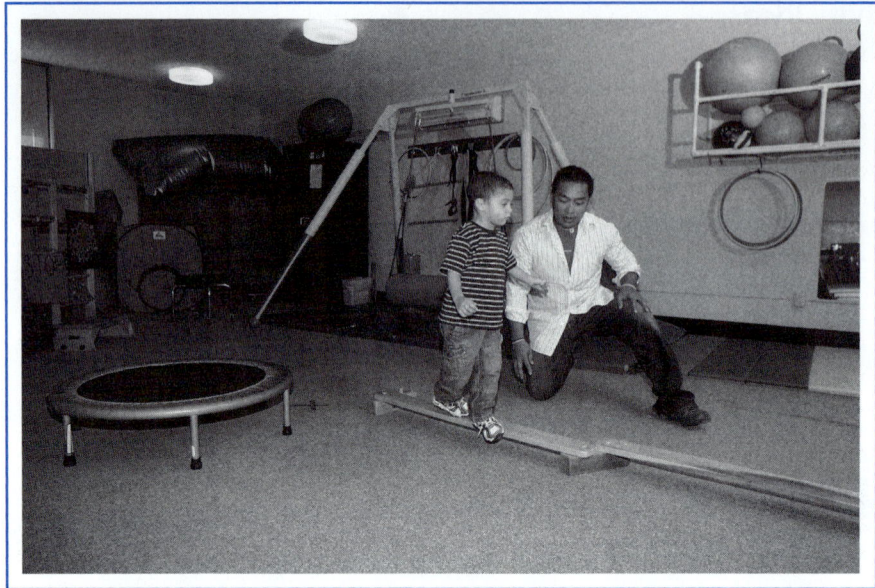

The young child is becoming more coordinated and can balance on smaller surfaces.

(Adolph, Vereijken, & Shrout, 2003). Their eye-hand coordination is more accurate, so they can reach and grasp objects, but they still have difficulty using hands and fingers independently. They are able to fit objects together and like to put them together and pull them apart. Toddlers may use either their right or left hand, but most still have not firmly established handedness. These children are visually fascinated with some new items and carefully observe novel objects. They use a spoon when eating and are learning to use a fork. Some children this age have all 20 baby teeth. These children should learn to brush their own teeth. Many children this age exhibit signs of being ready for toilet learning.

SUGGESTIONS FOR IMPLEMENTING CURRICULUM—PHYSICAL DEVELOPMENT

CHILD BEHAVIOR	MATERIALS	EXAMPLES OF CAREGIVER STRATEGIES
Muscular Control *MOVEMENT*		
Bends at waist	objects to drop and pick up: pail and plastic rings	Play game with child. Observe appropriateness of materials, interest of child.

(continued)

CHILD BEHAVIOR	MATERIALS	EXAMPLES OF CAREGIVER STRATEGIES
Climbs	low objects: steps up to slide, tires	Select safe materials and safe height.
Jumps	two- to three-step equipment	Keep floor or ground space clear where jumping. Block off higher levels so jump is safe distance for muscles and balance.
Stands on one foot	song for lifting one foot	Make up rhyme or song about standing on one foot. Child will stand on one foot for only a few seconds. Provide feedback and encourage child to repeat or try again.
ARM		
Throws	target: large paper sack or plastic basin; objects: Nerf™ ball, yarn ball	Provide space for child to throw objects at target. Decorate target so child is aiming at hoop or door.
HAND		
Touches	textured objects: sand paper, fur, corduroy, egg carton bottom, juice can	Make feely box. Allow child to pull out objects to touch and see. Label objects and textures for child.
Twists	jars and cans with lids; large plastic nuts and bolts	Provide objects that twist on and off easily.
Eating		
Uses spoon	spoon that fits child's hand	Provide food that can be spooned easily.
Is learning to use fork	fork that fits child's hand	Provide food that will stay on fork.
Uses fingers		Cut solid food in small pieces so it can be picked up with fingers.
Teeth		
Has all 20 baby teeth Brushes teeth	toothbrush, toothpaste	Assist with toothpaste and water.
Elimination		
May show interest in and readiness for toilet learning	potty chair, training pants; slacks, leggings easy to remove	Show child where potty chair is. Encourage child to use it. Provide feedback to child when he or she does. Avoid pushing child. Many show interest in toileting months before they are ready for actual transition to toilet learning. Review Chapter 3 to understand child who is ready for consistent toilet learning.

Cognitive and Language Development

Cognitive Development

Many children between 24 and 30 months are entering Piaget's preoperational stage of cognitive development. The first substage of the preoperational stage is preconceptual, which occurs from about two to four years of age. These children can mentally sort some objects and actions. The mental symbols are partly detached from experience. Early nonverbal classifications are called *graphic collections*, in which children can focus on figurative properties. These children form some verbal preconcepts, but the meaning of words may fluctuate from one time to another. Verbal reasoning is from the particular to the particular.

Preconceptual children are constructing and organizing knowledge about a wide range of areas in their world. They are beginning to classify objects and to develop very limited ideas of quantity, number, space, and time. Due to their preference for routines and sameness, their sense of time is based more on what happens after an event rather than on an understanding of *later* or minutes of time passage.

The development of the symbolic function occurs in the preconceptual stage. It involves the following mental representations, presented here in increasing order of complexity. In the child's search for hidden objects the object remains permanent (does not cease to exist) in the child's thinking even when the child cannot see it. These experiences form the basis for more specific representational thinking. In *deferred imitation* the child imitates another person's behavior even when that person is no longer present. A child engaged in symbolic play may give the caregiver a stone and tell the caregiver to "eat this apple"; the stone represents the real object. The child's *drawings* may be scribbles, experiments with the media, or they may begin to be representations; a child may point to a mark he or she has made on a piece of paper and say his or her own name. Mental images are pictures in the mind with which children can carry out action sequences internally. Language is used easily to represent objects or behaviors. As children develop language, they internalize words, meanings, mental images, and thoughts; from a Vygotskian perspective, language plays a critical role in cognitive development. This internalization of thoughts permits toddlers to use private speech to guide and regulate their behaviors (see Chapter 2).

Children at this age are active explorers, seeking information through manipulating and observing their world. As problem solvers, they now move beyond trial and error to mental manipulation of ideas and physical manipulation of objects to construct their reasoning.

When there is only one "right" way to play, opportunities for experimentations and new discovery are limited. Open-ended materials, such as common household objects, recycled items, tools, cooking utensils, and gadgets are particularly fascinating because adults use them. Nesting and stacking objects and containers for dumping and pouring are examples of good mental stimulators. They require active handling and teaching about relationships such as top, middle, bottom, small, big, bigger, and biggest. Large hollow and wooden unit blocks of different sizes are the best toys of all (Healy, 2004; Hewitt, 2001).

spotlight on research

Adult Depression and Infant Cognitive Development

This text has discussed in previous chapters the importance of quality infant-parent interactions. When adults are attuned to infants, the infants have better social-emotional developmental outcomes. Mothers who are depressed tend to have more difficulty in creating and maintaining positive, synchronous interactions (see Wanless, Rosenkoetter, & McClelland, 2008, for a review). But, do such interactions impact other areas of development?

Feldman and Eidelman (2009) studied 126 infant-mother pairs from birth-age five. All of these infants had a healthy low-risk, yet premature birth. Mothers were asked to report their depressive symptoms prior to being discharged from the hospital. Mother-infant interactions were captured on video-tape at six, twelve, and twenty-four months of age. Those tapes were analyzed for maternal sensitivity (e.g., positive affect, acknowledgement of child communication) and child social engagement (e.g., social initiation, gaze, alertness). Cognitive development was measured by the Bayley Scales of Infant Development at six, twelve, and twenty-four months of age and the Wechsler Preschool and Primary Scale of Intelligence at five years. The results of the analyses showed that maternal depression impacted the children's cognitive development. More specifically, those mothers reporting more symptoms of depression had children who showed slower rates of cognitive growth from infancy through five years of age. In contrast, another longitudinal study examining the relationship between maternal depression and cognitive outcomes found a weak relationship, even though maternal depression was negatively related to parenting behaviors (Kiernan & Huerta, 2008).

Wanless, et al., (2008), in their review of literature, examined current studies on *paternal* depression and discovered that the research results are somewhat mixed. For example, some studies demonstrated that fathers who were depressed spent less time in parenting, including playful and cognitively stimulating activities while others found no different in parental behaviors. Research by Roggman and colleagues (see Spotlight on Research box in Chapter 3) uncovered the importance of participating in Early Head Start programs on fathers' ability to create complex play situations with their toddlers. Thus, it appears that paternal interaction is important to their infants' and toddlers' cognitive outcomes and adults who are depressed have more difficulty in being engaged with their young child.

Teachers should be supportive of all families and children in their care. Making available information on mental health resources to everyone on a regular basis reduces the need for families to seek assistance in finding the help they may need. In the United States, seeking mental health support is still viewed as a sign of weakness. Infant and toddler professionals should advocate for such behavior as a sign of strength and should create policies and practices for their own school/classroom from a strength-based perspective that emphasizes resilience and protective factors over symptomatic behaviors (Lamb-Parker, LeBuffe, Powell, & Halpern, 2008).

SUGGESTIONS FOR IMPLEMENTING CURRICULUM—COGNITIVE DEVELOPMENT

CHILD BEHAVIOR	EXAMPLES OF CAREGIVER STRATEGIES
Piaget's Preoperational Stage, Preconceptual Substage	
NONVERBAL CLASSIFICATION	
Makes graphic collections	Allow child to create own classifications.
VERBAL PRECONCEPTS	
Uses words differently at different times	Listen and ask for clarification of words used differently.

(continued)

CHILD BEHAVIOR	EXAMPLES OF CAREGIVER STRATEGIES
Uses words with private meanings	Listen to child's words in context; reword or question to find meaning.
Begins to label classes of objects	Repeat and identify class of object. Extend child's label to include other objects.
Focuses on one attribute	Reinforce classifications. Child has not yet formed stable classes of objects.
VERBAL REASONING	
Reasons from particular to particular	Understand and accept child's classification of behaviors that seem alike. Ask for clarification if needed.
QUANTITY	
Understands *some, more, gone, big*	Use quantity words in context with objects. Respond and expand on child's use.
NUMBER	
Understands *more*	Use objects to identify *more*.
SPACE	
Understands *up, down, behind, under, over*	Use spatial-position words with actions, e.g., "I will lift you up. I am putting you down on the floor."
TIME	
Understands *now, soon*	Label actions in terms of time, e.g., "Let's wash your hands now."

Language Development

Children of this age are rapidly increasing their vocabulary. Their vocabulary may include as many as 200 to 300 words. This is a time for grammatical (e.g., functional or space) words (refer back to Chapter 11).

> . . . more new space words are added to the child's vocabulary in the six-month period from two to two-and-a-half than in any other six-month period. . . . The increase in use of two space words combined gives exactness to location: "right home," "way up," "in here," "under the table." (Ames & Ilg, 1980, p. 89)

As toddlers move from telegraphic speech to communicating complete ideas through sentences, they begin to use subject-verb-object sentences and include grammatical or function words, such as *on*, *in*, *a*, and *the*. Anisfeld (1984) says that they *construct* sentences; they do not reproduce sentences from memory. Thus, the child has to think and select words that express his or her ideas in ways others can understand. This may not be smooth, as the toddler has to plan and coordinate all the parts (words) of the sentences. The more words used, the more difficult it is for the toddler to construct a sentence. While toddlers learn to use word order patterns common to their language based on their interactions with more skilled others, they cannot tell you the basic rule or principle of word order they are using. These are abstract principles.

Anisfeld has identified several mental associations that toddlers have to construct in order to effectively engage in verbal conversations:

- **Demonstrative naming:** The first word in a demonstrative naming phrase points out an object, the second names it, e.g., "this ball" or "here spoon."
- **Attribution:** Children give objects a specific attribute, often using an adjective-noun combination, e.g., "blue shoes." The attribute *blue* distinguishes one particular pair of shoes from all other items in a class of things called *shoes*.
- **Possession:** Children make special associations between a person and an object, often using a two-word phrase, e.g., "mommy chair."
- **Action:** Action sentences separate the action from the actor and from the object and explore the relations among these three. Children's descriptions of their own or other's actions at this age include sentences like "I ride trike" and "I jump."
- **Recurrence:** A recurrence sentence tells of a thing or event that happens again. Children often use "more" to express this, for example, "more juice," "more ride."
- **Negation:** The negative sentences of children this age usually say that something desired or expected is not there or has disappeared or that the child cannot, is not permitted to, or does not want to do something. A child may say, "no car" or "no hit."

Children also extend their construction of language to include two ways of forming new words. They begin to use the plural and the past tense forms of words. By now children understand that there is more than one hand, or eye, or foot. They listen to others talking and learn that the word changes when referring to more than one hand. They then construct their words to include plurals, for example, *hands*, *eyes*, and so forth. However, at this age they apply the same plural rule to all words, making words such as *foots*. Applying the same rule to all of one kind of words is called overregularization. When children can distinguish between what is happening now and what has happened previously, they can begin to use some words that are in the past tense, such as "I jumped." They also overregularize past tense forms, constructing words like "goed" and "seed."

Children also have to learn prosodic patterning or how to use the appropriate stress and intonation to express their specific ideas. They learn emphasis and rhythm of word parts, words, and sentences along with the words themselves and syntax. For example, "*my* ball" means something different from "my *ball*."

Books contain language patterns that serve as examples to children who are busily constructing language; therefore, you should read to children often. Children can also tell the story when they have books with pictures. These experiences provide practice in putting thoughts into oral language. Books are selected frequently by

The repetitive lyrics of a song help a child to learn proper word patterns.

spotlight *on practice*

Voices from the Field

I am a preservice teacher at a local university as well as an Assistant Teacher in a toddler room. I have been learning about language and cognitive development of toddlers and decided to try out a learning experience with the children. I planned a game with two parts. First, I would name a body part and have the children point to that part of their body. If they were successful, I would then point to a body part and see if they could name it. The second part of the game should be more challenging, but it would help me to authentically assess their language and concept development.

When invited to play a game with me, three different children told me "no" and went to play elsewhere. Finally, Armani came over to me and sat on my lap. I began the game. She easily pointed to all of the body parts that I named. She was able to label her belly and head when I pointed, but not her nose, before getting bored and moving on to another area. I then noticed Sam playing with Mr. Potato Head®. I went over and picked up different body parts, asked "What is this?" while holding up the arm. Sam said "Hand." Then, I asked, "Do you have one of these too?" He said "No." Then, I said "Well, why not?" Sam said, "Because it does not match." I said, "Do you have fingers?" He said "Yes" and showed me where they were. Then I said, "Does the Potato Head arm have fingers?" Sam said "Yes" I looked at him and said, "Well what is this?" and pointed at the hand. Sam replied, "A hand." I asked, "Do you have a hand?" He smiled and said "Yes." He looked at me and said, "They are the same."

(Box continues)

> **voices** *(continued)*
>
> While my plan did not go exactly as planned, I was able to have positive interactions with two different children. I learned that teachers should find ways to deliver their plans in ways that match what the toddlers want to accomplish. I also learned that Armani knew the labels of belly and head while Sam knew the label of hand. Sam independently compared his body parts to those on a toy.

toddlers, so teachers must have available a wide variety of high-quality books. Books should represent different genders, races, ethnicities, and life-styles in accurate, non-biased manners (Pelo, 2008). Selecting books can be challenging; however, there are many resources available. Staub & Dell'Antonia (2006) suggest that you pay close attention to what aspects of a book engage a child (e.g., colors, busy or simple pictures, animal or human characters, labels or story line, books by same author) and then look for those characteristics in another book. They advise not to overlook the obvious such as a favorite animal (refer to Spotlight on Practice, Chapter 14). Local librarians can also provide invaluable assistance when selecting books for young children.

Written language is becoming more a part of the children's world. They see print at home, at the grocery store, out the bus window, and in other homes or centers. They look at the print in a book as the caregiver reads the story or tells the story line. They see their own names on each of their own papers. They are eager to make their own marks.

Writing opportunities can be provided to children in several ways. Create a writing center and have recycled paper, printer paper, pencils, pens, crayons, and markers readily available. Toddlers should be able to self-select and self-regulate the use of these materials with your guidance. Provide opportunities to write on an easel or chalkboard. If you do not have a chalkboard available, make your own by painting a section of a low wall with chalkboard paint. Select the location carefully so that it will get a lot of use and is easily cleaned. Thick, soft chalk, while it is messier, makes dark marks more easily. Thin, regular-size chalk breaks easily and can cause frustration (Lamme, 1984).

With repeated practice, some toddlers may begin to do controlled scribbling or even representative drawings. Controlled scribbling has several characteristics.

> Gradually, after much playing around with markers, chalk, and crayons, your child's scribbles become more controlled. He begins to see the relationship between the marks he is making on paper and the writing utensil in his hand. His scribbles are more systematic.... The lines go up and down ... or in circles. Dots may surround the picture.... He systematically scribbles with each marker in the box.... Later, as part of the scribble pattern, circles, triangles, arrows, and squares may emerge. (Lamme, 1984, pp. 39–40)

reading checkpoint

Before moving on with your reading, make sure that you can answer the following questions about the material discussed so far.

1. Write an example for each of the following language patterns:
   a. demonstrative naming
   b. attribution
   c. possession
   d. action sentences
   e. recurrence
   f. negation

SUGGESTIONS FOR IMPLEMENTING CURRICULUM—LANGUAGE DEVELOPMENT

CHILD BEHAVIOR	MATERIALS	EXAMPLES OF CAREGIVER STRATEGIES
Uses demonstrative naming	toys, objects	Point to and label objects, e.g., "a foot," "a hand," "the nose." Extend to sentences: "Mary has a foot. This is a foot."
Uses attribution	toys, objects	Combine labels, e.g., "red car," "big book." Extend to sentences: "Ray has the red car; Twila has the green car."
Uses possession	toys, objects	Identify and label: "Roger's shoe, Jenny's shoe."
Uses action	toys, objects	Identify and label own and child's actions: "Urvi sits on the floor." "Stewart is eating."
Uses recurrence		Use word patterns that indicate repeating or additional, e.g., at snack ask each child if he or she wants *more* apple.
Learns word order		Use proper word order, e.g., "The truck moves." Extend child's "Move truck" to "Yes, the truck moves."
Learns prosodic patterning		Use expression when talking. Accent the proper syllables. The child will imitate you.
Uses subject-verb pattern		Use whole sentences. Expand the child's sentences.
Uses verb-object pattern		Use whole sentences. Expand the child's sentences.
Omits function words		Use whole sentences. Expand the child's sentences.
Selects and uses books	picture books, storybooks	Read aloud. Listen to the child "read."
Controls scribbling	markers, crayons, chalk, chalkboard, paper	Provide materials and space. Write labels and notes to the child. Share the child's scribbling.

Emotional Development

Feelings about the self continue to develop for children between 24 and 30 months of age. Emotional development includes positive and negative self-image, competence, and acceptance. Children this age are becoming more independent while simultaneously recognizing their need for help. They attempt to please and show affection. At 24 months they make fewer demands and are better able to express themselves. They can attend for longer and longer periods of time as they fully engage their minds and bodies in learning. However, by 30 months these easier-going children can seem to suddenly become more demanding and more possessive about their things. They become frustrated, say "no" to almost everything, and have temper tantrums. They may suddenly want help with things they previously could do and want to do things they are not able to do. In quick succession they may be aggressive, then shy, then act like a baby. They cannot handle too many choices and many demand sameness and consistency. In fact, meeting their need for sameness may well be the best way to handle the 30-month-old. *Routines* provide children this age with consistency and security. They may be affectionate at one moment and want no affection the next. Here, the caregiver's skills of being well organized, consistent, and flexible (as discussed in earlier chapters) may be challenged. Be sure to use plenty of the three *A*s for your own benefit, as well as that of the children.

We have tried to point out some of the behavioral components of healthy development in toddlerhood, a stage during which a child works on becoming an autonomous being capable of competently functioning in an environment appropriately geared to his or her needs and abilities. It should be clear that children who are given sufficient opportunities to explore, use their senses, be physically active, use expressive materials, and develop language skills may often—through the very nature of these activities—be destructive, messy, noisy, impudent, and defiant.

Friends show affection for each other.

These behaviors reflect directly the crisis they are experiencing in regard to their identity development: autonomy versus shame and doubt. During these times, early childhood educators must demonstrate respect for the toddler while providing extra helpings of the three *A*s in order to meet the toddlers' developmental needs. Even when frustrated by the toddlers' inconsistent behaviors, teachers should continue to use positive guidance strategies (see Chapter 6), because successfully resolving this emotional crisis is vital for subsequent development.

SUGGESTIONS FOR IMPLEMENTING CURRICULUM—EMOTIONAL DEVELOPMENT

CHILD BEHAVIOR	EXAMPLES OF CAREGIVER STRATEGIES
Types of Emotions and Feelings	
Feels comfortable with self	Provide experiences which appropriately challenge children; when they succeed, they often feel pleased with themselves.
Feels positive self-worth	Give the child positive feedback. Reinforce other people's reflections of the child as a worthy person.
Feels negative self-worth	Be sensitive to the child's frustrations with tasks and with social encounters. Provide reassurance of the child's worth.
Control of Emotions and Feelings	
Expresses emotions	Accept the child's feelings as honest rather than manipulative.

Social Development

Twenty-four-month-olds enjoy the company of other children; they are beginning to interact while playing. Because toddlers still have some difficulty sharing, they continue to engage in parallel play. It is possible to involve children this age in group activities, such as painting individual pictures while sitting at the same table. Facilitating interactions between the toddlers will contribute to the toddlers initiating and engaging in cooperative interactions. By 30 months these children interact with each other, but may often quarrel over possessions rather than participate in a cooperative effort.

Play, according to child development experts, offers children a way to discover who they are and who they can be (Elkind, 2007; Honig, 2005). Toddlers become graceful and coordinated as they dance with scarves, explore gender roles as they play superheroes, and learn to control impulses and persist at difficult tasks through play (Honig, 2005). Children who are given the chance to enjoy a variety of experiences of play—role-playing, make-believe play, social play with peers, individual creative and artistic play, dyadic play with an adult—not only develop emotionally, physically, cognitively, and socially but also become self-actualized (Tobin & Davidson, 1989).

With continued assistance, toddlers recognize emotions in others and may help with tasks such as chores. Following a routine may allow the caregiver to gain some cooperation in tasks and cleaning up. However, many toddlers desire to be helpful outside of routines. They want to help you sweep the floor, clean up spilled paint, or water the classroom plants. Accepting their offers to volunteer promotes their social as well as emotional development—they learn to see themselves as capable, helpful persons. We understand that cleaning up the mess or completing the chore on your own would take less time. However, the benefits of patiently teaching such skills will last a lifetime.

Children of this age are certainly television and video viewers (Weber & Singer, 2004). A parent survey revealed that "By 23 months of age, 100 percent of the children in the sample watched television and 90 percent watched videos. . . . children typically watched videos for 25 minutes per day and those who watched television programs did so for more than one hour per day" (Weber & Singer, p. 32). While the parents also noted that many of them watched every television program with their child (47 percent), it is unclear what developmental benefits there are for the toddlers. Teachers need to discuss with parents the importance of reading daily with their child. If half an hour or more is devoted to watching television or videos, this time might be more wisely spent on shared reading activities given the developmental and educational outcomes associated with that strategy (Dodici, Draper, & Peterson, 2003; Lawhon & Cobb, 2002; Rosenkoetter & Barton, 2002). In any case, television and videos have no place in an educational setting for infants and toddlers. There is no evidence that "media can be integrated into the lives of very young children in a developmentally appropriate way" (Weber & Singer, 2004, p. 36).

SUGGESTIONS FOR IMPLEMENTING CURRICULUM—SOCIAL DEVELOPMENT

CHILD BEHAVIOR	EXAMPLES OF CAREGIVER STRATEGIES
Self	
Realizes own skills	Provide materials and equipment that child can use to own satisfaction. Provide challenging materials that child can use.
Others	
Shows independence	Allow child to accomplish as many tasks as possible by self. Assist when asked or when you anticipate you are needed.
Acts to please adult	Provide verbal and nonverbal positive feedback to child. Recognize child's need for your attention and approval. Plan activities child can help you with (e.g., clean-up).
Shows feelings to others	Show feelings to child. Show appropriate actions with feelings, e.g., *happy*: laugh, physical excitement; *sad*: hug, pat, listen. Provide feedback when he or she uses those behaviors.
Recognizes emotions in others	Label children's behaviors. Verbalize about feelings of others. Provide appropriate responses to behaviors. Provide feedback when child identifies or responds to others' emotions.

(continued)

CHILD BEHAVIOR	EXAMPLES OF CAREGIVER STRATEGIES
Understands *mine* and *yours*	Reinforce possession by child and others. It is *mine* while the speaker is using it.
Starts to share	Provide materials and equipment so some sharing is necessary. Provide feedback when child shares. Verbalize reasons for sharing. Recognize, however, that not all children can share yet.
Helps others	Provide opportunities for purposeful helping: clean-up, passing out items, assisting with clothing. Thank child for helping behaviors. Accept toddlers' offers to assist when they volunteer.
Engages in parallel play	Plan space and materials so children can play close to others without having to interact in play.
Engages in cooperative interactions	Engage the toddlers in conversations as they enjoy parallel play. Describe, for example, what each child is doing with materials (how alike and how different).

reading checkpoint

Before moving on with your reading, make sure that you can answer the following questions about the material discussed so far.

1. List two developing social accomplishments of a child 24 to 30 months old.
2. Describe a situation in which a child is asserting independence. How should the teacher respond to the child's actions?

SUMMARY

After several months of using mental trial and error, toddlers are ready to use mental manipulation to solve problems. The use of open-ended materials such as blocks, recycled lids, or paper and pencils promote their verbal and mathematical reasoning skills. While their cognitive skills are growing, it can seem that they are regressing emotionally. However, the demonstration of dependent behaviors, making more frequent demands, and challenging your requests are all typical behaviors as they resolve the identity crisis of autonomy versus shame and doubt. Consistently being patient and applying heavy doses of the three *A*s will assist everyone in moving towards a successful resolution of this crisis.

key terms

action sentences
attribution
demonstrative naming
mental images

negation
overregularization
possession
preconceptual

preoperational stage
prosodic patterning
recurrence
search for hidden objects

case study
Ming

Ming is a sweet 26-month-old who comes from a low-income family. The Department of Social Services provides her child care free of charge because of the severe poverty of her family. She often comes to the program without having eaten and insufficiently dressed for the weather. Her 24-year-old mother is a day laborer with three other small children.

Ming's teacher, Ms. Tao, has known from daily interactions that her mother has limited English proficiency. When the first parent conference was held, she called on the services of another parent who is bilingual. While explaining her observations of Ming's development in all areas, she learned that Ming's mother was overwhelmed with all of the information. She slowed down and focused on what she believed were the most important pieces of information about Ming. For example, she shared that Ming was on target with her language and cognitive development, but is often hungry and tired. Working together, through the interpreter, they created a plan to help Ming get more sleep. The teacher also provided information on community resources such as a local food bank in case the family didn't have access to enough food resources. Imagine that you co-teach with Ms. Tao.

1. What impact does a lack of food have on a child's development? Would you expect Ming to be on target with her cognitive and language skills? Why or why not?
2. What do you think about the teacher providing Ming's mother with information on the food bank? Would you have done this differently? Why or why not?
3. What supports at both school and in the home could be provided to help Ming stay on track with her development? What supports could be given to help Ming's family?

QUESTIONS AND EXPERIENCES FOR REFLECTION

1. Observe a child 24 to 30 months old for 15 minutes during playtime and record your observations using a running record (Appendix A). Then,
    a. Categorize the child's social behaviors.
    b. List ways in which the child used preconceptual classification.
    c. List the kinds of representations the child used.

2. Make a theme picture book. Use it with a child. Observe the child's emotional reactions. Observe the child's language. Involve the child in rereading the book.

3. Use a commercially prepared puppet to engage a child 24 to 30 months old in pretend play. Record as many observations as you can after the experience to:
    a. analyze the child's responses and
    b. evaluate the effectiveness of your strategies for facilitating the pretend play.

REFERENCES

Adolph, K. E., Vereijken, B., & Shrout, P. E. (2003). What changes in infant walking and why. *Child Development, 74*(2), 475–497.

Ames, L. B. & Ilg, F. L. (1980). *Your two-year-old: Terrible or tender?* New York: Delacorte Press.

Anisfeld, M. (1984). *Language development from birth to three.* Hillsdale, NJ: Lawrence Erlbaum Associates.

Dodici, B. J., Draper, D. C., & Peterson, C. A. (2003). Early parent-child interactions and early literacy development. *Topics in Early Childhood Special Education, 23*(3), 124–36.

Elkind, D. (2007). *The power of play: How spontaneous, imaginative activities lead to happier, healthier children.* Cambridge, MA: Da Capo Press.

Feldman, R. & Eidelman, A. I. (2009). Biological and environmental initial conditions shape the trajectories of cognitive and social-emotional development across the first years of life. *Developmental Science, 12* (1), 194–200.

Healy, J. (2004). *Your child's growing mind: A guide to learning and brain development from birth to adolescence* (3rd ed.). New York: Broadway Books.

Hewitt, K. (2001). Blocks as a tool for learning: A historical and contemporary perspective. *Young Children, 56*(1), 6–13.

Honig, A. S. (2005, April). What infants, toddlers, and preschoolers learn from play: A dozen ideas. Paper presented at the American Montessori Society meeting, Chicago, IL.

Kiernan, K. E. & Huerta, M. C. (2008). Economic deprivation, maternal depression, parenting and children's cognitive and emotional development in early childhood. *The British Journal of Sociology, 59* (4), 783–806.

Lamb-Parker, F., LeBuffe, P., Powell, G., & Halpern, E. (2008). A strength-based, systemic mental health approach to support children's social and emotional development. *Infants and Young Children, 21* (1), 49–55.

Lamme, L. L. (1984). *Growing up writing*. Washington, DC: Acropolis Books.

Lawhon, T. & Cobb, J. B. (2002). Routines that build emergent literacy skills in infants, toddlers, and preschoolers. *Early Childhood Education Journal, 30*(2), 113–118.

Pelo, A. (Ed.). (2008). *Rethinking early childhood education*. Milwaukee, WI: Rethinking Schools Publication.

Roggman, L. A., Boyce, L. K., Cook, G. A., Christiansen, K., & Jones, D. (2004). Playing With Daddy: Social Toy Play, Early Head Start, and Developmental Outcomes. *Fathering, 2* (1), 83–108.

Rosenkoetter, S., & Barton, L. R. (2002). Bridges to literacy: Early routines that promote later school success. *Zero to Three, 22*(4), 33–38.

Spinrad, T. & Stifter, C. A. (2006). Toddlers' empathy-related responding to distress: Predictions from negative emotionality and maternal behavior in infancy. *Infancy, 10*(2), 97–121.

Straub, S. & Dell'Antonia, K. J. (2006). *Reading with babies, toddlers, and twos: A guide to choosing, reading, and loving books together*. Naperville, IL: Sourcebooks, Inc.

Tobin, W. & Davidson, D. (1989). *Preschool in three cultures*. New Haven, CT: Yale University.

Weber, D. S. & Singer, D. G. (2004). The media habits of infants and toddlers: Findings from a parent survey. *Zero to Three, 25*(1), 30–36.

Wanless, S. B. Rosenkoetter, S. E., & McClelland, M. M. (2008). Paternal depression and infant cognitive development: Implications for research and intervention. *Infants and Young Children, 21* (2), 134–141.

For additional activities, web links, and other resources, please visit our website at www.cengage.com/education/swim

chapter 16

THE CHILD FROM THIRTY TO THIRTY-SIX MONTHS OF AGE

learning objectives

After reading this chapter, you should be able to:

- Identify and record sequences of change in the physical, cognitive/language emotional, and social development of children from 30 to 36 months of age.
- Select materials appropriate to the development of children at that age level.
- Devise strategies appropriate to children at that developmental level.

chapter outline

- Materials and Activities
- Caregiver Strategies to Enhance Development
  Physical Development
  Cognitive and Language Development
  Emotional Development
  Social Development
- Case Study: Juan
- Summary: Closing Note

Juan's Story

Juan, 35 months old, is playing in the play yard. He sits on a Big Wheel tricycle and rolls backward, gets off and runs around with other children, picks at the ground and finds a grub, which he takes to show the caregiver. Juan walks around showing the grub to others, sits on a small trike, takes the grub and puts it by a tree trunk, sits on the ground, climbs a tree, climbs down and runs after a soccer ball, plops down on the Big Wheel, gets up and then kicks a soccer ball back and forth with another child. Later he plays with another grub. When asked where the grub is, he stops, puts his hands up in the air and says, "He dead." He finds another grub and shows it to the caregiver, saying, "He sleep. Wake up, grub." The bug moves and rolls up again. Juan says, "He sleep."

MATERIALS AND ACTIVITIES

Children this age are active, eager learners. They practice newly acquired skills and develop new ones. They like large muscle activity and are developing their fine muscles for more controlled manipulation of objects. They enjoy imaginative play and exploring their world. Their play incorporates their imagination, their language, and their understanding of themselves and others. They construct sentences to share their ideas. They represent their ideas in play and language, and they recognize pictures. They listen to stories and enjoy participating in rhymes, fingerplays, music, and singing.

Types of Materials

riding toys	markers, crayons, chalk, pens
wagon	wooden beads and string
trucks for hauling	rhythm instruments
rocking boat	CDs
tunnel, barrel to crawl through and on	tapes
	dramatic play props
cardboard blocks	puppets
wooden unit block set	books
wooden people	materials to explore—feel, measure, use
wooden animals	

Examples of Homemade Materials

PROP BOXES

Gather props for a specific story or role. For example, put a stethoscope, white shirt, and small pad of paper in a shoebox for doctor props. In a larger box put a child-size firefighter's hat, boots, and poncho. Gather the materials based on your observations of the children's play. Select items that will enhance and promote development.

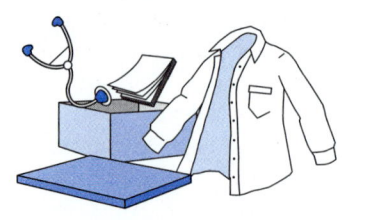

FIGURE 16–1

(continued)

chapter 16 THE CHILD FROM THIRTY TO THIRTY-SIX MONTHS OF AGE

PUPPETS

Use cardboard tubes from paper towels. Cut paper to make face. Child uses markers or crayons to make face and clothes features. Glue face on tube.

BOOK: JOURNAL

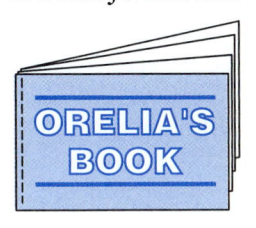

Sew or staple sheets of unlined paper together. Each morning ask child to identify one toy he or she wants to play with or an activity to do. Write a sentence identifying what the child chose. Allow the child to scribble and draw on the page. Read the sentence to the child. Label journal with the child's name. To promote partnerships with families, send the journal home each Friday. Encourage the family members to add sentences and illustrations for the days the child is not at school.

WOODEN PEOPLE OR ANIMALS

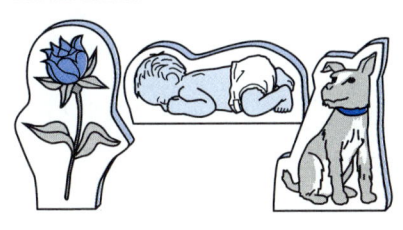

Draw or cut out of a magazine pictures of people: infants, children, adults; firefighter, police officer, doctor; or animals or other objects, such as cars or houses.

Glue pictures on a piece of 1-inch-thick white pine board. With a jigsaw, cut around the outside of the picture on three sides, cutting the bottom straight across. Sand the edges smooth. Apply two coats of nontoxic sealer. The object will stand up by itself.

FIGURE 16-1 *(continued)*

Activity Ideas

Keeping records of formal and informal observations will assist you in planning appropriate experiences for each child. Plan for a holistic curriculum. Identify the children's interests. Use these to focus your daily and weekly plans. You will mostly want to plan individual activities, but some short small-group activities may be included, such as reading or telling a story, singing a song, saying a rhyme, or doing a fingerplay. Any small-group activity would also be appropriate for use with individuals. In addition, short- and long-term projects which carry ideas from one day to another provide a mechanism for toddlers to develop important dispositions and knowledge. Working on an ongoing project naturally results in challenges and problems to be solved. Therefore, projects assist toddlers in developing the disposition of discipline or the ability to maintain energy in and focus on an activity in the face of obstacles in order to reach a desired aim (Glassman & Whaley, 2000). Building on the children's interests and working towards an aim are both necessary conditions for quality education. "Children who are not emotionally engaged with the material they are learning and by the teachers who instruct them, cannot grow intellectually" (Olfman, 2008, p. 62).

CAREGIVER STRATEGIES TO ENHANCE DEVELOPMENT

Physical Development

Children of this age are increasing their stability in both fast and slow movements, running and walking. They can walk backward. They run quickly and usually maintain their balance. They can alternate feet going upstairs. They can master a tricycle. They jump up and down, they jump off objects, and they jump forward. They can twist and turn to dress and undress, and they can use their small muscles to hold clothes and begin buttoning, snapping, and zippering. They practice their physical skills. Right- or left-handedness is now established, though children use both hands in many activities.

At this age children can establish sleep routines that they can do themselves in the child care setting. Before nap they can go to the bathroom and wash their hands. They can sit on their cots, take their own shoes off, and put the shoes under the cot. They can lie down with their heads near the top of the cot. When they awaken, they can go to the bathroom and return to put on their shoes. If others are still sleeping, they can choose a quiet activity, such as looking at books or listening to a story or music with earphones.

Most children are fully engaged in toilet learning by 36 months of age. They need to wear clothes they can remove quickly and easily. They need easy access to the bathroom, and they need occasional questions and reminders to go to the bathroom.

SUGGESTIONS FOR IMPLEMENTING CURRICULUM—PHYSICAL DEVELOPMENT	
CHILD BEHAVIOR	**EXAMPLES OF CAREGIVER STRATEGIES**
Muscular Control	
MOVEMENT AND COORDINATION	
Walks evenly	Provide uncluttered floor space.
Runs	Provide space and games for appropriate running.
Jumps in place and forward	Play games and sing songs that encourage jumping.
Dances to music	Play favorite music and provide scarves for moving rhythmically.
Dresses and undresses self with assistance	Allow time for child to manipulate clothes. Demonstrate how to hold button and buttonholes, zipper and cloth, and so on.
Uses fine motor coordination	Turns one page at a time.

(continued)

CHILD BEHAVIOR	EXAMPLES OF CAREGIVER STRATEGIES
HAND	
Has established handedness	Allow child to select hand to use.
Sleeping	
Assists with preparation routines	Plan time in schedule for children to do as much of the routines as possible. It takes longer for a child to wash and dry hands alone than if you help, but child needs to be independent and to develop skills. Help with tight snaps and so on.
Elimination	
Is in process of or has completed toilet learning	Provide reminders and assistance when needed. Assist with clothes and hand washing when needed. Clean up area. *Wash your hands.*

spotlight *on research*

Culturally Appropriate Assessment

As a teacher, you are not trained to screen and diagnose developmental delays or other special needs. You will need to understand, however, the ethical use of observational and screening tools. The National Association for the Education of Young Children's position statement on ethical conduct (2005) includes the use of assessment data to make decisions regarding the care and education of young children. This statement included the following ideals regarding the assessment of children:

I-1.6—To use assessment instruments and strategies that are appropriate for the children to be assessed, that are used only for the purposes for which they were designed, and that have the potential to benefit children.

I-1.7—To use assessment information to understand and support children's development and learning, to support instruction, and to identify children who may need additional services.

The statement also sets out the ideal that each child's culture, language, ethnicity, and family structure are recognized and valued in the program (I-1.10). Taking these three ideas together suggests that teachers should intentionally advocate for culturally appropriate screening of infants and toddlers. Unfortunately, this is easier said than done.

Most screening tools have been validated with white, middle-class populations with little investigation of the cultural aspects of screening (Lyman, Njoroge, & Willis, 2007). For example, Sturner, Albus, Thomas, and Howard (2007) argue for the revision of the Diagnostic Classification of Mental Health and Developmental Disorders of Infancy and Early Childhood. They want the assessment to be graduated more finely to classify a range of symptomatology. In addition, they would like the tool refined to assess the families' strengths more accurately, not just their weaknesses. While these are excellent modifications for this assessment instrument, none of the changes address the cultural bias which most certainly is present in it.

Autism is a rising concern for early intervention specialists, teachers, and families in the United States. Much research has been conducted to create reliable and valid assessment tools that accurately diagnose autism during infancy and toddlerhood. For example, the Quantitative CHecklist for Autism in Toddlers (Q-CHAT) was validated on a large sample of toddlers with and without a history of autism (Allison et al., 2008). The Modified CHecklist for Autism in Toddlers (M-CHAT) compared older and younger toddlers of low- and high-risk for autism (Pandey et al., 2008). In addition, the Autism Diagnostic Observation Schedule (ADOS) and Autism Observation Scale for Infants (AOSI) were used to classify infants who were at high-risk for autism

(Box continues)

spotlight *(continued)*

because a sibling had previously been diagnosed with the disorder (Brian et al., 2008). However, like the infant mental health example provided above, little attention seems to be placed on insuring accuracy of assessment in regards to cultural appropriateness.

Teachers must work with the clinicians who use the tools to insure the assessment data accurately reflect what is known about the families' cultural background and practices. Clinicians may be unaware of potential stereotyping that may come as a result of their using assessments designed for a particular population with culturally diverse individuals/families (Lyman et al., 2007). These authors go on to say that "screening for risks to development involves a complex interaction of the dynamics of the parent-child relationship, the effects of culture on those dynamics and growth, and cultural definitions of normalcy and risk" (p. 48). Each individual culture may have different expectations and definitions of what is considered developmentally on target. Therefore, teachers must help others to see that each assessment used was designed, and the results of each assessment are interpreted, through a particular cultural lens. By openly acknowledging the ethnocentricity of our assessment tools and taking steps to be more culturally competent in our screening, we can better assist children from all ethnic groups with having a chance to grow up healthy (Lyman et al., 2007).

Cognitive and Language Development

Cognitive Development

Children at this age are curious, exploring problem-solvers. They are seeking to discover what makes things tick, what objects are made of, and how actions happen. As discussed previously, they use observing, questioning, manipulating, classifying, and measuring to learn about their world. According to Piaget, there are three different types of knowledge that children construct or learn.

Children construct physical knowledge by moving objects and observing changes in objects. They observe the effects of their pulling, pushing, rolling, kicking, jumping, blowing, sucking, throwing, swinging, twirling, balancing, and dropping objects. Knowledge about physical events requires inferences drawn from observations. The source of physical knowledge is partly in the object, and the reaction depends on its properties (DeVries, 2000). Offer materials and activities that help children discover the physical characteristics of objects.

In the preconceptual stage children may attempt to put objects in an order, like biggest to smallest buttons, but unless the materials present cues, such as fitting together, the children may not be able to determine the logic of ordering. Arranging objects in a series, or seriation, is guesswork for young children because they do not understand the relationships in a series of objects. However, physical knowledge about the properties of objects develops through their continued interactions with materials.

The second type of knowledge children construct, logico-mathematical knowledge, is gained by discovering relationships among objects. Comparisons of quantity, number, space, and time are explorations in relating two or more objects or events in a new and abstract way. Children can seek relationships among any kinds

Blocks, pegs, and other manipulatives provide cues to young children for mathematical concepts such as one-to-one correspondence and sorting.

of materials. Games and activities that use the invented relationships help stimulate and reinforce their constructions. For example, providing a group of objects to sort and classify might lead a child to notice color relationships.

Children learn the third type of knowledge, social-arbitrary knowledge, from other people through various forms of communication (DeVries, 2000). They learn the names of objects, meanings of words, and days of the week, for example, from others. They learn the classroom rules from their caregivers, who bear the major responsibility in the child care program for providing this type of information and helping the child construct social-arbitrary knowledge.

Because toddlers still reason prelogically, adults and children construct experiences differently. Even if both a child and an adult were present during the same experience, each would learn and experience something different. Jane Healy, in her book *Your Child's Growing Mind* (2004), gives several ways to help "bridge the schema" gaps (p. 57), or fill in missing information.

1. As you solve problems together, talk through your own questions. "I wonder how I should start?" "Could I put them together?" "Is it working?" "What's going to happen?" "How did I do?"
2. Ask the child similar questions. Phrase them simply and give the child plenty of time to think and answer.

3. Let the child repeat each solution several times to understand it.
4. Encourage understanding. Ask "Why do you think that happened?" "Why did (or didn't) that work?"

Interacting in this manner not only bridges informational gaps but also, by its very nature, engages toddlers emotionally and intellectually. Older toddlers need curriculum, environments, and interactions that engage them emotionally and intellectually because successfully completing a challenge provides valuable information about their capabilities. Carefully planning learning experiences that give value to the tools of the learning disciplines (e.g., mathematics, social studies) gives curriculum intellectual integrity (Bredekamp & Copple, 1997). Toddlers should be given opportunities to investigate scientific topics they have questions about (e.g., living creatures, microorganisms, gravity; see, for example, Youngquist, 2004) and use scientific tools/processes such as observing, recording, and testing hypotheses. They should have daily experiences with mathematical concepts such as solving problems, measurement, and geometry. These experiences can be completed separately or integrated into learning experiences and projects (see Chapter 9). An example of an integrated learning experience would be cooking. When caregivers provide opportunities for cooking, toddlers gain cognitive skills (e.g., transformations), mathematics skills (e.g., measuring), literacy skills (e.g., written communication for providing information), and life skills (e.g., making healthy food choices; Colker, 2005; Darbyshire, 2004; Houts, 2002).

When young children continually make new discoveries, they become enthusiastic learners.

A note of caution should be introduced here. In no case should toddlers be forced or required to engage in these activities. These learning experiences should be among the many choices in the environment. Moreover, designing curriculum in this manner ensures that the content is contextualized at all times.

SUGGESTIONS FOR IMPLEMENTING CURRICULUM—COGNITIVE DEVELOPMENT	
CHILD BEHAVIOR	**EXAMPLES OF CAREGIVER STRATEGIES**
Piaget's Preoperational Stage, Preconceptual Substage	
NONVERBAL CLASSIFICATION	
Makes graphic collections	Encourage child to use art media to represent objects, ideas, etc. Listen to child's explanation of his or her own classification system.
VERBAL PRECONCEPTS	
Uses words differently at different times	Observe context of talk. Ask for clarification of meaning if necessary.
Labels objects in one class	Remember that child's meaning may not be as inclusive as yours. Determine exactly what child meant.
VERBAL REASONING	
Thinks one action is like another action	Observe the behavior that precedes a child's talking. Determine how child is forming relationships among his or her actions.
Reasons from effect to cause	Think backward from action to previous action to understand child's reasoning.
QUANTITY	
Understands *some, more, gone, big*	Use words labeling quantity. They are a part of the daily experiences.
NUMBER	
Understands *more*	Use words labeling number as a comparative. Use daily situations, e.g., "There are more rocks in this pail than in that pail."
SPACE	
Understands *up, down, behind, under, over*	Label child's actions when child is moving into different positions in space, e.g., "Merrilee is behind the box. Ashton is under the box."
TIME	
Understands *now, soon, before, after*	Use time words in daily experiences, e.g., "We wash our hands before we eat." "We go to the bathroom after naptime."

Language Development

Children this age continue to increase their vocabulary. Their daily experiences provide opportunities for them to construct meanings of new objects and to extend previously learned concepts. The labeling process is now part of children's construction of the identity of objects.

Dramatic play with peers is becoming more prevalent.

Older toddlers continue to overregularize words. However, more and more of their plural words are formed correctly. These children are very gradually constructing concepts of time, and most of their new time words come during this period. The past is still an abstraction they are attempting to understand grammatically. They still overregularize past tense verbs, saying things like, "Jim bited me" and "I bringed these out."

Sentence length increases as children increase their use and familiarity with frequently used vocabulary, word order patterns, and stress and intonation patterns. They speak more complete sentences and are able to express several ideas in a sequence of sentences.

Dramatic play provides opportunities to combine language with imagination. Children of this age can describe their actions and say what they think others might say. They are mastering their language and fitting it into a social context (Honig, 2005).

Books play an increasingly important role. Reading aloud provides examples of language patterns. Reading the pictures encourages self-expression; talking about the story or the pictures facilitates comprehension of the language. Having these experiences fosters larger vocabularies and better storytelling abilities in the children.

The ability to produce or express language during the toddler years has been associated with larger vocabularies and better reading outcomes during the early elementary years (Rescorla, 2002; see also Pullen & Justice, 2003). While the pathways are not completely understood, adult styles of interactions and literacy

Frequent reading of books stimulates the toddlers to re-read and re-tell familiar ones and also create new stories of their own.

behaviors at home and at school are believed to play significant roles in literacy outcomes (Britto & Brooks-Gunn, 2001; Dodici, Draper, & Peterson, 2003; Murray & Yingling, 2000; Williams & Rask, 2003). Teachers must develop partnerships with families to support and enhance the language and literacy development of children. While many strategies exist for helping parents read to children at home (Darling & Westberg, 2004), creating literacy bags that contain high-quality children's literature and a guidebook for parents with, for example, questions for discussion has been shown to increase both the quality and frequency of reading books at home for older children (Dever & Burts, 2002). Logically, if parents are helped early on to carve out time daily to read to their infants and toddlers, greater literacy outcomes might be gained (see, for example, Raikes et al., 2006).

Literacy also involves learning to communicate ideas in writing. **Scribbling** continues as the child is involved in the writing process. Each child is developing scribbling at his or her own rate. Children are scribblers from the time they hold a writing tool until after they learn to write their names. There is a progression to their scribbles which moves from random scribbling, to controlled scribbling, to the naming of scribbling, to writing mock letters and words, to learning, finally, how to write. It is important not to underestimate the value of scribbling as a foundation for writing (Lamme, 1984, p. 37).

You model many uses of writing for children. You write their names on their artwork papers, and dictated sentences on the pages of a classroom story. You write a note to their family members. You write charts about daily experiences, such as the growth steps of beans the children planted. In this way, the children experience meaningful uses of writing.

✓ reading checkpoint

Before moving on with your reading, make sure that you can answer the following questions about the material discussed so far.

1. Write one example of a child's statement using a word that for the child has a meaning different from the one adults give the word.
2. Compare how children learn physical knowledge, logico-mathematical knowledge, and social-arbitrary knowledge.

SUGGESTIONS FOR IMPLEMENTING CURRICULUM—LANGUAGE DEVELOPMENT

CHILD BEHAVIOR	MATERIALS	EXAMPLES OF CAREGIVER STRATEGIES
Increases vocabulary		
Associates word and object		Introduce new objects to see and feel and use. Label objects and actions with single words and use in sentences.
Improves syntax		
Experiments with word order		Repeat child's sentence, using proper word order.
Makes two- and three-word sentences		Respond to child's meaning. Extend the sentence.
Uses longer sentences		Respond to child's meaning. Commend his or her ideas.
Improves word forms		
Uses plurals		Use correct plural form. When child says "foots," restate the word, e.g., "See your feet."
Uses past tense		Use correct past tense. When child says "He bited me," restate: "He bit you? Show me where he bit you."
Improves reading skills		
Listens to stories, "reads" pictures and storybooks	recordings, pictures, picture books	Read aloud. Listen to child "read." Use expression. Tell or read story line.
Uses controlled scribbling	markers, chalk, crayons, pencil, paper	Write to child. Write notes to child and others. Label objects. Write dictated sentences.

Emotional Development

Between 30 and 36 months, children let you know how they feel and then may move beyond their anger or happiness to express a wide variety of different feelings. They express their emotions and feelings strongly, but they are becoming more skilled at expressing their emotions in a socially acceptable manner. However, significant differences exist in how different cultures socialize children to express emotions. According to Day and Parlakian (2004), the following attributes of emotional expression tend to vary across cultures:

a. The intensity of emotional expression
b. The loudness or volume of speech
c. The directness of questions
d. The directness of eye contact
e. The degree to which touching is involved
f. The use of gestures
g. The amount of personal space desired

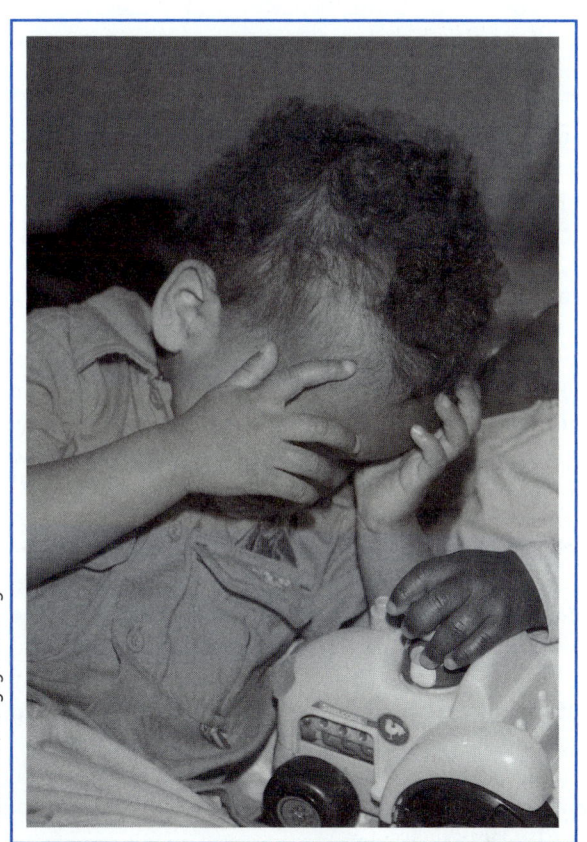

Toddlers begin to express self-conscious emotions such as shame and guilt.

Thus, teachers should be aware of and respect the differences that children bring with them to school. The goal is not to establish consistency among the children in the room but rather to provide cultural continuity from home to school (Day & Parlakian, 2004).

Within this context of cultural differences, toddlers, like older children, express negativism in several ways. Sometimes negative behavior is a way of asserting themselves and their independence. They may begin or continue to display physical aggression (Baillargeon et al., 2007; Fagot & Leve, 1998; Tremblay et al., 2004). Their widening world presents many new experiences. Older toddlers may use aggression in their attempts to assert some control over their world.

Because of the link between aggression and concurrent and future mental health issues, child development and early childhood experts are particularly concerned about aggression in toddlers (see, for example, Collins et al., 2003). Much research has been conducted to understand the causes of aggression and patterns of trajectories. Tremblay et al. (2004) found that the best predictors of high, stable physical aggression were maternal variables (e.g., history of antisocial behavior during mother's school years, early childbearing, and coercive parenting behavior) and family variables (e.g., low income and family dysfunction). Similarly, both parent coercion during home observations and marital status predicted externalizing behavior during kindergarten (Fagot & Leve, 1998). These authors also investigated how child characteristics and behaviors predicted outcomes at five years of age; while child playgroup behaviors at 18 months were predictive of later externalizing behaviors, boys' behaviors were also correlated with reports of problems at home and school. Thus, differential patterns of stability and predictability have been found for boys and girls (see also Baillargeon et al., 2007; Gill & Calkins, 2003; Hays, Castle, & Davies, 2000).

The strong display of emotions carries over to children's work in the classroom. Toddlers of this age are enthusiastic learners, enjoying themselves and their discoveries. Their developing mastery of skills enhances their feelings of competence, self-worth, and acceptance of self. Dispositions such as discipline or persistence in continuing a task (see beginning of chapter) enables children to discover many things. As they continue their exploration for several hours, days, or even weeks, the persistence will enable them to accomplish enough to have the feeling of "I did it" or "See what I found out." Children generally discover the love of learning when they are offered developmentally appropriate choices and are positively encouraged for their decisions by the caregiver who combines the three *A*s of child care: Attention, Approval, and Attunement. This love of learning is obvious when the child has a long attention span and displays great persistence in finishing a task. A short attention span, however, limits a child's exposure and involvement in many activities. Early childhood educators must devote a great deal of time to observing the children's interests so that experiences can be planned that engage the toddlers. Doing so will assist with the toddlers' abilities to attend and therefore to learn. Optimal learning occurs when children are provided experiences that are hands-on, minds-on, and feelings-on (NAEYC, 1998).

At about 33 months the child will begin to think in terms of her own past and may pretend to be a baby again. This regression may be a need based on her own development or the presence of a new baby in the family. Whatever the cause, these toddlers need lots of the three *A*s and the time and patience to regain their proper place in their environment. In addition, the ability to focus on the past allows the opportunity for toddlers to reflect on their recent behaviors. For children this age, reflection must be supported by concrete products such as photographs and artifacts such as drawings or sculptures. Holsington (2002) discovered that taking photographs of block play assisted children with asking questions, thinking through problems, and making connections between building experiences.

At around 36 months, depending upon temperament, children's emotional responses become calmer. They become less resistant and use words like *yes* and *will* to replace the earlier *no* and *won't*. The three-year-old is generally a happy, secure and somewhat conforming person. Often you will hear the child repeat back to you the three *A*s that you have given him or her over and over again.

Toddlers can also be encouraged to display caring behaviors (i.e., their own use of the three *A*s) and responsibility through class pets. Teachers should select a pet only after she has learned of any allergies. Sometimes teachers select pets that tend to be allergy free, such as fish. Toddlers should be closely supervised in the beginning and until they demonstrate the ability to care for the pet appropriately. Set specific,

Class pets help to develop caring behaviors as well as responsibility.

positively worded limits so that expected behaviors are clear. Telling a child to "Be nice" is not specific enough. It is better to say, "Pet the bunny on her back. She likes to be petted from her head to her tail." If a class pet is not possible, consider inviting the children to share their pets from home.

SUGGESTIONS FOR IMPLEMENTING CURRICULUM—EMOTIONAL DEVELOPMENT	
CHILD BEHAVIOR	**EXAMPLES OF CAREGIVER STRATEGIES**
Types of Emotions and Feelings	
Reacts strongly	Accept child's initial response. Help child keep within bounds of appropriate behavior, e.g., let child express anger by vigorously riding a Big Wheel for a while or drawing an angry picture.
Acts negatively	Rephrase suggestions to child. Stimulate interest in a different activity. Describe emotions child is feeling.
Learns enthusiastically	Reinforce child's excitement with learning. Provide opportunities for challenging, developmental, and content-rich experiences.
Masters skills	Provide toys, equipment, and materials that the child needs to use often to master skills.
Control of Emotions and Feelings	
Is physically aggressive	Provide activities for child to work out feelings and the need to control, such as using a puppet for imaginary play or letting the child be a leader in a structured activity. Have the child paint, draw, use clay, dance, or go outdoors to run, jump, and yell.

Social Development

Egocentrism continues to be present in the preconceptual substage. Even though young children can distinguish themselves from others, they are only slowly developing the ideas that follow from this. They are just beginning to understand that others have feelings. They assume that when they speak, everyone understands the exact meaning of their words; they do not realize that others may give different meanings to the same words or experiences.

Young children interpret changes in appearance to mean changes in the basic object or person. "Preconceptual children generally do not see things or people as having a core and consistent identity over time" (Cowan, 1978, p. 133). This fluctuation includes their concepts of self. "They seem to have little idea that their 'self' of a few days ago is relevant to what is happening now, today" (p. 133).

Children continue to identify their "selfness" within their world. Their toys are a part of themselves, and they remain very possessive of the toys and materials they are using. However, their strengthening sense of self also provides a foundation for expanding interactions with others. Children this age are increasingly aware of others as individuals. They use adults as resources, seeking assistance from them when they decide they need help. They become directive with others, exerting control over people, animals, and toys as they learn ways to control their world. Children this age sometimes recognize others' needs and may help with tasks or initiate or respond with assistance.

The children's self-control is increasing. Their desire for instant gratification is being restricted, so they sometimes accept delayed gratification. They may take turns occasionally. At times they may decide to share, and they may play cooperatively for short periods of time. The research strongly suggests that what begins to ingrain the deepest sense of these prosocial qualities in that child is the felt experience, over and over and over again, of cooperation; the experience of having an important adult put aside his or her own needs to meet the child's very real needs; the experience of that important adult showing empathy, concern, respect, and nurturance toward the baby or toddler (Wolf, 1986).

SUGGESTIONS FOR IMPLEMENTING CURRICULUM—SOCIAL DEVELOPMENT

CHILD BEHAVIOR	EXAMPLES OF CAREGIVER STRATEGIES
Self	
Acts possessive	Provide enough toys and materials so child can control use of some of them for a time.
Others	
Seeks assistance	Allow child to use you as a resource. Help where needed. Do not take over.
Directs others	Provide opportunities for child to display leadership skills with peers.
Helps others	Praise child's spontaneous helping. Ask for assistance so child can help with routines and so forth.
Control of Self	
Plays cooperatively	Provide toys, materials, and time.
Shares	Encourage by providing opportunities to share, e.g., when eating orange or apple slices.
Takes turns	Use daily routines to help control wasting time, e.g., taking turns to wash hands.

✓ reading checkpoint

Before moving on with your reading, make sure that you can answer the following questions about the material discussed so far.

1. What are the benefits to children of having a class pet?
2. Provide two examples of cultural differences in expressing emotions. Describe which aspects of emotional expression those differences reflect.
3. Describe how you would assist a child in demonstrating ownership of toys or security items.

spotlight on curriculum

This textbook has provided you with guidance on how to create emergent, responsive curricula for infants and toddlers. We believe that the best way to create curricula for very young children is to develop it yourself based on careful observations of the children in your care. We also realize that there are some curriculum models that can provide you with additional structure and direction. If you were to select and implement a particular given model, it should only be done after careful consideration and investigation of the theories used to build the program. A program model should provide you with guidance (as this textbook has) without causing you to merely implement a series of predetermined curriculum activities.

There are a number of high-quality program models that might be useful to you as a classroom teacher or as a child care program; yet, this section will feature only a few for which information is readily available on the World Wide Web. *High/Scope for Infants and Toddlers, Creative Curriculum for Infants, Toddlers, and Twos*, and the *Waldorf Curriculum* all build on the understanding that children are active meaning-makers who need open-ended materials to explore and develop their minds. Hence, play is a fundamental aspect of all of these models. In addition, planning for positive social interactions among adults and children is a significant component in each model.

Research is available for each program model. Of course, careful attention to who conducted the research and how outcomes were measured are important when evaluating the data and conclusions drawn. Some research comparing program models, such as Edwards (2002), is not affiliated with any particular program model and thus might be considered more objective.

SUMMARY

Older toddlers, those 30 to 36 months of age, are especially energetic in learning. They want to know more. They want to be a "big kid." They are beginning to demonstrate some capabilities, such as dressing and undressing, that are equivalent to preschool children. Thus, as they should be provided challenging learning experiences that build on and stretch their capabilities. For example, as toddlers are able to care for their basic needs, they are now ready to care for another living creature. Having a classroom pet can assist in the development of important cognitive, language, emotional, and social skills.

key terms

discipline
dramatic play
scribbling
seriation

case study

Juan

Juan has exhibited average or above-average growth in all areas except language. In his home, his parents and four siblings speak only Spanish. After discovering this, Juan's teacher Paul wanted his Developmental Profile to be completed again for his primary language. Rosa, a Spanish-speaking teacher in the program, agreed to assist.

(Box continues)

The results of this profile differ significantly from the first one for language development. His language skills were assessed at the 34-month level, right as expected. Paul and Rosa prepared for the upcoming family-teacher conference by organizing their observations and interpretations and thinking of questions they could ask Juan's parents in order to establish a plan for supporting Juan's development. Based on previous conversations, Paul knew that Juan's parents were concerned about his language skills. He opened the conference by welcoming the family and immediately had Rosa share her observations. Juan's parents were significantly relieved to understand that he is progressing as expected in his home language. They both felt it was necessary, however, to place specific attention on his learning English.

Paul and Rosa worked with Juan's family to design a plan that supported all areas of development, including learning English as his second language.

1. What problems might have been created if Paul did not know that Spanish was the primary language spoken in the home? How might this have significantly altered the development of Juan's plan?
2. Why are assessments, especially those involving language, best conducted in the child's home language?
3. What supports should Paul offer to Juan and his family?

QUESTIONS AND EXPERIENCES FOR REFLECTION

1. Observe one child for 10 minutes in a play yard. Write a list of the child's activities. Identify equipment and materials used.

2. Observe a child for 10 minutes in a play yard. Tally the times the child shares a toy or equipment. Tally the times the child plays *with* another child.

3. Observe a caregiver for five minutes. Write down the dialogue the caregiver has with a child or with several children. Categorize the caregiver's statements that mirror, support, or respond to the child's statements.

4. Observe children at play. List the language and actions that indicate their developing concepts of quantity, number, space, and time.

5. Plan and use one activity with a child to facilitate the child's construction of physical knowledge and one to facilitate logico-mathematical knowledge.

REFERENCES

Allison, C., Baron-Cohen, S., Wheelwright, S., Charman, T., Richler, J., Pasco, G., et al. (2008). The Q-CHAT (Quantitative CHecklist for Autism in Toddlers): A normally distributed quantitative measure of autistic traits at 18–24 months of age: Preliminary report. *Journal of Autism & Developmental Disorders, 38*(8), 1414–1425.

Baillargeon, R. H., Zoccolillo, M., Keenan, K., Cote, S., Perusse, D., Wu, H., et al. (2007). Gender differences in physical aggression: A prospective population-based survey of children before and after 2 years of age. *Developmental Psychology, 43*(1), 13–26.

Bredekamp, S., & Copple, C. (Eds.). (1997). *Developmentally appropriate practice in early childhood programs* (Rev. ed.). Washington, DC: National Association for the Education of Young Children.

Brian, J., Bryson, S. E., Garon, N., Roberts, W., Smith, I. M., Szatmari, P., et al. (2008). Clinical assessment of autism in high-risk 18-month-olds. *Autism: The International Journal of Research & Practice, 12*(5), 433–456.

Britto, P. R., & Brooks-Gunn, J. (2001). Beyond shared book reading: Dimensions of home literacy and low-income African American preschoolers' skills. *New Directions for Child and Adolescent Development, Summer* (92), 73–89.

Colker, L. (2005). *The cooking book: Fostering young children's learning and delight.* Washington, DC: National Association for the Education of Young Children.

Collins, R., Mascia, J., Kendall, R., Golden, O., Schock, L., & Parlakian, R. (2003). Promoting mental health in child care settings: Caring for the whole child. *Zero to Three, 23*(4), 39–45.

Cowan, P. A. (1978). *Piaget with feeling.* New York: Holt, Rinehart & Winston.

Darbyshire, J. (2004). *Everyday learning: Vol. 2, No. 4. Everyday learning in the kitchen.* S. Wales (Series Ed.) & P. Linke (Vol. Ed.). Watson, ACT: Early Childhood Australia, Inc.

Darling, S., & Westberg, L. (2004). Parent involvement in children's acquisition of reading. *The Reading Teacher, 57*(8), 774–776.

Day, M., & Parlakian, R. (2004). *How culture shapes social-emotional development: Implications for practice in infant-family programs.* Washington, DC: Zero to Three.

Dever, M. T., & Burts, D. C. (2002). An evaluation of family literacy bags as a vehicle for parent involvement. *Early Child Development and Care, 172*(4), 359–370.

DeVries, R. (2000). Vygotsky, Piaget, and education: A reciprocal assimilation of theories and educational practices [Electronic version]. *New Ideas in Psychology, 18*(2–3), 187–213.

Dodici, B. J., Draper, D. C., & Peterson, C. A. (2003). Early parent-child interactions and early literacy development. *Topics in Early Childhood Special Education, 23*(3), 124–136.

Edwards, C. P. (2002). Three approaches from Europe: Waldorf, Montessori, and Reggio Emilia. *Early Childhood Research and Practice, 4*(1). Retrieved March 23, 2009, from http://ecrp.uiuc.edu/v4n1/edwards.html

Fagot, B. I., & Leve, L. D. (1998). Teacher ratings of externalizing behavior at school entry for boys and girls: Similar early predictors and different correlates. *Journal of Child Psychology and Psychiatry and Allied Disciplines, 39*(4), 555–566.

Gill, K. L., & Calkins, S. D. (2003). Do aggressive/destructive toddlers lack concern for others? Behavioral and physiological indicators of empathic responding in 2-year-old children. *Developmental and Psychopathology, 15*(1), 55–71.

Glassman, M., & Whaley, K. (2000). Dynamic aims: The use of long-term projects in early childhood classrooms in light of Dewey's educational philosophy. *Early Childhood Research & Practice, 2*(1). Retrieved May 14, 2009, from http://ecrp.uiuc.edu/v2n1/glassman.html

Hays, D. F., Castle, J., & Davies, L. (2000). Toddlers' use of force against familiar peers: A precursor of serious aggression? *Child Development, 71*(2), 457–467.

Healy, J. (2004). *Your child's growing mind: A guide to learning and brain development from birth to adolescence* (3rd ed.). New York: Broadway Books.

Holsington, C. (2002). Using photographs to support children's science inquiry. *Young Children, 57*(5), 26–32.

Honig, A. S. (2005, April). What infants, toddlers, and preschoolers learn from play: A dozen ideas. Paper presented at the American Montessori Society meeting, Chicago, IL.

Houts, A. (2002). *Cooking around the calendar with kids: Holiday and seasonal food and fun.* Maryville, MO: Snaptail Press.

Lamme, L. L. (1984). *Growing up writing.* Washington, DC: Acropolis Books.

Lyman, D. R., Njoroge, W. F. M., & Willis, D. W. (2007). Early childhood psychosocial screening in culturally diverse populations: A survey of clinical experience with the Ages and Stages Questionnaires: Social-Emotional (ASQ: SE). *Zero to Three, 27*(5), 46–54.

Murray, A. D., & Yingling, J. L. (2000). Competence in language at 24 months: Relations with attachment security and home stimulation. *Journal of Genetic Psychology, 161*(2), 133–140.

National Association for the Education of Young Children (NAEYC). (1998). *Tools for teaching developmentally appropriate practice* [Video series]. Washington, DC: Author.

National Association for the Education of Young Children (NAEYC). (2005). Position statement: Code of ethical conduct and statement of commitment. Washington, DC: Author. Retrieved December 12, 2006, from http://www.naeyc.org/about/positions/pdf/PSETH05.PDF

Olfman, S. (2008). What about play? In A. Pelo (Ed.), *Rethinking early childhood education* (pp. 61–64). Milwaukee, WI: Rethinking Schools Publication.

Pandey, J., Verbalis, A., Robins, D. L., Boorsetin, H., Klin, A., Babitz, T., et al. (2008). Screening for autism in older and younger toddlers with the Modified Checklist for Autism in Toddlers. *Autism: The International Journal of Research & Practice, 12*(5), 513–535.

Pullen, P. C., & Justice, L. M. (2003). Enhancing phonological awareness, print awareness, and oral language skills in preschool children. *Intervention in School and Clinic, 39*(2), 87–98.

Raikes, H., Pan, B. A., Luze, G., Tamis-LeMonda, C. S., Brooks-Gunn, J., Constantine, J., et al. (2006). Mother-child bookreading in low-income families: Correlates and outcomes during the first three years of life. *Child Development, 77*(4), 924–953.

Rescorla, L. (2002, April). Language and reading outcomes to age 9 in late-talking toddlers. *Journal of Speech, Language, and Hearing Research, 45*, 360–371.

Sturner, R., Albus, K., Thomas, J., & Howard, B. (2007). A proposed adaptation of DC: 0-3R for primary care, developmental research, and prevention of mental disorders. *Infant Mental Health Journal, 28*(1), 1–11.

Tremblay, R. E., Nagin, D. S., Seguin, J. R., Zoccolillo, M., Zelazo, P. D., Boivin, M., et al. (2004). Physical aggression during early childhood: Trajectories and predictors. *Pediatrics, 114*(1), e43–e50.

Williams, M., & Rask, H. (2003). Literacy through play: How families with able children support their literacy development. *Early Child Development and Care, 173*(5), 527–533.

Wolf, D. P. (1986). *Connecting: Friendship in the lives of young children and their teachers.* Washington, DC: Exchange Press.

Youngquist, J. (2004). From medicine to microbes: A project investigation of health. *Young Children, 59*(2), 28–32.

ADDITIONAL RESOURCES

Epstein, A. S. (2009). *Me, you, us: Social-emotional learning in preschool.* Ypsilanti, MI: HighScope Press.

Glenn, H. S., & Nelsen, J. (2000). *Raising self-reliant children in a self-indulgent world: Seven building blocks for developing capable young people* (Rev. ed.). New York: Three Rivers Press.

Hyson, M. (2004). *The emotional development of young children: Building an emotion-centered curriculum* (2nd ed.). New York: Teachers College Press.

Nelsen, J., Erwin, C., & Duffy, R. A. (2007). *Positive discipline: The first three years* (2nd ed.). New York: Three Rivers Press.

SUMMARY: CLOSING NOTE

Even now in the twenty-first century the huge gap between humankind's intellectual development and emotional development is obvious. With the advent of an operational definition and curricula for teaching emotional intelligence and research suggesting only moderate correlation with cognitive intelligence, we now have the knowledge and skills necessary to improve the humanity of the next generation. As a caregiver of infants and toddlers, you have an essential role in ensuring that our youngest citizens learn how to interact humanely and intimately with other people, develop sound mental health and healthy self-esteem, maintain a balance between thinking and feeling, and improve the quality of life.

You are in the unique position to assist the field of early childhood education and the greater society in changing from an exclusive emphasis on cognitive skills to a greater emphasis on being emotionally healthy and socially at ease when in the presence of others. By placing importance on the emotional and social development of children, as well as the other major areas of physical and cognition, you can significantly help create a social structure in which compassion, understanding, and ethical behavior are valued and practiced.

Caregivers of children from birth through the toddler age are in an ideal position to lay the foundation for emotionally and socially intelligent individuals. Your abilities to practice the three *A*s and care for young children sensitively will promote optimal development for individuals; in the process, society will truly be affected. Congratulations on your choice of the most important position in society!

For additional activities, web links, and other resources, please visit our website at www.cengage.com/education/swim

APPENDIX A
Tools for Observing and Recording

appendix outline

Running Record

Anecdotal Record

Developmental Prescriptions (Combination of Checklist and Rating Scale)
    Approximately Birth to Four Months of Age
    Approximately Four to Eight Months of Age
    Approximately Eight to Twelve Months of Age
    Approximately Twelve to Eighteen Months of Age
    Approximately Eighteen to Twenty-four Months of Age
    Approximately Twenty-four to Thirty Months of Age
    Approximately Thirty to Thirty-six Months of Age

Indoor Safety Checklist

Playground Safety Checklist

Running Record

Context	Observations (behavioral descriptions of what you see and hear)	Analysis/Interpretations/Questions

Anecdotal Record

Child's name: Age:

Observer's name: Date:

Setting:

What actually happened/What I saw:

Reflection/Interpretation/Questions:

Child's name: Age:

Observer's name: Date:

Setting:

What actually happened/What I saw:

Reflection/Interpretation/Questions:

Developmental Prescriptions (Combination of Checklist and Rating Scale)

Approximately Birth to Four Months of Age

Child behavior	Date first observed	Practicing	Proficient
Physical Development			
MUSCULAR CONTROL			
Reflex			
Grasp reflex			
Startle reflex			
Tonic neck reflex			
Head and neck			
Turns head			
Holds head upright with support			
Lifts head slightly when on stomach			
Holds head to sides and middle			
Holds up head when on back and on stomach			
Holds head without support			
Trunk			
Holds up chest			
Sits with support			
May attempt to raise self			
May fuss if left lying down with little chance to sit up			
Holds up chest and shoulders			
Leg			
Rolls from stomach to back			
Arm			
Moves randomly			
Reaches			

Child behavior	Date first observed	Practicing	Proficient
Hand			
Opens and closes			
Keeps hands open			
Plays with hands			
Uses hands to grasp object			
Whole hand and fingers against thumb			
Thumb and forefinger			
Holds and moves object			
Eye-hand coordination			
Moves arm toward object; may miss it			
Reaches hand to object; may grab or miss it			
SEEING			
Focuses eight inches from eyes			
Follows with eyes			
See objects beyond eight inches			
Looks from object to object			
Looks around; focuses on object; then continues visual searching			
HEARING			
Responds to voice and range of sounds			
Reacts to hearing low- and high-pitched sounds			
Locates source of sound			
SLEEPING			
Sleeps much of the day and night			
Takes a long morning nap and a long afternoon nap			
May have irregular sleep habits			
EATING AND ELIMINATION			
Establishes regular time for eating and bowel movements			

(continued)

Approximately Birth to Four Months of Age *(continued)*

Child behavior	Date first observed	Practicing	Proficient
Cognitive Development			
SENSORIMOTOR SUBSTAGE 1			
Reflexive actions			
Passive to active search			
SENSORIMOTOR SUBSTAGE 2			
Small, gradual changes come from repetition			
Coordination of behaviors, e.g., looking toward sound			
Puts hand, object in mouth and sucks on it			
Moves hand, object to see it			
Produces a pleasurable motor activity and repeats activity			
OBJECT PERMANENCE			
Follows moving object with eyes until object disappears			
Looks where object disappeared			
Loses interest and turns away			
Language Development			
LANGUAGE INITIATION–RESPONSE			
Initiates making sounds			
Responds vocally to another person			
Makes sound, repeats sound, continues practicing sound and lengthening it			
Imitates a few sounds he or she already knows			
Experiments with sounds			
Coos in vowel-like sounds			
Adds pitch to cooing			

Child behavior	Date first observed	Practicing	Proficient
CRYING			
Cries apparently automatically in distress, frustration			
Cries differently to express hunger, discomfort, anger			
Cries less as vocalizing increases			|//

Emotional Development

Child behavior	Date first observed	Practicing	Proficient
TYPES OF EMOTIONS and FEELINGS			
Shows excitement			
Shows stress			
Shows enjoyment			
Shows anger			
Shows fear			
Protests			
CONTROL OF EMOTIONS AND FEELINGS			
Cries			
Increases sounds (talking)			
Reflects sounds (talking)			
Comforted by holding			
TEMPERAMENT (LIST BEHAVIORS TO INDICATE BASIC APPROACH)			
Activity level			
Regularity			
Response to new situations: Approach or withdrawal			
Adaptability to change in routine			
Sensory threshold			
Positive or negative mood			
Intensity of response			
Distractibility			
Persistence and attention span			

(continued)

Approximately Birth to Four Months of Age *(continued)*

Child behavior	Date first observed	Practicing	Proficient
Social Development			
ATTACHMENT			
Shows special closeness to family members			
Develops familiarity with one primary caregiver			
SELF			
Becomes aware of hands and feet			
Smiles spontaneously			
Smiles at people (social smile)			
INTERACTIONS WITH OTHERS			
Interacts with people			
Laughs			
Initiates talking to others			

Additional Observations of Child:

Approximately Four to Eight Months of Age

Child behavior	Date first observed	Practicing	Proficient
Physical Development			

MUSCULAR CONTROL

- Head and neck
  - Holds head up independently
  - Holds head in midline position
  - Holds head up when on back, stomach, and sitting

- Trunk
  - Holds up chest, shoulders; arches back, hips
  - Sits with support
    - *May attempt to raise self*
    - *May fuss if left lying down with little chance to sit up*
  - Leans back and forth
  - Sits in a chair
  - Sits unsupported for short time
  - Pushes self to sitting position

- Leg
  - Straightens legs when standing
  - Stamps feet when standing
  - Rolls from back to stomach
  - Raises self to hands and knees
  - Stands with support
  - Pulls self to standing

- Locomotion
  - Kicks against surface to move
  - Rocks on hands and knees
  - Creeps on stomach
  - Uses legs to pull, push self when sitting

(continued)

Approximately Four to Eight Months of Age *(continued)*

Child behavior	Date first observed	Practicing	Proficient
Arm			
Visually directs reaching, hitting			
Throws objects			
Hand			
Picks up object with one hand; passes it to the other hand			
Uses objects in both hands			
Grasps and releases objects			
Drops objects			
EATING			
Begins solid foods (new tongue and swallowing technique)			
Drinks from cup (new tongue and swallowing technique)			
Eats at "mealtimes"—solid foods, milk, juice			
Feeds self finger foods			
TEETH			
First teeth emerge: two middle lower, two middle upper			
Cognitive Development			
SENSORIMOTOR SUBSTAGE 3			
Repeats interesting action			
Refines hand-eye coordination			
Looks for object, reaches for it, and accurately touches it			
Imitates behavior he or she can see or hear			
OBJECT PERMANENCE			
Searches visually (not manually) for short time when object disappears			
Sees part of object; looks for whole object			

Child behavior	Date first observed	Practicing	Proficient
Language Development			
Babbles syllable-like sounds			
Responds to talking by cooing, babbling, smiling			
Imitates sounds			
Looks when name is called			
Babbles conversation with others			
Reflects happiness, unhappiness in sounds made			
Babbles two- and three-syllable sounds			
Varies intensity, volume, pitch, and rhythm			
Emotional Development			
TYPES OF EMOTIONS AND FEELINGS			
Shows pleasure in watching others			
Shows pleasure in repetitive play			
Shows depression			
Shows fear: of strangers, of falling down			
Shows frustration with stimulation overload			
Shows happiness, delight, joy, humor			
Shows frustration, anger, and/or rage			
CONTROL OF EMOTIONS AND FEELINGS			
Sometimes stops crying when talked to, sung to			
TEMPERAMENT (LIST BEHAVIORS TO INDICATE BASIC APPROACH)			
Activity level			
Regularity			
Response to new situations: Approach or withdrawal			
Adaptability to change in routine			
Sensory threshold			

(continued)

Approximately Four to Eight Months of Age *(continued)*

Child behavior	Date first observed	Practicing	Proficient
Positive or negative mood			
Intensity of response			
Distractibility			
Persistence and attention span			

Social Development

ATTACHMENT

    Shows strong attachment to family members

    Differentiates response to family members

    Shows intense pleasure and frustration to person with whom attached

SELF

    Seeks independence in actions

    Plays self-designed games

INTERACTIONS WITH OTHERS

    Imitates others

    Plays with people

    Seeks family's and/or caregiver's attention by movement, sounds, smiles, cries

    Follows family members and/or caregiver to be in same room

    Acts shy with some strangers

Approximately Eight to Twelve Months of Age

Child behavior	Date first observed	Practicing	Proficient
Physical Development			
MUSCULAR CONTROL			
Trunk and leg			
Stands holding onto furniture or hand			
Stands without assistance			
Sits from standing			
Squats and stands			
Locomotion			
Crawls			
Steps forward			
Crawls up steps			
Steps sideways			
Walks with help			
Climbs on furniture			
Hand			
Brings both hands to middle of body			
Uses finger to poke			
Carries objects in hands			
Holds and uses pen and crayon			
Uses one hand to hold object, one hand to reach and explore			
Stacks blocks with dominant hand			
Takes off clothes			
EATING			
Holds bottle			
Holds cup			
Holds and uses spoon			
Uses fingers to eat most food			
Starts establishing food preferences			

(continued)

Approximately Eight to Twelve Months of Age *(continued)*

Child behavior	Date first observed	Practicing	Proficient
Cognitive Development			
SENSORIMOTOR SUBSTAGE 4			
Differentiates goals			
Can focus on reaching and focus on toy			
Object permanence			
Child knows object exists when it is no longer visible; child seeks toy that rolls behind object			
Causality			
Understands that others cause actions			
Imitation and play			
Imitates others' actions in play			
Language Development			
Shouts			
Labels object sounds			
Uses names: *mama, dada*			
Responds to familiar sounds			
Responds to familiar words			
Repeats syllables, words, e.g., *bye-bye*			
Engages in babble conversations			
Repeats, practices word over and over			
Says one or two words			
Emotional Development			
TYPES OF EMOTIONS AND FEELINGS			
May have tantrums			
Rejects items, situations			
Develops preferences for toys, people			
Shows independence—helps with feeding and dressing self			
Shows affection			

Child behavior	Date first observed	Practicing	Proficient
CONTROL OF EMOTIONS AND FEELINGS			
Obeys commands: No-No, Stop			
Sometimes inhibits own behavior			
TEMPERAMENT (LIST BEHAVIORS TO INDICATE BASIC APPROACH)			
Activity level			
Regularity			
Response to new situations: Approach or withdrawal			
Adaptability to change in routine			
Sensory threshold			
Positive or negative mood			
Intensity of response			
Distractibility			
Persistence and attention span			
Social Development			
May fear strangers			
Keeps family members or caregiver in sight			
Focuses on own pleasure; may not consider others			
Imitates play			
Shows ownership of people			
Shows ownership of materials			
May become shy, clinging			
May demand attention			

Approximately Twelve to Eighteen Months of Age

Child behavior	Date first observed	Practicing	Proficient
Physical Development			
MUSCULAR CONTROL			
Locomotion			
May prefer crawling to walking			
Walks alone			
Climbs up stairs with help			
Climbs down stairs with help			
Climbs over objects			
Hand			
Shows hand preference			
Rolls and catches objects			
Eye-hand coordination			
Scribbles			
Helps in dressing, undressing			
Cognitive Development			
SENSORIMOTOR DEVELOPMENT: SUBSTAGE 5			
Object permanence			
Watches toy hidden and moved			
Looks for it where moved			
Causality			
Investigates cause and effect			
Sees self as causal agent			
Explores various ways things happen			
Employs active trial and error to solve problems			
Experiments			
Imitation and play			
Turns play with imitation into rituals			

Child behavior	Date first observed	Practicing	Proficient
Language Development			
Imitates sounds of other people, objects			
Responds to word and gesture conversation			
Responds to many questions and commands child cannot say			
Engages in jargon (babbling with a real word inserted)			
Uses word approximation for some words			
Uses words in immediate context			
Looks at board books independently			
Identifies family members in photographs			
Uses markers			
Emotional Development			
TYPES OF EMOTIONS AND FEELINGS			
Expresses emotions in behavior and language			
Recognizes emotions in others			
Expresses sense of humor			
Displays negativism			
May have tantrums			
Uses play to express emotions, resolve conflicts			
Seeks dependency, security with family and caregiver			
Seeks to expand independence			
CONTROL OF EMOTIONS AND FEELINGS			
Begins to understand right and wrong			
Reinforces desired behavior			

(continued)

Approximately Twelve to Eighteen Months of Age *(continued)*

Child behavior	Date first observed	Practicing	Proficient
TEMPERAMENT (LIST BEHAVIORS TO INDICATE BASIC APPROACH)			
Activity level			
Regularity			
Response to new situations: Approach or withdrawal			
Adaptability to change in routine			
Sensory threshold			
Positive or negative mood			
Intensity of response			
Distractibility			
Persistence and attention span			
Social Development			
SELF			
Has concept of self			
Is egocentric: understands only own viewpoint			
OTHERS			
Seeks presence of family or caregiver			
Plays games			
Acts differently toward different people			
Uses variety of behaviors to gain attention			
May be shy with some people			
Engages in parallel play			

Approximately Eighteen to Twenty-four Months of Age

Child behavior	Date first observed	Practicing	Proficient
Physical Development			
MUSCULAR CONTROL			
Locomotion			
Walks backward			
Walks sideways			
Runs with stops and starts			
Jumps with both feet			
Kicks object			
Walks up and down stairs holding railing; both feet to one step			
Pushes and pulls objects while walking			
Climbs			
Pedals cycle			
Arm			
Throws object at target			
Hand			
Grasps and releases with developing finger muscles			
Pulls zippers			
Scribbles			
Increases wrist flexibility, turns wrist to turn object			
Turns book pages			
Digs with tool			
Makes individual marks with crayon or pen			
TEETH			
Uses toothbrush			

(continued)

Approximately Eighteen to Twenty-four Months of Age *(continued)*

Child behavior	Date first observed	Practicing	Proficient
Cognitive Development			
SENSORIMOTOR DEVELOPMENT: SUBSTAGE 6			
Mental trial and error			
Tries out ideas mentally, based on past concrete experiences			
Object permanence			
Sees object disappear, remembers object, and figures out where it went			
Deferred imitation and symbolization			
Imitates past events			
Engages in symbolic play			
Uses symbolic play to resolve conflict			
Uses symbolic play to try on roles			
Language Development			
Uses language to reflect own meaning; expects others to have same meaning			
Expands vocabulary rapidly, labeling objects			
Points to objects and pictures named by others			
Learns social words—*hello, please, thank you*			
Uses language to express needs, desires			
Uses language to direct others			
Asks questions			
Uses nouns, verbs, pronouns			
Is learning prepositions			
Calls self by name			
Follows directions of one step or two steps			
Uses telegraphic speech (two- to three-word sentences)			
"Reads" books			

Child behavior	Date first observed	Practicing	Proficient
Listens to stories and rhymes			
Scribbles			
Emotional Development			
TYPES OF EMOTIONS AND FEELINGS			
Views internal feelings and external behavior as same			
Shows one or more emotions at same time			
Seeks approval			
May develop new fears			
Increases fantasy			
May increase aggressiveness			
Seeks security in routines			
May become shy again			
Sometimes rejects family members or caregivers			
CONTROL OF EMOTIONS AND FEELINGS			
Uses reactions of others as a controller of own behavior			
May resist change			
Moves to extremes, from lovable to demanding and stubborn			
TEMPERAMENT (LIST BEHAVIORS TO INDICATE BASIC APPROACH)			
Activity level			
Regularity			
Response to new situations: Approach or withdrawal			
Adaptability to change in routine			
Sensory threshold			
Positive or negative mood			
Intensity of response			
Distractibility			
Persistence and attention span			

(continued)

Approximately Eighteen to Twenty-four Months of Age *(continued)*

Child behavior	Date first observed	Practicing	Proficient
Social Development			
SELF			
Shows strong ownership by identifying materials as belonging to self			
Uses *I, mine, me, you*			
OTHERS			
Begins to be aware of others' feelings			
Believes people have changes in identity			
Interacts with other children; expands social relationships			
Looks to others for help			
Imitates tasks of others			
Wants to help, assists with tasks			
May do opposite of what is requested			
Engages in parallel play			

Approximately Twenty-four to Thirty Months of Age

Child behavior	Date first observed	Practicing	Proficient
Physical Development			
MUSCULAR CONTROL			
Movement			
Bends at waist			
Climbs			
Jumps			
Stands on one foot			
Is learning to use fork			
ELIMINATION			
May show interest in learning to use toilet			
Cognitive Development			
PREOPERATIONAL STAGE: PRECONCEPTUAL			
Nonverbal classification			
Makes graphic collections			
Verbal preconcepts			
Uses words differently at different times			
Uses words with private meanings			
Labels objects in one class			
Focuses on one attribute			
Verbal reasoning			
Reasons from particular to particular			
Quantity			
Understands some, more, gone, big			
Number			
Understands more			
Space			
Understands up, down, behind, under, over			
Time			
Understands now, soon			

(continued)

Approximately Twenty-four to Thirty Months of Age *(continued)*

Child behavior	Date first observed	Practicing	Proficient
Language Development			
Uses demonstrative naming			
Uses attribution			
Uses possession			
Uses action			
Uses recurrence			
Uses negation			
Learns prosodic patterning			
Uses subject-verb combinations			
Uses verb-object			
May use subject-verb-object			
Selects and reads books			
Uses controlled scribbling			
Emotional Development			
TYPES OF EMOTIONS AND FEELINGS			
Self-esteem			
Feels comfortable with self			
Feels positive self-worth			
Feels negative self-worth			
CONTROL OF EMOTIONS AND FEELINGS			
Independently expresses many emotions in socially acceptable manner			
TEMPERAMENT (LIST BEHAVIORS TO INDICATE BASIC APPROACH)			
Activity level			
Regularity			
Response to new situations: Approach or withdrawal			
Adaptability to change in routine			
Sensory threshold			
Positive or negative mood			

Child behavior	Date first observed	Practicing	Proficient
Intensity of response			
Distractibility			
Persistence and attention span			
Social Development			
SELF			
Realizes own skills			
Identifies self as boy or girl			
OTHERS			
Acts to please adult			
Recognizes the difference between *mine* and *yours*.			
Shares, but not consistently			
Helps others			
Engages in parallel play			
May engage in brief episodes of cooperative play			

Approximately Thirty to Thirty-six Months of Age

Child behavior	Date first observed	Practicing	Proficient
Physical Development			
MOVEMENT AND COORDINATION			
Runs smoothly			
Jumps in place and forward			
Has firmly established handedness			
ELIMINATION			
Is in process of or has completed toilet learning			
Cognitive Development			
PREOPERATIONAL STAGE: PRECONCEPTUAL			
Nonverbal classification			
Makes graphic collections			
Verbal reasoning			
Thinks one action is like another action			
Reasons from effect to cause			
Time			
Understands now, soon, before, after			
Language Development			
Has vocabulary of over 200 words			
Creates longer sentences			
Includes functional words (e.g., *a, an, the*)			
Uses plurals with accuracy and overregularization			
Uses past tense with accuracy and overregularization			
Listens to stories, "reads" pictures, storybooks			

Child behavior	Date first observed	Practicing	Proficient
Emotional Development			
TYPES OF EMOTIONS AND FEELINGS			
Reacts strongly			
Acts negatively			
Learns enthusiastically			
CONTROL OF EMOTIONS AND FEELINGS			
Is physically aggressive			
TEMPERAMENT (LIST BEHAVIORS TO INDICATE BASIC APPROACH)			
Activity level			
Regularity			
Response to new situations: Approach or withdrawal			
Adaptability to change in routine			
Sensory threshold			
Positive or negative mood			
Intensity of response			
Distractibility			
Persistence and attention span			
Social Development			
SELF			
Acts possessive			
OTHERS			
Seeks assistance			
Directs others			
Helps others			
CONTROL OF SELF			
Plays cooperatively			
Shares			
Takes turns			

Indoor Safety Checklist

Item	Yes/No	Corrections/ Comments	Date correction made
General Environment			
Floors are smooth and have a nonskid surface.			
Pipes and radiators are inaccessible to children or are covered to prevent contact.			
Hot tap water temperature for hand washing is 110°F–115°F or less.			
Electrical cords are out of children's reach and are kept out of doorways and traffic paths.			
Unused electrical outlets are covered by furniture or shock stops.			
Medicines, cleansers, and aerosols are kept in a locked place, where children are unable to see and reach them.			
All windows have screens that stay in place when used; expandable screens are not used.			
Windows can be opened only six inches or less from the bottom.			
Drawers are kept closed to prevent tripping or bumps.			
Trash is covered at all times.			
Walls and ceilings are free of peeling paint and cracked or falling plaster; center has been inspected for lead paint.			
There are no disease-bearing animals, such as turtles, parrots, or cats.			
Children are always supervised.			
There is no friable (crumbly) asbestos releasing into the air.			
Equipment and Toys			
Toys and play equipment are checked often for sharp edges, small parts, and sharp points.			
All toys are painted with lead-free paint.			
Toys are put away when not in use.			
Toy chests have lightweight lids or no lids.			
Art materials are nontoxic, and have either the AP or the CP label.			
Curtains, pillows, blankets, and soft toys are made of flame-resistant material.			

Item	Yes/No	Corrections/ Comments	Date correction made
Hallways and Stairs			
Stairs and stairways are free of boxes, toys, and other clutter.			
Stairways are well lit.			
The right-hand railing on the stairs is at child height and does not wobble when held; there is a railing or wall on both sides of stairways.			
Stairway gates are in place when appropriate.			
Closed doorways to unsupervised or unsafe areas are always locked unless this prevents emergency evacuation.			
Staff are able to watch for strangers entering the building.			
Kitchen			
Trash is kept away from areas where food is prepared or stored.			
Trash is stored away from the furnace and water heater.			
Pest strips are *not* used; pesticides for crawling insects are applied by a certified pest control operator.			
Cleansers and other poisonous products are stored in their original containers, away from food and out of children's reach.			
Food preparation surfaces are clean and free of cracks and chips.			
Electrical cords are placed where people will not trip over them or pull them.			
There are no sharp or hazardous cooking utensils within children's reach (e.g., knives).			
Pot handles are always turned in toward the back of the stove during cooking.			
The fire extinguisher can be reached easily in an emergency.			
All staff know how to use the fire extinguisher correctly.			

(continued)

Indoor Safety Checklist *(continued)*

Item	Yes/No	Corrections/ Comments	Date correction made
Bathrooms			
Stable step stools are available when needed.			
Electrical outlets are covered with shock stops or outlet covers.			
Cleaning products, soap, and disinfectant are stored in a locked place, out of children's reach.			
Floors are smooth and have a nonskid surface.			
The trash container is emptied daily and kept clean.			
Hot water for hand washing is 110°F–115°F.			
Emergency Preparation			
All staff understand their roles and responsibilities in case of emergency.			
At least one staff person is always present who is certified in first aid and CPR for infants and children.			
The first aid kit is checked regularly for supplies and is kept where it can be reached easily by staff in an emergency.			
Smoke detectors and other alarms are checked regularly to make sure they are working.			
Each room and hallway has a fire escape route posted in clear view.			
Emergency procedures and telephone numbers are posted near each phone in clear view.			
Children's emergency phone numbers are kept near the phone, where they can be reached quickly.			
All exits are clearly marked and are free of clutter.			
Doors open in the direction of all exit travel.			
Cots are placed so that walkways are clear for evacuation in an emergency.			

Source: Statewide Comprehensive Injury Prevention Program (SCIPP), Massachusetts Department of Public Health.

Playground Safety Checklist

Item	Yes/No	Corrections/ Comments	Date correction made
All Equipment			
Nuts, bolts, or screws that stick out are covered with masking tape or sanded down.			
Metal equipment is free from rust or chipping paint.			
Wood equipment is free from splinters or rough surfaces, sharp edges, and pinching/crushing parts.			
Nuts and bolts are tight.			
Anchors for equipment are stable and buried below ground level.			
Equipment is in its proper place and is not bent with use.			
Children who use equipment are of the age/developmental level for which the equipment was designed.			
Ground Surface			
All play equipment has 8–12 inches of shock-absorbing material underneath (e.g., pea gravel or wood chips).			
Surfaces are raked weekly to prevent them from becoming packed down and to find hidden hazards (e.g., litter, sharp objects, animal feces).			
Stagnant pools of water are not present on the surface.			
There is no exposed concrete where equipment is anchored.			
Spacing			
Swing sets are at least nine feet from other equipment.			
Swings are at least 1½ feet from each other.			
Slides have a 2½- to 3-yard run-off space.			
There is at least eight feet of space between equipment items.			

(continued)

Playground Safety Checklist *(continued)*

Item	Yes/No	Corrections/ Comments	Date correction made
Boundaries between equipment items are visible to children (e.g., painted lines or low bushes).			
Play areas for bike riding, games, and boxes are separate from other equipment.			
Swing sets are at least six feet from walls and fences, walkways, and other play areas; there is a barrier to prevent children from getting into traffic (e.g., when chasing a ball).			
Slides			
Slides are six feet in height or less.			
Side rims are at least 2½ inches high.			
Slides have an enclosed platform at the top for children to rest and get into position for sliding.			
Slide ladders have handrails on both sides and flat steps.			
There is a flat surface at the bottom of the slide for slowing down.			
Metal slides are shaded to prevent burns.			
Wood slides are waxed, or oiled with linseed oil.			
The slide incline is equal to or less than 30 degrees.			
Steps and rungs are 7–11 inches apart to accommodate children's leg and arm reach.			
Climbing Equipment			
Ladders of different heights are available for children of different ages and sizes.			
Bars stay in place when grasped.			
The maximum height from which a child can fall is 7½ feet.			
Climbers have regularly spaced footholds from top to bottom.			
There is an easy, safe "way out" for children when they reach the top.			

Item	Yes/No	Corrections/ Comments	Date correction made
Equipment is dry before children are allowed to use it.			
Rungs are painted in bright or contrasting colors so children will see them.			
Swings			
Chair swings are available for children under age five.			
Canvas sling and saddle seats are available for older children.			
S-shaped or open-ended hooks have been removed.			
Hanging rings are less than five inches or more than 10 inches in diameter (smaller or larger than child's head).			
The point at which seat and chain meet is exposed.			
Sandboxes			
Sandboxes are located in a shaded spot; only sterilized sand is used.			
Sandbox is securely covered, if accessible to pets or other animals.			
The frame is sanded and smooth, without splinters or rough surfaces.			
The sand is raked at least every two weeks to check for debris and to provide exposure to air and sun.			
The sandbox has proper drainage.			
Poisonous plants and berries are removed from play area.			
There is a source of clean drinking water available in the play area.			
There is shade.			
The entire play area can be seen easily for good supervision.			

Source: Recommendations of Statewide Comprehensive Injury Prevention Program (SCIPP), Massachusetts Department of Public Health.

APPENDIX B
Developmental Profile and Instructions

INSTRUCTIONS

Copy the Developmental Profile form (Figure B–1). Create a profile for each infant and/or toddler in your care by following these instructions.

1. Write the child's name, date(s) of assessment(s), and date of birth (D. O. B.) on the profile. (Use the Sample Developmental Profile in Figure B–2 as an example.)
2. Calculate chronological age (C. A.) using the following method:

		Year	Month	Day
Assessment	=	2007	2	24
D. O. B.	=	2006	2	21
C. A.	=	1 (12 mo.)	0	3

3. Place the C. A. in months in the middle shaded C. A. row on the profile and put one-month intervals at each row for children with chronological ages from 1 to 17 months and two-month intervals for chronological ages from 18 months up (see Figure B–2 for an example).
4. Write the child behaviors assessed from the Developmental Prescription (Appendix A) under each major Developmental Area on the profile (see Sample Profile in Figure B–2).
5. Observe how the child performs on each skill and place an X in the row representing the monthly development for each listed child behavior.
6. Connect the *X*s to illustrate graphically the child's development.
7. Write notes on strengths and weaknesses shown by the profile.

appendix B DEVELOPMENTAL PROFILE AND INSTRUCTIONS   **475**

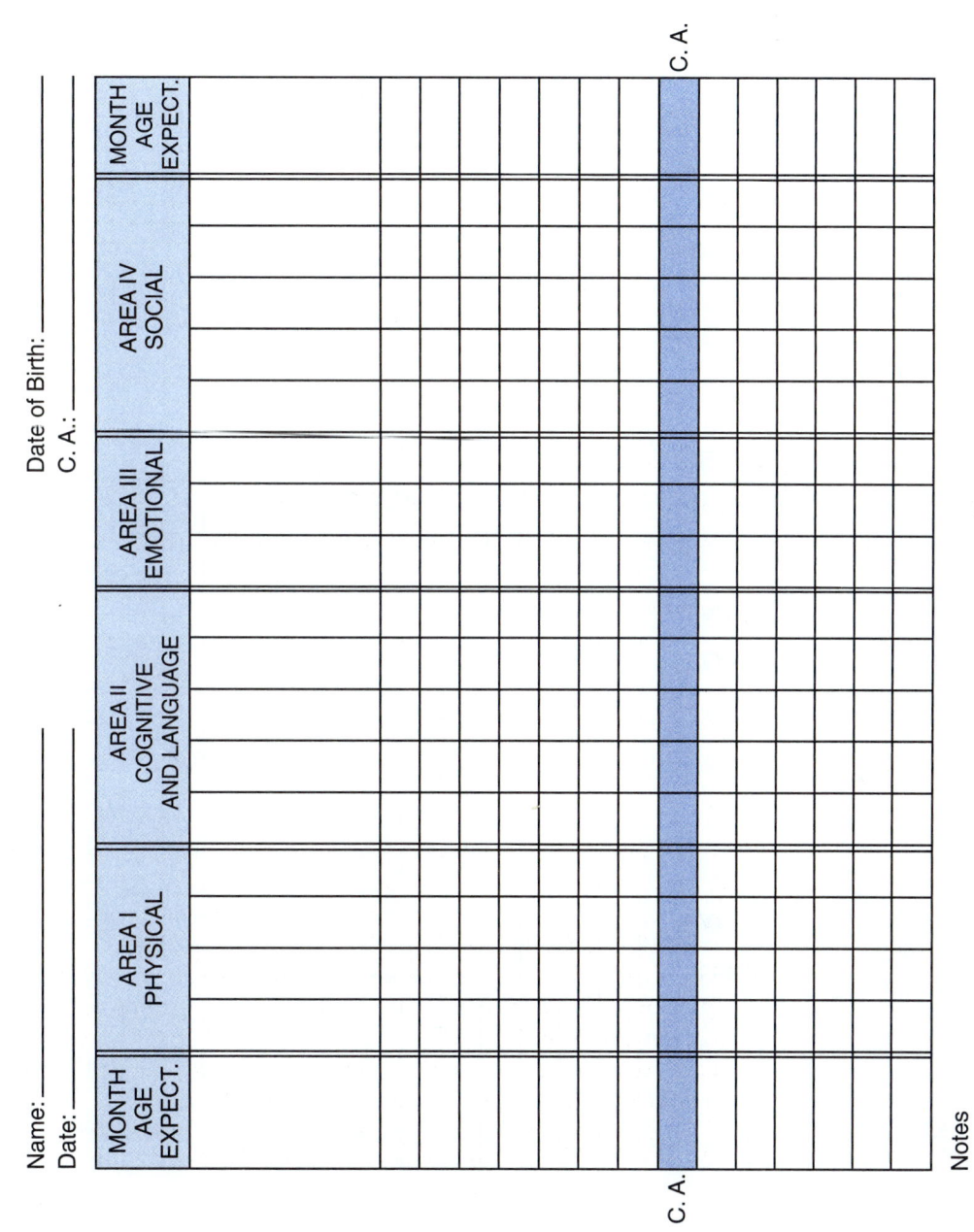

FIGURE B-1 Blank Developmental Profile

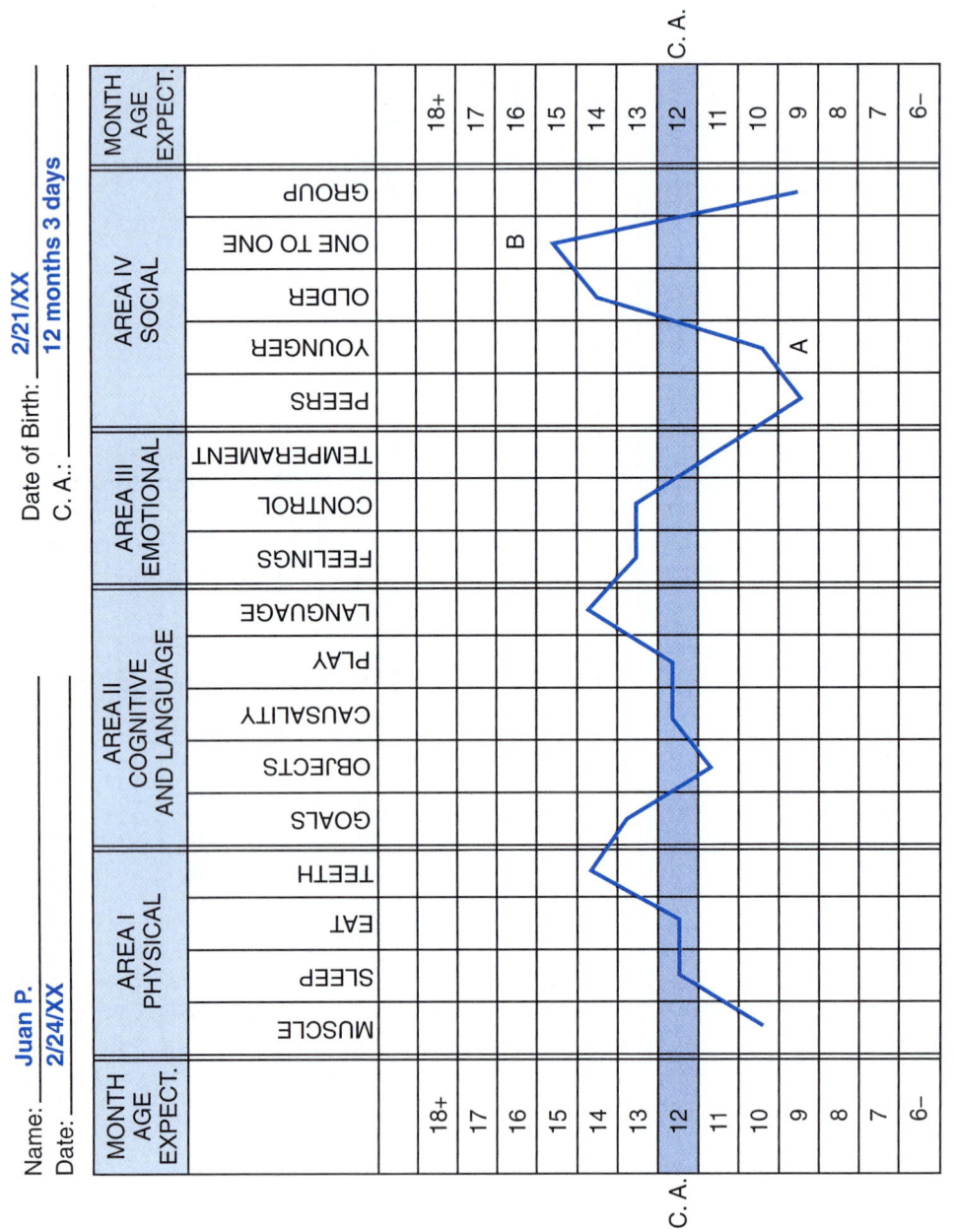

476 appendix B DEVELOPMENTAL PROFILE AND INSTRUCTIONS

Name: Juan P.
Date: 2/24/XX
Date of Birth: 2/21/XX
C. A.: 12 months 3 days

MONTH AGE EXPECT.	AREA I PHYSICAL				AREA II COGNITIVE AND LANGUAGE					AREA III EMOTIONAL			AREA IV SOCIAL					MONTH AGE EXPECT.
	MUSCLE	SLEEP	EAT	TEETH	GOALS	OBJECTS	CAUSALITY	PLAY	LANGUAGE	FEELINGS	CONTROL	TEMPERAMENT	PEERS	YOUNGER	OLDER	ONE TO ONE	GROUP	
18+																		18+
17																		17
16																B		16
15																		15
14																		14
13																		13
12 C.A.																		**12 C.A.**
11																		11
10																		10
9														A				9
8																		8
7																		7
6−																		6−

Notes: A = Juan has a little problem dealing with a group—sometimes is overwhelmed.
B = He responds very well to one to one adult attention.

FIGURE B-2 Sample of Completed Developmental Profile

APPENDIX C
Standards for Infant/Toddler Caregivers

This section provides specific information about standards for practicing or preservice teachers. Covered in this appendix are the six CDA Competency Areas and five NAEYC Standards for Early Childhood Professional Preparation: Initial Licensure Programs. Table C–1, which was initially provided in Chapter 5, is included to remind you of the relationships between these two sets of teacher standards.

Appendix Overview

CDA Competency Standards for Infant/Toddler Caregivers in Center-based Programs
NAEYC Standards for Early Childhood Professional Preparation: Initial Licensure Programs
NAEYC Initial Licensure Standards Summary

CDA COMPETENCY STANDARDS FOR INFANT/ TODDLER CAREGIVERS IN CENTER-BASED PROGRAMS

The CDA Competency Standards are the national standards used to evaluate a caregiver's performance with children and families during the CDA assessment process. The Competency Standards are divided into six **competency goals,** which are statements of a general purpose or goal for caregiver behavior. The competency goals are common to all child care settings. The six goals are defined in more detail in 13 **functional areas,** which describe the major tasks or functions that a caregiver must complete in order to carry out the competency goal (see Table C–2).

TABLE C–1 OVERLAP OF THE CDA AND NAEYC STANDARDS

CDA Competency Areas	NAEYC Teacher Preparation Standards					
	1. Promoting child development and learning	2. Building family and community relationships	3. Observing, documenting, and assessing	4. Teaching and learning	5. Becoming a professional
I. Safe, healthy learning environment	X			X	
II. Advance physical and intellectual competence	X			X	
III. Support social and emotional development; positive guidance	X			X	
IV. Positive and productive relationships with families		X			
V. Well-run, purposeful program			X		
VI. Commitment to professionalism					X

Table C–2 CDA COMPETENCY GOALS AND FUNCTIONAL AREAS

I. To establish and maintain a safe, healthy learning environment.
1. **Safe:** Candidate provides a safe environment to prevent and reduce injuries.
2. **Healthy:** Candidate promotes good health and nutrition and provides an environment that contributes to the prevention of illness.
3. **Learning Environment:** Candidate uses space, relationships, materials, and routines as resources for constructing an interesting, secure, and enjoyable environment that encourages play, exploration, and learning.

II. To advance physical and intellectual competence.
4. **Physical:** Candidate provides a variety of equipment, activities, and opportunities to promote the physical development of children.
5. **Cognitive:** Candidate provides activities and opportunities that encourage curiosity, exploration, and problem solving appropriate to the development levels and learning styles of children.
6. **Communication:** Candidate actively communicates with children and provides opportunities and support for children to understand, acquire, and use verbal and nonverbal means of communicating thoughts and feelings.
7. **Creative:** Candidate provides opportunities that stimulate children to play with sound, rhythm, language, materials, space, and ideas in individual ways and to express their creative abilities.

III. To support social and emotional development and provide positive guidance.
8. **Self:** Candidate provides physical and emotional security for each child and **helps** each child to know, accept, and take pride in himself or herself and to develop a sense of independence.
9. **Social:** Candidate helps each child feel accepted in the group, helps children learn to communicate and get along with others, and encourages feelings of empathy and mutual respect among children and adults.
10. **Guidance:** Candidate provides a supportive environment in which children can begin to learn and practice appropriate and acceptable behaviors as individuals and as a group.

IV. To establish positive and productive relationships with families.
11. **Families:** Candidate maintains an open, friendly, and cooperative relationship with each child's family, encourages their involvement in the program, and supports the child's relationship with his or her family.

V. To ensure a well-run, purposeful program responsive to particular needs.
12. **Program Management:** Candidate is a manager who uses all available resources to ensure an effective operation. The Candidate is a competent organizer, planner, record keeper, communicator, and a cooperative coworker.

VI. To maintain a commitment to professionalism.
13. **Professionalism:** Candidate makes decisions based on knowledge of early childhood theories and practices. Candidate promotes quality in child care services. Candidate takes advantage of opportunities to improve competence, both for personal and professional growth for the benefit of children and families.

Each functional area is explained by a *developmental context*, which presents a brief overview of child development from birth to three years and provides a rationale for the functional area definition and examples of competent caregiver behavior that follow. Three different developmental levels are identified: young infants (birth–8 months), mobile infants (9–17 months), and toddlers (18–36 months). Children develop at different rates, and descriptions of these levels emphasize the unique characteristics and needs of children at each stage of development.

Each functional area is further explained by a list of sample caregiver behaviors (not included here). These examples describe behavior that demonstrates that a caregiver is acting in a competent way or exhibiting a skill in a particular functional area. During the assessment process, most candidates will exhibit other competent behavior, and a competent candidate might not demonstrate all the examples listed under a functional area. The examples are organized according to developmental stages of children from birth to three years, in order to emphasize the importance of the special skills needed to work with young infants, mobile infants, and toddlers. Special bilingual specialization examples are presented for several functional areas.

The samples of caregiver competency included in the standards should serve as a basis for recognizing other, more specific behaviors that are important to the individual candidate. CDA candidates and individuals conducting or participating in CDA training will be able to think of many different ways to demonstrate skill in the six competency goals and 13 functional areas.

Competent caregivers integrate their work and constantly adapt their skills—always thinking of the development of the whole child. In all functional areas, it is important for competent caregivers to individualize their work with each child while meeting the needs of the group. In every area, too, caregivers must promote multiculturalism, support families with different languages, and meet the needs of children with special needs. And, while demonstrating skills and knowledge, competent caregivers must also demonstrate personal qualities, such as flexibility and a positive style of communicating with young children and working with families.

The Council for Early Childhood Professional Recognition has designed both training and assessment systems for persons interested in the CDA credential. For more information, contact

> Council for Professional Recognition
> 2460 16th St., NW
> Washington, DC 20009
> Telephone: (202) 265-9090 or (800) 424-4310
> Fax: (202) 265-9161
> http://www.cdacouncil.org/

NAEYC STANDARDS FOR EARLY CHILDHOOD PROFESSIONAL PREPARATION: INITIAL LICENSURE PROGRAMS

The National Association for the Education of Young Children (NAEYC) has designed standards for teacher preparation programs at the Associate, Initial, and Advanced levels. The NAEYC Standards for Early Childhood Professional Preparation are the national standards used to evaluate teacher preparation programs. This process involves evaluating the pre-service teacher's performance with children and families during annual program reviews. The standards are divided into five categories and, occasionally, subcategories.

These standards were created to assist NAEYC with meeting the mission of improving the quality of services for children and families birth through age eight. Teacher preparation standards are just one avenue for tackling this monumental task of helping children learn and develop well. Accreditation standards for early childhood programs, guidelines for developmentally appropriate practices, curriculum content and assessment, teacher preparation standards, and a system for financing early childhood education all work together to create this context.

Because programs educate teachers to participate in a wide range of diverse settings and programs, e.g., private nursery school programs, center- and family-based child care programs, kindergartens, public school programs, early intervention programs including Early Head Start and Head Start, and so on, standards cannot be rigid or "one size fits all."

The following page outlines and summarizes the five standards for early childhood professional preparation: initial level. Refer to the entire document for more specific guidelines and examples for each standard. More information about each set of standards can be downloaded from the NAEYC website at http://www.naeyc.org/files/ecada/file/2003%20NAEYC%20Assoc%20Deg%20Progs.pdf (associate), http://www.naeyc.org/files/ncate/file/initiallicensure.pdf (initial), or http://www.naeyc.org/files/ncate/file/advanced_standards.pdf (advanced). Please note that the standards are currently under revision. They are expected to receive final approval and be disseminated in the fall of 2009.

NAEYC INITIAL LICENSURE STANDARDS SUMMARY

NAEYC Initial Licensure Standards

Standard 1. Promoting Child Development and Learning
Candidates use their understanding of young children's characteristics and needs, and of multiple interacting influences on children's development and learning, to create environments that are healthy, respectful, supportive, and challenging for all children.

Standard 2. Building Family and Community Relationships
Candidates know about, understand, and value the importance and complex characteristics of children's families and communities. They use this understanding to create respectful, reciprocal relationships that support and empower families, and to involve all families in their children's development and learning.

Standard 3. Observing, Documenting, and Assessing to Support Young Children and Families
Candidates know about and understand the goals, benefits, and uses of assessment. They know about and use systematic observations, documentation, and other effective assessment strategies in a responsible way, in partnership with families and other professionals, to influence children's development and learning positively.

Standard 4. Teaching and Learning
Candidates integrate their understanding of and relationships with children and families; their understanding of developmentally effective approaches to teaching and learning; and their knowledge of academic disciplines to design, implement, and evaluate experiences that promote positive development and learning for all children.

Sub-Standard 4a. Connecting with children and families
Candidates know, understand, and use positive relationships and supportive interactions as the foundation for their work with young children.

Sub-Standard 4b. Using developmentally effective approaches
Candidates know, understand, and use a wide array of effective approaches, strategies, and tools to influence children's development and learning positively.

Sub-Standard 4c. Understanding content knowledge in early education
Candidates understand the importance of each content area in young children's learning. They know the essential concepts, inquiry tools, and structure of content areas including academic subjects and can identify resources to deepen their understanding.

Sub-Standard 4d. Building meaningful curriculum
Candidates use their own knowledge and other resources to design, implement, and evaluate meaningful, challenging curricula that promote comprehensive developmental and learning outcomes for all young children.

Standard 5. Becoming a Professional
Candidates identify and conduct themselves as members of the early childhood profession. They know and use ethical guidelines and other professional standards related to early childhood practice. They are continuous, collaborative learners who demonstrate knowledgeable, reflective, and critical perspectives on their work, making informed decisions that integrate knowledge from a variety of sources. They are informed advocates for sound educational practices and policies.

Source: NAEYC Standards for Early Childhood Professional Preparation Initial Licensure Programs. © The National Association for the Education of Young Children.

Glossary

A

abstract An idea not existing in the real world; the basis of a concept.

accommodation Piaget's process of changing or altering skills to better fit the requirements of a task.

accreditation Process of demonstrating and validating the presence of indicators of quality as set out by national standards.

action sentence In language development, action sentences separate the action from the actor and object and explore the relations among these three.

active listening The skill required to simply "feed back" the deeper felt message (not words) of the sender in the words of the receiver.

adaptation A change in behavior that helps the child survive in his or her environment; described by Piaget as a cognitive skill.

ages and stages A use of chronological age as it relates to a level of development clearly distinguishable from the previous level.

alert times Times during the day when a child is attending and attracted to the world around him or her.

ambivalent attachment A form of connection between infant and primary caregiver in which the infant simultaneously seeks and resists emotionally and physically connecting with the caregiver.

anecdotal record A brief narrative account of one event written using descriptive language.

approval One of the three *A*s of child care; feedback that a person is accepted as he or she is.

assessment The process of gathering data about young children, usually through observations, and analyzing it; the results of assessments are used to inform educational decisions.

assimilation Piaget's way of explaining how children refine cognitive structures into schemes.

attachment theory A theory that infants are born needing an emotional attachment to their primary caregiver.

attention One of the three *A*s of child care; focusing sensory modalities (e.g., visual, auditory) on a specific child.

attribution Children give objects a symbol with meaning.

attunement One of the three *A*s of child care; feedback that is *in tune with* or responsive to the behaviors or moods being currently displayed by the child.

avoidant attachment One of the types of attachment between infants and primary caregiver that is related to inconsistent and insensitive caregiver attention.

B

babbling Prelanguage speech with which the baby explores the variety of sounds.

baby signing Nonverbal language using gestures and expressions with infants.

483

behaviorism School of psychology that studies stimuli, responses, and rewards that influence behavior.

bias A prejudgment concerning the style and forms of a specific culture.

brain plasticity When one part of the brain is damaged, other parts take over the functions of the damaged parts.

C

calibrating Carefully observing the specific behaviors demonstrated by another during an interaction in order to build rapport.

cardiopulmonary resuscitation (CPR) Lifesaving technique of manually starting and maintaining a human heartbeat.

caregiver See **early childhood educator.**

caring community of learners One of the five guidelines for developmentally appropriate practice that focuses on creating a classroom context that supports the development of caring, inclusive relationships for everyone involved.

cause and effect In sensorimotor development, observation allows a child to identify the relationship between an action and its effect.

center-based care Child care provided away from home for more than six children for some part of the day or night.

certification A form of regulation for professional child care; standards vary by state.

checklist A method for recording observational data that notes the presence of specific, predetermined skills or behaviors.

child-centered Designing a learning environment and curriculum with children at the center, rather than an adult.

Child Development Associate (CDA) A credential provided by the Council for Early Childhood Professional Recognition when a person has provided evidence of meeting the national standards for caregiver performance.

child-directed speech Adjustments adults make in their tone, volume, and speech patterns to capture and sustain focal attention from an infant.

child-proof To ensure a safe environment by removing potential hazards.

choices A guidance technique where the adult provides at least two acceptable options from which the child can choose; minimizes confrontations and helps the child learn to choose wisely.

choke tube Plastic tube used to determine safe sizes of objects for child play.

classical conditioning Association of an unconditioned stimulus with a conditioned stimulus that evokes specific conditioned or unconditioned responses.

cognitive developmental theory Piaget's theory that children construct knowledge and awareness through manipulation and exploration of their environment.

cognitive disequilibrium Piaget's term for children's cognitive reaction when placed in new and unfamiliar situations in which old schemes no longer work well.

cognitive equilibrium Piaget's term for a cognitive state in which a child's schemes work to explain the child's environment.

cognitive functions Refers to a broad class of the functions to name, indicate, describe, and/or comment.

consequences The natural and/or logical outcomes of actions.

context bound A characteristic of early language in which an infant only understands a word in the context where it was originally learned.

continuity of care Having the same teachers work with the same group of children and families for more than one year, ideally for three years.

cooing The second stage of vocalization in infants from birth to four months old, which resembles vowel-like sounds.

CPR See **cardiopulmonary resuscitation.**

crawling Strategy for mobility where the infant or toddler moves on hands and knees while using arms and legs in opposition.

cultural diversity Differences within groups of people that should be valued and celebrated.

culture Values and beliefs held in common by a group of people.

curriculum Everything that occurs during the course of the day with infants and toddlers; planned learning experiences and routine care.

D

daily plans An approach to curriculum in which planned learning experiences are designed daily based on specific observations of the children.

deferred imitation Imitation of another person's behavior even when that person is no longer present.

demand feeding Providing solid or liquid foods when an infant or toddler is hungry.

demonstrative naming In language development, a process in which the first word points out an object and the second names it (e.g., "this ball").

descriptive phrasing A technique for reporting observations, which involves using words or phrases to describe observable behaviors.

development Operationally defined as general sequences and patterns of growth and maturity.

developmental perspective Teacher and/or program emphasis, in both home-based care and child care centers, on the developmental capabilities of children.

developmentally appropriate practice Process of making educational decisions about the well-being and education of young children based on information or knowledge about child development and learning; the needs, interests, and strengths of each individual child in the group; and the social and cultural contexts in which the individual children live.

disability A condition resulting from a loss of physical functioning; or difficulties in learning and social adjustment that significantly interfere with normal growth and development.

discipline 1) Approach to teaching appropriate behavior and setting limits on inappropriate behavior; 2) The ability to focus on an activity in the face of obstacles in order to reach a desired outcome.

discovery The opportunity to find interesting items and examine them closely, to be facilitated as part of environmental design.

disequilibrium An internal mental state which motivates learning because the child is uncomfortable and seeks to make sense of what he or she has observed or experienced.

disorder A disturbance in normal functioning (mental, physical, or psychological).

disoriented attachment A form of attachment between infant and primary caregiver in which the infant has usually been traumatized by severe or prolonged abandonment.

documentation Any activity that generates a performance record with sufficient detail to help others understand the behavior observed.

documentation panel A visual and written explanation of children's learning displayed to others (family members, children, colleagues, and/or community members).

double substitution Pretend play in which two materials are transformed, within a single act, into something they are not in reality.

dramatic play A form of play that provides opportunities to combine language with imagination.

E

early childhood educator A professional who holds specialized knowledge in the care and education of young children.

Early Head Start programs Federally supported programs for low-income families with children birth to three years of age.

early intervention Comprehensive services for infants and toddlers who have special rights or are at risk of acquiring a disability. Services may include education, health care, and/or social and psychological assistance.

ecological systems theory Bronfenbrenner's theory of nested environmental systems that influence the development and behavior of people.

egocentric Toddlers see the world from their own point of view; in the first year and a half of life their bodies and the objects they play with are perceived to be part of *self*.

elimination The process of excreting urine and feces from the body.

emotional detachment A situation arising from physical or emotional abuse in which the infant or toddler fails to create enduring emotional bonds with others.

emotional development The ability in infants to express and regulate pleasure, happiness, fear, and frustration.

emotional intelligence Skills learned early in life that are necessary for healthy emotional development, good relationships, and fulfillment in life experiences.

emotional regulation Learning to control and manage strong emotions in a socially and culturally acceptable manner.

empathy Sensitivity to what others feel, need, or want; the fundamental relationship skill present at birth.

equilibration The movement from equilibrium to disequilibrium and back to equilibrium again.

equilibrium A state of homeostasis or balance which reflects how an infant's or toddler's current cognitive schemes work to explain his or her environment.

ethology The study of behavior patterns and character development.

evolutionary theory The theory that child development is genetically determined and happens automatically.

exceptional A term describing any individual whose physical, mental, or behavioral performance deviates so substantially from the average (higher or lower) that additional support is required to meet the individual's needs.

exosystem Bronfenbrenner's term for the influences that are not a direct part of a child's experience but influence development, such as parent education.

experience-dependent Type of motor neuron pathway that waits for environmental experiences before being activated.

experience-expectant Type of motor neuron pathway that apparently expects specific stimuli at birth.

F

facilitate To help another person with an experience that she/he cannot do independently at that time.

family-based care Care and education provided to a small group of children in a home setting.

family-caregiver conferences Periodic meetings between family members and caregiver to review documentation and interpretation of each child's developmental progress as well as to create plans for supporting development in the future.

family grouping Method for grouping children where children are of different ages.

fear Physical and psychological reaction to threat.

fetal alcohol effect (FAE) or fetal alcohol syndrome (FAS) Growth delays, facial abnormalities, mental retardation, impulsivity, and behavioral problems resulting from exposure to alcohol during prenatal development. Outcomes for FAE are less severe than those resulting from FAS.

fine motor control The ability to control small muscles such as those in the hands and fingers.

finger foods Foods that older infants and toddlers can easily feed to themselves such as crackers or dry cereal.

flexibility Component of environment design that reflects changes in response to the individual child and each group of children living in the environment.

G

good touch Term for respectful, sensitive, and pleasurable touch.

goodness of fit The temperamental match between very young children and their caregivers.

grammatical words Function words that have little meaning on their own yet affect the meaning of other words (e.g., articles, prepositions, or conjunctions).

gross motor control The control of large muscle activity.

group family child care Care provided for 6 to 12 children in a home setting; usually has two or more caregivers.

guide To direct toward a desirable goal.

H

Head Start programs Federally supported child care programs for low-income families with children three to five years of age.

hearing Physical and neurological process of bringing sound into the nervous system.

high active Infant temperament type in which infant may kick, wriggle, and jerk, requiring the caregiver to provide more assistance while the infant learns to sit up.

holistic care A type of care that considers the whole child, including physical, emotional, social, verbal, and cognitive development.

home-school journal A notebook or journal in which teachers and family members write notes about key happenings and which they send back and forth on a daily or weekly basis.

home visit A meeting in the child's home providing an opportunity for the caregiver to see how the family members and child relate to each other in the home setting.

human immunodeficiency virus (HIV) infection Immune disease that attacks white blood cells and is transmitted through open sores or other bodily fluid sources.

I

I statements Expressions about one's own thoughts and feelings without judging the other person.

identity An infant's or toddler's self-constructed definition of who she or he is.

image of the child Beliefs about children that teachers hold; these beliefs are examined for how they impact teacher-child interactions, management of the environment, and selection of teaching strategies.

imitation Mimicking or copying someone else's behavior; a normal stage of play.

in-home care Child care that takes place in the child's home.

individual constructivism Piaget's belief that each person individually creates new understandings, interpretations, and realities through interactions with materials, equipment, and people in their environment.

infant A child from birth to walking.

inserimento A period of gradual "settling in" or "transition and adjustment" that includes strategies for building relationships and community among adults and children when the child is first entering a Reggio Emilia (Italy)–inspired child care program.

instrumental function In language development for 18- to 24-month-olds, refers to the broad class of functions to request, reject, manipulate, and comment.

interactional synchrony A sensitively tuned "emotional dance," in which interactions are mutually rewarding to caregiver and infant.

interpretive phrasing A form of reporting that makes judgments without providing observable data to justify the conclusions.

intersubjectivity Vygotsky's term to explain how children and adults come to understand each other by adjusting perceptions to fit the other person's map of the world.

J

jargon Language term which refers to the mixing of one real word with strings of babble.

L

labeling Naming objects for association and language development.

language Visual and auditory symbols representing objects and ideas.

language development Acquisition of one's first language; during 8 to 12 months of age, an infant's use of combinations of sounds, babbling, and words to converse with self and others.

learning The acquisition of new information through experiences, investigation, or interactions with another.

learning center A particular part of the environment where materials and equipment are organized to promote and encourage a specific type of learning; for example, music or science.

lexical words Words that have a concrete or abstract connection to objects or events (e.g., nouns, verbs, and adverbs).

licensing regulations Official rules on teacher-child ratios, safety, health, and zoning that an individual or organization must follow to be granted a license to provide care for children.

limits Positively worded statements about desired or acceptable behavior that help children acquire appropriate behaviors for a particular setting.

locomotion The attempt to gain stability when moving forward or upwards (e.g., crawling and walking) against the force of gravity.

locus of control The extent to which a person perceives his or her life as within his or her own control.

logico-mathematical knowledge Knowledge that is individually constructed by each child and involves identifying relationships between objects.

low active Infant temperament style of little movement; caregivers may leave the baby in one position longer than they do with infants who are high active.

M

macrosystem Bronfenbrenner's term for influences on development from the general culture, including laws and customs.

make-believe play Vygotsky's term for using imagination to act out internal concepts of how the world functions and how rules are formed.

manipulation Includes reaching, grasping, and releasing objects; in the first year of development the control of objects moves from reflexive to voluntary.

maturation Naturally unfolding course of growth and development.

medically fragile A subgroup of health disorders for individuals who are at risk for medical emergencies and often require specialized support (e.g., feeding tubes).

memory the process of storing and recalling stimuli at a later time.

mental images Pictures in the mind with which children can carry out action sequences internally.

mesosystem Bronfenbrenner's term for the second level of influence for the child that involves interactions among microsystems, such as a teacher in a child care center and family members.

metacognition Awareness of one's own thought processes.

microsystem Bronfenbrenner's term for the innermost level of influence found in the immediate surrounding of the child, such as parents or an early childhood educator.

milestones Specific behaviors common to an entire population that are used to track development and are observed when they are first or consistently manifested.

mirroring A communication technique of repeating exactly what is said without adding or interpreting any of the speaker's words.

motivation An internal drive that moves someone to action.

multiple disabilities Children who have more than one identified exceptionality; typically they have severe educational needs that are not easily accommodated with programs designed for just one special right.

muscular control Gaining conscious control over muscles so that behaviors such as reaching, grabbing, and releasing can occur when the infant or toddler wants them to.

N

National Association for the Education of Young Children (NAEYC) Professional organization that offers professional resources and development for early childhood educators, as well as recognition for programs that represent high-quality care.

National Association for Family Child Care (NAFCC) An association offering professional recognition and distinction to family child care providers whose services represent high-quality child care.

nature Biological and genetic foundations that influence development and learning.

negation Language strategy used to communicate that something desired or expected is not there or that the child cannot, is not permitted to, or does not want to do something.

negative reinforcers Consequences for a behavior that have the effect of decreasing the frequency or duration of the behavior.

noble savage Rousseau's term for a young child, born with a natural morality or sense of right and wrong.

nonverbal signal Any feedback given visually without the use of auditory stimuli.

normative approach Observing large numbers of children to establish average or normal expectations of when a particular skill or ability is present.

nurture Environmental factors that influence development and learning.

O

object permanence Starting at 8 to 12 months, infants remember that people and objects exist even if they are currently out of sight.

observational learning In child development, a way in which children learn through attending (watching) the behaviors of others.

omnipotent The sense of being unaware of any physical limitations and feeling above physical laws.

organization A process of rearranging new sets of information (schemes) and linking them to other established schemes, resulting in an expanded cognitive system.

original sin Belief by Puritans, for example, that infants are born bad and must be tamed by harsh, restrictive child-rearing practices.

over-regularization Strategy of applying one standard grammatical rule to an irregular word, e.g., "goed" for the past tense of *go*.

overgeneralize The use of one word to mean many different things.

P

pacing Matching complementary behavior to that of another person to build rapport.

parallel play Type of play in which older infants and toddlers engage with similar materials and share physical space but do not interact with one another.

parenting styles The caregiving style of a child's parents and other family members.

partnerships Alliances with family and community members to support and enhance the well-being and learning of young children.

passive influences Influences that affect a person without the necessity of interaction, such as television.

perspective-taking Acquiring the skills for recognizing and responding to the perspectives of others; not a skill to be expected of infants and toddlers, but the foundations for skills should be set.

philosophy Set of educational beliefs that guide behaviors and decision-making for individual teachers and groups of teachers (e.g., programs).

phonemic features Sounds usually associated with letter symbols.

phonology Understanding the basic sounds of the language and how they are combined to make words.

physical development The acquisition of skills and control of fine and gross motor muscles; occurs rapidly for children age 8 to 18 months as they learn to crawl, stand with support, and walk independently.

physical knowledge Knowledge constructed through the direct interaction with materials.

pincer grasp The physical skill of using the thumb and pointer finger to grasp objects.

planned experiences Curricular experiences designed to enhance and support the individual learning needs, interests, and abilities of the children in an early childhood program.

portfolio Tool for collecting, storing, and documenting what you know about a child and her development and learning.

positive reinforcer Consequences for behavior that have the effect of increasing the frequency or duration of the behavior.

positive self-talk The internalization of positive messages we hear about ourselves from others.

possession Children make special associations between a person and an object, often using a two-word phrase; e.g., "mommy chair" to indicate possession.

pragmatics An understanding of how to engage in communication with others that is socially acceptable and effective.

preconceptual The first substage of Piaget's preoperational stage of cognitive development, in which children can mentally sort some objects and actions.

preoperational stage Piaget's second stage of cognitive development, during which toddlers and preschoolers reason based on perception.

pretend other A child's make-believe other person or object.

pretend self Pretend play directed toward self in which pretense is apparent.

primary caregiving system Method of organizing work in which one teacher is primarily responsible for half of the children and the other teacher is primarily responsible for the rest.

private speech Vygotsky's term for internal dialogue that children use for self-guidance and understanding.

problem solving A guidance technique where the adult assists two or more children with identifying a problem, brainstorming solutions, then selecting, following through with, and evaluating the resolution.

progettazione Italian term that is loosely translated as "flexible planning."

project An ongoing investigation which provokes infants, toddlers, and teachers to construct knowledge.

prosodic patterning Communication strategy in which toddlers learn how to use the appropriate stress and intonation to express their specific ideas.

psychoanalytic theory Freud's theory of personality development, including psychosexual stages.

psychosocial theory Erikson's stage theory of development, including trust, autonomy, identity, and intimacy.

R

rapport building Using the strategies of **calibrating** and **pacing** to establish harmonious agreement between two people.

rating scale Method of recording observational data similar to checklists, but that lists frequencies (e.g., never, seldom, always) or qualities of characteristics or activities (e.g., eats using fingers, eats using spoon, eats using fork).

recurrence A language concept about repetition that young children often express with *more*, e.g., "more ride."

referral Assisting families with locating agencies or professionals who can provide additional support and/or services.

regression Temporary movement back to earlier stages of development after higher levels have been accomplished.

relationships The human need for companionship and close emotional bonds; teachers must consider this need when designing learning environments.

representation Methods for telling others what you think or believe, including but not limited to storytelling, drawing, painting, sculpting with clay or wire.

respect A feeling of high regard for someone and a willingness to treat him or her accordingly.

rights of children The belief that children do not just have needs for adults to deal with but rather rights to appropriate care and education.

role-playing When children represent their ideas by acting them out using props such as puppets, dolls, or other dramatic play materials.

routine care Strategies for meeting the basic needs (e.g., hunger, cleanliness) of infants and toddlers.

running record A long narrative account of a significant period of time for a child, a group, or an activity written using descriptive language.

S

scaffolding A term describing incremental steps in learning and development from simple to complex.

schemes Piaget's concept to explain cognitive patterns of actions used to learn new information.

scribbling Nonsense writing marks that are a precursor to writing.

search for hidden objects The object remains permanent (does not cease to exist) in the child's thinking even when the child cannot see it.

secure attachment A connection between infant and primary caregiver in which the infant feels safe and responds warmly to the caregiver.

self-awareness Sensory-grounded information regarding one's existence; what a person sees, hears, and feels in the body related to self.

self-esteem Personal judgment of worthiness based on an evaluation of having, or not, particular valued characteristics or abilities.

self-health Focus on the physical, social, emotional, and cognitive factors within oneself; taking good care of oneself.

self-recognition Conscious awareness of self as different from others and the environment; occurs first usually between 9 and 15 months of age.

self-regulation The skills necessary to direct and control one's own behavior in socially and culturally appropriate ways.

self-responsibility Taking over responsibility for fulfilling some of one's own needs.

self-soothing Comforting and making oneself at ease.

semantics The study of meaning in language, including concepts.

sense of agency In development of self, the awareness that the child can affect other people, places, and things.

senses principle The need for an environment to be pleasing to the senses, e.g., offering natural light and appealing art to look at.

sensorimotor stage Piaget's first stage of cognitive development, which is focused on motor activity and coordination of movements.

sensory threshold Individual differences in how children respond to environmental stimuli, such as noise when sleeping.

separation and individuation The process of defining self as separate from others, which starts in infancy and continues throughout childhood.

separation anxiety Fear exhibited at the loss of physical or emotional connection with the primary caregiver.

seriation Ordering items in sequence based on criteria such as color, length, or size (e.g., small, medium, large).

sleep Most newborns sleep between 11 and 21 hours a day. Infant sleep is not a continuous activity.

social learning theories A body of theory that adds social influences to behaviorism to explain development.

social-arbitrary knowledge Culturally constructed knowledge (e.g., language, values, rules) that is passed on or transmitted from one person to another through social interactions.

sociocultural theory Vygotsky's theory on development, which predicts how cultural values, beliefs, and concepts are passed from one generation to the next.

solitary play Playing alone; a child may look at other children and play near them, but children do not yet interact.

special education Specially designed instruction provided to children in all settings (such as the classroom, the home, and hospitals or community agencies).

special rights The right that a child has to education that is individualized to address her or his strengths as well as areas of developing potential.

stability Within the first month, infants can lift their heads; by the third month they are using their arms to push against the floor to raise their heads and chests.

stages Normal patterns of development that most people go through in maturation, first described by Jean-Jacques Rousseau.

stimuli The initial energy behind a need that creates an action.

stranger anxiety Fear exhibited by older infants and toddlers (begins typically around nine months of age) toward people who are different or unknown; demonstrates their growing cognitive abilities.

substitution Using a "meaningless" object in a creative or imaginative manner or using an object in a pretense act in a way that differs from how the child has previously used the object.

sudden infant death syndrome (SIDS) A tragic event in which a young child dies after going to sleep for a nap or at bedtime with no prior indication of discomfort.

survival of the fittest Darwin's theory that only the best-adapted members of a species are able to continue to thrive.

symbolic play Children's symbolic representations of objects, feelings, or ideas.

synchrony See **interactional synchrony**.

syntax How words combine into understandable phrases and sentences.

T

tabula rasa Locke's term, Latin for "blank slate," which implies that infants are a blank screen at birth and are completely molded by the influences of the environment.

teaching A process of active instruction and interactions that provides materials and guidance so that learning can occur.

teething Begins in infants approximately four to eight months old and refers to teeth breaking through the gums.

telegraphic speech When infants and toddlers combine two or three words into a sentence including only key words (e.g., "go daddy").

temper tantrum Angry emotional outburst and frustrated behavior when an infant or toddler suddenly wants to do things he or she may not do and does not want to do things he or she can do.

temperament Physical, emotional, and social personality traits and characteristics.

toddler A child between 10 and 36 months of age.

toilet learning The developmental process for gaining control of bladder and bowels; complex process involving physical, cognitive, social, emotional, and language skills.

transparency A component of environmental design that allows you to supervise easily because see-through materials (such as fabrics or decorated acrylic) are used to divide spaces.

trial and error An approach to exploration during which the child utilizes a number of strategies and observes the results of these actions.

U

universal precautions Medical term for a series of standard procedures used to keep the patient and staff as healthy and safe as possible during physical care.

W

walking Upright locomotion; initially executed with support from an adult or furniture and then usually occurring without support around the child's first birthday.

weekly plans Approach to curriculum where experiences are planned on a weekly basis based on specific observations of the children.

Y

you statements Sentences that give advice to or judgment about another person, often closing off further communication.

young infant A child between birth and eight months of age.

Z

zone of proximal development Vygotsky's term for a range of tasks that a child is developmentally ready to learn.

Index

A

Acceptance, child's feeling of, 80, 371, 412, 432
Accommodation, 43
Accreditation, 124
Acquired Immune Deficiency Syndrome (AIDS), 58
ACT (Adults and Children Together) Against Violence, 19
Active alert sleep, 39
Active listening, 179–180
  with families, 182–187
Active sleep, 39
Activities
  birth to 6 months, *92*, 293, 299–300, 304–306
  eighteen to 24 months, 377–378
  eight to twelve months, *92*, 334–335
  four to eight months, 313–315
  infants, 87
  levels, 73–74
  physical knowledge and, 47
  pretense, 49
  30 to 36 months of age, *92*, 420–422
  toddlers, 88
  twelve to eighteen months, *92*, 356–358
  24 to 30 months of age, 40, *92*, 399–403
  See also Play
Activity level, *73*–74
Action sentences, 409
Adaptation, 43, *73*
Ad Council, 19
Adult depression and infant cognitive development case study, 407
Advocacy, 125–126, 228–229
African Americans, 60
Agency, sense of, 85
Aggression, 78, 84, 89
AIDS, 20, 58
AIDS case study, 246–247
Ainsworth, M. D., 86, 106, 112, 307, 329
Albus, K, 423
Alert times, 39, 273
Aloof, 81
American Academy of Child and Adolescent Psychiatry (AACAP), 94

American Academy of Pediatrics, 57
American Association on Intellectual and Developmental Disabilities, 58
American Association on Mental Retardation, 58
The American Dental Association (ADA), 36
American Medical Association (AMA), 57
American Psychological Association, 94
American Public Health Association, 244
The American Red Cross, 236
Anecdotal records, 134, *136*
Anisfeld, M., 299, 301, 324, 342, 343, 344, 385, 408, 409
Anti-bias Classroom (Hall), 258
Anti-Bias Curriculum (Derman-Sparks and A.B.C. Task Force), 257–258
Anti-Bias Curriculum: Tools for Empowering Young Children (Derman-Sparks), 257
Approach behavior, 74
Approval, 69, *164*. *See also* Three As of child care
Aronson, S. S., 246, 268
Arrival time, 263
Assessment, 7–8, 137–138, 141–142, 423–424
Assimilation, 43
Association for Childhood Education International, 126
At-risk children, 57
  biologically, 57
  environmentally, 95
  families with, 192–195
Attachment disorder, 94
Attachment-in-the-making phase, 85
Attachment theory
  birth to four months, 307–309
  caregiver role, 85–88, 106–109
  continuity of care, 16
  controversies, 13
  developmental influences of, 11, 307–309
  disorder, 94
  family education, 188
  family grouping, 16
  histories, 86–87

importance of, 86–86
overview, 11, 13, 16, 18
phases, 85–86
secure versus insecure patterns, 86
social development, 85–88, 307–309, 328–331
styles, 86
Attention, 69, 76, 109–111. *See also* Three As of child care
Attention span, 74
Attribution, 409
Attunement, 69. *See also* Three As of child care
Authentic documentation, 137–139
Autism, 94
Autism Spectrum Disorders, 94
Autonomy, 69
Avoidant attachment, 106

B

Babbling, 52, 324, *325*, *345*, *366*
Baby Signs, 54
Back to Sleep Campaign, 235
Bandura, Albert, 11
Bank Street College, 257
Barton, L. R., 386, 389, 415
Bayley Scales of Infant Development, 407
Behaviorism, 10
Belmont, M. J., 10
Beyond the Whiteness of Whiteness (Lazarre), 257
Bias, 257–258
Bidirectional influences, 23
Binet, Alfred, 9
Biofeedback, 269
Biologically at-risk children, 57
Birch, H. G., 72, 73
Birth to 36 months, 28–65, 355–374
  activities, *92*
  birth to four months, 287–310
  children with special needs, 54–59
  cognitive/language development, 42–54
  developmental needs of, 29–42, 213–215
  eighteen to 24 months, 35, *36*, 40, 44, 48, 72, 79, 86, 94, *238*, 376–396

493

494 INDEX

Birth to 36 months *(continued)*
   eight to twelve months, 7–8, *36*, 44, *238*, 333–353
   emotional development, 35, 67–83
   four to eight months, *36*, 44, 71, *238*, 312–332
   physical development, 29–42
   social development, 83–93
   30 to 36 months, *36*, 38, 43–45, 53, 70, 71, 72, 85, *92*, *238*, 420–440
   twelve to eighteen months, 7–8, 32, 33, *36*, 79, 141, *238*, 355–374
   24 to 30 months, 33, *36*, 38, 40, 43, 44, 53, 71, 85, *92*, *238*, 399–417
Bodily fluids, 241–242
Body
   feeling states and, 67–68
   movement and classroom design, 212, 213, 221
   weight, 33–34
Body language. *See* Nonverbal communication
Bonding, 71–72
Bowlby, John, 11
Brain development, 30–33
   birth to 24 months, 30
   caregiver influence, 32–33
   overview, 31–32
   plasticity, 31
   recent research, 31
   twelve to eighteen months, 32
   24 months and over, 32
Brain plasticity, 31
Breast-feeding case study, 298, 331
Bredekamp, S., 106, 123, 124, 152, 176, 210, 212, 216, 218, 221, 275, 363, 426
Bronfenbrenner, Urie, 12–13, 15, 23
Bruner, Jerome, 43, 291

C

Calibrating, 177
California, Easter Seals Child Development Center Network, 258
Care and education plans, 142
Caregivers
   advocacy strategies, 19, 125–126, 228–229
   assessments, 141–143, 423–424
   attachment behavior, 11–12, 16, 18, 307–309

caring attitude, 112, 122, 152
children with special rights, 54–59, 93–96
development-enhancing strategies, 7, 32, 50
   appropriate practices, 123–124, 176
   cognitive/language development, 43, 297–303, 321–326, 341–346, 362–366, 382–389, 406–412, 424–430
   cultural diversity, 22
   Developmental Prescription, 38, 71
   Developmental Profile, 7–9, 142
   emotional development, 77, 303–307, 326–328, 347–349, 367–371, 389–*391*, 412–*414*, 431–434
   physical development, 32, 33–34, 37, 291–297, 316–321, 336–341, 359–*362*, 379–382, 403–405, 422–424
   research, 86–87, 89, 107–108, 123, 128–129
   social development, 82–83, 85, 307–309, 328–331, 349–351, 371–372, 391–394, 414–416, 434–436
evaluations, 141–143
families' relationships with, 123
   additional support for, 191–198
   communication, 181–191
   conferences, 188–190
   curriculum, 254–255
   feeding relationship, 298
   home visits, 190–191
   interactions, 6, 20, 84, 125, 299, 343, 407
   partnership, 19, 187–191, 228–229
   principles, 23–24, 153–154
knowledge acquisition, 21–22, 123–126
language development and, 53, 54
mental health, 94, 121–123
neurological growth, impact on children, 33
newborns, 23
observations influence on decisions, 130–141
physical health, 121–123
professional preparation, 126–128
as professionals, 122–123
respectful attitude, 122
responsiveness of, 11, 14

routine care, 18
self-awareness influenced by, 71, 76–77
self-care, 122
self-image, 121–122
temperament, 75–76, 326–328
three As and, 69, 106–109
of toddlers, 6, 18, 23, 356
See also Caregiving
Caregiving
   attachment and, 11–12, 16, 18, 106–107, 307–309
   care setting influences, 259–261
   custodial care versus, 143
   educational philosophy, 260–261
   empathy influenced by, 78
   importance of, 71–72, 86–88, 104–105
   locus of control and, 88–91
   partnership, 124–125, 187–191, 228–229
   physical development influenced by, 32, 33–34, 37
   principles of, 6, 153–154
   program implementation, 124
   respectful attitudes, 113
   self-esteem influenced by, 9, 80, 82
   styles, 78, 177
   teacher education's impact on, 41, 128–130
   temperament influenced by, 75–76, 326–328
   ten principles of, 6
   three As and, 69, 106–109
   time factors in, 18–19
   See also Caregivers; Primary caregiving system
Caring, caregivers' attitude of, 122, 152
Caring community of learners, 152
Castle, J., 47, 391, 432
Caucasian American children, 14
Causality, *342*, *363–364*
Cause and effect, 362
CDA. *See* Child Development Associate
Centers for Disease Control and Prevention (CDC), 94
Central nervous system (CNS), 57
Cerebral cortex, 32, 33
Cerebral palsy, 57
Checklists, 136–*137*
Chess, S., 72, 73, 75
Child abuse/neglect, 20, 68, 95, 194–195
The Child Advocate, *126*

INDEX 495

Child care centers
  case study, 24
  curriculum influence of, 227, 260
  family, 259
  indoor equipment, 245
  influences from, 259–261
  material waste and, 228
  not-for-profit, 187
  on-site, 254
  policy boards, 187
  safety of, 246
  staff, 198
  time and, 260
Child care environment, 149–172, 215–225
  age-appropriate materials, 18, 143, 230–233, 244
  boundaries, 213, *225*
  child's perspective, 215–225
    discovery, 224
    documentation, 139, 221–222
    environmental design, *225*
    flexibility, 218
    identity, 58, 71–72, 219–221
    independence, 72, 80, 110–111, 223
    influences from, 261–262
    limits, 166–168
    morality, 89
    movement, 221, 291–292
    overview, 215–216
    relationships, *92*, 165–166, 218–219
    representation, 218–219, 223
    senses, 222–223
    transparency, 216–218
  curriculum influence of, 227, 252–262
  design principles, 206, 216–*225*
  emotional, 82–83
  equipment/materials, 143, 230–234, 237–*238*, 242–246
  family grouping, 16, 18
  intelligence, influencing factors, 76, 105, 298
  management of, 211
  messy versus dry, 210–211
  noisy versus quiet, 211–212
  observation of, 130–141
  organization of, 244–246
  pathways, 213, *225*
  physical, 82–83, 229–230
  review/assessment of, 229–230
  safe/secure, 212–213, 235–246
  society's perspective, 227–229
    curricular changes, 227
    environmental changes, 226–227
    partnerships/advocacy, 228–229
  stimulating, 212
  teacher's perspective, 210–215
    basic needs, 213–215
    environmental design, *225*
    learning centers, 206–215, *225*
    security, 212–213
    use of space, 210–212
  trust, 69–70, 111–112
Child Care Health Handbook, 236
Child-centered caregiving, 9, 23
Child development and care
  associate certificate for, 127
  cultural diversity, 21–23
  current needs/trends, 15–21, 23
  current theories, 4–5, 11–13, 20
  Developmental Profile, 7–9
  historical theories, 9–14
  theories of, 9–21
  See also Development
Child Development Associate (CDA), 127
Child Development Associate Certificate, 127–*128*
Child-directed speech, 53
Child Welfare League of America, *126*
Choices, 168–169
Choke tube, 234
Classical conditioning, 10
Classical music, 230
Classroom. *See* Child care environment
Clear-cut attachment phase, 86
Cleft lip/palate, and socio-emotional development, 35
Cognitive constructivism, 43
Cognitive developmental theory
  Piaget's, 11, 42–45, 72, *322*, *342*, *363*–*364*, *427*
  Vygotsky's, 48–51
Cognitive disorders, 58
Cognitive function of language, 45–46, 385
Cognitive/language development, 42–54, 297–303, 321–326, 341–346, 362–367, 406–412
  birth to four months, 43–44, 297–303
  cognitive functions, 45–46, 385
  cognitive structures, 46
  eighteen to 24 months, 44, 48, *382*–*384*
  eight to twelve months, 44, 341–346
  four to eight months, 43, 44, 321–326
  infants, 44, 52–53
  knowledge construction, 43, 46
  knowledge types, 46–48
  language development, 51–54
  nine to twelve months, 44, 53
  Piaget's theory, 11, 43–45, 72, *322*, *342*, *363*–*364*
  play, 48–*49*
  stages, 43–45
  strategies for enhancing, 297–303, 321–326, 341–346, 362–366, 382–*384*, 406–412
  30 to 36 months, 43–45, 53, 424–430
  twelve to eighteen months, 44, 362–366
  24 to 30 months, 42–54, 406–412
  See also Language development
Colleagues, communication with, 198–200
Communication, 176–201
  children and, 160–166
    emotional regulation, 77, 160, 163–164
    labeling/expressing feelings, 160–163
    perspective-taking, 165–166
  with colleagues, 198–200
    collaboration, 199
    decision-making, 200
    feedback, 199
    listening, 198
    support, 199–200
  daily communication log, 140
  with families, 181–198
    active listening, 182–187
    at-risk families, 192–195
    caregiver conferences, 188–190
    classroom design for, 123–124
    education of, 188
    expectations, 185–187
    feelings, 185
    grandparents as parents, 191–192
    home visits, 190–191
    information gathering, 183
    information sharing, 184
    partnering with, 187–188, 228–229
    teacher's perspective, 181–182
    teenage parents, 195–198
  process, 176–177
  skills
    active listening, 179–180
    I versus you statements, 178–179
    mirroring, 180–181
    rapport building, 177–178
Communication disorders, 58–59, 94

496 INDEX

Compact fluorescent lightbulbs (CFLs), 226
Conferences, family-caregiver, 188–190
Consequences, 168
Constructivism
  cognitive, 43, 362
  social, 43
Consumer Product Safety Commission, 243, 244
Context-bound words, 344–345
Continuity of care, 16, 18, 24, 107, 154, 216
Controlling caregiver style, 157–158
Cooing, 52, 301, *325*
Coopersmith, S., 80
Coordination, as cognitive development stage, 44
Copple, C., 106, 123, 124, 152, 176, 185, 210, 212, 218, 221, 223, 275, 291, 363, 426
Cortisol, 32
Council for Exceptional Children, 58
Council for Professional Recognition, 127
Cowan, P. A., 45, 434
Crawling, 37, 166, 336
Creative Curriculum for Infants, Toddlers, and Twos, 436
Creative Resources for the Anti-bias Classroom, 258
Crying, and sleep patterns, 39
Cultural diversity
  assessments, appropriate, 423–424
  bias and, 256–259
  case study, 24
  communication and, 177
  curriculum influence of, 255–259
  emotional expressions, 431–432
  guidelines, 258–259
  research and, 257–258
  valuing, 21–23
Culture, curriculum influence of, 255–259
Curiosity, 67, 77, 111, 343–344. *See also* Discovery
Curriculum, 251–283
  birth to four months, 290–310
  case study, 282–283
  cognitive/language development, 42–54, 297–303, 321–326, 341–346, 362–366, 424–430
  definition, 252
  educational philosophy and, 260–261
  eighteen to 24 months, 379–396
  eight to twelve months, 251–283, 336–353

emotional development, 67–82, 303–306, 326–328, 347–349, 367–370, 431–434
  feedback, 179–180, 281
  four to eight months, 35–*36*, 67–83, 315–332
individualizing, 252–*253*
infants, 252
influences, 253–281
  child care setting, 257, 259–261
  children, 261–262
  culture, 255–259
  parents, 259
  society, 253–255
overview, 252
physical development, 263, 266, 274, 291–297, 316–321, 336–341, 359–*362*, 379–*382*, 422–424
planned learning experiences, 273–281
  daily plans, 275
  weekly plans, 275–277
routine care, 262–273
social development, 253–254, 307–309, 328–332, 349–*351*, 371–*372*, 434–436
30 to 36 months, 271, 424–430
36 to 42 months, 271
twelve to eighteen months, 251–283, 359–374
24 to 30 months, 251–283
Custodial care, 143

D

Daily communication log, 140
Daily plans, 275
Darwin, Charles, 9
Davies, L., 391, 432
Decision-making, 187
  caregiver-family partnership, 187
  staff, 200
Decroly, Ovide, 153
Deferred imitation, 342, *384*
Dell'Antonia, K. J., 411
Demand feeding, 266
Demonstrative naming, 409
Dental eruption chart, *36*
Descriptive phrasing, 133–134
Detached caregiver style, 78, 86
Development
  assessment of, 7–9, 423–424
  birth to four months, 285–310
  definition, 29

eighteen to 24 months, 29–42, 379–394
  eight to twelve months, 29–42, 336–352
  four to eight months, 29–42
  learning versus, 29–*30*, 59
  needs, 129, 213–215
  overview of, 4–5
  strategies for enhancing, 50, 290–309, 315–331, 336–352, 379–394, 403–416
  30 to 36 months, 29–42, 420–440
  twelve to eighteen months, 29–42, 336–352, 359–374
  24 to 30 months, 29–42, 403–416
  universal versus unique, *13*
  See also Child development and care; Development domains; specific types
Developmentally appropriate practices
  guidelines for, 176
  outcomes of, 128–129
  scope of, 123–124
Developmental perspective, 1–24
  case study, 24
  cultural diversity and, 21–23
  current trends in, 15–21
  infant to toddler, education, 1–23, 129, 153–156
  overview, 4–5
  theories, 9–14
  using a, 5–7
  See also Developmental Profile
Developmental Prescription, 38, 71
Developmental Profile, 7–9
  eighteen to months, 7–*8*
  eight to twelve months, 7–*8*
  four to eight months, 7–*8*
  30 to 36 months, 7–*8*, 436–437
  security and trust, 71
  twelve to eighteen months, 7–*8*
  24 to 30 months, 7–*8*
  using, 7–9
Development domains, 6–7
  cognitive/language, 6, 42–54
  defined by Goleman, 76–79
  emotional, 6, 35, 76–78
  physical, 6, 29–41
  social, 6, 82–*92*, 253–254
  theoretical contributions, 9–14, 35, 42–51, 76–78
Devries, R., 47, 424, 425
Dewey, John, 105
Diapering, 18, 268–271

INDEX   497

Differentiation, as phase in individuation, 44, 71
Disabilities
  definition, 56
  cognitive and developmental, 58
  hearing, 57–58
  language and communication, 58–59
  medically fragile, 58
  motor, 57
  multiple, 94–95
  visual, 57
Discipline, 157–160
  choices, 168–169
  consequences, 168
  definition, 157
  disposition enhancing projects, 421
  labeling expressed emotions, 160–163
  limits, 166–168
  mental models, 158–160
  perspective-taking, 164–166
  principles, 153–154
  problem solving, 169–170
  redirection, 169
  regulating emotions, 163–164
Discovery, classroom design for, 224. *See also* Curiosity
Disequilibrium, 43
Disorder, 56
Disoriented attachment, 107
Distractibility, *73*
Diversity and the New Teacher: Learning from experience in urban schools, 258
Documentation, classroom design for, 221–222
Documentation panels, 139
Doubt, 69
Down syndrome, 58
Down Syndrome Association, 58
Dramatic play, 58, 428
Drew, C. J., 56, 58, 60, 94, 95, 95
Drowsiness, as sleep pattern, 39
Dynamic systems theory, 37

E

Early childhood educators. *See* Caregivers
Early Head Start, 20–21, 94, 95
Early intervention, 56
Easter Seals California Child Development Center Network, 258

Eating, 266–267, 317–318
  birth to four months, 297
  classroom design for, 213–214
  curriculum planning for, 266–267
  eighteen to 24 months, 266–267, *382*
  eight to twelve months, 266–267, *340–341*
  four to eight months, 266–267, 317–318, *321*
  twelve to eighteen months, 266–267, *361–362*
  24 to 30 months, 266–267, *405*
Ecological systems theory, 12, 13, 15, 110
Educating citizens in a multicultural society (Banks), 258
Educational philosophy, 260–261
Egan, M. W., 56, 58, 60, 94, 95, 95
Egocentrism, 81, 371
Eidelman, A. I., 407
Eighteen to 24 months, 376–396
  cognitive/language development, 42–54, 382–*384*
  Developmental Profile, 7–9
  development-enhancing strategies, 29–42, 382–394
  emotional development, 35–*36*, 67–83, 389–*391*
  equipment/materials, *238*
  language development, 44, 384–389
  materials/activities, 143, 377–378
  physical development, 29–42, 379–382
  reapproachment subphase, 72
  social development, 83–93, 253–254, 391–394
  special needs children, 94
Eight to twelve months, 333–354
  cognitive/language development, 44, 341–346
  Developmental Profile, 7–*8*
  development-enhancing strategies, 29–42, 336–352
  emotional development, 35–*36*, 67–83, 85–86, 347–349
  equipment/materials, *238*
  materials/activities, 143, 334–335
  physical development, 29–42, 336–341, *342*
  sensorimotor stage, 44
  social development, 83–93, 253–254, 349–351
Elimination, 29, 41, 270, *405*, *423*
Emergency procedures, 235

Emotional contagion, 78
Emotional detachment, 68
Emotional development, 67–82, 303–306, 326–328, 347–349, 367–371
  birth to four months, 67–82, 303–306
  bonding and separation-individuation theory, 71–72
  case study, 96–97
  cleft lop/palate case study and, 35
  eighteen to 24 months, 389–*391*
  eight to twelve months, 67–82, 85–86, 347–349
  emotional intelligence, 76–80
  expressions, 431–432
  fear, 326, *328*, 349
  feelings, 67–68, *328*, 369
  fifteen to eighteen months, 72
  four to eight months, 326–328
  metacognition, 76
  patterns, 67–82
  psychosocial theory, 68–71
  regulation, 77, 163–164, *306*, *328*, *370*, *414*
  security/trust, 69
  self-awareness, 76
  self-esteem, 80–82
  strategies for enhancing, 303–306, 326–328, 347–349, 367–371, 389–*391*, 403–416, 431–434
  temperament, 72–76, *306*, 326–328
  ten to fifteen months, 67–82, 85, 87
  30 to 36 months, 67–82, 85, 431–434
  36 months and beyond, 68
  twelve to eighteen months, 367–371
  24 to 30 months, 67–82, 85, 412–414
  types of, 306, 328, 349, 369, 414
Emotional intelligence, 76–80
Emotional intelligence (Goleman), 76
Emotional regulation, 77, 163–164
Emotional talk, 160–162
Emotion-centered, 162–163
Empathy, 78
Enlightened self-interest, 81
Environment. *See* Child care environment
Environmental design principles, 206
Environmental factors
  adverse, 20
  alcohol (FAE, FAS), 95
  brain development, 4–5, 13, 31–33
  crises and, 14
  genetic code and, 5, 31
  individual potential influenced by, 5, 11, 84

498 INDEX

Environmental factors *(continued)*
  infant and toddler problems, 95, 169–170
  patterns of development, 13
  physical, 229–230
  temperament, 72–73, 326–328
  See also Caregiving
Environmentally at-risk children, 95, 192–195
Equilibration, 43
Equilibrium, 43
Equipment, 230–234
  age-appropriate, 230–233, 244
  at-risk children, 55
  basic, *231*
  cost, 232–234
  fall surface, 244–245
  guide for analyzing, *238*
  maintenance, 245
  selection, 230–234
  supervision of, 244
  types, *237*
Erikson, Erik, 9–10
Erikson's stages of development, 68–71
Ethnographic reports, 134
Ethology, 11, 85–86, 112
Everyday Acts Against Racism (Reddy), 258
Evolutionary theory, 67–68
Exceptional children, 56
Exosystem, 12, 19
Expectations
  for caregivers, 67, 70
  for children, 8–9, 38
  for family members, 84, 185–187, 254
Experience-dependent neuron pathways, 33
Experience-expectant neuron pathways, 33
Exploratory levels of play, *49*

F

Familiar objects, 212
Families
  assessment/education of, 188
  attachment histories, 11, 86–87
  attachment roles, 11–13
  beliefs in, 110
  caregivers' relationships with, 19, 176–201
  as child experts, 19
  communication, 181–187
  conferences, 188–190
  curriculum, 254–256
    expectations, 185–186, 254
    home visits, 190–191
    partnership, 19, 187–191, 228–229
    principles, 23–24, 153–154
  competency goals, 176
  cultural differences in, 256, 257, 258
  definition, 176n
  expectations, 254–256
  facts and figures on, in the United States, *17*
  feeding relationship, 298
  groupings, 16–21
  Individualized Family Service Plan, 95
  interactions, 6, 84
  knowledge acquisition of, 123
  low income, 254
  partnering with, 187–191, 228–229
  requiring additional support
    at-risk children, 57, 192–195
    child abuse/neglect in, 20, 68, 95, 194–195
    grandparents as parents, 191–192
    teenage parents, 195–198
    statistics on, *17*
  styles of, 255, 260
  See also Parents
Family child care homes, 259
Family grouping, 16–21
Father-child interactions, 84, 257
Fear, 10, 78, 91, 112, 176, 326, *349, 369*
Feedback
  active listening and, 179–180
  colleagues and, 179
  on curriculum, 281
  rapport building, 177
  reactionary, 179–180
  sharing, 199
  sheets, 189
Feeding relationship, 298
Feelings, 67–68
  caregiver-family communication about, 185, 199
  control of, *370, 391*
  emotional development, 303–304, 412–414
  evolution of, 67–68
  labeling/expressing, 160–163
  primary emotions, 161
  types of, *308, 328, 349, 369, 414, 434*
  visual chart, *161*
  See also entries beginning Emotional
Feldman, R., 407

Fetal alcohol syndrome/fetal alcohol effect (FAS/FAE), 95
Fine motor control, 37
Finger foods, 267, 318
Fire drills, 235
First aid, 236, 240–241
Florida, 17
Flow, 77–78
Food. *See* Eating
Forebrain, 31–32
Four to eight months, 312–332
  cognitive/language development, 42–54, 321–326
  Developmental Profile, 7–9
  development-enhancing strategies, 29–42, 315–332
  emotional development, 35–36, 67–83, 326–328
  equipment/materials, *238*, materials/activities, 143, 313–315
  language development, 43, 44, 321–326
  physical development, 29–42, 316–321
  separation-individuation, 71
  social development, 83–93, 253–254, 328–331
Fox, N. A., 114, 158–159, 304
Franyo, G. A., 76
Freud, Sigmund, 9
Functional ability, *49*

G

General developmental disorders, 58
Gerber, Magda, 6, 15
Gesell, Arnold, 9, 13
Gestural communication, 53
Goleman, Daniel, 76–78
Goodness-of-fit model, adult-child, 75, 327
Good Samaritan Law, 240
Grammatical words, 325
Grandparents as parents, 191–192
Green environment, *229*
Gross motor control, 37
Guidance strategies, positive, 368–369. *See also* Childcare environment
Guilt, 69, 82, 183, 185, 255

H

Hall, G. Stanley, 9
Handedness, 380, *381*, 404, 422, *423*
Hand washing, 214, 220, 271–272

Hardman, M. L., 56, 58, 60, 94, 95, 95
Hay, D. F., 81, 370, 391, 432
Head Start, 21, 57, 165, 190, 362
Health
    classroom environment and, 235–246
    emergency procedures, 235
    first aid, 236, 240–241
    Human Immunodeficiency Virus (HIV) Infection, 243
    immunization, 236, *239*
    injuries, 243–246
    policies, 235–236, 241, 246
    services, 13, *17*, 19, 56, 57, 58, 95
    symptoms of severe illness, 236
    universal precautions, 241–243
Healthy caregiver style, 78
Healy, Jane, 297, 322, 425
Hearing development, 34, 57–58, 291, 299, *320*
Hearing disabilities, 57–58
Hepatitis B, 241
Herr, J., 33, 53, 184, 193, 234, 268, 308, 389
High active children, 74, 327
High/Scope for Infants and Toddlers, 436
Hindbrain, 31–32
HIV infection, 243
Holsington, C., 433
Homemade materials, 233–234
    birth to four months, 289–290
    eighteen to 24 months, 378
    eight to twelve months, 334–335
    four to eight months, 313–315
    overview, 233–234
    30 to 36 months, 420–421
    twelve to eighteen months, 358
    24 to 30 months
Home-school journals, 139–140
Home-school relationship. *See* Families: caregivers' relationships with
Home visits, 190–191
Human Immunodeficiency Virus (HIV) infection, 243
Hyson, M. C., 4, 76, 78, 127, 162, 163, 169

I

Identity, child's, 58, 71–72, 219–221
Illness, symptoms of severe, 236
Imitation, 11, *342, 364*
The Immigrant Child Advocacy Center, *126*
Immunization, 236, *239*

Independence, child's, *92,* 110–111, 209–210, 223
Individual constructivism, 362
Individualized Family Service Plan, 95
Individual rights, 55
Individuals with Disabilities Education Act (IDEA), 54, 94
Individuation, 71–72
Infants. *See* Birth to eight months; Eight to twelve months; Four to eight months
Infant persistence, 343
Infant-Toddler Specialists of Indiana (ITSI), 127–128
Information gathering/sharing, 183–184
Initiative, 69
Injuries, 243–246
Insensitivity, 81
Inserimento (transition/adjustment period), 155–156
Instrumental function of language, 51–54, 385
Interactional synchrony, 79, 116
Interactional synchrony case study, 116
International Reading Association, 19
Interpretative phrasing, 133–134
Intersubjectivity, 50
I statements, 178–179

J

Jargon, 53

K

Kamii, C., 47
Kantor, R., 277, 281, 382
King, Andre, 258
Knowledge, types of, 46–47
Knowing, development of, 46

L

Lamme, Linda, 344, 345, 366, 387, 411
Language development
    birth to four months, 297–303
    caregivers impact on, 53
    eighteen to 24 months, 44, 51–54, 384–389
    eight to twelve months, 341–346
    four to eight months, 43–44, 51–54, 315–332
    infants, 44, 52–53
    nine to twelve months, 44, 53, 51–54

    strategies for enhancing, 53–54, 297–303, 321–326, 341–346, 362–367, 384–389, 406–412, 424–430
    theories, 52
    30 to 36 months, 51–54
    twelve to eighteen months, 51–54, 362–367
    24 to 30 months, 43, 44, 53, 51–54, 406–412
    See also Cognitive/language development
Language disorders, 58
Learning, 29
    definition, 29
    development versus, 29–*30*, 59
    skills needed for, 126
    standards for, *128*
    toilet, 40–41
    See also Planned learning experiences
Learning centers, 207–210, 277
    boundaries, 213, *225*
    combining, 218
    curriculum planning, 142, 277
    design perspective, *225,* 277
    flexibility and, 218
    independence versus dependence, 209–210
    indoor, 206–207, 211, 245
    location of, 207, 212, 215
    materials, 143
    number of work spaces, 208
    outdoor, 207–208, 211, *231,* 240, 245
    placement of, 223
    rotating, 218
Learning environment. *See* Child care environment
Least restrictive environment, 55
Lexical words, 325
Libidinal object constancy, 71, 72
Licensing regulations, 123–124
Light, classroom design for, 226
Light-emitting diodes (LEDs), 226
Limits, setting of, 166–168
Listening
    active, 179–180
    to colleagues, 198
    to families, 182–187
Little Folks Child Care Center, 24
Locke, John, 9
Locomotion
    defined, 37
    eighteen to 24 months, 380–382

Locomotion *(continued)*
    eight to twelve months, *339*,
    four to eight months, 316–317, *319*, 329
    strategies to enhance development, 336
    twelve to eighteen months, 361
Locus of control, 88–91
Logical consequences, 168
Logico-mathematical knowledge, 47, 424–425
Loizou, E., 129
Looping, 16
Low active children, 73–74, 327

M

Macrosystem, 13
Mahler, Margaret, 71–72
Make-believe play, 50–51
Makin, L., 345
Manipulation, 37, 317
Marshall, P. J., 39, 304
Maryland Committee for Children, 233–234
Massachusetts Department of Public Health, 245
Mastery, versus approval, *164*
Mastery climate, 152
Materials
    access to, 226–227
    age-appropriate, 230–233, 244
    amount of, 217, 233
    birth to four months, 288–290
    choke tube, 234
    cost, 232–233, 234
    culturally diverse, 23
    curriculum planning and, 208, 246, *253*, 261, 263–264, *276–277*
    eighteen to 24 months, *49*, 377–378
    eight to twelve month, 334–335
    four to eight months, *49*, 313–315
    guide for analyzing, *238*
    homemade, 233–234, 289–290, 313–315, 334–335, 358, 378, 400–403, 420–421
    management of, 230–234
    open-ended, 208–209, 218, 223, 225, *264*, 277, 406, 436
    organization of, 244–246
    real objects, 208, *225*, *237*
    selection, 230–234
    30 to 36 months, *49*, 420–422
    twelve to eighteen months, *49*, 356–358
    24 to 30 months, *49*, 399–403
    types, *237*, 289, 313, 334, 357, 377, 400, 420
Maturational perspective, 9, 71
Maturation, 9, 71
May, N., 277, 281,
Medically fragile children, 58
Mental health disorders, 94
Mental images, 406
Mental models, 158–160
Merril Palmer Institute Child Development Lab, 257
Mesosystem, 12, 16, 19
Metacognition, 76–77
Microsystem, 12, 16
Midbrain, 31, 78
Milestones
    assessment and, 7, 136, 139, 141–142
    children with disorders, 58
    definition, 7
    developmental, 38, 85
    motor development, 37–38
    physical, 34
    social development, *92*
Mirroring, 180–181
Modeling, 11–*12*, 22, 158–160, 436
Modified CHecklist for Autism in Toddlers (M-CHAT), 423
Moods, 73
Moral development, 81, 89, 215–216
Motivation, 77–78
Motor development, 37–38
    birth to four months, 37, 291–292, *294–295*
    eighteen to 24 months, 38
    eight to twelve months, 37, 336–341
    fine motor control, 37
    four to eight months, 37, 316–321
    gross motor control, 37
    milestones, 37
    30 to 36 months, 38
    twelve to eighteen months, 37, 359–*362*
    24 to 30 months, 38
Motor disabilities, 57
Movement, classroom design for, 221
Multiple disabilities, 94–95
Muscular control
    birth to four months, *294–295*
    development, 291, 293, *294–295*, *318–320*, *360–362*, *380–382*, *404–405*, *422–423*
    eighteen to 24 months, *380–382*
    eight to twelve months, 336, *338–341*
    four to eights months, *318–320*,
    30 to 36 months, *422–423*
    twelve to eighteen months, *360–362*
    24 to 30 months, *404–405*
Music, 67, 132, 211–213, 230
Myelin, 30
Myelomeningocele, 57

N

Nap time, 116, 142–143, 215, 263–265
Narcissism, 81
Narratives, 134
National Association for Family Child Care (NAFCC), 124, *126*
National Association for Nursery Education (NANE), 362
National Association for the Education of Young Children (NAEYC), 4, 19, 124, 127, *128*
National Association of Child Care Resource and Referral Agencies (NACCRRA), 4, *126*, 274–275
National Association of the Deaf, 58
The National Children's Advocacy Center, *126*
National Council for Accreditation of Teacher Education (NCATE), 20
National Council for Exceptional Children, 57
National Family Child Care Association (NFCCA), 4
National Resource Center for Health and Safety in Child Care, 244–245
National Society for Children and Adults with Autism, 94
National Society for the Prevention of Blindness, 57
Natural selection, 9
Nature versus nurture, 29
Negation, 409
Negative reinforcers, 10
Neurological development, 29–33
Neuroscience imaging techniques, 11
Noble savages, 9
Noise, 10, 34, 211–212, 222
Nonverbal classification stage, 45, *407*, *427*
Nonverbal communication
    active listening and, 161, 176–179
    learning enhancement, 54
    rapport building and, 177–178

Normal autistic phase, in individuation, 71
Normative approach, 9
"No," saying, 72, 134, 168, 368
Novel objects, 212
Number stage, 45, *408*, *427*

O

Obama, President, 21
Object permanence, 72, *322*, 341–342, *363*, *384*
Observations, 130–141
   assessment of, 141–142
   authentication of, 137–139
   of caregivers, 130–132
   development and, 290
   methods of, 42–43, 130, 132–137, 139–141
   objects of, 131–132
   rating scales, 137
   reasons for, 130–131
   recording findings, 132–133
   self-, 76
   uses of, 142–143
Observational learning, 11
Omnipotence, 72
Open-ended materials, 208–209, 218, 223, 232, 237, *364*, 406
Organization
   cognitive function of, 43, 385
   defined, 43
   family- and work-life issues, 254
   improvements in, 131
   principles, 154
Original sin, 9
Outdoor safety, 243–246
Overgeneralization (language), 365–366
Over-regularization (language), 409, 428

P

Pacific Oaks College, 257
Pacing, 177
Pain, role of, 67
Parallel play, *92*, 170, 371–372
Parents
   assessment/education of, 188
   attachment histories, 11, 86–87
   competency goals, 176
   cultural expectations of, 255–256
   curriculum influence of, 255–256
   depression, influence on cognitive development, 407
   eating, 297
   feeding relationship, 298
   grandparents as, 191–192
   HIV-infected children, 243
   military deployment and, 191–192
   parental incarceration, 193–194
   perfect, 255
   quality time and, 373
   styles of parenting, 16, 260
   teenage, 195–198
   work-at-home, 331–332
   See also Families
Partnerships
   advocacy and, 228–229
   community agencies and organizations, 124–125
   with families, 4–5, 187–191, 228–229
   interventions, 59
   for knowledge acquisition, 16, 124–125
   overview, 124–125
Peers
   conflict with, 392–393
   interactions of toddlers case study, 370
   relationship development, 83
Persistence, *73*–74
Personality, 68, 71–72, 81
Perspective-taking, 165–166
Philosophy, educational, 260–261
Phonology, 51
Physical development, 29–41, 291–297, 316–321, 336–341, 359–*362*
   birth to four months, 33, 35, 37, 39, 40, 43, *294–296*
   eighteen to 24 months, 379–382
   eight to twelve months, 33, 34, 37, 291–297, 336–341
   elimination, 29, 41, 270, *405*, *423*
   four to eight months, 35, 36, 37, 316–321
   hearing, 34, *320*
   motor development, 37–38
   neurology, 29–33
   physical growth, 33–34, 359–*362*
   sight, 32, 295, *320*, *296*
   sleep, 39–40, 215, 292–293, 297, *320*, *340*, *361*, *382*, *423*
   strategies for enhancing, 50, 291–297, 316–321, 336–341, 359–*362*, 379–382, 403–405, 422–424
   teething, 35–37, 318, *321*
   30 to 36 months, 36, 38, 422–424
   toilet learning, 40–41
   twelve to eighteen months, 34, 35, 37, 40, 359–*362*
   24 to 30 months, 33, 38, 40, 403–405
   vision, 35
Physical growth, 33–34
Physical knowledge, 46–47
Piaget, Jean, 11, 42–44
Pincer grasp, 337
Planned experiences, 275
Planned learning experiences, 273–281
   alert times, 273
   daily plans, 142, 275
   feedback, 281
   guidelines, 274–275
   learning centers, 277
   planned experiences, 275
   progettazione, 277
   projects, 277–281
   schedules, 142–143, 263–273
   30 to 36 months, 271
   weekly plans, 275–277
Play, 48–*49*, 215, *342*, *364*
Playground safety, 244–246
Policy boards, child care center, 187
Portfolios, 138
Positive attitudes, 81
Positive guidance strategies, 368
Positive reinforcers, 10
Positive self-talk, 164
Possession, 409
Posture, 177
Poverty, 16–*17*, 20
Powell, Dunlap, and Fox's mental model, 158–160
Practicing, as phase in individuation, 71
Pragmatics, 51
Preattachment phase, 85
Preconceptual stage, 45, 406–*408*, 434
Prelogical thinking, 42
Preoperational stage, 44–45, 406–*408*
Primary caregivers. *See* Caregivers
Primary caregiving system, 18, 24, 87, 188, 350
Primary Scale of Intelligence, 407
Private speech, 50, 406
Progettazione (flexible planning), 277–278
Projects, 277–281
Prosocial behaviors, 91–92
Prosodic patterning, 409–410
Prunes, synapses, 31

INDEX

Psychoanalytic theory, 9
Psychosocial theory, 9–10, 68–71
Punishment, 10, 89, 157, 211

Q

Quantitative CHecklist for Autism in Toddlers (Q-CHAT), 423
Quantity stage, 45, *408*, *427*
Quiet, in classroom, 211–212
Quiet alert, sleep pattern, 39
Quiet sleep, 39

R

Rapid eye movement. *See* REM (rapid eye movement)
Rapport building, 177–178
Rapprochement, as phase in individuation, 71, 72
Rating scales, 137
Reading, 194, 206, 207, 365–366, 428, *430*
Reading aloud, 344–345
Recchia, S. L., 129
Reciprocal relationship phase, 86
Recording
    classroom design for, 140
    importance of, 112–113, 121, 133
    methods of, 132, 139, 227
Recurrence, 409
Recycling center, 234
Red flags, in assessment, 95, 142
Redirection, 169
Reflective self, 5, 139, 153, 281, 389, 433
Reflex, 33, 44, *294*
Reggio Emilia
    curricular planning, 277–278
    history of, 153
    image of the child, 154–155
    inserimento (transition/adjustment period), 155–156
    philosophy of, 55, 153–154
    projects, 154
    rights of children, 15, 55, 153
Regression, 347
Regularity, *73*
Relating, 15
Relationship development, 82–86
    boundaries, 82–86
    classroom design for, 218–219
    emotional intelligence and, 76–80
    father-child interactions, 84

REM (Rapid eye movement), 39–40
Representation, as cognitive development stage, 44
Representation, classroom design for, 218–219, 223
Reproduction, as cognitive development stage, 44
Resistant attachment, 107
Resources and Instruction for Staff Excellence (RISE), 158
Respect
    cautions regarding, 112
    definition, 111
    development and education, 15
    feelings and, 185
    for infants, 6, 81–82, 88, 113, 114
    relationship development, 82–83
    rights of children and, 90, 111, 122
    self-esteem and, 80, 82
Responses, *73*, *164*
reSTORE, recycling center, 234
Rest time. *See* Nap time
Rights of children, 15, 54–59, 93–96, 111
Rinaldi, C., 111, 139, 155, 277–278
Role playing, 383
Roots and Wings (York), 258
Rosenkoetter, S., 386, 389, 407, 415
Rousseau, Jean-Jacques, 9
Routine care, 262–273, 413
    arrival, 263
    daily communication log, 140
    diapering/toileting, 18, 268–271
    eating, 18, 266–267, 297, 317–318, *321*, *340–341*, *361–362*, *405*
    end of day, 273
    events form, *140*
    feedback and, 281
    hand washing, 214, 220, 271–272
    and physical/sexual abuse, 195
    sleeping, 18, 215, 263–265, 292–293, 297, *320*, *340*, *361*, *382*, *423*
    toothbrushing, 37, 272–273
    waking, 39, 265
Running records, 134–*135*

S

Safety
    classroom environment, 235–243
    emergency procedures, 235
    health and, 235–243
    outdoor, 244–246
Sandboxes, 47, 245

Sanderson, M., 277, 281, 382
Scaffolding
    curriculum 252
    definition of, 13, 50
    development, 170, 382
    positive self-talk and, 164
    zone of proximal development (ZPD), 110
Schedules, 142–143, *239*, 263–273
Schemes, 43
Schumann, M. J., 265
Scribbling, 38, 345, 387, *388*, 411, *412*, 429–430
Scripts, 22
Search for hidden objects, 275, 406
Secure attachment, 86, 88, 105–109, 112
Security, 69–71, 212–213, 262, 303. *See also* Safety
Seeking Educational Equity and Diversity (SEED) Project, 258
Self-awareness, 68, 71, 72, 76, 77
Self-concept, 9, 71, 80, 85, 87, *92*, 104
Self-confidence, 69
Self-constancy, 72
Self-control, 51, 88–91, 435
Self-doubt, 82
Self-efficacy, 76, 169
Self, Environment, Child model, 158
Self-esteem, 9, 72, 80–82, 383
Self-expression, 91, 428
Self-health, 116
Self-image
    caregiver's, 121–122
    child's, 154–155, 412
Self-interest, 81
Selfish actions, 68, 81
Selfless caregiver style, 81
Self-recognition, 85, *330*
Self-regulation, 51, 69, 77, 78, 84, 160
Self-responsibility, 69, 77, 80–81, 88–91
Self-soothing, 77, 163, 395
Self-talk, positive, 85, 164
Self-worth, 81, 166, 389, *414*, 432
Semantics, 51
Sense of agency, 85
Senses, classroom design for, 222–223
Sensitivity, 71, 81
Sensorimotor stage, 43–44
    birth to four months, 299–*300*
    eighteen to 24 months, *383–384*
    eight to twelve months, *342*
    four to eight months, *321–322*
    twelve to eighteen months, *363–364*

INDEX 503

Sensory tables, 208, 211, 218
Sensory threshold, *73*, 304
Separation anxiety, 72, 86, 107
Separation-individuation, 71–72
Seriation, 424
Shame, 69, 82, 367, 414
Sickle cell anemia (SCA) case study, 60
Sight, 34, 35, 57, 295, *320*, *296*
Sign language, 32, 54, 58
Skinner, B. F., 10
Sleep apnea, 39
Sleep development, 39–40, 292–293
   birth to four months, 292–293, 297
   eighteen to months, 263–265, *382*
   eight to twelve months, 263–265, *340*
   four to eight months, 263–265, *320*
   infant to toddler, 40, 263–265
   newborns, 39–40
   patterns, 39
   30 to 36 months, 263–265, *423*
   twelve to eighteen months, 263–265, *361*
Sleeping, in child care. *See* Nap time
Smiling, 87, *92*, 109–110, 114
Social-arbitrary knowledge, 47
Social constructivism, 43
Social development, 82–*92*, 253–254, 307–309, 328–332, 349–351, 371–372
   attachment, 86–88, 307–309, *330*
   birth to four months, 85, 92, 253–254, 307–309
   eighteen to 24 months, 391–394
   eight to twelve months, 85–86, 253–254, 349–351
   empathy, 78
   four to eight months, 328–332
   locus of control, 88–91
   milestones, *92*
   prosocial behaviors, 91–92
   relationships, 82–86
   strategies for enhancing, 82, 89, 92, 307–309, 328–332, 349–351, 371–372, 391–394, 414–416, 434–436
   30 to 36 months, 253–254, 434–436
   twelve to eighteen months, 92, 253–254, 371–372
   24 to 36 months, 86, *92*, 253–254, 414–416
Social intelligence (Goleman), 76
Social learning theories, 11, 85

Society, curriculum influence of, 227, 253–254
Sociocultural theory, 13. *See also* Vygotsky's cognitive development theory
Solitary play, 371
Space management, 45, 210–212, *408*, *427*
Special education, 56
Special needs children, 54–59, 93–95
   birth to eighteen months, 94
   categories of, 57–59
   eighteen to 24 months, 94
   emotional and social development, 93–95
   functional ability of, *56*
   identification of, 54
   interventions and, 55, 56
   rights of, 54–55
   resources for, 58, 59
   teachers responsibilities, 95
   team approach to, 59
   terminology for, *56*
Speech, in infants. 50–54, 324, 343, 384. *See also* Language development; specific types
Spina bifida, 5
Spinrad, T., 77, 78, 400
Spoiling children, 87, 88, 112
Stability (movement), 37, 292, 336, 379, 422
Staff. *See* Colleagues
Stages of child development, 9
   Erikson and, 9–10, 68–71, 112
   Piaget and, 11, 43–45, 72, *300*, *322*, *342*, 360, *363–364*, *383–384*, *406–408*, *427*
   Rousseau and, 9
   of sleep, 39
   universal, 13
Standards, *127–128*
State, definition of, 39
Staub, S., 411
Stifter, C. A., 400
Stimulating learning environment, 84, 212–213
Stimuli, 32–33, *73*
Stranger anxiety, *92*, 97, 326
Strange Situation, 86
Sturner, R., 423
Sudden infant death syndrome (SIDS), 39–40
Survival of the fittest, 9

Swim, T. J., 33, 53, 55111, 129, 139, 143, 155, 157, 170, 184, 193, 234, 262, 268, 275, 277, 281, 308, 368, 389
Symbolic play, 84, 383–*384*
Symptoms of severe illness, 236
Syntax, 51, 409, *430*

T

Tabula rasa, 9
Tantrums, 35, 162–163, *349*, 368–*369*, 395, 413
Task analysis, 202
Teacher education, 20, 128–130
Teachers. *See* Caregivers
Teaching/Learning Anti-racism (Derman-Sparks and Phillips), 258
Teenage parents, 195–198
Teething, 35–37, 318, *321*, *382*, *341*, 352
Telegraphic speech, 53, 384–385
Television viewing, 301, 415
Temperament, 72–76, 326–328
Terrible twos, 168
Theories
   bonding and separation-individuation theory, 71–72
   child development and care, 9–14
   cognitive/language development, 29, 37, 42–51
   development domain, 6–7, 76–79
   dynamic systems, 37
   ecological systems, 12, 13, 15, 110
   emotional development, 6, 35, 76–78
   evolutionary theory, 67–68
   infant and toddler needs, 129
   Piaget's theory, 11, 43–45, 72, *322*, *342*, *363–364*
   physical development, 6
   psychoanalytic theory, 9
   psychosocial theory, 9–10, 68–71
   sociocultural theory, 13
   social development, *6*
   See also Attachment theory; Cognitive developmental theory; specific types; Reggio Emilia; Vygotsky's cognitive development theory
30 to 36 months, 420–440
   activities, 40, *92*
   bonding/separation-individuation theory, 71, 72

30 to 36 months, *(continued)*
    cognitive/language development, 42–54, 424–430
    Developmental Profile, 7–9
    development-enhancing strategies, 29–42
    emotional development, 67–83, 431–434
    equipment/materials, *238*
    Erikson's theory, 70
    materials/activities, 143, 420–422
    milestones, 85, *92*
    movement activities, 38
    physical development, 29–42, 422–424
    social development, 83–93, 253–254, 434–436
    teeth, 36
Thomas, A., 72, 73
Thomas, J., 423
Thomson Delmar Learning, 257
Three As of child care (Attention, Approval, Attunement), 103–119
    approval, 69, 76, 111–112, *164*
    attachment and, 106–109
    attention, 69, 76, 109–111
    attunement, 69, 76, 112–114
    basis of, 104–105
    caregivers and, 69, 106–109, 304–305, 413
    child abuse or neglect and, 194
    cognitive development and, 107, 110
    domains and, 76–79
    emotional development and, 69, 105, 107, 112, 304–305, 368–369, 389
    emotional intelligence and, 76
    family child care homes and, 259
    guidance strategies, 368
    physical development, 304–305
    regression and, 433
    security and, 109
    self-esteem and, 383
    teaching concept of, 71, 104
    as tools, 105–106
    using, 114–115
    value of, 111, 112
    versus stress, 69
Time management, 260, *408*, *427*
Time stage, 45, *408*, *427*
Time techniques, for recording and tracking, 139
Toddlers. *See* Twelve to eighteen months

Toileting
    classroom design for, 213–214
    curriculum planning for, 268–271
Toilet learning, 40–41
    Toothbrushing, 272–273
Transactional theories, 23
Transparency, 216–218
Tremblay, R. E., 432
Trial and error, 44, 48, 270, 363, *383–384*
Trust, 69–70, 76, 87, 112
Twelve to eighteen months, 355–374
    activities, *92*
    caregivers, 79, 136, 142–142, 356
    cerebral cortex, 32
    cognitive/language development, 42–54, 326–366
    Developmental Profile, 7–8
    development-enhancing strategies, 29–42, 359–373
    emotional development, 35–36, 67–83, 367–370
    materials/activities, *49*, 143, *238*, 356–358
    physical development, 29–42, 359–362
    social development, 83–93, *92*, 371–373
24 to 30 months, 399–417
    activities, *92*
    brain development, 32
    cognitive/language development, 42–54, 406–412
    development-enhancing strategies, 29–42
    emotional development, 67–83, 412–414
    equipment/materials, *238*
    language development, 43, 44, 53
    materials/activities, *49*, 143, 399–403
    physical development, 29–42, 403–405
    social development, 83–93, *92*, 253–254, 414–416

U

Underprivileged child case study, 201–202
Universal precautions, 241–243
Universal versus unique development, *13*

V

Vecchi, V., 206
Verbal
    preconcepts, 45, *407–408*, *427*
    reasoning, 45, *408*
Violence, 19
Vision development, 35
Visual disabilities, 57
Vocabulary, 52–53, 105, 365, 384, 408, *430*
Vocalization, 53, 252, 301, 307, 309, 325
Voices for America's Children, *126*
Vygotsky, Lev Semenovich, 48–51, 109
Vygotsky's cognitive development theory, 48–51

W

Waking, 39, 139, 265–266
Waldorf Curriculum, 436
Wanless, S. B., 407
Warning signs, in assessment, 142
Water tables, *231*
Watson, John, 10
Watson, L.R., 94
Webbing, 279–*280*
Wechsler Preschool, 407
Weekly plans, 275–277
Welfare reform, 20–21
What if all the kids are white? (Derman-Sparks and Ramsey), 258
Withdrawal behavior, 74
Word forms, *430*
Writing, 218, 221, 223, 279, 345, 366, 411, 429–430
Wurm, J., 155, 280, 281

Y

Your Child's Growing Mind, 297, 322, 425
You statements, 178–179

Z

Zero to three case study, 315
Zone of proximal development (ZPD), 50, 110–111